D0147296

The Editor

Paul R. Petrie is Professor of English at Southern Connecticut State University. He is the author of *Conscience and Purpose: Fiction and Social Consciousness in Howells, Jewett, Chesnutt, and Cather*, and of essays on Howells, Wharton, Chesnutt, Jewett, Cather, and Hawthorne. He has also edited the Broadview edition of W. D. Howells's *An Imperative Duty*.

NORTON CRITICAL EDITIONS
AMERICAN REALISM & REFORM

ALCOTT, LITTLE WOMEN
ALGER, RAGGED DICK
ANDERSON, WINESBURG, OHIO
CHESNUTT, THE CONJURE STORIES
CHESNUTT, THE MARROW OF TRADITION
CHOPIN, THE AWAKENING
CRANE, MAGGIE: A GIRL OF THE STREETS
CRANE, THE RED BADGE OF COURAGE
DOUGLASS, NARRATIVE OF THE LIFE OF FREDERICK DOUGLASS
DREISER, SISTER CARRIE
DU BOIS, THE SOULS OF BLACK FOLK
EMERSON, EMERSON'S PROSE AND POETRY
FULLER, WOMAN IN THE NINETEENTH CENTURY
HAWTHORNE, THE BLITHEDALE ROMANCE
HAWTHORNE, THE HOUSE OF THE SEVEN GABLES
HAWTHORNE, NATHANIEL HAWTHORNE'S TALES
HAWTHORNE, THE SCARLET LETTER AND OTHER WRITINGS
HOWELLS, THE RISE OF SILAS LAPHAM
JACOBS, INCIDENTS IN THE LIFE OF A SLAVE GIRL
JAMES, THE AMBASSADORS
JAMES, THE AMERICAN
JAMES, THE PORTRAIT OF A LADY
JAMES, TALES OF HENRY JAMES
JAMES, THE TURN OF THE SCREW
JAMES, THE WINGS OF THE DOVE
LINCOLN, LINCOLN'S SELECTED WRITINGS
MELVILLE, THE CONFIDENCE-MAN
MELVILLE, MELVILLE'S SHORT NOVELS
MELVILLE, MOBY-DICK
MELVILLE, PIERRE
MONTGOMERY, ANNE OF GREEN GABLES
MOODIE, ROUGHING IT IN THE BUSH
NORRIS, MCTEAGUE
NORTHUP, TWELVE YEARS A SLAVE
POE, THE SELECTED WRITINGS OF EDGAR ALLAN POE
RIIS, HOW THE OTHER HALF LIVES
SINCLAIR, THE JUNGLE
STOWE, UNCLE TOM'S CABIN
THOREAU, WALDEN, CIVIL DISOBEDIENCE, AND OTHER WRITINGS
TWAIN, ADVENTURES OF HUCKLEBERRY FINN
TWAIN, THE ADVENTURES OF TOM SAWYER
TWAIN, A CONNECTICUT YANKEE IN KING ARTHUR'S COURT
TWAIN, PUDD'NHEAD WILSON AND THOSE EXTRAORDINARY TWINS
WASHINGTON, UP FROM SLAVERY
WHARTON, THE AGE OF INNOCENCE
WHARTON, ETHAN FROME
WHARTON, THE HOUSE OF MIRTH
WHITMAN, LEAVES OF GRASS AND OTHER WRITINGS

For a complete list of Norton Critical Editions, visit
wwnorton.com/nortoncriticals

A NORTON CRITICAL EDITION

W. D. Howells

THE RISE OF SILAS LAPHAM

AUTHORITATIVE TEXT

CONTEXTS

CRITICISM

Edited by

PAUL R. PETRIE

SOUTHERN CONNECTICUT STATE UNIVERSITY

W • W • NORTON & COMPANY • *New York • London*

W. W. Norton & Company has been independent since its founding in 1923, when William Warder Norton and Mary D. Herter Norton first published lectures delivered at the People's Institute, the adult education division of New York City's Cooper Union. The firm soon expanded its program beyond the Institute, publishing books by celebrated academics from America and abroad. By midcentury, the two major pillars of Norton's publishing program—trade books and college texts—were firmly established. In the 1950s, the Norton family transferred control of the company to its employees, and today—with a staff of four hundred and a comparable number of trade, college, and professional titles published each year—W. W. Norton & Company stands as the largest and oldest publishing house owned wholly by its employees.

Copyright © 2018 by W.W. Norton & Company, Inc.

All rights reserved
Printed in the United States of America

Library of Congress Cataloging-in-Publication Data

Names: Howells, William Dean, 1837–1920, author. | Petrie, Paul R., 1964–editor.
Title: The rise of Silas Lapham : authoritative text, contexts, criticism / W. D. Howells ; edited by Paul R. Petrie.
Description: First edition. | New York : W. W. Norton & Company, [2018] | Series: A Norton critical edition | Includes bibliographical references.
Identifiers: LCCN 2018006268 | **ISBN 9780393922424 (pbk.)**
Subjects: LCSH: Boston (Mass.)—Fiction. | Businessmen—Fiction. | Rich people—Fiction. | Socialites—Fiction. | Domestic fiction. | Psychological fiction. | Howells, William Dean, 1837–1920. Rise of Silas Lapham.
Classification: LCC PS2025 .R5 2018 | DDC 813/.4—dc23 LC record available at https://lccn.loc.gov/2018006268

W. W. Norton & Company, Inc., 500 Fifth Avenue, New York, NY 10110
wwnorton.com
W. W. Norton & Company Ltd., 15 Carlisle Street, London W1D 3BS

1 2 3 4 5 6 7 8 9 0

Contents

Criticism

Introduction

The Rise of Silas Lapham (1884–85) occupies a pivotal place both in W. D. Howells's career and in his body of work. Written three years after his resignation from the editorship of the prestigious Boston-based *Atlantic Monthly* magazine, where he had worked (first as assistant editor) since 1866, the novel represents some of the first fruits of his decision to take the risk of supporting himself and his family of five solely on the basis of his writing, without the fiscal insurance provided by a salaried position. Even so, Howells was already well embarked on a personal epoch of success virtually unprecedented for a professional author in the United States. Benefiting from the rapid expansion of the newly lucrative publishing industry in the post–Civil War decades, Howells was among the first American writers to devise ways of supporting themselves primarily on the basis of their literary writing, taking advantage of a seemingly insatiable consumer demand for new fiction. "If I were two W.D.H.'s," Howells jokingly wrote to his father in the late autumn of 1882, "I could not supply the magazines' demand for that writer in England and America."[1] Increasingly well known on both sides of the Atlantic, first as an editor, essayist, and travel writer and more recently as a novelist, Howells was poised for further success as he began writing his new novel during the spring and summer of 1884. When the first installments of his work-in-progress began serial publication in *The Century Illustrated Monthly* that fall, they began what would become his biggest publishing success to date. From November 1884 through August 1885, readers eagerly awaited each new installment in Howells's tale of a Vermont farmer turned Boston millionaire-industrialist and of his and his family's anxious negotiations of the social and moral quandaries created by their unexpected economic ascent.

The rising arc of Howells's fortunes as a professional man of letters tracks closely with his development as a fiction writer and an aesthetic theorist. *Lapham* (pronounced "Lap-um") was Howells's

1. Unpublished letter to William Cooper Howells, November 5, 1882, in the Harvard College library. Quoted in Edwin H. Cady, *The Road to Realism: The Early Years 1837–1885 of William Dean Howells* (Syracuse UP, 1956), pp. 229–30.

tenth novel,[2] and in it he doubled down on the increasingly well-developed set of artistic principles that had guided his editorial decisions at the *Atlantic* as well as the creation of his recent fiction. Beginning with relatively straightforward notions of a new, anti-romantic literature (devised in part during long talks with his fellow literary aspirant Henry James when both men were living in Cambridge, Massachusetts, in the latter 1860s), Howells's ideas gained more concrete and specific form as he exercised them in his editorial and book-reviewing work for the *Atlantic Monthly* and, increasingly, in his own fiction. After Howells signed an unprecedentedly lucrative publishing contract with Harper Brothers the year after *The Rise of Silas Lapham*, he confirmed in short order his role as the preeminent American voice for the new literary Realism,[3] expressing his aesthetic ideas in the monthly *Editor's Study* columns he authored for the widely influential *Harper's* magazine. Intensifying the campaign he had begun during the *Atlantic* years and extended in his fiction, Howells used his new publishing venue to introduce readers to groundbreaking literary voices from Europe as well as to new writers from virtually every region of the United States. While his range of reading recommendations was remarkably varied, the thread that ran through almost all his reviews was the case he made for a new literature based on close, empirical observation of commonplace, everyday experience instead of on the imitation of conventional literary models and modes. Against the unflaggingly popular entertainments afforded by sentimental and "romanticistic" fiction,[4] which in Howells's view seriously misrepresented the real world inhabited by his readers and himself, Howells called for a literature that would be more true to life as lived and observed. Instead of a literature dedicated to spurious moral uplift by way of painting life as it should be rather than as it actually is, Howells argued that fiction should engage its readers in genuine ethical deliberation by

2. Some ambiguity arises from the fact that Howells himself seems to have regarded his second novel, *A Chance Acquaintance* (1873), rather than its predecessor *Their Wedding Journey* (1871) as his first, perhaps because of the earlier work's generic hybridity, combining travel writing with fiction. Further muddling the count is the fact that Howells had finished writing *Indian Summer*, the novel published next after *Silas Lapham*, before *Lapham* had completed its serial run in *Century* magazine in summer 1885.
3. While Howells's friend and fellow Realist Henry James was, during the 1870s and 1880s, as closely identified with the movement in the public mind as Howells ("It was our Howells-and-James epoch," Henry Adams would later recall), and while James and Mark Twain would come to share that role in the twentieth century, it was Howells whose frequent and ubiquitous advocacy in the periodical press for Realist literary principles and writers (including James and Twain) made him the preeminent public spokesperson for the movement.
4. Howells coined the term (which is drawn from the text of his lecture titled "Novel-Writing and Novel-Reading"; see p. 319) to distinguish between the popular fiction targets of his criticism and the artistically respectable Romances of (for instance) Nathaniel Hawthorne, which Howells recognized as a serious, independent literary genre operating under its own rules of engagement with extra-literary realities.

depicting characters much like themselves engaged in personal, domestic, and social circumstances like their own. Popular fiction, he argued, worked practical and moral harm on readers who mistook its idealized fantasies for reality; the new Realism would help readers understand the social, moral, and cognitive complexities of their own and others' lives. Only thus, reasoned Howells, could the aesthetics of fiction serve constructive social and ethical purposes in a modern society undergoing a chaotic reordering of traditional patterns of human interrelationship under the unrelenting pressures of urbanization, industrialization, large-scale immigration, and comprehensive economic reorganization.

As Howells developed these aesthetic ideas in his book reviews, he simultaneously enacted and tested them in his fiction. He frequently embedded internal commentary in his novels about the relationship between reality and its representation in literature, seeking to understand and manage the endless cultural feedback loop by which individuals' perceptions of external realities—material, relational, and social—were influenced and mediated by prior artistic portrayals. In much the same way that later generations would worry about the effects of electronic social media, the Internet, film, and television on our individual and collective sense of reality, Howells routinely used his fiction to draw critical attention to the ways people's fiction-reading habits impinged, for better and worse, on their perceptions of self and world and on the conduct of their personal relationships. While advocating for and demonstrating what he believed to be an aesthetically and ethically superior mode of artistic interaction with reality, he nevertheless always maintained awareness that every literary representation, no matter how successfully "realistic," remained (to borrow the title of Harold H. Kolb's book about American literary Realism) a mediated "illusion of life" and not life itself. In *The Rise of Silas Lapham*, this set of concerns is front and center from very early in the novel, as characters repeatedly discuss the books they have been reading and how the content of these fictions tallies—or doesn't—with their own lives and experiences. The most prominent example of this fictional meta-discourse is the imaginary sentimental romance novel titled *Tears, Idle Tears*, which becomes a key point of conversation in the novel's pivotal dinner party scene in Chapter XIV. When the basic scenario of that novel suddenly reappears, in cosmetically altered form, in the lives of Howells's own characters, they and readers alike are engaged in what becomes a long, complicated, and ultimately open-ended consideration of the uses and effects of fiction's virtual realities in the lives of actual readers.

A major strand of that discourse is centrally and intensively concerned with gender. As a canny literary businessman, Howells was acutely aware that the primary readership for fiction, including his own, was made up of women. Struggling from early in his career to devise creative ways of evading or altering readers' conventional expectations concerning what he and Henry James took to calling "the everlasting young man and young woman"[5] in contemporary fiction, Howells contended repeatedly with the problematic relations between literary art and gender conventions. Consequently, one of *Silas Lapham*'s subplots centers on Lapham's daughter Penelope, who finds herself unexpectedly inhabiting a courtship situation seemingly drawn directly from the pages of *Tears, Idle Tears*, the novel that she has been reading and—until that point—ridiculing. Howells was acutely sensitive to the psychic vulnerability of middle-class American women, who were relentlessly subjected to a pervasive gender ideology that assigned to them the thankless roles of moral self-sacrifice and self-effacement. In Howells's own life, the predicament was made ever-present by the illness of his elder daughter, Winifred, whose chronic bouts of listlessness, depression, loss of appetite, and stomach pain—symptoms of the illness then known as neurasthenia or female hysteria—were diagnosed as essentially psychosomatic in origin.[6] Using Penelope Lapham as his test case, Howells revealed the dangerous power of the era's prevailing gender ideology, exerted through the widely popular genre of sentimental fiction, to warp the moral and emotional health of his young women readers.

In this and other ways, Howells consistently thought of literary art as inseparable from its social, political, and moral effects. As his literary-aesthetic principles pushed into progressively deeper political and social-ethical waters during the decade of *Silas Lapham*, so too did his novels. While his earlier novels had already begun addressing questions of social difference and division in American society, *The Rise of Silas Lapham* addressed these issues with new urgency and intensity.[7] *Lapham* engages with the problematic persistence of social class distinctions in an officially (if incompletely) democratic and egalitarian American society, one that seemed to offer individuals an unprecedented potential for upward mobility

5. The phrase appears in "Novel-Writing and Novel-Reading."
6. Winny died in 1889 under the care of the internationally famous American physician S. Weir Mitchell, the inventor of the "rest cure" for neurasthenics best-known in our time as the target of Charlotte Perkins Gilman's short story "The Yellow Wall-paper." Ambiguous evidence drawn primarily from Howells's correspondence suggests the possibility of a physical cause for Winny's illness—a possibility that became a further source of torment for Howells and his wife after Winny's death.
7. *A Chance Acquaintance* (1873), which recounts the troubled progress of the relationship between a young Bostonian man of established upper-class pedigree and a young woman of rural, midwestern, and decidedly middle-class provenance, may be the most direct antecedent to *Silas Lapham* in this regard, but its investigation of this shared subject matter is relatively modest in its scope and ambition.

while at the same time subtly yet unmistakably limiting that possibility. In exploring these topics, Howells drew deeply on personal experience. Born in 1847 and raised in a succession of small towns in a rural Ohio only a generation removed from statehood, Howells was educated (like Benjamin Franklin and Howells's close friend Mark Twain) primarily in the print shop, working as typesetter, copy editor, and factotum for his printer-publisher-editor father. From these quintessentially humble midwestern roots, Howells had risen to both economic success and social acceptance into the tight-knit circle of polite society in his adoptive home of Boston, then still widely considered to be the citadel of American high culture. But Howells's successes never quite erased a lingering sense of himself as an outsider in the Athens of America, and his uneasiness with his own status sharpened his sensitivity to social difference and the subtle enforcements of class boundaries. That sense of mild alienation found expression, for instance, in his lifelong habit of frequently changing residence—as though no single home, not even those he had designed and built for himself, could give him a stable feeling of belonging.[8]

In *The Rise of Silas Lapham*, such feelings of cultural alienation gain imaginative expression partly on the basis of regional differences akin to Howells's own: Lapham is a transplanted Vermont farmer (although, as more than one critic has noticed, he speaks and carries himself suspiciously more like a midwesterner than a New Englander) who must find his place in the alien environs of New England's major metropolis. But the Laphams' escalating anxieties about their social status in their adoptive home are only secondarily a matter of regional culture; the main source of their discomfort is a matter of social class. As Lapham seeks to ratify his entrepreneurial success by winning entrance for his family into the inner circle of Boston's elite (represented in the novel primarily by the Coreys, whose acceptance the Laphams simultaneously covet and disdain), the novel charts the complex relationship between economic success and class status. The Laphams' acquisition of the material trappings of upper-class status—most prominently registered by the grand house "on the water side of Beacon," in the fashionable new Back Bay neighborhood of the city (see maps on pp. 367–70), that Lapham

8. Another telling episode in Howells's unsettled relationship to Boston's cultural and social elite was his anguished sense of complicity in his friend Mark Twain's widely publicized send-up of established New England literary elders Oliver Wendell Holmes Sr., Ralph Waldo Emerson, and Henry Wadsworth Longfellow. In a speech delivered at a gala dinner given by the *Atlantic* in December 1877 to mark Holmes's seventieth birthday, Twain caricatured the three as drunken and disheveled travelers, unwanted guests in a bemused California miner's cabin. Howells had introduced Twain's presentation, and letters and accounts written by the two men after the event reveal the extent of their conflicted attitudes as outsiders who had made good in the seat of eastern American civilization.

is in the process of building—only very equivocally wins for them the higher social status in the eyes of Boston's old-money "Brahmin" class that they remain ambivalent about desiring.[9]

The complexities of the Laphams' lives in the liminal space between classes are portrayed with minutely detailed descriptions of comparative manners and mores, speech patterns and body language, habits of thought, and actuating assumptions about character and conduct. To his mastery of the tools of the novelist of manners, Howells added new depths of psychological observation and insight. Exploring in detail the acute psychoemotional dis-ease created by the Laphams' ambiguous social situation, the novel probes the sources and effects of social behavior in and on individual psychology. Characters are consistently drawn as complex intermixtures of conscious and subconscious motivation, thought and emotion, moral agency and social training. Howells's meticulous representations of human psychology earned for him among a first generation of readers and reviewers both admiration and, in many instances, opprobrium. For more conventional readers, Howells's approach to characterization seemed coldly analytical, too "scientific" to allow readers the close and warm identification with characters that earlier fictional norms had taught them to expect.

Howells's more unsympathetic readers faulted the novelist, as well, for his unapologetic offering of the unvarnished, unidealized Laphams as the focus of his novel: characters whose class status, occupation, language, and manners, judged according to conventional canons of literary taste, should have disqualified them from serious literary representation in the pages of polite literature. While Lapham, as an essentially middle-class figure, is certainly not a member of the "dangerous classes" that reformer Charles Loring Brace had only recently helped teach genteel readers to fear,[1] Howells's decision to focus literary attention on such *déclassé* subjects as the "ungrammatical" Laphams was nonetheless pioneering, opening the way for depictions of the urban and rural working poor in the next decades by literary Naturalists such as Stephen Crane, Frank Norris, and Theodore Dreiser. Howells's focus in *Silas Lapham* is essentially and deliberately on the middle class, despite the great wealth of his *nouveau riche* protagonist and his inclusion of figures occupying both higher and lower social niches than the Laphams themselves. But an audience reading his novel in the wake of the

9. Brahmins are the highest, priestly caste in Hindu society (primarily in India). In an 1860 *Atlantic Monthly* article, Oliver Wendell Holmes Sr. borrowed the term "Brahmin caste" to characterize eastern Massachusetts' longest established, socially elite families as an unofficial and benign intellectual and moral aristocracy for New England.
1. Charles Loring Brace, *The Dangerous Classes of New York, and Twenty Years' Work among Them*, Wynkoop and Hallenbeck, 1872.

"Long Depression" of the 1870s, which had exposed deep and worsening cultural and economic fault lines in American society, would have been well aware that the Laphams' anxious middle-class quest to rise into the genteel classes was fully contiguous with more extreme manifestations of Gilded Age social division. While the novel makes only one brief foray into the ghetto, it nevertheless clearly registers the deepening segregation of Boston, like other large American cities of the period, into inner-city tenement districts for poor wage-laborers and fashionable "streetcar suburbs" for middle-class professionals and capitalists. The novel's events, moreover, unfold across a clearly mapped late-nineteenth-century Boston, where the Laphams' and Coreys' respective places of residence, work, and leisure are routinely deployed by the author and interpreted by the characters as signifiers of their relative status within an unmistakably unsettled social and cultural order.

More extreme manifestations of class division also make brief appearances in the novel, most notably in the central dinner party scene, when Bromfield Corey notes with irony that while Boston's social elites vacation in Bar Harbor and Newport, leaving their Beacon Hill mansions empty, the city's laborers spend their summer crammed densely into unsafe and unsanitary tenement housing just a few blocks away. Howells's original inclusion in this passage of a reference to the newly invented explosive, dynamite, which had already been put to use as an instrument of violent political protest in Europe, caused a prepublication uproar in the offices of *Century* magazine. At the requests of his editor and publisher, Howells removed the reference, apparently willingly, but its original inclusion was an indication of where the author's politics and aesthetics were headed. In 1887, when eight men were arrested and tried in connection with a bomb thrown during a labor protest in Chicago's Haymarket Square, Howells risked his reputation and his livelihood by publicly decrying the political show trial that resulted in their convictions and death sentences despite clearly insufficient evidence. "[A]fter fifty years of optimistic content with 'civilization' and its ability to come out all right in the end," he wrote to his friend and fellow novelist Henry James in 1888, "I now abhor it, and feel that it is coming out all wrong in the end, unless it bases itself anew on a real equality."[2] The result, in artistic terms, was the succession of "economic" novels of the later 1880s and 1890s, works that extended the range of Howells's representations of social difference and division, addressing issues of class, labor, and capitalism even more directly than had *Silas Lapham*.

2. October 10, 1888, *Selected Letters of W.D. Howells,* Volume 3: *1882–1891*, Twayne, 1980, p. 231.

The preceding paragraphs suggest some of the reasons for this novel's longevity. Another reason is the balance the novel achieves between the author's penchant for formal, thematic, and ethical open-endedness, on the one hand, and the still-prevailing expectation among readers and many critics (formed under the long shadow of mid-twentieth-century formalist criticism) that a successful novel is characterized by thematic unity and formal closure. One implication of Howells's commitment to Realism was a deep and abiding suspicion of neatly contrived and resolved plotlines, which he saw as symptoms of a novel's "literosity"[3] that might interfere with its higher calling to represent life as lived and observed rather than as filtered through earlier literary conventions. One contemporary reviewer of *Silas Lapham*, for instance, quipped that "in defiance of his own dictum, Mr. Howells has contrived to tell a very good story,"[4] obliquely referencing a not infrequently heard complaint about the supposed plotlessness of Howells's fiction. In the decades following publication and onward into the mid-twentieth-century academic "Howells revival," Howells's perceived success in formally and thematically uniting and balancing *Silas Lapham*'s plot and subplots has been a major ground for praise from readers and critics. Howells would give fuller rein later in his career to his impulse to sacrifice the well-made plot for the sake of what he judged to be the more important goals of accurate social, psychological, and material representation. But in his mid-career works, of which *Silas Lapham* is a prime example, he made something of a specialty of seeming to grant, while not quite completely denying, the kinds of affective and formal closure that his readers demanded. While *Silas Lapham*'s plot appears to resolve Lapham's business, social, and moral quandaries, the narrator's and Lapham's own pronouncements at the end of the novel leave the precise terms of those resolutions remarkably, if surreptitiously, unresolved. Similarly, the novel's handling of its courtship plot ends where such plots are conventionally expected to end, in marriage, while subtly tempering the normally attendant social and emotional resolutions by way of a series of caveats and prospective complications in the new couple's future life together. The novel thus walks a shadowy line between adherence to nineteenth-century readers' expectations and understated experimentation with narrative conventions, along lines that would become increasingly common in the next century.

Howells's literary reputation would suffer a precipitous decline during the early decades of the twentieth century, a casualty of shifting literary fashions and of a devastating series of public attacks by

3. The term appears frequently in Howells' *Editor's Study* columns.
4. See [A Want of Perception as to Climax], on p. 405.

a generation of self-consciously "modern" writers (including Sinclair Lewis, Van Wyck Brooks, and Gertrude Atherton, among others) who found in the culturally iconic figure of Howells a convenient symbol for all they loathed about their American-Victorian cultural inheritance. The academic "Howells Revival" of the mid-twentieth century would only partly rehabilitate the author's standing, in and out of the university. But despite the fact that Howells's name shows little sign of returning to the "household word" status it enjoyed during the decades surrounding the turn of the century, *The Rise of Silas Lapham*—the only one of Howells's books to remain continuously in print since first publication—has retained a secure place in the body of Howells's work and in the canon of American literature. Generally considered a high point in its author's career, *Silas Lapham* seems assured of retaining that status even as much of the rest of Howells's writing undeservedly slips further from the mainstream of academic and popular regard. *The Rise of Silas Lapham* continues to speak, in Howells's characteristically rational, incisive, ironic, yet sympathetic and humorous voice, to a society just as deeply riven by class divisions, just as stymied by the persistence of caste in an ostensibly democratic and aspirational nation, and just as hampered by its citizens' dim half-consciousness of the mechanisms by which social inequalities are produced and maintained, as Howells and his readers were. *The Rise of Silas Lapham* continues to be for us, and about us.

Acknowledgments

Thanks are due to my friends and colleagues in the English Department at Southern Connecticut State University who at various stages in the creation of this volume graciously offered their insights and opinions on sundry matters pertaining to both content and form as well as commiserating with me as I experienced the inevitable travails of editorship. In particular, I would like to thank Charles Baraw, Joel Dodson, Scott Ellis, Nicole Fluhr, and Cynthia Stretch for their patience with the endless stream of trial balloons and what-if scenarios I sent in their direction during the book's construction. Farther afield, Professors Hildegard Hoeller and Anne K. Phillips generously and usefully shared their experiences as Norton Critical Edition editors. The librarians and staff of the Hilton C. Buley library at SCSU, especially interlibrary loan supervisor Beth Paris, were crucial to my research, as were Nan Card at the Rutherford B. Hayes Presidential Library and Museums, Mary Haegert at the Houghton Library at Harvard University, and Sue Hodson, Stephanie Arias, and Samuel Wylie at the Huntington Library, San Marino, California. I am grateful to my department chair Michael Shea, the members of the department and university sabbatical committees, SCSU's president, the Board of Regents of the Connecticut State Colleges & Universities for supporting work on this volume by granting me an indispensable semester of sabbatical leave, and the SCSU School of Arts & Sciences for generous funding. Closer to home, thanks are perpetually owing to Allison T. Hild for her expert guidance and unfailing emotional support. Thanks too to Maxwell P. H. Petrie and Claudia T. H. Petrie, for contributing valuable student's-eye perspectives on portions of the text.

I owe the opportunity to edit this book to John Kelly and Carol Bemis at W. W. Norton; profound thanks also to Thea Goodrich and Rachel Goodman for their patience, good humor, and exceptionally clear guidance during all phases of the editorial process. My fellow members of the William Dean Howells Society offered encouragement and some specific suggestions as I pondered the difficult decisions about what to include and what to reluctantly leave out of this new edition of the novel; the Society's generous grant helped defray the cost of republication permission fees. Last, thanks are due to the many scholars who have written so very engagingly and insightfully about *Silas Lapham* over the decades: rereading the scholarly work of the mid-twentieth-century Howells Revival alongside the criticism produced since the appearance of the first Norton Critical Edition of the novel in 1982 establishes the continuing vitality of the novel itself as well as the enormous debt owed by younger scholars to a now rapidly retiring generation of Howellsians. In particular, I would like to acknowledge the editor of the original Norton *Lapham*: Don L. Cook's sterling work in that edition offered a powerful model for its successor. I can only hope that the new edition will prove to be as useful for readers, students, and teachers as Professor Cook's has been for the past three and a half decades.

This volume is dedicated to the memory of Professor Michael T. "Timo" Gilmore (1942–2014), late of Brandeis University, whose untimely passing prevented him from completing what should have been his edition instead of mine.

A Note on the Text

Before its publication as a book in the summer of 1885, *The Rise of Silas Lapham* had been published in monthly installments in *The Century Illustrated Monthly Magazine* from November 1884 through August 1885. Howells's novel shared space during parts of its run in *Century* with two other landmark works: Henry James's *The Bostonians* and Mark Twain's *Adventures of Huckleberry Finn*. The rapid expansion of periodical publishing during the later part of the nineteenth century had accustomed contemporary audiences to reading long fiction in weekly or monthly installments, and writers, including Howells, learned to manage these publication breaks to aesthetic advantage, planning plot and structure with one eye on piquing and maintaining audience interest from one installment to the next. The enforced hiatuses between magazine issues were thus an integral part of the reading experience for *Silas Lapham*'s first readers, and there is no small value in reading the novel with an awareness of its original division into monthly installments. Toward that end, bracketed headings in the text of the novel in this volume indicate the beginnings of each successive installment, and the table that follows shows how each set of chapters first appeared serially.

***Century* Issue**	**Chapters**
November 1884	I & II
December 1884	III, IV, & V
January 1885	VI, VII, & VIII
February 1885	IX & X
March 1885	XI & XII
April 1885	XIII & XIV
May 1885	XV, XVI, XVII, & XVIII
June 1885	XIX, XX, & XXI
July 1885	XXII, XXIII, XXIV, & XXV
August 1885	XXVI & XXVII

The text in this volume is the novel as it originally appeared in *Century*, which was the basis for the novel's first publication as a book when its magazine serialization ended. According to the editors of the definitive scholarly edition of the novel (volume 12 in Indiana University Press's *A Selected Edition of W. D. Howells*), in the absence of the novel's no longer extant manuscript, the magazine text is the closest we have to a definitive version of the work. The publication process followed by Howells and his publishers on both sides of the Atlantic (David Douglas in Edinburgh and Ticknor & Company in Boston) ensured that Howells amended and approved page proofs of each month's installment before their publication in *Century*. These revised proofs became the basis not only of the magazine text but also of the first British and American editions of the completed book. Howells did make a few, mostly minor revisions of the magazine text before its book publication, but errors introduced when the type was reset for the printing of the book, and again when the printing plates were shipped from England to the United States for reuse in manufacturing the American edition, make the magazine version the preferred copy-text for the novel. A more detailed account of the novel's publication history may be found in David J. Nordloh's excellent "Textual Commentary" in the *Selected Edition*, which also includes extensive textual apparatus chronicling all substantive differences among the various published versions of the novel. See also Walter J. Meserve's equally illuminating "Introduction," in the same volume.

A few of the more significant changes Howells made in the novel either during his revision of proofs before *Century* publication or between magazine and book publication have been noted in the footnotes in this edition. The two most noteworthy sets of revisions—one in which Silas Lapham and his wife, Persis, discuss Jewish residency in their Boston neighborhood and its effect on property values, and another in which the host of a Beacon Hill dinner party expresses bafflement at the fact that the urban poor refrain from using dynamite to blow up the vacant mansions of the city's wealthier citizens while they are away on vacation—have likewise been noted in the footnotes, and the variant texts have been included elsewhere in the volume for easy comparison.

Cover illustration featuring W. D. Howells, *Harper's Weekly* magazine (June 19, 1886). Courtesy of Archives & Special Collections at the Thomas J. Dodd Research Center, University of Connecticut Library.

The Text of

THE RISE OF SILAS LAPHAM

The Rise of Silas Lapham

[FIRST INSTALLMENT—NOVEMBER 1884]

I.

When Bartley Hubbard went to interview Silas Lapham for the "Solid Men of Boston" series, which he undertook to finish up in "The Events," after he replaced their original projector on that newspaper, Lapham received him in his private office by previous appointment.

"Walk right in!" he called out to the journalist, whom he caught sight of through the door of the counting-room.

He did not rise from the desk at which he was writing, but he gave Bartley his left hand for welcome, and he rolled his large head in the direction of a vacant chair. "Sit down! I'll be with you in just half a minute."

"Take your time," said Bartley, with the ease he instantly felt. "I'm in no hurry." He took a note-book from his pocket, laid it on his knee, and began to sharpen a pencil.

"There!" Lapham pounded with his great hairy fist on the envelope he had been addressing. "William!" he called out, and he handed the letter to a boy who came to get it. "I want that to go right away. Well, sir," he continued, wheeling round in his leather cushioned swivel-chair, and facing Bartley, seated so near that their knees almost touched, "so you want my life, death, and Christian sufferings, do you, young man?"

"That's what I'm after," said Bartley. "Your money or your life."

"I guess you wouldn't want my life without the money," said Lapham, as if he were willing to prolong these moments of preparation.

"Take 'em both," Bartley suggested. "Don't want your money without your life, if you come to that. But you're just one million times more interesting to the public than if you hadn't a dollar; and you know that as well as I do, Mr. Lapham. There's no use beating about the bush."

"No," said Lapham, somewhat absently. He put out his huge foot and pushed the ground-glass door shut between his little den and the book-keepers, in their larger den outside.

"In personal appearance," wrote Bartley in the sketch for which he now studied his subject, while he waited patiently for him to continue, "Silas Lapham is a fine type of the successful American. He has a square, bold chin, only partially concealed by the short, reddish-gray beard, growing to the edges of his firmly closing lips. His nose is short and straight; his forehead good, but broad rather than high; his eyes blue, and with a light in them that is kindly or sharp according to his mood. He is of medium height, and fills an average arm-chair with a solid bulk, which, on the day of our interview, was unpretentiously clad in a business suit of blue serge. His head droops somewhat from a short neck, which does not trouble itself to rise far from a pair of massive shoulders."

"I don't know as I know just where you want me to begin," said Lapham.

"Might begin with your birth; that's where most of us begin," replied Bartley.

A gleam of humorous appreciation shot into Lapham's blue eyes.

"I didn't know whether you wanted me to go quite so far back as that," he said. "But there's no disgrace in having been born, and I was born in the State of Vermont, pretty well up under the Canada line—so well up, in fact, that I came very near being an adoptive citizen; for I was bound to be an American of *some* sort, from the word Go! That was about—well, let me see!—pretty near sixty years ago: this is '75, and that was '20. Well, say I'm fifty-five years old; and I've *lived* 'em, too; not an hour of waste time about *me*, anywheres! I was born on a farm, and—"

"Worked in the fields summers and went to school winters: regulation thing?" Bartley cut in.

"Regulation thing," said Lapham, accepting this irreverent version of his history somewhat dryly.

"Parents poor, of course," suggested the journalist. "Any barefoot business? Early deprivations of any kind, that would encourage the youthful reader to go and do likewise? Orphan myself, you know," said Bartley, with a smile of cynical good comradery.

Lapham looked at him silently, and then said with quiet self-respect, "I guess if you see these things as a joke, my life wont inter*est* you."

"Oh, yes, it will," returned Bartley, unabashed. "You'll see; it'll come out all right." And in fact it did so, in the interview which Bartley printed.

"Mr. Lapham," he wrote, "passed rapidly over the story of his early life, its poverty and its hardships, sweetened, however, by the recollections of a devoted mother, and a father who, if somewhat her inferior in education, was no less ambitious for the advancement of his children. They were quiet, unpretentious people, religious, after the fashion of that time, and of sterling morality, and they taught their children the simple virtues of the Old Testament and Poor Richard's Almanac."[1]

Bartley could not deny himself this gibe; but he trusted to Lapham's unliterary habit of mind for his security in making it, and most other people would consider it sincere reporter's rhetoric.

"You know," he explained to Lapham, "that we have to look at all these facts as material, and we get the habit of classifying them. Sometimes a leading question will draw out a whole line of facts that a man himself would never think of." He went on to put several queries, and it was from Lapham's answers that he generalized the history of his childhood. "Mr. Lapham, although he did not dwell on his boyish trials and struggles, spoke of them with deep feeling and an abiding sense of their reality." This was what he added in the interview, and by the time he had got Lapham past the period where risen Americans are all pathetically alike in their narrow circumstances, their sufferings, and their aspirations, he had beguiled him into forgetfulness of the check he had received, and had him talking again in perfect enjoyment of his autobiography.

"Yes, sir," said Lapham, in a strain which Bartley was careful not to interrupt again, "a man never sees all that his mother has been to him till it's too late to let her know that he sees it. Why, *my* mother—" he stopped. "It gives me a lump in the throat," he said apologetically, with an attempt at a laugh. Then he went on: "She was a little, frail thing, not bigger than a good-sized intermediate school-girl; but she did the whole work of a family of boys, and boarded the hired men besides. She cooked, swept, washed, ironed, made and mended from daylight till dark—and from dark till daylight, I was going to say; for I don't know how she got any time for sleep. But I suppose she did. She got time to go to church, and to teach us to read the Bible, and to misunderstand it in the old way. She was *good*. But it aint her on her knees in church that comes back to me so much like the sight of an angel, as her on her knees before me at night, washing my poor, dirty little feet, that I'd run bare in all day, and making me decent for bed. There were six of us boys; it seems to me we were all of a size; and she was just so careful with all of us. I can feel her hands on my feet yet!" Bartley looked at Lapham's No. 10 boots and softly whistled through his teeth. "We were patched all over; but we wa'n't ragged. *I* don't know how she got through it. She didn't seem to think it was anything; and I guess it was no more than my father expected of her. *He* worked like a horse in doors and out—up at

1. Published annually by Benjamin Franklin from 1732 to 1758, the almanac included practical moral maxims promoting virtues like thrift and hard work.

daylight, feeding the stock, and groaning round all day with his rheumatism, but not stopping."

Bartley hid a yawn over his note-book, and probably, if he could have spoken his mind, he would have suggested to Lapham that he was not there for the purpose of interviewing his ancestry. But Bartley had learned to practice a patience with his victims which he did not always feel, and to feign an interest in their digressions till he could bring them up with a round turn.

"I tell you," said Lapham, jabbing the point of his penknife into the writing-pad on the desk before him, "when I hear women complaining nowadays that their lives are stunted and empty, I want to tell 'em about my *mother's* life. *I* could paint it out for 'em."

Bartley saw his opportunity at the word paint, and cut in. "And you say, Mr. Lapham, that you discovered this mineral paint on the old farm yourself?"

Lapham acquiesced in the return to business. "*I* didn't discover it," he said, scrupulously. "My father found it one day, in a hole made by a tree blowing down. There it was, laying loose in the pit, and sticking to the roots that had pulled up a big cake of dirt with 'em. *I* don't know what give him the idea that there was money in it, but he did think so from the start. I guess, if they'd had the word in those days, they'd considered him pretty much of a crank about it. He was trying as long as he lived to get that paint introduced; but he couldn't make it go. The country was so poor they couldn't paint their houses with anything; and father hadn't any facilities. It got to be a kind of joke with us; and I guess that paint-mine[2] did as much as any one thing to make us boys clear out as soon as we got old enough. All my brothers went West and took up land; but I hung on to New England, and I hung on to the old farm, not because the paint-mine was on it, but because the old house was—and the graves. Well," said Lapham, as if unwilling to give himself too much credit, "there wouldn't been any market for it, anyway. You can go through that part of the State and buy more farms than you can shake a stick at for less money than it cost to build the barns on 'em. Of course, it's turned out a good thing. I keep the old house up in good shape, and we spend a month or so there every summer. M' wife kind of likes it, and the girls. Pretty place; sightly all round it. I've got a force of men at work there the whole time, and I've got a man and his wife in the house. Had a family meeting there last year; the whole connection from out West. There!" Lapham rose from his seat and took down a large warped, unframed photograph from the top of his desk,

2. A mineral deposit used to produce paint. Lapham explains the manufacturing process and the paint's composition later in the chapter.

passing his hand over it, and then blowing vigorously upon it, to clear it of the dust. "There we are, *all* of us."

"I don't need to look twice at *you*," said Bartley, putting his finger on one of the heads.

"Well, that's Bill," said Lapham, with a gratified laugh. "He's about as brainy as any of us, I guess. He's one of their leading lawyers, out Dubuque way; been judge of the Common Pleas once or twice. That's his son—just graduated at Yale—alongside of my youngest girl. Good-looking chap, aint he?"

"*She's* a good-looking chap," said Bartley, with prompt irreverence. He hastened to add, at the frown which gathered between Lapham's eyes, "What a beautiful creature she is! What a lovely, refined, sensitive face! And she looks *good*, too."

"She *is* good," said the father, relenting.

"And, after all, that's about the best thing in a woman," said the potential reprobate. "If my wife wasn't good enough to keep both of us straight, I don't know what would become of me."

"My other daughter," said Lapham, indicating a girl with eyes that showed large, and a face of singular gravity. "Mis' Lapham," he continued, touching his wife's effigy with his little finger. "My brother Willard and his family—farm at Kankakee.[3] Hazard Lapham and his wife—Baptist preacher in Kansas. Jim and his three girls—milling business at Minneapolis. Ben and his family—practicing medicine in Fort Wayne."

The figures were clustered in an irregular group in front of an old farm-house, whose original ugliness had been smartened up with a coat of Lapham's own paint and heightened with an incongruous piazza. The photographer had not been able to conceal the fact that they were all decent, honest-looking, sensible people, with a very fair share of beauty among the young girls; some of these were extremely pretty, in fact. He had put them into awkward and constrained attitudes, of course; and they all looked as if they had the instrument of torture which photographers call a headrest under their occiputs.[4] Here and there an elderly lady's face was a mere blur; and some of the younger children had twitched themselves into wavering shadows, and might have passed for spirit photographs of their own little ghosts.[5] It was the standard family-group photograph, in which most Americans have figured at some time or other; and Lapham exhibited a just satisfaction in it. "I presume," he mused aloud, as he put

3. A town in northeastern Illinois.
4. The backs of their heads.
5. Literally, the effect produced when an object moves during photographic exposure. Some people believed that photography recorded evidence of a spiritual dimension of reality.

it back on top of his desk, "that we sha'n't soon get together again, all of us."

"And you say," suggested Bartley, "that you staid right along on the old place, when the rest cleared out West?"

"No-o-o-o," said Lapham, with a long, loud drawl; "I cleared out West too, first off. Went to Texas. Texas was all the cry in those days. But I got enough of the Lone Star in about three months, and I come back with the idea that Vermont was good enough for me."

"Fatted calf business?"[6] queried Bartley, with his pencil poised above his note-book.

"I presume they were glad to see me," said Lapham, with dignity. "Mother," he added gently, "died that winter, and I staid on with father. I buried him in the spring; and then I came down to a little place called Lumberville, and picked up what jobs I could get. I worked round at the saw-mills, and I was ostler[7] awhile at the hotel—I always *did* like a good horse. Well, I *wa'n't* exactly a college graduate, and I went to school odd times. I got to driving the stage after while, and by and by I *bought* the stage and run the business myself. Then I hired the tavern-stand, and—well, to make a long story short, then I got married. Yes," said Lapham, with pride, "I married the school-teacher. We did pretty well with the hotel, and my wife she was always at me to paint up. Well, I put it off, and *put* it off, as a man will, till one day I give in, and says I, 'Well, *let's* paint up. Why, Pert,'—m'wife's name's Persis,[8]—'I've got a whole paint-mine out on the farm. Let's go out and look at it.' So we drove out. I'd let the place for seventy-five dollars a year to a shif'less kind of a Kanuck[9] that had come down that way; and I'd hated to see the house with him in it; but we drove out one Saturday afternoon, and we brought back about a bushel of the stuff in the buggy-seat, and I tried it crude, and I tried it burnt; and I liked it. M' wife she liked it, too. There wa'n't any painter by trade in the village, and I mixed it myself. Well, sir, that tavern's got that coat of paint on it yet, and it haint ever had any other, and I don't know's it ever will. Well, you know, I felt as if it was a kind of a harumscarum experiment, all the while; and I presume I shouldn't have tried it, but I kind of liked to do it because father'd always set so much store by his paint-mine. And when I'd got the first coat on,"—Lapham called it *cut*,—"I presume I must have set as much as half an hour, looking at it and thinking how he would have enjoyed it. I've had my share of luck in this world,

6. In the New Testament parable of the prodigal son (Luke 15.11–32), the father kills a fatted calf to celebrate his son's return home.
7. Stableman; also spelled "hostler."
8. Lapham's wife is named for a Christian woman praised by the apostle Paul in Romans 16.12.
9. Canadian (slang), sometimes used derisively; usually spelled "Canuck."

and I aint a-going to complain on my *own* account, but I've noticed that most things get along too late for most people. It made me feel bad, and it took all the pride out my success with the paint, thinking of father. Seemed to me I might 'a' taken more interest in it when he was by to see; but we've got to live and learn. Well, I called my wife out,—I'd tried it on the back of the house, you know,—and she left her dishes,—I can remember she came out with her sleeves rolled up and set down alongside of me on the trestle,—and says I, 'What do you think, Persis?' And says she, 'Well, you haint got a paint-mine, Silas Lapham; you've got a *gold*-mine.' She always was just so enthusiastic about things. Well, it was just after two or three boats had burnt up out West, and a lot of lives lost, and there was a great cry about non-inflammable paint, and I guess that was what was in her mind. 'Well, I guess it aint any gold-mine, Persis,' says I; 'but I guess it *is* a paint-mine. I'm going to have it analyzed, and if it turns out what I think it is, I'm going to work it. And if father hadn't had such a long name, I should call it the Nehemiah Lapham Mineral Paint. But, any rate, every barrel of it, and every keg, and every bottle, and every package, big or little, has got to have the initials and figures N. L. f. 1835, S. L. t. 1855, on it. Father found it in 1835, and I tried it in 1855.'"

"'S. T.—1860—X.' business," said Bartley.

"Yes," said Lapham, "but I hadn't heard of Plantation Bitters then, and I hadn't seen any of the fellow's labels.[1] I set to work and I got a man down from Boston; and I carried him out to the farm, and he analyzed it—made a regular job of it. Well, sir, we built a kiln, and we kept a lot of that paint-ore red-hot for forty-eight hours; kept the Kanuck and his family up, firing. The presence of iron in the ore showed with the magnet from the start; and when he came to test it, he found out that it contained about seventy-five per cent. of the peroxide of iron."

Lapham pronounced the scientific phrases with a sort of reverent satisfaction, as if awed through his pride by a little lingering uncertainty as to what peroxide was. He accented it as if it were purr-ox-*eyed;* and Bartley had to get him to spell it.

"Well, and what then?" he asked, when he had made a note of the percentage.

"What then?" echoed Lapham. "Well, then, the fellow set down and told me, 'You've got a paint here,' says he, 'that's going to drive every other mineral paint out of the market. Why,' says he, 'it'll drive 'em right into the Back Bay!'[2] Of course, *I* didn't know what the Back

1. The label on bottles of Drake's Plantation Bitters, a popular medicinal tonic, included markings similar to those adorning containers of Lapham's paint.
2. A vast expanse of tidal wetlands adjacent to the Charles River estuary, bordering the peninsular city of Boston on the southwest. During the time period recounted in the

Bay was then; but I begun to open my eyes; thought I'd had 'em open before, but I guess I hadn't. Says he, 'That paint has got hydraulic cement in it, and it can stand fire and water and acids'; he named over a lot of things. Says he, 'It'll mix easily with linseed oil, whether you want to use it boiled or raw; and it aint a-going to crack nor fade any; and it aint a-going to scale. When you've got your arrangements for burning it properly, you're going to have a paint that will stand like the everlasting hills, in every climate under the sun.' Then he went into a lot of particulars, and I begun to think he was drawing a long bow,[3] and meant to make his bill accordingly. So I kept pretty cool; but the fellow's bill didn't amount to anything hardly—said I might pay him after I got going; young chap, and pretty easy; but every word he said was gospel. Well, I aint a-going to brag up my paint; I don't suppose you came here to hear me blow——"

"Oh, yes, I did," said Bartley. "That's what I want. Tell all there is to tell, and I can boil it down afterward. A man can't make a greater mistake with a reporter than to hold back anything out of modesty. It may be the very thing we want to know. What we want is the whole truth, and more; we've got so much modesty of our own that we can temper almost any statement."

Lapham looked as if he did not quite like this tone, and he resumed a little more quietly. "Oh, there isn't really very much more to say about the paint itself. But you can use it for almost anything where a paint is wanted, inside or out. It'll prevent decay, and it'll stop it, after it's begun, in tin or iron. You can paint the inside of a cistern or a bath-tub with it, and water wont hurt it; and you can paint a steam-boiler with it, and heat wont. You can cover a brick wall with it, or a railroad car, or the deck of a steam-boat, and you can't do a better thing for either."

"Never tried it on the human conscience, I suppose," suggested Bartley.

"No, sir," replied Lapham, gravely. "I guess you want to keep that as free from paint as you can, if you want much use of it. I never cared to try any of it on mine." Lapham suddenly lifted his bulk up out of his swivel-chair, and led the way out into the wareroom beyond the office partitions, where rows and ranks of casks, barrels, and kegs stretched dimly back to the rear of the building, and diffused an honest, clean, wholesome smell of oil and paint. They were labeled and branded as containing each so many pounds of Lapham's Mineral Paint, and each bore the mystic devices, *N. L. f. 1835—S. L. t. 1855.* "There!" said Lapham, kicking one of

novel, it was in the process of being filled to support the new, upscale residential neighborhood that bears its name.

3. Exaggerating or lying.

the largest casks with the toe of his boot, "that's about our biggest package; and here," he added, laying his hand affectionately on the head of a very small keg, as if it were the head of a child, which it resembled in size, "this is the smallest. We used to put the paint on the market dry, but now we grind every ounce of it in oil—very best quality of linseed oil—and warrant it. We find it gives more satisfaction. Now, come back to the office, and I'll show you our fancy brands."

It was very cool and pleasant in that dim wareroom, with the rafters showing overhead in a cloudy perspective, and darkening away into the perpetual twilight at the rear of the building; and Bartley had found an agreeable seat on the head of a half-barrel of the paint, which he was reluctant to leave. But he rose and followed the vigorous lead of Lapham back to the office, where the sun of a long summer afternoon was just beginning to glare in at the window. On shelves opposite Lapham's desk were tin cans of various sizes, arranged in tapering cylinders, and showing, in a pattern diminishing toward the top, the same label borne by the casks and barrels in the wareroom. Lapham merely waved his hand toward these; but when Bartley, after a comprehensive glance at them, gave his whole attention to a row of clean, smooth jars, where different tints of the paint showed through flawless glass, Lapham smiled and waited in pleased expectation.

"Hello!" said Bartley. "That's pretty!"

"Yes," assented Lapham, "it is rather nice. It's our latest thing, and we find it takes with customers first-rate. Look here!" he said, taking down one of the jars, and pointing to the first line of the label.

Bartley read, "THE PERSIS BRAND," and then he looked at Lapham and smiled.

"After *her*, of course," said Lapham. "Got it up and put the first of it on the market her last birthday. She was pleased."

"I should think she might have been," said Bartley, while he made a note of the appearance of the jars.

"I don't know about your mentioning it in your interview," said Lapham, dubiously.

"That's going into the interview, Mr. Lapham, if nothing else does. Got a wife myself, and I know just how you feel." It was in the dawn of Bartley's prosperity on the "Boston Events," before his troubles with Marcia had seriously begun.[4]

"Is that so?" said Lapham, recognizing with a smile another of the vast majority of married Americans; a few hate their wives, but nearly

4. Readers would have recognized Bartley and Marcia Hubbard, as well as this brief synopsis of their story, from Howells's earlier novel, *A Modern Instance* (1882).

all the rest think them supernal in intelligence and capability. "Well," he added, "we must see about that. Where'd you say you lived?"

"We don't live; we board. Mrs. Nash, 13 Canary Place."

"Well, we've all got to commence that way," suggested Lapham, consolingly.

"Yes; but we've about got to the end of our string. I expect to be under a roof of my own on Clover street before long. I suppose," said Bartley, returning to business, "that you didn't let the grass grow under your feet much after you found out what was in your paint-mine?"

"No, sir," answered Lapham, withdrawing his eyes from a long stare at Bartley, in which he had been seeing himself a young man again, in the first days of his married life. "I went right back to Lumberville and sold out everything, and put all I could rake and scrape together into paint. And Mis' Lapham was with me every time. No hang back about *her*. I tell you she was a *woman*!"

Bartley laughed. "That's the sort most of us marry."

"No, we don't," said Lapham. "Most of us marry silly little girls grown up to *look* like women."

"Well, I guess that's about so," assented Bartley, as if upon second thought.

"If it hadn't been for her," resumed Lapham, "the paint wouldn't have come to anything. I used to tell her it wa'n't the seventy-five per cent. of purr-ox-eyed of iron in the *ore* that made that paint go; it was the seventy-five per cent. of purr-ox-eyed of iron in *her*."

"Good!" cried Bartley. "I'll tell Marcia that."

"In less'n six months there wa'n't a board-fence, nor a bridge-girder, nor a dead wall, nor a barn, nor a face of rock in that whole region that didn't have 'Lapham's Mineral Paint—Specimen' on it in the three colors we begun by making."[5] Bartley had taken his seat on the window-sill, and Lapham, standing before him, now put up his huge foot close to Bartley's thigh; neither of them minded that.

"I've heard a good deal of talk about that S. T.—1860—X. man, and the stove-blacking man, and the kidney-cure man, because they advertised in that way; and I've read articles about it in the papers; but I don't see where the joke comes in, exactly. So long as the people that own the barns and fences don't object, I don't see what the public has got to do with it. And I never saw anything so very sacred about a big rock, along a river or in a pasture that it wouldn't do to put mineral paint on it in three colors. I wish some of the people that talk about the landscape, and *write* about it, had to bu'st one of them rocks *out* of the landscape with powder, or dig a hole to bury

5. Nineteenth-century farmers often leased large rocks or the walls of their barns to advertisers.

it in, as we used to have to do up on the farm; I guess they'd sing a little different tune about the profanation of scenery. There aint any man enjoys a sightly bit of nature—a smooth piece of interval, with half a dozen good-sized wine-glass elms in it—more than *I* do. But I aint a-going to stand up for every big ugly rock I come across, as if we were all a set of dumn Druids.[6] I say the landscape was made for man, and not man for the landscape."

"Yes," said Bartley, carelessly; "it was made for the stove-polish man and the kidney-cure man."

"It was made for any man that knows how to use it," Lapham returned, insensible to Bartley's irony. "Let 'em go and live with nature in the *winter*, up there along the Canada line, and I guess they'll get enough of her for one while. Well—where was I?"

"Decorating the landscape," said Bartley.

"Yes, sir; I started right there at Lumberville, and it give the place a start, too. You wont find it on the map now; and you wont find it in the gazetteer. I give a pretty good lump of money to build a town-hall, about five years back, and the first meeting they held in it they voted to change the name,—Lumberville *wa'n't* a name,—and it's Lapham now."

"Isn't it somewhere up in that region that they get the old Brandon red?" asked Bartley.

"We're about fifty miles from Brandon.[7] The Brandon's a good paint," said Lapham, conscientiously. "Like to show you round up at our place some odd time, if you get off."

"Thanks. I should like it first-rate. Works there?"

"Yes; Works there. Well, sir, just about the time I got started, the war broke out; and it knocked my paint higher than a kite. The thing dropped perfectly dead. I presume that if I'd had any sort of influence, I might have got it into government hands, for gun-carriages and army-wagons, and may be on board government vessels. But I hadn't, and we had to face the music. I was about broken-hearted, but m'wife she looked at it another way. '*I* guess it's a providence,' says she. 'Silas, I guess you've got a country that's worth fighting for. Any rate, you better go out and give it a chance.' Well, sir, I went. I knew she meant business. It might kill her to have me go, but it would kill her sure if I staid. She was one of that kind. I went. Her last words was, 'I'll look after the paint, Si.' We hadn't but just one little girl then,—boy'd died,—and Mis' Lapham's mother was livin' with us; and I knew if times *did* anyways come up again, m'wife'd know just what to do. So I went. I got through; and you can call me

6. The professional and priestly caste of Iron Age Celtic peoples in Europe; they were often associated with Stonehenge and with nature worship. "Dumn": a more polite version of *damn*.
7. A town in east-central Vermont.

Colonel, if you want to. Feel there!" Lapham took Bartley's thumb and forefinger and put them on a bunch in his leg, just above the knee. "Anything hard?"

"Ball?"

Lapham nodded. "Gettysburg. That's my thermometer. If it wa'n't for that, I shouldn't know enough to come in when it rains."

Bartley laughed at a joke which betrayed some evidences of wear. "And when you came back, you took hold of the paint and rushed it."

"I took hold of the paint and rushed it—all I could," said Lapham, with less satisfaction than he had hitherto shown in his autobiography. "But I found that I had got back to another world. The day of small things was past, and I don't suppose it will ever come again in this country. My wife was at me all the time to take a partner—somebody with capital; but I couldn't seem to bear the idea. That paint was like my own blood to me. To have anybody else concerned in it was like—well, I don't know what. I saw it was the thing to do; but I tried to fight it off, and I tried to joke it off. I used to say, 'Why didn't you take a partner yourself, Persis, while I was away?' And she'd say, 'Well, if you hadn't come back, I should, Si.' Always *did* like a joke about as well as any woman *I* ever saw. Well, I had to come to it. I took a partner." Lapham dropped the bold blue eyes with which he had been till now staring into Bartley's face, and the reporter knew that here was a place for asterisks in his interview, if interviews were faithful. "He had money enough," continued Lapham, with a suppressed sigh; "but he didn't know anything about paint. We hung on together for a year or two. And then we quit."

"And he had the experience," suggested Bartley, with companionable ease.

"I had some of the experience too," said Lapham, with a scowl; and Bartley divined, through the freemasonry of all who have sore places in their memories, that this was a point which he must not touch again.

"And since that, I suppose, you've played it alone."

"I've played it alone."

"You must ship some of this paint of yours to foreign countries, Colonel?" suggested Bartley, putting on a professional air.

"We ship it to all parts of the world. It goes to South America, lots of it. It goes to Australia, and it goes to India, and it goes to China, and it goes to the Cape of Good Hope. It'll stand any climate. Of course, we don't export these fancy brands much. They're for home use. But we're introducing them elsewhere. Here." Lapham pulled open a drawer, and showed Bartley a lot of labels in different languages—Spanish, French, German, and Italian. "We expect to do a good business in all those countries. We've got our agencies in

Cadiz now, and in Paris, and in Hamburg, and in Leghorn. It's a thing that's bound to make its way. Yes, sir. Wherever a man has got a ship, or a bridge, or a dock, or a house, or a car, or a fence, or a pig-pen, anywhere in God's universe, to paint, that's the paint for him, and he's bound to find it out sooner or later. You pass a ton of that paint dry through a blast-furnace, and you'll get a quarter of a ton of pig-iron. I believe in my paint. I believe it's a blessing to the world. When folks come in, and kind of smell round, and ask me what I mix it with, I always say, 'Well, in the first place, I mix it with *Faith*, and after that I grind it up with the best quality of boiled linseed oil that money will buy.'"

Lapham took out his watch and looked at it, and Bartley perceived that his audience was drawing to a close. "'F you ever want to run down and take a look at our Works, pass you over the road,"—he called it *rud*,—"and it sha'n't cost you a cent."

"Well, may be I shall, sometime," said Bartley. "Good afternoon, Colonel."

"Good afternoon. Or—hold on! My horse down there yet, William?" he called to the young man in the counting-room, who had taken his letter at the beginning of the interview. "Oh! All right!" he added, in response to something the young man said. "Can't I set you down somewhere, Mr. Hubbard? I've got my horse at the door, and I can drop you on my way home. I'm going to take Mis' Lapham to look at a house I'm driving piles for, down on the New Land."

"Don't care if I do," said Bartley.

Lapham put on a straw hat, gathered up some papers lying on his desk, pulled down its rolling cover, turned the key in it, and gave the papers to an extremely handsome young woman at one of the desks in the outer office. She was stylishly dressed, as Bartley saw, and her smooth, yellow hair was sculpturesquely waved over a low, white forehead. "Here," said Lapham, with the same prompt, gruff kindness that he had used in addressing the young man, "I want you should put these in shape, and give me a type-writer copy to-morrow."

"What an uncommonly pretty girl!" said Bartley, as they descended the rough stairway and found their way out to the street, past the dangling rope of a block and tackle wandering up into the cavernous darkness overhead.

"She does her work," said Lapham, shortly.

Bartley mounted to the left side of the open buggy standing at the curb-stone, and Lapham, gathering up the hitching-weight, slid it under the buggy-seat and mounted beside him.

"No chance to speed a horse here, of course," said Lapham, while the horse with a spirited gentleness picked her way, with a high, long action, over the pavement of the street. The streets were all narrow, and most of them crooked, in that quarter of the town; but at the end of one the spars of a vessel penciled themselves delicately against the cool blue of the afternoon sky. The air was full of a smell pleasantly compounded of oakum,[8] of leather, and of oil. It was not the busy season, and they met only two or three trucks heavily straggling toward the wharf with their long string teams; but the cobblestones of the pavement were worn with the dint of ponderous wheels, and discolored with iron-rust from them; here and there, in wandering streaks over its surface, was the gray stain of the salt water with which the street had been sprinkled.

After an interval of some minutes, which both men spent in looking round the dashboard from opposite sides to watch the stride of the horse, Bartley said, with a light sigh, "I had a colt once down in Maine that stepped just like that mare."

"Well!" said Lapham, sympathetically recognizing the bond that this fact created between them. "Well, now, I tell you what you do. You let me come for you 'most any afternoon, now, and take you out over the Milldam,[9] and speed this mare a little. I'd like to show you what this mare can do. Yes, I would."

"All right," answered Bartley; "I'll let you know my first day off."

"Good," cried Lapham.

"Kentucky?" queried Bartley.

"No, sir. I don't ride behind anything but Vermont; never did. Touch of Morgan,[1] of course; but you can't have much Morgan in a horse if you want speed. Hambletonian[2] mostly. Where'd you say you wanted to get out?"

"I guess you may put me down at the 'Events' office, just round the corner here. I've got to write up this interview while it's fresh."

"All right," said Lapham, impersonally assenting to Bartley's use of him as material.

He had not much to complain of in Bartley's treatment, unless it was the strain of extravagant compliment which it involved. But the flattery was mainly for the paint, whose virtues Lapham did not believe could be overstated, and himself and his history had been treated with as much respect as Bartley was capable of showing any one. He made a very picturesque thing of the discovery of the paint-mine. "Deep in the heart of the virgin forests of Vermont, far up toward the line of the Canadian snows, on a desolate mountain-side, where an autumnal storm had done its wild work, and the great trees, strewn hither and thither, bore witness to its violence, Nehemiah

8. Loose fibers tarred for use in caulking.
9. A long causeway extending from the western terminus of Beacon Street and linking Boston to its neighbors across the Back Bay (see maps on pp. 367–70).
1. Breed of horse valued for its combination of speed, strength, and endurance.
2. A breed of trotting horse famous for its speed.

Lapham discovered, just forty years ago, the mineral which the alchemy of his son's enterprise and energy has transmuted into solid ingots of the most precious of metals. The colossal fortune of Colonel Silas Lapham lay at the bottom of a hole which an uprooted tree had dug for him, and which for many years remained a paint-mine of no more appreciable value than a soap-mine."

Here Bartley had not been able to deny himself his grin; but he compensated for it by the high reverence with which he spoke of Colonel Lapham's record during the war of the rebellion, and of the motives which impelled him to turn aside from an enterprise in which his whole heart was engaged and take part in the struggle. "The Colonel bears imbedded in the muscle of his right leg a little memento of the period in the shape of a minie-ball, which he jocularly referred to as his thermometer, and which relieves him from the necessity of reading 'The Probabilities'[3] in his morning paper. This saves him just so much time; and for a man who, as he said, has not a moment of waste time on him anywhere, five minutes a day are something in the course of a year. Simple, clear, bold, and straightforward in mind and action, Colonel Silas Lapham, with a prompt comprehensiveness and a never-failing business sagacity, is, in the best sense of that much-abused term, one of nature's noblemen, to the last inch of his five eleven and a half. His life affords an example of single-minded application and unwavering perseverance which our young business men would do well to emulate. There is nothing showy or meretricious about the man. He believes in mineral paint, and he puts his heart and soul into it. He makes it a religion; though we would not imply that it *is* his religion. Colonel Lapham is a regular attendant at the Rev. Dr. Langworthy's church. He subscribes liberally to the Associated Charities, and no good object or worthy public enterprise fails to receive his support. He is not now actively in politics, and his paint is not partisan; but it is an open secret that he is, and always has been, a stanch Republican. Without violating the sanctities of private life, we cannot speak fully of various details which came out in the free and unembarrassed interview which Colonel Lapham accorded our representative. But we may say that the success of which he is justly proud he is also proud to attribute in great measure to the sympathy and energy of his wife—one of those women who, in whatever walk of life, seem born to honor the name of American Woman, and to redeem it from the national reproach of Daisy Millerism.[4] Of Colonel Lapham's family, we will simply add that it consists of two young lady daughters.

3. I.e., the weather forecast. "Minie-ball": a bullet for a muzzle-loading rifle, used extensively in the Civil War.
4. *Daisy Miller,* a popular but controversial novella by Henry James (1843–1916), tells the story of an innocent but indiscreet American young woman who is ostracized by the

"The subject of this very inadequate sketch is building a house on the water side of Beacon street, after designs by one of our leading architectural firms, which, when complete, will be one of the finest ornaments of that exclusive avenue. It will, we believe, be ready for the occupancy of the family sometime in the spring."

When Bartley had finished his article, which he did with a good deal of inward derision, he went home to Marcia, still smiling over the thought of Lapham, whose burly simplicity had peculiarly amused him.

"He regularly turned himself inside out to me," he said, as he sat describing his interview to Marcia.

"Then I know you could make something nice out of it," said his wife; "and that will please Mr. Witherby."

"Oh, yes, I've done pretty well; but I couldn't let myself loose on him the way I wanted to. Confound the limitations of decency, anyway! I should like to have told just what Colonel Lapham thought of landscape advertising in Colonel Lapham's own words. I'll tell you one thing, Marsh: he had a girl there at one of the desks that you wouldn't let *me* have within gunshot of *my* office. Pretty? It aint any name for it!" Marcia's eyes began to blaze, and Bartley broke out into a laugh, in which he arrested himself at sight of a formidable parcel in the corner of the room.

"Hello! What's that?"

"Why, *I* don't know what it is," replied Marcia, tremulously. "A man brought it just before you came in, and I didn't like to open it."

"Think it was some kind of infernal machine?" asked Bartley, getting down on his knees to examine the package. "*Mrs.* B. Hubbard, heigh?" He cut the heavy hemp string with his penknife. "We must look into this thing. I should like to know who's sending packages to Mrs. Hubbard in my absence." He unfolded the wrappings of paper, growing softer and finer inward, and presently pulled out a handsome square glass jar, through which a crimson mass showed richly. "The Persis Brand!" he yelled. "I knew it!"

"Oh, what is it, Bartley?" quavered Marcia. Then, courageously drawing a little nearer: "Is it some kind of jam?" she implored.

"Jam? No!" roared Bartley. "It's *paint!* It's mineral paint—Lapham's paint!"

"Paint?" echoed Marcia, as she stood over him while he stripped their wrappings from the jars which showed the dark blue, dark

expatriate colony in Rome because of her failure to conform to genteel codes of behavior. The story provoked widespread and in some cases scandalized discussion of the characteristics of the contemporary American girl and of American mores and manners. James's novella was not published until 1878, but Lapham earlier in this chapter says that the year is 1875. See p. 307 for Howells's defense of this and other perceived anachronisms in his novel.

green, light brown, dark brown, and black, with the dark crimson, forming the gamut of color of the Lapham paint. Don't *tell* me it's paint that *I* can use, Bartley!"

"Well, I shouldn't advise you to use much of it—just at present," said her husband. "But it's paint that you can use in moderation."

Marcia cast her arms round his neck and kissed him. "O Bartley, I think I'm the happiest girl in the world! I was just wondering what I should do. There are places in that Clover street house that need touching up so dreadfully. I shall be very careful. You needn't be afraid I shall overdo. But this just saves my life. Did you *buy* it, Bartley? You know we couldn't afford it, and you oughtn't to have done it! And what does the Persis Brand mean?"

"Buy it?" cried Bartley. "No! The old fool's sent it to you as a present. You'd better wait for the facts before you pitch into me for extravagance, Marcia. Persis is the name of his wife; and he named it after her because it's his finest brand. You'll see it in my interview. Put it on the market her last birthday for a surprise to her."

"What old fool?" faltered Marcia.

"Why, Lapham—the mineral paint man."

"Oh, what a good man!" sighed Marcia from the bottom of her soul. "Bartley! you *wont* make fun of him, as you do of some of those people? *Will* you?"

"Nothing that *he*'ll ever find out," said Bartley, getting up and brushing off the carpet-lint from his knees.

II.

After dropping Bartley Hubbard at the "Events" building, Lapham drove on down Washington street to Nankeen Square at the South End,[1] where he had lived ever since the mistaken movement of society in that direction ceased. He had not built, but had bought very cheap of a terrified gentleman of good extraction who discovered too late that the South End was not the thing, and who in the eagerness of his flight to the Back Bay threw in his carpets and shades for almost nothing. Mrs. Lapham was even better satisfied with their bargain than the Colonel himself, and they had lived in Nankeen Square for twelve years. They had seen the saplings planted in the pretty oval round which the houses were built flourish up into sturdy young trees, and their two little girls in the same period had grown into young ladies; the Colonel's tough frame had expanded into

1. Built on reclaimed marshland along Boston Neck on the southeastern shore of Back Bay beginning in 1849, the South End (not to be confused with South Boston, farther to the east) became a center of Irish immigrant settlement in the years after the Civil War. The fictional Nankeen Square appears to be modeled on Chester Square, one of a number of South End residential developments consisting of townhouses overlooking parkland situated in the center of the street.

the bulk which Bartley's interview indicated; and Mrs. Lapham, while keeping a more youthful outline, showed the sharp print of the crow's-foot at the corners of her motherly eyes, and certain slight creases in her wholesome cheeks. The fact that they lived in an unfashionable neighborhood was something that they had never been made to feel to their personal disadvantage, and they had hardly known it till the summer before this story opens, when Mrs. Lapham and her daughter Irene had met some other Bostonians far from Boston, who made it memorable. They were people whom chance had brought for the time under a singular obligation to the Lapham ladies, and they were gratefully recognizant of it. They had ventured—a mother and two daughters—as far as a rather wild little Canadian watering-place on the St. Lawrence, below Quebec, and had arrived some days before their son and brother was expected to join them. Two of their trunks had gone astray, and on the night of their arrival the mother was taken violently ill. Mrs. Lapham came to their help, with her skill as nurse, and with the abundance of her own and her daughter's wardrobe, and a profuse, single-hearted kindness. When a doctor could be got at, he said that but for Mrs. Lapham's timely care, the lady would hardly have lived. He was a very effusive little Frenchman, and fancied he was saying something very pleasant to everybody.

A certain intimacy inevitably followed, and when the son came he was even more grateful than the others. Mrs. Lapham could not quite understand why he should be as attentive to her as to Irene; but she compared him with other young men about the place, and thought him nicer than any of them. She had not the means of a wider comparison; for in Boston, with all her husband's prosperity, they had not had a social life. Their first years there were given to careful getting on Lapham's part, and careful saving on his wife's. Suddenly the money began to come so abundantly that she need not save; and then they did not know what to do with it. A certain amount could be spent on horses, and Lapham spent it; his wife spent on rich and rather ugly clothes and a luxury of household appointments. Lapham had not yet reached the picture-buying stage of the rich man's development, but they decorated their house with the costliest and most abominable frescoes; they went upon journeys, and lavished upon cars and hotels; they gave with both hands to their church and to all the charities it brought them acquainted with; but they did not know how to spend on society. Up to a certain period Mrs. Lapham had the ladies of her neighborhood in to tea, as her mother had done in the country in her younger days. Lapham's idea of hospitality was still to bring a heavy-buying customer home to potluck; neither of them imagined dinners.

Their two girls had gone to the public schools, where they had not got on as fast as some of the other girls; so that they were a year behind in graduating from the grammar-school, where Lapham thought that they had got education enough. His wife was of a different mind; she would have liked them to go to some private school for their finishing. But Irene did not care for study; she preferred housekeeping, and both the sisters were afraid of being snubbed by the other girls, who were of a different sort from the girls of the grammar-school; these were mostly from the parks and squares, like themselves. It ended in their going part of a year. But the elder had an odd taste of her own for reading, and she took some private lessons, and read books out of the circulating library; the whole family were amazed at the number she read, and rather proud of it.

They were not girls who embroidered or abandoned themselves to needle-work. Irene spent her abundant leisure in shopping for herself and her mother, of whom both daughters made a kind of idol, buying her caps and laces out of their pin-money, and getting her dresses far beyond her capacity to wear. Irene dressed herself very stylishly, and spent hours on her toilet every day. Her sister had a simpler taste, and, if she had done altogether as she liked, might even have slighted dress. They all three took long naps every day, and sat hours together minutely discussing what they saw out of the window. In her self-guided search for self-improvement, the elder sister went to many church lectures on a vast variety of secular subjects, and usually came home with a comic account of them, and that made more matter of talk for the whole family. She could make fun of nearly everything; Irene complained that she scared away the young men whom they got acquainted with at the dancing-school sociables. They were, perhaps, not the wisest young men.

The girls had learned to dance at Papanti's;[2] but they had not belonged to the private classes. They did not even know of them, and a great gulf divided them from those who did. Their father did not like company, except such as came informally in their way; and their mother had remained too rustic to know how to attract it in the sophisticated city fashion. None of them had grasped the idea of European travel; but they had gone about to mountain and seaside resorts, the mother and the two girls, where they witnessed the spectacle which such resorts present throughout New England, of multitudes of girls, lovely, accomplished, exquisitely dressed, humbly glad of the presence of any sort of young man; but the Laphams had no skill or courage to make themselves noticed, far less courted by the solitary invalid, or clergyman, or artist. They lurked helplessly

2. Boston's premiere dance academy founded in 1837 by Lorenzo Papanti (1799–1873), an expatriate Italian.

about in the hotel parlors, looking on and not knowing how to put themselves forward. Perhaps they did not care a great deal to do so. They had not a conceit of themselves, but a sort of content in their own ways that one may notice in certain families. The very strength of their mutual affection was a barrier to worldly knowledge; they dressed for one another; they equipped their house for their own satisfaction; they lived richly to themselves, not because they were selfish, but because they did not know how to do otherwise. The elder daughter did not care for society, apparently. The younger, who was but three years younger, was not yet quite old enough to be ambitious of it. With all her wonderful beauty, she had an innocence almost vegetable. When her beauty, which in its immaturity was crude and harsh, suddenly ripened, she bloomed and glowed with the unconsciousness of a flower; she not merely did not feel herself admired, but hardly knew herself discovered. If she dressed well, perhaps too well, it was because she had the instinct of dress; but till she met this young man who was so nice to her at Baie St. Joan,[3] she had scarcely lived a detached, individual life, so wholly had she depended on her mother and her sister for her opinions, almost her sensations. She took account of everything he did and said, pondering it, and trying to make out exactly what he meant, to the inflection of a syllable, the slightest movement or gesture. In this way she began for the first time to form ideas which she had not derived from her family, and they were none the less her own because they were often mistaken.

One of the things which he partly said, partly looked, and which was altogether casual, she repeated to her mother, and they canvassed it, as they did all things relating to these new acquaintances, and made it part of a novel point of view which they were acquiring. It was something that Mrs. Lapham especially submitted to her husband when they got home; she asked him if it were true, and if it made any difference.

"It makes a difference in the price of property," replied the Colonel, promptly. "But as long as we don't want to sell, it don't matter."

"Why, Silas Lapham," said his wife, "do you mean to tell me that this house is worth less than we gave for it?"

"It's worth a good deal less. You see, they *have* got in—and pretty thick, too—it's no use denying it. And when they get in, they send down the price of property. Of course, there aint any sense in it; *I* think it's all dumn foolishness. It's cruel, and folks ought to be ashamed. But there it is. You tell folks that the Saviour himself was one, and the twelve apostles, and all the prophets,—I don't know but

3. In the book version of the novel, Howells changed the fictional Baie St. Joan to Baie St. Paul, an actual resort town on the St. Lawrence River in Quebec.

what Adam was—guess he *was,*—and it don't make a bit of difference. They send down the price of real estate. Prices begin to shade when the first one gets in."

Mrs. Lapham thought the facts over a few moments. "Well, what do we care, so long as we're comfortable in our home? And they're just as nice and as good neighbors as can be."

"Oh, it's all right as far as I'm concerned," said Lapham.[4] "Who did you say those people were that stirred you up about it?"

Mrs. Lapham mentioned their name. Lapham nodded his head. "Do you know them? What business is he in?"

"I guess he aint in anything," said Lapham.

"They were very nice," said Mrs. Lapham, impartially.

"Well, they'd ought to be," returned the Colonel. "Never done anything else."

"They didn't seem stuck up," urged his wife.

"They no need to—with you. I could buy him and sell him, twice over."

This answer satisfied Mrs. Lapham rather with the fact than with her husband. "Well, I guess I wouldn't brag, Silas," she said.

In the winter the ladies of this family, who returned to town very late, came to call on Mrs. Lapham. They were again very polite. But the mother let drop, in apology for their calling almost at nightfall, that the coachman had not known the way exactly.

"Nearly all our friends are on the New Land or on the Hill."[5]

There was a barb in this that rankled after the ladies had gone; and on comparing notes with her daughter, Mrs. Lapham found that a barb had been left to rankle in her mind also.

"They said they had never been in this part of the town before."

Upon a strict search of her memory, Irene could not report that the fact had been stated with anything like insinuation, but it was that which gave it a more penetrating effect.

"Oh, well, of course," said Lapham, to whom these facts were referred. "Those sort of people haven't got much business up our way, and they don't come. It's a fair thing all round. We don't trouble the Hill or the New Land much."

"We know where they are," suggested his wife, thoughtfully.

"Yes," assented the Colonel. "*I* know where they are. I've got a lot of land over on the Back Bay."

"You have?" eagerly demanded his wife.

4. Howells removed this passage (beginning with "One of the things . . .") from the book edition of the novel, along with a shorter passage on the same topic later in the chapter. See Howells's correspondence with Cyrus L. Sulzberger, founding editor of *The American Hebrew* (pp. 305–7), along with the variant versions of the text (pp. 303–5).

5. I.e., the upscale Back Bay neighborhood of Boston then being reclaimed from the marshes and Beacon Hill, the other, older prestigious section of the city, adjacent to the Back Bay north of Boston Common and the Public Garden.

"Want me to build on it?" he asked in reply, with a quizzical smile. "I guess we can get along here for a while."

This was at night. In the morning Mrs. Lapham said:

"I suppose we ought to do the best we can for the children, in every way."

"I supposed we always had," replied her husband.

"Yes, we have, according to our light."

"Have you got some new light?"

"I don't know as it's light. But if the girls are going to keep on living in Boston and marry here, I presume we ought to try to get them into society, some way; or ought to do something."

"Well, who's ever done more for their children than we have?" demanded Lapham, with a pang at the thought that he could possibly have been outdone. "Don't they have everything they want? Don't they dress just as you say? Don't you go everywhere with 'em? Is there ever anything going on that's worth while that they don't see it or hear it? *I* don't know what you mean. Why don't you get them into society? There's money enough!"

"There's got to be something besides money, I guess," said Mrs. Lapham, with a hopeless sigh. "I presume we didn't go to work just the right way about their schooling. We ought to have got them into some school where they'd have got acquainted with city girls—girls who could help them along. Nearly everybody at Miss Smillie's was from somewhere else."

"Well, it's pretty late to think about that now," grumbled Lapham.

"And we've always gone our own way, and not looked out for the future. We ought to have gone out more, and had people come to the house. Nobody comes."

"Well, is that my fault? I guess nobody ever makes people welcomer."

"We ought to have invited company more."

"Why don't you do it now? If it's for the girls, I don't care if you have the house full all the while."

Mrs. Lapham was forced to a confession full of humiliation. "I don't know who to ask."

"Well, you can't expect me to tell you."

"No; we're both country people, and we've kept our country ways, and we don't, either of us, know what to do. You've had to work so hard, and your luck was so long coming, and then it came with such a rush, that we haven't had any chance to learn what to do with it. It's just the same with Irene's looks; I didn't expect she was ever going to have any, she *was* such a plain child, and, all at once, she's blazed out this way. As long as it was Pen that didn't seem to care for society, I didn't give much mind to it. But I can see it's going to be different with Irene. I don't believe but what we're in the wrong neighborhood."

"Well," said the Colonel, "there aint a prettier lot on the Back Bay than mine. It's on the water side of Beacon,[6] and it's twenty-eight feet wide and a hundred and fifty deep. Let's build on it."

Mrs. Lapham was silent awhile. "No," she said finally; "we've always got along well enough here, and I guess we better stay."

At breakfast she said, casually: "Girls, how would you like to have your father build on the New Land?"

The girls said they did not know. It was more convenient to the horse-cars where they were.

Mrs. Lapham stole a look of relief at her husband, and nothing more was said of the matter.

The mother of the family who had called upon Mrs. Lapham brought her husband's cards, and when Mrs. Lapham returned the visit she was in some trouble about the proper form of acknowledging the civility. The Colonel had no card but a business card, which advertised the principal depot and the several agencies of the mineral paint; and Mrs. Lapham doubted, till she wished to goodness that she had never seen nor heard of those people, whether to ignore her husband in the transaction altogether, or to write his name on her own card. She decided finally upon this measure, and she had the relief of not finding the family at home. As far as she could judge, Irene seemed to suffer a little disappointment from the fact.

For several months there was no communication between the families. Then there came to Nankeen Square a lithographed circular from the people on the Hill, signed in ink by the mother, and affording Mrs. Lapham an opportunity to subscribe for a charity of undeniable merit and acceptability. She submitted it to her husband, who promptly drew a check for five hundred dollars.

She tore it in two. "I will take a check for a hundred, Silas," she said.

"Why?" he asked, looking up guiltily at her.

"Because a hundred is enough; and I don't want to show off before them."

"Oh, I thought may be you did. Well, Pert," he added, having satisfied human nature by the preliminary thrust, "I guess you're about right. When do you want I should begin to build on Beacon street?"

6. Lapham's Back Bay lot "on the water side of Beacon" is closely modeled on a house purchased by Howells at 302 Beacon Street (which he describes using the identical phrase in a letter to Henry James; see p. 291) and extensively renovated under his direction during the writing of the novel. At the time of the novel's events in the mid-1870s, Beacon Street had been extended just a few blocks west from the original shoreline of the Back Bay at the Boston Common, so Lapham's lot was on newly reclaimed land very near where Beacon Street became the Mill Dam and crossed the unfilled part of the bay.

He handed her the new check, where she stood over him, and then leaned back in his chair and looked up at her.

"I don't want you should begin at all. What do you mean, Silas?" She rested against the side of his desk.

"Well, I don't know as I mean anything. But shouldn't you like to build? Everybody builds, at least once in a life-time."

"Where is your lot? In the Diphtheria District?"[7]

Up to a certain point in their prosperity Mrs. Lapham had kept strict account of all her husband's affairs; but as they expanded, and ceased to be of the retail nature with which women successfully grapple, the intimate knowledge of them made her nervous. There was a period in which she felt that they were being ruined, but the crash had not come; and, since his great success, she had abandoned herself to a blind confidence in her husband's judgment, which she had hitherto felt needed her revision. He came and went, day by day, unquestioned. He bought and sold and got gain. She knew that he would tell her if ever things went wrong, and he knew that she would ask him whenever she was anxious.

"No, it aint in the Diphtheria District," said Lapham, rather enjoying the insinuation. "I looked after that when I was trading; and I guess there's more diphtheria in the name than anything else, anyway. I got that lot for *you,* Pert; I thought you'd want to build on the Back Bay some day."

"Pshaw!" said Mrs. Lapham, deeply pleased inwardly, but not going to show it, as she would have said. "I guess you want to build there yourself." She insensibly got a little nearer to her husband. They liked to talk to each other in that blunt way; it is the New England way of expressing perfect confidence and tenderness.

"Well, I guess I do," said Lapham, not insisting upon the unselfish view of the matter. "I always did like the water side of Beacon. There aint a sightlier place in the world for a house. And some day there's bound to be a drive-way all along behind them houses, between them and the water, and then a lot there is going to be worth the gold that will cover it—*coin.* I've had offers for that lot, Pert, twice over what I give for it. Yes, I *have.* Don't you want to ride over there some afternoon with me and see it?"

"I'm satisfied where we be, Si," said Mrs. Lapham, recurring to the parlance of her youth in her pathos at her husband's kindness. She sighed anxiously, for she felt the trouble a woman knows in view of any great change. They had often talked of altering over the house in which they lived, but they had never come to it; and they had often

7. Because the Back Bay was built on and adjacent to tidal marshes, some thought the site unhealthy. In the book version of the novel, Howells softened the effect by removing Persis's reference to "the Diphtheria District" and replacing it with the milder assertion, "They say it's unhealthy over there."

talked of building, but it had always been a house in the country that they had thought of. "I wish you had sold that lot."

"I haint," said the Colonel, briefly.

"I don't know as I feel much like changing our way of living."

"Guess we could live there pretty much as we live here. There's all kinds of people on Beacon street; you mustn't think they're all big-bugs. I know one party that lives in a house he built to sell, and his wife don't keep any girl. You can have just as much style there as you want, or just as little. I guess we live as well as most of 'em now, and set as good a table. And if you come to style, I don't know as anybody has got more of a right to put it on than what we have."

"Well, I don't want to build on Beacon street, Si," said Mrs. Lapham, gently.

"Just as you please, Persis. I aint in any hurry to leave."

Mrs. Lapham stood flapping the check which she held in her right hand against the edge of her left. "A Mr. Liliengarten has bought the Gordon house across the square," she said, thoughtfully.

"Well, I'm agreeable. I suppose he's got the money to pay for it."

"Oh, yes, they've all got money," sighed Mrs. Lapham.[8] "What are you going to do this afternoon?"

"I'm going to take a turn on the Brighton road," said the Colonel.

"I don't believe but what I should like to go along," said his wife.

"All right. You haint ever rode behind that mare yet, Pert, and I want you should see me let her out once. They say the snow's all packed down already, and the going is A 1."

At four o'clock in the afternoon, with a cold, red winter sunset before them, the Colonel and his wife were driving slowly down Beacon street in the light, high-seated cutter,[9] where, as he said, they were a pretty tight fit. He was holding the mare in till the time came to speed her, and the mare was springily jolting over the snow, looking intelligently from side to side, and cocking this ear and that, while from her nostrils, her head tossing easily, she blew quick, irregular whiffs of steam.

"Gay, aint she?" proudly suggested the Colonel.

"She *is* gay," assented his wife.

They met swiftly dashing sleighs, and let them pass on either hand, down the beautiful avenue narrowing with an admirably even skyline in the perspective. They were not in a hurry. The mare jounced easily along, and they talked of the different houses on either side of the way. They had a crude taste in architecture, and they admired the worst. There were women's faces at many of the handsome windows, and once in a while a young man on the

8. This is the second passage concerning Jews and property values excised by Howells before the serial version of the novel was republished in book form. See p. 23, n. 4.
9. A small, sporty, horse-drawn sleigh.

pavement caught his hat suddenly from his head, and bowed in response to some salutation from within.

"I don't think our girls would look very bad behind one of those big panes," said the Colonel.

"No," said his wife, dreamily.

"Where's the *young* man? Did he come with them?"

"No; he was to spend the winter with a friend of his that has a ranch in Texas. I guess he's got to do something."

"Yes; gentlemaning as a profession has got to play out in a generation or two."

Neither of them spoke of the lot, though Lapham knew perfectly well what his wife had come with him for, and she was aware that he knew it. The time came when he brought the mare down to a walk, and then slowed up almost to a stop, while they both turned their heads to the right and looked at the vacant lot, through which showed the frozen stretch of the Back Bay, a section of the Long Bridge, and the roofs and smoke-stacks of Charlestown.[1]

"Yes, it's sightly," said Mrs. Lapham, lifting her hand from the reins, on which she had unconsciously laid it.

Lapham said nothing, but he let the mare out a little.

The sleighs and cutters were thickening round them. On the Milldam it became difficult to restrict the mare to the long, slow trot into which he let her break. The beautiful landscape widened to right and left of them, with the sunset redder and redder, over the low, irregular hills before them. They crossed the Milldam into Longwood,[2] and here, from the crest of the first upland, stretched two endless lines, in which thousands of cutters went and came. Some of the drivers were already speeding their horses, and these shot to and fro on inner lines, between the slowly moving vehicles on either side of the road. Here and there a burly mounted policeman, bulging over the pommel of his McClellan saddle,[3] jolted by, silently gesturing and directing the course, and keeping it all under the eye of the law. It was what Bartley Hubbard called "a carnival of fashion and gayety on the Brighton road," in his account of it. But most of the people in those elegant sleighs and cutters had so little the air of the great world that one knowing it at all must have wondered where they and their money came from; and the gayety of the

1. Located across the Charles River to the north of Boston, the town would have been visible downriver from Lapham's building lot, past the Long Bridge, which crossed the Charles River from Beacon Hill to Cambridge.
2. Traveling west, the Laphams pass from the end of Beacon Street onto the Mill Dam, crossing the Back Bay into the Longwood section of Brookline, Boston's nearest suburb to the west and from there intersecting the Brighton Road leading farther northwestward into the Allston/Brighton district, newly annexed to the city in 1873.
3. A saddle designed by Civil War General George B. McClellan (1826–1885), who led the Union Army during 1861 and 1862. "Pommel": the raised front of a saddle.

men, at least, was expressed, like that of Colonel Lapham, in a grim, almost fierce, alertness; the women wore an air of courageous apprehension. At a certain point the Colonel said, "I'm going to let her out, Pert," and he lifted and then dropped the reins lightly on the mare's back.

She understood the signal, and, as an admirer said, "she laid down to her work." Nothing in the immutable iron of Lapham's face betrayed his sense of triumph, as the mare left everything behind her on the road. Mrs. Lapham, if she felt fear, was too busy holding her flying wraps about her, and shielding her face from the scud of ice flung from the mare's heels, to betray it; except for the rush of her feet, the mare was as silent as the people behind her; the muscles of her back and thighs worked more and more swiftly, like some mechanism responding to an alien force, and she shot to the end of the course, grazing a hundred encountered and rival sledges in her passage, but unmolested by the policemen, who probably saw that the mare and the Colonel knew what they were about, and, at any rate, were not the sort of men to interfere with trotting like that. At the end of the heat Lapham drew her in, and turned off on a side street into Brookline.

"Tell you what, Pert," he said, as if they had been quietly jogging along, with time for uninterrupted thought since he last spoke, "I've about made up my mind to build on that lot."

"All right, Silas," said Mrs. Lapham; "I suppose you know what you're about. Don't build on it for me, that's all."

When she stood in the hall at home, taking off her things, she said to the girls, who were helping her, "Some day your father will get killed with that mare."

"Did he speed her?" asked Penelope, the elder. She was named after her grandmother, who had in her turn inherited from another ancestress the name of the Homeric matron[4] whose peculiar merits won her a place even among the Puritan Faiths, Hopes, Temperances, and Prudences. Penelope was the girl whose odd, serious face had struck Bartley Hubbard in the photograph of the family group Lapham showed him on the day of the interview. Her large eyes, like her hair, were brown; they had the peculiar look of nearsighted eyes which is called mooning; her complexion was of a dark pallor.

Her mother did not reply to a question which might be considered already answered. "He says he's going to build on that lot of his," she next remarked, unwinding the long veil which she had tied round her neck to hold her bonnet on. She put her hat and cloak on

4. I.e., the wife of Odysseus in Homer's *Odyssey,* who ingeniously resisted her many suitors while faithfully waiting twenty years for her husband's return from the Trojan War.

the hall table, to be carried upstairs later, and they all went in to tea: creamed oysters, birds, hot biscuit, two kinds of cake, and dishes of stewed and canned fruit and honey. The women dined alone at one, and the Colonel at the same hour down-town. But he liked a good hot meal when he got home in the evening. The house flared with gas, and the Colonel, before he sat down, went about shutting the registers, through which a welding heat came voluming up from the furnace.

"I'll be the death of that nigger[5] *yet,*" he said, "if he don't stop making on such a fire. The only way to get any comfort out of your furnace is to take care of it yourself."

"Well," answered his wife from behind the tea-pot, as he sat down at table with this threat, "there's nothing to prevent you, Si. And you can shovel the snow, too, if you want to—till you get over to Beacon street, anyway."

"I guess I can keep my own sidewalk on Beacon street clean, if I take the notion."

"I should like to see you at it," retorted his wife.

"Well, you keep a sharp lookout, and may be you will."

Their taunts were really expressions of affectionate pride in each other. They liked to have it, give and take, that way, as they would have said, right along.

"A man can be a man on Beacon street as well as anywhere, I guess."

"Well, I'll do the wash, as I used to in Lumberville," said Mrs. Lapham. "I presume you'll let me have set tubs, Si. You know I aint so young, any more."[6] She passed Irene a cup of Oolong tea,—none of them had a sufficiently cultivated palate for Souchong,[7]—and the girl handed it to her father.

"Papa," she asked, "you don't really mean that you are going to build over there?"

"Don't I? You wait and see," said the Colonel, stirring his tea.

"I don't believe you do," pursued the girl.

"Is that so? I presume you'd hate to have me. Your mother does." He said *doos,* of course.

Penelope took the word. "I go in for it. I don't see any use in not enjoying money, if you've got it *to* enjoy. That's what it's for, I suppose; though you mightn't always think so." She had a slow, quaint way of talking, that seemed a pleasant personal modification of some

5. In the book version of the novel, Howells changed Lapham's "nigger" to the marginally less offensive (for the time) *darkey.* Both words highlight Lapham's vulgarity.
6. Persis is requesting permanently installed laundry equipment to replace older, more cumbersome, portable washtubs and washboards.
7. Lapsang Souchong and Oolong are both varieties of tea from China.

ancestral Yankee drawl, and her voice was low and cozy, and so far from being nasal that it was a little hoarse.

"I guess the ayes has it, Pen," said her father. "How would it do to let Irene and your mother stick in the old place here, and us go into the new house?" At times the Colonel's grammar failed him.

The matter dropped, and the Laphams lived on as before, with joking recurrences to the house on the water side of Beacon. The Colonel seemed less in earnest than any of them about it; but that was his way, his girls said; you never could tell when he really meant a thing.

[SECOND INSTALLMENT—DECEMBER 1884]

III.

Toward the end of the winter there came a newspaper addressed to Miss Irene Lapham; it proved to be a Texas newspaper, with a complimentary account of the ranch of the Hon. Loring G. Stanton, which the representative of the journal had visited.

"It must be his friend," said Mrs. Lapham, to whom her daughter brought the paper; "the one he's staying with."

The girl did not say anything, but she carried the paper to her room, where she scanned every line of it for another name. She did not find it, but she cut the notice out and stuck it into the side of her mirror, where she could read it every morning when she brushed her hair, and the last thing at night when she looked at herself in the glass just before turning off the gas. Her sister often read it aloud, standing behind her and rendering it with elocutionary effects.

"The first time I ever heard of a love-letter in the form of a puff to a cattle-ranch. But perhaps that's the style on the Hill."

Mrs. Lapham told her husband of the arrival of the paper, treating the fact with an importance that he refused to see in it.

"How do you know the fellow sent it, anyway?" he demanded.

"Oh, I know he did."

"I don't see why he couldn't write to 'Rene, if he really meant anything."

"Well, I guess that wouldn't be their way," said Mrs. Lapham; she did not at all know what their way would be.

When the spring opened Colonel Lapham showed that he had been in earnest about building on the New Land. His idea of a house was a brown-stone front, four stories high, and a French roof with an air-chamber above.[1] Inside, there was to be a reception-room on the street and a dining-room back. The parlors were to be on the

1. I.e., a Mansard roof; a four-sided, double-pitched roof, the lower pitch being almost vertical and pierced by dormer windows to create an extra story of living space under the roof.

second floor, and finished in black walnut or parti-colored paint. The chambers were to be on the three floors above, front and rear, with side rooms over the front door. Black walnut was to be used everywhere except in the attic, which was to be painted and grained to look like black walnut. The whole was to be very high-studded, and there were to be handsome cornices and elaborate center-pieces throughout,[2] except, again, in the attic.

These ideas he had formed from the inspection of many new buildings which he had seen going up, and which he had a passion for looking into. He was confirmed in his ideas by a master-builder who had put up a great many houses on the Back Bay as a speculation, and who told him that if he wanted to have a house in the style, that was the way to have it.

The beginnings of the process by which Lapham escaped from the master-builder and ended in the hands of an architect are so obscure that it would be almost impossible to trace them. But it all happened, and Lapham promptly developed his ideas of black-walnut finish, high-studding, and cornices. The architect was able to conceal the shudder which they must have sent through him. He was skillful, as nearly all architects are, in playing upon that simple instrument Man. He began to touch Colonel Lapham's stops.

"Oh, certainly, have the parlors high-studded. But you've seen some of those pretty, old-fashioned country-houses, haven't you, where the entrance-story is very low-studded?"

"Yes," Lapham assented.

"Well, don't you think something of that kind would have a very nice effect? Have the entrance-story low-studded, and your parlors on the next floor as high as you please. Put your little reception-room here beside the door, and get the whole width of your house frontage for a square hall, and an easy low-tread staircase running up three sides of it. I'm sure Mrs. Lapham would find it much pleasanter." The architect caught toward him a scrap of paper lying on the table at which they were sitting and sketched his idea. "Then have your dining-room behind the hall, looking on the water."

He glanced at Mrs. Lapham, who said, "Of course," and the architect went on:

"That gets you rid of one of those long, straight, ugly staircases,"—until that moment Lapham had thought a long, straight staircase the chief ornament of a house,—"and gives you an effect of amplitude and space."

"That's so!" said Mrs. Lapham. Her husband merely made a noise in his throat.

2. Architectural details indicating Lapham is sparing no expense in the building of his house. "High-studded": meaning the ceilings would be very high. "Cornices": decorative moldings running along the top edges of the walls.

"Then, were you thinking of having your parlors together, connected by folding doors?" asked the architect deferentially.

"Yes, of course," said Lapham. "They're always so, aint they?"

"Well, nearly," said the architect. "I was wondering how would it do to make one large square room at the front, taking the whole breadth of the house, and, with this hall-space between, have a music-room back for the young ladies?"

Lapham looked helplessly at his wife, whose quicker apprehension had followed the architect's pencil with instant sympathy. "First-rate!" she cried.

The Colonel gave way. "I guess that would do. It'll be kind of odd, wont it?"

"Well, I don't know," said the architect. "Not so odd, I hope, as the other thing will be a few years from now." He went on to plan the rest of the house, and he showed himself such a master in regard to all the practical details that Mrs. Lapham began to feel a motherly affection for the young man, and her husband could not deny in his heart that the fellow seemed to understand his business. He stopped walking about the room, as he had begun to do when the architect and Mrs. Lapham entered into the particulars of closets, drainage, kitchen arrangements, and all that, and came back to the table. "I presume," he said, "you'll have the drawing-room finished in black walnut?"

"Well, yes," replied the architect, "if you like. But some less expensive wood can be made just as effective with paint. Of course you can paint black walnut, too."

"Paint it?" gasped the Colonel.

"Yes," said the architect quietly. "White, or a little off white."

Lapham dropped the plan he had picked up from the table. His wife made a little move toward him of consolation or support.

"Of course," resumed the architect, "I know there has been a great craze for black walnut. But it's an ugly wood; and for a drawing-room there is really nothing like white paint. We should want to introduce a little gold here and there. Perhaps we might run a painted frieze[3] round under the cornice—garlands of roses on a gold ground; it would tell wonderfully in a white room."

The Colonel returned less courageously to the charge. "I presume you'll want Eastlake[4] mantel-shelves and tiles?" He meant this for a sarcastic thrust at a prevailing foible of the profession.

3. A horizontal decorative band.

4. The Eastlake movement in home design, started by the English designer Charles Locke Eastlake (1836–1906) and popular in the post–Civil War United States, aimed to simplify overelaborate styles of Victorian era ornamentation by introducing less ornate geometric designs, delicate spindles, and low-relief carvings. Eastlake's *Hints on Household Taste* (1868) had been published in its first American edition in 1872, in Boston.

"Well, no," gently answered the architect. "I was thinking perhaps a white marble chimney-piece, treated in the refined Empire style,[5] would be the thing for that room."

"White marble!" exclaimed the Colonel. "I thought that had gone out long ago."

"Really beautiful things can't go out. They may disappear for a little while, but they must come back. It's only the ugly things that stay out after they've had their day."

Lapham could only venture very modestly, "Hard-wood floors?"

"In the music-room, of course," consented the architect.

"And in the drawing-room?"

"Carpet. Some sort of moquette,[6] I should say. But I should prefer to consult Mrs. Lapham's taste in that matter."

"And in the other rooms?"

"Oh, carpets, of course."

"And what about the stairs?"

"Carpet. And I should have the rail and banisters white—banisters turned or twisted."

The Colonel said under his breath, "Well, I'm dumned!" but he gave no utterance to his astonishment in the architect's presence. When he went at last,—the session did not end till eleven o'clock,—Lapham said, "Well, Pert, I guess that fellow's fifty years behind, or ten years ahead. I wonder what the Ongpeer style is?"

"I don't know. I hated to ask. But he seemed to understand what he was talking about. I declare, he knows what a woman wants in a house better than she does herself."

"And a man's simply nowhere in comparison," said Lapham. But he respected a fellow who could beat him at every point, and have a reason ready, as this architect had; and when he recovered from the daze into which the complete upheaval of all his preconceived notions had left him, he was in a fit state to swear by the architect. It seemed to him that he had discovered the fellow (as he always called him) and owned him now, and the fellow did nothing to disturb this impression. He entered into that brief but intense intimacy with the Laphams which the sympathetic architect holds with his clients. He was privy to all their differences of opinion and all their disputes about the house. He knew just where to insist upon his own ideas, and where to yield. He was really building several other houses, but he gave the Laphams the impression that he was doing none but theirs.

The work was not begun till the frost was thoroughly out of the ground, which that year was not before the end of April. Even then it did not proceed very rapidly. Lapham said they might as well take

5. A Neoclassical style identified with the reign of the French emperor Napoleon and characterized by elaborate but delicate ornamentation.
6. A thick, woven, velvety fabric often used for carpeting.

their time to it; if they got the walls up and the thing closed in before the snow flew, they could be working at it all winter. It was found necessary to dig for the kitchen; at that point the original salt marsh lay near the surface, and before they began to put in the piles for the foundation they had to pump. The neighborhood smelt like the hold of a ship after a three years' voyage. People who had cast their fortunes with the New Land went by professing not to notice it; people who still "hung on to the Hill" put their handkerchiefs to their noses, and told each other the old terrible stories of the material used in filling up the Back Bay.

Nothing gave Lapham so much satisfaction in the whole construction of his house as the pile-driving. When this began, early in the summer, he took Mrs. Lapham every day in his buggy and drove round to look at it; stopping the mare in front of the lot, and watching the operation with even keener interest than the little loafing Irish boys who superintended it in force. It pleased him to hear the portable engine chuckle out a hundred thin whiffs of steam, in carrying the big iron weight to the top of the framework above the pile, then seem to hesitate, and cough once or twice in pressing the weight against the detaching apparatus. There was a moment in which the weight had the effect of poising before it fell; then it dropped with a mighty whack on the iron-bound head of the pile and drove it a foot into the earth.

"By gracious!" he would say, "there aint anything like that in *this* world for *business*, Persis!"

Mrs. Lapham suffered him to enjoy the sight twenty or thirty times before she said, "Well, now drive on, Si."

By the time the foundation was in and the brick walls had begun to go up, there were so few people left in the neighborhood that she might indulge with impunity her husband's passion for having her clamber over the floor-timbers and the skeleton staircases with him. Many of the householders had boarded up their front doors before the buds had begun to swell and the assessor to appear in early May; others had followed soon; and Mrs. Lapham was as safe from remark as if she had been in the depth of the country. Ordinarily she and her girls left town early in July, going to one of the hotels at Nantasket,[7] where it was convenient for the Colonel to get to and from his business by the boat. But this summer they were all lingering a few weeks later, under the novel fascination of the new house, as they called it, as if there were no other in the world.

Lapham drove there with his wife after he had set Bartley Hubbard down at the "Events" office, but on this day something

7. A resort area in Hull, Massachusetts, situated on a peninsula on the south shore of Massachusetts Bay and easily accessible by boat from Boston.

happened that interfered with the solid pleasure they usually took in going over the house. As the Colonel turned from casting anchor at the mare's head with the hitching-weight, after helping his wife to alight, he encountered a man to whom he could not help speaking, though the man seemed to share his hesitation if not his reluctance at the necessity. He was a tallish, thin man, with a dust-colored face, and a dead, clerical air, which somehow suggested at once feebleness and tenacity.

Mrs. Lapham held out her hand to him.

"Why, Mr. Rogers!" she exclaimed, and then, turning toward her husband, seemed to refer the two men to each other. They shook hands, but Lapham did not speak. "I didn't know you were in Boston," pursued Mrs. Lapham. "Is Mrs. Rogers with you?"

"No," said Mr. Rogers, with a voice which had the flat, succinct sound of two pieces of wood clapped together. "Mrs. Rogers is still in Chicago."

A little silence followed, and then Mrs. Lapham said:

"I presume you are quite settled out there."

"No; we have left Chicago. Mrs. Rogers has merely remained to finish up a little packing."

"Oh, indeed! Are you coming back to Boston?"

"I cannot say as yet. We some think of so doing."

Lapham turned away and looked up at the building. His wife pulled a little at her glove, as if embarrassed or even pained. She tried to make a diversion.

"We are building a house," she said, with a meaningless laugh.

"Oh, indeed," said Mr. Rogers, looking up at it.

Then no one spoke again, and she said, helplessly:

"If you come to Boston, I hope I shall see Mrs. Rogers."

"She will be happy to have you call," said Mr. Rogers.

He touched his hat-brim, and made a bow forward rather than in Mrs. Lapham's direction.

She mounted the planking that led into the shelter of the bare brick walls, and her husband slowly followed. When she turned her face toward him her cheeks were burning, and tears that looked hot stood in her eyes.

"You left it all to me!" she cried. "Why couldn't you speak a word?"

"I hadn't anything to say to him," replied Lapham sullenly.

They stood awhile, without looking at the work which they had come to enjoy, and without speaking to each other.

"I suppose we might as well go on," said Mrs. Lapham at last, as they returned to the buggy. The Colonel drove recklessly toward the Milldam. His wife kept her veil down and her face turned from him. After a time she put her handkerchief up under her veil and wiped her eyes, and he set his teeth and squared his jaw.

"I don't see how he always manages to appear just at the moment when he seems to have gone fairly out of our lives, and blight everything," she whimpered.

"I supposed he was dead," said Lapham.

"Oh, don't *say* such a thing! It sounds as if you wished it."

"Why do you mind it? What do you let him blight everything for?"

"I can't help it, and I don't believe I ever shall. I don't know as his being dead would help it any. I can't ever see him without feeling just as I did at first."

"I tell you," said Lapham, "it was a perfectly square thing. And I wish, once for all, you would quit bothering about it. My conscience is easy as far as he's concerned, and it always was."

"And I can't look at him without feeling as if you'd ruined him, Silas."

"Don't look at him, then," said her husband with a scowl. "I want you should recollect in the first place, Persis, that I never wanted a partner."

"If he hadn't put his money in when he did, you'd 'a' broken down."

"Well, he got his money out again, and more too," said the Colonel with a sulky weariness.

"He didn't want to take it out."

"I gave him his choice: buy out or go out."

"You know he couldn't buy out then. It was no choice at all."

"It was a business chance."

"No; you had better face the truth, Silas. It was no chance at all. You crowded him out. A man that had saved you! No, you had got greedy, Silas. You had made your paint your god, and you couldn't bear to let anybody else share in its blessings."

"I tell you he was a drag and a brake on me from the word go. You say he saved me. Well, if I hadn't got him out he'd 'a' ruined me sooner or later. So it's an even thing, as far forth as that goes."

"No, it aint an even thing, and you know it, Silas. Oh, if I could only get you once to acknowledge that you did wrong about it, then I should have some hope. I don't say you meant wrong exactly, but you took an advantage. Yes, you took an advantage! You had him where he couldn't help himself, and then you wouldn't show him any mercy."

"I'm sick of this," said Lapham. "If you'll 'tend to the house, I'll manage my business without your help."

"You were very glad of my help once."

"Well, I'm tired of it now. Don't meddle."

"I *will* meddle. When I see you hardening yourself in a wrong thing, it's time for me to meddle, as you call it, and I will. I can't ever get you to own up the least bit about Rogers, and I feel as if it was hurting you all the while."

"What do you want I should own up about a thing for when I don't feel wrong? I tell you Rogers haint got anything to complain of, and that's what I told you from the start. It's a thing that's done every day. I was loaded up with a partner that didn't know anything, and couldn't do anything, and I unloaded; that's all."

"You unloaded just at the time when you knew that your paint was going to be worth about twice what it ever had been; and you wanted all the advantage for yourself."

"I had a right to it. I made the success."

"Yes, you made it with Rogers's money; and when you'd made it you took his share of it. I guess you thought of that when you saw him, and that's why you couldn't look him in the face."

At these words Lapham lost his temper.

"I guess you don't want to ride with me any more to-day," he said, turning the mare abruptly round.

"I'm as ready to go back as what you are," replied his wife. "And don't you ask me to go to that house with you any more. You can sell it, for all me. I sha'n't live in it. There's blood on it."

IV.

The silken texture of the marriage tie bears a daily strain of wrong and insult to which no other human relation can be subjected without lesion; and sometimes the strength that knits society together might appear to the eye of faltering faith the curse of those immediately bound by it. Two people by no means reckless of each other's rights and feelings, but even tender of them for the most part, may tear at each other's heart-strings in this sacred bond with perfect impunity; though if they were any other two they would not speak or look at each other again after the outrages they exchange. It is certainly a curious spectacle, and doubtless it ought to convince an observer of the divinity of the institution. If the husband and wife are blunt, outspoken people like the Laphams, they do not weigh their words; if they are more refined, they weigh them very carefully, and know accurately just how far they will carry, and in what most sensitive spot they may be planted with most effect.

Lapham was proud of his wife, and when he married her it had been a rise in life for him. For a while he stood in awe of his good fortune, but this could not last, and he simply remained supremely satisfied with it. The girl who had taught school with a clear head and a strong hand was not afraid of work; she encouraged and helped him from the first, and bore her full share of the common burden. She had health, and she did not worry his life out with peevish complaints and vagaries; she had sense and principle, and in their simple lot she did what was wise and right. Their marriage was hallowed by an early sorrow: they lost their boy, and it was years before they could look each other in the face and speak of him. No one gave up more than they when they gave up each other, and Lapham went to the war. When he came back and began to work, her zeal and courage formed the spring of his enterprise. In that affair of the partnership she had tried to be his conscience, but perhaps she would have defended him if he had accused himself; it was one of those things in this life which seem destined to await justice, or at least judgment, in the next. As he said, Lapham had dealt fairly by his partner in money; he had let Rogers take more money out of the business than he put into it; he had, as he said, simply forced out of it a timid and inefficient participant in advantages which he had created. But Lapham had not created them all. He had been dependent at one time on his partner's capital. It was a moment of terrible trial. Happy is the man forever after who can choose the ideal, the unselfish part in such an exigency! Lapham could not rise to it. He did what he could maintain to be perfectly fair. The wrong, if any, seemed to be condoned to him, except when from time to time his wife brought it up. Then all the question stung and burned anew, and had to be reasoned out and put away once more. It seemed to have an inextinguishable vitality. It slept, but it did not die.

His course did not shake Mrs. Lapham's faith in him. It astonished her at first, and it always grieved her that he could not see that he was acting solely in his own interest. But she found excuses for him, which at times she made reproaches. She vaguely perceived that his paint was something more than business to him; it was a sentiment, almost a passion. He could not share its management and its profit with another without a measure of self-sacrifice far beyond that which he must make with something less personal to him. It was the poetry of that nature, otherwise so intensely prosaic; and she understood this, and for the most part forbore. She knew him good and true and blameless in all his life, except for this wrong, if it were a wrong; and it was only when her nerves tingled intolerably with some chance renewal of the pain she had suffered that she shared her anguish with him in true wifely fashion.

With those two there was never anything like an explicit reconciliation. They simply ignored a quarrel; and Mrs. Lapham had only to say a few days after at breakfast, "I guess the girls would like to go round with you this afternoon, and look at the new house," in order to make her husband grumble out as he looked down into his coffee-cup, "I guess we better all go, hadn't we?"

"Well, I'll see," she said.

There was not really a great deal to look at when Lapham arrived on the ground in his four-seated open phaeton. But the walls were up, and the studding had already given skeleton shape to the interior. The floors were roughly boarded over, and the stairways were in place, with provisional treads rudely laid. They had not begun to lath and plaster yet, but the clean, fresh smell of the mortar in the walls mingling with the pungent fragrance of the pine shavings neutralized the Venetian odor that drew in over the water. It was pleasantly shady there, though for the matter of that the heat of the morning had all been washed out of the atmosphere by a tide of east wind setting in at noon, and the thrilling, delicious cool of a Boston summer afternoon bathed every nerve.

The foreman went about with Mrs. Lapham, showing her where the doors were to be; but Lapham soon tired of this, and having found a pine stick of perfect grain, he abandoned himself to the pleasure of whittling it in what was to be the reception-room, where he sat looking out on the street from what was to be the bay-window. Here he was presently joined by his girls, who, after locating their own room on the water side above the music-room, had no more wish to enter into details than their father.

"Come and take a seat in the bay-window, ladies," he called out to them, as they looked in at him through the ribs of the wall. He jocosely made room for them on the trestle on which he sat.

They came gingerly and vaguely forward, as young ladies do when they wish not to seem to be going to do a thing they have made up their minds to do. When they had taken their places on their trestle, they could not help laughing with scorn, open and acceptable to their father; and Irene curled her chin up, in a little way she had, and said, "How ridiculous!" to her sister.

"Well, I can tell you what," said the Colonel, in fond enjoyment of their young-ladyishness, "your mother wasn't ashamed to sit with me on a trestle when I called her out to look at the first coat of my paint that I ever tried on a house."

"Yes; we've heard that story," said Penelope, with easy security of her father's liking what she said. "We were brought up on that story."

"Well, it's a good story," said her father.

At that moment a young man came suddenly in range, who began to look up at the signs of building as he approached. He dropped his eyes in coming abreast of the bay-window, where Lapham sat with his girls, and then his face lightened, and he took off his hat and bowed to Irene. She rose mechanically from the trestle, and her face lightened too. She was a very pretty figure of a girl, after our fashion of girls, round and slim and flexible, and her face was admirably regular. But her great beauty—and it was very great—was in her coloring. This was of an effect for which there is no word but delicious, as we use it of fruit or flowers. She had red hair, like her father in his earlier days, and the tints of her cheeks and temples were such as suggested May-flowers and apple-blossoms and peaches. Instead of the gray that often dulls this complexion, her eyes were of a blue at once intense and tender, and they seemed to burn on what they looked at with a soft, lambent flame. It was well understood by her sister and mother that her eyes always expressed a great deal more than Irene ever thought or felt; but this is not saying that she was not a very sensible girl and very honest.

The young man faltered perceptibly, and Irene came a little forward, and then there gushed from them both a smiling exchange of greeting, of which the sum was that he supposed she was out of town, and that she had not known that he had got back. A pause ensued, and flushing again in her uncertainty as to whether she ought or ought not to do it, she said, "My father, Mr. Corey; and my sister."

The young man took off his hat again, showing his shapely head, with a line of wholesome sunburn ceasing where the recently and closely clipped hair began. He was dressed in a fine summer check, with a blue white-dotted neckerchief, and he had a white hat, in which he looked very well when he put it back on his head. His whole dress seemed very fresh and new, and, in fact, he had cast aside his Texan habiliments only the day before.

"How do you do, sir?" said the Colonel, stepping to the window, and reaching out of it the hand which the young man advanced to take. "Wont you come in? We're at home here. House I'm building."

"Oh, indeed?" returned the young man; and he came promptly up the steps, and through its ribs into the reception-room.

"Have a trestle?" asked the Colonel, while the girls exchanged little shocks of terror and amusement at the eyes.

"Thank you," said the young man, simply, and sat down.

"Mrs. Lapham is upstairs interviewing the carpenter, but she'll be down in a minute."

"I hope she's quite well," said Corey. "I supposed—I was afraid she might be out of town."

"Well, we are off to Nantasket next week. The house kept us in town pretty late."

"It must be very exciting, building a house," said Corey to the elder sister.

"Yes, it is," she assented, loyally refusing in Irene's interest the opportunity of saying anything more.

Corey turned to the latter. "I suppose you've all helped to plan it?"

"Oh, no; the architect and mamma did that."

"But they allowed the rest of us to agree, when we were good," said Penelope.

Corey looked at her, and saw that she was shorter than her sister, and had a dark complexion.

"It's very exciting," said Irene.

"Come up," said the Colonel, rising, "and look round if you'd like to."

"I should like to, very much," said the young man.

He helped the young ladies over crevasses of carpentry and along narrow paths of planking, on which they had made their way unassisted before. The elder sister left the younger to profit solely by these offices as much as possible. She walked between them and her father, who went before, lecturing on each apartment and taking the credit of the whole affair more and more as he talked on.

"There!" he said, "we're going to throw out a bay-window here, so as get the water all the way up and down. This is my girls' room," he added, looking proudly at them both.

It seemed terribly intimate. Irene blushed deeply and turned her head away.

But the young man took it all, apparently, as simply as their father. "What a lovely lookout," he said. The Back Bay spread its glassy sheet before them, empty but for a few smaller boats and a large schooner, with her sails close-reefed and dripping like snow from her yards, which a tug was rapidly towing toward Cambridge. The carpentry of that city, embanked and embowered in foliage, shared the picturesqueness of Charlestown in the distance.

"Yes," said Lapham, "I go in for using the best rooms in your house yourself. If people come to stay with you, they can put up with the second best. Though we don't intend to have any second best. There aint going to be an unpleasant room in the whole house, from top to bottom."

"Oh, I wish papa wouldn't brag so!" breathed Irene to her sister, where they stood a little apart looking away together.

The Colonel went on. "No, sir," he swelled out, "I have gone in for making a regular job of it. I've got the best architect in Boston, and I'm building a house to suit myself. And if money can do it, I guess I'm going to be suited."

"It seems very delightful," said Corey, "and very original."

"Yes, sir. That fellow hadn't talked five minutes before I saw that he knew what he was about every time."

"I wish mamma would come!" breathed Irene again. "I shall certainly go through the floor if papa says anything more."

"They are making a great many very pretty houses nowadays," said the young man. "It's very different from the old-fashioned building."

"Well," said the Colonel, with a large toleration of tone and a deep breath that expanded his ample chest, "we spend more on our houses nowadays. I started out to build a forty-thousand-dollar house. Well, sir! that fellow has got me in for more than sixty thousand already, and I doubt if I get out of it much under a hundred. You can't have a nice house for nothing. It's just like ordering a picture of a painter. You pay him enough, and he can afford to paint you a first-class picture; and if you don't, he can't. That's all there is of it. Why, they tell me that A. T. Stewart[1] gave one of those French fellows sixty thousand dollars for a little seven-by-nine picture the other day. Yes, sir, give an architect money enough and he'll give you a nice house, every time."

"I've heard that they're sharp at getting money to realize their ideas," assented the young man with a laugh.

"Well, I should say so!" exclaimed the Colonel. "They come to you with an improvement that you can't resist. It has good looks and common sense and everything in its favor, and it's like throwing money away to refuse. And they always manage to get you when your wife is around, and then you're helpless."

The Colonel himself set the example of laughing at this joke, and the young man joined him less obstreperously. The girls turned, and he said: "I don't think I ever saw this view to better advantage. It's surprising how well the Memorial Hall[2] and the Cambridge spires work up, over there. And the sunsets must be magnificent."

Lapham did not wait for them to reply.

"Yes, sir, it's about the sightliest view I know of. I always did like the water side of Beacon. Long before I owned property here, or ever expected to, m'wife and I used to ride down this way, and stop the buggy to get this view over the water. When people talk to me about the Hill, I can understand 'em. It's snug, and it's old-fashioned, and it's where they've always lived. But when they talk about Commonwealth Avenue,[3] I don't know what they mean. It don't hold a candle to the water side of Beacon. You've got just as much wind over there, and you've got just as much dust, and all the view you've got is the view across the street. No, sir! When you come to the Back Bay at all, give me the water side of Beacon."

"Oh, I think you're quite right," said the young man. "The view here is everything."

Irene looked "I wonder what papa is going to say next!" at her sister, when their mother's voice was heard overhead, approaching the opening in the floor where the stairs were to be; and she presently appeared, with one substantial foot a long way ahead. She was followed by the carpenter, with his rule sticking out of his overalls pocket, and she was still talking to him about some

1. Alexander Turney Stewart (1803–1876), an Irish-born businessman who made a fortune in the wholesale and retail dry goods business in New York City.
2. A Victorian Gothic building on the Harvard University campus, erected in honor of Harvard men who had fought for the Union in the Civil War.
3. A wide, Parisian-style parkway running parallel to Beacon Street two blocks to the south, away from the Charles River.

measurements they had been taking, when they reached the bottom, so that Irene had to say, "Mamma, Mr. Corey," before Mrs. Lapham was aware of him.

He came forward with as much grace and speed as the uncertain footing would allow, and Mrs. Lapham gave him a stout squeeze of her comfortable hand.

"Why, Mr. Corey! When did you get back?"

"Yesterday. It hardly seems as if I *had* got back. I didn't expect to find you in a new house."

"Well, you are our first caller. I presume you wont expect I should make excuses for the state you find it in. Has the Colonel been doing the honors?"

"Oh, yes. And I've seen more of your house than I ever shall again, I suppose."

"Well, I hope not," said Lapham, "There'll be several chances to see us in the old one yet, before we leave."

He probably thought this a neat, off-hand way of making the invitation, for he looked at his womankind as if he might expect their admiration.

"Oh, yes, indeed!" said his wife. "We shall be very glad to see Mr. Corey, any time."

"Thank you; I shall be glad to come."

He and the Colonel went before, and helped the ladies down the difficult descent. Irene seemed less sure-footed than the others; she clung to the young man's hand an imperceptible moment longer than need be, or else he detained her. He found opportunity of saying, "It's so pleasant seeing you again," adding, "All of you."

"Thank you," said the girl. "They must all be glad to have you at home again."

Corey laughed.

"Well, I suppose they would be, if they were at home to have me. But the fact is, there's nobody in the house but my father and myself, and I'm only on my way to Bar Harbor."[4]

"Oh! Are they there?"

"Yes; it seems to be the only place where my mother can get just the combination of sea and mountain air that she wants."

"We go to Nantasket—it's convenient for papa; and I don't believe we shall go anywhere else this summer, mamma's so taken up with building. We do nothing but talk house; and Pen says we eat and sleep house. She says it would be a sort of relief to go and live in tents for a while."

"She seems to have a good deal of humor," the young man ventured, upon the slender evidence.

4. A highly fashionable resort town on Mount Desert Island in Maine.

The others had gone to the back of the house a moment, to look at some suggested change. Irene and Corey were left standing in the doorway. A lovely light of happiness played over her face and etherealized its delicious beauty. She had some ado to keep herself from smiling outright, and the effort deepened the dimples in her cheeks; she trembled a little, and the pendants shook in the tips of her pretty ears.

The others came back directly, and they all descended the front steps together. The Colonel was about to renew his invitation, but he caught his wife's eye, and, without being able to interpret its warning exactly, was able to arrest himself, and went about gathering up the hitching-weight, while the young man handed the ladies into the phaeton. Then he lifted his hat, and the ladies all bowed, and the Laphams drove off, Irene's blue ribbons fluttering backward from her hat, as if they were her clinging thoughts.

"So that's young Corey, is it?" said the Colonel, letting the stately stepping, tall coupé horse make his way homeward at will with the phaeton. "Well, he aint a bad-looking fellow, and he's got a good, fair and square, honest eye. But I don't see how a fellow like that, that's had every advantage in this world, can hang round home and let his father support him. Seems to me, if I had his health and his education, I should want to strike out and do something for myself."

The girls on the back seat had hold of each other's hands, and they exchanged electrical pressures at the different points their father made.

"I presume," said Mrs. Lapham, "that he was down in Texas looking after something."

"He's come back without finding it, I guess."

"Well, if his father has the money to support him, and don't complain of the burden, I don't see why *we* should."

"Oh, I know it's none of my business; but I don't like the principle. I like to see a man *act* like a man. I don't like to see him taken care of like a young lady. Now, I suppose that fellow belongs to two or three clubs, and hangs around 'em all day, lookin' out the window,—I've seen 'em,—instead of tryin' to hunt up something to do for an honest livin'."

"If I was a young man," Penelope struck in, "I would belong to twenty clubs, if I could find them, and I would hang around them all, and look out the window till I dropped."

"Oh, you would, would you?" demanded her father, delighted with her defiance, and twisting his fat head around over his shoulder to look at her. "Well, you wouldn't do it on *my* money, if you were a son of *mine*, young lady."

"Oh, you wait and see," retorted the girl.

This made them all laugh. But the Colonel recurred seriously to the subject that night, as he was winding up his watch preparatory to putting it under his pillow.

"I could make a man of that fellow, if I had him in the business with me. There's stuff in him. But I spoke up the way I did because I didn't choose Irene should think I would stand any kind of a loafer 'round—I don't care who he is, or how well educated or brought up. And I guess, from the way Pen spoke up, that 'Rene saw what I was driving at."

The girl, apparently, was less anxious about her father's ideas and principles than about the impression which he had made upon the young man. She had talked it over and over with her sister before they went to bed, and she asked in despair, as she stood looking at Penelope brushing out her hair before the glass,

"Do you suppose he'll think papa always talks in that bragging way?"

"He'll be right if he does," answered her sister. "It's the way father always does talk. You never noticed it so much, that's all. And I guess if he can't make allowance for father's bragging, he'll be a little too good. *I* enjoyed hearing the Colonel go on."

"I know you did," returned Irene in distress. Then she sighed. "Didn't you think he looked very nice?"

"Who? The Colonel?" Penelope had caught up the habit of calling her father so from her mother, and she used his title in all her jocose and perverse moods.

"You know very well I don't mean papa," pouted Irene.

"Oh! Mr. Corey! Why didn't you say Mr. Corey if you meant Mr. Corey? If I meant Mr. Corey, I should say Mr. Corey. It isn't swearing! Corey, Corey, Co——"

Her sister clapped her hand over her mouth. "Will you *hush*, you wretched thing?" she whimpered. "The whole house can hear you."

"Oh, yes, they can hear me all over the square. Well, I think he looked well enough for a plain youth, who hadn't taken his hair out of curl-papers for some time."

"It *was* clipped pretty close," Irene admitted; and they both laughed at the drab effect of Mr. Corey's skull, as they remembered it. "Did you like his nose?" asked Irene, timorously.

"Ah, now you're *coming* to something," said Penelope. "I don't know whether, if I had so much of a nose, I should want it all Roman."

"I don't see how you can expect to have a nose part one kind and part another," argued Irene.

"Oh, *I* do. Look at mine!" She turned aside her face, so as to get a three-quarters view of her nose in the glass, and crossing her hands, with the brush in one of them, before her, regarded it judicially. "Now, my nose started Grecian, but changed its mind before it got over the bridge, and concluded to be snub the rest of the way."

"You've got a very pretty nose, Pen," said Irene, joining in the contemplation of its reflex in the glass.

"Don't say that in hopes of getting me to compliment *his,* Mrs."— she stopped, and then added deliberately—"C.!"

Irene also had her hair-brush in her hand, and now she sprang at her sister and beat her very softly on the shoulder with the flat of it. "You mean thing!" she cried, between her shut teeth, blushing hotly.

"Well, *D.,* then," said Penelope. "You've nothing to say against D.? Though I think C. is just as nice an initial."

"Oh!" cried the younger, for all expression of unspeakable things.

"I think he has very good eyes," admitted Penelope.

"Oh, he *has!* And didn't you like the way his sack-coat set? So close to him, and yet free—kind of peeling away at the lapels?"

"Yes, I should say he was a young man of great judgment. He knows how to choose his tailor."

Irene sat down on the edge of a chair. "It was so nice of you, Pen, to come in, that way, about clubs."

"Oh, I didn't mean anything by it except opposition," said Penelope. "I couldn't have father swelling on so, without saying something."

"How he *did* swell!" sighed Irene. "Wasn't it a relief to have mamma come down, even if she did seem to be all stocking at first?"

The girls broke into a wild giggle and hid their faces in each other's necks. "I thought I *should* die," said Irene.

"'It's just like ordering a painting,'" said Penelope, recalling her father's talk, with an effect of dreamy absent-mindedness. "'You give the painter money enough, and he can afford to paint you a first-class picture. Give an architect money enough, and he'll give you a first-class house, every time.'"

"Oh, wasn't it awful!" moaned her sister. "No one would ever have supposed that he had fought the very idea of an architect for weeks, before he gave in."

Penelope went on. "'I always did like the water side of Beacon— long before I owned property there. When you come to the Back Bay at all, give me the water side of Beacon.'"

"Ow-w-w-w!" shrieked Irene. "*Do* stop!"

The door of their mother's chamber opened below, and the voice of the real Colonel called, "What are you doing up there, girls? Why don't you go to bed?"

This extorted nervous shrieks from both of them. The Colonel heard a sound of scurrying feet, whisking drapery, and slamming doors. Then he heard one of the doors opened again, and Penelope said, "I was only repeating something you said when you talked to Mr. Corey."

"Very well, now," answered the Colonel. "You postpone the rest of it till to-morrow at breakfast, and see that you're up in time to let *me* hear it."

V.

At the same moment young Corey let himself in at his own door with his latch-key, and went to the library, where he found his father turning the last leaves of a story in the "Revue des Deux Mondes."[1] He was a white-mustached old gentleman, who had never been able to abandon his *pince-nez*[2] for the superior comfort of spectacles, even in the privacy of his own library. He knocked the glasses off as his son came in, and looked up at him with lazy fondness, rubbing the two red marks that they always leave on the side of the nose.

"Tom," he said, "where did you get such good clothes?"

"I stopped over a day in New York," replied the son, finding himself a chair. "I'm glad you like them."

"Yes, I always do like your clothes, Tom," returned the father thoughtfully, swinging his glasses. "But I don't see how you can afford 'em. *I* can't."

"Well, sir," said the son, who dropped the sir into his speech with his father, now and then, in an old-fashioned way that was rather charming, "you see I have an indulgent parent."

"Smoke?" suggested the father, pushing toward his son a box of cigarettes, from which he had taken one.

"No, thank you," said the son. "I've dropped that."

"Ah, is that so?" The father began to feel about on the table for matches, in the purblind fashion of elderly men. His son rose, lighted one, and handed it to him. "Well,—oh, thank you, Tom!—I believe some statisticians prove that if you will give up smoking you can dress very well on the money your tobacco costs, even if you haven't got an indulgent parent. But I'm too old to try. Though, I confess, I should rather like the clothes. Whom did you find at the club?"

"There were a lot of fellows there," said young Corey, watching the accomplished fumigation of his father in an absent way.

"It's astonishing what a hardy breed the young club-men are," observed his father. "All summer through, in weather that sends the sturdiest female flying to the sea-shore, you find the clubs filled with young men, who don't seem to mind the heat in the least."

"Boston isn't a bad place, at the worst, in summer," said the son, declining to take up the matter in its ironical shape.

1. *Review of the Two Worlds*, a stylish magazine of literature and culture originating in Paris.
2. Pinch-nose (French); i.e., templeless eyeglasses that clip to the bridge of the nose.

"I dare say it isn't, compared with Texas," returned the father, smoking tranquilly on. "But I don't suppose you find many of your friends in town outside of the club."

"No; you're requested to ring at the rear door, all the way down Beacon street and up Commonwealth Avenue. It's rather a blank reception for the returning prodigal."

"Ah, the prodigal must take his chance if he comes back out of season. But I'm glad to have you back, Tom, even as it is, and I hope you're not going to hurry away. You must give your energies a rest."

"I'm sure you never had to reproach me with abnormal activity," suggested the son, taking his father's jokes in good part.

"No, I don't know that I have," admitted the elder. "You've always shown a fair degree of moderation, after all. What do you think of taking up next? I mean after you have embraced your mother and sisters at Mount Desert. Real estate? It seems to me that it is about time for you to open out as a real-estate broker. Or did you ever think of matrimony?"

"Well, not just in that way, sir," said the young man. "I shouldn't quite like to regard it as a career, you know."

"No, no. I understand that. And I quite agree with you. But you know I've always contended that the affections could be made to combine pleasure and profit. I wouldn't have a man marry for money,—that would be rather bad,—but I don't see why, when it comes to falling in love, a man shouldn't fall in love with a rich girl as easily as a poor one. Some of the rich girls are very nice, and I should say that the chances of a quiet life with them were rather greater. They've always had everything, and they wouldn't be so ambitious and uneasy. Don't you think so?"

"It would depend," said the son, "upon whether a girl's people had been rich long enough to have given her position before she married. If they hadn't, I don't see how she would be any better than a poor girl in that respect."

"Yes, there's sense in that. But the suddenly rich are on a level with any of us nowadays. Money buys position at once. I don't say that it isn't all right. The world generally knows what it's about, and knows how to drive a bargain. I dare say it makes the new rich pay too much. But there's no doubt but money is to the fore now. It is the romance, the poetry of our age. It's the thing that chiefly strikes the imagination. The Englishmen who come here are more curious about the great new millionaires than about any one else, and they respect them more. It's all very well. I don't complain of it."

"And you would like a rich daughter-in-law, quite regardless, then?"

"Oh, not quite so bad as that, Tom," said his father. "A little youth, a little beauty, a little good sense and pretty behavior—one mustn't object to those things; and they go just as often with money as without it. And I suppose I should like her people to be rather grammatical."

"It seems to me that you're exacting, sir," said the son. "How can you expect people who have been strictly devoted to business to be grammatical? Isn't that rather too much?"

"Perhaps it is. Perhaps you're right. But I understood your mother to say that those benefactors of hers, whom you met last summer, were very passably grammatical."

"The father isn't."

The elder, who had been smoking with his profile toward his son, now turned his face full upon him. "I didn't know you had seen him?"

"I hadn't until to-day," said young Corey, with a little heightening of his color. "But I was walking down street this afternoon, and happened to look round at a new house some one was putting up, and I saw the whole family in the window. It appears that Mr. Lapham is building the house."

The elder Corey knocked the ash of his cigarette into the holder at his elbow. "I am more and more convinced, the longer I know you, Tom, that we are descended from Giles Corey. The gift of holding one's tongue seems to have skipped me, but you have it in full force. I can't say just how you would behave under *peine forte et dure,* but under ordinary pressure you are certainly able to keep your own counsel. Why didn't you mention this encounter at dinner? You weren't asked to plead to an accusation of witchcraft."[3]

"No, not exactly," said the young man. "But I didn't quite see my way to speaking of it. We had a good many other things before us."

"Yes, that's true. I suppose you wouldn't have mentioned it now if I hadn't led up to it, would you?"

"I don't know, sir. It was rather on my mind to do so. Perhaps it was I who led up to it."

His father laughed. "Perhaps you did, Tom; perhaps you did. Your mother would have known you were leading up to something, but I'll confess that I didn't. What is it?"

"Nothing very definite. But do you know that in spite of his syntax I rather liked him?"

The father looked keenly at the son; but unless the boy's full confidence was offered, Corey was not the man to ask it. "Well?" was all that he said.

"I suppose that in a new country one gets to looking at people a little out of our tradition; and I dare say that if I hadn't passed a winter in Texas I might have found Colonel Lapham rather too much."

3. Accused of witchcraft during the Salem trials of 1692, Giles Corey (1621–1692) refused to plead either innocent or guilty and was sentenced to be crushed to death by rocks, a punishment known as "*peine forte et dure*" (strong and hard pain; French).

"You mean that there are worse things in Texas?"

"Not that exactly. I mean that I saw it wouldn't be quite fair to test him by our standards."

"This comes of the error which I have often deprecated," said the elder Corey. "In fact I am always saying that the Bostonian ought never to leave Boston. Then he knows—and then only—that there can *be* no standard but ours. But we are constantly going away, and coming back with our convictions shaken to their foundations. One man goes to England, and returns with the conception of a grander social life; another comes home from Germany with the notion of a more searching intellectual activity; a fellow just back from Paris has the absurdest ideas of art and literature; and you revert to us from the cowboys of Texas, and tell us to our faces that we ought to try Papa Lapham by a jury of his peers. It ought to be stopped—it ought, really. The Bostonian who leaves Boston ought to be condemned to perpetual exile."

The son suffered the father to reach his climax with smiling patience. When he asked finally, "What are the characteristics of Papa Lapham that place him beyond our jurisdiction?" the younger Corey crossed his long legs, and leaned forward to take one of his knees between his hands.

"Well, sir, he bragged, rather."

"Oh, I don't know that bragging should exempt him from the ordinary processes. I've heard other people brag in Boston."

"Ah, not just in that personal way—not about money."

"No, that was certainly different."

"I don't mean," said the young fellow, with the scrupulosity which people could not help observing and liking in him, "that it was more than an indirect expression of satisfaction in the ability to spend."

"No. I should be glad to express something of the kind myself, if the facts would justify me."

The son smiled tolerantly again. "But if he was enjoying his money in that way, I didn't see why he shouldn't show his pleasure in it. It might have been vulgar, but it wasn't sordid. And I don't know that it was vulgar. Perhaps his successful strokes of business were the romance of his life——"

The father interrupted with a laugh. "The girl must be uncommonly pretty. What did she seem to think of her father's brag?"

"There were two of them," answered the son evasively.

"Oh, two! And is the sister pretty, too?"

"Not pretty, but rather interesting. She is like her mother."

"Then the pretty one isn't the father's pet?"

"I can't say, sir. I don't believe," added the young fellow, "that I can make you see Colonel Lapham just as I did. He struck me as very simple-hearted and rather wholesome. Of course he could be tiresome; we all can; and I suppose his range of ideas is limited. But he is a force, and not a bad one. If he hasn't got over being surprised at the effect of rubbing his lamp[4]——"

"Oh, one could make out a case. I suppose you know what you are about, Tom. But remember that we are Essex County[5] people, and that in savor we are just a little beyond the salt of the earth. I will tell you plainly that I don't like the notion of a man who has rivaled the hues of nature in her wildest haunts with the tints of his mineral paint; but I don't say there are not worse men. He isn't to my taste, though he might be ever so much to my conscience."

"I suppose," said the son, "that there is nothing really to be ashamed of in mineral paint. People go into all sorts of things."

His father took his cigarette from his mouth and once more looked his son full in the face. "Oh, is *that* it?"

"It has crossed my mind," admitted the son. "I must do something. I've wasted time and money enough. I've seen much younger men all through the West and Southwest taking care of themselves. I don't think I was particularly fit for anything out there, but I am ashamed to come back and live upon you, sir."

His father shook his head with an ironical sigh. "Ah, we shall never have a real aristocracy while this plebeian reluctance to live upon a parent or a wife continues the animating spirit of our youth. It strikes at the root of the whole feudal system. I really think you owe me an apology, Tom. I supposed you wished to marry the girl's money, and here you are, basely seeking to go into business with her father."

Young Corey laughed again like a son who perceives that his father is a little antiquated, but keeps a filial faith in his wit. "I don't know that it's quite so bad as that; but the thing had certainly crossed my mind. I don't know how it's to be approached, and I don't know that it's at all possible. But I confess that I 'took to' Colonel Lapham from the moment I saw him. He looked as if he 'meant business,' and I mean business too."

The father smoked thoughtfully. "Of course people do go into all sorts of things, as you say, and I don't know that one thing is more ignoble than another, if it's decent, and large enough. In my time you would have gone into the China trade or the India trade—though *I* didn't; and a little later cotton would have been your manifest destiny—though it wasn't mine; but now a man may do almost anything. The real-estate business *is* pretty full. Yes, if you have a deep inward vocation for it, I don't see why mineral paint shouldn't do.

4. Corey alludes to the Middle Eastern folktale of Aladdin, wherein rubbing a magic lamp produces a genie who must obey the orders of the lamp's owner.
5. Corey lays claim to special merit on the basis of family origins in one of the four original "shires" of the Massachusetts Bay Colony established in 1643. Essex County lies northeast of Boston.

I fancy it's easy enough approaching the matter. We will invite Papa Lapham to dinner, and talk it over with him."

"Oh, I don't think that would be exactly the way, sir," said the son, smiling at his father's patrician unworldliness.

"No? Why not?"

"I'm afraid it would be a bad start. I don't think it would strike him as business-like."

"I don't see why he should be punctilious, if we're not."

"Ah, we might say that if he were making the advances."

"Well, perhaps you are right, Tom. What is your idea?"

"I haven't a very clear one. It seems to me I ought to get some business friend of ours, whose judgment he would respect, to speak a good word for me."

"Give you a character?"

"Yes. And of course I must go to Colonel Lapham. My notion would be to inquire pretty thoroughly about him, and then, if I liked the look of things, to go right down to Republic street and let him see what he could do with me, if anything."

"That sounds tremendously practical to me, Tom, though it may be just the wrong way. When are you going down to Mount Desert?"

"To-morrow, I think, sir," said the young man. "I shall turn it over in my mind while I'm off."

The father rose, showing something more than his son's height, with a very slight stoop, which the son's figure had not. "Well," he said, whimsically, "I admire your spirit, and I don't deny that it is justified by necessity. It's a consolation to think that while I've been spending and enjoying, I have been preparing the noblest future for you—a future of industry and self-reliance. You never could draw, but this scheme of going into the mineral-paint business shows that you have inherited something of my feeling for color."

The son laughed once more, and waiting till his father was well on his way upstairs, turned out the gas and then hurried after him and preceded him into his chamber. He glanced over it, to see that everything was there, to his father's hand. Then he said, "Good-night, sir," and the elder responded, "Good-night, my son," and the son went to his own room.

Over the mantel in the elder Corey's room hung a portrait which he had painted of his own father, and now he stood a moment and looked at this as if struck by something novel in it. The resemblance between his son and the old India merchant, who had followed the trade from Salem to Boston when the larger city drew it away from the smaller, must have been what struck him. Grandfather and grandson had both the Roman nose which appears to have flourished chiefly at the formative period of the republic, and which occurs more rarely in the descendants of the conscript fathers, though it still characterizes the profiles of a good many Boston ladies. Bromfield Corey had not inherited it, and he had made his straight nose his defense when the old merchant accused him of a want of energy. He said, "What could a man do whose unnatural father had left his own nose away from him?" This amused but did not satisfy the merchant. "You must do something," he said; "and it's for you to choose. If you don't like the India trade, go into something else. Or, take up law or medicine. No Corey yet ever proposed to do nothing." "Ah, then, it's quite time one of us made a beginning," urged the man who was then young, and who was now old, looking into the somewhat fierce eyes of his father's portrait. He had inherited as little of the fierceness as of the nose, and there was nothing predatory in his son either, though the aquiline beak had come down to him in such force. Bromfield Corey liked his son Tom for the gentleness which tempered his energy.

"Well, let us compromise," he seemed to be saying to his father's portrait. "I will travel." "Travel? How long? "the keen eyes demanded. "Oh, indefinitely. I wont be hard with you, father." He could see the eyes soften, and the smile of yielding come over his father's face; the merchant could not resist a son who was so much like his dead mother. There was some vague understanding between them that Bromfield Corey was to come back and go into business after a time, but he never did so. He traveled about over Europe, and traveled handsomely, frequenting good society everywhere, and getting himself presented at several courts, at a period when it was a distinction to do so. He had always sketched, and with his father's leave he fixed himself at Rome, where he remained studying art and rounding the being inherited from his Yankee progenitors, till there was very little left of the ancestral angularities. After ten years he came home and painted that portrait of his father. It was very good, if a little amateurish, and he might have made himself a name as a painter of portraits if he had not had so much money. But he had plenty of money, though by this time he was married and beginning to have a family. It was absurd for him to paint portraits for pay, and ridiculous to paint them for nothing; so he did not paint them at all. He continued a dilettante, never quite abandoning his art, but working at it fitfully, and talking more about it than working at it. He had his theory of Titian's[6] method; and now and then a Bostonian insisted upon buying a picture of him. After a while he hung it more and more inconspicuously, and said apologetically, "Oh, yes! that's one of Bromfield Corey's things. It has nice qualities, but it's amateurish."

6. Tiziano Vicelli (c. 1490–1576), Renaissance Italian painter of the Venetian school known for his innovative use of color.

In process of time the money seemed less abundant. There were shrinkages of one kind and another, and living had grown much more expensive and luxurious. For many years he talked about going back to Rome, but he never went, and his children grew up in the usual way. Before he knew it his son had him out to his class-day spread at Harvard,[7] and then he had his son on his hands. The son made various unsuccessful provisions for himself, and still continued upon his father's hands, to their common dissatisfaction, though it was chiefly the younger who repined. He had the Roman nose and the energy without the opportunity, and at one of the reversions his father said to him, "You ought not to have that nose, Tom; then you would do very well. You would go and travel, as I did."

Lapham and his wife lay awake talking after he had quelled the disturbance in his daughters' room overhead; and their talk was not altogether of the new house.

"I tell you," he said, "if I had that fellow in the business with me I would make a man of him."

"Well, Silas Lapham," returned his wife, "I do believe you've got mineral paint on the brain. Do you suppose a fellow like young Corey, brought up the way he's been, would touch mineral paint with a ten-foot pole?"

"Why not? "haughtily asked the Colonel.

"Well, if you don't know already, there's no use trying to tell you."

[THIRD INSTALLMENT—JANUARY 1885]

VI.

The Coreys had always had a house at Nahant,[1] but after letting it for a season or two they found they could get on without it, and sold it at the son's instance, who foresaw that if things went on as they were going, the family would be straitened to the point of changing their mode of life altogether. They began to be of the people of whom it was said that they staid in town very late; and when the ladies did go away, it was for a brief summering in this place and that. The father remained at home altogether; and the son joined them in the intervals of his enterprises, which occurred only too often.

At Bar Harbor, where he now went to find them, after his winter in Texas, he confessed to his mother that there seemed no very good opening there for him. He might do as well as Loring Stanton, but

7. An annual event for graduating seniors and their families at Harvard's commencement.

1. A long-established vacation retreat on a peninsula on the north shore of Massachusetts Bay, almost directly across the bay from the less fashionable Nantasket, where the Laphams summer.

he doubted if Stanton was doing very well. Then he mentioned the new project which he had been thinking over. She did not deny that there was something in it, but she could not think of any young man who had gone into such a business as that, and it appeared to her that he might as well go into a patent medicine or a stove-polish.

"There was one of his hideous advertisements," she said, "painted on a reef that we saw as we came down."

Corey smiled. "Well, I suppose, if it was in a good state of preservation, that is proof positive of the efficacy of the paint on the hulls of vessels."

"It's very distasteful to me, Tom," said his mother; and if there was something else in her mind, she did not speak more plainly of it than to add: "It's not only the kind of business, but the kind of people you would be mixed up with."

"I thought you didn't find them so very bad," suggested Corey.

"I hadn't seen them in Nankeen Square then."

"You can see them on the water side of Beacon street when you go back."

Then he told of his encounter with the Lapham family in their new house. At the end his mother merely said, "It is getting very common down there," and she did not try to oppose anything further to his scheme.

The young man went to see Colonel Lapham shortly after his return to Boston. He paid his visit at Lapham's office, and if he had studied simplicity in his summer dress he could not have presented himself in a figure more to the mind of a practical man. His hands and neck still kept the brown of the Texan suns and winds, and he looked as business-like as Lapham himself.

He spoke up promptly and briskly in the outer office, and caused the pretty girl to look away from her copying at him. "Is Mr. Lapham in?" he asked; and after that moment for reflection which an array of bookkeepers so addressed likes to give the inquirer, a head was lifted from a ledger and nodded toward the inner office.

Lapham had recognized the voice, and he was standing, in considerable perplexity of mind, to receive Corey, when the young man opened his painted glass door. It was a hot afternoon, and Lapham was in his shirtsleeves. Scarcely a trace of the boastful hospitality with which he had welcomed Corey to his house a few days before lingered in his present address. He looked at the young man's face, as if he expected him to dispatch whatever unimaginable affair he had come upon.

"Wont you sit down? How are you? You'll excuse me," he added, in brief allusion to the shirt-sleeves. "I'm about roasted."

Corey laughed. "I wish you'd let me take off *my* coat."

"Why, *take* it off!" cried the Colonel, with instant pleasure. There is something in human nature which causes the man in his shirt-sleeves to wish all other men to appear in the same dishabille.

"I will, if you ask me after I've talked with you two minutes," said the young fellow, companionably pulling up the chair offered him toward the desk where Lapham had again seated himself. "But perhaps you haven't got two minutes to give me?"

"Oh, yes, I have," said the Colonel. "I was just going to knock off. I can give you twenty, and then I shall have fifteen minutes to catch the boat."

"All right," said Corey. "I want you to take me into the mineral paint business."

The Colonel sat dumb. He twisted his thick neck, and looked round at the door to see if it was shut. He would not have liked to have any of those fellows outside hear him, but there is no saying what sum of money he would not have given if his wife had been there to hear what Corey had just said.

"I suppose," continued the young man, "I could have got several people whose names you know to back my industry and sobriety, and say a word for my business capacity. But I thought I wouldn't trouble anybody for certificates till I found whether there was a chance, or the ghost of one, of your wanting me. So I came straight to you."

Lapham gathered himself together as well as he could. He had not yet forgiven Corey for Mrs. Lapham's insinuation that he would feel himself too good for the mineral paint business; and though he was dispersed by that astounding shot at first, he was not going to let any one even hypothetically despise his paint with impunity. "How do you think I am going to take you on?" They took on hands at the works; and Lapham put it as if Corey were a hand coming to him for employment. Whether he satisfied himself by this or not, he reddened a little after he had said it.

Corey answered, ignorant of the offense: "I haven't a very clear idea, I'm afraid; but I've been looking a little into the matter from the outside——"

"I hope you haint been paying any attention to that fellow's stuff in the 'Events'?"[2] Lapham interrupted. Since Bartley's interview had appeared, Lapham had regarded it with very mixed feelings. At first it gave him a glow of secret pleasure, blended with doubt as to how his wife would like the use Bartley had made of her in it. But she had not seemed to notice it much, and Lapham had experienced the gratitude of the man who escapes. Then his girls had begun to make fun of it; and though he did not mind Penelope's jokes much,

2. The fictitious newspaper first introduced in Chapter I is published for a mass readership and would not be read by people of the Coreys' higher social standing.

he did not like to see that Irene's gentility was wounded. Business friends met him with the kind of knowing smile about it that implied their sense of the fraudulent character of its praise—the smile of men who had been there and who knew how it was themselves. Lapham had his misgivings as to how his clerks and underlings looked at it; he treated them with stately severity for a while after it came out, and he ended by feeling rather sore about it. He took it for granted that everybody had read it.

"I don't know what you mean," replied Corey. "I don't see the 'Events' regularly."

"Oh, it was nothing. They sent a fellow down here to interview me, and he got everything about as twisted as he could."

"I believe they always do," said Corey. "I hadn't seen it. Perhaps it came out before I got home."

"Perhaps it did."

"My notion of making myself useful to you was based on a hint I got from one of your own circulars."

Lapham was proud of those circulars; he thought they read very well. "What was that?"

"I could put a little capital into the business," said Corey, with the tentative accent of a man who chances a thing. "I've got a little money, but I didn't imagine you cared for anything of that kind."

"No, sir, I don't," returned the Colonel bluntly. "I've had one partner, and one's enough."

"Yes," assented the young man, who doubtless had his own ideas as to eventualities—or perhaps rather had the vague hopes of youth. "I didn't come to propose a partnership. But I see that you are introducing your paint into the foreign markets, and there I really thought I might be of use to you, and to myself, too."

"How?" asked the Colonel scantly.

"Well, I know two or three languages pretty well. I know French, and I know German, and I've got a pretty fair sprinkling of Spanish."

"You mean that you can talk them?" asked the Colonel, with the mingled awe and slight that such a man feels for such accomplishments.

"Yes; and I can write an intelligible letter in either of them."

Lapham rubbed his nose. "It's easy enough to get all the letters we want translated."

"Well," pursued Corey, not showing his discouragement if he felt any, "I know the countries where you want to introduce this paint of yours. I've been there. I've been in Germany and France, and I've been in South America and Mexico; I've been in Italy, of course. I believe I could go to any of those countries and place it to advantage."

Lapham had listened with a trace of persuasion in his face, but now he shook his head.

"It's placing itself as fast as there's any call for it. It wouldn't pay us to send anybody out to look after it. Your salary and expenses would eat up about all we should make on it."

"Yes," returned the young man intrepidly, "if you had to pay me any salary and expenses."

"You don't propose to work for nothing?"

"I propose to work for a commission." The Colonel was beginning to shake his head again, but Corey hurried on. "I haven't come to you without making some inquiries about the paint, and I know how it stands with those who know best. I believe in it."

Lapham lifted his head and looked at the young man, deeply moved.

"It's the best paint in God's universe," he said, with the solemnity of prayer.

"It's the best in the market," said Corey; and he repeated, "I believe in it."

"You believe in it," began the Colonel, and then he stopped. If there had really been any purchasing power in money, a year's income would have bought Mrs. Lapham's instant presence. He warmed and softened to the young man in every way, not only because he must do so to any one who believed in his paint, but because he had done this innocent person the wrong of listening to a defamation of his instinct and good sense, and had been willing to see him suffer for a purely supposititious offense.

Corey rose.

"You mustn't let me outstay my twenty minutes," he said, taking out his watch. "I don't expect you to give a decided answer on the spot. All that I ask is that you'll consider my proposition."

"Don't hurry," said Lapham. "Sit still! I want to tell you about this paint," he added, in a voice husky with the feeling that his hearer could not divine. "I want to tell you *all* about it."

"I could walk with you to the boat," suggested the young man.

"Never mind the boat! I can take the next one. Look here!" The Colonel pulled open a drawer, as Corey sat down again, and took out a photograph of the locality of the mine. "Here's where we get it. This photograph don't half do the place justice," he said, as if the imperfect art had slighted the features of a beloved face. "It's one of the sightliest places in the country, and here's the very spot"—he covered it with his huge forefinger—"where my father found that paint, more than forty—years—ago. Yes, sir!"

He went on, and told the story in unsparing detail, while his chance for the boat passed unheeded, and the clerks in the outer office hung up their linen office coats and put on their seersucker or flannel street coats. The young lady went, too, and nobody was left but the porter, who made from time to time a noisy demonstration of fastening a distant blind, or putting something in place. At last the Colonel roused himself from the autobiographical delight of the history of his paint. "Well, sir, that's the story."

"It's an interesting story," said Corey, with a long breath, as they rose together, and Lapham put on his coat.

"That's what it is," said the Colonel. "Well!" he added, "I don't see but what we've got to have another talk about this thing. It's a surprise to me, and I don't see exactly how you're going to make it pay."

"I'm willing to take the chances," answered Corey. "As I said, I believe in it. I should try South America first. I should try Chili."

"Look here!" said Lapham, with his watch in his hand. "I like to get things over. We've just got time for the six o'clock boat. Why don't you come down with me to Nantasket? I can give you a bed as well as not. And then we can finish up."

The impatience of youth in Corey responded to the impatience of temperament in his elder.

"Why, I don't see why I shouldn't," he allowed himself to say. "I confess I should like to have it finished up myself, if it could be finished up in the right way."

"Well, we'll see. Dennis!" Lapham called to the remote porter, and the man came. "Want to send any word home?" he asked Corey.

"No; my father and I go and come as we like, without keeping account of each other. If I don't come home, he knows that I'm not there. That's all."

"Well, that's convenient. You'll find you can't do that when you're married. Never mind, Dennis," said the Colonel.

He had time to buy two newspapers on the wharf before he jumped on board the steam-boat with Corey. "Just made it," he said; "and that's what I like to do. I can't stand it to be aboard much more than a minute before she shoves out." He gave one of the newspapers to Corey as he spoke, and set him the example of catching up a camp-stool on their way to that point on the boat which his experience had taught him was the best. He opened his paper at once and began to run over its news, while the young man watched the spectacular recession of the city, and was vaguely conscious of the people about him, and of the gay life of the water round the boat. The air freshened; the craft thinned in number; they met larger sail, lagging slowly inward in the afternoon light; the islands of the bay waxed and waned as the steamer approached and left them behind.

"I hate to see them stirring up those Southern fellows again," said the Colonel, speaking into the paper on his lap. "Seems to me it's time to let those old issues go."

"Yes," said the young man. "What are they doing now?"

"Oh, stirring up the Confederate brigadiers in Congress.[3] I don't like it. Seems to me, if our party haint got any other stock-in-trade, we better shut up shop altogether." Lapham went on, as he scanned his newspaper, to give his ideas of public questions, in a fragmentary way, while Corey listened patiently, and waited for him to come back to business. He folded up his paper at last, and stuffed it into his coat pocket. "There's one thing I always make it a rule to do," he said, "and that is to give my mind a complete rest from business while I'm going down on the boat. I like to get the fresh air all through me, soul and body. I believe a man can give his mind a rest, just the same as he can give his legs a rest, or his back. All he's got to do is to use his will-power. Why, I suppose, if I hadn't adopted some such rule, with the strain I've had on me for the last ten years, I should 'a' been a dead man long ago. That's the reason I like a horse. You've got to give your mind to horse; you can't help it, unless you want to break your neck; but a boat's different, and there you got to use your willpower. You got to take your mind right up and put it where you want it. I make it a rule to read the paper on the boat—Hold on!" he interrupted himself to prevent Corey from paying his fare to the man who had come round for it. "I've got tickets. And when I get through the paper, I try to get somebody to talk to, or I watch the people. It's an astonishing thing to me where they all come from. I've been riding up and down on these boats for six or seven years, and I don't know but very few of the faces I see on board. Seems to be a perfectly fresh lot every time. Well, of course! Town's full of strangers in the summer season, anyway, and folks keep coming down from the country. They think it's a great thing to get down to the beach, and they've all heard of the electric light on the water, and they want to see it. But you take faces now! The astonishing thing to me is not what a face tells, but what it don't tell. When you think of what a man is, or a woman is, and what most of 'em have been through before they get to be thirty, it seems as if their experience would burn right through. But it don't. I like to watch the couples, and try to make out which are engaged, or going to be, and which are married, or better be. But half the time I can't make any sort of guess. Of course, where they're young and kittenish, you can tell; but where they're anyways on, you can't. Heigh?"

"Yes, I think you're right," said Corey, not perfectly reconciled to philosophy in the place of business, but accepting it as he must.

"Well," said the Colonel, "I don't suppose it was meant we should know what was in each other's minds. It would take a man out of

3. When predominantly Southern Democrats gained a majority in the House of Representatives for the first time since before the Civil War in the election of 1874, Republicans mocked them by "waving the bloody shirt" to symbolize the South's rebellion.

his own hands. As long as he's in his own hands, there's some hopes of his doing something with himself; but if a fellow has been found out—even if he hasn't been found out to be so very bad—it's pretty much all up with him. No, sir. I don't want to know people through and through."

The greater part of the crowd on board—and, of course, the boat was crowded—looked as if they might not only be easily but safely known. There was little style and no distinction among them; they were people who were going down to the beach for the fun or the relief of it, and were able to afford it. In face they were commonplace, with nothing but the American poetry of vivid purpose to light them up, where they did not wholly lack fire. But they were nearly all shrewd and friendly-looking, with an apparent readiness for the humorous intimacy native to us all. The women were dandified in dress, according to their means and taste, and the men differed from each other in degrees of indifference to it. To a straw-hatted population, such as ours is in summer, no sort of personal dignity is possible. We have not even the power over observers which comes from the fantasticality of an Englishman when he discards the conventional dress. In our straw hats and our serge or flannel sacks we are no more imposing than a crowd of boys.

"Some day," said Lapham, rising as the boat drew near the wharf of the final landing, "there's going to be an awful accident on these boats. Just look at that jam."

He meant the people thickly packed on the pier, and under strong restraint of locks and gates, to prevent them from rushing on board the boat and possessing her for the return trip before she had landed her Nantasket passengers.

"Overload 'em every time," he continued, with a sort of dry, impersonal concern at the impending calamity, as if it could not possibly include him. "They take about twice as many as they ought to carry, and about ten times as many as they could save if anything happened. Yes, sir, it's bound to come. Hello! There's my girl!" He took out his folded newspaper and waved it toward a group of phaetons and barouches[4] drawn up on the pier a little apart from the pack of people, and a lady in one of them answered with a flourish of her parasol.

When he had made his way with his guest through the crowd, she began to speak to her father before she noticed Corey. "Well, Colonel, you've improved your last chance. We've been coming to every boat since four o'clock,—or Jerry has,—and I told mother that I would come myself once, and see if *I* couldn't fetch you; and if I failed, you could walk next time. You're getting perfectly spoiled."

4. Two different kinds of carriages.

The Colonel enjoyed letting her scold him to the end before he said, with a twinkle of pride in his guest and satisfaction in her probably being able to hold her own against any discomfiture, "I've brought Mr. Corey down for the night with me, and I was showing him things all the way, and it took time."

The young fellow was at the side of the open beach-wagon, making a quick, gentlemanly bow, and Penelope Lapham was cozily drawling, "Oh, how do you do, Mr. Corey?" before the Colonel had finished his explanation.

"Get right in there, alongside of Miss Lapham, Mr. Corey," he said, pulling himself up into the place beside the driver. "No, no," he had added quickly, at some signs of polite protest in the young man, "I don't give up the best place to anybody. Jerry, suppose you let me have hold of the leathers a minute."

This was his way of taking the reins from the driver; and in half the time he specified, he had skillfully turned the vehicle on the pier, among the crooked lines and groups of foot-passengers, and was spinning up the road toward the stretch of verandaed hotels and restaurants in the sand along the shore. "Pretty gay down here," he said, indicating all this with a turn of his whip, as he left it behind him. "But I've got about sick of hotels; and this summer I made up my mind that I'd take a cottage. Well, Pen, how are the folks?" He looked half-way round for her answer, and with the eye thus brought to bear upon her he was able to give her a wink of supreme content. The Colonel, with no sort of ulterior design, and nothing but his triumph over Mrs. Lapham definitely in his mind, was feeling, as he would have said, about right.

The girl smiled a daughter's amusement at her father's boyishness. "I don't think there's much change since morning. Did Irene have a headache when you left?"

"No," said the Colonel.

"Well, then, there's that to report."

"Pshaw!" said the Colonel, with vexation in his tone.

"I'm sorry Miss Irene isn't well," said Corey politely.

"I think she must have got it from walking too long on the beach. The air is so cool here that you forget how hot the sun is."

"Yes, that's true," assented Corey.

"A good night's rest will make it all right," suggested the Colonel, without looking round. "But you girls have got to look out."

"If you're fond of walking," said Corey, "I suppose you find the beach a temptation."

"Oh, it isn't so much that," returned the girl. "You keep walking on and on because it's so smooth and straight before you. We've been here so often that we know it all by heart—just how it looks at high tide, and how it looks at low tide, and how it looks after a storm.

We're as well acquainted with the crabs and stranded jelly-fish as we are with the children digging in the sand and the people sitting under umbrellas. I think they're always the same, all of them."

The Colonel left the talk to the young people. When he spoke next it was to say, "Well, here we are!" and he turned from the highway and drove up in front of a brown cottage with a vermilion roof, and a group of geraniums clutching the rock that cropped up in the loop formed by the road. It was treeless and bare all round, and the ocean, unnecessarily vast, weltered away a little more than a stone's cast from the cottage. A hospitable smell of supper filled the air, and Mrs. Lapham was on the veranda, with that demand in her eyes for her belated husband's excuses, which she was obliged to check on her tongue at sight of Corey.

VII.

The exultant Colonel swung himself lightly down from his seat. "I've brought Mr. Corey with me," he nonchalantly explained.

Mrs. Lapham made their guest welcome, and the Colonel showed him to his room, briefly assuring himself that there was nothing wanting there. Then he went to wash his own hands, carelessly ignoring the eagerness with which his wife pursued him to their chamber.

"What gave Irene a headache?" he asked, making himself a fine lather for his hairy paws.

"Never you mind Irene," promptly retorted his wife. "How came he to come? Did you press him? If you *did*, I'll never forgive you, Silas!"

The Colonel laughed, and his wife shook him by the shoulder to make him laugh lower. " 'Sh!" she whispered. "Do you want him to hear *every* thing? *Did* you urge him?"

The Colonel laughed the more. He was going to get all the good out of this. "No, I didn't urge him. Seemed to want to come."

"I don't believe it. Where did you meet him?"

"At the office."

"What office?"

"Mine."

"Nonsense! What was he doing there?"

"Oh, nothing much."

"What did he come for?"

"Come for? Oh! He *said* he wanted to go into the mineral paint business."

Mrs. Lapham dropped into a chair, and watched his bulk shaken with smothered laughter. "Silas Lapham," she gasped, "if you try to get off any more of those things on me——"

The Colonel applied himself to the towel. "Had a notion he could work it in South America. *I* don't know what he's up to."

"Never mind!" cried his wife. "I'll get even with you *yet*."

"So I told him he had better come down and talk it over," continued the Colonel, in well-affected simplicity. "I knew he wouldn't touch it with a ten-foot pole."

"Go on!" threatened Mrs. Lapham.

"Right thing to do, wa'n't it?"

A tap was heard at the door, and Mrs. Lapham answered it. A maid announced supper. "Very well," she said, "come to tea now. But I'll make you pay for this, Silas."

Penelope had gone to her sister's room as soon as she entered the house.

"Is your head any better, 'Rene?" she asked.

"Yes, a little," came a voice from the pillows. "But I shall not come to tea. I don't want anything. If I keep still, I shall be all right by morning."

"Well, I'm sorry," said the elder sister. "He's come down with father."

"He hasn't! Who?" cried Irene, starting up in simultaneous denial and demand.

"Oh, well, if you say he hasn't, what's the use of my telling you who?"

"Oh, how can you treat me so!" moaned the sufferer. "What do you mean, Pen?"

"I guess I'd better not tell you," said Penelope, watching her like a cat playing with a mouse. "If you're not coming to tea, it would just excite you for nothing."

The mouse moaned and writhed upon the bed.

"Oh, I wouldn't treat *you* so!"

The cat seated herself across the room and asked quietly:

"Well, what could you do if it *was* Mr. Corey? You couldn't come to tea, you say. But *he*'ll excuse you. *I*'ve told him you had a headache. Why, of course you can't come! It would be too barefaced. But you needn't be troubled, Irene; I'll do my best to make the time pass pleasantly for him." Here the cat gave a low titter, and the mouse girded itself up with a momentary courage and self-respect.

"I should think you would be ashamed to come here and tease me so."

"I don't see why you shouldn't believe me," argued Penelope. "Why shouldn't he come down with father, if father asked him? and he'd be sure to if he thought of it. I don't see any p'ints about that frog that's any better than any other frog."[1]

1. Penelope's words are a minimally altered quotation from a character in "Jim Smiley and His Jumping Frog" (1865), a wildly popular early story by Mark Twain (Samuel L. Clemens, 1835–1910), in which a stranger wins a bet on a frog-jumping contest by pouring lead shot down the throat of his opponent's frog to weigh it down. Penelope is joking that she cannot see much difference between Tom and any other man.

The sense of her sister's helplessness was too much for the tease; she broke down in a fit of smothered laughter, which convinced her victim that it was nothing but an ill-timed joke.

"Well, Pen, I wouldn't use you so," she whimpered.

Penelope threw herself on the bed beside her.

"Oh, poor Irene! He *is* here. It's a solemn fact." And she caressed and soothed her sister, while she choked with laughter. "You must get up and come out. I don't know what brought him here, but here he *is*."

"It's too late now," said Irene, desolately. Then she added, with a wilder despair: "What a fool I was to take that walk!"

"Well," coaxed her sister, "come out and get some tea. The tea will do you good."

"No, no; I can't come. But send me a cup here."

"Yes, and then perhaps you can see him later in the evening."

"I shall not see him at all."

An hour after Penelope came back to her sister's room and found her before her glass. "You might as well have kept still, and been well by morning, 'Rene," she said. "As soon as we were done father said, 'Well, Mr. Corey and I have got to talk over a little matter of business, and we'll excuse you, ladies.' He looked at mother in a way that I guess was pretty hard to bear. 'Rene, you ought to have heard the Colonel swelling at supper. It would have made you feel that all he said the other day was nothing."

Mrs. Lapham suddenly opened the door.

"Now, see here, Pen," she said, as she closed it behind her, "I've had just as much as I can stand from your father, and if you don't tell me this instant what it all means——"

She left the consequences to imagination, and Penelope replied, with her mock soberness:

"Well, the Colonel does seem to be on his high horse, ma'am. But you mustn't ask me what his business with Mr. Corey is, for I don't know. All that I know is that I met them at the landing, and that they conversed all the way down—on literary topics."

"Nonsense! What do you think it is?"

"Well, if you want my candid opinion, I think this talk about business is nothing but a blind. It seems a pity Irene shouldn't have been up to receive him," she added.

Irene cast a mute look of imploring at her mother, who was too much preoccupied to afford her the protection it asked.

"Your father said he wanted to go into the business with him."

Irene's look changed to a stare of astonishment and mystification, but Penelope preserved her imperturbability.

"Well, it's a lucrative business, I believe."

"Well, I don't believe a word of it!" cried Mrs. Lapham. "And so I told your father."

"Did it seem to convince him?" inquired Penelope.

Her mother did not reply. "I know one thing," she said. "He's got to tell me every word, or there'll be no sleep for him *this* night."

"Well, ma'am," said Penelope, breaking down in one of her queer laughs, "I shouldn't be a bit surprised if you were right."

"Go on and dress, Irene," ordered her mother, "and then you and Pen come out into the parlor. They can have just two hours for business, and then we must all be there to receive him. You haven't got headache enough to hurt you."

"Oh, it's all gone now," said the girl.

At the end of the limit she had given the Colonel, Mrs. Lapham looked into the dining-room, which she found blue with his smoke.

"I think you gentlemen will find the parlor pleasanter now, and we can give it up to you."

"Oh, no, you needn't," said her husband. "We've got about through." Corey was already standing, and Lapham rose too. "I guess we can join the ladies now. We can leave that little point till to-morrow."

Both of the young ladies were in the parlor when Corey entered with their father, and both were frankly indifferent to the few books and the many newspapers scattered about on the table where the large lamp was placed. But after Corey had greeted Irene he glanced at the novel under his eye, and said, in the dearth that sometimes befalls people at such times: "I see you're reading 'Middlemarch.' Do you like George Eliot?"[2]

"Who?" asked the girl.

Penelope interposed. "I don't believe Irene's read it yet. I've just got it out of the library; I heard so much talk about it. I wish she would let you find out a little about the people for yourself," she added. But here her father struck in:

"I can't get the time for books. It's as much as I can do to keep up with the newspapers; and when night comes, I'm tired, and I'd rather go out to the theater, or a lecture, if they've got a good stereopticon[3] to give you views of the places. But I guess we all like a play better than 'most anything else. I want something that'll make me laugh. I don't believe in tragedy. I think there's enough of that in real life without putting it on the stage. Seen 'Joshua Whitcomb'?"[4]

2. Pen name of Mary Ann Evans (1819–1880). Her novel *Middlemarch: A Study of Provincial Life* (1871–72), offered a Realist depiction of English small-town life, including attention to contemporary social issues related to class, gender and marriage, and political reform. Two of its principal plot lines concern young people (Dorothea Brooke and Tertius Lydgate) whose excessive idealism causes them to make disastrous marriage decisions.
3. A slide projector used for entertainment and educational purposes.
4. A comic New England rustic character popularized on the stage by American playwright and actor Henry Denman Thompson (1833–1911).

The whole family joined in the discussion, and it appeared that they all had their opinions of the plays and actors. Mrs. Lapham brought the talk back to literature. "I guess Penelope does most of our reading."

"Now, mother, you're not going to put it all on me!" said the girl, in comic protest.

Her mother laughed, and then added, with a sigh: "I used to like to get hold of a good book when I was a girl; but we weren't allowed to read many novels in those days. My mother called them all *lies*. And I guess she wasn't so very far wrong about some of them."

"They're certainly fictions," said Corey, smiling.

"Well, we do buy a good many books, first and last," said the Colonel, who probably had in mind the costly volumes which they presented to one another on birthdays and holidays. "But I get about all the reading I want in the newspapers. And when the girls want a novel, I tell 'em to get it out of the library. That's what the library's for. Phew!" he panted, blowing away the whole unprofitable subject. "How close you women-folks like to keep a room! You go down to the sea-side or up to the mountains for a change of air, and then you cork yourselves into a room so tight you don't have any air at all. Here! You girls get on your bonnets and go and show Mr. Corey the view of the hotels from the rocks."

Corey said that he should be delighted. The girls exchanged looks with each other, and then with their mother. Irene curved her pretty chin in comment upon her father's incorrigibility, and Penelope made a droll mouth, but the Colonel remained serenely content with his finesse. "I got 'em out of the way," he said, as soon as they were gone, and before his wife had time to fall upon him, "because I've got through my talk with him, and now I want to talk with *you*. It's just as I said, Persis; he wants to go into the business with me."

"It's lucky for you," said his wife, meaning that now he would not be made to suffer for attempting to hoax her. But she was too intensely interested to pursue that matter further. "What in the world do you suppose he means by it?"

"Well, I should judge by his talk that he had been trying a good many different things since he left college, and he haint found just the thing he likes—or the thing that likes him. It aint so easy. And now he's got an idea that he can take hold of the paint and push it in other countries—push it in Mexico and push it in South America. He's a splendid Spanish scholar,"—this was Lapham's version of Corey's modest claim to a smattering of the language,—"and he's been among the natives enough to know their ways. And he believes in the paint," added the Colonel.

"I guess he believes in something else besides the paint," said Mrs. Lapham.

"What do you mean?"

"Well, Silas Lapham, if you can't see *now* that he's after Irene, I don't know what ever *can* open your eyes. That's all."

The Colonel pretended to give the idea silent consideration, as if it had not occurred to him before. "Well, then, all I've got to say is, that he's going a good way round. I don't say you're wrong, but if it's Irene, I don't see why he should want to go off to South America to get her. And that's what he proposes to do. I guess there's some paint about it too, Persis. He says he believes in it,"—the Colonel devoutly lowered his voice,—"and he's willing to take the agency on his own account down there, and run it for a commission on what he can sell."

"Of course! He isn't going to take hold of it any way so as to feel beholden to you. He's got too much pride for that."

"He aint going to take hold of it at all, if he don't mean paint in the first place and Irene afterward. I don't object to him, as I know, either way, but the two things wont mix; and I don't propose he shall pull the wool over my eyes—or anybody else. But, as far as heard from, up to date, he means paint first, last, and all the time. At any rate, I'm going to take him on that basis. He's got some pretty good ideas about it, and he's been stirred up by this talk, just now, about getting our manufactures into the foreign markets. There's an overstock in everything, and we've got to get rid of it, or we've got to shut down till the home demand begins again. We've had two or three such flurries before now, and they didn't amount to much. They say we can't extend our commerce under the high tariff system we've got now, because there aint any sort of reciprocity on our side,—we want to have the other fellows show all the reciprocity,—and the English have got the advantage of us every time.[5] I don't know whether it's so or not; but I don't see why it should apply to my paint. Anyway, he wants to try it, and I've about made up my mind to let him. Of course I aint going to let him take all the risk. I believe in the paint *too,* and I shall pay his expenses anyway."

"So you want another partner after all?" Mrs. Lapham could not forbear saying.

"Yes, if that's your idea of a partner. It isn't mine," returned her husband dryly.

"Well, if you've made up your mind, Si, I suppose you're ready for advice," said Mrs. Lapham.

The Colonel enjoyed this. "Yes, I *am.* What have you got to say against it?"

5. Lapham's comments, including his doubts about tariff policies, accord with the economic facts of the "Long Depression" of 1873–79, a period of prolonged economic contraction, high unemployment, wage stagnation, and elevated rates of business and bank failure.

"I don't know as I've got anything. I'm satisfied if you are."

"Well?"

"When is he going to start for South America?"

"I shall take him into the office awhile. He'll get off some time in the winter. But he's got to know the business first."

"Oh, indeed! Are you going to take him to board in the family?"

"What are you after, Persis?"

"Oh, nothing! I presume he will feel free to visit in the family, even if he don't board with us."

"I presume he will."

"And if he don't use his privileges, do you think he'll be a fit person to manage your paint in South America?"

The Colonel reddened consciously. "I'm not taking him on that basis."

"Oh, yes, you are! You may pretend you aint to yourself, but you mustn't pretend so to me. Because I know you."

The Colonel laughed. "Pshaw!" he said.

Mrs. Lapham continued: "I don't see any harm in hoping that he'll take a fancy to her. But if you really think it wont do to mix the two things, I advise you not to take Mr. Corey into the business. It will do all very well if he *does* take a fancy to her; but if he don't, you know how you'll feel about it. And I know you well enough, Silas, to know that you can't do him justice if that happens. And I don't think it's right you should take this step unless you're pretty sure. I can see that you've set your heart on this thing——"

"I haven't set my heart on it at all," protested Lapham.

"And if you can't bring it about, you're going to feel unhappy over it," pursued his wife, regardless of his protest.

"Oh, very well," he said. "If you know more about what's in my mind than I do, there's no use arguing, as I can see."

He got up, to carry off his consciousness, and sauntered out of the door on to his piazza. He could see the young people down on the rocks, and his heart swelled in his breast. He had always said that he did not care what a man's family was, but the presence of young Corey as an applicant to him for employment, as his guest, as the possible suitor of his daughter, was one of the sweetest flavors that he had yet tasted in his success. He knew who the Coreys were very well, and, in his simple, brutal way, he had long hated their name as a symbol of splendor which, unless he should live to see at least three generations of his descendants gilded with mineral paint, he could not hope to realize in his own. He was acquainted in a business way with the tradition of old Phillips Corey, and he had heard a great many things about the Corey who had spent his youth abroad and his father's money everywhere, and done nothing but say smart things. Lapham could not see the smartness of some of them which had been repeated to him. Once he had encountered the fellow, and it seemed to Lapham that the tall, slim, white-mustached man, with the slight stoop, was everything that was offensively aristocratic. He had bristled up aggressively at the name when his wife told how she had made the acquaintance of the fellow's family the summer before, and he had treated the notion of young Corey's caring for Irene with the contempt which such a ridiculous superstition deserved. He had made up his mind about young Corey beforehand; yet when he met him he felt an instant liking for him, which he frankly acknowledged, and he had begun to assume the burden of his wife's superstition, of which she seemed now ready to accuse him of being the inventor.

Nothing had moved his thick imagination like this day's events since the girl who taught him spelling and grammar in the school at Lumberville had said she would have him for her husband.

The dark figures, stationary on the rocks, began to move, and he could see that they were coming toward the house. He went indoors so as not to appear to have been watching them.

VIII.

A week after she had parted with her son at Bar Harbor, Mrs. Corey suddenly walked in upon her husband in their house in Boston. He was at breakfast, and he gave her the patronizing welcome with which the husband who has been staying in town all summer receives his wife when she drops down upon him from the mountains or the sea-side. For a little moment she feels herself strange in the house, and suffers herself to be treated like a guest, before envy of his comfort vexes her back into possession and authority. Mrs. Corey was a lady, and she did not let her envy take the form of open reproach.

"Well, Anna, you find me here in the luxury you left me to. How did you leave the girls?"

"The girls were well," said Mrs. Corey, looking absently at her husband's brown velvet coat, in which he was so handsome. No man had ever grown gray more beautifully. His hair, while not remaining dark enough to form a theatrical contrast with his mustache, was yet some shades darker, and, in becoming a little thinner, it had become a little more gracefully wavy. His skin had the pearly tint which that of elderly men sometimes assumes, and the lines which time had traced upon it were too delicate for the name of wrinkles. He had never had any personal vanity, and there was no consciousness in his good looks now.

"I am glad of that. The boy I have with me," he returned; "that is, when he *is* with me."

"Why, where is he?" demanded the mother.

"Probably carousing with the boon Lapham somewhere. He left me yesterday afternoon to go and offer his allegiance to the Mineral Paint King, and I haven't seen him since."

"Bromfield!" cried Mrs. Corey. "Why didn't you stop him?"

"Well, my dear, I'm not sure that it isn't a very good thing."

"A good thing? It's horrid!"

"No, I don't think so. It's decent. Tom had found out—without consulting the landscape, which I believe proclaims it everywhere——"

"Hideous!"

"That it's really a good thing; and he thinks that he has some ideas in regard to its dissemination in the parts beyond seas."

"Why shouldn't he go into something else?" lamented the mother.

"I believe he has gone into nearly everything else, and come out of it. So there is a chance of his coming out of this. But as I had nothing to suggest in place of it, I thought it best not to interfere. In fact, what good would my telling him that mineral paint was nasty have done? I dare say *you* told him it was nasty."

"Yes! I did."

"And you see with what effect, though he values your opinion three times as much as he values mine. Perhaps you came up to tell him again that it was nasty?"

"I feel very unhappy about it. He is throwing himself away. Yes, I should like to prevent it if I could!"

The father shook his head.

"If Lapham hasn't prevented it, I fancy it's too late. But there may be some hopes of Lapham. As for Tom's throwing himself away, I don't know. There's no question but he is one of the best fellows under the sun. He's tremendously energetic, and he has plenty of the kind of sense which we call horse; but he isn't brilliant. No, Tom is not brilliant. I don't think he would get on in a profession, and he's instinctively kept out of everything of the kind. But he has got to do something. What shall he do? He says mineral paint, and really I don't see why he shouldn't. If money is fairly and honestly earned, why should we pretend to care what it comes out of, when we don't really care? That superstition is exploded everywhere."

"Oh, it isn't the paint alone," said Mrs. Corey; and then she perceptibly arrested herself, and made a diversion in continuing: "I wish he had married some one."

"With money?" suggested her husband. "From time to time I have attempted Tom's corruption from that side, but I suspect Tom has a conscience against it, and I rather like him for it. I married for love myself," said Corey, looking across the table at his wife.

She returned his look tolerantly, though she felt it right to say, "What nonsense!"

"Besides," continued her husband, "if you come to money, there is the paint princess. She will have plenty."

"Ah, that's the worst of it," sighed the mother. "I suppose I could get on with the paint——"

"But not with the princess? I thought you said she was a very pretty, well-behaved girl?"

"She is very pretty, and she is well-behaved; but there is nothing of her. She is insipid; she is very insipid."

"But Tom seemed to like her flavor, such as it was?"

"How can I tell? We were under a terrible obligation to them, and I naturally wished him to be polite to them. In fact, I asked him to be so."

"And he was too polite?"

"I can't say that he was. But there is no doubt that the child is extremely pretty."

"Tom says there are two of them. Perhaps they will neutralize each other."

"Yes, there is another daughter," assented Mrs. Corey. "I don't see how you can joke about such things, Bromfield," she added.

"Well, I don't either, my dear, to tell you the truth. My hardihood surprises me. Here is a son of mine whom I see reduced to making his living by a shrinkage in values. It's very odd," interjected Corey, "that some values should have this peculiarity of shrinking. You never hear of values in a picture shrinking; but rents, stocks, real estate—all those values shrink abominably. Perhaps it might be argued that one should put all his values into pictures; I've got a good many of mine there."

"Tom needn't earn his living," said Mrs. Corey, refusing her husband's jest. "There's still enough for all of us."

"That is what I have sometimes urged upon Tom. I have proved to him that with economy, and strict attention to business, he need do nothing as long as he lives. Of course he would be somewhat restricted, and it would cramp the rest of us; but it is a world of sacrifices and compromises. He couldn't agree with me, and he was not in the least moved by the example of persons of quality in Europe, which I alleged in support of the life of idleness. It appears that he wishes to do something—to do something for himself. I am afraid that Tom is selfish."

Mrs. Corey smiled wanly. Thirty years before, she had married the rich young painter in Rome, who said so much better things than he painted—charming things, just the things to please the fancy of a girl who was disposed to take life a little too seriously and practically. She saw him in a different light when she got him home to Boston; but he had kept on saying the charming things, and he had not done much else. In fact, he had fulfilled the promise of his youth. It was a good trait in him that he was not actively but only passively extravagant. He was not adventurous with his money; his tastes were as simple as an Italian's; he had no expensive habits. In the process of time he had grown to lead a more and more secluded life. It was hard to get him out anywhere, even to dinner. His patience with their narrowing circumstances had a pathos which she felt the more the more she came into charge of their joint life. At times it seemed too bad that the children and their education and pleasures should cost so much. She knew, besides, that if it had not been for them she would have gone back to Rome with him, and lived princely there for less than it took to live respectably in Boston.

"Tom hasn't consulted me," continued his father, "but he has consulted other people. And he has arrived at the conclusion that mineral paint is a good thing to go into. He has found out all about it, and about its founder or inventor. It's quite impressive to hear him talk. And if he must do something for himself, I don't see why his egotism shouldn't as well take that form as another. Combined with the paint princess, it isn't so agreeable; but that's only a remote possibility, for which your principal ground is your motherly solicitude. But even if it were probable and imminent, what could you do? The chief consolation that we American parents have in these matters is that we can do nothing. If we were Europeans, even English, we should take some cognizance of our children's love affairs, and in some measure teach their young affections how to shoot. But it is our custom to ignore them until they have shot, and then they ignore us. We are altogether too delicate to arrange the marriages of our children; and when they have arranged them we don't like to say anything, for fear we should only make bad worse. The right way is for us to school ourselves to indifference. That is what the young people have to do elsewhere, and that is the only logical result of our position here. It is absurd for us to have any feeling about what we don't interfere with."

"Oh, people do interfere with their children's marriages very often," said Mrs. Corey.

"Yes, but only in a half-hearted way, so as not to make it disagreeable for themselves if the marriages go on in spite of them, as they're pretty apt to do. Now, my idea is that I ought to cut Tom off with a shilling. That would be very simple, and it would be economical. But you would never consent, and Tom wouldn't mind it."

"I think our whole conduct in regard to such things is wrong," said Mrs. Corey.

"Oh, very likely. But our whole civilization is based upon it. And who is going to make a beginning? To which father in our acquaintance shall I go and propose an alliance for Tom with his daughter? I should feel like an ass. And will you go to some mother, and ask her sons in marriage for our daughters? You would feel like a goose. No; the only motto for us is, Hands off altogether."

"I shall certainly speak to Tom when the time comes," said Mrs. Corey.

"And I shall ask leave to be absent from your discomfiture, my dear," answered her husband.

The son returned that afternoon, and confessed his surprise at finding his mother in Boston. He was so frank that she had not quite the courage to confess in turn why she had come, but trumped up an excuse.

"Well, mother," he said promptly, "I have made an engagement with Mr. Lapham."

"Have you, Tom?" she asked faintly.

"Yes. For the present I am going to have charge of his foreign correspondence, and if I see my way to the advantage I expect to find in it, I am going out to manage that side of his business in South America and Mexico. He's behaved very handsomely about it. He says that if it appears for our common interest, he shall pay me a salary as well as a commission. I've talked with Uncle Jim, and he thinks it's a good opening."

"Your Uncle Jim does?" queried Mrs. Corey in amaze.

"Yes; I consulted him the whole way through, and I've acted on his advice."

This seemed an incomprehensible treachery on her brother's part.

"Yes; I thought you would like to have me. And besides, I couldn't possibly have gone to any one so well fitted to advise me."

His mother said nothing. In fact, the mineral paint business, however painful its interest, was, for the moment, superseded by a more poignant anxiety. She began to feel her way cautiously toward this.

"Have you been talking about your business with Mr. Lapham all night?"

"Well, pretty much," said her son, with a guiltless laugh. "I went to see him yesterday afternoon, after I had gone over the whole ground with Uncle Jim, and Mr. Lapham asked me to go down with him and finish up."

"Down?" repeated Mrs. Corey.

"Yes, to Nantasket. He has a cottage down there."

"At Nantasket?" Mrs. Corey knitted her brows a little. "What in the world can a cottage at Nantasket be like?"

"Oh, very much like a 'cottage' anywhere. It has the usual allowance of red roof and veranda. There are the regulation rocks by the sea; and the big hotels on the beach about a mile off, flaring away with electric lights and roman-candles at night. We didn't have them at Nahant."

"No," said his mother. "Is Mrs. Lapham well? And her daughter?"

"Yes, I think so," said the young man. "The young ladies walked me down to the rocks in the usual way after dinner, and then I came back and talked paint with Mr. Lapham till midnight. We didn't settle anything till this morning coming up on the boat."

"What sort of people do they seem to be at home?"

"What sort? Well, I don't know that I noticed." Mrs. Corey permitted herself the first part of a sigh of relief; and her son laughed, but apparently not at her. "They're just reading 'Middlemarch.' They say there's so much talk about it. Oh, I suppose they're very good people. They seemed to be on very good terms with each other."

"I suppose it's the plain sister who's reading 'Middlemarch.'"

"Plain? Is she plain?" asked the young man, as if searching his consciousness. "Yes, it's the older one who does the reading, apparently. But I don't believe that even she overdoes it. They like to talk better. They reminded me of Southern people in that." The young man smiled, as if amused by some of his impressions of the Lapham family. "The living, as the country people call it, is tremendously good. The Colonel—he's a colonel—talked of the coffee as his wife's coffee, as if she had personally made it in the kitchen, though I believe it was merely inspired by her. And there was everything in the house that money could buy. But money has its limitations."

This was a fact which Mrs. Corey was beginning to realize more and more unpleasantly in her own life; but it seemed to bring her a certain comfort in its application to the Laphams. "Yes, there is a point where taste has to begin," she said.

"They seemed to want to apologize to me for not having more books," said Corey. "I don't know why they should. The Colonel said they bought a good many books, first and last; but apparently they don't take them to the sea-side."

"I dare say they *never* buy a *new* book. I've met some of these moneyed people lately, and they lavish on every conceivable luxury, and then borrow books, and get them in the cheap paper editions."

"I fancy that's the way with the Lapham family," said the young man, smilingly. "But they are very good people. The other daughter is humorous."

"Humorous?" Mrs. Corey knitted her brows in some perplexity. "Do you mean like Mrs. Sayre?"[1] she asked, naming the lady whose name must come into every Boston mind when humor is mentioned.

"Oh, no; nothing like that. She never says anything that you can remember; nothing in flashes or ripples; nothing the least literary. But it's a sort of droll way of looking at things; or a droll medium through which things present themselves. I don't know. She tells what she's seen, and mimics a little."

1. She remains unidentified.

"Oh," said Mrs. Corey, coldly. After a moment she asked: "And is Miss Irene as pretty as ever?"

"She's a wonderful complexion," said the son, unsatisfactorily. "I shall want to be by when father and Colonel Lapham meet," he added, with a smile.

"Ah, yes, your father!" said the mother, in that way in which a wife at once compassionates and censures her husband to their children.

"Do you think it's really going to be a trial to him?" asked the young man, quickly.

"No, no, I can't say it is. But I confess I wish it was some other business, Tom."

"Well, mother, I don't see why. The principal thing looked at now is the amount of money; and while I would rather starve than touch a dollar that was dirty with any sort of dishonesty——"

"Of course you would, my son!" interposed his mother, proudly.

"I shouldn't at all mind its having a little mineral paint on it. I'll use my influence with Colonel Lapham—if I ever have any—to have his paint scraped off the landscape."

"I suppose you wont begin till the autumn."

"Oh, yes, I shall," said the son, laughing at his mother's simple ignorance of business. "I shall begin to-morrow morning."

"To-morrow morning!"

"Yes. I've had my desk appointed already, and I shall be down there at nine in the morning to take possession."

"Tom!" cried his mother, "why do you think Mr. Lapham has taken you into business so readily? I've always heard that it was so hard for young men to get in."

"And do you think I found it easy with him? We had about twelve hours' solid talk."

"And you don't suppose it was any sort of—personal consideration?"

"Why, I don't know exactly what you mean, mother. I suppose he likes me."

Mrs. Corey could not say just what she meant. She answered, ineffectually enough:

"Yes. You wouldn't like it to be a favor, would you?"

"I think he's a man who may be trusted to look after his own interest. But I don't mind his beginning by liking me. It'll be my own fault if I don't make myself essential to him."

"Yes," said Mrs. Corey.

"Well," demanded her husband, at their first meeting after her interview with their son, "what did you say to Tom?"

"Very little, if anything. I found him with his mind made up, and it would only have distressed him if I had tried to change it."

"That is precisely what I said, my dear."

"Besides, he had talked the matter over fully with James, and seems to have been advised by him. I can't understand James."

"Oh! it's in regard to the paint, and not the princess, that he's made up his mind. Well, I think you were wise to let him alone, Anna. We represent a faded tradition. We don't really care what business a man is in, so it is large enough, and he doesn't advertise offensively; but we think it fine to affect reluctance."

"Do you really feel so, Bromfield?" asked his wife, seriously.

"Certainly I do. There was a long time in my misguided youth when I supposed myself some sort of porcelain; but it's a relief to be of the common clay, after all, and to know it. If I get broken, I can be easily replaced."

"If Tom must go into such a business," said Mrs. Corey, "I'm glad James approves of it."

"I'm afraid it wouldn't matter to Tom if he didn't; and I don't know that I should care," said Corey, betraying the fact that he had perhaps had a good deal of his brother-in-law's judgment in the course of his life. "You had better consult him in regard to Tom's marrying the princess."

"There is no necessity at present for that," said Mrs. Corey, with dignity. After a moment, she asked, "Should you feel quite so easy if it were a question of that, Bromfield?"

"It would be a little more personal."

"You feel about it as I do. Of course, we have both lived too long, and seen too much of the world, to suppose we can control such things. The child is good, I haven't the least doubt, and all those things can be managed so that they wouldn't disgrace us. But she has had a certain sort of bringing up. I should prefer Tom to marry a girl with another sort, and this business venture of his increases the chances that he wont. That's all."

"'Tis not so deep as a well, nor so wide as a church door, but 'twill serve.'"[2]

"I shouldn't like it."

"Well, it hasn't happened yet."

"Ah, you never can realize anything beforehand."

"Perhaps that has saved me some suffering. But you have at least the consolation of two anxieties at once. I always find that a great advantage. You can play one off against the other."

Mrs. Corey drew a long breath as if she did not experience the suggested consolation; and she arranged to quit, the following afternoon, the scene of her defeat, which she had not had the courage to make a battle-field. Her son went down to see her off on the boat,

2. A slightly altered version of Mercutio's reference to his fatal wound in Shakespeare's *Romeo and Juliet* (3.1.92–93).

after spending his first day at his desk in Lapham's office. He was in a gay humor, and she departed in a reflected gleam of his good spirits. He told her all about it, as he sat talking with her at the stern of the boat, lingering till the last moment, and then stepping ashore, with as little waste of time as Lapham himself, on the gang-plank which the deck-hands had laid hold of. He touched his hat to her from the wharf to reassure her of his escape from being carried away with her, and the next moment his smiling face hid itself in the crowd.

He walked on smiling up the long wharf, encumbered with trucks and hacks and piles of freight, and, taking his way through the deserted business streets beyond this bustle, made a point of passing the door of Lapham's warehouse, on the jambs of which his name and paint were lettered in black on a square ground of white. The door was still open, and Corey loitered a moment before it, tempted to go upstairs and fetch away some foreign letters which he had left on his desk, and which he thought he might finish up at home. He was in love with his work, and he felt the enthusiasm for it which nothing but the work we can do well inspires in us. He believed that he had found his place in the world, after a good deal of looking, and he had the relief, the repose, of fitting into it. Every little incident of the momentous, uneventful day was a pleasure in his mind, from his sitting down at his desk, to which Lapham's boy brought him the foreign letters, till his rising from it an hour ago. Lapham had been in view within his own office, but he had given Corey no formal reception, and had, in fact, not spoken to him till toward the end of the forenoon, when he suddenly came out of his den with some more letters in his hand, and after a brief "How d'ye do?" had spoken a few words about them, and left them with him. He was in his shirt-sleeves again, and his sanguine person seemed to radiate the heat with which he suffered. He did not go out to lunch, but had it brought to him in his office, where Corey saw him eating it before he left his own desk to go out and perch on a swinging seat before the long counter of a down-town restaurant. He observed that all the others lunched at twelve, and he resolved to anticipate his usual hour. When he returned; the pretty girl who had been clicking away at a type-writer all the morning was neatly putting out of sight the evidences of pie from the table where her machine stood, and was preparing to go on with her copying. In his office Lapham lay asleep in his armchair, with a newspaper over his face.

Now, while Corey lingered at the entrance to the stairway, these two came down the stairs together, and he heard Lapham saying, "Well, then, you better get a divorce."

He looked red and excited, and the girl's face, which she veiled at sight of Corey, showed traces of tears. She slipped round him into the street.

But Lapham stopped, and said, with the show of no feeling but surprise: "Hello, Corey! Did you want to go up?"

"Yes; there were some letters I hadn't quite got through with."

"You'll find Dennis up there. But I guess you better let them go till to-morrow. I always make it a rule to stop work when I'm done."

"Perhaps you're right," said Corey, yielding.

"Come along down as far as the boat with me. There's a little matter I want to talk over with you."

It was a business matter, and related to Corey's proposed connection with the house.

The next day the head book-keeper, who lunched at the long counter of the same restaurant with Corey, began to talk with him about Lapham. Walker had not apparently got his place by seniority; though, with his bald head, and round, smooth face, one might have taken him for a plump elder, if he had not looked equally like a robust infant. The thick, drabbish-yellow mustache was what arrested decision in either direction, and the prompt vigor of all his movements was that of a young man of thirty, which was really Walker's age. He knew, of course, who Corey was, and he had waited for a man who might look down on him socially to make the overtures toward something more than business acquaintance; but, these made, he was readily responsive, and drew freely on his philosophy of Lapham and his affairs.

"I think about the only difference between people in this world is that some know what they want, and some don't. Well, now," said Walker, beating the bottom of his salt-box to make the salt come out, "the old man knows what he wants every time. And generally he gets it. Yes, sir, he generally gets it. He knows what he's about, but I'll be blessed if the rest of us do half the time. Anyway, we don't till he's ready to let us. You take my position in most business houses. It's confidential. The head book-keeper knows right along pretty much everything the house has got in hand. I'll give you my word *I* don't. He may open up to you a little more in your department, but, as far as the rest of us go, he don't open up any more than an oyster on a hot brick. They say he had a partner once; I guess he's dead. *I* wouldn't like to be the old man's partner. Well, you see, this paint of his is like his heart's blood. Better not try to joke him about it. I've seen people come in occasionally and try it. They didn't get much fun out of it."

While he talked, Walker was plucking up morsels from his plate, tearing off pieces of French bread from the long loaf, and feeding them into his mouth in an impersonal way, as if he were firing up an engine.

"I suppose he thinks," suggested Corey, "that if he doesn't tell, nobody else will."

Walker took a draught of beer from his glass, and wiped the foam from his mustache.

"Oh, but he carries it too far! It's a weakness with him. He's just so about everything. Look at the way he keeps it up about that type-writer girl of his. You'd think she was some princess traveling incognito. There isn't one of us knows who she is, or where she came from, or who she belongs to. He brought her and her machine into the office one morning, and set 'em down at a table, and that's all there is about it, as far as we're concerned. It's pretty hard on the girl, for I guess she'd like to talk; and to any one that didn't know the old man—" Walker broke off and drained his glass of what was left in it.

Corey thought of the words he had overheard from Lapham to the girl. But he said, "She seems to be kept pretty busy."

"Oh, yes," said Walker; "there aint much loafing round the place, in any of the departments, from the old man's down. That's just what I say. He's got to work just twice as hard, if he wants to keep everything in his own mind. But he aint afraid of work. That's one good thing about him. And Miss Dewey has to keep step with the rest of us. But she don't look like one that would take to it naturally. Such a pretty girl as that generally thinks she does enough when she looks her prettiest."

"She's a pretty girl," said Corey, non-committally. "But I suppose a great many pretty girls have to earn their living."

"Don't any of 'em like to do it," returned the book-keeper. "They think it's a hardship, and I don't blame 'em. They have got a right to get married, and they ought to have the chance. And Miss Dewey's smart, too. She's as bright as a biscuit. I guess she's had trouble. I shouldn't be much more than half surprised if Miss Dewey wasn't Miss Dewey, or hadn't always been. Yes, sir," continued the book-keeper, who prolonged the talk as they walked back to Lapham's warehouse together, "I don't know exactly what it is,—it isn't any one thing in particular,—but I should say that girl had been married. I wouldn't speak so freely to any of the rest, Mr. Corey,—I want you to understand that,—and it isn't any of my business, anyway; but that's my opinion."

Corey made no reply, as he walked beside the book-keeper, who continued:

"It's curious what a difference marriage makes in people. Now, I know that I don't look any more like a bachelor of my age than I do like the man in the moon, and yet I couldn't say where the difference came in, to save me. And it's just so with a woman. The minute you catch sight of her face, there's something in it that tells you whether she's married or not. What do you suppose it is?"

"I'm sure I don't know," said Corey, willing to laugh away the topic. "And from what I read occasionally of some people who go about repeating their happiness, I shouldn't say that the intangible evidences were always unmistakable."

"Oh, of course," admitted Walker, easily surrendering his position. "All signs fail in dry weather. Hello! What's that?" He caught Corey by the arm, and they both stopped.

At a corner, half a block ahead of them, the summer noon solitude of the place was broken by a bit of drama. A man and woman issued from the intersecting street, and at the moment of coming into sight the man, who looked like a sailor, caught the woman by the arm, as if to detain her. A brief struggle ensued, the woman trying to free herself, and the man half coaxing, half scolding. The spectators could now see that he was drunk; but before they could decide whether it was a case for their interference or not, the woman suddenly set both hands against the man's breast and gave him a quick push. He lost his footing and tumbled into a heap in the gutter. The woman faltered an instant, as if to see whether he was seriously hurt, and then turned and ran.

When Corey and the book-keeper reëntered the office, Miss Dewey had finished her lunch, and was putting a sheet of paper into her type-writer. She looked up at them with her eyes of turquoise blue, under her low white forehead, with the hair neatly rippled over it, and then began to beat the keys of her machine.

[FOURTH INSTALLMENT—FEBRUARY 1885]

IX.

Lapham had the pride which comes of self-making, and he would not openly lower his crest to the young fellow he had taken into his business. He was going to be obviously master in his own place to every one; and during the hours of business he did nothing to distinguish Corey from the half-dozen other clerks and book-keepers in the outer office, but he was not silent about the fact that Bromfield Corey's son had taken a fancy to come to him. "Did you notice that fellow at the desk facing my type-writer girl? Well, sir, that's the son of Bromfield Corey—old Phillips Corey's grandson. And I'll say this for him, that there isn't a man in the office that looks after his work better. There isn't anything he's too good for. He's right here at nine every morning, before the clock gets in the word. I guess it's his grandfather coming out in him. He's got charge of the foreign correspondence. We're pushing the paint everywhere." He flattered himself that he did not lug the matter in. He had been warned against that by his wife, but he had the right to do Corey justice, and his brag took the form of illustration. "Talk about training for business—I tell you it's all in the man himself! I used to believe in what old Horace Greeley[1] said about college graduates being the poorest kind of horned cattle; but I've changed my mind a little. You take that fellow Corey. He's been through Harvard, and he's had about every advantage that a fellow could have. Been everywhere, and talks half a dozen languages like English. I suppose he's got money enough to live without lifting a hand, any more than his father does; son of Bromfield Corey, you know. But the thing was in him. He's a natural-born business man; and I've had many a fellow with me that had come up out of the street, and worked hard all his life, without ever losing his original opposition to the thing. But Corey likes it. I believe the fellow would like to stick at that desk of his night and day. I don't know where he got it. I guess it must be his grandfather, old Phillips Corey; it often skips a generation, you know. But what I say is, a thing has got to be born in a man; and if it ain't born in him, all the privations in the world won't put it there, and if it is, all the college training won't take it out."

Sometimes Lapham advanced these ideas at his own table, to a guest whom he had brought to Nantasket for the night. Then he suffered exposure and ridicule at the hands of his wife, when opportunity offered. She would not let him bring Corey down to Nantasket at all.

"No, indeed!" she said. "I am not going to have them think we're running after him. If he wants to see Irene, he can find out ways of doing it for himself."

"Who wants him to see Irene?" retorted the Colonel angrily.

"I do," said Mrs. Lapham. "And I want him to see her without any of your connivance, Silas. I'm not going to have it said that I put my girls *at* anybody. Why don't you invite some of your other clerks?"

"He ain't just like the other clerks. He's going to take charge of a part of the business. It's quite another thing."

"Oh, indeed!" said Mrs. Lapham vexatiously. "Then you *are* going to take a partner."

"I shall ask him down if I choose!" returned the Colonel, disdaining her insinuation.

His wife laughed with the fearlessness of a woman who knows her husband.

"But you won't choose when you've thought it over, Si." Then she applied an emollient to his chafed surface. "Don't you suppose I feel as you do about it? I know just how proud you are, and I'm not going to have you do anything that will make you feel meeching[2] afterward. You just let things take their course. If he wants Irene, he's

1. A prominent newspaper editor (1811–1872), who popularized the slogan, "Go West, young man, and grow up with the country"; he was a presidential candidate in 1872.
2. Cringing, skulking, cowardly.

going to find out some way of seeing her; and if he don't, all the plotting and planning in the world isn't going to make him."

"Who's plotting?" again retorted the Colonel, shuddering at the utterance of hopes and ambitions which a man hides with shame, but a woman talks over as freely and coolly as if they were items of a milliner's bill.

"Oh, not *you!*" exulted his wife. "I understand what *you* want. You want to get this fellow, who is neither partner nor clerk, down here to talk business with him. Well, now, you just talk business with him at the office."

The only social attention which Lapham succeeded in offering Corey was to take him in his buggy, now and then, for a spin out over the Milldam. He kept the mare in town, and on a pleasant afternoon he liked to knock off early, as he phrased it, and let the mare out a little. Corey understood something about horses, though in a passionless way, and he would have preferred to talk business when obliged to talk horse. But he deferred to his business superior with the sense of discipline which is innate in the apparently insubordinate American nature. If Corey could hardly have helped feeling the social difference between Lapham and himself, in his presence he silenced his traditions, and showed him all the respect that he could have exacted from any of his clerks. He talked horse with him, and when the Colonel wished he talked house. Besides himself and his paint Lapham had not many other topics; and if he had a choice between the mare and the edifice on the water side of Beacon street, it was just now the latter. Sometimes, in driving in or out, he stopped at the house, and made Corey his guest there, if he might not at Nantasket; and one day it happened that the young man met Irene there again. She had come up with her mother alone, and they were in the house, interviewing the carpenter as before, when the Colonel jumped out of his buggy and cast anchor at the pavement. More exactly, Mrs. Lapham was interviewing the carpenter, and Irene was sitting in the bow-window on a trestle, and looking out at the driving. She saw him come up with her father, and bowed and blushed. Her father went on upstairs to find her mother, and Corey pulled up another trestle which he found in the back part of the room. The first floorings had been laid throughout the house, and the partitions had been lathed so that one could realize the shape of the interior.

"I suppose you will sit at this window a good deal," said the young man.

"Yes, I think it will be very nice. There's so much more going on than there is in the Square."

"It must be very interesting to you to see the house grow."

"It is. Only it doesn't seem to grow so fast as I expected."

"Why, I'm amazed at the progress your carpenter has made every time I come."

The girl looked down, and then lifting her eyes she said, with a sort of timorous appeal:

"I've been reading that book since you were down at Nantasket."

"Book?" repeated Corey, while she reddened with disappointment. "Oh, yes. 'Middlemarch.' Did you like it?"

"I haven't got through with it yet. Pen has finished it."

"What does she think of it?"

"Oh, I think she likes it very well. I haven't heard her talk about it much. Do you like it?"

"Yes; I liked it immensely. But it's several years since I read it."

"I didn't know it was so old. It's just got into the Seaside Library," she urged, with a little sense of injury in her tone.

"Oh, it hasn't been out such a very great while," said Corey, politely. "It came a little before 'Daniel Deronda.'"[3]

The girl was again silent. She followed the curl of a shaving on the floor with the point of her parasol.

"Do you like that Rosamond Vincy?"[4] she asked, without looking up.

Corey smiled in his kind way.

"I didn't suppose she was expected to have any friends. I can't say I liked her. But I don't think I disliked her so much as the author does. She's pretty hard on her good-looking"—he was going to say girls, but as if that might have been rather personal, he said—"people."

"Yes, that's what Pen says. She says she doesn't give her any chance to be good. She says she should have been just as bad as Rosamond if she had been in her place."

The young man laughed. "Your sister is very satirical, isn't she?"

"I don't know," said Irene, still intent upon the convolutions of the shaving. "She keeps us laughing. Papa thinks there's nobody that can talk like her." She gave the shaving a little toss from her, and took the parasol up across her lap. The unworldliness of the Lapham girls did not extend to their dress; Irene's costume was very stylish, and she governed her head and shoulders stylishly. "We are going to have the back room upstairs for a music-room and library," she said abruptly.

"Yes?" returned Corey. "I should think that would be charming."

"We expected to have book-cases, but the architect wants to build the shelves in."

The fact seemed to be referred to Corey for his comment.

3. Eliot's last completed novel, published in 1876.
4. The self-absorbed beauty in *Middlemarch*, unhappily married to the idealistic physician Lydgate.

"It seems to me that would be the best way. They'll look like part of the room then. You can make them low, and hang your pictures above them."

"Yes, that's what he said." The girl looked out of the window in adding, "I presume with nice bindings it will look very well."

"Oh, nothing furnishes a room like books."

"No. There will have to be a good many of them."

"That depends upon the size of your room and the number of your shelves."

"Oh, of course! I presume," said Irene, thoughtfully, "we shall have to have Gibbon."

"If you want to read him," said Corey, with a laugh of sympathy for an imaginable joke.

"We had a great deal about him at school. I believe we had one of his books. Mine's lost, but Pen will remember."

The young man looked at her, and then said, seriously, "You'll want Greene, of course, and Motley, and Parkman."

"Yes. What kind of writers are they?"

"They're historians, too."

"Oh, yes; I remember now. That's what Gibbon was. Is it Gibbon or Gibbons?"

The young man decided the point with apparently superfluous delicacy. "Gibbon, I think."[5]

"There used to be so many of them," said Irene, gayly. "I used to get them mixed up with each other, and I couldn't tell them from the poets. Should you want to have poetry?"

"Yes; I suppose some edition of the English poets."

"We don't any of us like poetry. Do you like it?"

"I'm afraid I don't very much," Corey owned. "But, of course, there was a time when Tennyson[6] was a great deal more to me than he is now."

"We had something about him at school, too. I think I remember the name. I think we ought to have *all* the American poets."

"Well, not all. Five or six of the best: you want Longfellow and Bryant and Whittier and Holmes and Emerson and Lowell."[7]

5. Tom suggests standard authors in poetry and history, while Irene favors popular fiction and drama. English historian Edward Gibbon (1737–1794) wrote the six-volume *History of the Decline and Fall of the Roman Empire* (1776–88). George Washington Greene (1811–1883), John Lothrop Motley (1814–1877), and Francis Parkman (1823–1893) were all highly regarded American historians.
6. Alfred, Lord Tennyson (1809–1892), the preeminent poet of Victorian England, served as poet laureate from 1850 until his death.
7. Tom's list of American poets includes, in addition to the prominent Transcendentalist poet and essayist Ralph Waldo Emerson (1803–1882), the "Fireside" or "Schoolroom" poets whose works were standard fare in 19th-century American schoolbooks and parlors: Henry Wadsworth Longfellow (1807–1882), William Cullen Bryant (1794–1878), John Greenleaf Whittier (1807–1892), Oliver Wendell Holmes Sr. (1809–1894), and

The girl listened attentively, as if making mental note of the names. "And Shakspere," she added. "Don't you like Shakspere's plays?"

"Oh, yes, very much."

"I used to be perfectly crazy about his plays. Don't you think 'Hamlet' is splendid? We had ever so much about Shakspere. Weren't you perfectly astonished when you found out how many other plays of his there were? I always thought there was nothing but 'Hamlet' and 'Romeo and Juliet' and 'Macbeth' and 'Richard III.' and 'King Lear,' and that one that Robeson and Crane[8] have—oh, yes! 'Comedy of Errors.'"

"Those are the ones they usually play," said Corey.

"I presume we shall have to have Scott's[9] works," said Irene, returning to the question of books.

"Oh, yes."

"One of the girls used to think he was *great.* She was always talking about Scott." Irene made a pretty little, amiably contemptuous mouth. "He isn't American, though?" she suggested.

"No," said Corey; "he's Scotch, I believe."

Irene passed her glove over her forehead. "I always get him mixed up with Cooper.[1] Well, papa has got to get them. If we have a library, we have got to have books in it. Pen says it's perfectly ridiculous having one. But papa thinks whatever the architect says is right. He fought him hard enough at first. I don't see how any one can keep the poets and the historians and novelists separate in their mind. Of course papa will buy them if we say so. But I don't see how I'm ever going to tell him which ones." The joyous light faded out of her face and left it pensive.

"Why, if you like," said the young man, taking out his pencil, "I'll put down the names we've been talking about."

He clapped himself on his breast pockets to detect some lurking scrap of paper.

"Will you?" she cried delightedly. "Here! take one of my cards," and she pulled out her card-case. "The carpenter writes on a three-cornered block and puts it into his pocket, and it's so uncomfortable

---

James Russell Lowell (1819–1891). As assistant editor (beginning in 1866) and editor (1871–81) of the Boston-based *Atlantic Monthly* magazine (where he had succeeded Lowell), Howells was personally acquainted with all of these writers and, in some cases, had published their later writings.

8. I.e., Stuart Robson (not "Robeson"; 1836–1903) and William Henry Crane (1845–1928), American actors who starred in a long-running production of Shakespeare's *Comedy of Errors.*

9. Sir Walter Scott (1771–1832), Scottish poet and novelist, who wrote the tremendously popular series of historical romances collectively known as the Waverley novels, including *Rob Roy, Ivanhoe,* and *Kenilworth.*

1. James Fenimore Cooper (1789–1851), often described as the "American Scott," wrote the Leatherstocking Tales, novels recounting the 18th-century adventures of an American frontiersman and his Native American friends and enemies.

he can't help remembering it. Pen says she's going to adopt the three-cornered-block plan with papa."

"Thank you," said Corey. "I believe I'll use your card." He crossed over to her, and after a moment sat down on the trestle beside her. She looked over the card as he wrote. "Those are the ones we mentioned, but perhaps I'd better add a few others."

"Oh, thank you," she said, when he had written the card full on both sides. "He has got to get them in the nicest binding, too. I shall tell him about their helping to furnish the room, and then he can't object." She remained with the card, looking at it rather wistfully.

Perhaps Corey divined her trouble of mind.

"If he will take that to any book-seller, and tell him what bindings he wants, he will fill the order for him."

"Oh, thank you very much," she said, and put the card back into her card-case with great apparent relief. Then she turned her lovely face toward the young man, beaming with the triumph a woman feels in any bit of successful manœuvring, and began to talk with recovered gayety of other things, as if, having got rid of a matter annoying out of all proportion to its importance, she was now going to indemnify herself.

Corey did not return to his own trestle. She found another shaving within reach of her parasol, and began poking that with it, and trying to follow it through its folds. Corey watched her awhile.

"You seem to have a great passion for playing with shavings," he said. "Is it a new one?"

"New what?"

"Passion."

"I don't know," she said, dropping her eyelids, and keeping on with her effort. She looked shyly aslant at him. "Perhaps you don't approve of playing with shavings?"

"Oh, yes, I do. I admire it very much. But it seems rather difficult. I've a great ambition to put my foot on the shaving's tail and hold it for you."

"Well," said the girl.

"Thank you," said the young man. He did so, and now she ran her parasol point easily through it. They looked at each other and laughed. "That was wonderful. Would you like to try another?" he asked.

"No, I thank you," she replied. "I think one will do."

They both laughed again, for whatever reason or no reason, and then the young girl became sober. To a girl everything a young man does is of significance; and if he holds a shaving down with his foot while she pokes through it with her parasol, she must ask herself what he means by it.

"They seem to be having rather a long interview with the carpenter to-day," said Irene, looking vaguely toward the ceiling. She turned with polite ceremony to Corey. "I'm afraid you're letting them keep you. You mustn't."

"Oh, no. You're letting me stay," he returned.

She bridled, and bit her lip for pleasure. "I presume they will be down before a great while. Don't you like the smell of the wood and the mortar? It's so fresh."

"Yes, it's delicious." He bent forward and picked up from the floor the shaving with which they had been playing, and put it to his nose. "It's like a flower. May I offer it to you?" he asked, as if it had been one.

"Oh, thank you, thank you!" She took it from him and put it into her belt, and then they both laughed once more.

Steps were heard descending. When the elder people reached the floor where they were sitting, Corey rose and presently took his leave.

"What makes you so solemn, 'Rene?" asked Mrs. Lapham.

"Solemn?" echoed the girl. "I'm not a *bit* solemn. What *can* you mean?"

Corey dined at home that evening, and as he sat looking across the table at his father, he said, "I wonder what the average literature of non-cultivated people is."

"Ah," said the elder, "I suspect the average is pretty low even with cultivated people. You don't read a great many books yourself, Tom."

"No, I don't," the young man confessed. "I read more books when I was with Stanton, last winter, than I had since I was a boy. But I read them because I must—there was nothing else to do. It wasn't because I was fond of reading. Still, I think I read with some sense of literature and the difference between authors. I don't suppose that people generally do that; I have met people who had read books without troubling themselves to find out even the author's name, much less trying to decide upon his quality. I suppose that's the way the vast majority of people read."

"Yes. If authors were not almost necessarily recluses, and ignorant of the ignorance about them, I don't see how they could endure it. Of course they are fated to be overwhelmed by oblivion at last, poor fellows; but to see it weltering all round them while they are in the very act of achieving immortality must be tremendously discouraging. I don't suppose that we who have the habit of reading, and at least a nodding acquaintance with literature, can imagine the bestial darkness of the great mass of people—even people whose houses are rich, and whose linen is purple and fine. But occasionally we get glimpses of it. I suppose you found the latest publications lying all about in Lapham cottage when you were down there?"

Young Corey laughed. "It wasn't exactly cumbered with them."

"No?"

"To tell the truth, I don't suppose they ever buy books. The young ladies get novels that they hear talked of out of the circulating library."

"Had they knowledge enough to be ashamed of their ignorance?"

"Yes, in certain ways—to a certain degree."

"It's a curious thing, this thing we call civilization," said the elder, musingly. "We think it is an affair of epochs and of nations. It's really an affair of individuals. One brother will be civilized and the other a barbarian. I've occasionally met young girls who were so brutally, insolently, willfully indifferent to the arts which make civilization that they ought to have been clothed in the skins of wild beasts and gone about barefoot with clubs over their shoulders. Yet they were of polite origin, and their parents were at least respectful of the things that these young animals despised."

"I don't think that is exactly the case with the Lapham family," said the son, smiling. "The father and mother rather apologized about not getting time to read, and the young ladies by no means scorned it."

"They are quite advanced!"

"They are going to have a library in their Beacon street house."

"Oh, poor things! How are they ever going to get the books together?"

"Well, sir," said the son, coloring a little, "*I* have been indirectly applied to for help."

"You, Tom!" His father dropped back in his chair and laughed.

"I recommended the standard authors," said the son.

"Oh, I never supposed your *prudence* would be at fault, Tom!"

"But seriously," said the young man, generously smiling in sympathy with his father's enjoyment, "they're not unintelligent people. They are very quick, and they are shrewd and sensible."

"I have no doubt that some of the Sioux are so. But that is not saying that they are civilized. All civilization comes through literature now, especially in our country. A Greek got his civilization by talking and looking, and in some measure a Parisian may still do it. But we, who live remote from history and monuments, we must read or we must barbarize. Once we were softened, if not polished, by religion; but I suspect that the pulpit counts for much less now in civilizing."

"They're enormous devourers of newspapers, and theater-goers; and they go a great deal to lectures. The Colonel prefers them with the stereopticon."

"They might get a something in that way," said the elder, thoughtfully. "Yes, I suppose one must take those things into account—especially the newspapers and the lectures. I doubt if the theater is a factor in civilization among us. I dare say it doesn't deprave a great deal, but from what I've seen of it I should say that it was intellectually degrading. Perhaps they might get some sort of lift from it; I don't know. Tom!" he added, after a moment's reflection. "I really think I ought to see this patron of yours. Don't you think it would be rather decent in me to make his acquaintance?"

"Well, if you have the fancy, sir," said the young man. "But there's no sort of obligation. Colonel Lapham would be the last man in the world to want to give our relation any sort of social character. The meeting will come about in the natural course of things."

"Ah, I didn't intend to propose anything immediate," said the father. "One can't do anything in the summer, and I should prefer your mother's superintendence. Still, I can't rid myself of the idea of a dinner. It appears to me that there ought to be a dinner."

"Oh, pray don't feel that there's any necessity."

"Well," said the elder, with easy resignation, "there's at least no hurry."

"There is one thing I don't like," said Lapham, in the course of one of those talks which came up between his wife and himself concerning Corey, "or at least I don't understand it; and that's the way his father behaves. I don't want to force myself on any man; but it seems to me pretty queer the way he holds off. I should think he would take enough interest in his son to want to know something about his business. What is he afraid of?" demanded Lapham angrily. "Does he think I'm going to jump at a chance to get in with him, if he gives me one? He's mightily mistaken if he does. *I* don't want to know him."

"Silas," said his wife, making a wife's free version of her husband's words, and replying to their spirit rather than their letter, "I hope you never said a word to Mr. Corey to let him know the way you feel."

"I never mentioned his father to him!" roared the Colonel. "That's the way I feel about it!"

"Because it would spoil everything. I wouldn't have them think we cared the least thing in the world for their acquaintance. We shouldn't be a bit better off. We don't know the same people they do, and we don't care for the same kind of things."

Lapham was breathless with resentment of his wife's implication. "Don't I tell you," he gasped, "that I don't want to know them? Who began it? They're friends of yours if they're anybody's."

"They're distant acquaintances of mine," returned Mrs. Lapham quietly; "and this young Corey is a clerk of yours. And I want we should hold ourselves so that when they get ready to make the advances we can meet them half-way or not, just as we choose."

"That's what grinds me," cried her husband. "Why should we wait for them to make the advances? Why shouldn't we make 'em? Are they any better than we are? My note of hand would be worth ten times what Bromfield Corey's is on the street to-day. And I made *my* money. I haven't loafed my life away."

"Oh, it isn't what you've got, and it isn't what you've done exactly. It's what you are."

"Well, then, what's the difference?"

"None that really amounts to anything, or that need give you any trouble, if you don't think of it. But he's been all his life in society, and he knows just what to say and what to do, and he can talk about the things that society people like to talk about, and you—can't."

Lapham gave a furious snort. "And does that make him any better?"

"No. But it puts him where he can make the advances without demeaning himself, and it puts you where you can't. Now, look here, Silas Lapham! You understand this thing as well as I do. You know that I appreciate you, and that I'd sooner die than have you humble yourself to a living soul. But I'm not going to have you coming to me, and pretending that you can meet Bromfield Corey as an equal on his own ground. You can't. He's got a better education than you, and if he hasn't got more brains than you, he's got different. And he and his wife, and their fathers and grandfathers before 'em, have always had a high position, and you can't help it. If you want to know them, you've got to let them make the advances. If you don't, all well and good."

"I guess," said the chafed and vanquished Colonel, after a moment for swallowing the pill, "that they'd have been in a pretty fix if you'd waited to let them make the advances last summer."

"That was a different thing altogether. I didn't know who they were, or may be I should have waited. But all I say now is that if you've got young Corey into business with you, in hopes of our getting into society with his father, you better ship him at once. For I ain't going to have it on that basis."

"Who wants to have it on that basis?" retorted her husband.

"Nobody, if you don't," said Mrs. Lapham tranquilly.

Irene had come home with the shaving in her belt, unnoticed by her father, and unquestioned by her mother. But her sister saw it at once, and asked her what she was doing with it.

"Oh, nothing," said Irene, with a joyful smile of self-betrayal, taking the shaving carefully out, and laying it among the laces and ribbons in her drawer.

"Hadn't you better put it in water, 'Rene? It'll be all wilted by morning," said Pen.

"You mean thing!" cried the happy girl. "It isn't a flower!"

"Oh, I thought it was a whole bouquet. Who gave it to you?"

"I sha'n't tell you," said Irene saucily.

"Oh, well, never mind. Did you know Mr. Corey had been down here this afternoon, walking on the beach with me?"

"He wasn't—he wasn't at all! He was at the house with *me*. There! I've caught you fairly."

"Is that so?" drawled Penelope. "Then I never could guess who gave you that precious shaving."

"No, you couldn't!" said Irene, flushing beautifully. "And you may guess, and you may guess, and you may guess!" With her lovely eyes she coaxed her sister to keep on teasing her, and Penelope continued the comedy with the patience that women have for such things.

"Well, I'm not going to try, if it's no use. But I didn't know it had got to be the fashion to give shavings instead of flowers. But there's some sense in it. They can be used for kindlings when they get old, and you can't do anything with old flowers. Perhaps he'll get to sending 'em by the barrel."

Irene laughed for pleasure in this tormenting. "Oh, Pen, I want to tell you how it all happened."

"Oh, he *did* give it to you, then? Well, I guess I don't care to hear."

"You shall, and you've got to!" Irene ran and caught her sister, who feigned to be going out of the room, and pushed her into a chair. "There, now!" She pulled up another chair, and hemmed her in with it. "He came over, and sat down on the trestle alongside of me——"

"What? As close as you are to me now?"

"You wretch! I will *give* it to you! No, at a proper distance. And here was this shaving on the floor, that I'd been poking with my parasol——"

"To hide your embarrassment."

"Pshaw! I wasn't a bit embarrassed. I was just as much at my ease! And then he asked me to let him hold the shaving down with his foot, while I went on with my poking. And I said yes he might——"

"What a bold girl! You said he might hold a shaving down for you?"

"And then—and then—" continued Irene, lifting her eyes absently, and losing herself in the beatific recollection, "and then—Oh, yes! Then I asked him if he didn't like the smell of pine shavings. And then he picked it up, and said it smelt like a flower. And then he asked if he might offer it to me—just for a joke, you know. And I took it, and stuck it in my belt. And we had such a laugh! We got into a regular gale. And oh, Pen, what do you suppose he meant by it?" She suddenly caught herself to her sister's breast, and hid her burning face on her shoulder.

"Well, there used to be a book about the language of flowers. But I never knew much about the language of shavings, and I can't say exactly——"

"Oh, don't—*don't,* Pen!" and here Irene gave over laughing, and began to sob in her sister's arms.

"Why, 'Rene!" cried the elder girl.

"You *know* he didn't mean anything. He doesn't care a bit about me. He hates me! He despises me! Oh, what shall I do?"

A trouble passed over the face of the sister as she silently comforted the child in her arms; then the drolling light came back into her eyes. "Well, 'Rene, *you* haven't got to do *any*thing. That's one advantage girls have got—if it *is* an advantage. I'm not always sure."

Irene's tears turned to laughing again. When she lifted her head it was to look into the mirror confronting them, where her beauty showed all the more brilliant for the shower that had passed over it. She seemed to gather courage from the sight.

"It must be awful to have to *do,*" she said, smiling into her own face. "I don't see how they ever can."

"Some of 'em can't—especially when there's such a tearing beauty around."

"Oh, pshaw, Pen! You know that isn't so. You've got a real pretty mouth, Pen," she added thoughtfully, surveying the feature in the glass, and then pouting her own lips for the sake of that effect on them.

"It's a useful mouth," Penelope admitted; "I don't believe I could get along without it now, I've had it so long."

"It's got such a funny expression—just the mate of the look in your eyes; as if you were just going to say something ridiculous. He said, the very first time he saw you, that he knew you were humorous."

"Is it possible? It must be so, if the Grand Mogul said it. Why didn't you tell me so before, and not let me keep on going round just like a common person?"

Irene laughed as if she liked to have her sister take his praises in that way rather than another. "I've got such a stiff, prim kind of mouth," she said, drawing it down, and then looking anxiously at it.

"I hope you didn't put on that expression when he offered you the shaving. If you did, I don't believe he'll ever give you another splinter."

The severe mouth broke into a lovely laugh, and then pressed itself in a kiss against Penelope's cheek.

"There! Be done, you silly thing! I'm not going to have you accepting *me* before I've offered myself, *anyway.*" She freed herself from her sister's embrace, and ran from her round the room.

Irene pursued her, in the need of hiding her face against her shoulder again. "Oh, Pen! Oh, Pen!" she cried.

The next day, at the first moment of finding herself alone with her eldest daughter, Mrs. Lapham asked, as if knowing that Penelope must have already made it subject of inquiry: "What was Irene doing with that shaving in her belt yesterday?"

"Oh, just some nonsense of hers with Mr. Corey. He gave it to her at the new house." Penelope did not choose to look up and meet her mother's grave glance.

"What do you think he meant by it?"

Penelope repeated Irene's account of the affair, and her mother listened without seeming to derive much encouragement from it.

"He doesn't seem like one to flirt with her," she said at last. Then, after a thoughtful pause: "Irene is as good a girl as ever breathed, and she's a perfect beauty. But I should hate the day when a daughter of mine was married for her beauty."

"You're safe as far as I'm concerned, mother."

Mrs. Lapham smiled ruefully. "She isn't really equal to him, Pen. I misdoubted that from the first, and it's been borne in upon me more and more ever since. She hasn't mind enough."

"I didn't know that a man fell in love with a girl's intellect," said Penelope quietly.

"Oh, no. He hasn't fallen in love with Irene at all. If he had, it wouldn't matter about the intellect."

Penelope let the self-contradiction pass.

"Perhaps he has, after all."

"No," said Mrs. Lapham. "She pleases him when he sees her. But he doesn't try to see her."

"He has no chance. You won't let father bring him here."

"He would find excuses to come without being brought, if he wished to come," said the mother. "But she isn't in his mind enough to make him. He goes away and doesn't think anything more about her. She's a child. She's a good child, and I shall always say it; but she's nothing but a child. No, she's got to forget him."

"Perhaps that won't be so easy."

"No, I presume not. And now your father has got the notion in his head, and he will move heaven and earth to bring it to pass. I can see that he's always thinking about it."

"The Colonel has a will of his own," observed the girl, rocking to and fro where she sat looking at her mother.

"I wish we had never met them!" cried Mrs. Lapham. "I wish we had never thought of building! I wish he had kept away from your father's business!"

"Well, it's too late now, mother," said the girl. "Perhaps it isn't so bad as you think."

"Well, we must stand it, anyway," said Mrs. Lapham, with the grim antique Yankee submission.

"Oh, yes, we've got to stand it," said Penelope, with the quaint modern American fatalism.

X.

It was late June, almost July, when Corey took up his life in Boston again, where the summer slips away so easily. If you go out of town early, it seems a very long summer when you come back in October; but if you stay, it passes swiftly, and, seen foreshortened in its flight, seems scarcely a month's length. It has its days of heat, when it is very hot, but for the most part it is cool, with baths of the east wind that seem to saturate the soul with delicious freshness. Then there are stretches of gray, westerly weather, when the air is full of the sentiment of early autumn, and the frying of the grasshopper in the blossomed weed of the vacant lots on the Back Bay is intershot with the carol of crickets; and the yellowing leaf on the long slope of Mt. Vernon street smites the sauntering observer with tender melancholy. The caterpillar, gorged with the spoil of the lindens on Chestnut,[1] and weaving his own shroud about him in his lodgment on the brickwork, records the passing of summer by mid-July; and if after that comes August, its breath is thick and short, and September is upon the sojourner before he has fairly had time to philosophize the character of the town out of season.

But it must have appeared that its most characteristic feature was the absence of everybody he knew. This was one of the things that commended Boston to Bromfield Corey during the summer; and if his son had any qualms about the life he had entered upon with such vigor, it must have been a relief to him that there was scarcely a soul left to wonder or pity. By the time people got back to town the fact of his connection with the mineral paint man would be an old story, heard afar off with different degrees of surprise, and considered with different degrees of indifference. A man has not reached the age of twenty-six in any community where he was born and reared without having had his capacity pretty well ascertained; and in Boston the analysis is conducted with an unsparing thoroughness which may fitly impress the un-Bostonian mind, darkened by the popular superstition that the Bostonians blindly admire one another. A man's qualities are sifted as closely in Boston as they doubtless were in Florence or Athens; and, if final mercy was shown in those cities because a man was, with all his limitations, an Athenian or Florentine, some abatement might as justly be made in Boston for like reason. Corey's powers had been gauged in college, and he had not given his world reason to think very differently of him since he came out of college. He was rated as an energetic fellow, a little indefinite in aim, with the smallest amount of inspiration that can save a man

1. Mt. Vernon and Chestnut are streets on Beacon Hill, near Boston Common and the Public Garden.

from being commonplace. If he was not commonplace, it was through nothing remarkable in his mind, which was simply clear and practical, but through some combination of qualities of the heart that made men trust him, and women call him sweet—a word of theirs which conveys otherwise indefinable excellences. Some of the more nervous and excitable said that Tom Corey was as sweet as he could live; but this perhaps meant no more than the word alone. No man ever had a son less like him than Bromfield Corey. If Tom Corey had ever said a witty thing, no one could remember it; and yet the father had never said a witty thing to a more sympathetic listener than his own son. The clear mind which produced nothing but practical results reflected everything with charming lucidity; and it must have been this which endeared Tom Corey to every one who spoke ten words with him. In a city where people have good reason for liking to shine, a man who did not care to shine must be little short of universally acceptable without any other effort for popularity; and those who admired and enjoyed Bromfield Corey loved his son. Yet, when it came to accounting for Tom Corey, as it often did in a community where every one's generation is known to the remotest degrees of cousinship, they could not trace his sweetness to his mother, for neither Anna Bellingham nor any of her family, though they were so many blocks of Wenham ice[2] for purity and rectangularity, had ever had any such savor; and, in fact, it was to his father, whose habit of talk wronged it in himself, that they had to turn for this quality of the son's. They traced to the mother the traits of practicality and common sense in which he bordered upon the commonplace, and which, when they had dwelt upon them, made him seem hardly worth the close inquiry they had given him.

While the summer wore away he came and went methodically about his business, as if it had been the business of his life, sharing his father's bachelor liberty and solitude, and expecting with equal patience the return of his mother and sisters in the autumn. Once or twice he found time to run down to Mt. Desert and see them; and then he heard how the Philadelphia and New York people were getting in everywhere, and was given reason to regret the house at Nahant which he had urged to be sold. He came back and applied himself to his desk with a devotion that was exemplary rather than necessary; for Lapham made no difficulty about the brief absences which he asked, and set no term to the apprenticeship that Corey was serving in the office before setting off upon that mission to South America in the early winter, for which no date had yet been fixed.

2. Wenham Lake, in Essex County, was world famous for its translucent ice, which was sold commercially for use in food refrigeration.

The summer was a dull season for the paint as well as for everything else. Till things should brisk up, as Lapham said, in the fall, he was letting the new house take a great deal of his time. Æsthetic ideas had never been intelligibly presented to him before, and he found a delight in apprehending them that was very grateful to his imaginative architect. At the beginning, the architect had foreboded a series of mortifying defeats and disastrous victories in his encounters with his client; but he had never had a client who could be more reasonably led on from one outlay to another. It appeared that Lapham required but to understand or feel the beautiful effect intended, and he was ready to pay for it. His bull-headed pride was concerned in a thing which the architect made him see, and then he believed that he had seen it himself, perhaps conceived it. In some measure the architect seemed to share his delusion, and freely said that Lapham was very suggestive. Together they blocked out windows here, and bricked them up there; they changed doors and passages; pulled down cornices and replaced them with others of different design; experimented with costly devices of decoration, and went to extravagant lengths in novelties of finish. Mrs. Lapham, beginning with a woman's adventurousness in the unknown region, took fright at the reckless outlay at last, and refused to let her husband pass a certain limit. He tried to make her believe that a far-seeing economy dictated the expense; and that if he put the money into the house, he could get it out any time by selling it. She would not be persuaded.

"I don't want you should sell it. And you've put more money into it now than you'll ever get out again, unless you can find as big a goose to buy it, and that isn't likely. No, sir! You just stop at a hundred thousand, and don't you let him get you a cent beyond. Why, you're perfectly bewitched with that fellow! You've lost your head, Silas Lapham, and if you don't look out you'll lose your money too."

The Colonel laughed; he liked her to talk that way, and promised he would hold up awhile.

"But there's no call to feel anxious, Pert. It's only a question what to do with the money. I can reinvest it; but I never had so much of it to spend before."

"Spend it, then," said his wife; "don't throw it away! And how came you to have so much more money than you know what to do with, Silas Lapham?" she added.

"Oh, I've made a very good thing in stocks lately."

"In stocks? When did you take up gambling for a living?"

"Gambling? Stuff! What gambling? Who said it was gambling?"

"You have; many a time."

"Oh, yes, buying and selling on a margin. But this was a *bona fide* transaction. I bought at forty-three for an investment, and I sold at a hundred and seven; and the money passed both times."

"Well, you better let stocks alone," said his wife, with the conservatism of her sex. "Next time you'll buy at a hundred and seven and sell at forty-three. Then where'll you be?"

"Left," admitted the Colonel.

"You better stick to paint awhile yet."

The Colonel enjoyed this, too, and laughed again with the ease of a man who knows what he is about. A few days after that he came down to Nantasket with the radiant air which he wore when he had done a good thing in business and wanted his wife's sympathy. He did not say anything of what had happened till he was alone with her in their own room; but he was very gay the whole evening, and made several jokes which Penelope said nothing but very great prosperity could excuse: they all understood these moods of his.

"Well, what is it, Silas?" asked his wife when the time came. "Any more big-bugs wanting to go into the mineral paint business with you?"

"Something better than that."

"I could think of a good many better things," said his wife, with a sigh of latent bitterness. "What's this one?"

"I've had a visitor."

"Who?"

"Can't you guess?"

"I don't want to try. Who was it?"

"Rogers."

Mrs. Lapham sat down with her hands in her lap, and stared at the smile on her husband's face, where he sat facing her.

"I guess you wouldn't want to joke on that subject, Si," she said, a little hoarsely, "and you wouldn't grin about it unless you had some good news. I don't know what the miracle is, but if you could tell quick——"

She stopped like one who can say no more.

"I will, Persis," said her husband, and with that awed tone in which he rarely spoke of anything but the virtues of his paint. "He came to borrow money of me, and I lent him it. That's the short of it. The long——"

"Go on," said his wife, with gentle patience.

"Well, Pert, I was never so much astonished in my life as I was to see that man come into my office. You might have knocked me down with—I don't know what."

"I don't wonder. Go on!"

"And he was as much embarrassed as I was. There we stood, gaping at each other, and I hadn't hardly sense enough to ask him to take a chair. I don't know just how we got at it. And I don't remember just how it was that he said he came to come to me. But he had got hold of a patent right that he wanted to go into on a large scale, and there he was wanting me to supply him the funds."

"Go on!" said Mrs. Lapham, with her voice further in her throat.

"I never felt the way you did about Rogers, but I know how you always did feel, and I guess I surprised him with my answer. He had brought along a lot of stock as security——"

"You didn't take it, Silas!" his wife flashed out.

"Yes, I did, though," said Lapham. "You wait. We settled our business, and then we went into the old thing, from the very start. And we talked it all over. And when we got through we shook hands. Well, I don't know when it's done me so much good to shake hands with anybody."

"And you told him—you owned up to him that you were in the wrong, Silas?"

"No, I didn't," returned the Colonel, promptly; "for I wasn't. And before we got through, I guess he saw it the same as I did."

"Oh, no matter! so you had the chance to show how you felt."

"But I never felt that way," persisted the Colonel. "I've lent him the money, and I've kept his stocks. And he got what he wanted out of me."

"Give him back his stocks!"

"No, I sha'n't. Rogers came to borrow. He didn't come to beg. You needn't be troubled about his stocks. They're going to come up in time; but just now they're so low down that no bank would take them as security, and I've got to hold them till they do rise. I hope you're satisfied now, Persis," said her husband; and he looked at her with the willingness to receive the reward of a good action which we all feel when we have performed one. "I lent him the money you kept me from spending on the house."

"Truly, Si? Well, I'm satisfied," said Mrs. Lapham, with a deep, tremulous breath. "The Lord has been good to you, Silas," she continued, solemnly. "You may laugh if you choose, and I don't know as *I* believe in his interfering a great deal; but I believe he's interfered this time; and I tell you, Silas, it ain't always he gives people a chance to make it up to others in this life. I've been afraid you'd die, Silas, before you got the chance; but he's let you live to make it up to Rogers."

"I'm glad to be let live," said Lapham, stubbornly; "but I hadn't anything to make up to Milton K. Rogers. And if God has let me live for that——"

"Oh, say what you please, Si! Say what you please, now you've done it! I sha'n't stop you. You've taken the one spot—the one *speck*—off you that was ever there, and I'm satisfied."

"There wa'n't ever any speck there," Lapham held out, lapsing more and more into his vernacular; "and what I done, I done for you, Persis."

"And I thank you for your own soul's sake, Silas."

"I guess my soul's all right," said Lapham.

"And I want you should promise me one thing more."

"Thought you said you were satisfied?"

"I am. But I want you should promise me this: that you won't let anything tempt you—anything!—to ever trouble Rogers for that money you lent him. No matter what happens—no matter if you lose it all. Do you promise?"

"Why, I don't ever *expect* to press him for it. That's what I said to myself when I lent it. And of course I'm glad to have that old trouble healed up. I don't *think* I ever did Rogers any wrong, and I never did think so; but if I *did* do it—*if* I did—I'm willing to call it square, if I never see a cent of my money back again."

"Well, that's all," said his wife.

They did not celebrate his reconciliation with his old enemy—for such they had always felt him to be since he ceased to be an ally—by any show of joy or affection. It was not in their tradition, as stoical for the woman as for the man, that they should kiss or embrace each other at such a moment. She was content to have told him that he had done his duty, and he was content with her saying that. But before she slept she found words to add that she always feared the selfish part he had acted toward Rogers had weakened him, and left him less able to overcome any temptation that might beset him; and that was one reason why she could never be easy about it. Now she should never fear for him again.

This time he did not explicitly deny her forgiving impeachment.

"Well, it's all past and gone now, anyway; and I don't want you should think anything more about it."

He was man enough to take advantage of the high favor in which he stood when he went up to town, and to abuse it by bringing Corey down to supper. His wife could not help condoning the sin of disobedience in him at such a time. Penelope said that between the admiration she felt for the Colonel's boldness and her mother's forbearance, she was hardly in a state to entertain company that evening; but she did what she could.

Irene liked being talked to better than talking, and when her sister was by she was always, tacitly or explicitly, referring to her for confirmation of what she said. She was content to sit and look pretty as she looked at the young man and listened to her sister's drolling. She laughed, and kept glancing at Corey to make sure that he was understanding her. When they went out on the veranda to see the moon on the water, Penelope led the way and Irene followed.

They did not look at the moonlight long. The young man perched on the rail of the veranda, and Irene took one of the red-painted rocking-chairs where she could conveniently look at him and at her sister, who sat leaning forward lazily and running on, as the phrase is. That low, crooning note of hers was delicious; her face, glimpsed now and then in the moonlight as she turned it or lifted it a little, had a fascination which kept his eye. Her talk was very unliterary, and its effect seemed hardly conscious. She was far from epigram in her funning. She told of this trifle and that; she sketched the characters and looks of people who had interested her, and nothing seemed to have escaped her notice; she mimicked a little, but not much; she suggested, and then the affair represented itself as if without her agency. She did not laugh; when Corey stopped, she made a soft cluck in her throat, as if she liked his being amused, and went on again.

The Colonel, left alone with his wife for the first time since he had come from town, made haste to take the word. "Well, Pert, I've arranged the whole thing with Rogers, and I hope you'll be satisfied to know that he owes me twenty thousand dollars, and that I've got security from him to the amount of a fourth of that, if I was to force his stocks to a sale."

"How came he to come down with you?" asked Mrs. Lapham.

"Who? Rogers?"

"Mr. Corey."

"Corey? Oh!" said Lapham, affecting not to have thought she could mean Corey. "He proposed it."

"Likely!" jeered his wife, but with perfect amiability.

"It's so," protested the Colonel. "We got talking about a matter just before I left, and he walked down to the boat with me; and then he said if I didn't mind he guessed he'd come along down and go back on the return boat. Of course I couldn't let him do that."

"It's well for you you couldn't."

"And I couldn't do less than bring him here to tea."

"Oh, certainly not."

"But he ain't going to stay the night—unless," faltered Lapham, "you want him to."

"Oh, of course, *I* want him to! I guess he'll stay, probably."

"Well, you know how crowded that last boat always is, and he can't get any other now."

Mrs. Lapham laughed at the simple wile. "I hope you'll be just as well satisfied, Si, if it turns out he doesn't want Irene after all."

"Pshaw, Persis! What are you always bringing that up for?" pleaded the Colonel. Then he fell silent, and presently his rude, strong face was clouded with an unconscious frown.

"There!" cried his wife, startling him from his abstraction. "I see how you'd feel; and I hope that you'll remember who you've got to blame."

"I'll risk it," said Lapham, with the confidence of a man used to success.

From the veranda the sound of Penelope's lazy tone came through the closed windows, with joyous laughter from Irene and peals from Corey.

"Listen to that!" said her father within, swelling up with inexpressible satisfaction. "That girl can talk for twenty, right straight along. She's better than a circus any day. I wonder what she's up to now."

"Oh, she's probably getting off some of those yarns of hers, or telling about some people. She can't step out of the house without coming back with more things to talk about than most folks would bring back from Japan. There ain't a ridiculous person she's ever seen but what she's got something from them to make you laugh at; and I don't believe we've ever had anybody in the house since the girl could talk that she hain't got some saying from, or some trick that'll pint 'em out so't you can see 'em and hear 'em. Sometimes I want to stop her; but when she gets into one of her gales there ain't any standing up against her. I guess it's lucky for Irene that she's got Pen there to help entertain her company. I can't ever feel down where Pen is."

"That's so," said the Colonel. "And I guess she's got about as much culture as any of them. Don't you?"

"She reads a great deal," admitted her mother. "She seems to be at it the whole while. I don't want she should injure her health, and sometimes I feel like snatchin' the books away from her. I don't know as it's good for a girl to read so much, anyway, especially novels. I don't want she should get notions."

"Oh, I guess Pen'll know how to take care of herself," said Lapham.

"She's got sense enough. But she ain't so practical as Irene. She's more up in the clouds—more of what you may call a dreamer. Irene's wide-awake every minute; and I declare, any one to see these two together when there's anything to be done, or any lead to be taken, would say Irene was the oldest, nine times out of ten. It's only when they get to talking that you can see Pen's got twice as much brains."

"Well," said Lapham, tacitly granting this point, and leaning back in his chair in supreme content. "Did you ever see much nicer girls anywhere?"

His wife laughed at his pride. "I presume they're as much swans as anybody's geese."

"No; but honestly, now!"

"Oh, they'll do; but don't you be silly, if you can help it, Si."

The young people came in, and Corey said it was time for his boat. Mrs. Lapham pressed him to stay, but he persisted, and he would not let the Colonel send him to the boat; he said he would rather walk. Outside, he pushed along toward the boat, which presently he could see lying at her landing in the bay, across the sandy tract to the left of the hotels. From time to time he almost stopped in his rapid walk, as a man does whose mind is in a pleasant tumult; and then he went forward at a swifter pace.

"She's charming!" he said, and he thought he had spoken aloud. He found himself floundering about in the deep sand, wide of the path; he got back to it, and reached the boat just before she started. The clerk came to take his fare, and Corey looked radiantly up at him in his lantern-light, with a smile that he must have been wearing a long time; his cheek was stiff with it. Once some people who stood near him edged suddenly and fearfully away, and then he suspected himself of having laughed outright.

[FIFTH INSTALLMENT—MARCH 1885]

XI.

Corey put off his set smile with the help of a frown, of which he first became aware after reaching home, when his father asked:

"Anything gone wrong with your department of the fine arts today, Tom?"

"Oh, no—no, sir," said the son, instantly relieving his brows from the strain upon them, and beaming again. "But I was thinking whether you were not perhaps right in your impression that it might be well for you to make Colonel Lapham's acquaintance before a great while."

"Has he been suggesting it in any way?" asked Bromfield Corey, laying aside his book and taking his lean knee between his clasped hands.

"Oh, not at all!" the young man hastened to reply. "I was merely thinking whether it might not begin to seem intentional, your not doing it."

"Well, Tom, you know I have been leaving it altogether to you——"

"Oh, I understand, of course, and I didn't mean to urge anything of the kind——"

"You are so very much more of a Bostonian than I am, you know, that I've been waiting your motion in entire confidence that you would know just what to do, and when to do it. If I had been left quite to my own lawless impulses, I think I should have called upon your *padrone*[1] at once. It seems to me that *my* father would have

1. Patron or boss (Italian).

found some way of showing that he expected as much as that from people placed in the relation to him that we hold to Colonel Lapham."

"Do you think so?" asked the young man.

"Yes. But you know I don't pretend to be an authority in such matters. As far as they go, I am always in the hands of your mother and you children."

"I'm very sorry, sir. I had no idea I was overruling your judgment. I only wanted to spare you a formality that didn't seem quite a necessity yet. I'm very sorry," he said again, and this time with more comprehensive regret. "I shouldn't like to have seemed remiss with a man who has been so considerate of me. They are all very good-natured."

"I dare say," said Bromfield Corey, with the satisfaction which no elder can help feeling in disabling the judgment of a younger man, "that it won't be too late if I go down to your office with you to-morrow."

"No, no. I didn't imagine your doing it at once, sir."

"Ah, but nothing can prevent me from doing a thing when once I take the bit in my teeth," said the father, with the pleasure which men of weak will sometimes take in recognizing their weakness. "How does their new house get on?"

"I believe they expect to be in it before New Year's."

"Will they be a great addition to society?" asked Bromfield Corey, with unimpeachable seriousness.

"I don't quite know what you mean," returned the son, a little uneasily.

"Ah, I see that you do, Tom."

"No one can help feeling that they are all people of good sense and—right ideas."

"Oh, that won't do. If society took in all the people of right ideas and good sense, it would expand beyond the calling capacity of its most active members. Even your mother's social conscientiousness could not compass it. Society is a very different sort of thing from good sense and right ideas. It is based upon them, of course, but the airy, graceful, winning superstructure which we all know demands different qualities. Have your friends got these qualities,—which may be felt, but not defined?"

The son laughed. "To tell you the truth, sir, I don't think they have the most elemental ideas of society, as we understand it. I don't believe Mrs. Lapham ever gave a dinner."

"And with all that money!" sighed the father.

"I don't believe they have the habit of wine at table. I suspect that when they don't drink tea and coffee with their dinner, they drink ice-water."

"Horrible!" said Bromfield Corey.

"It appears to me that this defines them."

"Oh, yes. There are people who give dinners, and who are not cognoscible.[2] But people who have never yet given a dinner, how is society to assimilate them?"

"It digests a great many people," suggested the young man.

"Yes; but they have always brought some sort of sauce piquante with them. Now, as I understand you, these friends of yours have no such sauce."

"Oh, I don't know about that!" cried the son.

"Oh, rude, native flavors, I dare say. But that isn't what I mean. Well, then, they must spend. There is no other way for them to win their way to general regard. We must have the Colonel elected to the Ten O'clock Club,[3] and he must put himself down in the list of those willing to entertain. Any one can manage a large supper. Yes, I see a gleam of hope for him in that direction."

In the morning Bromfield Corey asked his son whether he should find Lapham at his place as early as eleven.

"I think you might find him even earlier. I've never been there before him. I doubt if the porter is there much sooner."

"Well, suppose I go with you, then?"

"Why, if you like, sir," said the son, with some deprecation.

"Oh, the question is, will *he* like?"

"I think he will, sir"; and the father could see that his son was very much pleased.

Lapham was rending an impatient course through the morning's news when they appeared at the door of his inner room. He looked up from the newspaper spread on the desk before him, and then he stood up, making an indifferent feint of not knowing that he knew Bromfield Corey by sight.

"Good-morning, Colonel Lapham," said the son, and Lapham waited for him to say further, "I wish to introduce my father."

Then he answered "Good-morning," and added rather sternly for the elder Corey, "How do you do, sir? Will you take a chair?" and he pushed him one.

They shook hands and sat down, and Lapham said to his subordinate, "Have a seat"; but young Corey remained standing, watching them in their observance of each other with an amusement which was a little uneasy. Lapham made his visitor speak first by waiting for him to do so.

"I'm glad to make your acquaintance, Colonel Lapham, and I ought to have come sooner to do so. My father in your place would

2. Knowable (literally); here used figuratively, to mean acknowledgeable, in a social sense.
3. A fictional example of one of the gentlemen's social and dining clubs popular among Boston's professional and intellectual class. Howells himself belonged to at least two such organizations, one known simply as The Club and another, more exclusive one called the Saturday Club.

have expected it of a man in my place at once, I believe. But I can't feel myself altogether a stranger as it is. I hope Mrs. Lapham is well? And your daughter?"

"Thank you," said Lapham, "they're quite well."

"They were very kind to my wife——"

"Oh, that was nothing!" cried Lapham. "There's nothing Mrs. Lapham likes better than a chance of that sort. Mrs. Corey and the young ladies well?"

"Very well, when I heard from them. They're out of town."

"Yes, so I understood," said Lapham, with a nod toward the son. "I believe Mr. Corey, here, told Mrs. Lapham." He leaned back in his chair, stiffly resolute to show that he was not incommoded by the exchange of these civilities.

"Yes," said Bromfield Corey. "Tom has had the pleasure which I hope for of seeing you all. I hope you're able to make him useful to you here?" Corey looked round Lapham's room vaguely, and then out at the clerks in their railed inclosure, where his eye finally rested on an extremely pretty girl, who was operating a type-writer.

"Well, sir," replied Lapham, softening for the first time with this approach to business, "I guess it will be our own fault if we don't. By the way, Corey," he added, to the younger man, as he gathered up some letters from his desk, "here's something in your line. Spanish or French, I guess."

"I'll run them over," said Corey, taking them to his desk.

His father made an offer to rise.

"Don't go," said Lapham, gesturing him down again. "I just wanted to get him away a minute. I don't care to say it to his face,—I don't like the principle,—but since you ask me about it, I'd just as lief say that I've never had any young man take hold here equal to your son. I don't know as you care——"

"You make me very happy," said Bromfield Corey. "Very happy indeed. I've always had the idea that there was something in my son, if he could only find the way to work it out. And he seems to have gone into your business for the love of it."

"He went to work in the right way, sir! He told me about it. He looked into it. And that paint is a thing that will bear looking into."

"Oh, yes. You might think he had invented it, if you heard him celebrating it."

"Is that so?" demanded Lapham, pleased through and through. "Well, there ain't any other way. You've got to believe in a thing before you can put any heart in it. Why, I had a partner in this thing once, along back just after the war, and he used to be always wanting to tinker with something else. 'Why,' says I, 'you've got the best thing in God's universe now. Why ain't you satisfied?' I had to get rid of him at last. I stuck to my paint, and that fellow's drifted round pretty much all over the whole country, whittling his capital down all the while, till here the other day I had to lend him some money to start him new. No, sir, you've got to believe in a thing. And I believe in your son. And I don't mind telling you that, so far as he's gone, he's a success."

"That's very kind of you."

"No kindness about it. As I was saying the other day to a friend of mine, I've had many a fellow right out of the street that had to work hard all his life, and didn't begin to take hold like this son of yours."

Lapham expanded with profound self-satisfaction. As he probably conceived it, he had succeeded in praising, in a perfectly casual way, the supreme excellence of his paint, and his own sagacity and benevolence; and here he was sitting face to face with Bromfield Corey, praising his son to him, and receiving his grateful acknowledgments as if he were the father of some office-boy whom Lapham had given a place half out of charity.

"Yes, sir, when your son proposed to take hold here, I didn't have much faith in his ideas, that's the truth. But I had faith in him, and I saw that he meant business from the start. I could see it was born in him. Any one could."

"I'm afraid he didn't inherit it directly from me," said Bromfield Corey; "but it's in the blood, on both sides."

"Well, sir, we can't help those things," said Lapham, compassionately. "Some of us have got it, and some of us haven't. The idea is to make the most of what we *have* got."

"Oh, yes; that is the idea. By all means."

"And you can't ever tell what's in you till you try. Why, when I started this thing, I didn't more than half understand my own strength. I wouldn't have said, looking back, that I could have stood the wear and tear of what I've been through. But I developed as I went along. It's just like exercising your muscles in a gymnasium. You can lift twice or three times as much after you've been in training a month as you could before. And I can see that it's going to be just so with your son. His going through college won't hurt him,—he'll soon slough all that off,—and his bringing up won't; don't be anxious about it. I noticed in the army that some of the fellows that had the most go-ahead were fellows that hadn't ever had much more to do than girls before the war broke out. Your son will get along."

"Thank you," said Bromfield Corey, and smiled—whether because his spirit was safe in the humility he sometimes boasted, or because it was triply armed in pride against anything the Colonel's kindness could do.

"He'll get along. He's a good businessman and he's a fine fellow. *Must* you go?" asked Lapham, as Bromfield Corey now rose more resolutely. "Well, glad to see you. It was natural you should want to come and see what he was about, and I'm glad you did. I should have felt just so about it. Here is some of our stuff," he said, pointing out the various packages in his office, including the Persis Brand.

"Ah, that's very nice, very nice indeed," said his visitor. "That color through the jar—very rich—delicious. Is Persis Brand a name?"

Lapham blushed.

"Well, Persis is. I don't know as you saw an interview that fellow published in the 'Events' awhile back?"

"What is the 'Events'?"

"Well, it's that new paper Witherby's started."

"No," said Bromfield Corey, "I haven't seen it. I read 'The Daily,'" he explained; by which he meant "The Daily Advertiser,"[4] the only daily there is in the old-fashioned Bostonian sense.

"He put a lot of stuff in my mouth that I never said," resumed Lapham; "but that's neither here nor there, so long as you haven't seen it. Here's the department your son's in," and he showed him the foreign labels. Then he took him out into the warehouse to see the large packages. At the head of the stairs, where his guest stopped to nod to his son and say "Good-bye, Tom," Lapham insisted upon going down to the lower door with him. "Well, call again," he said in hospitable dismissal. "I shall always be glad to see you. There ain't a great deal doing at this season." Bromfield Corey thanked him, and let his hand remain perforce in Lapham's lingering grasp. "If you ever like to ride after a good horse——" the Colonel began.

"Oh, no, no, no; thank you! The better the horse, the more I should be scared. Tom has told me of your driving!"

"Ha, ha, ha!" laughed the Colonel. "Well! every one to his taste. Well, good-morning, sir!" and he suffered him to go.

"Who is the old man blowing to this morning?" asked Walker, the book-keeper, making an errand to Corey's desk.

"My father."

"Oh! That your father? I thought he must be one of your Italian correspondents that you'd been showing round, or Spanish."

In fact, as Bromfield Corey found his way at his leisurely pace up through the streets on which the prosperity of his native city was founded, hardly any figure could have looked more alien to its life. He glanced up and down the façades and through the crooked vistas like a stranger, and the swarthy fruiterer of whom he bought an apple, apparently for the pleasure of holding it in his hand, was not surprised that the purchase should be transacted in his own tongue.

Lapham walked back through the outer office to his own room without looking at Corey, and during the day he spoke to him only

4. Boston's oldest newspaper, founded in 1813, was read by members of the city's old, socially established families.

of business matters. That must have been his way of letting Corey see that he was not overcome by the honor of his father's visit. But he presented himself at Nantasket with the event so perceptibly on his mind that his wife asked: "Well, Silas, has Rogers been borrowing any more money of you? I don't want you should let that thing go too far. You've done enough."

"You needn't be afraid. I've seen the last of Rogers for one while." He hesitated, to give the fact an effect of no importance. "Corey's father called this morning."

"Did he?" said Mrs. Lapham, willing to humor his feint of indifference. "Did *he* want to borrow some money too?"

"Not as I understood." Lapham was smoking at great ease, and his wife had some crocheting on the other side of the lamp from him.

The girls were on the piazza looking at the moon on the water again. "There's no man in it to-night," Penelope said, and Irene laughed forlornly.

"What *did* he want, then?" asked Mrs. Lapham.

"Oh, I don't know. Seemed to be just a friendly call. Said he ought to have come before."

Mrs. Lapham was silent awhile. Then she said: "Well, I hope you're satisfied now."

Lapham rejected the sympathy too openly offered. "I don't know about being satisfied. I wa'n't in any hurry to see him."

His wife permitted him this pretense also. "What sort of a person is he, anyway?"

"Well, not much like his son. There's no sort of business about him. I don't know just how you'd describe him. He's tall; and he's got white hair and a mustache; and his fingers are very long and limber. I couldn't help noticing them as he sat there with his hands on the top of his cane. Didn't seem to be dressed very much, and acted just like anybody. Didn't talk much. Guess I did most of the talking. Said he was glad I seemed to be getting along so well with his son. He asked after you and Irene; and he said he couldn't feel just like a stranger. Said you had been very kind to his wife. Of course I turned it off. Yes," said Lapham thoughtfully, with his hands resting on his knees, and his cigar between the fingers of his left hand, "I guess he meant to do the right thing, every way. Don't know as I ever saw a much pleasanter man. Dunno but what he's about the pleasantest man I ever did see." He was not letting his wife see in his averted face the struggle that revealed itself there—the struggle of stalwart achievement not to feel flattered at the notice of sterile elegance, not to be sneakingly glad of its amiability, but to stand up and look at it with eyes on the same level. God, who made us so much like himself, but out of the dust, alone knows when that struggle will end. The time had been when Lapham could not have imagined any worldly splendor which his dollars could not buy if he chose to spend them for it; but his wife's half discoveries, taking form again in his ignorance of the world, filled him with helpless misgiving. A cloudy vision of something unpurchasable, where he had supposed there was nothing, had cowed him in spite of the burly resistance of his pride.

"I don't see why he shouldn't be pleasant," said Mrs. Lapham. "He's never done anything else."

Lapham looked up consciously, with an uneasy laugh. "Pshaw, Persis! you never forget anything!"

"Oh, I've got more than that to remember. I suppose you asked him to ride after the mare?"

"Well," said Lapham, reddening guiltily, "he said he was afraid of a good horse."

"Then, of course, you hadn't asked him." Mrs. Lapham crocheted in silence, and her husband leaned back in his chair and smoked.

At last he said, "I'm going to push that house forward. They're loafing on it. There's no reason why we shouldn't be in it by Thanksgiving. I don't believe in moving in the dead of winter."

"We can wait till spring. We're very comfortable in the old place," answered his wife. Then she broke out on him: "What are you in such a hurry to get into that house for? Do you want to invite the Coreys to a house-warming?"

Lapham looked at her without speaking.

"Don't you suppose I can see through you? I declare, Silas Lapham, if I didn't know different, I should say you *were* about the biggest fool! Don't you know *any*thing? Don't you know that it wouldn't do to ask those people to our house before they've asked us to theirs? They'd laugh in our faces!"

"I don't believe they'd laugh in our faces. What's the difference between our asking them and their asking us?" demanded the Colonel, sulkily.

"Oh, well! If you don't see!"

"Well, I *don't* see. But *I* don't want to ask them to the house. I suppose, if I want to, I can invite him down to a fish dinner at Taft's."

Mrs. Lapham fell back in her chair, and let her work drop in her lap with that "Tckk!" in which her sex knows how to express utter contempt and despair.

"What's the matter?"

"Well, if you *do* such a thing, Silas, I'll never speak to you again! It's no *use!* It's *no* use! I did think, after you'd behaved so well about Rogers, I might trust you a little. But I see I can't. I presume as long as you live you'll have to be nosed about like a perfect—*I* don't know what!"

"What are you making such a fuss about?" demanded Lapham, terribly crest-fallen, but trying to pluck up a spirit. "I haven't done anything yet. I can't ask your advice about anything any more without having you fly out. Confound it! I shall do as I please after this."

But as if he could not endure that contemptuous atmosphere, he got up, and his wife heard him in the dining-room pouring himself out a glass of ice-water, and then heard him mount the stairs to their room, and slam its door after him.

"Do you know what your father's wanting to do now?" Mrs. Lapham asked her eldest daughter, who lounged into the parlor a moment with her wrap stringing from her arm, while the younger went straight to bed. "He wants to invite Mr. Corey's father to a fish dinner at Taft's!"[5]

Penelope was yawning with her hand on her mouth; she stopped, and, with a laugh of amused expectance, sank into a chair, her shoulders shrugged forward.

"Why! what in the world has put the Colonel up to that?"

"Put him up to it! There's that fellow, who ought have come to see him long ago, drops into his office this morning, and talks five minutes with him, and your father is flattered out of his five senses. He's crazy to get in with those people, and I shall have a perfect battle to keep him within bounds."

"Well, Persis, ma'am, you can't say but what you began it," said Penelope.

"Oh, yes, I began it," confessed Mrs. Lapham. "Pen," she broke out, "what do you suppose he means by it?"

"Who? Mr. Corey's father? What does the Colonel think?"

"Oh, the Colonel!" cried Mrs. Lapham. She added tremulously: "Perhaps he *is* right. He *did* seem to take a fancy to her last summer, and now if he's called in that way—" She left her daughter to distribute the pronouns aright, and resumed: "Of course, I should have said once that there wasn't any question about it. I should have said so last year; and I don't know what it is keeps me from saying so now. I suppose I know a little more about things than I did; and your father's being so bent on it sets me all in a twitter. He thinks his money can do everything. Well, I don't say but what it can, a good many. And 'Rene is as good a child as ever there was; and I don't see but what she's pretty-appearing enough to suit any one. She's pretty-behaved, too; and she *is* the most capable girl. I presume young men don't care very much for such things nowadays; but there ain't a great many girls can go right into the kitchen, and make such a custard as she did yesterday. And look at the way she does, through

5. A popular restaurant situated on Point Shirley, across Boston Harbor east of the city, and specializing in fish and game.

the whole house! She can't seem to go into a room without the things fly right into their places. And if she had to do it to-morrow, she could make all her own dresses a great deal better than them we pay to do it. I don't say but what he's about as nice a fellow as ever stepped. But there! I'm ashamed of going on so."

"Well, mother," said the girl after a pause, in which she looked as if a little weary of the subject, "why do you worry about it? If it's to be it'll be, and if it isn't——"

"Yes, that's what I tell your father. But when it comes to myself, I see how hard it is for him to rest quiet. I'm afraid we shall all do something we'll repent of afterwards."

"Well, ma'am," said Penelope, "*I* don't intend to do anything wrong; but if I do, I promise not to be sorry for it. I'll go that far. And I think I wouldn't be sorry for it beforehand, if I were in your place, mother. Let the Colonel go on! He likes to manœuvre, and he isn't going to hurt any one. The Corey family can take care of themselves, I guess."

She laughed in her throat, drawing down the corners of her mouth, and enjoying the resolution with which her mother tried to fling off the burden of her anxieties. "Pen! I believe you're right. You always do see things in such a light! There! I don't care if he brings him down every day."

"Well, ma'am," said Pen, "I don't believe 'Rene would, either. She's just so indifferent!"

The Colonel slept badly that night, and in the morning Mrs. Lapham came to breakfast without him.

"Your father ain't well," she reported. "He's had one of his turns."

"*I* should have thought he had two or three of them," said Penelope, "by the stamping round I heard. Isn't he coming to breakfast?"

"Not just yet," said her mother. "He's asleep, and he'll be all right if he gets his nap out. I don't want you girls should make any great noise."

"Oh, we'll be quiet enough," returned Penelope. "Well, I'm glad the Colonel isn't sojering. At first I thought he might be sojering."[6] She broke into a laugh, and, struggling indolently with it, looked at her sister. "You don't think it'll be necessary for anybody to come down from the office and take orders from him while he's laid up, do you, mother?" she inquired.

"Pen!" cried Irene. "He'll be well enough to go up on the ten o'clock boat," said the mother, sharply.

"I think papa works too hard all through the summer. Why don't you make him take a rest, mamma?" asked Irene.

"Oh, take a rest! The man slaves harder every year. It used to be so that he'd take a little time off now and then; but I declare, he

6. Soldiering (slang).

hardly ever seems to breathe now away from his office. And this year he says he doesn't intend to go down to Lapham, except to see after the works for a few days. *I* don't know what to do with the man any more! Seems as if the more money he got, the more he wanted to get. It scares me to think what would happen to him if he lost it. I know one thing," concluded Mrs. Lapham. "He shall not go back to the office to-day."

"Then he won't go up on the ten o'clock boat," Pen reminded her.

"No, he won't. You can just drive over to the hotel as soon as you're through, girls, and telegraph that he's not well, and won't be at the office till to-morrow. I'm not going to have them send anybody down here to bother him."

"That's a blow," said Pen. "I didn't know but they might send——" she looked demurely at her sister—"Dennis!"

"Mamma!" cried Irene.

"Well, I declare, there's no living with this family any more," said Penelope.

"There, Pen, be done!" commanded her mother. But perhaps she did not intend to forbid her teasing. It gave a pleasant sort of reality to the affair that was in her mind, and made what she wished appear not only possible but probable.

Lapham got up and lounged about, fretting and rebelling as each boat departed without him, through the day; before night he became very cross, in spite of the efforts of the family to soothe him, and grumbled that he had been kept from going up to town. "I might as well have gone as not," he repeated, till his wife lost her patience.

"Well, you shall go to-morrow, Silas, if you have to be carried to the boat."

"I declare," said Penelope, "the Colonel don't pet worth a cent."[7]

The six o'clock boat brought Corey. The girls were sitting on the piazza, and Irene saw him first.

"Oh, Pen!" she whispered, with her heart in her face; and Penelope had no time for mockery before he was at the steps.

"I hope Colonel Lapham isn't ill," he said, and they could hear their mother engaged in a moral contest with their father indoors.

"Go and put on your coat! I say you shall! It don't matter *how* he sees you at the office, shirt-sleeves or not. You're in a gentleman's house now—or you ought to be—and you sha'n't see company in your dressing-gown."

Penelope hurried in to subdue her mother's anger.

"Oh, he's very much better, thank you!" said Irene, speaking up loudly to drown the noise of the controversy.

7. I.e., he is too irritable to be soothed.

"I'm glad of that," said Corey, and when she led him indoors the vanquished Colonel met his visitor in a double-breasted frock-coat, which he was still buttoning up. He could not persuade himself at once that Corey had not come upon some urgent business matter, and when he was clear that he had come out of civility, surprise mingled with his gratification that he should be the object of solicitude to the young man. In Lapham's circle of acquaintance they complained when they were sick, but they made no womanish inquiries after one another's health, and certainly paid no visits of sympathy till matters were serious. He would have enlarged upon the particulars of his indisposition if he had been allowed to do so; and after tea, which Corey took with them, he would have remained to entertain him if his wife had not sent him to bed. She followed him to see that he took some medicine she had prescribed for him, but she went first to Penelope's room, where she found the girl with a book in her hand, which she was not reading.

"You better go down," said the mother. "I've got to go to your father, and Irene is all alone with Mr. Corey; and I know she'll be on pins and needles without you're there to help make it go off."

"She'd better try to get along without me, mother," said Penelope soberly. "I can't always be with them."

"Well," replied Mrs. Lapham, "then *I* must. There'll be a perfect Quaker meeting[8] down there."

"Oh, I guess 'Rene will find something to say if you leave her to herself. Or if she don't, *he* must. It'll be all right for you to go down when you get ready; but I sha'n't go till toward the last. If he's coming here to see Irene—and I don't believe he's come on father's account—he wants to see her and not me. If she can't interest him alone, perhaps he'd as well find it out now as any time. At any rate, I guess you'd better make the experiment. You'll know whether it's a success if he comes again."

"Well," said the mother, "may be you're right. I'll go down directly. It does seem as if he did mean something, after all."

Mrs. Lapham did not hasten to return to her guest. In her own girlhood it was supposed that if a young man seemed to be coming to see a girl, it was only common sense to suppose that he wished to see her alone; and her life in town had left Mrs. Lapham's simple traditions in this respect unchanged. She did with her daughter as her mother would have done with her.

Where Penelope sat with her book, she heard the continuous murmur of voices below, and after a long interval she heard her mother descend. She did not read the open book that lay in her lap, though

8. Quaker worship services were held in silence until a congregant felt a call from the divine spirit to speak.

she kept her eyes fast on the print. Once she rose and almost shut the door, so that she could scarcely hear; then she opened it wide again with a self-disdainful air, and resolutely went back to her book, which again she did not read. But she remained in her room till it was nearly time for Corey to return to his boat.

When they were alone again, Irene made a feint of scolding her for leaving her to entertain Mr. Corey.

"Why! didn't you have a pleasant call?" asked Penelope.

Irene threw her arms round her. "Oh, it was a *splendid* call! I didn't suppose I could make it go off so well. We talked nearly the whole time about you!"

"I don't think *that* was a very interesting subject."

"He kept asking about you. He asked everything. You don't know how much he thinks of you, Pen. Oh, Pen! what do you think made him come? Do you think he really did come to see how papa was?" Irene buried her face in her sister's neck.

Penelope stood with her arms at her side, submitting. "Well," she said, "I don't think he did, altogether."

Irene, all glowing, released her. "Don't you—don't you *really?* Oh! Pen, don't you think he *is* nice? Don't you think he's handsome? Don't you think I behaved horridly when we first met him this evening, not thanking him for coming? I know he thinks I've no manners. But it seemed as if it would be thanking him for coming to see me. Ought I to have asked him to come again, when he said good-night? I didn't; I couldn't. Do you believe he'll think I don't want him to? You don't believe he would keep coming if he didn't—want to——"

"He hasn't kept coming a great deal, yet," suggested Penelope.

"No; I know he hasn't. But if he—if he should?"

"Then I should think he wanted to."

"Oh, would you—*would* you? Oh, how good you always are, Pen! And you always say what you think. I wish there was some one coming to see you too. That's all that I don't like about it. Perhaps——He was telling about his friend there in Texas——"

"Well," said Penelope, "his friend couldn't call often from Texas. You needn't ask Mr. Corey to trouble about me, 'Rene. I think I can manage to worry along, if you're satisfied."

"Oh, I *am,* Pen. When do you suppose he'll come again?" Irene pushed some of Penelope's things aside on the dressing-case, to rest her elbow and talk at ease. Penelope came up and put them back.

"Well, not to-night," she said; "and if that's what you're sitting up for——"

Irene caught her round the neck again, and ran out of the room.

The Colonel was packed off on the eight o'clock boat the next morning; but his recovery did not prevent Corey from repeating his visit in a week. This time Irene came radiantly up to Penelope's room, where she had again withdrawn herself. "You must come down, Pen," she said. "He's asked if you're not well, and mamma says you've got to come."

After that Penelope helped Irene through with her calls, and talked them over with her far into the night after Corey was gone. But when the impatient curiosity of her mother pressed her for some opinion of the affair, she said, "You know as much as I do, mother."

"Don't he ever say anything to you about her—praise her up, any?"

"He's never mentioned Irene to me."

"He hasn't to me, either," said Mrs. Lapham, with a sigh of trouble. "Then what makes him keep coming?"

"I can't tell you. One thing, he says there isn't a house open in Boston where he's acquainted. Wait till some of his friends get back, and then if he keeps coming, it'll be time to inquire."

"Well!" said the mother; but as the weeks passed she was less and less able to attribute Corey's visits to his loneliness in town, and turned to her husband for comfort.

"Silas, I don't know as we ought to let young Corey keep coming so. I don't quite like it, with all his family away."

"He's of age," said the Colonel. "He can go where he pleases. It don't matter whether his family's here or not."

"Yes, but if they don't want he should come? Should you feel just right about letting him?"

"How're you going to stop him? I swear, Persis, I don't know what's got over you! What is it? You didn't use to be so. But to hear you talk, you'd think those Coreys were too good for this world, and we wa'n't fit for 'em to walk on."

"I'm not going to have 'em say we took an advantage of their being away and tolled him on."[9]

"I should like to *hear* 'em say it!" cried Lapham. "Or anybody!"

"Well," said his wife, relinquishing this point of anxiety, "I can't make out whether he cares anything for her or not. And Pen can't tell either; or else she won't."

"Oh, I guess he cares for her, fast enough," said the Colonel.

"I can't make out that he's said or done the first thing to show it."

"Well, I was better than a year getting *my* courage up."

"Oh, that was different," said Mrs. Lapham, in contemptuous dismissal of the comparison, and yet with a certain fondness. "I guess, if he cared for her, a fellow in his position wouldn't be long getting up his courage to speak to Irene."

Lapham brought his fist down on the table between them.

9. Led him on.

"Look here, Persis! Once for all, now, don't you ever let me hear you say anything like that again! I'm worth nigh on to a million, and I've made it every cent myself; and my girls are the equals of anybody, I don't care who it is. He ain't the fellow to take on any airs; but if he ever tries it with me, I'll send him to the right about mighty quick. I'll have a talk with him, if——"

"No, no; don't do that!" implored his wife. "I didn't mean anything. I don't know as I meant *any*thing. He's just as unassuming as he can be, and I think Irene's a match for anybody. You just let things go on. It'll be all right. You never can tell how it is with young people. Perhaps *she's* offish. Now you ain't—you ain't going to say anything?"

Lapham suffered himself to be persuaded, the more easily, no doubt, because after his explosion he must have perceived that his pride itself stood in the way of what his pride had threatened. He contented himself with his wife's promise that she would never again present that offensive view of the case, and she did not remain without a certain support in his sturdy self-assertion.

XII.

Mrs. Corey returned with her daughters in the early days of October, having passed three or four weeks at Intervale[1] after leaving Bar Harbor. They were somewhat browner than they were when they left town in June, but they were not otherwise changed. Lily, the elder of the girls, had brought back a number of studies of kelp and toadstools, with accessory rocks and rotten logs, which she would never finish up and never show any one, knowing the slightness of their merit. Nanny, the younger, had read a great many novels with a keen sense of their inaccuracy as representations of life, and had seen a great deal of life with a sad regret for its difference from fiction. They were both nice girls, accomplished, well dressed of course, and well-enough looking; but they had met no one at the seaside or the mountains whom their taste would allow to influence their fate, and they had come home to the occupations they had left, with no hopes and no fears to distract them.

In the absence of these they were fitted to take the more vivid interest in their brother's affairs, which they could see weighed upon their mother's mind after the first hours of greeting.

"Oh, it seems to have been going on, and your father has never written a word about it," she said, shaking her head.

"What good would it have done?" asked Nanny, who was little and fair, with rings of light hair that filled a bonnet-front very prettily;

1. A stylish vacation destination in New Hampshire's White Mountains.

she looked best in a bonnet. "It would only have worried you. He could not have stopped Tom; you couldn't, when you came home to do it."

"I dare say papa didn't know much about it," suggested Lily. She was a tall, lean, dark girl, who looked as if she were not quite warm enough, and whom you always associated with wraps of different æsthetic effect after you had once seen her.

It is a serious matter always to the women of his family when a young man gives them cause to suspect that he is interested in some other woman. A son-in-law or brother-in-law does not enter the family; he need not be caressed or made anything of; but the son's or brother's wife has a claim upon his mother and sisters which they cannot deny. Some convention of their sex obliges them to show her affection, to like or to seem to like her, to take her to their intimacy, however odious she may be to them. With the Coreys it was something more than an affair of sentiment. They were by no means poor, and they were not dependent money-wise upon Tom Corey; but the mother had come, without knowing it, to rely upon his sense, his advice in everything, and the sisters, seeing him hitherto so indifferent to girls, had insensibly grown to regard him as altogether their own till he should be released, not by his marriage, but by theirs, an event which had not approached with the lapse of time. Some kinds of girls—they believed that they could readily have chosen a kind—might have taken him without taking him from them; but this generosity could not be hoped for in such a girl as Miss Lapham.

"Perhaps," urged their mother, "it would not be so bad. She seemed an affectionate little thing with her mother, without a great deal of character, though she was so capable about some things."

"Oh, she'll be an affectionate little thing with Tom too, you may be sure," said Nanny. "And that characterless capability becomes the most intense narrow-mindedness. She'll think we were against her from the beginning."

"She has no cause for that," Lily interposed, "and we shall not give her any."

"Yes, we shall," retorted Nanny. "We can't help it; and if we can't, her own ignorance would be cause enough."

"I can't feel that she's altogether ignorant," said Mrs. Corey, justly.

"Of course she can read and write," admitted Nanny.

"I can't imagine what he finds to talk about with her," said Lily.

"Oh, *that's* very simple," returned her sister. "They talk about themselves, with occasional references to each other. I have heard people 'going on' on the hotel piazzas. She's embroidering, or knitting, or tatting,[2] or something of that kind; and he says she seems

2. A lace-making method.

quite devoted to needle-work; and she says, yes, she has a perfect passion for it, and everybody laughs at her for it; but she can't help it, she always was so from a child, and supposes she always shall be,—with remote and minute particulars. And she ends by saying that perhaps he does not like people to tat, or knit, or embroider, or whatever. And he says, oh, yes, he does; what could make her think such a thing? but for his part he likes boating rather better, or if you're in the woods camping. Then she lets him take up one corner of her work, and perhaps touch her fingers; and that encourages him to say that he supposes nothing could induce her to drop her work long enough to go down on the rocks, or out among the huckleberry bushes; and she puts her head on one side, and says she doesn't know really. And then they go, and he lies at her feet on the rocks, or picks huckleberries and drops them in her lap, and they go on talking about themselves, and comparing notes to see how they differ from each other. And——"

"That will do, Nanny," said her mother.

Lily smiled autumnally. "Oh, disgusting!"

"Disgusting? Not at all!" protested her sister. "It's very amusing when you see it, and when you do it——"

"It's always a mystery what people see in each other," observed Mrs. Corey, severely.

"Yes," Nanny admitted, "but I don't know that there is much comfort for us in the application."

"No, there isn't," said her mother.

"The most that we can do is to hope for the best till we know the worst. Of course we shall make the best of the worst when it comes."

"Yes, and perhaps it would not be so very bad. I was saying to your father when I was here in July that those things can always be managed. You must face them as if they were nothing out of the way, and try not to give any cause for bitterness among ourselves."

"That's true. But I don't believe in too much resignation beforehand. It amounts to concession," said Nanny.

"Of course we should oppose it in all proper ways," returned her mother.

Lily had ceased to discuss the matter. In virtue of her artistic temperament, she was expected not to be very practical. It was her mother and her sister who managed, submitting to the advice and consent of Corey what they intended to do.

"Your father wrote me that he had called on Colonel Lapham at his place of business," said Mrs. Corey, seizing her first chance of approaching the subject with her son.

"Yes," said Corey. "A dinner was father's idea, but he came down to a call, at my suggestion."

"Oh," said Mrs. Corey, in a tone of relief, as if the statement threw a new light on the fact that Corey had suggested the visit. "He said so little about it in his letter that I didn't know just how it came about."

"I thought it was right they should meet," explained the son, "and so did father. I was glad that I suggested it, afterward; it was extremely gratifying to Colonel Lapham."

"Oh, it was quite right in every way. I suppose you have seen something of the family during the summer."

"Yes, a good deal. I've been down at Nantasket rather often."

Mrs. Corey let her eyes droop. Then she asked: "Are they well?"

"Yes, except Lapham himself, now and then. I went down once or twice to see him. He hasn't given himself any vacation this summer; he has such a passion for his business that I fancy he finds it hard being away from it at any time, and he's made his new house an excuse for staying——"

"Oh, yes, his house! Is it to be something fine?"

"Yes; it's a beautiful house. Seymour is doing it."

"Then, of course, it will be very handsome. I suppose the young ladies are very much taken up with it; and Mrs. Lapham."

"Mrs. Lapham, yes. I don't think the young ladies care so much about it."

"It must be for them. Aren't they ambitious?" asked Mrs. Corey, delicately feeling her way.

Her son thought awhile. Then he answered with a smile:

"No, I don't really think they are. They are unambitious, I should say." Mrs. Corey permitted herself a long breath. But her son added, "It's the parents who are ambitious for them," and her respiration became shorter again.

"Yes," she said.

"They're very simple, nice girls," pursued Corey. "I think you'll like the elder, when you come to know her."

When you come to know her. The words implied an expectation that the two families were to be better acquainted.

"Then she is more intellectual than her sister?" Mrs. Corey ventured.

"Intellectual?" repeated her son. "No; that isn't the word, quite. Though she certainly has more mind."

"The younger seemed very sensible."

"Oh, sensible, yes. And as practical as she's pretty. She can do all sorts of things, and likes to be doing them. Don't you think she's an extraordinary beauty?"

"Yes—yes, she is," said Mrs. Corey, at some cost.

"She's good, too," said Corey, "and perfectly innocent and transparent. I think you will like her the better the more you know her."

"I thought her very nice from the beginning," said the mother, heroically; and then nature asserted itself in her. "But I should be afraid that she might perhaps be a little bit tiresome at last; her range of ideas seemed so extremely limited."

"Yes, that's what I was afraid of. But, as a matter of fact, she isn't. She interests you by her very limitations. You can see the working of her mind, like that of a child. She isn't at all conscious even of her beauty."

"I don't believe young men can tell whether girls are conscious or not," said Mrs. Corey. "But I am not saying the Miss Laphams are not—" Her son sat musing, with an inattentive smile on his face. "What is it?"

"Oh, nothing. I was thinking of Miss Lapham and something she was saying. She's very droll, you know."

"The elder sister? Yes, you told me that. Can you see the workings of her mind too?"

"No; she's everything that's unexpected." Corey fell into another revery, and smiled again; but he did not offer to explain what amused him, and his mother would not ask.

"I don't know what to make of his admiring the girl so frankly," she said afterward to her husband. "That couldn't come naturally till after he had spoken to her, and I feel sure that he hasn't yet."

"You women haven't risen yet—it's an evidence of the backwardness of your sex—to a conception of the Bismarck idea in diplomacy.[3] If a man praises one woman, you still think he's in love with another. Do you mean that because Tom didn't praise the elder sister so much, he *has* spoken to *her*?"

Mrs. Corey refused the consequence, saying that it did not follow. "Besides, he did praise her."

"You ought to be glad that matters are in such good shape, then. At any rate, you can do absolutely nothing."

"Oh! I know it," sighed Mrs. Corey. "I wish Tom would be a little opener with me."

"He's as open as it's in the nature of an American-born son to be with his parents. I dare say if you'd ask him plumply what he meant in regard to the young lady, he would have told you—if he knew."

"Why, don't you think he does know, Bromfield?"

"I'm not at all sure he does. You women think that because a young man dangles after a girl, or girls, he's attached to them. It doesn't at all follow. He dangles because he must, and doesn't know what to do with his time, and because they seem to like it. I dare say that

3. Otto Von Bismarck (1815–1898), the German "Iron Chancellor," was famous for his relentlessness and directness in conducting diplomacy.

Tom has dangled a good deal in this instance because there was nobody else in town."

"Do you really think so?"

"I throw out the suggestion. And it strikes me that a young lady couldn't do better than stay in or near Boston during the summer. Most of the young men are here, kept by business through the week, with evenings available only on the spot, or a few miles off. What was the proportion of the sexes at the seashore and the mountains?"

"Oh, twenty girls at least for even an excuse of a man. It's shameful."

"You see, I am right in one part of my theory. Why shouldn't I be right in the rest?"

"I wish you were. And yet I can't say that I do. Those things are very serious with girls. I shouldn't like Tom to have been going to see those people if he meant nothing by it."

"And you wouldn't like it if he did. You are difficult, my dear." Her husband pulled an open newspaper toward him from the table.

"I feel that it wouldn't be at all like him to do so," said Mrs. Corey, going on to entangle herself in her words, as women often do when their ideas are perfectly clear. "Don't go to reading, please, Bromfield! I am really worried about this matter. I must know how much it means. I can't let it go on so. I don't see how you can rest easy without knowing."

"I don't in the least know what's going to become of me when I die; and yet I sleep well," replied Bromfield Corey, putting his newspaper aside.

"Ah, but this is a very different thing."

"So much more serious? Well, what can you do? We had this out when you were here in the summer, and you agreed with me then that we could do nothing. The situation hasn't changed at all."

"Yes, it has; it has continued the same," said Mrs. Corey, again expressing the fact by a contradiction in terms. "I think I must ask Tom outright."

"You know you can't do that, my dear."

"Then why doesn't he tell us?"

"Ah, that's what *he* can't do, if he's making love to Miss Irene—that's her name, I believe—on the American plan. He will tell us after he has told *her*. That was the way I did. Don't ignore our own youth, Anna. It was a long while ago, I'll admit."

"It was very different," said Mrs. Corey, a little shaken.

"I don't see how. I dare say Mamma Lapham knows whether Tom is in love with her daughter or not; and no doubt Papa Lapham knows it at second hand. But we shall not know it until the girl herself does. Depend upon that. Your mother knew, and she told your father; but my poor father knew nothing about it till we were engaged; and I had been hanging about—dangling, as you call it——"

"No, no; *you* called it that."

"Was it I?—for a year or more."

The wife could not refuse to be a little consoled by the image of her young love which the words conjured up, however little she liked its relation to her son's interest in Irene Lapham. She smiled pensively. "Then you think it hasn't come to an understanding with them yet?"

"An understanding? Oh, probably."

"An explanation, then?"

"The only logical inference from what we've been saying is that it hasn't. But I don't ask you to accept it on that account. May I read now, my dear?"

"Yes, you may read now," said Mrs. Corey, with one of those sighs which perhaps express a feminine sense of the unsatisfactoriness of husbands in general, rather than a personal discontent with her own.

"Thank you, my dear; then I think I'll smoke too," said Bromfield Corey, lighting a cigar.

She left him in peace, and she made no further attempt upon her son's confidence. But she was not inactive for that reason. She did not, of course, admit to herself, and far less to others, the motive with which she went to pay an early visit to the Laphams, who had now come up from Nantasket to Nankeen Square. She said to her daughters that she had always been a little ashamed of using her acquaintance with them to get money for her charity, and then seeming to drop it. Besides, it seemed to her that she ought somehow to recognize the business relation that Tom had formed with the father; they must not think that his family disapproved of what he had done.

"Yes, business is business," said Nanny, with a laugh. "Do you wish us to go with you again?"

"No; I will go alone this time," replied the mother with dignity.

Her coupé[4] now found its way to Nankeen Square without difficulty, and she sent up a card, which Mrs. Lapham received in the presence of her daughter Penelope.

"I presume I've got to see her," she gasped.

"Well, don't look so guilty, mother," joked the girl; "you haven't been doing anything so *very* wrong."

"It seems as if I *had*. I don't know what's come over me. I wasn't afraid of the woman before, but now I don't seem to feel as if I could look her in the face. He's been coming here of his own accord, and I fought against his coming long enough, goodness knows. I didn't want him to come. And as far forth as that goes, we're as

4. A two-door, enclosed carriage.

respectable as they are; and your father's got twice their money, any day. We no need to go begging for their favor. I guess they were glad enough to get him in with your father."

"Yes, those are all good points, mother," said the girl; "and if you keep saying them over, and count a hundred every time before you speak, I guess you'll worry through."

Mrs. Lapham had been fussing distractedly with her hair and ribbons, in preparation for her encounter with Mrs. Corey. She now drew in a long quivering breath, stared at her daughter without seeing her, and hurried downstairs. It was true that when she met Mrs. Corey before she had not been awed by her; but since then she had learned at least her own ignorance of the world, and she had talked over the things she had misconceived and the things she had shrewdly guessed so much that she could not meet her on the former footing of equality. In spite of as brave a spirit and as good a conscience as woman need have, Mrs. Lapham cringed inwardly, and tremulously wondered what her visitor had come for. She turned from pale to red, and was hardly coherent in her greetings; she did not know how they got to where Mrs. Corey was saying exactly the right things about her son's interest and satisfaction in his new business, and keeping her eyes fixed on Mrs. Lapham's, reading her uneasiness there, and making her feel, in spite of her indignant innocence, that she had taken a base advantage of her in her absence to get her son away from her and marry him to Irene. Then, presently, while this was painfully revolving itself in Mrs. Lapham's mind, she was aware of Mrs. Corey's asking if she was not to have the pleasure of seeing Miss Irene.

"No; she's out, just now," said Mrs. Lapham. "I don't know just when she'll be in. She went to get a book." And here she turned red again, knowing that Irene had gone to get the book because it was one that Corey had spoken of.

"Oh! I'm sorry," said Mrs. Corey. "I had hoped to see her. And your other daughter, whom I never met?"

"Penelope?" asked Mrs. Lapham, eased a little. "She is at home. I will go and call her." The Laphams had not yet thought of spending their superfluity on servants who could be rung for; they kept two girls and a man to look after the furnace, as they had for the last ten years. If Mrs. Lapham had rung in the parlor, her second girl would have gone to the street door to see who was there. She went upstairs for Penelope herself, and the girl, after some rebellious derision, returned with her.

Mrs. Corey took account of her, as Penelope withdrew to the other side of the room after their introduction, and sat down, indolently submissive on the surface to the tests to be applied, and following Mrs. Corey's lead of the conversation in her odd drawl.

"You young ladies will be glad to be getting into your new house," she said, politely.

"I don't know," said Penelope. "We're so used to this one."

Mrs. Corey looked a little baffled, but she said sympathetically, "Of course, you will be sorry to leave your old home."

Mrs. Lapham could not help putting in on behalf of her daughters: "I guess if it was left to the girls to say, we shouldn't leave it at all."

"Oh, indeed!" said Mrs. Corey; "are they so much attached? But I can quite understand it. My children would be heart-broken too if we were to leave the old place." She turned to Penelope. "But you must think of the lovely new house, and the beautiful position."

"Yes, I suppose we shall get used to them too," said Penelope, in response to this didactic consolation.

"Oh, I could even imagine your getting very fond of them," pursued Mrs. Corey, patronizingly. "My son has told me of the lovely outlook you're to have over the water. He thinks you have such a beautiful house. I believe he had the pleasure of meeting you all there when he first came home."

"Yes, I think he was our first visitor."

"He is a great admirer of your house," said Mrs. Corey, keeping her eyes very sharply, however politely, on Penelope's face, as if to surprise there the secret of any other great admiration of her son's that might helplessly show itself.

"Yes," said the girl, "he's been there several times with father; and he wouldn't be allowed to overlook any of its good points."

Her mother took a little more courage from her daughter's tranquillity.

"The girls make such fun of their father's excitement about his building, and the way he talks it into everybody."

"Oh, indeed!" said Mrs. Corey, with civil misunderstanding and inquiry.

Penelope flushed, and her mother went on: "I tell him he's more of a child about it than any of them."

"Young people are very philosophical nowadays," remarked Mrs. Corey.

"Yes, indeed," said Mrs. Lapham. "I tell them they've always had everything, so that nothing's a surprise to them. It was different with us in our young days."

"Yes," said Mrs. Corey, without assenting.

"I mean the Colonel and myself," explained Mrs. Lapham.

"Oh, yes—*yes!*" said Mrs. Corey.

"I'm sure," the former went on, rather helplessly, "*we* had to work hard enough for everything we got. And so we appreciated it."

"So many things were not done for young people then," said Mrs. Corey, not recognizing the early-hardships stand-point of

Mrs. Lapham. "But I don't know that they are always the better for it now," she added, vaguely, but with the satisfaction we all feel in uttering a just commonplace.

"It's rather hard living up to blessings that you've always had," said Penelope.

"Yes," replied Mrs. Corey, distractedly, and coming back to her slowly from the virtuous distance to which she had absented herself. She looked at the girl searchingly again, as if to determine whether this were a touch of the drolling her son had spoken of. But she only added: "You will enjoy the sunsets on the Back Bay so much."

"Well, not unless they're new ones," said Penelope. "I don't believe I could promise to enjoy any sunsets that I was used to, a great deal."

Mrs. Corey looked at her with misgiving, hardening into dislike. "No," she breathed, vaguely. "My son spoke of the fine effect of the lights about the hotel from your cottage at Nantasket," she said to Mrs. Lapham.

"Yes, they're splendid!" exclaimed that lady. "I guess the girls went down every night with him to see them from the rocks."

"Yes," said Mrs. Corey, a little dryly; and she permitted herself to add: "He spoke of those rocks. I suppose both you young ladies spend a great deal of your time on them when you're there. At Nahant my children were constantly on them."

"Irene likes the rocks," said Penelope. "I don't care much about them,—especially at night."

"Oh, indeed! I suppose you find it quite as well looking at the lights comfortably from the veranda."

"No; you can't see them from the house."

"Oh," said Mrs. Corey. After a perceptible pause, she turned to Mrs. Lapham. "I don't know what my son would have done for a breath of sea air this summer, if you had not allowed him to come to Nantasket. He wasn't willing to leave his business long enough to go anywhere else."

"Yes, he's a born business man," responded Mrs. Lapham enthusiastically. "If it's born in you, it's bound to come out. That's what the Colonel is always saying about Mr. Corey. He says it's born in him to be a business man, and he can't help it." She recurred to Corey gladly because she felt that she had not said enough of him when his mother first spoke of his connection with the business. "I don't believe," she went on excitedly, "that Colonel Lapham has ever had anybody with him that he thought more of."

"You have *all* been very kind to my son," said Mrs. Corey in acknowledgment, and stiffly bowing a little, "and we feel greatly indebted to you. Very much so."

At these grateful expressions Mrs. Lapham reddened once more, and murmured that it had been very pleasant to them, she was sure.

She glanced at her daughter for support, but Penelope was looking at Mrs. Corey, who doubtless saw her from the corner of her eyes, though she went on speaking to her mother.

"I was sorry to hear from him that Mr.—Colonel?—Lapham had not been quite well this summer. I hope he's better now?"

"Oh, yes, indeed," replied Mrs. Lapham; "he's all right now. He's hardly ever been sick, and he don't know how to take care of himself. That's all. We don't any of us; we're all so well."

"Health is a great blessing," sighed Mrs. Corey.

"Yes, so it is. How is your oldest daughter?" inquired Mrs. Lapham. "Is she as delicate as ever?"

"She seems to be rather better since we returned." And now Mrs. Corey, as if forced to the point, said bunglingly that the young ladies had wished to come with her, but had been detained. She based her statement upon Nanny's sarcastic demand; and, perhaps seeing it topple a little, she rose hastily, to get away from its fall. "But we shall hope for some—some other occasion," she said vaguely, and she put on a parting smile, and shook hands with Mrs. Lapham and Penelope, and then, after some lingering commonplaces, got herself out of the house.

Penelope and her mother were still looking at each other, and trying to grapple with the effect or purport of the visit, when Irene burst in upon them from the outside.

"Oh, mamma! wasn't that Mrs. Corey's carriage just drove away?"

Penelope answered with her laugh. "Yes! You've just missed the most delightful call, 'Rene. So easy and pleasant every way. Not a bit stiff! Mrs. Corey was so friendly! She didn't make *me* feel at all as if she'd bought me, and thought she'd given too much; and mother held up her head as if she were all wool and a yard wide,[5] and she would just like to have anybody deny it."

In a few touches of mimicry she dashed off a sketch of the scene: her mother's trepidation, and Mrs. Corey's well-bred repose and polite scrutiny of them both. She ended by showing how she herself had sat huddled up in a dark corner, mute with fear.

"If she came to make us say and do the wrong thing, she must have gone away happy; and it's a pity you weren't here to help, Irene. I don't know that I aimed to make a bad impression, but I guess I succeeded—even beyond my deserts." She laughed; then suddenly she flashed out in fierce earnest. "If I missed doing anything that could make me as hateful to her as she made herself to me——" She checked herself, and began to laugh. Her laugh broke, and the tears started into her eyes; she ran out of the room, and up the stairs.

"What—what does it mean?" asked Irene, in a daze.

5. I.e., high-quality goods.

Mrs. Lapham was still in the chilly torpor to which Mrs. Corey's call had reduced her. Penelope's vehemence did not rouse her. She only shook her head absently, and said, "I don't know."

"Why should Pen care what impression she made? I didn't suppose it would make any difference to her whether Mrs. Corey liked her or not."

"I didn't, either. But I could see that she was just as nervous as she could be, every minute of the time. I guess she didn't like Mrs. Corey any too well from the start, and she couldn't seem to act like herself."

"Tell me about it, mamma," said Irene, dropping into a chair.

Mrs. Corey described the interview to her husband on her return home. "Well, and what are your inferences?" he asked.

"They were extremely embarrassed and excited—that is, the mother. I don't wish to do her injustice, but she certainly behaved consciously."

"You made her feel so, I dare say, Anna. I can imagine how terrible you must have been, in the character of an accusing spirit, too ladylike to say anything. What did you hint?"

"I hinted nothing," said Mrs. Corey, descending to the weakness of defending herself. "But I saw quite enough to convince me that the girl is in love with Tom, and the mother knows it."

"That was very unsatisfactory. I supposed you went to find out whether Tom was in love with the girl. Was she as pretty as ever?"

"I didn't see her; she was not at home; I saw her sister."

"I don't know that I follow you quite, Anna. But no matter. What was the sister like?"

"A thoroughly disagreeable young woman."

"What did she do?"

"Nothing. She's far too sly for that. But that was the impression."

"Then you didn't find her so amusing as Tom does?"

"I found her pert. There's no other word for it. She says things to puzzle you and put you out."

"Ah, that was worse than pert, Anna; that was criminal. Well, let us thank heaven the younger one is so pretty."

Mrs. Corey did not reply directly. "Bromfield," she said, after a moment of troubled silence, "I have been thinking over your plan, and I don't see why it isn't the right thing."

"What is my plan?" inquired Bromfield Corey.

"A dinner."

Her husband began to laugh. "Ah, you overdid the accusing-spirit business, and this is reparation." But Mrs. Corey hurried on, with combined dignity and anxiety:

"We can't ignore Tom's intimacy with them—it amounts to that; it will probably continue even if it's merely a fancy, and we must seem to know it; whatever comes of it, we can't disown it. They are very simple, unfashionable people, and unworldly; but I can't say that they are offensive, unless—unless," she added, in propitiation of her husband's smile, "unless the father—how *did* you find the father?" she implored.

"He will be very entertaining," said Corey, "if you start him on his paint. What was the disagreeable daughter like? Shall you have her?"

"She's little and dark. We must have them all," Mrs. Corey sighed. "Then you don't think a dinner would do?"

"Oh, yes, I do. As you say, we can't disown Tom's relation to them, whatever it is. We had much better recognize it, and make the best of the inevitable. I think a Lapham dinner would be delightful." He looked at her with delicate irony in his voice and smile, and she fetched another sigh, so deep and sore now that he laughed outright. "Perhaps," he suggested, "it would be the best way of curing Tom of his fancy, if he has one. He has been seeing her with the dangerous advantages which a mother knows how to give her daughter in the family circle, and with no means of comparing her with other girls. You must invite several other very pretty girls."

"Do you really think so, Bromfield?" asked Mrs. Corey, taking courage a little. "That might do." But her spirits visibly sank again. "I don't know any other girl half so pretty."

"Well, then, better bred."

"She is very lady-like, very modest, and pleasing."

"Well, more cultivated."

"Tom doesn't get on with such people."

"Oh, you *wish* him to marry her, I see."

"No, no——"

"Then you'd better give the dinner to bring them together, to promote the affair."

"You know I don't want to do that, Bromfield. But I feel that we must do something. If we don't, it has a clandestine appearance. It isn't just to them. A dinner won't leave us in any worse position, and may leave us in a better. Yes," said Mrs. Corey, after another thoughtful interval, "we must have them—have them all. It could be very simple."

"Ah, you can't give a dinner under a bushel,[6] if I take your meaning, my dear. If we do this at all, we mustn't do it as if we were ashamed of it. We must ask people to meet them."

6. In Jesus's Sermon on the Mount, he calls on his followers to be "the light of the world," illustrating his point with a pair of metaphors: "A city that is set on an hill cannot be hid. Neither do men light a candle, and put it under a bushel, but on a candlestick; and it giveth light unto all that are in the house" (Matthew 5.14–15).

"Yes," sighed Mrs. Corey. "There are not many people in town yet," she added, with relief that caused her husband another smile. "There really seems a sort of fatality about it," she concluded, religiously.

"Then you had better not struggle against it. Go and reconcile Lily and Nanny to it as soon as possible."

Mrs. Corey blanched a little. "But don't you think it will be the best thing, Bromfield?"

"I do indeed, my dear. The only thing that shakes my faith in the scheme is the fact that I first suggested it. But if you have adopted it, it must be all right, Anna. I can't say that I expected it."

"No," said his wife, "it wouldn't do."

[sixth installment—april 1885]

XIII.

Having distinctly given up the project of asking the Laphams to dinner, Mrs. Corey was able to carry it out with the courage of sinners who have sacrificed to virtue by frankly acknowledging its superiority to their intended transgression. She did not question but the Laphams would come; and she only doubted as to the people whom she should invite to meet them. She opened the matter with some trepidation to her daughters, but neither of them opposed her; they rather looked at the scheme from her own point of view, and agreed with her that nothing had really yet been done to wipe out the obligation to the Laphams helplessly contracted the summer before, and strengthened by that ill-advised application to Mrs. Lapham for charity. Not only the principal of their debt of gratitude remained, but the accruing interest. They said, What harm could giving the dinner possibly do them? They might ask any or all of their acquaintance without disadvantage to themselves; but it would be perfectly easy to give the dinner just the character they chose, and still flatter the ignorance of the Laphams. The trouble would be with Tom, if he were really interested in the girl; but he could not say anything if they made it a family dinner; he could not feel anything. They had each turned in her own mind, as it appeared from a comparison of ideas, to one of the most comprehensive of those cousinships which form the admiration and terror of the adventurer in Boston society. He finds himself hemmed in and left out at every turn by ramifications that forbid him all hope of safe personality in his comments on people; he is never less secure than when he hears some given Bostonian denouncing or ridiculing another. If he will be advised, he will guard himself from concurring in these criticisms, however just they appear, for the probability is that their object is a cousin of not more than one remove from the censor. When the alien hears a group of Boston ladies calling one another, and speaking of all their gentlemen friends, by the familiar abbreviations of their Christian names, he must feel keenly the exile to which he was born; but he is then, at least, in comparatively little danger; while these latent and tacit cousinships open pitfalls at every step around him, in a society where Middlesexes have married Essexes and produced Suffolks for two hundred and fifty years.[1]

These conditions, however, so perilous to the foreigner, are a source of strength and security to those native to them. An uncertain acquaintance may be so effectually involved in the meshes of such a cousinship, as never to be heard of outside of it; and tremendous stories are told of people who have spent a whole winter in Boston, in a whirl of gayety, and who, the original guests of the Suffolks, discover upon reflection that they have met no one but Essexes and Middlesexes.

Mrs. Corey's brother James came first into her mind, and she thought with uncommon toleration of the easy-going, uncritical good-nature of his wife. James Bellingham had been the adviser of her son throughout, and might be said to have actively promoted his connection with Lapham. She thought next of the widow of her cousin, Henry Bellingham, who had let her daughter marry that Western steamboat man, and was fond of her son-in-law; she might be expected at least to endure the paint-king and his family. The daughters insisted so strongly upon Mrs. Bellingham's son, Charles, that Mrs. Corey put him down—if he were in town; he might be in Central America; he got on with all sorts of people. It seemed to her that she might stop at this: four Laphams, five Coreys, and four Bellinghams were enough.

"That makes thirteen," said Nanny. "You can have Mr. and Mrs. Sewell."

"Yes, that is a good idea," assented Mrs. Corey. "He is our minister, and it is very proper."

"I don't see why you don't have Robert Chase. It is a pity he shouldn't see her—for the color."

"I don't quite like the idea of that," said Mrs. Corey; "but we can have him too, if it won't make too many." The painter had married into a poorer branch of the Coreys, and his wife was dead. "Is there any one else?"

"There is Miss Kingsbury."[2]

1. Howells alludes, in terms that suggest the complex lineages of the British nobility, to three of the four longest-established counties in Massachusetts, whose founding families' interrelationships were similarly convoluted. Elsewhere Howells humorously noted that these family ties created "admiration and terror" for the uninformed "adventurer in Boston society" because he never knew whether he was saying the wrong thing about someone's relative.
2. Both Clara Kingsbury and the Reverend and Mrs. Sewell were recurring Howells characters: Clara had appeared in *A Modern Instance* (1882) and would reappear in *An Imperative Duty* (1891). The Sewells play an important role in *The Minister's Charge* (1887).

"We have had her so much. She will begin to think we are using her."

"She won't mind; she's so good-natured."

"Well, then," the mother summed up, "there are four Laphams, five Coreys, four Bellinghams, one Chase, and one Kingsbury—fifteen. Oh! and two Sewells. Seventeen. Ten ladies and seven gentlemen. It doesn't balance very well, and it's too large."

"Perhaps some of the ladies won't come," suggested Lily.

"Oh, the ladies always come," said Nanny.

Their mother reflected. "Well, I will ask them. The ladies will refuse in time to let us pick up some gentlemen somewhere; some more artists. Why! we must have Mr. Seymour, the architect; he's a bachelor, and he's building their house, Tom says."

Her voice fell a little when she mentioned her son's name, and she told him of her plan, when he came home in the evening, with evident misgiving.

"What are you doing it for, mother?" he asked, looking at her with his honest eyes.

She dropped her own in a little confusion. "I won't do it at all, my dear," she said, "if you don't approve. But I thought——You know we have never made any proper acknowledgment of their kindness to us at Baie St. Paul. Then in the winter, I'm ashamed to say, I got money from her for a charity I was interested in; and I hate the idea of merely *using* people in that way. And now your having been at their house this summer—we can't seem to disapprove of that; and your business relations to him——"

"Yes, I see," said Corey. "Do you think it amounts to a dinner?"

"Why, I don't know," returned his mother. "We shall have hardly any one out of our family connection."

"Well," Corey assented, "it might do. I suppose what you wish is to give them a pleasure."

"Why, certainly. Don't you think they'd like to come?"

"Oh, they'd like to come; but whether it would be a pleasure after they were here is another thing. I should have said that if you wanted to have them, they would enjoy better being simply asked to meet our own immediate family."

"That's what I thought of in the first place, but your father seemed to think it implied a social distrust of them; and we couldn't afford to have that appearance, even to ourselves."

"Perhaps he was right."

"And besides, it might seem a little significant."

Corey seemed inattentive to this consideration. "Whom did you think of asking?" His mother repeated the names. "Yes, that would do," he said, with a vague dissatisfaction.

"I won't have it at all, if you don't wish, Tom."

"Oh, yes, have it; perhaps you ought. Yes, I dare say it's right. What did you mean by a family dinner seeming significant?"

His mother hesitated. When it came to that, she did not like to recognize in his presence the anxieties that had troubled her. But "I don't know," she said, since she must. "I shouldn't want to give that young girl, or her mother, the idea that we wished to make more of the acquaintance than—than you did, Tom."

He looked at her absent-mindedly, as if he did not take her meaning. But he said, "Oh, yes, of course," and Mrs. Corey, in the uncertainty in which she seemed destined to remain concerning this affair, went off and wrote her invitation to Mrs. Lapham. Later in the evening, when they again found themselves alone, her son said, "I don't think I understood you, mother, in regard to the Laphams. I think I do now. I certainly don't wish you to make more of the acquaintance than I have done. It wouldn't be right; it might be very unfortunate. Don't give the dinner!"

"It's too late now, my son," said Mrs. Corey. "I sent my note to Mrs. Lapham an hour ago." Her courage rose at the trouble which showed in Corey's face. "But don't be annoyed by it, Tom. It isn't a family dinner, you know, and everything can be managed without embarrassment. If we take up the affair at this point, you will seem to have been merely acting for us; and they can't possibly understand anything more."

"Well, well! Let it go! I dare say it's all right. At any rate, it can't be helped now."

"I don't wish to help it, Tom," said Mrs. Corey, with a cheerfulness which the thought of the Laphams had never brought her before. "I am sure it is quite fit and proper, and we can make them have a very pleasant time. They are good, inoffensive people, and we owe it to ourselves not to be afraid to show that we have felt their kindness to us, and his appreciation of you."

"Well," consented Corey. The trouble that his mother had suddenly cast off was in his tone; but she was not sorry. It was quite time that he should think seriously of his attitude toward these people if he had not thought of it before, but, according to his father's theory, had been merely dangling.

It was a view of her son's character that could hardly have pleased her in different circumstances; yet it was now unquestionably a consolation if not wholly a pleasure. If she considered the Laphams at all, it was with the resignation which we feel at the evils of others, even when they have not brought them on themselves.

Mrs. Lapham, for her part, had spent the hours between Mrs. Corey's visit and her husband's coming home from business in reaching the same conclusion with regard to Corey; and her spirits were at the lowest when they sat down to supper. Irene was downcast with her; Penelope was purposely gay; and the Colonel was beginning, after his first plate of the boiled ham,—which, bristling with cloves, rounded its bulk on a wide platter before him,—to take note of the surrounding mood, when the door-bell jingled peremptorily, and the girl left waiting on the table to go and answer it. She returned at once with a note for Mrs. Lapham, which she read, and then, after a helpless survey of her family, read again.

"Why, what *is* it, mamma?" asked Irene; while the Colonel, who had taken up his carving-knife for another attack on the ham, held it drawn half across it.

"Why, *I* don't know what it *does* mean," answered Mrs. Lapham tremulously, and she let the girl take the note from her.

Irene ran it over, and then turned to the name at the end with a joyful cry and a flush that burned to the top of her forehead. Then she began to read it once more.

The Colonel dropped his knife and frowned impatiently, and Mrs. Lapham said, "You read it out loud, if you know what to make of it, Irene." But Irene, with a nervous scream of protest, handed it to her father, who performed the office.

"DEAR MRS. LAPHAM:

"Will you and General Lapham——"

"I didn't know I was a general," grumbled Lapham. "I guess I shall have to be looking up my back pay. Who is it writes this, anyway?" he asked, turning the letter over for the signature.

"Oh, never mind. Read it through!" cried his wife, with a kindling glance of triumph at Penelope, and he resumed:

"—and your daughters give us the pleasure of your company at dinner on Thursday, the 28th, at half-past six.

"Yours sincerely,

"ANNA B. COREY."

The brief invitation had been spread over two pages, and the Colonel had difficulties with the signature which he did not instantly surmount. When he had made out the name and pronounced it, he looked across at his wife for an explanation.

"*I* don't know what it all means," she said, shaking her head and speaking with a pleased flutter. "She was here this afternoon, and I should have said she had come to see how bad she *could* make us feel. I declare, I never felt so put down in my life by anybody."

"Why, what did she do? What did she say?" Lapham was ready, in his dense pride, to resent any affront to his blood, but doubtful, with the evidence of this invitation to the contrary, if any affront had been offered. Mrs. Lapham tried to tell him, but there was really nothing tangible; and when she came to put it into words, she could not make out a case. Her husband listened to her excited attempt, and then he said, with judicial superiority, "*I* guess nobody's been trying to make you feel bad, Persis. What would she go right home and invite you to dinner for, if she'd acted the way you say?"

In this view it did seem improbable, and Mrs. Lapham was shaken. She could only say, "Penelope felt just the way I did about it."

Lapham looked at the girl, who said, "Oh, *I* can't prove it! I begin to think it never happened. I guess it didn't."

"Humph!" said her father, and he sat frowning thoughtfully awhile—ignoring her mocking irony, or choosing to take her seriously. "You can't really put your finger on anything," he said to his wife, "and it ain't likely there *is* anything. Anyway, she's done the proper thing by you now."

Mrs. Lapham faltered between her lingering resentment and the appeals of her flattered vanity. She looked from Penelope's impassive face to the eager eyes of Irene. "Well—just as you *say,* Silas. I don't know as she *was* so very bad. I guess may be she was embarrassed some——"

"That's what I told you, mamma, from the start," interrupted Irene. "Didn't I tell you she didn't mean anything by it? It's just the way she acted at Baie St. Paul, when she got well enough to realize what you'd done for her!"

Penelope broke into a laugh. "Is *that* her way of showing her gratitude? I'm sorry I didn't understand that before."

Irene made no effort to reply. She merely looked from her mother to her father with a grieved face for their protection, and Lapham said, "When we've done supper, you answer her, Persis. Say we'll come."

"With one exception," said Penelope.

"What do you mean?" demanded her father, with a mouth full of ham.

"Oh, nothing of importance. Merely that I'm not going."

Lapham gave himself time to swallow his morsel, and his rising wrath went down with it. "I guess you'll change your mind when the time comes," he said. "Anyway, Persis, you say we'll all come, and then, if Penelope don't want to go, you can excuse her after we get there. That's the best way."

None of them, apparently, saw any reason why the affair should not be left in this way, or had a sense of the awful and binding nature of a dinner-engagement. If she believed that Penelope would not finally change her mind and go, no doubt Mrs. Lapham thought that Mrs. Corey would easily excuse her absence. She did not find it so simple a matter to accept the invitation. Mrs. Corey had said "Dear Mrs. Lapham," but Mrs. Lapham had her doubts whether it would not be a servile imitation to say "Dear Mrs. Corey" in return; and she was tormented as to the proper phrasing throughout and the precise temperature which she should impart to her politeness. She wrote an unpracticed, uncharacteristic round hand, the same in which she used to set the children's copies at school, and she subscribed herself, after some hesitation between her husband's given name and her own, "Yours truly, Mrs. S. Lapham."

Penelope had gone to her room, without waiting to be asked to advise or criticise; but Irene had decided upon the paper, and, on the whole, Mrs. Lapham's note made a very decent appearance on the page.

When the furnace-man came, the Colonel sent him out to post it in the box at the corner of the square. He had determined not to say anything more about the matter before the girls, not choosing to let them see that he was elated; he tried to give the effect of its being an every-day sort of thing, abruptly closing the discussion with his order to Mrs. Lapham to accept; but he had remained swelling behind his newspaper during her prolonged struggle with her note, and he could no longer hide his elation when Irene followed her sister upstairs.

"Well, Pers," he demanded, "what do you say now?"

Mrs. Lapham had been sobered into something of her former misgiving by her difficulties with her note. "Well, I don't know what *to* say. I declare, I'm all mixed up about it, and I don't know as we've begun as we can carry out in promising to go. I presume," she sighed, "that we can *all* send some excuse at the last moment, if we don't want to go."

"I guess we can carry out, and I guess we sha'n't want to send any excuse," bragged the Colonel. "If we're ever going to be anybody at all, we've got to go and see how it's done. I presume we've got to give some sort of party when we get into the new house, and this gives the chance to ask 'em back again. You can't complain now but what they've made the advances, Persis?"

"No," said Mrs. Lapham, lifelessly; "I wonder why they wanted to do it. Oh, I suppose it's all right," she added in deprecation of the anger with her humility which she saw rising in her husband's face; "but if it's all going to be as much trouble as that letter, I'd rather be whipped. *I* don't know what I'm going to wear; or the girls, either. I do wonder—I've heard that people go to dinner in low-necks. Do you suppose it's the custom?"

"How should *I* know?" demanded the Colonel. "I guess you've got clothes enough. Any rate, you needn't fret about it. You just go round to White's, or Jordan & Marsh's,[3] and ask for a dinner dress. I guess

3. R. H. White and Jordan & Marsh were prominent Boston department stores.

that'll settle it; they'll know. Get some of them imported dresses. I see 'em in the window every time I pass; lots of 'em."

"Oh, it ain't the dress!" said Mrs. Lapham. "I don't suppose but what we could get along with that; and I want to do the best we can for the children; but *I* don't know what we're going to talk about to those people when we get there. We haven't got anything in common with them. Oh, I don't say they're any better," she again made haste to say in arrest of her husband's resentment. "I don't believe they are; and I don't see why they should be. And there ain't anybody has got a better right to hold up their head than you have, Silas. You've got plenty of money, and you've made every cent of it."

"I guess I shouldn't amounted to much without you, Persis," interposed Lapham, moved to this justice by her praise.

"Oh, don't talk about *me!*" protested the wife. "Now that you've made it all right about Rogers, there ain't a thing in this world against you. But still, for all that, I can see—and I can feel it when I can't see it—that we're different from those people. They're well-meaning enough, and they'd excuse it, I presume, but we're too old to learn to be like them."

"The children ain't," said Lapham, shrewdly.

"No, the children ain't," admitted his wife, "and that's the only thing that reconciles me to it."

"You see how pleased Irene looked when I read it?"

"Yes, she was pleased."

"And I guess Penelope'll think better of it before the time comes."

"Oh, yes, we do it for them. But whether we're doing the best thing for 'em, goodness knows. I'm not saying anything against *him.* Irene'll be a lucky girl to get him, if she wants him. But there! I'd ten times rather she was going to marry such a fellow as *you* were, Si, that had to make every inch of his own way, and she had to help him. It's *in* her!"

Lapham laughed aloud for pleasure in his wife's fondness; but neither of them wished that he should respond directly to it. "I guess, if it wa'n't for me, he wouldn't have a much easier time. But don't you fret! It's all coming out right. That dinner ain't a thing for you to be uneasy about. It'll pass off perfectly easy and natural."

Lapham did not keep his courageous mind quite to the end of the week that followed. It was his theory not to let Corey see that he was set up about the invitation, and when the young man said politely that his mother was glad they were able to come, Lapham was very short with him. He said yes, he believed that Mrs. Lapham and the girls were going. Afterward he was afraid Corey might not understand that he was coming too; but he did not know how to approach the subject again, and Corey did not, so he let it pass. It worried him to see all the preparation that his wife and Irene were making, and he tried to laugh at them for it; and it worried him to find that Penelope was making no preparation at all for herself, but only helping the others. He asked her what should she do if she changed her mind at the last moment and concluded to go, and she said she guessed she should not change her mind, but if she did, she would go to White's with him and get him to choose her an imported dress, he seemed to like them so much. He was too proud to mention the subject again to her.

Finally, all that dress-making in the house began to scare him with vague apprehensions in regard to his own dress. As soon as he had determined to go, an ideal of the figure in which he should go presented itself to his mind. He should not wear any dress-coat, because, for one thing, he considered that a man looked like a fool in a dress-coat, and, for another thing, he had none—had none on principle. He would go in a frock-coat and black pantaloons, and perhaps a white waistcoat, but a black cravat, anyway. But as soon as he developed this ideal to his family, which he did in pompous disdain of their anxieties about their own dress, they said he should not go so. Irene reminded him that he was the only person without a dress-coat at a corps-reunion dinner which he had taken her to some years before, and she remembered feeling awfully about it at the time. Mrs. Lapham, who would perhaps have agreed of herself, shook her head with misgiving. "I don't see but what you'll have to get you one, Si," she said. "I don't believe they *ever* go without 'em to a private house."

He held out openly, but on his way home the next day, in a sudden panic, he cast anchor before his tailor's door and got measured for a dress-coat. After that he began to be afflicted about his waistcoat, concerning which he had hitherto been airily indifferent. He tried to get opinion out of his family, but they were not so clear about it as they were about the frock. It ended in their buying a book of etiquette, which settled the question adversely to a white waistcoat. The author, however, after being very explicit in telling them not to eat with their knives, and above all not to pick their teeth with their forks,—a thing which he said no lady or gentleman ever did,—was still far from decided as to the kind of cravat Colonel Lapham ought to wear: shaken on other points, Lapham had begun to waver also concerning the black cravat. As to the question of gloves for the Colonel, which suddenly flashed upon him one evening, it appeared never to have entered the thoughts of the etiquette man, as Lapham called him. Other authors on the same subject were equally silent, and Irene could only remember having heard, in some vague sort of way, that gentlemen did not wear gloves so much any more.

Drops of perspiration gathered on Lapham's forehead in the anxiety of the debate; he groaned, and he swore a little in the compromise profanity which he used.

"I declare," said Penelope, where she sat purblindly sewing on a bit of dress for Irene, "the Colonel's clothes are as much trouble as anybody's. Why don't you go to Jordan & Marsh's and order one of the imported dresses for yourself, father?" That gave them all the relief of a laugh over it, the Colonel joining in piteously.

He had an awful longing to find out from Corey how he ought to go. He formulated and repeated over to himself an apparently careless question, such as, "Oh, by the way, Corey, where do you get your gloves?" This would naturally lead to some talk on the subject, which would, if properly managed, clear up the whole trouble. But Lapham found that he would rather die than ask this question, or any question that would bring up the dinner again. Corey did not recur to it, and Lapham avoided the matter with positive fierceness. He shunned talking with Corey at all, and suffered in grim silence.

One night, before they fell asleep, his wife said to him, "I was reading in one of those books to-day, and I don't believe but what we've made a mistake if Pen holds out that she won't go."

"Why?" demanded Lapham, in the dismay which beset him at every fresh recurrence to the subject.

"The book says that it's very impolite not to answer a dinner invitation promptly. Well, we've done that all right,—at first I didn't know but what we had been a little too quick, may be,—but then it says if you're not going, that it's the height of rudeness not to let them know at once, so that they can fill your place at the table."

The Colonel was silent for a while. "Well, I'm dumned," he said finally, "if there seems to be any end to this thing. If it was to do over again, I'd say no for all of us."

"I've wished a hundred times they hadn't asked us; but it's too late to think about that *now.* The question is, what are we going to do about Penelope?"

"Oh, I guess she'll go, at the last moment."

"She says she won't. She took a prejudice against Mrs. Corey that day, and she can't seem to get over it."

"Well, then, hadn't you better write in the morning, as soon as you're up, that she ain't coming?"

Mrs. Lapham sighed helplessly. "I shouldn't know how to get it in. It's so late now; I don't see how I could have the face."

"Well, then, she's got to go, that's all."

"She's set she won't."

"And I'm set she shall," said Lapham, with the loud obstinacy of a man whose women always have their way.

Mrs. Lapham was not supported by the sturdiness of his proclamation.

But she did not know how to do what she knew she ought to do about Penelope, and she let matters drift. After all, the child had a right to stay at home if she did not wish to go. That was what Mrs. Lapham felt, and what she said to her husband next morning, bidding him let Penelope alone, unless she chose herself to go. She said it was too late now to do anything, and she must make the best excuse she could when she saw Mrs. Corey. She began to wish that Irene and her father would go and excuse her too. She could not help saying this, and then she and Lapham had some unpleasant words.

"Look here!" he cried. "Who wanted to go in for these people in the first place? Didn't you come home full of 'em last year, and want me to sell out here and move some-wheres else because it didn't seem to suit 'em? And now you want to put it all on me! I ain't going to stand it."

"Hush!" said his wife. "Do you want to raise the house? I *didn't* put it on you, as you say. You took it on yourself. Ever since that fellow happened to come into the new house that day, you've been perfectly crazy to get in with them. And now you're so afraid you shall do something wrong before 'em, you don't hardly dare to say your life's your own. I declare, if you pester me any more about those gloves, Silas Lapham, I won't go."

"Do you suppose I want to go on my own account?" he demanded furiously.

"No," she admitted. "Of course I don't. I know very well that you're doing it for Irene; but, for goodness gracious sake, don't worry our lives out, and make yourself a perfect laughing-stock before the children."

With this modified concession from her, the quarrel closed in sullen silence on Lapham's part. It was the night before the dinner, and the question of his gloves was still unsettled, and in a fair way to remain so. He had bought a pair, so as to be on the safe side, perspiring in company with the young lady who sold them, and who helped him try them on at the shop; his nails were still full of the powder which she had plentifully peppered into them in order to overcome the resistance of his blunt fingers. But he was uncertain whether he should wear them. They had found a book at last that said the ladies removed their gloves on sitting down at table, but it said nothing about gentlemen's gloves. He left his wife where she stood half hook-and-eyed at her glass in her new dress, and went down to his own den beyond the parlor. Before he shut his door he caught a glimpse of Irene trailing up and down before the long mirror in *her* new dress, followed by the seamstress on her knees; the woman had her mouth full of pins, and from time to time she made Irene stop till she could put one of the pins into her train; Penelope sat in a corner criticising and counseling. It made Lapham sick, and he despised himself and all his brood for the trouble they were taking. But another glance gave him a sight of the young girl's face in the mirror, beautiful and radiant with happiness; and his heart melted again with paternal tenderness and pride. It was going to be a great pleasure to Irene, and Lapham felt that she was bound to cut out anything there. He was vexed with Penelope that she was not going, too; he would have liked to have those people hear her talk. He held his door a little open, and listened to the things she was "getting off" there to Irene. He showed that he felt really hurt and disappointed about Penelope, and the girl's mother made her console him the next evening before they all drove away without her. "You try to look on the bright side of it, father. I guess you'll see that it's best I didn't go when you get there. Irene needn't open her lips, and they can all see how pretty she is; but they wouldn't know how smart I was unless I talked, and may be then they wouldn't."

This thrust at her father's simple vanity in her made him laugh; and then they drove away, and Penelope shut the door, and went upstairs with her lips firmly shutting in a sob.

XIV.

The Coreys were one of the few old families who lingered in Bellingham Place, the handsome, quiet old street which the sympathetic observer must grieve to see abandoned to boarding-houses.[1] The dwellings are stately and tall, and the whole place wears an air of aristocratic seclusion, which Mrs. Corey's father might well have thought assured when he left her his house there at his death. It is one of two evidently designed by the same architect who built some houses in a characteristic taste on Beacon street opposite the Common. It has a wooden portico, with slender fluted columns, which have always been painted white, and which, with the delicate moldings of the cornice, form the sole and sufficient decoration of the street front; nothing could be simpler, and nothing could be better. Within, the architect has again indulged his preference for the classic; the roof of the vestibule, wide and low, rests on marble columns, slim and fluted like the wooden columns without, and an ample staircase climbs in a graceful, easy curve from the tessellated pavement.[2] Some carved Venetian *scrigni*[3] stretched along the wall; a rug lay at

1. Beacon Hill includes many short residential courts, providing access to interior lots from the larger through streets. One such street on the north side of Revere Street is labeled Bellingham Place on modern maps, but older maps show it as Hills Court, and it is likely that Howells's Bellingham Place is fictional. The Coreys' residence appears to be in the vicinity of Chestnut and Revere Streets and Louisburg Square (where the Howells family lived before buying a house "on the water side of Beacon" in Back Bay), just north of Boston Common and the Public Garden.
2. A mosaic floor treatment incorporating small pieces of stone, glass, or tile into larger geometric patterns.
3. A casket or chest for storing valuables (Italian).

the foot of the stairs; but otherwise the simple adequacy of the architectural intention had been respected, and the place looked bare to the eyes of the Laphams when they entered. The Coreys had once kept a man, but when young Corey began his retrenchments the man had yielded to the neat maid who showed the Colonel into the reception-room and asked the ladies to walk up two flights.

He had his charges from Irene not to enter the drawing-room without her mother, and he spent five minutes in getting on his gloves, for he had desperately resolved to wear them at last. When he had them on, and let his large fists hang down on either side, they looked, in the saffron tint which the shop-girl said his gloves should be of, like canvased hams. He perspired with doubt as he climbed the stairs, and while he waited on the landing for Mrs. Lapham and Irene to come down from above, before going into the drawing-room, he stood staring at his hands, now open and now shut, and breathing hard. He heard quiet talking beyond the *portière*[4] within, and presently Tom Corey came out.

"Ah, Colonel Lapham! Very glad to see you."

Lapham shook hands with him and gasped, "Waiting for Mis' Lapham," to account for his presence. He had not been able to button his right glove, and he now began, with as much indifference as he could assume, to pull them both off, for he saw that Corey wore none. By the time he had stuffed them into the pocket of his coat-skirt his wife and daughter descended.

Corey welcomed them very cordially too, but looked a little mystified. Mrs. Lapham knew that he was silently inquiring for Penelope, and she did not know whether she ought to excuse her to him first or not. She said nothing, and after a glance toward the regions where Penelope might conjecturably be lingering, he held aside the *portière* for the Laphams to pass, and entered the room with them.

Mrs. Lapham had decided against low-necks on her own responsibility, and had intrenched herself in the safety of a black silk, in which she looked very handsome. Irene wore a dress of one of those shades which only a woman or an artist can decide to be green or blue, and which to other eyes looks both or neither, according to their degrees of ignorance. If it was more like a ball dress than a dinner dress, that might be excused to the exquisite effect. She trailed, a delicate splendor, across the carpet in her mother's somber wake, and the consciousness of success brought a vivid smile to her face. Lapham, pallid with anxiety lest he should somehow disgrace himself, giving thanks to God that he should have been spared the shame of wearing gloves where no one else did, but at the same

4. A doorway curtain (French).

time despairing that Corey should have seen him in them, had an unwonted aspect of almost pathetic refinement.

Mrs. Corey exchanged a quick glance of surprise and relief with her husband as she started across the room to meet her guests, and in her gratitude to them for being so irreproachable, she threw into her manner a warmth that people did not always find there. "General Lapham?" she said, shaking hands in quick succession with Mrs. Lapham and Irene, and now addressing herself to him.

"No, ma'am, only Colonel," said the honest man, but the lady did not hear him. She was introducing her husband to Lapham's wife and daughter, and Bromfield Corey was already shaking his hand and saying he was very glad to see him again, while he kept his artistic eye on Irene, and apparently could not take it off. Lily Corey gave the Lapham ladies a greeting which was physically rather than socially cold, and Nanny stood holding Irene's hand in both of hers a moment, and taking in her beauty and her style with a generous admiration which she could afford, for she was herself faultlessly dressed in the quiet taste of her city, and looking very pretty. The interval was long enough to let every man present confide his sense of Irene's beauty to every other; and then, as the party was small, Mrs. Corey made everybody acquainted. When Lapham had not quite understood, he held the person's hand, and, leaning urbanely forward, inquired, "What name?" He did that because a great man to whom he had been presented on the platform at a public meeting had done so to him, and he knew it must be right.

A little lull ensued upon the introductions, and Mrs. Corey said quietly to Mrs. Lapham, "Can I send any one to be of use to Miss Lapham?" as if Penelope must be in the dressing-room.

Mrs. Lapham turned fire-red, and the graceful forms in which she had been intending to excuse her daughter's absence went out of her head. "She isn't upstairs," she said, at her bluntest, as country people are when embarrassed. "She didn't feel just like coming tonight. I don't know as she's feeling very well."

Mrs. Corey emitted a very small "O!"—very small, very cold,—which began to grow larger and hotter and to burn into Mrs. Lapham's soul before Mrs. Corey could add, "I'm very sorry. It's nothing serious, I hope?"

Robert Chase, the painter, had not come, and Mrs. James Bellingham was not there, so that the table really balanced better without Penelope; but Mrs. Lapham could not know this, and did not deserve to know it. Mrs. Corey glanced round the room, as if to take account of her guests, and said to her husband, "I think we are all here, then," and he came forward and gave his arm to Mrs. Lapham. She perceived then that in their determination not to be the first to come, they had been the last, and must have kept the others waiting for them.

Lapham had never seen people go down to dinner arm-in-arm before, but he knew that his wife was distinguished in being taken out by the host, and he waited in jealous impatience to see if Tom Corey would offer his arm to Irene. He gave it to that big girl they called Miss Kingsbury, and the handsome old fellow whom Mrs. Corey had introduced as her cousin took Irene out. Lapham was startled from the misgiving in which this left him by Mrs. Corey's passing her hand through his arm, and he made a sudden movement forward, but felt himself gently restrained. They went out the last of all; he did not know why, but he submitted, and when they sat down he saw that Irene, although she had come in with that Mr. Bellingham, was seated beside young Corey, after all.

He fetched a long sigh of relief when he sank into his chair and felt himself safe from error if he kept a sharp lookout and did only what the others did. Bellingham had certain habits which he permitted himself, and one of these was tucking the corner of his napkin into his collar; he confessed himself an uncertain shot with a spoon, and defended his practice on the ground of neatness and common sense. Lapham put his napkin into his collar too, and then, seeing that no one but Bellingham did it, became alarmed and took it out again slyly. He never had wine on his table at home, and on principle he was a prohibitionist; but now he did not know just what to do about the glasses at the right of his plate. He had a notion to turn them all down, as he had read of a well-known politician's doing at a public dinner, to show that he did not take wine; but, after twiddling with one of them a moment, he let them be, for it seemed to him that would be a little too conspicuous, and he felt that every one was looking. He let the servant fill them all, and he drank out of each, not to appear odd. Later, he observed that the young ladies were not taking wine, and he was glad to see that Irene had refused it, and that Mrs. Lapham was letting it stand untasted. He did not know but he ought to decline some of the dishes, or at least leave most of some on his plate, but he was not able to decide; he took everything and ate everything.

He noticed that Mrs. Corey seemed to take no more trouble about the dinner than anybody, and Mr. Corey rather less; he was talking busily to Mrs. Lapham, and Lapham caught a word here and there that convinced him she was holding her own. He was getting on famously himself with Mrs. Corey, who had begun with him about his new house; he was telling her all about it, and giving her his ideas. Their conversation naturally included his architect across the table; Lapham had been delighted and secretly surprised to find the fellow there; and at something Seymour said the talk spread suddenly, and the pretty house he was building for Colonel Lapham became the general theme. Young Corey testified to its loveliness, and the architect said laughingly that if he had been able to make a nice thing of it, he owed it to the practical sympathy of his client.

"Practical sympathy is good," said Bromfield Corey; and, slanting his head confidentially to Mrs. Lapham, he added, "Does he bleed your husband, Mrs. Lapham? He's a terrible fellow for appropriations!"

Mrs. Lapham laughed, reddening consciously, and said she guessed the Colonel knew how to take care of himself. This struck Lapham, then draining his glass of sauterne,[5] as wonderfully discreet in his wife.

Bromfield Corey leaned back in his chair a moment. "Well, after all, you can't say, with all your modern fuss about it, that you do much better now than the old fellows who built such houses as this."

"Ah," said the architect, "nobody can do better than well. Your house is in perfect taste; you know I've always admired it; and I don't think it's at all the worse for being old-fashioned. What we've done is largely to go back of the hideous style that raged after they forgot how to make this sort of house. But I think we may claim a better feeling for structure. We use better material, and more wisely; and by and by we shall work out something more characteristic and original."

"With your chocolates and olives, and your clutter of bric-à-brac?"

"All that's bad, of course, but I don't mean that. I don't wish to make you envious of Colonel Lapham, and modesty prevents my saying that his house is prettier,—though I may have my convictions,—but it's better built. All the new houses are better built. Now, your house——"

"Mrs. Corey's house," interrupted the host, with a burlesque haste in disclaiming responsibility for it that made them all laugh. "*My* ancestral halls are in Salem, and I'm told you couldn't drive a nail into their timbers; in fact, I don't know that you would want to do it."

"I should consider it a species of sacrilege," answered Seymour, "and I shall be far from pressing the point I was going to make against a house of Mrs. Corey's."

This won Seymour the easy laugh, and Lapham silently wondered that the fellow never got off any of those things to him.

"Well," said Corey, "you architects and the musicians are the true and only artistic creators. All the rest of us, sculptors, painters,

5. A French sweet white wine.

novelists, and tailors, deal with forms that we have before us; we try to imitate, we try to represent. But you two sorts of artists create form. If you represent, you fail. Somehow or other you do evolve the camel out of your inner consciousness."[6]

"I will not deny the soft impeachment," said the architect, with a modest air.

"I dare say. And you'll own that it's very handsome of me to say this, after your unjustifiable attack on Mrs. Corey's property."

Bromfield Corey addressed himself again to Mrs. Lapham, and the talk subdivided itself as before. It lapsed so entirely away from the subject just in hand, that Lapham was left with rather a good idea, as he thought it, to perish in his mind, for want of a chance to express it. The only thing like a recurrence to what they had been saying was Bromfield Corey's warning Mrs. Lapham, in some connection that Lapham lost, against Miss Kingsbury. "She's worse," he was saying, "when it comes to appropriations than Seymour himself. Depend upon it, Mrs. Lapham, she will give you no peace of your mind, now she's met you, from this out. Her tender mercies are cruel;[7] and I leave you to supply the context from your own scriptural knowledge. Beware of her, and all her works.[8] She calls them works of charity; but heaven knows whether they are. It don't stand to reason that she gives the poor *all* the money she gets out of people. I have my own belief"—he gave it in a whisper for the whole table to hear—"that she spends it for champagne and cigars."

Lapham did not know about that kind of talking; but Miss Kingsbury seemed to enjoy the fun as much as anybody, and he laughed with the rest.

"You shall be asked to the very next debauch of the committee, Mr. Corey; then you won't dare expose us," said Miss Kingsbury.

"I wonder you haven't been down upon Corey to go to the Chardon street[9] home and talk with your indigent Italians in their native tongue," said Charles Bellingham. "I saw in the 'Transcript'[1] the other night that you wanted some one for the work."

6. Corey uses the example of a camel, a singularly unique creature, to illustrate his point that composers and architects "create form" directly from their "inner consciousness" instead of re-presenting already existent forms as artists working in mimetic art forms do.
7. Proverbs 12.10: "A righteous man regardeth the life of his beast: but the tender mercies of the wicked are cruel."
8. Corey refers to the baptismal rite in the Episcopal Church's Book of Common Prayer, in which an infant's parents are asked whether they "renounce the devil and all his works."
9. A street bordering the North End, a neighborhood that had played host to successive waves of immigrants culminating in an influx of Italians beginning in the 1870s.
1. The highly respectable *Boston Evening Transcript* was an afternoon newspaper published between 1830 and 1941.

"We did think of Mr. Corey," replied Miss Kingsbury; "but we reflected that he probably wouldn't talk with them at all; he would make them keep still to be sketched, and forget all about their wants."

Upon the theory that this was a fair return for Corey's pleasantry, the others laughed again.

"There is one charity," said Corey, pretending superiority to Miss Kingsbury's point, "that is so difficult I wonder it hasn't occurred to a lady of your courageous invention."

"Yes?" said Miss Kingsbury. "What is that?"

"The occupation, by deserving poor of neat habits, of all the beautiful, airy, wholesome houses that stand empty the whole summer long, while their owners are away in their lowly cots beside the sea."

"Yes, that is terrible," replied Miss Kingsbury, with quick earnestness, while her eyes grew moist. "I have often thought of our great, cool houses standing useless here, and the thousands of poor creatures stifling in their holes and dens, and the little children dying for wholesome shelter. How cruelly selfish we are!"

"That is a very comfortable sentiment, Miss Kingsbury," said Corey, "and must make you feel almost as if you had thrown open No. 931 to the whole North End. But I am serious about this matter. I spend my summers in town, and I occupy my own house, so that I can speak impartially and intelligently; and I tell you that in some of my walks on the Hill and down on the Back Bay, nothing but the surveillance of the local policeman prevents me from personally affronting[2] those long rows of close-shuttered, handsome, brutally insensible houses. If I were a poor man, with a sick child pining in some garret or cellar at the North End, I should break into one of them, and camp out on the grand piano."

"Surely, Bromfield," said his wife, "you don't consider what havoc such people would make with the furniture of a nice house!"

"That is true," answered Corey, with meek conviction. "I never thought of that."

"And if you were a poor man with a sick child, I doubt if you'd have so much heart for burglary as you have now," said James Bellingham.[3]

2. Instead of "personally affronting," Howells had originally wanted Corey to contemplate "applying dynamite" to the empty Beacon Street houses, but that language was removed from the novel before publication, under pressure from *Century* magazine's publisher and its editor. Their correspondence with Howells about this passage appears later in this volume, along with the variant versions of the text. Two years later, Howells would risk his reputation and livelihood by publicly protesting the politically motivated convictions and subsequent death sentences assigned to eight anarchists for their unsubstantiated roles in a dynamite bombing that killed several policemen during a labor demonstration in Chicago's Haymarket Square in 1886.

3. Originally, Howells had not included Bellingham in this exchange. Instead, Corey had said "I never thought of the furniture. Probably a poor man with a dying child would consider it, and would not break into the house after all." (See the previous note.)

"It's wonderful how patient they are," said Mr. Sewell, the minister. "The spectacle of the hopeless luxury and comfort the hardworking poor man sees around him must be hard to bear at times."

Lapham wanted to speak up and say that he had been there himself, and knew how such a man felt. He wanted to tell them that generally a poor man was satisfied if he could make both ends meet; that he didn't envy any one his good luck, if he had earned it, so long as he wasn't running under himself. But before he could get the courage to address the whole table, Sewell added, "I suppose he don't always think of it."

"But some day he *will* think about it," said Corey. "In fact, we rather invite him to think about it, in this country."

"My brother-in-law," said Charles Bellingham, with the pride a man feels in a mentionably remarkable brother-in-law, "has no end of fellows at work under him out there at Omaha, and he says it's the fellows from countries where they've been kept from thinking about it that are discontented. The Americans never make any trouble. They seem to understand that so long as we give unlimited opportunity, nobody has a right to complain."

"What do you hear from Leslie?" asked Mrs. Corey, turning from these profitless abstractions to Mrs. Bellingham.

"You know," said that lady in a lower tone, "that there is another baby?"

"No! I hadn't heard of it!"

"Yes; a boy. They have named him after his uncle."

"Yes," said Charles Bellingham, joining in. "He is said to be a noble boy and to resemble me."

"All boys of that tender age are noble," said Corey, "and look like anybody you wish them to resemble. Is Leslie still homesick for the bean-pots of her native Boston?"

"She is getting over it, I fancy," replied Mrs. Bellingham. "She's very much taken up with Mr. Blake's enterprises, and leads a very exciting life. She says she's like people who have been home from Europe three years; she's past the most poignant stage of regret, and hasn't reached the second, when they feel that they *must* go again."

Lapham leaned a little toward Mrs. Corey, and said of a picture which he saw on the wall opposite, "Picture of your daughter, I presume?"

"No; my daughter's grandmother. It's a Stuart Newton;[4] he painted a great many Salem beauties. She was a Miss Polly Burroughs. My daughter *is* like her, don't you think?" They both looked at Nanny Corey and then at the portrait. "Those pretty old-fashioned dresses

4. Gilbert Stuart Newton (1794–1835), society portraitist and nephew of the famous George Washington portraitist Gilbert Stuart (1755–1828).

are coming in again. I'm not surprised you took it for her. The others"—she referred to the other portraits more or less darkling on the walls—"are my people; mostly Copleys."[5]

These names, unknown to Lapham, went to his head like the wine he was drinking; they seemed to carry light for the moment, but a film of deeper darkness followed. He heard Charles Bellingham telling funny stories to Irene and trying to amuse the girl; she was laughing and seemed very happy. From time to time Bellingham took part in the general talk between the host and James Bellingham and Miss Kingsbury and that minister, Mr. Sewell. They talked of people mostly; it astonished Lapham to hear with what freedom they talked. They discussed these persons unsparingly; James Bellingham spoke of a man known to Lapham for his business success and great wealth as not a gentleman; his cousin Charles said he was surprised that the fellow had kept from being governor so long.

When the latter turned from Irene to make one of these excursions into the general talk, young Corey talked to her; and Lapham caught some words from which it seemed that they were speaking of Penelope. It vexed him to think she had not come; she could have talked as well as any of them; she was just as bright; and Lapham was aware that Irene was not as bright, though when he looked at her face, radiant with its young beauty and happiness, he said to himself that it did not make any difference. He felt that he was not holding up his end of the line, however. When some one spoke to him he could only summon a few words of reply, that seemed to lead to nothing; things often came into his mind appropriate to what they were saying, but before he could get them out they were off on something else; they jumped about so, he could not keep up; but he felt, all the same, that he was not doing himself justice.

At one time the talk ran off upon a subject that Lapham had never heard talked of before; but again he was vexed that Penelope was not there, to have her say; he believed that her say would have been worth hearing.

Miss Kingsbury leaned forward and asked Charles Bellingham if he had read "Tears, Idle Tears,"[6] the novel that was making such a sensation; and when he said no, she said she wondered at him. "It's perfectly heart-breaking, as you'll imagine from the name; but there's such a dear old-fashioned hero and heroine in it, who keep dying for each other all the way through and making the most wildly

5. The Copley name would have been familiar to Bostonians primarily because of John Singleton Copley (1738–1815), the Boston-born colonial portrait painter after whom the Back Bay's Copley Square was named.
6. Howells's imaginary novel borrows its title from a popular lyric poem by Tennyson, itself part of a longer narrative poem about gender called *The Princess: A Medley* (1847).

satisfactory and unnecessary sacrifices for each other. You feel as if you'd done them yourself."

"Ah, that's the secret of its success," said Bromfield Corey. "It flatters the reader by painting the characters colossal, but with his chin and lips, so that he feels himself of their supernatural proportions. You've read it, Nanny?"

"Yes," said his daughter. "It ought to have been called 'Slop, Idle Slop.'"

"Oh, not quite *slop,* Nanny," pleaded Miss Kingsbury.

"It's astonishing," said Charles Bellingham, "how we do like the books that go for our heart-strings. And I really suppose that you can't put a more popular thing than self-sacrifice into a novel. We do like to see people suffering sublimely."

"There was talk some years ago," said James Bellingham, "about novels going out."

"They're just coming in!" cried Miss Kingsbury.

"Yes," said Mr. Sewell, the minister. "And I don't think there ever was a time when they formed the whole intellectual experience of more people. They do greater mischief than ever."

"Don't be envious, parson," said the host.

"No," answered Sewell. "I should be glad of their help. But those novels with old-fashioned heroes and heroines in them—excuse me, Miss Kingsbury—are ruinous!"

"Don't you feel like a moral wreck, Miss Kingsbury?" asked the host.

But Sewell went on: "The novelists might be the greatest possible help to us if they painted life as it is, and human feelings in their true proportion and relation, but for the most part they have been and are altogether noxious."

This seemed sense to Lapham; but Bromfield Corey asked: "But what if life as it is isn't amusing? Aren't we to be amused?"

"Not to our hurt," sturdily answered the minister. "And the self-sacrifice painted in most novels like this——"

"Slop, Idle Slop?" suggested the proud father of the inventor of the phrase.

"Yes—is nothing but psychical suicide, and is as wholly immoral as the spectacle of a man falling upon his sword."

"Well, I don't know but you're right, parson," said the host; and the minister, who had apparently got upon a battle-horse of his, careered onward in spite of some tacit attempts of his wife to seize the bridle.

"Right? To be sure I am right. The whole business of love, and love-making and marrying, is painted by the novelists in a monstrous disproportion to the other relations of life. Love is very sweet, very pretty——"

"Oh, *thank* you, Mr. Sewell," said Nanny Corey in a way that set them all laughing.

"But it's the affair, commonly, of very young people, who have not yet character and experience enough to make them interesting. In novels it's treated, not only as if it were the chief interest of life, but the sole interest of the lives of two ridiculous young persons; and it is taught that love is perpetual, that the glow of a true passion lasts forever; and that it is sacrilege to think or act otherwise."

"Well, but isn't that true, Mr. Sewell?" pleaded Miss Kingsbury.

"I have known some most estimable people who had married a second time," said the minister, and then he had the applause with him. Lapham wanted to make some open recognition of his good sense, but could not.

"I suppose the passion itself has been a good deal changed," said Bromfield Corey, "since the poets began to idealize it in the days of chivalry."

"Yes; and it ought to be changed again," said Mr. Sewell.

"What! Back?"

"I don't say that. But it ought to be recognized as something natural and mortal, and divine honors, which belong to righteousness alone, ought not to be paid it."

"Oh, you ask too much, parson," laughed his host, and the talk wandered away to something else.

It was not an elaborate dinner; but Lapham was used to having everything on the table at once, and this succession of dishes bewildered him; he was afraid perhaps he was eating too much. He now no longer made any pretense of not drinking his wine, for he was thirsty, and there was no more water, and he hated to ask for any. The ice-cream came, and then the fruit. Suddenly Mrs. Corey rose and said across the table to her husband, "I suppose you will want your coffee here." And he replied, "Yes; we'll join you at tea."

The ladies all rose, and the gentlemen got up with them. Lapham started to follow Mrs. Corey, but the other men merely stood in their places, except young Corey, who ran and opened the door for his mother. Lapham thought with shame that it was he who ought to have done that; but no one seemed to notice, and he sat down again gladly, after kicking out one of his legs which had gone to sleep.

They brought in cigars with coffee, and Bromfield Corey advised Lapham to take one that he chose for him. Lapham confessed that he liked a good cigar about as well as anybody, and Corey said: "These are new. I had an Englishman here the other day who was smoking old cigars in the superstition that tobacco improved with age, like wine."

"Ah," said Lapham, "anybody who had ever lived off a tobacco country could tell him better than that." With the fuming cigar between his lips he felt more at home than he had before. He turned sidewise in his chair and, resting one arm on the back, intertwined the fingers of both hands, and smoked at large ease.

James Bellingham came and sat down by him. "Colonel Lapham, weren't you with the 96th Vermont when they charged across the river in front of Pickensburg,[7] and the rebel battery opened fire on them in the water?"

Lapham slowly shut his eyes and slowly dropped his head for assent, letting out a white volume of smoke from the corner of his mouth.

"I thought so," said Bellingham. "I was with the 85th Massachusetts, and I sha'n't forget that slaughter. We were all new to it still. Perhaps that's why it made such an impression."

"I don't know," suggested Charles Bellingham. "Was there anything much more impressive afterward? I read of it out in Missouri, where I was stationed at the time, and I recollect the talk of some old army men about it. They said that death-rate couldn't be beaten. I don't know that it ever was."

"About one in five of us got out safe," said Lapham, breaking his cigar-ash off on the edge of a plate. James Bellingham reached him a bottle of Apollinaris.[8] He drank a glass, and then went on smoking.

They all waited, as if expecting him to speak, and then Corey said: "How incredible those things seem already! You gentlemen *know* that they happened; but are you still able to believe it?"

"Ah, nobody *feels* that anything happened," said Charles Bellingham. "The past of one's experience doesn't differ a great deal from the past of one's knowledge. It isn't much more probable; it's really a great deal less vivid than some scenes in a novel that one read when a boy."

"I'm not sure of that," said James Bellingham.

"Well, James, neither am I," consented his cousin, helping himself from Lapham's Apollinaris bottle. "There would be very little talking at dinner if one only said the things that one was sure of."

The others laughed, and Bromfield Corey remarked thoughtfully, "What astonishes the craven civilian in all these things is the abundance—the superabundance—of heroism. The cowards were the exception; the men that were ready to die, the rule."

"The woods were full of them," said Lapham, without taking his cigar from his mouth.

7. A fictitious battle. The 96th Vermont and 85th Massachusetts regiments (mentioned later) are also fictitious.
8. A German sparkling mineral water.

"That's a nice little touch in 'School,'" interposed Charles Bellingham, "where the girl says to the fellow who was at Inkerman,[9] 'I should think you would be so proud of it,' and he reflects awhile, and says, 'Well, the fact is, you know, there were so many of us.'"

"Yes, I remember that," said James Bellingham, smiling for pleasure in it. "But I don't see why you claim the credit of being a craven civilian, Bromfield," he added, with a friendly glance at his brother-in-law, and with the willingness Boston men often show to turn one another's good points to the light in company; bred so intimately together at school and college and in society, they all know these points. "A man who was out with Garibaldi in '48," continued James Bellingham.

"Oh, a little amateur red-shirting,"[1] Corey interrupted in deprecation. "But even if you choose to dispute my claim, what has become of all the heroism? Tom, how many club men do you know who would think it sweet and fitting to die for their country?"[2]

"I can't think of a great many at the moment, sir," replied the son, with the modesty of his generation.

"And I couldn't in '61," said his uncle. "Nevertheless they were there."

"Then your theory is that it's the occasion that is wanting," said Bromfield Corey. "But why shouldn't civil-service reform, and the resumption of specie payment, and a tariff for revenue only, inspire heroes?[3] They are all good causes."

"It's the occasion that's wanting," said James Bellingham, ignoring the *persiflage*. "And I'm very glad of it."

"So am I," said Lapham, with a depth of feeling that expressed itself in spite of the haze in which his brain seemed to float. There was a great deal of the talk that he could not follow; it was too quick for him; but here was something he was clear of. "I don't want to see any more men killed in my time." Something serious, something somber must lurk behind these words, and they waited for Lapham to say more; but the haze closed round him again, and he remained silent, drinking Apollinaris.

9. French and British troops routed the Russians in the Battle of Inkerman (1854), during the Crimean War. "School": an 1869 drama by the English playwright Thomas William Robertson (1829–1871).
1. The Red Shirts fought under the leadership of Giuseppe Garibaldi (1807–1882) against occupying forces from Austria and France during the failed Italian Revolution of 1848.
2. Corey alludes to lines from an ode by the Latin poet Horace: "*Dulce et decorum est pro patria mori*" (It is sweet and fitting to die for one's country).
3. Corey names a number of contested political issues of the 1870s. "Civil-service reform": sought to replace patronage and nepotism with competitive exams to win government employment. "Specie payment": the Specie Payment Resumption Act of 1875 restored the gold standard for U.S. currency. "Tariff for revenue only": proposed to replace protectionist tariff rates established during the Civil War with lower rates designed only to recoup government expenses.

"We non-combatants were notoriously reluctant to give up fighting," said Mr. Sewell, the minister; "but I incline to think Colonel Lapham and Mr. Bellingham may be right. I dare say we shall have the heroism again if we have the occasion. Till it comes, we must content ourselves with the every-day generosities and sacrifices. They make up in quantity what they lack in quality, perhaps."

"They're not so picturesque," said Bromfield Corey. "You can paint a man dying for his country, but you can't express on canvas a man fulfilling the duties of a good citizen."

"Perhaps the novelists will get at him by and by," suggested Charles Bellingham. "If I were one of these fellows, I shouldn't propose to myself anything short of that."

"What: the commonplace?" asked his cousin.

"Commonplace? The commonplace is just that light, impalpable, aerial essence which they've never got into their confounded books yet. The novelist who could interpret the common feelings of commonplace people would have the answer to 'the riddle of the painful earth'[4] on his tongue."

"Oh, not so bad as that, I hope," said the host; and Lapham looked from one to the other, trying to make out what they were at. He had never been so up a tree before.

"I suppose it isn't well for us to see human nature at white heat habitually," continued Bromfield Corey, after a while. "It would make us vain of our species. Many a poor fellow in that war and in many another has gone into battle simply and purely for his country's sake, not knowing whether, if he laid down his life, he should ever find it again, or whether, if he took it up hereafter, he should take it up in heaven or hell. Come, parson!" he said, turning to the minister, "what has ever been conceived of omnipotence, of omniscience, so sublime, so divine as that?"

"Nothing," answered the minister, quietly. "God has never been imagined at all. But if you suppose such a man as that was Authorized, I think it will help you to imagine what God must be."

"There's sense in that," said Lapham. He took his cigar out of his mouth, and pulled his chair a little toward the table, on which he placed his ponderous fore-arms. "I want to tell you about a fellow I had in my own company when we first went out. We were all privates to begin with; after a while they elected me captain—I'd had the tavern stand, and most of 'em knew me. But Jim Millon never got to be anything more than corporal; corporal when he was killed." The others arrested themselves in various attitudes of attention, and remained listening to Lapham with an interest that profoundly flattered him. Now, at last, he felt that he was holding up his end of the

4. A line from Tennyson's poem "The Palace of Art" (1833).

rope. "I can't say he went into the thing from the highest motives, altogether; our motives are always pretty badly mixed, and when there's such a hurrah-boys as there was then, you can't tell which is which. I suppose Jim Millon's wife was enough to account for his going, herself. She was a pretty bad assortment," said Lapham, lowering his voice and glancing round at the door to make sure that it was shut, and she used to lead Jim *one* kind of life. "Well, sir," continued Lapham, synthetizing his auditors in that form of address, "that fellow used to save every cent of his pay and send it to that woman. Used to get me to do it for him. I tried to stop him. 'Why, Jim,' said I, 'you know what she'll do with it.' 'That's so, Cap,' says he, 'but I don't know what she'll do without it.' And it did keep her straight—straight as a string—as long as Jim lasted. Seemed as if there was something mysterious about it. They had a little girl,—about as old as my oldest girl,—and Jim used to talk to me about her. Guess he done it as much for her as for the mother; and he said to me before the last action we went into, 'I should like to turn tail and run, Cap. I ain't comin' out o' this one. But I don't suppose it would do.' 'Well, not for you, Jim,' said I. 'I want to live,' he says; and he bust out crying right there in my tent. 'I want to live for poor Molly and Zerrilla'—that's what they called the little one; I dunno where they got the name. 'I ain't ever had half a chance; and now she's doing better, and I believe we should get along after this.' He set there cryin' like a baby. But he wa'n't no baby when he went into action. I hated to look at him after it was over, not so much because he'd got a ball that was meant for me by a sharp-shooter—he saw the devil takin' aim, and he jumped to warn me—as because he didn't look like Jim; he looked like—fun; all desperate and savage. I guess he died hard."

The story made its impression, and Lapham saw it. "Now I say," he resumed, as if he felt that he was going to do himself justice, and say something to heighten the effect his story had produced. At the same time, he was aware of a certain want of clearness. He had the idea, but it floated vague, elusive, in his brain. He looked about as if for something to precipitate it in tangible shape.

"Apollinaris?" asked Charles Bellingham, handing the bottle from the other side. He had drawn his chair closer than the rest to Lapham's, and was listening with great interest. When Mrs. Corey asked him to meet Lapham he accepted gladly. "You know I go in for that sort of thing, Anna. Since Leslie's affair[5] we're rather bound to do it. And I think we meet these practical fellows too little. There's

5. Charles Bellingham apparently refers to his sister, whose marriage to a "Western steamboat man" had suggested to Mrs. Corey in the previous chapter the appropriateness of inviting Bellingham and his mother to the Lapham dinner.

always something original about them." He might naturally have believed that the reward of his faith was coming.

"Thanks, I will take some of this wine," said Lapham, pouring himself a glass of Madeira[6] from a black and dusty bottle caressed by a label bearing the date of the vintage. He tossed off the wine, unconscious of its preciousness, and waited for the result. That cloudiness in his brain disappeared before it, but a mere blank remained. He not only could not remember what he was going to say, but he could not recall what they had been talking about. They waited, looking at him, and he stared at them in return. After a while he heard the host saying, "Shall we join the ladies?"

Lapham went, trying to think what had happened. It seemed to him a long time since he had drunk that wine.

Miss Corey gave him a cup of tea, where he stood aloof from his wife, who was talking with Miss Kingsbury and Mrs. Sewell; Irene was with Miss Nanny Corey. He could not hear what they were talking about; but if Penelope had come he knew that she would have done them all credit. He meant to let her know how he felt about her behavior when he got home. It was a shame for her to miss such a chance. Irene was looking beautiful, as pretty as all the rest of them put together, but she was not talking, and Lapham perceived that at a dinner party you ought to talk. He was himself conscious of having talked very well. He now wore an air of great dignity, and, in conversing with the other gentlemen, he used a grave and weighty deliberation. Some of them wanted him to go into the library. There he gave his ideas of books. He said he had not much time for anything but the papers; but he was going to have a complete library in his new place. He made an elaborate acknowledgment to Bromfield Corey of his son's kindness in suggesting books for his library; he said that he had ordered them all, and that he meant to have pictures. He asked Mr. Corey who was about the best American painter going now. "I don't set up to be a judge of pictures, but I know what I like," he said. He lost the reserve which he had maintained earlier, and began to boast. He himself introduced the subject of his paint, in a natural transition from pictures; he said Mr. Corey must take a run up to Lapham with him some day, and see the Works; they would interest him, and he would drive him round the country; he kept most of his horses up there, and he could show Mr. Corey some of the finest Jersey[7] grades in the country. He told about his brother William, the judge at Dubuque; and a farm he had out there that paid for itself every year in wheat. As he cast off all fear, his voice rose, and he hammered his arm-chair with the thick of his

6. A costly, amber-colored, fortified Portuguese wine, often served as a dessert.
7. A high-quality breed of dairy cattle.

hand for emphasis. Mr. Corey seemed impressed; he sat perfectly quiet, listening, and Lapham saw the other gentlemen stop in their talk every now and then to listen. After this proof of his ability to interest them, he would have liked to have Mrs. Lapham suggest again that he was unequal to their society, or to the society of anybody else. He surprised himself by his ease among men whose names had hitherto overawed him. He got to calling Bromfield Corey by his surname alone. He did not understand why young Corey seemed so preoccupied, and he took occasion to tell the company how he had said to his wife the first time he saw that fellow that he could make a man of him if he had him in the business; and he guessed he was not mistaken. He began to tell stories of the different young men he had had in his employ. At last he had the talk altogether to himself; no one else talked, and he talked unceasingly. It was a great time; it was a triumph.

He was in this successful mood when word came to him that Mrs. Lapham was going; Tom Corey seemed to have brought it, but he was not sure. Anyway, he was not going to hurry. He made cordial invitations to each of the gentlemen to drop in and see him at his office, and would not be satisfied till he had exacted a promise from each. He told Charles Bellingham that he liked him, and assured James Bellingham that it had always been his ambition to know him, and that if any one had said when he first came to Boston that in less than ten years he should be hobnobbing with Jim Bellingham, he should have told that person he lied. He would have told anybody he lied that had told him ten years ago that a son of Bromfield Corey would have come and asked him to take him into the business. Ten years ago he, Silas Lapham, had come to Boston, a little worse off than nothing at all, for he was in debt for half the money that he had bought out his partner with, and here he was now worth a million, and meeting you gentlemen like one of you. And every cent of that was honest money,—no speculation,—every copper of it for value received. And here, only the other day, his old partner, who had been going to the dogs ever since he went out of the business, came and borrowed twenty thousand dollars of him! Lapham lent it because his wife wanted him to: she had always felt bad about the fellow's having to go out of the business.

He took leave of Mr. Sewell with patronizing affection, and bade him come to him if he ever got into a tight place with his parish work; he would let him have all the money he wanted; he had more money than he knew what to do with. "Why, when your wife sent to mine last fall," he said, turning to Mr. Corey, "I drew my check for five hundred dollars, but my wife wouldn't take more than one hundred; said she wasn't going to show off before Mrs. Corey. I call that a pretty good joke on Mrs. Corey. I must tell her how Mrs. Lapham done her out of a cool four hundred dollars."

He started toward the door of the drawing-room to take leave of the ladies; but Tom Corey was at his elbow, saying, "I think Mrs. Lapham is waiting for you below, sir," and in obeying the direction Corey gave him toward another door he forgot all about his purpose, and came away without saying good-night to his hostess.

Mrs. Lapham had not known how soon she ought to go, and had no idea that in her quality of chief guest she was keeping the others. She staid till eleven o'clock, and was a little frightened when she found what time it was; but Mrs. Corey, without pressing her to stay longer, had said it was not at all late. She and Irene had had a perfect time. Everybody had been very polite; on the way home they celebrated the amiability of both the Miss Coreys and of Miss Kingsbury. Mrs. Lapham thought that Mrs. Bellingham was about the pleasantest person she ever saw; she had told her all about her married daughter who had married an inventor and gone to live in Omaha—a Mrs. Blake.

"If it's that car-wheel Blake," said Lapham, proudly, "I know all about him. I've sold him tons of the paint."

"Pooh, papa! How you do smell of smoking!" cried Irene.

"Pretty strong, eh?" laughed Lapham, letting down a window of the carriage. His heart was throbbing wildly in the close air, and he was glad of the rush of cold that came in, though it stopped his tongue, and he listened more and more drowsily to the rejoicings that his wife and daughter exchanged. He meant to have them wake Penelope up and tell her what she had lost; but when he reached home he was too sleepy to suggest it. He fell asleep as soon as his head touched the pillow, full of supreme triumph.

But in the morning his skull was sore with the unconscious, night-long ache; and he rose cross and taciturn. They had a silent breakfast. In the cold gray light of the morning the glories of the night before showed poorer. Here and there a painful doubt obtruded itself and marred them with its awkward shadow. Penelope sent down word that she was not well, and was not coming to breakfast, and Lapham was glad to go to his office without seeing her.

He was severe and silent all day with his clerks, and peremptory with customers. Of Corey he was slyly observant, and as the day wore away he grew more restively conscious. He sent out word by his office-boy that he would like to see Mr. Corey for a few minutes after closing. The type-writer girl had lingered too, as if she wished to speak with him, and Corey stood in abeyance as she went toward Lapham's door.

"Can't see you to-night, Zerrilla," he said bluffly, but not unkindly. "Perhaps I'll call at the house, if it's important."

"It is," said the girl, with a spoiled air of insistence.

"Well," said Lapham; and, nodding to Corey to enter, he closed the door upon her. Then he turned to the young man and demanded: "Was I drunk last night?"

[SEVENTH INSTALLMENT—MAY 1885]

XV.

Lapham's strenuous face was broken up with the emotions that had forced him to this question: shame, fear of the things that must have been thought of him, mixed with a faint hope that he might be mistaken, which died out at the shocked and pitying look in Corey's eyes.

"Was I drunk?" he repeated. "I ask you, because I was never touched by drink in my life before, and I don't know." He stood with his huge hands trembling on the back of his chair, and his dry lips apart, as he stared at Corey.

"That is what every one understood, Colonel Lapham," said the young man. "Every one saw how it was. Don't——"

"Did they talk it over after I left?" asked Lapham, vulgarly.

"Excuse me," said Corey, blushing, "my father doesn't talk his guests over with one another." He added, with youthful superfluity, "You were among gentlemen."

"I was the only one that wasn't a gentleman there!" lamented Lapham. "I disgraced you! I disgraced my family! I mortified your father before his friends!" His head dropped. "I showed that I wasn't fit to go with you. I'm not fit for any decent place. What did I say? What did I do?" he asked, suddenly lifting his head and confronting Corey. "Out with it! If you could bear to see it and hear it, I had ought to bear to know it!"

"There was nothing—really nothing," said Corey. "Beyond the fact that you were not quite yourself, there was nothing whatever. My father *did* speak of it to me," he confessed, "when we were alone. He said that he was afraid we had not been thoughtful of you, if you were in the habit of taking only water; I told him I had not seen wine at your table. The others said nothing about you."

"Ah, but what did they think!"

"Probably what we did: that it was purely a misfortune—an accident."

"I wasn't fit to be there," persisted Lapham. "Do you want to leave?" he asked, with savage abruptness.

"Leave?" faltered the young man.

"Yes; quit the business? Cut the whole connection?"

"I haven't the remotest idea of it!" cried Corey in amazement. "Why in the world should I?"

"Because you're a gentleman, and I'm not, and it ain't right I should be over you. If you want to go, I know some parties that would be glad to get you. I will give you up if you want to go before anything worse happens, and I sha'n't blame you. I can help you to something better than I can offer you here, and I will."

"There's no question of my going, unless you wish it," said Corey. "If you do——"

"Will you tell your father," interrupted Lapham, "that I had a notion all the time that I was acting the drunken blackguard, and that I've suffered for it all day? Will you tell him I don't want him to notice me if we ever meet, and that I know I'm not fit to associate with gentlemen in anything but a business way, if I am that?"

"Certainly, I shall do nothing of the kind," retorted Corey. "I can't listen to you any longer. What you say is shocking to me—shocking in a way you can't think."

"Why, man!" exclaimed Lapham, with astonishment; "if *I* can stand it, *you* can!"

"No," said Corey, with a sick look, "that doesn't follow. You may denounce yourself, if you will; but I have my reasons for refusing to hear you—my reasons why I *can't* hear you. If you say another word I must go away."

"*I* don't understand you," faltered Lapham, in bewilderment, which absorbed even his shame.

"You exaggerate the effect of what has happened," said the young man. "It's enough, more than enough, for you to have mentioned the matter to me, and I think it's unbecoming in me to hear you."

He made a movement toward the door, but Lapham stopped him with the tragic humility of his appeal. "Don't go yet! I can't let you. I've disgusted you,—I see that; but I didn't mean to. I—I take it back."

"Oh, there's nothing to take back," said Corey, with a repressed shudder for the abasement which he had seen. "But let us say no more about it—think no more. There wasn't one of the gentlemen present last night who didn't understand the matter precisely as my father and I did, and that fact must end it between us two."

He went out into the larger office beyond, leaving Lapham helpless to prevent his going. It had become a vital necessity with him to think the best of Lapham, but his mind was in a whirl of whatever thoughts were most injurious. He thought of him the night before in the company of those ladies and gentlemen, and he quivered in resentment of his vulgar, braggart, uncouth nature. He recognized his own allegiance to the exclusiveness to which he was born and bred, as a man perceives his duty to his country when her rights are invaded. His eye fell on the porter going about in his shirt-sleeves to make the place fast for the night, and he said to himself that

Dennis was not more plebeian than his master; that the gross appetites, the blunt sense, the purblind ambition, the stupid arrogance were the same in both, and the difference was in a brute will that probably left the porter the gentler man of the two. The very innocence of Lapham's life in the direction in which he had erred wrought against him in the young man's mood: it contained the insult of clownish inexperience. Amidst the stings and flashes of his wounded pride, all the social traditions, all the habits of feeling, which he had silenced more and more by force of will during the past months, asserted their natural sway, and he rioted in his contempt of the offensive boor, who was even more offensive in his shame than in his trespass. He said to himself that he was a Corey, as if that were somewhat; yet he knew that at the bottom of his heart all the time was that which must control him at last, and which seemed sweetly to be suffering his rebellion, secure of his submission in the end. It was almost with the girl's voice that it seemed to plead with him, to undo in him, effect by effect, the work of his indignant resentment, to set all things in another and fairer light, to give him hopes, to suggest palliations, to protest against injustices. It *was* in Lapham's favor that he was so guiltless in the past, and now Corey asked himself if it were the first time he could have wished a guest at his father's table to have taken less wine; whether Lapham was not rather to be honored for not knowing how to contain his folly where a veteran transgressor might have held his tongue. He asked himself, with a thrill of sudden remorse, whether, when Lapham humbled himself in the dust so shockingly, he had shown him the sympathy to which such *abandon* had the right; and he had to own that he had met him on the gentlemanly ground, sparing himself and asserting the superiority of his sort, and not recognizing that Lapham's humiliation came from the sense of wrong, which he had helped to accumulate upon him by superfinely standing aloof and refusing to touch him.

He shut his desk and hurried out into the early night, not to go anywhere, but to walk up and down, to try to find his way out of the chaos, which now seemed ruin, and now the materials out of which fine actions and a happy life might be shaped. Three hours later he stood at Lapham's door.

At times what he now wished to do had seemed forever impossible, and again it had seemed as if he could not wait a moment longer. He had not been careless, but very mindful of what he knew must be the feelings of his own family in regard to the Laphams, and he had not concealed from himself that his family had great reason and justice on their side in not wishing him to alienate himself from their common life and associations. The most that he could urge to himself was that they had not all the reason and justice; but he had hesitated and delayed because they had so much. Often he could not make it appear right that he should merely please himself in what chiefly concerned himself. He perceived how far apart in all their experiences and ideals the Lapham girls and his sisters were; how different Mrs. Lapham was from his mother; how grotesquely unlike were his father and Lapham; and the disparity had not always amused him.

He had often taken it very seriously, and sometimes he said that he must forego the hope on which his heart was set. There had been many times in the past months when he had said that he must go no farther, and as often as he had taken this stand he had yielded it, upon this or that excuse, which he was aware of trumping up. It was part of the complication that he should be unconscious of the injury he might be doing to some one besides his family and himself; this was the defect of his diffidence; and it had come to him in a pang for the first time when his mother said that she would not have the Laphams think she wished to make more of the acquaintance than he did; and then it had come too late. Since that he had suffered quite as much from the fear that it might not be as that it might be so; and now, in the mood, romantic and exalted, in which he found himself concerning Lapham, he was as far as might be from vain confidence. He ended the question in his own mind by affirming to himself that he was there, first of all, to see Lapham and give him an ultimate proof of his own perfect faith and unabated respect, and to offer him what reparation this involved for that want of sympathy—of humanity—which he had shown.

XVI.

The Nova Scotia second-girl[1] who answered Corey's ring said that Lapham had not come home yet.

"Oh," said the young man, hesitating on the outer step.

"I guess you better come in," said the girl. "I'll go and see when they're expecting him."

Corey was in the mood to be swayed by any chance. He obeyed the suggestion of the second-girl's patronizing friendliness, and let her shut him into the drawing-room, while she went upstairs to announce him to Penelope.

"Did you tell him father wasn't at home?"

"Yes. He seemed so kind of disappointed, I told him to come in, and I'd see when he *would* be in," said the girl, with the human interest which sometimes replaces in the American domestic the servile deference of other countries.

1. A house servant who performs lighter work. Nova Scotia is an east-coast Canadian province.

A gleam of amusement passed over Penelope's face, as she glanced at herself in the glass. "Well," she cried, finally, dropping from her shoulders the light shawl in which she had been huddled over a book when Corey rang, "I will go down."

"All right," said the girl, and Penelope began hastily to amend the disarray of her hair, which she tumbled into a mass on the top of her little head, setting off the pale dark of her complexion with a flash of crimson ribbon at her throat. She moved across the carpet once or twice with the quaint grace that belonged to her small figure, made a dissatisfied grimace at it in the glass, caught a handkerchief out of a drawer and slid it into her pocket, and then descended to Corey.

The Lapham drawing-room in Nankeen Square was in the parti-colored paint which the Colonel had hoped to repeat in his new house: the trim of the doors and windows was in light green and the panels in salmon; the walls were a plain tint of French gray paper, divided by gilt moldings into broad panels with a wide stripe of red velvet paper running up the corners; the chandelier was of massive imitation bronze; the mirror over the mantel rested on a fringed mantel-cover of green reps, and heavy curtains of that stuff hung from gilt lambrequin[2] frames at the window; the carpet was of a small pattern in crude green, which, at the time Mrs. Lapham bought it, covered half the new floors in Boston. In the paneled spaces on the walls were some stone-colored landscapes, representing the mountains and cañons of the West, which the Colonel and his wife had visited on one of the early official railroad excursions. In front of the long windows looking into the square were statues, kneeling figures which turned their backs upon the company within doors, and represented allegories of Faith and Prayer to people without. A white marble group of several figures, expressing an Italian conception of Lincoln Freeing the Slaves,—a Latin negro and his wife,—with our Eagle flapping his wings in approval, at Lincoln's feet, occupied one corner, and balanced the what-not[3] of an earlier period in another. These phantasms added their chill to that imparted by the tone of the walls, the landscapes, and the carpets, and contributed to the violence of the contrast when the chandelier was lighted up full glare, and the heat of the whole furnace welled up from the registers into the quivering atmosphere on one of the rare occasions when the Laphams invited company.

Corey had not been in this room before; the family had always received him in what they called the sitting-room. Penelope looked

2. A curtain or drapery hung at the top and sides of a window. "Reps": pieces of ribbed fabric.
3. Shelves for displaying decorative objects.

into this first, and then she looked into the parlor, with a smile that broke into a laugh as she discovered him standing under the single burner, which the second-girl had lighted for him in the chandelier.

"I don't understand how you came to be put in there," she said, as she led the way to the cozier place, "unless it was because Alice thought you were only here on probation, anyway. Father hasn't got home yet, but I'm expecting him every moment; I don't know what's keeping him. Did the girl tell you that mother and Irene were out?"

"No, she didn't say. It's very good of you to see me." She had not seen the exaltation which he had been feeling, he perceived with half a sigh; it must all be upon this lower level; perhaps it was best so. "There was something I wished to say to your father——I hope," he broke off, "you're better to-night."

"Oh, yes, thank you," said Penelope, remembering that she had not been well enough to go to dinner the night before.

"We all missed you very much."

"Oh, thank you! I'm afraid you wouldn't have missed me if I had been there."

"Oh, yes, we should," said Corey, "I assure you."

They looked at each other.

"I really think I believed I was saying something," said the girl.

"And so did I," replied the young man. They laughed rather wildly, and then they both became rather grave.

He took the chair she gave him, and looked across at her, where she sat on the other side of the hearth, in a chair lower than his, with her hands dropped in her lap, and the back of her head on her shoulders as she looked up at him. The soft-coal fire in the grate purred and flickered; the drop-light cast a mellow radiance on her face. She let her eyes fall, and then lifted them for an irrelevant glance at the clock on the mantel.

"Mother and Irene have gone to the Spanish Students' concert."

"Oh, have they?" asked Corey; and he put his hat, which he had been holding in his hand, on the floor beside his chair.

She looked down at it for no reason, and then looked up at his face for no other, and turned a little red. Corey turned a little red himself. She who had always been so easy with him now became a little constrained.

"Do you know how warm it is out-of-doors?" he asked.

"No; is it warm? I haven't been out all day."

"It's like a summer night."

She turned her face towards the fire, and then started abruptly. "Perhaps it's too warm for you here?"

"Oh, no, it's very comfortable."

"I suppose it's the cold of the last few days that's still in the house. I was reading with a shawl on when you came."

"I interrupted you."

"Oh, no. I had finished the book. I was just looking over it again."

"Do you like to read books over?"

"Yes; books that I like at all."

"What was it?" asked Corey.

The girl hesitated. "It has rather a sentimental name. Did you ever read it?—'Tears, Idle Tears.'"

"Oh, yes; they were talking of that last night; it's a famous book with ladies. They break their hearts over it. Did it make you cry?"

"Oh, it's pretty easy to cry over a book," said Penelope, laughing; "and that one *is* very natural till you come to the main point. Then the naturalness of all the rest makes that seem natural too; but I guess it's rather forced."

"Her giving him up to the other one?"

"Yes; simply because she happened to know that the other one had cared for him first. Why should she have done it? What right had she?"

"I don't know. I suppose that the self-sacrifice——"

"But it *wasn't* self-sacrifice—or not self-sacrifice alone. She was sacrificing him, too; and for some one who couldn't appreciate him half as much as she could. I'm provoked with myself when I think how I cried over that book—for I did cry. It's silly—it's wicked for any one to do what that girl did. Why can't they let people have a chance to behave reasonably in stories?"

"Perhaps they couldn't make it so attractive," suggested Corey, with a smile.

"It would be novel, at any rate," said the girl. "But so it would in real life, I suppose," she added.

"I don't know. Why shouldn't people in love behave sensibly?"

"That's a very serious question," said Penelope, gravely. "*I* couldn't answer it," and she left him the embarrassment of supporting an inquiry which she had certainly instigated herself. She seemed to have finally recovered her own ease in doing this. "Do you admire our autumnal display, Mr. Corey?"

"Your display?"

"The trees in the square. *We* think it's quite equal to an opening at Jordan & Marsh's."

"Ah, I'm afraid you wouldn't let me be serious even about your maples."

"Oh, yes, I should—if you like to be serious."

"Don't you?"

"Well, not about serious matters. That's the reason that book made me cry."

"You make fun of everything. Miss Irene was telling me last night about you."

"Then it's no use for me to deny it so soon. I must give Irene a talking to."

"I hope you won't forbid her to talk about you!"

She had taken up a fan from the table, and held it, now between her face and the fire, and now between her face and him. Her little visage, with that arch, lazy look in it, topped by its mass of dusky hair, and dwindling from the full cheeks to the small chin, had a Japanese effect in the subdued light, and it had the charm which comes to any woman with happiness. It would be hard to say how much of this she perceived that he felt. They talked about other things awhile, and then she came back to what he had said. She glanced at him obliquely round her fan, and stopped moving it. "Does Irene talk about me?" she asked.

"I think so—yes. Perhaps it's only I who talk about you. You must blame me if it's wrong," he returned.

"Oh, I didn't say it was wrong," she replied. "But I hope if you said anything very bad of me, you'll let me know what it was, so that I can reform——"

"No, don't change, please!" cried the young man.

Penelope caught her breath, but went on resolutely, "Or rebuke you for speaking evil of dignities." She looked down at the fan, now flat in her lap, and tried to govern her head, but it trembled, and she remained looking down. Again they let the talk stray, and then it was he who brought it back to themselves, as if it had not left them.

"I have to talk *of* you," said Corey, "because I get to talk *to* you so seldom."

"You mean that I do all the talking, when we're—together?" She glanced sidewise at him; but she reddened after speaking the last word.

"We're so seldom together," he pursued.

"I don't know what you mean——"

"Sometimes I've thought—I've been afraid—that you avoided me."

"Avoided you?"

"Yes! Tried not to be alone with me."

She might have told him that there was no reason why she should be alone with him, and that it was very strange he should make this complaint of her. But she did not. She kept looking down at the fan, and then she lifted her burning face and looked at the clock again. "Mother and Irene will be sorry to miss you," she gasped.

He instantly rose and came towards her. She rose too, and mechanically put out her hand. He took it as if to say good-night. "I didn't mean to send you away," she besought him.

"Oh, I'm not going," he answered, simply. "I wanted to say—to say that it's I who make her talk about you. To say I—There is something I want to say to you; I've said it so often to myself that I feel as if you must know it." She stood quite still, letting him keep her hand, and questioning his face with a bewildered gaze. "You *must* know—she must have told you—she must have guessed——" Penelope turned white, but outwardly quelled the panic that sent the blood to her heart. "I—I didn't expect—I hoped to have seen your father—but I must speak now, whatever—I love you!"

She freed her hand from both of those he had closed upon it, and went back from him across the room with a sinuous spring. "*Me!*" Whatever potential complicity had lurked in her heart, his words brought her only immeasurable dismay.

He came towards her again. "Yes, *you*. Who else?"

She fended him off with an imploring gesture. "I thought—I—it was——"

She shut her lips tight, and stood looking at him where he remained in silent amaze. Then her words came again, shudderingly. "Oh, what have you done?"

"Upon my soul," he said, with a vague smile, "I don't know. I hope no harm?"

"Oh, don't laugh!" she cried, laughing hysterically herself. "Unless you want me to think you the greatest wretch in the world!"

"I?" he responded. "For heaven's sake tell me what you mean!"

"You know I can't tell you. Can you say—can you put your hand on your heart and say that—you—say you never meant—that you meant me—all along?"

"Yes!—Yes! Who else? I came here to see your father, and to tell him that I wished to tell you this—to ask him——But what does it matter? You must have known it—you must have seen—and it's for you to answer me. I've been abrupt, I know, and I've startled you; but if you love me, you can forgive that to my loving you so long before I spoke."

She gazed at him with parted lips.

"Oh, mercy! What shall I do? If it's true—what you say—you must go!" she said. "And you must never come any more. Do you promise that?"

"Certainly not," said the young man. "Why should I promise such a thing—so abominably wrong? I could obey if you didn't love me——"

"Oh, I don't! Indeed I don't! Now will you obey?"

"No. I don't believe you."

"Oh!"

He possessed himself of her hand again.

"My love—my dearest! What is this trouble, that you can't tell it? It can't be anything about yourself. If it is anything about any one else, it wouldn't make the least difference in the world, no matter what it was. I would be only too glad to show by any act or deed I could that nothing could change me towards you."

"Oh, you don't understand!"

"No, I don't. You must tell me."

"I will never do that."

"Then I will stay here till your mother comes, and ask her what it is."

"Ask *her*?"

"Yes! Do you think I will give you up till I know why I must?"

"You force me to it! Will you go if I tell you, and never let any human creature know what you have said to me?"

"Not unless you give me leave."

"That will be never. Well, then——" She stopped, and made two or three ineffectual efforts to begin again. "No, no! I can't. You must go!"

"I will not go!"

"You said you—loved me. If you do, you will go."

He dropped the hands he had stretched towards her, and she hid her face in her own.

"There!" she said, turning it suddenly upon him. "Sit down there. And will you promise me—on your honor—not to speak—not to try to persuade me—not to—touch me? You won't touch me?"

"I will obey you, Penelope."

"As if you were never to see me again? As if I were dying?"

"I will do what you say. But I shall see you again; and don't talk of dying. This is the beginning of life——"

"No. It's the end," said the girl, resuming at last something of the hoarse drawl which the tumult of her feeling had broken into those half-articulate appeals. She sat down too, and lifted her face towards him. "It's the end of life for me, because I know now that I must have been playing false from the beginning. You don't know what I mean, and I can never tell you. It isn't my secret—it's some one else's. You—you must never come here again. I can't tell you why, and you must never try to know. Do you promise?"

"You can forbid me. I must do what you say."

"I do forbid you, then. And you shall not think I am cruel——"

"How could I think that?"

"Oh, how hard you make it!"

Corey laughed for very despair. "Can I make it easier by disobeying you?"

"I know I am talking crazily. But I'm not crazy."

"No, no," he said, with some wild notion of comforting her; "but try to tell me this trouble! There is nothing under heaven—no calamity, no sorrow—that I wouldn't gladly share with you, or take all upon myself if I could!"

"I know! But this you can't. Oh, my——"

"Dearest! Wait! Think! Let me ask your mother—your father——"

She gave a cry.

"No! If you do that, you will make me hate you! Will you——"

The rattling of a latch-key was heard in the outer door.

"Promise!" cried Penelope.

"Oh, I promise!"

"Good-bye!" She suddenly flung her arms round his neck, and, pressing her cheek tight against his, flashed out of the room by one door as her father entered it by another.

Corey turned to him in a daze. "I—I called to speak with you—about a matter——But it's so late now. I'll—I'll see you to-morrow."

"No time like the present," said Lapham, with a fierceness that did not seem referable to Corey. He had his hat still on, and he glared at the young man out of his blue eyes with a fire that something else must have kindled there.

"I really can't, now," said Corey, weakly. "It will do quite as well to-morrow. Goodnight, sir."

"Good-night," answered Lapham abruptly, following him to the door, and shutting it after him. "I think the devil must have got into pretty much everybody to-night," he muttered, coming back to the room, where he put down his hat. Then he went to the kitchen-stairs and called down, "Hello, Alice! I want something to eat!"

XVII.

"What's the reason the girls never get down to breakfast any more?" asked Lapham when he met his wife at the table in the morning. He had been up an hour and a half, and he spoke with the severity of a hungry man. "It seems to me they don't amount to *any*thing. Here I am, at my time of life, up the first one in the house. I ring the bell for the cook at quarter-past six every morning, and the breakfast is on the table at half-past seven right along, like clock-work, but I never see anybody but you till I go to the office."

"Oh, yes, you do, Si," said his wife, soothingly. "The girls are nearly always down. But they're young, and it tires them more than it does us to get up early."

"They can rest afterwards. They don't do anything after they *are* up," grumbled Lapham.

"Well, that's your fault, ain't it? You oughtn't to have made so much money, and then they'd have had to work." She laughed at Lapham's Spartan mood, and went on to excuse the young people. "Irene's been up two nights hand running,[1] and Penelope says she ain't well. What makes you so cross about the girls? Been doing something you're ashamed of?"

1. Successively, in a row.

"I'll tell you when I've been doing anything to be ashamed of," growled Lapham.

"Oh, no, you won't!" said his wife, jollily. "You'll only be hard on the rest of us. Come, now, Si; what is it?"

Lapham frowned into his coffee with sulky dignity, and said, without looking up, "I wonder what that fellow wanted here last night?"

"What fellow?"

"Corey. I found him here when I came home, and he said he wanted to see me; but he wouldn't stop."

"Where was he?"

"In the sitting-room."

"Was Pen there?"

"*I* didn't see her."

Mrs. Lapham paused, with her hand on the cream-jug. "Why, what in the land *did* he want? Did he say he wanted you?"

"That's what he said."

"And then he wouldn't stay?"

"No."

"Well, then, I'll tell you just what it is, Silas Lapham. He came here"—she looked about the room and lowered her voice—"to see you about Irene, and then he hadn't the courage."

"I guess he's got courage enough to do pretty much what he wants to," said Lapham, glumly. "All I know is, he was here. You better ask Pen about it, if she ever gets down."

"I guess I sha'n't wait for her," said Mrs. Lapham; and, as her husband closed the front door after him, she opened that of her daughter's room and entered abruptly.

The girl sat at the window, fully dressed, and as if she had been sitting there a long time. Without rising, she turned her face towards her mother. It merely showed black against the light, and revealed nothing till her mother came close to her with successive questions. "Why, how long have you been up, Pen? Why don't you come to your breakfast? Did you see Mr. Corey when he called last night? Why, what's the matter with you? What have you been crying about?"

"Have I been crying?"

"Yes! Your cheeks are all wet!"

"I thought they were on fire. Well, I'll tell you what's happened." She rose and then fell back in her chair. "Lock the door!" she ordered, and her mother mechanically obeyed. "I don't want Irene in here. There's nothing the matter. Only, Mr. Corey offered himself to me last night."

Her mother remained looking at her, helpless, not so much with amaze, perhaps, as dismay.

"Oh, I'm not a ghost! I wish I was! You had better sit down, mother. You have got to know all about it."

Mrs. Lapham dropped nervelessly into the chair at the other window, and while the girl went slowly but briefly on, touching only the vital points of the story, and breaking at times into a bitter drollery, she sat as if without the power to speak or stir.

"Well, that's all, mother. I should say I had dreamt it, if I had slept any last night; but I guess it really happened."

The mother glanced round at the bed, and said, glad to occupy herself delayingly with the minor care: "Why, you have been sitting up all night! You will kill yourself."

"I don't know about killing myself, but I've been sitting up all night," answered the girl. Then, seeing that her mother remained blankly silent again, she demanded, "Why don't you blame me, mother? Why don't you say that I led him on, and tried to get him away from her? Don't you believe I did?"

Her mother made her no answer, as if these ravings of self-accusal needed none. "Do you think," she asked, simply, "that he got the idea you cared for him?"

"He knew it! How could I keep it from him? I said I didn't—at first!"

"It was no use," sighed the mother. "You might as well said you did. It couldn't help Irene any, if you didn't."

"I always tried to help her with him, even when I——"

"Yes, I know. But she never was equal to him. I saw that from the start; but I tried to blind myself to it. And when he kept coming——"

"You never thought of me!" cried the girl, with a bitterness that reached her mother's heart. "I was nobody! I couldn't feel! No one could care for me!" The turmoil of despair, of triumph, of remorse and resentment, which filled her soul, tried to express itself in the words.

"No," said the mother humbly. "I didn't think of you. Or I didn't think of you enough. It did come across me sometimes that maybe——But it didn't seem as if——And your going on so for Irene——"

"You let me go on. You made me always go and talk with him for her, and you didn't think I would talk to him for myself. Well, I didn't!"

"I'm punished for it. When did you—begin to care for him?"

"How do I know? What difference does it make? It's all over now, no matter when it began. He won't come here any more, unless I let him." She could not help betraying her pride in this authority of hers, but she went on anxiously enough: "What will you say to Irene? She's safe as far as I'm concerned; but if he don't care for her, what will you do?"

"I don't know what to do," said Mrs. Lapham. She sat in an apathy from which she apparently could not rouse herself. "I don't see as anything can be done."

Penelope laughed in a pitying derision.

"Well, let things go on then. But they won't *go* on."

"No, they won't go on," echoed her mother. "She's pretty enough, and she's capable; and your father's got the money—I don't know what I'm saying! She ain't equal to him, and she never was. I kept feeling it all the time, and yet I kept blinding myself."

"If he had ever cared for her," said Penelope, "it wouldn't have mattered whether she was equal to him or not. *I'm* not equal to him either."

Her mother went on: "I might have thought it was you; but I had got set——Well! I can see it all clear enough, now it's too late. *I* don't know what to do."

"And what do you expect *me* to do?" demanded the girl. "Do you want *me* to go to Irene and tell her that I've got him away from her?"

"Oh, good Lord!" cried Mrs. Lapham. "What shall I do? What do you want I should do, Pen?"

"Nothing for me," said Penelope. "I've had it out with myself. Now do the best you can for Irene."

"I couldn't say you had done wrong, if you was to marry him to-day."

"Mother!"

"No, I couldn't. I couldn't say but what you had been good and faithful all through, and you had a perfect right to do it. There ain't any one to blame. He's behaved like a gentleman, and I can see now that he never thought of her, and that it was you all the while. Well, marry him, then! He's got the right, and so have you."

"What about Irene? I don't want you to talk about me. I can take care of myself."

"She's nothing but a child. It's only a fancy with her. She'll get over it. She hain't really got her heart set on him."

"She's got her heart set on him, mother. She's got her whole life set on him. You know that."

"Yes, that's so," said the mother, as promptly as if she had been arguing to that rather than the contrary effect.

"If I could give him to her, I would. But he isn't mine to give." She added in a burst of despair, "He isn't mine to keep!"

"Well," said Mrs. Lapham, "she has got to bear it. I don't know what's to come of it all. But she's got to bear her share of it." She rose and went toward the door.

Penelope ran after her in a sort of terror. "You're not going to tell Irene?" she gasped, seizing her mother by either shoulder.

"Yes, I am," said Mrs. Lapham. "If she's a woman grown, she can bear a woman's burden."

"I can't let you tell Irene," said the girl, letting fall her face on her mother's neck. "Not Irene," she moaned. "I'm afraid to let you. How can I ever look at her again?"

"Why, you haven't done anything, Pen," said her mother, soothingly.

"I wanted to! Yes, I must have done something. How could I help it? I did care for him from the first, and I must have tried to make him like me. Do you think I did? No, no! You mustn't tell Irene! Not—not—yet! Mother! Yes! I did try to get him from her!" she cried, lifting her head, and suddenly looking her mother in the face with those large dim eyes of hers. "What do you think? Even last night! It was the first time I ever had him all to myself, for myself, and I know now that I tried to make him think that I was pretty and—funny. And I didn't try to make him think of her. I knew that I pleased him, and I tried to please him more. Perhaps I could have kept him from saying that he cared for me; but when I saw he did—I must have seen it—I couldn't. I had never had him to myself, and for myself, before. I needn't have seen him at all, but I wanted to see him; and when I was sitting there alone with him, how do I know what I did to let him feel that I cared for him? Now, will you tell Irene? I never thought he did care for me, and never expected him to. But I liked him. Yes—I did like him! Tell her that! Or else *I* will."

"If it was to tell her he was dead," began Mrs. Lapham, absently.

"How easy it would be!" cried the girl in self-mockery. "But he's worse than dead to her; and so am I. I've turned it over a million ways, mother; I've looked at it in every light you can put it in, and I can't make anything but misery out of it. You can see the misery at the first glance, and you can't see more or less if you spend your life looking at it." She laughed again, as if the hopelessness of the thing amused her. Then she flew to the extreme of self-assertion. "Well, I *have* a right to him, and he has a right to me. If he's never done anything to make her think he cared for her,—and I know he hasn't; it's all been our doing,—then he's free and I'm free. We can't make her happy, whatever we do; and why shouldn't I——No, that won't do! I reached that point before!" She broke again into her desperate laugh. "*You* may try now, mother!"

"I'd best speak to your father first——"

Penelope smiled a little more forlornly than she had laughed.

"Well, yes; the Colonel will have to know. It isn't a trouble that I can keep to myself exactly. It seems to belong to too many other people."

Her mother took a crazy encouragement from her return to her old way of saying things.

"Perhaps he can think of something."

"Oh, I don't doubt but the Colonel will know just what to do!"

"You mustn't be too down-hearted about it. It—it'll all come right——"

"You tell Irene that, mother."

Mrs. Lapham had put her hand on the door-key; she dropped it, and looked at the girl with a sort of beseeching appeal for the comfort she could not imagine herself. "Don't look at me, mother," said Penelope, shaking her head. "You know that if Irene were to die without knowing it, it wouldn't come right for me."

"Pen!"

"I've read of cases where a girl gives up the man that loves her so as to make some other girl happy that the man doesn't love. That might be done."

"Your father would think you were a fool," said Mrs. Lapham, finding a sort of refuge in her strong disgust for the pseudo-heroism. "No! If there's to be any giving up, let it be by the one that sha'n't make anybody but herself suffer. There's trouble and sorrow enough in the world, without *making* it on purpose!"

She unlocked the door, but Penelope slipped round and set herself against it. "Irene shall not give up!"

"I will see your father about it," said the mother. "Let me out now——"

"Don't let Irene come here!"

"No. I will tell her that you haven't slept. Go to bed now, and try to get some rest. She isn't up herself yet. You must have some breakfast."

"No; let me sleep if I can. I can get something when I wake up. I'll come down if I can't sleep. Life has got to go on. It does when there's a death in the house, and this is only a little worse."

"Don't you talk nonsense!" cried Mrs. Lapham, with angry authority.

"Well, a little better, then," said Penelope, with meek concession.

Mrs. Lapham attempted to say something, and could not. She went out and opened Irene's door. The girl lifted her head drowsily from her pillow. "Don't disturb your sister when you get up, Irene. She hasn't slept well——"

"*Please* don't talk! I'm almost *dead* with sleep!" returned Irene. "Do go, mamma! I sha'n't disturb her." She turned her face down in the pillow, and pulled the covering up over her ears.

The mother slowly closed the door and went down-stairs, feeling bewildered and baffled almost beyond the power to move. The time had been when she would have tried to find out why this judgment had been sent upon her. But now she could not feel that the innocent suffering of others was inflicted for her fault; she shrank instinctively from that cruel and egotistic misinterpretation of the mystery of pain and loss. She saw her two children, equally if differently dear to her, destined to trouble that nothing could avert, and she could not blame either of them; she could not blame the means of this misery to them; he was as innocent as they, and though her heart was sore against him in this first moment, she could still be just to him in it. She was a woman who had been used to seek the light by striving; she had hitherto literally worked to it. But it is the curse of prosperity that it takes work away from us, and shuts that door to hope and health of spirit. In this house, where everything had come to be done for her, she had no tasks to interpose between her and her despair. She sat down in her own room and let her hands fall in her lap,—the hands that had once been so helpful and busy,—and tried to think it all out. She had never heard of the fate that was once supposed to appoint the sorrows of men irrespective of their blamelessness or blame, before the time when it came to be believed that sorrows were penalties; but in her simple way she recognized something like that mythic power when she rose from her struggle with the problem, and said aloud to herself, "Well, the witch is in it." Turn which way she would, she saw no escape from the misery to come—the misery which had come already to Penelope and herself, and that must come to Irene and her father. She started when she definitely thought of her husband, and thought with what violence it would work in every fiber of his rude strength. She feared that, and she feared something worse—the effect which his pride and ambition might seek to give it; and it was with terror of this, as well as the natural trust with which a woman must turn to her husband in any anxiety at last, that she felt she could not wait for evening to take counsel with him. When she considered how wrongly he might take it all, it seemed as if it were already known to him, and she was impatient to prevent his error.

She sent out for a messenger, whom she dispatched with a note to his place of business: "Silas, I should like to ride with you this afternoon. Can't you come home early? Persis." And she was at dinner with Irene, evading her questions about Penelope, when answer came that he would be at the house with the buggy at half-past two. It is easy to put off a girl who has but one thing in her head; but, though Mrs. Lapham could escape without telling anything of Penelope, she could not escape seeing how wholly Irene was engrossed with hopes now turned so vain and impossible. She was still talking of that dinner, of nothing but that dinner, and begging for flattery of herself and praise of him, which her mother had till now been so ready to give.

"Seems to me you don't take very much interest, mamma!" she said, laughing and blushing, at one point.

"Yes,—yes, I do," protested Mrs. Lapham, and then the girl prattled on.

"I guess I shall get one of those pins that Nanny Corey had in her hair. I think it would become me, don't you?"

"Yes; but, Irene—I don't like to have you go on so, till—unless he's said something to show—You oughtn't to give yourself up to thinking——" But at this the girl turned so white, and looked such reproach at her, that she added, frantically: "Yes, get the pin. It is just the thing for you! But don't disturb Penelope. Let her alone till I get back. I'm going out to ride with your father. He'll be here in half an hour. Are you through? Ring, then. Get yourself that fan you saw the other day. Your father won't say anything; he likes to have you look well. I could see his eyes on you half the time the other night."

"I should have liked to have Pen go with me," said Irene, restored to her normal state of innocent selfishness by these flatteries. "Don't you suppose she'll be up in time? What's the matter with her that she didn't sleep?"

"I don't know. Better let her alone."

"Well," submitted Irene.

XVIII.

Mrs. Lapham went away to put on her bonnet and cloak, and she was waiting at the window when her husband drove up. She opened the door and ran down the steps. "Don't get out; I can help myself in," and she clambered to his side, while he kept the fidgeting mare still with voice and touch.

"Where do you want I should go?" he asked, turning the buggy.

"Oh, I don't care. Out Brookline way, I guess. I wish you hadn't brought this fool of a horse," she gave way, petulantly. "I wanted to have a talk."

"When I can't drive this mare and talk too, I'll sell out altogether," said Lapham. "She'll be quiet enough when she's had her spin."

"Well," said his wife; and while they were making their way across the city to the Milldam she answered certain questions he asked about some points in the new house.

"I should have liked to have you stop there," he began; but she answered so quickly, "Not to-day," that he gave it up and turned his horse's head westward, when they struck Beacon street.

He let the mare out, and he did not pull her in till he left the Brighton road and struck off under the low boughs that met above one of the quiet streets of Brookline, where the stone cottages, with here and there a patch of determined ivy on their northern walls, did what they could to look English amid the glare of the autumnal foliage. The smooth earthen track under the mare's hoofs was scattered with flakes of the red and yellow gold that made the air luminous around them, and the perspective was gay with innumerable tints and tones.

"Pretty sightly," said Lapham, with a long sigh, letting the reins lie loose in his vigilant hand, to which he seemed to relegate the whole charge of the mare. "I want to talk with you about Rogers, Persis. He's been getting in deeper and deeper with me; and last night he pestered me half to death to go in with him in one of his schemes. I ain't going to blame anybody, but I hain't got very much confidence in Rogers. And I told him so last night."

"Oh, don't talk to me about Rogers!" his wife broke in. "There's something a good deal more important than Rogers in the world, and more important than your business. It seems as if you couldn't think of anything else—that and the new house. Did you suppose I wanted to ride so as to talk Rogers with you?" she demanded, yielding to the necessity a wife feels of making her husband pay for her suffering, even if he has not inflicted it. "I declare——"

"Well, hold on, now!" said Lapham. "What *do* you want to talk about? I'm listening."

His wife began, "Why, it's just this, Silas Lapham!" and then she broke off to say, "Well, you may wait, now—starting me wrong, when it's hard enough anyway."

Lapham silently turned his whip over and over in his hand and waited.

"Did you suppose," she asked at last, "that that young Corey had been coming to see Irene?"

"I don't know what I supposed," replied Lapham sullenly. "You always said so." He looked sharply at her under his lowering brows.

"Well, he hasn't," said Mrs. Lapham; and she replied to the frown that blackened on her husband's face, "And I can tell you what, if you take it in that way I sha'n't speak another word."

"Who's takin' it what way?" retorted Lapham savagely. "What are you drivin' at?"

"I want you should promise that you'll hear me out quietly."

"I'll hear you out if you'll give me a chance. I haven't said a word yet."

"Well, I'm not going to have you flying into forty furies, and looking like a perfect thunder-cloud at the very start. I've had to bear it, and you've got to bear it too."

"Well, let me have a chance at it, then."

"It's nothing to blame anybody about, as I can see, and the only question is, what's the best thing to do about it. There's only one thing we can do; for if he don't care for the child, nobody wants to make him. If he hasn't been coming to see her, he hasn't, and that's all there is to it."

"No, it ain't!" exclaimed Lapham.

"There!" protested his wife.

"If he hasn't been coming to see her, what *has* he been coming for?"

"He's been coming to see Pen!" cried the wife. "*Now* are you satisfied?" Her tone implied that he had brought it all upon them; but at the sight of the swift passions working in his face to a perfect comprehension of the whole trouble, she fell to trembling, and her broken voice lost all the spurious indignation she had put into it. "Oh, Silas! what are we going to do about it? I'm afraid it'll kill Irene."

Lapham pulled off the loose driving-glove from his right hand with the fingers of his left, in which the reins lay. He passed it over his forehead, and then flicked from it the moisture it had gathered there. He caught his breath once or twice, like a man who meditates a struggle with superior force and then remains passive in its grasp.

His wife felt the need of comforting him, as she had felt the need of afflicting him. "I don't say but what it can be made to come out all right in the end. All I say is, I don't see my way clear yet."

"What makes you think he likes Pen?" he asked, quietly.

"He told her so last night, and she told me this morning. Was he at the office today?"

"Yes, he was there. I haven't been there much myself. He didn't say anything to me. Does Irene know?"

"No; I left her getting ready to go out shopping. She wants to get a pin like the one Nanny Corey had on."

"Oh, my Lord!" groaned Lapham.

"It's been Pen from the start, I guess, or almost from the start. I don't say but what he was attracted some by Irene at the *very* first; but I guess it's been Pen ever since he saw her; and we've taken up with a notion, and blinded ourselves with it. Time and again I've had my doubts whether he cared for Irene any; but I declare to goodness, when he kept coming, I never hardly thought of Pen, and I couldn't help believing at last he *did* care for Irene. Did it ever strike you he might be after Pen?"

"No. I took what you said. I supposed you knew."

"Do you blame me, Silas?" she asked timidly.

"No. What's the use of blaming? We don't either of us want anything but the children's good. What's it all of it for, if it ain't for that? That's what we've both slaved for all our lives."

"Yes, I know. Plenty of people *lose* their children," she suggested.

"Yes, but that don't comfort me any. I never was one to feel good because another man felt bad. How would you have liked it if some one had taken comfort because his boy lived when ours died? No, I can't do it. And this is worse than death, someways. That comes and it goes; but this looks as if it was one of those things that had come to stay. The way I look at it, there ain't any hope for anybody. Suppose we don't want Pen to have him; will that help Irene any, if he don't want her? Suppose we don't want to let him have either; does that help either?"

"You talk," exclaimed Mrs. Lapham, "as if our say was going to settle it. Do you suppose that Penelope Lapham is a girl to take up with a fellow that her sister is in love with, and that she always thought was in love with her sister, and go off and be happy with him? Don't you believe but what it would come back to her, as long as she breathed the breath of life, how she'd teased her about him, as I've heard Pen tease Irene, and helped to make her think he was in love with her, by showing that she thought so herself? It's ridiculous!"

Lapham seemed quite beaten down by this argument. His huge head hung forward over his breast; the reins lay loose in his moveless hand; the mare took her own way. At last he lifted his face and shut his heavy jaws.

"Well?" quavered his wife.

"Well," he answered, "if he wants her, and she wants him, I don't see what that's got to do with it." He looked straight forward, and not at his wife.

She laid her hands on the reins. "Now, you stop right here, Silas Lapham! If I thought that—if I really believed you could be willing to break that poor child's heart, and let Pen disgrace herself by marrying a man that had as good as killed her sister, just because you wanted Bromfield Corey's son for a son-in-law——"

Lapham turned his face now, and gave her a look. "You had better *not* believe that, Persis! Get up!" he called to the mare, without glancing at her, and she sprang forward. "I see you've got past being any use to yourself on this subject."

"Hello!" shouted a voice in front of him. "Where the devil you goin' to?"

"Do you want to *kill* somebody?" shrieked his wife.

There was a light crash, and the mare recoiled her length, and separated their wheels from those of the open buggy in front which Lapham had driven into. He made his excuses to the occupant; and the accident relieved the tension of their feelings and left them far from the point of mutual injury which they had reached in their common trouble and their unselfish will for their children's good.

It was Lapham who resumed the talk. "I'm afraid we can't either of us see this thing in the right light. We're too near to it. I wish to the Lord there was somebody to talk to about it."

"Yes," said his wife; "but there ain't anybody."

"Well, I dunno," suggested Lapham, after a moment; "why not talk to the minister of your church? May be he could see some way out of it."

Mrs. Lapham shook her head hopelessly. "It wouldn't do. I've never taken up my connection with the church, and I don't feel as if I'd got any claim on him."

"If he's anything of a man, or anything of a preacher, you *have* got a claim on him," urged Lapham; and he spoiled his argument by adding, "I've contributed enough *money* to his church."

"Oh, that's nothing," said Mrs. Lapham. "I ain't well enough acquainted with Dr. Langworthy, or else I'm *too* well. No; if I was to ask any one, I should want to ask a total stranger. But what's the use, Si? Nobody could make us see it any different from what it is, and I don't know as I should want they should."

It blotted out the tender beauty of the day and weighed down their hearts ever more heavily within them. They ceased to talk of it a hundred times, and still came back to it. They drove on and on. It began to be late. "I guess we better go back, Si," said his wife; and as he turned without speaking, she pulled her veil down and began to cry softly behind it, with low little broken sobs.

Lapham started the mare up and drove swiftly homeward. At last his wife stopped crying and began trying to find her pocket. "Here, take mine, Persis," he said kindly offering her his handkerchief, and she took it and dried her eyes with it. "There was one of those fellows there the other night," he spoke again, when his wife leaned back against the cushions in peaceful despair, "that I liked the looks of about as well as any man I ever saw. I guess he was a pretty good man. It was that Mr. Sewell." He looked at his wife, but she did not say anything. "Persis," he resumed, "I can't bear to go back with nothing settled in our minds. I can't bear to let you."

"We must, Si," returned his wife, with gentle gratitude. Lapham groaned. "Where does he live?" she asked.

"On Bolingbroke street.[1] He gave me his number."

"Well, it wouldn't do any good. What could he say to us?"

"Oh, I don't know as he could say anything," said Lapham hopelessly; and neither of them said anything more till they crossed the Milldam and found themselves between the rows of city houses.

"Don't drive past the new house, Si," pleaded his wife. "I couldn't bear to see it. Drive—drive up Bolingbroke street. We might as well see where he *does* live."

"Well," said Lapham. He drove along slowly. "That's the place," he said finally, stopping the mare and pointing with his whip.

"It wouldn't do any good," said his wife, in a tone which he understood as well as he understood her words. He turned the mare up to the curbstone.

"You take the reins a minute," he said, handing them to his wife.

He got down and rang the bell, and waited till the door opened; then he came back and lifted his wife out. "He's in," he said.

1. The street is fictional, but its name takes its cue from the actual cross-streets near Lapham's Beacon Street address, which are named for English aristocratic houses (Gloucester, Hereford, Exeter, and so on).

He got the hitching-weight from under the buggy-seat and made it fast to the mare's bit.

"Do you think she'll stand with that?" asked Mrs. Lapham.

"I guess so. If she don't, no matter."

"Ain't you afraid she'll take cold," she persisted, trying to make delay.

"Let her!" said Lapham. He took his wife's trembling hand under his arm, and drew her to the door.

"He'll think we're crazy," she murmured, in her broken pride.

"Well, we *are*," said Lapham. "Tell him we'd like to see him alone awhile," he said to the girl who was holding the door ajar for him, and she showed him into the reception-room, which had been the Protestant confessional for many burdened souls before their time, coming, as they did, with the belief that they were bowed down with the only misery like theirs in the universe; for each one of us must suffer long to himself before he can learn that he is but one in a great community of wretchedness which has been pitilessly repeating itself from the foundation of the world.

They were as loath to touch their trouble when the minister came in as if it were their disgrace; but Lapham did so at last, and, with a simple dignity which he had wanted in his bungling and apologetic approaches, he laid the affair clearly before the minister's compassionate and reverent eye. He spared Corey's name, but he did not pretend that it was not himself and his wife and their daughters who were concerned.

"I don't know as I've got any right to trouble you with this thing," he said, in the moment while Sewell sat pondering the case, "and I don't know as I've got any warrant for doing it. But, as I told my wife here, there was something about you—I don't know whether it was anything you *said* exactly—that made me feel as if you could help us. I guess I didn't say so much as that to her; but that's the way I felt. And here we are. And if it ain't all right——"

"Surely," said Sewell, "it's all right. I thank you for coming—for trusting your trouble to me. A time comes to every one of us when we can't help ourselves, and then we must get others to help us. If people turn to me at such a time, I feel sure that I was put into the world for something—if nothing more than to give my pity, my sympathy."

The brotherly words, so plain, so sincere, had a welcome in them that these poor outcasts of sorrow could not doubt.

"Yes," said Lapham huskily, and his wife began to wipe the tears again under her veil.

Sewell remained silent, and they waited till he should speak. "We can be of use to one another here, because we can always be wiser for some one else than we can for ourselves. We can see another's sins and errors in a more merciful light—and that is always a fairer light—than we can our own; and we can look more sanely at others' afflictions." He had addressed these words to Lapham; now he turned to his wife. "If some one had come to you, Mrs. Lapham, in just this perplexity, what would you have thought?"

"I don't know as I understand you," faltered Mrs. Lapham.

Sewell repeated his words, and added, "I mean, what do you think some one else ought to do in your place?"

"Was there ever any poor creatures in such a strait before?" she asked, with pathetic incredulity.

"There's no new trouble under the sun," said the minister.

"Oh, if it was any one else, I should say—I should say—Why, of course! I should say that their duty was to let——" She paused.

"One suffer instead of three, if none is to blame?" suggested Sewell. "That's sense, and that's justice. It's the economy of pain which naturally suggests itself, and which would insist upon itself, if we were not all perverted by traditions which are the figment of the shallowest sentimentality. Tell me, Mrs. Lapham, didn't this come into your mind when you first learned how matters stood?"

"Why, yes, it flashed across me. But I didn't think it could be right."

"And how was it with you, Mr. Lapham?"

"Why, that's what *I* thought, of course. But I didn't see my way——"

"No," cried the minister, "we are all blinded, we are all weakened by a false ideal of self-sacrifice. It wraps us round with its meshes, and we can't fight our way out of it. Mrs. Lapham, what made you feel that it might be better for three to suffer than one?"

"Why, she did herself. I know she would die sooner than take him away from her."

"I supposed so!" cried the minister bitterly. "And yet she is a sensible girl, your daughter?"

"She has more common sense——"

"Of course! But in such a case we somehow think it must be wrong to use our common sense. I don't know where this false ideal comes from, unless it comes from the novels that befool and debauch almost every intelligence in some degree. It certainly doesn't come from Christianity, which instantly repudiates it when confronted with it. Your daughter believes, in spite of her common sense, that she ought to make herself and the man who loves her unhappy, in order to assure the lifelong wretchedness of her sister, whom he doesn't love, simply because her sister saw him and fancied him first! And I'm sorry to say that ninety-nine young people out of a hundred—oh, nine hundred and ninety-nine out of a thousand!—would consider that noble and beautiful and heroic; whereas you know at the bottom of your hearts that it would be foolish and cruel and revolting. You know what marriage is! And what it must be without love on both sides."

The minister had grown quite heated and red in the face.

"I lose all patience!" he went on vehemently. "This poor child of yours has somehow been brought to believe that it will kill her sister if her sister does not have what does not belong to her, and what it is not in the power of all the world, or any soul in the world, to give her. Her sister will suffer—yes, keenly!—in heart and in pride; but she will not die. You will suffer, too, in your tenderness for her; but you must do your duty. You must help her to give up. You would be guilty if you did less. Keep clearly in mind that you are doing right, and the only possible good. And God be with you!"

[EIGHTH INSTALLMENT—JUNE 1885]

XIX.

"He talked sense, Persis," said Lapham gently, as he mounted to his wife's side in the buggy and drove slowly homeward through the dusk.

"Yes, he talked sense," she admitted. But she added, bitterly, "I guess, if he had it to *do!* Oh, he's right, and it's got to be done. There ain't any other way for it. It's sense; and, yes, it's justice." They walked to their door after they left the horse at the livery stable around the corner, where Lapham kept it. "I want you should send Irene up to our room as soon as we get in, Silas."

"Why, ain't you going to have any supper first?" faltered Lapham, with his latch-key in the lock.

"No. I can't lose a minute. If I do, I sha'n't do it at all."

"Look here, Persis," said her husband tenderly, "let *me* do this thing."

"Oh, *you!*" said his wife, with a woman's compassionate scorn for a man's helplessness in such a case. "Send her right up. And I shall feel—" She stopped, to spare him.

Then she opened the door, and ran up to her room, without waiting to speak to Irene, who had come into the hall at the sound of her father's key in the door.

"I guess your mother wants to see you upstairs," said Lapham, looking away.

Her mother turned round and faced the girl's wondering look as Irene entered the chamber, so close upon her that she had not yet had time to lay off her bonnet; she stood with her wraps still on her arm.

"Irene!" she said harshly, "there is something you have got to bear. It's a mistake we've all made. He don't care anything for you. He never did. He told Pen so last night. He cares for her."

The sentences had fallen like blows. But the girl had taken them without flinching. She stood up immovable, but the delicate rose-light of her complexion went out and left her snow-white. She did not offer to speak.

"Why don't you say something?" cried her mother. "Do you want to kill me, Irene?"

"Why should I want to hurt *you*, mamma?" the girl replied steadily, but in an alien voice. "There's nothing to say. I want to see Pen a minute."

She turned and left the room. As she mounted the stairs that led to her own and her sister's rooms on the floor above, her mother helplessly followed. Irene went first to her own room at the front of the house, and then came out, leaving the door open and the gas flaring behind her. The mother could see that she had tumbled many things out of the drawers of her bureau upon the marble top.

She passed her mother, where she stood in the entry. "You can come too, if you want to, mamma," she said.

She opened Penelope's door without knocking, and went in. Penelope sat at the window, as in the morning. Irene did not go to her; but she went and laid a gold hair-pin on her bureau, and said, without looking at her, "There's a pin that I got to-day, because it was like his sister's. It won't become a dark person so well, but you can have it."

She stuck a scrap of paper in the side of Penelope's mirror. "There's that account of Mr. Stanton's ranch. You'll want to read it, I presume."

She laid a withered *boutonnière* on the bureau beside the pin. "There's his buttonhole bouquet. He left it by his plate, and I stole it."

She had a pine-shaving, fantastically tied up with a knot of ribbon, in her hand. She held it a moment; then, looking deliberately at Penelope, she went up to her, and dropped it in her lap without a word. She turned, and, advancing a few steps, tottered and seemed about to fall.

Her mother sprang forward with an imploring cry, "Oh, 'Rene, 'Rene, 'Rene!"

Irene recovered herself before her mother could reach her. "Don't touch me," she said icily. "Mamma, I'm going to put on my things. I want papa to walk with me. I'm choking here."

"I—I can't let you go out, Irene, child," began her mother.

"You've got to," replied the girl. "Tell papa to hurry his supper."

"Oh, poor soul! He doesn't want any supper. *He* knows it too."

"I don't want to talk about that. Tell him to get ready."

She left them once more.

Mrs. Lapham turned a hapless glance upon Penelope.

"Go and tell him, mother," said the girl. "I would, if I could. If she can walk, let her. It's the only thing for her." She sat still; she did not even brush to the floor the fantastic thing that lay in her lap, and that sent up faintly the odor of the sachet powder with which Irene liked to perfume her boxes.

Lapham went out with the unhappy child, and began to talk with her, crazily, incoherently enough.

She mercifully stopped him. "Don't talk, papa. I don't want any one should talk with me."

He obeyed, and they walked silently on and on. In their aimless course they reached the new house on the water side of Beacon, and she made him stop, and stood looking up at it. The scaffolding which had so long defaced the front was gone, and in the light of the gas-lamp before it all the architectural beauty of the façade was suggested, and much of the finely felt detail was revealed. Seymour had pretty nearly satisfied himself in that rich façade; certainly Lapham had not stinted him of the means.

"Well," said the girl, "I shall never live in it," and she began to walk on.

Lapham's sore heart went down, as he lumbered heavily after her. "Oh, yes, you will, Irene. You'll have lots of good times there yet."

"No," she answered, and said nothing more about it. They had not talked of their trouble at all, and they did not speak of it now. Lapham understood that she was trying to walk herself weary, and he was glad to hold his peace and let her have her way. She halted him once more before the red and yellow lights of an apothecary's window.

"Isn't there something they give you to make you sleep?" she asked vaguely. "I've got to sleep to-night!"

Lapham trembled. "I guess you don't want anything, Irene."

"Yes, I do! Get me something!" she retorted willfully. "If you don't, I shall die. I *must* sleep."

They went in, and Lapham asked for something to make a nervous person sleep. Irene stood poring over the show-case full of brushes and trinkets, while the apothecary put up the bromide, which he guessed would be about the best thing. She did not show any emotion; her face was like a stone, while her father's expressed the anguish of his sympathy. He looked as if he had not slept for a week; his fat eyelids drooped over his glassy eyes, and his cheeks and throat hung flaccid. He started as the apothecary's cat stole smoothly up and rubbed itself against his leg; and it was to him that the man said, "You want to take a tablespoonful of that as long as you're awake. I guess it won't take a great many to fetch you."

"All right," said Lapham, and paid and went out. "I don't know but I *shall* want some of it," he said, with a joyless laugh.

Irene came closer up to him and took his arm. He laid his heavy paw on her gloved fingers. After a while she said, "I want you should let me go up to Lapham to-morrow."

"To Lapham? Why, to-morrow's Sunday, Irene! You can't go to-morrow."

"Well, Monday, then. I can live through one day here."

"Well," said the father passively. He made no pretense of asking her why she wished to go, nor any attempt to dissuade her.

"Give me that bottle," she said, when he opened the door at home for her, and she ran up to her own room.

The next morning Irene came to breakfast with her mother; the Colonel and Penelope did not appear, and Mrs. Lapham looked sleep-broken and careworn.

The girl glanced at her. "Don't you fret about me, mamma," she said. "I shall get along." She seemed herself as steady and strong as rock.

"I don't like to see you keeping up so, Irene," replied her mother. "It'll be all the worse for you when you do break. Better give way a little at the start."

"I sha'n't break, and I've given way all I'm going to. I'm going to Lapham to-morrow,—I want you should go with me, mamma,—and I guess I can keep up one day here. All about it is, I don't want you should say anything, or *look* anything. And, whatever I do, I don't want you should try to stop me. And, the first thing, I'm going to take her breakfast up to her. Don't!" she cried, intercepting the protest on her mother's lips. "I shall not let it hurt Pen, if I can help it. She's never done a thing nor thought a thing to wrong me. I had to fly out at her last night; but that's all over now, and I know just what I've got to bear."

She had her way unmolested. She carried Penelope's breakfast to her, and omitted no care or attention that could make the sacrifice complete, with an heroic pretense that she was performing no unusual service. They did not speak, beyond her saying, in a clear, dry note, "Here's your breakfast, Pen," and her sister's answering, hoarsely and tremulously, "Oh, thank you, Irene." And, though two or three times they turned their faces toward each other while Irene remained in the room, mechanically putting its confusion to rights, their eyes did not meet. Then Irene descended upon the other rooms, which she set in order, and some of which she fiercely swept and dusted. She made the beds; and she sent the two servants away to church as soon as they had eaten their breakfast, telling them that she would wash their dishes. Throughout the morning her father and mother heard her about the work of getting dinner, with certain silences which represented the moments when she stopped and stood stock-still, and then, readjusting her burden, forced herself forward under it again.

They sat alone in the family-room, out of which their two girls seemed to have died. Lapham could not read his Sunday papers, and she had no heart to go to church, as she would have done earlier in life when in trouble. Just then she was obscurely feeling that the church was somehow to blame for that counsel of Mr. Sewell's on which they had acted.

"I should like to know," she said, having brought the matter up, "whether he would have thought it was such a light matter if it had been his own children. Do you suppose he'd have been so ready to act on his own advice if it *had* been?"

"He told us the right thing to do, Persis,—the only thing. We couldn't let it go on," urged her husband gently.

"Well, it makes me despise Pen! Irene's showing twice the character that she is, this very minute."

The mother said this so that the father might defend her daughter to her. He did not fail. "Irene's got the easiest part, the way I look at it. And you'll see that Pen'll know how to behave when the time comes."

"What do you want she should do?"

"I haven't got so far as that yet. What are we going to do about Irene?"

"What do you want Pen should do," repeated Mrs. Lapham, "when it comes to it?"

"Well, I don't want she should take him, for *one* thing," said Lapham.

This seemed to satisfy Mrs. Lapham as to her husband, and she said, in defense of Corey, "Why, I don't see what *he's* done. It's all been our doing."

"Never mind that now. What about Irene?"

"She says she's going to Lapham tomorrow. She feels that she's got to get away somewhere. It's natural she should."

"Yes. And I presume it will be about the best thing *for* her. Shall you go with her?"

"Yes."

"Well." He comfortlessly took up a newspaper again, and she rose with a sigh, and went to her room to pack some things for the morrow's journey.

After dinner, when Irene had cleared away the last trace of it in kitchen and dining-room with unsparing punctilio, she came downstairs, dressed to go out, and bade her father come to walk with her again. It was a repetition of the aimlessness of the last night's wanderings. They came back, and she got tea for them, and after that they heard her stirring about in her own room, as if she were busy about many things; but they did not dare to look in upon her, even after all the noises had ceased, and they knew she had gone to bed.

"Yes; it's a thing she's got to fight out by herself," said Mrs. Lapham.

"I guess she'll get along," said Lapham. "But I don't want you should misjudge Pen either. She's all right too. She ain't to blame."

"Yes, I know. But I can't work round to it all at once. I sha'n't misjudge her, but you can't expect me to get over it right away."

"Mamma," said Irene, when she was hurrying their departure the next morning, "what did she tell him when he asked her?"

"Tell him?" echoed the mother; and after a while she added, "She didn't tell him anything."

"Did she say anything about me?"

"She said he mustn't come here any more."

Irene turned and went into her sister's room. "Good-bye, Pen," she said, kissing her with an effect of not seeing or touching her. "I want you should tell him all about it. If he's half a man, he won't give up till he knows why you won't have him; and he has a right to know."

"It wouldn't make any difference. I couldn't have him after——"

"That's for you to say. But if you don't tell him about me, *I* will."

"'Rene!"

"Yes! You needn't say I cared for him. But you can say that you all thought he—cared for—me."

"Oh, Irene——"

"Don't!" Irene escaped from the arms that tried to cast themselves about her. "You are all right, Pen. You haven't done anything. You've helped me all you could. But I can't—yet."

She went out of the room and summoned Mrs. Lapham with a sharp "Now, mamma!" and went on putting the last things into her trunks.

The Colonel went to the station with them, and put them on the train. He got them a little compartment to themselves in the Pullman car; and as he stood leaning with his lifted hands against the sides of the doorway, he tried to say something consoling and hopeful: "I guess you'll have an easy ride, Irene. I don't believe it'll be dusty, any, after the rain last night."

"Don't you stay till the train starts, papa," returned the girl, in rigid rejection of his futilities. "Get off now."

"Well, if you want I should," he said, glad to be able to please her in anything. He remained on the platform till the cars started. He saw Irene bustling about in the compartment, making her mother comfortable for the journey; but Mrs. Lapham did not lift her head. The train moved off, and he went heavily back to his business.

From time to time during the day, when he caught a glimpse of him, Corey tried to make out from his face whether he knew what had taken place between him and Penelope. When Rogers came in about time of closing, and shut himself up with Lapham in his room, the young man remained till the two came out together and parted in their salutationless fashion.

Lapham showed no surprise at seeing Corey still there, and merely answered, "Well!" when the young man said that he wished to speak with him, and led the way back to his room.

Corey shut the door behind them. "I only wish to speak to you in case you know of the matter already; for otherwise I'm bound by a promise."

"I guess I know what you mean. It's about Penelope."

"Yes, it's about Miss Lapham. I am greatly attached to her—you'll excuse my saying it; I couldn't excuse myself if I were not."

"Perfectly excusable," said Lapham. "It's all right."

"Oh, I'm *glad* to hear you say that!" cried the young fellow joyfully. "I want you to believe that this isn't a new thing or an unconsidered thing with me—though it seemed so unexpected to her."

Lapham fetched a deep sigh. "It's all right as far as I'm concerned—or her mother. We've both liked you first-rate."

"Yes?"

"But there seems to be something in Penelope's mind—I don't know——" The Colonel consciously dropped his eyes.

"She referred to something—I couldn't make out what—but I hoped—I hoped—that with your leave I might overcome it—the barrier—whatever it was. Miss Lapham—Penelope—gave me the hope—that I was—wasn't—indifferent to her——"

"Yes, I guess that's so," said Lapham. He suddenly lifted his head, and confronted the young fellow's honest face with his own face, so different in its honesty. "Sure you never made up to any one else at the same time?"

"*Never!* Who could imagine such a thing? If that's all, I can easily——"

"I don't say that's all, nor that that's it. I don't want you should go upon that idea. I just thought, may be—you hadn't thought of it."

"No, I certainly hadn't thought of it! Such a thing would have been so impossible to me that I *couldn't* have thought of it; and it's so shocking to me now that I don't know what to say to it."

"Well, don't take it too much to heart," said Lapham, alarmed at the feeling he had excited; "I don't say she thought so. I was trying to guess—trying to——"

"If there is *any*thing I can say or do to convince you——"

"Oh, it ain't necessary to say anything. I'm all right."

"But Miss Lapham! I may see her again? I may try to convince her that——"

He stopped in distress, and Lapham afterwards told his wife that he kept seeing the face of Irene as it looked when he parted with her in the car; and whenever he was going to say yes, he could not open his lips. At the same time he could not help feeling that Penelope had a right to what was her own, and Sewell's words came back to him. Besides, they had already put Irene to the worst suffering. Lapham compromised, as he imagined.

"You can come round to-night and see *me*, if you want to," he said; and he bore grimly the gratitude that the young man poured out upon him.

Penelope came down to supper and took her mother's place at the head of the table.

Lapham sat silent in her presence as long as he could bear it. Then he asked, "How do you feel to-night, Pen?"

"Oh, like a thief," said the girl. "A thief that hasn't been arrested yet."

Lapham waited awhile before he said, "Well, now, your mother and I want you should hold up on that awhile."

"It isn't for you to say. It's something I *can't* hold up on."

"Yes, I guess you can. If I know what's happened, then what's happened is a thing that nobody is to blame for. And we want you should make the best of it, and not the worst. Heigh? It ain't going to help Irene any for you to hurt yourself—or anybody else; and I don't want you should take up with any such crazy notion. As far as heard from, you haven't stolen anything, and whatever you've got belongs to you."

"Has he been speaking to you, father?"

"Your mother's been speaking to me."

"Has *he* been speaking to you?"

"That's neither here nor there."

"Then he's broken his word, and I will never speak to him again!"

"If he was any such fool as to promise that he wouldn't talk to me on a subject"—Lapham drew a deep breath, and then made the plunge—"that I brought up——"

"Did you bring it up?"

"The same as brought up—the quicker he broke his word the better; and I want you should act upon that idea. Recollect that it's my business, and your mother's business, as well as yours, and we're going to have our say. He hain't done anything wrong, Pen, nor anything that he's going to be punished for. Understand that. He's got to have a reason, if you're not going to have him. I don't say you've got to have him; I want you should feel perfectly free about that; but I *do* say you've got to give him a reason."

"Is he coming here?"

"I don't know as you'd call it *coming*——"

"Yes, you do, father!" said the girl, in forlorn amusement at his shuffling.

"He's coming here to see *me*——"

"When's he coming?"

"I don't know but he's coming to-night."

"And you want I should see him?"

"I don't know but you'd better."

"All right. I'll see him."

Lapham drew a long, deep breath of suspicion inspired by this acquiescence. "What you going to do?" he asked presently.

"I don't know yet," answered the girl sadly. "It depends a good deal upon what *he* does."

"Well," said Lapham, with the hungriness of unsatisfied anxiety in his tone. When Corey's card was brought into the family-room where he and Penelope were sitting, he went into the parlor to find him. "I guess Penelope wants to see you," he said; and, indicating the family-room, he added, "She's in there," and did not go back himself.

Corey made his way to the girl's presence with open trepidation, which was not allayed by her silence and languor. She sat in the chair where she had sat the other night, but she was not playing with a fan now.

He came toward her, and then stood faltering. A faint smile quivered over her face at the spectacle of his subjection. "Sit down, Mr. Corey," she said. "There's no reason why we shouldn't talk it over quietly; for I know you will think I'm right."

"I'm sure of that," he answered hopefully. "When I saw that your father knew of it to-day, I asked him to let me see you again. I'm afraid that I broke my promise to you—technically——"

"It had to be broken."

He took more courage at her words. "But I've only come to do whatever you say, and not to be an—annoyance to you——"

"Yes, you have to know; but I couldn't tell you before. Now they all think I should."

A tremor of anxiety passed over the young man's face, on which she kept her eyes steadily fixed.

"We supposed it—it was—Irene——"

He remained blank a moment, and then he said with a smile of relief, of deprecation, of protest, of amazement, of compassion:

"*Oh!* Never! Never for an instant! How could you think such a thing? It was impossible! I never thought of her. But I see—I see! I can explain—no, there's nothing to explain! I have never knowingly done or said a thing from first to last to make you think that. I see how terrible it is!" he said; but he still smiled, as if he could not take it seriously. "I admired her beauty—who could help doing that?—and I thought her very good and sensible. Why, last winter in Texas, I told Stanton about our meeting in Canada, and we agreed—I only tell you to show you how far I always was from what you thought—that he must come North and try to see her, and—and—of course, it all sounds very silly!—and he sent her a newspaper with an account of his ranch in it——"

"She thought it came from you."

"Oh, good heavens! He didn't tell me till after he'd done it. But he did it for a part of our foolish joke. And when I met your sister again, I only admired her as before. I can see, now, how I must have seemed to be seeking her out; but it was to talk of you with her—I never talked of anything else if I could help it, except when I changed the subject because I was ashamed to be always talking of you. I see how distressing it is for all of you. But tell me that you believe me!"

"Yes, I must. It's all been our mistake——"

"It has indeed! But there's no mistake about my loving *you*, Penelope," he said; and the old-fashioned name, at which she had often mocked, was sweet to her from his lips.

"That only makes it worse!" she answered.

"Oh, no!" he gently protested. "It makes it better. It makes it right. How is it worse? How is it wrong?"

"Can't you see? You must understand all now! Don't you see that if she believed so too, and if she——" She could not go on.

"Did she—did your sister—think that too?" gasped Corey.

"She used to talk with me about you; and when you say you care for me now, it makes me feel like the vilest hypocrite in the world. That day you gave her the list of books, and she came down to Nantasket, and went on about you, I helped her to flatter herself—oh! I don't see how she can forgive me. But she knows I can never forgive myself! That's the reason she can do it. I can see now," she went on, "how I must have been trying to get you from her. I can't endure it! The only way is for me never to see you or speak to you again!" She laughed forlornly. "That would be pretty hard on you, if you cared."

"I do care—all the world!"

"Well, then, it would if you were going to keep on caring. You won't long, if you stop coming now."

"Is this all, then? Is it the end?"

"It's—whatever it is. I can't get over the thought of her. Once I thought I could, but now I see that I can't. It seems to grow worse. Sometimes I feel as if it would drive me crazy."

He sat looking at her with lack-luster eyes. The light suddenly came back into them. "Do you think I could love you if you had been false to her? I know you have been true to her, and truer still to yourself. I never tried to see her, except with the hope of seeing you too. I supposed she must know that I was in love with you. From the first time I saw you there that afternoon, you filled my fancy. Do you think I was flirting with the child, or—no, you *don't* think that! We have not done wrong. We have not harmed any one knowingly. We have a right to each other——"

"No! no! you must never speak to me of this again. If you do, I shall know that you despise me."

"But how will that help her? I don't love *her*."

"Don't say that to me! I have said that to myself too much."

"If you forbid me to love you, it won't make me love her," he persisted.

She was about to speak, but she caught her breath without doing so, and merely stared at him.

"I must do what you say," he continued. "But what good will it do her? You can't make her happy by making yourself unhappy."

"Do you ask me to profit by a wrong?"

"Not for the world. But there *is* no wrong!"

"There is something—I don't know what. There's a wall between us. I shall dash myself against it as long as I live; but that won't break it."

"Oh!" he groaned. "We have done no wrong. Why should we suffer from another's mistake as if it were our sin?"

"I don't know. But we must suffer."

"Well, then, I *will* not, for my part, and I will not let you. If you care for me——"

"You had no right to know it."

"You make it my privilege to keep you from doing wrong for the right's sake. I'm sorry, with all my heart and soul, for this error; but I can't blame myself, and I won't deny myself the happiness I haven't done anything to forfeit. I will never give you up. I will wait as long as you please for the time when you shall feel free from this mistake; but you shall be mine at last. Remember that. I might go away for months—a year, even; but that seems a cowardly and guilty thing, and I'm not afraid, and I'm not guilty, and I'm going to stay here and try to see you."

She shook her head. "It won't change anything. Don't you see that there's no hope for us?"

"When is she coming back?" he asked.

"I don't know. Mother wants father to come and take her out West for a while."

"She's up there in the country with your mother yet?"

"Yes."

He was silent; then he said, desperately:

"Penelope, she is very young; and perhaps—perhaps she might meet——"

"It would make no difference. It wouldn't change it for me."

"You are cruel—cruel to yourself, if you love me, and cruel to me. Don't you remember that night—before I spoke—you were talking of that book; and you said it was foolish and wicked to do as that girl did. Why is it different with you, except that you give me nothing, and can never give me anything when you take yourself away? If it were anybody else, I am sure you would say——"

"But it isn't anybody else, and that makes it impossible. Sometimes I think it might be if I would only say so to myself, and then all that I said to her about you comes up——"

"I will wait. It can't always come up. I won't urge you any longer now. But you will see it differently—more clearly. Good-bye—no! Good-night! I shall come again tomorrow. It will surely come right, and, whatever happens, you have done no wrong. Try to keep that in mind. I am so happy, in spite of all!"

He tried to take her hand, but she put it behind her. "No, no! I can't let you—yet!"

XX.

After a week Mrs. Lapham returned, leaving Irene alone at the old homestead in Vermont. "She's comfortable there—as comfortable as she can be anywheres, I guess," she said to her husband, as they drove together from the station, where he had met her in obedience to her telegraphic summons. "She keeps herself busy helping about the house; and she goes round amongst the hands in their houses. There's sickness, and you know how helpful she is where there's sickness. She don't complain any. I don't know as I've heard a word out of her mouth since we left home; but I'm afraid it'll wear on her, Silas."

"You don't look over and above well yourself, Persis," said her husband kindly.

"Oh, don't talk about me. What I want to know is whether you can't get the time to run off with her somewhere? I wrote to you about Dubuque. She'll work herself down, I'm afraid; and *then* I don't know as she'll be over it. But if she could go off, and be amused—see new people——"

"I could *make* the time," said Lapham, "if I had to. But, as it happens, I've got to go out West on business,—I'll tell you about it,—and I'll take Irene along."

"Good!" said his wife. "That's about the best thing I've heard yet. Where you going?"

"Out Dubuque way."

"Anything the matter with Bill's folks?"

"No. It's business."

"How's Pen?"

"I guess she ain't much better than Irene."

"He been about any?"

"Yes. But I can't see as it helps matters much."

"Tchk!" Mrs. Lapham fell back against the carriage cushions. "I declare, to see her willing to take the man that we all thought wanted her sister! I can't make it seem right."

"It's right," said Lapham stoutly; "but I guess she ain't willing; I wish she was. But there don't seem to be any way out of the thing, anywhere. It's a perfect snarl. But I don't want you should be anyways ha'sh with Pen."

Mrs. Lapham answered nothing; but when she met Penelope she gave the girl's wan face a sharp look, and began to whimper on her neck.

Penelope's tears were all spent. "Well, mother," she said, "you come back almost as cheerful as you went away. I needn't ask if 'Rene's in good spirits. We all seem to be overflowing with them. I suppose this is one way of congratulating me. Mrs. Corey hasn't been round to do it yet."

"Are you—are you engaged to him, Pen?" gasped her mother.

"Judging by my feelings, I should say not. I feel as if it was a last will and testament. But you'd better ask him when he comes."

"I can't bear to look at him."

"I guess he's used to that. He don't seem to expect to be looked at. Well! we're all just where we started. I wonder how long it will keep up?"

Mrs. Lapham reported to her husband when he came home at night—he had left his business to go and meet her, and then, after a desolate dinner at the house, had returned to the office again—that Penelope was fully as bad as Irene. "And she don't know how to work it off. Irene keeps doing; but Pen just sits in her room and mopes. She don't even read. I went up this afternoon to scold her about the state the house was in—you can see that Irene's away by the perfect mess; but when I saw her through the crack of the door I hadn't the heart. She sat there with her hands in her lap, just staring. And, my goodness! she *jumped* so when she saw me; and then she fell back, and began to laugh, and said she, 'I thought it was my ghost, mother!' I felt as if I should give way."

Lapham listened jadedly, and answered far from the point. "I guess I've got to start out there pretty soon, Persis."

"How soon?"

"Well, to-morrow morning."

Mrs. Lapham sat silent. Then, "All right," she said. "I'll get you ready."

"I shall run up to Lapham for Irene, and then I'll push on through Canada. I can get there about as quick."

"Is it anything you can tell me about, Silas?"

"Yes," said Lapham. "But it's a long story, and I guess you've got your hands pretty full as it is. I've been throwing good money after bad,—the usual way,—and now I've got to see if I can save the pieces."

After a moment Mrs. Lapham asked, "Is it—Rogers?"

"It's Rogers."

"I didn't want you should get in any deeper with him."

"No. You didn't want I should press him either; and I had to do one or the other. And so I got in deeper."

"Silas," said his wife, "I'm afraid I made you!"

"It's all right, Persis, as far forth as that goes. I was glad to make it up with him—I jumped at the chance. I guess Rogers saw that he had a soft thing in me, and he's worked it for all it was worth. But it'll all come out right in the end."

Lapham said this as if he did not care to talk any more about it. He added, casually, "Pretty near everybody but the fellows that owe *me* seem to expect me to do a cash business, all of a sudden."

"Do you mean that you've got payments to make, and that people are not paying *you*?"

Lapham winced a little. "Something like that," he said, and he lighted a cigar. "But when I tell you it's all right, I mean it, Persis. I ain't going to let the grass grow under my feet, though,—especially while Rogers digs the ground away from the roots."

"What are you going to do?"

"If it has to come to that, I'm going to squeeze him." Lapham's countenance lighted up with greater joy than had yet visited it since the day they had driven out to Brookline. "Milton K. Rogers is a rascal, if you want to know; or else all the signs fail. But I guess he'll find he's got his come-uppance." Lapham shut his lips so that the short, reddish-gray beard stuck straight out on them.

"What's he done?"

"What's he done? Well, now, I'll tell you what he's done, Persis, since you think Rogers is such a saint, and that I used him so badly in getting him out of the business. He's been dabbling in every sort of fool thing you can lay your tongue to,—wild-cat stocks, patent-rights, land speculations, oil claims,—till he's run through about everything. But he did have a big milling property out on the line of the P. Y. & X.,—saw-mills and grist-mills and lands,—and for the last eight years he's been doing a land-office business with 'em—business that would have made anybody else rich. But you can't make Milton K. Rogers rich, any more than you can fat a hide-bound colt. It ain't *in* him. He'd run through Vanderbilt, Jay Gould, and Tom Scott[1] rolled into one, in less than six months, give him a

1. Cornelius Vanderbilt (1794–1877), Jay Gould (1836–1892), and Thomas Alexander Scott (1823–1881) were Gilded Age "robber barons" who made immense fortunes building, investing, and speculating in railroads.

chance, and come out and want to borrow money of you. Well, he won't borrow any more money of *me*; and if he thinks I don't know as much about that milling property as he does, he's mistaken. I've taken his mills, but I guess I've got the inside track; Bill's kept me posted; and now I'm going out there to see how I can unload; and I sha'n't mind a great deal if Rogers is under the load when it's off, once."

"I don't understand you, Silas."

"Why, it's just this. The Great Lacustrine & Polar Railroad has leased the P. Y. & X.[2] for ninety-nine years,—*bought* it, practically,—and it's going to build car-works right by those mills, and it may want them. And Milton K. Rogers knew it when he turned 'em in on me."

"Well, if the road wants them, don't that make the mills valuable? You can get what you ask for them!"

"Can I? The P. Y. & X. is the only road that runs within fifty miles of the mills, and you can't get a foot of lumber nor a pound of flour to market any other way. As long as he had a little local road like the P. Y. & X. to deal with, Rogers could manage; but when it come to a big through line like the G. L. & P., he couldn't stand any chance at all. If such a road as that took a fancy to his mills, do you think it would pay what he asked? *No,* sir! He would take what the road offered, or else the road would tell him to carry his flour and lumber to market himself."

"And do you suppose he knew the G. L. & P. wanted the mills when he turned them in on you?" asked Mrs. Lapham, aghast, and falling helplessly into his alphabetical parlance.

The Colonel laughed scoffingly. "Well, when Milton K. Rogers don't know which side his bread's buttered on! I don't understand," he added thoughtfully, "how he's always letting it fall on the buttered side. But such a man as that is sure to have a screw loose in him somewhere."

Mrs. Lapham sat discomfited. All that she could say was, "Well, I want you should ask yourself whether Rogers would ever have gone wrong, or got into these ways of his, if it hadn't been for your forcing him out of the business when you did. I want you should think whether you're not responsible for everything he's done since."

"You go and get that bag of mine ready," said Lapham sullenly. "I guess I can take care of myself. And Milton K. Rogers too," he added.

That evening Corey spent the time after dinner in his own room, with restless excursions to the library, where his mother sat with his father and sisters, and showed no signs of leaving them. At last, in

2. Both railroads are imaginary; the name of the former satirizes the often grandiose titles of late-19th-century railroads and other corporations.

coming down, he encountered her on the stairs, going up. They both stopped consciously.

"I would like to speak with you, mother. I have been waiting to see you alone."

"Come to my room," she said.

"I have a feeling that you know what I want to say," he began there.

She looked up at him where he stood by the chimney-piece, and tried to put a cheerful note into her questioning "Yes?"

"Yes; and I have a feeling that you won't like it—that you won't approve of it. I wish you did—I wish you could!"

"I'm used to liking and approving everything you do, Tom. If I don't like this at once, I shall try to like it—you know that—for your sake, whatever it is."

"I'd better be short," he said, with a quick sigh. "It's about Miss Lapham." He hastened to add, "I hope it *isn't* surprising to you. I'd have told you before, if I could."

"No, it isn't surprising. I was afraid—I suspected something of the kind."

They were both silent in a painful silence.

"Well, mother?" he asked at last.

"If it's something you've quite made up your mind to——"

"It is!"

"And if you've already spoken to her——"

"I had to do that first, of course."

"There would be no use of my saying anything, even if I disliked it."

"You do dislike it!"

"No—no! I can't say that. Of course, I should have preferred it if you had chosen some nice girl among those that you had been brought up with—some friend or associate of your sisters, whose people we had known——"

"Yes, I understand that, and I can assure you that I haven't been indifferent to your feelings. I have tried to consider them from the first, and it kept me hesitating in a way that I'm ashamed to think of; for it wasn't quite right towards—others. But your feelings and my sisters' have been in my mind, and if I couldn't yield to what I supposed they must be, entirely——"

Even so good a son and brother as this, when it came to his love affair, appeared to think that he had yielded much in considering the feelings of his family at all.

His mother hastened to comfort him. "I know—I know. I've seen for some time that this might happen, Tom, and I have prepared myself for it. I have talked it over with your father, and we both agreed from the beginning that you were not to be hampered by our feeling. Still—it is a surprise. It must be."

"I know it. I can understand your feeling. But I'm sure that it's one that will last only while you don't know her well."

"Oh, I'm sure of that, Tom. I'm sure that we shall all be fond of her,—for your sake at first, even,—and I hope she'll like us."

"I am quite certain of that," said Corey, with that confidence which experience does not always confirm in such cases. "And your taking it as you do lifts a tremendous load off me."

But he sighed so heavily, and looked so troubled, that his mother said, "Well, now, you mustn't think of that any more. We wish what is for your happiness, my son, and we will gladly reconcile ourselves to anything that might have been disagreeable. I suppose we needn't speak of the family. We must both think alike about them. They have their—drawbacks, but they are thoroughly good people, and I satisfied myself the other night that they were not to be dreaded." She rose, and put her arm round his neck. "And I wish you joy, Tom! If she's half as good as you are, you will both be very happy." She was going to kiss him, but something in his looks stopped her—an absence, a trouble, which broke out in his words.

"I must tell you, mother! There's been a complication—a mistake—that's a blight on me yet, and that it sometimes seems as if we couldn't escape from. I wonder if you can help us! They all thought I meant—the other sister."

"Oh, Tom! But how *could* they?"

"I don't know. It seemed so glaringly plain—I was ashamed of making it so outright from the beginning. But they did. Even she did, herself!"

"But where could they have thought your eyes were—your taste? It wouldn't be surprising if any one were taken with that wonderful beauty; and I'm sure she's good too. But I'm astonished at them! To think you could prefer that little, black, odd creature, with her joking and——"

"*Mother!*" cried the young man, turning a ghastly face of warning upon her.

"What do you mean, Tom?"

"Did you—did—did *you* think so, too,—that it was *Irene* I meant?"

"Why, of course!"

He stared at her hopelessly.

"Oh, my son!" she said, for all comment on the situation.

"Don't reproach me, mother! I couldn't stand it."

"No. I didn't mean to do that. But how—*how* could it happen?"

"I don't know. When she first told me that they had understood it so, I laughed—almost—it was so far from me. But now, when you seem to have had the same idea—Did you all think so?"

"Yes."

They remained looking at each other. Then Mrs. Corey began: "It did pass through my mind once—that day I went to call upon them—that it might not be as we thought; but I knew so little of—of——"

"Penelope," Corey mechanically supplied.

"Is that her name?—I forgot—that I only thought of you in relation to her long enough to reject the idea; and it was natural, after our seeing something of the other one last year, that I might suppose you had formed some—attachment——"

"Yes; that's what they thought too. But I never thought of her as anything but a pretty child. I was civil to her because you wished it; and when I met her here again, I only tried to see her so that I could talk with her about her sister."

"You needn't defend yourself to *me*, Tom," said his mother, proud to say it to him in his trouble. "It's a terrible business for them, poor things," she added. "I don't know how they could get over it. But, of course, sensible people must see——"

"They haven't got over it. At least *she* hasn't. Since it's happened, there's been nothing that hasn't made me prouder and fonder of her! At first I *was* charmed with her—my fancy was taken; she delighted me—I don't know how; but she was simply the most fascinating person I ever saw. Now I never think of that. I only think how good she is—how patient she is with me, and how unsparing she is of herself. If she were concerned alone—if I were not concerned too—it would soon end. She's never had a thought for anything but her sister's feeling and mine from the beginning. I go there,—I know that I oughtn't, but I can't help it,—and she suffers it, and tries not to let me see that she is suffering it. There never was any one like her—so brave, so true, so noble. I won't give her up—I can't. But it breaks my heart when she accuses herself of what was all *my* doing. We spend our time trying to reason out of it, but we always come back to it at last, and I have to hear her morbidly blaming herself. Oh!"

Doubtless Mrs. Corey imagined some reliefs to this suffering, some qualifications of this sublimity in a girl she had disliked so distinctly; but she saw none in her son's behavior, and she gave him her further sympathy. She tried to praise Penelope, and said that it was not to be expected that she could reconcile herself at once to everything. "I shouldn't have liked it in her if she had. But time will bring it all right. And if she really cares for you——"

"I extorted that from her."

"Well, then, you must look at it in the best light you can. There is no blame anywhere, and the mortification and pain is something that must be lived down. That's all. And don't let what I said grieve you, Tom. You know I scarcely knew her, and I—I shall be sure to like any one you like, after all."

"Yes, I know," said the young man drearily. "Will you tell father?"

"If you wish."

"He must know. And I couldn't stand any more of this, just yet—any more mistake."

"I will tell him," said Mrs. Corey; and it was naturally the next thing for a woman who dwelt so much on decencies to propose: "We must go to call on her—your sisters and I. They have never seen her even; and she mustn't be allowed to think we're indifferent to her, especially under the circumstances."

"Oh, no! Don't go—not yet," cried Corey, with an instinctive perception that nothing could be worse for him. "We must wait—we must be patient. I'm afraid it would be painful to her now."

He turned away without speaking further; and his mother's eyes followed him wistfully to the door. There were some questions that she would have liked to ask him; but she had to content herself with trying to answer them when her husband put them to her.

There was this comfort for her always in Bromfield Corey, that he never was much surprised at anything, however shocking or painful. His standpoint in regard to most matters was that of the sympathetic humorist who would be glad to have the victim of circumstance laugh with him, but was not too much vexed when the victim could not. He laughed now when his wife, with careful preparation, got the facts of his son's predicament fully under his eye.

"Really, Bromfield," she said, "I don't see how you *can* laugh. Do you see any way out of it?"

"It seems to me that the way has been found already. Tom has told his love to the right one, and the wrong one knows it. Time will do the rest."

"If I had so low an opinion of them all as that, it would make me very unhappy. It's shocking to think of it."

"It is, upon the theory of ladies and all young people," said her husband, with a shrug, feeling his way to the matches on the mantel, and then dropping them with a sigh, as if recollecting that he must not smoke there. "I've no doubt Tom feels himself an awful sinner. But apparently he's resigned to his sin; he isn't going to give her up."

"I'm glad to say, for the sake of human nature, that *she* isn't resigned—little as I like her," cried Mrs. Corey.

Her husband shrugged again. "Oh, there mustn't be any indecent haste. She will instinctively observe the proprieties. But come, now, Anna! you mustn't pretend to me here, in the sanctuary of home, that practically the human affections don't reconcile themselves to any situation that the human sentiments condemn. Suppose the wrong sister had died: would the right one have had any scruple in marrying Tom, after they had both 'waited a proper time,' as the phrase is?"

"Bromfield, you're shocking!"

"Not more shocking than reality. You may regard this as a second marriage." He looked at her with twinkling eyes, full of the triumph the spectator of his species feels in signal exhibitions of human nature. "Depend upon it, the right sister will be reconciled; the wrong one will be consoled; and all will go merry as a marriage bell—a second marriage bell. Why, it's quite like a romance!" Here he laughed outright again.

"Well," sighed the wife, "I could almost wish the right one, as you call her, would reject Tom. I dislike her so much."

"Ah, now you're talking business, Anna," said her husband, with his hands spread behind the back he turned comfortably to the fire. "The whole Lapham tribe is distasteful to *me*. As I don't happen to have seen our daughter-in-law elect, I have still the hope—which you're disposed to forbid me—that she may not be quite so unacceptable as the others."

"Do you really feel so, Bromfield?" anxiously inquired his wife.

"Yes—I think I do"; and he sat down, and stretched out his long legs toward the fire.

"But it's very inconsistent of you to oppose the matter now, when you've shown so much indifference up to this time. You've told me, all along, that it was of no use to oppose it."

"So I have. I was convinced of that at the beginning, or my reason was. You know very well that I am equal to any trial, any sacrifice, day after to-morrow; but when it comes to-day it's another thing. As long as this crisis decently kept its distance, I could look at it with an impartial eye; but now that it seems at hand, I find that, while my reason is still acquiescent, my nerves are disposed to—excuse the phrase—kick. I ask myself, what have I done nothing for, all my life, and lived as a gentleman should, upon the earnings of somebody else, in the possession of every polite taste and feeling that adorns leisure, if I'm to come to this at last? And I find no satisfactory answer. I say to myself that I might as well have yielded to the pressure all round me, and gone to work, as Tom has."

Mrs. Corey looked at him forlornly, divining the core of real repugnance that existed in his self-satire.

"I assure you, my dear," he continued, "that the recollection of what I suffered from the Laphams at that dinner of yours is an anguish still. It wasn't their behavior,—they behaved well enough—or ill enough; but their conversation was terrible. Mrs. Lapham's range was strictly domestic; and when the Colonel got me in the library, he poured mineral paint all over me, till I could have been safely warranted not to crack or scale in any climate. I suppose we shall have to see a good deal of them. They will probably come here every Sunday night to tea. It's a perspective without a vanishing-point."

"It may not be so bad, after all," said his wife; and she suggested for his consolation that he knew very little about the Laphams yet.

He assented to the fact. "I know very little about them, and about my other fellow-beings. I dare say that I should like the Laphams better if I knew them better. But in any case, I resign myself. And we must keep in view the fact that this is mainly Tom's affair, and if his affections have regulated it to his satisfaction, we must be content."

"Oh, yes," sighed Mrs. Corey. "And perhaps it won't turn out so badly. It's a great comfort to know that you feel just as I do about it."

"I do," said her husband, "and more too."

It was she and her daughters who would be chiefly annoyed by the Lapham connection; she knew that. But she had to begin to bear the burden by helping her husband to bear his light share of it. To see him so depressed dismayed her, and she might well have reproached him more sharply than she did for showing so much indifference, when she was so anxious, at first. But that would not have served any good end now. She even answered him patiently when he asked her, "What did you say to Tom when he told you it was the other one?"

"What could I say? I could do nothing, but try to take back what I had said against her."

"Yes, you had quite enough to do, I suppose. It's an awkward business. If it had been the pretty one, her beauty would have been our excuse. But the plain one—what do you suppose attracted him in her?"

Mrs. Corey sighed at the futility of the question. "Perhaps I did her injustice. I only saw her a few moments. Perhaps I got a false impression. I don't think she's lacking in sense, and that's a great thing. She'll be quick to see that we don't mean unkindness, and can't, by anything we say or do, when she's Tom's wife." She pronounced the distasteful word with courage, and went on: "The pretty one might not have been able to see that. She might have got it into her head that we were looking down on her; and those insipid people are terribly stubborn. We can come to some understanding with *this* one; I'm sure of that." She ended by declaring that it was now their duty to help Tom out of his terrible predicament.

"Oh, even the Lapham cloud has a silver lining," said Corey. "In fact, it seems really to have all turned out for the best, Anna; though it's rather curious to find you the champion of the Lapham side, at last. Confess, now, that the right girl has secretly been your choice all along, and that while you sympathize with the wrong one, you rejoice in the tenacity with which the right one is clinging to her own!" He added with final seriousness, "It's just that she should, and, so far as I understand the case, I respect her for it."

"Oh, yes," sighed Mrs. Corey. "It's natural, and it's right." But she added, "I suppose they're glad of him on any terms."

"That is what I have been taught to believe," said her husband. "When shall we see our daughter-in-law elect? I find myself rather impatient to have that part of it over."

Mrs. Corey hesitated. "Tom thinks we had better not call, just yet."

"She has told him of your terrible behavior when you called before?"

"No, Bromfield! She couldn't be so vulgar as *that*?"

"But anything short of it?"

XXI.

Lapham was gone a fortnight. He was in a sullen humor when he came back, and kept himself shut close within his own den at the office the first day. He entered it in the morning without a word to his clerks as he passed through the outer room, and he made no sign throughout the forenoon, except to strike savagely on his desk-bell from time to time, and send out to Walker for some book of accounts or a letter-file. His boy confidentially reported to Walker that the old man seemed to have got a lot of papers round; and at lunch the book-keeper said to Corey, at the little table which they had taken in a corner together, in default of seats at the counter, "Well, sir, I guess there's a cold wave coming."

Corey looked up innocently, and said, "I haven't read the weather report."

"Yes, sir," Walker continued, "it's coming. Areas of rain along the whole coast, and increased pressure in the region of the private office. Storm-signals up at the old man's door now."

Corey perceived that he was speaking figuratively, and that his meteorology was entirely personal to Lapham. "What do you mean?" he asked, without vivid interest in the allegory, his mind being full of his own tragi-comedy.

"Why, just this: I guess the old man's takin' in sail. And I guess he's got to. As I told you the first time we talked about him, there don't any one know one-quarter as much about the old man's business as the old man does himself; and I ain't betraying any confidence when I say that I guess that old partner of his has got pretty deep into his books. I guess he's over head and ears in 'em, and the old man's gone in after him, and he's got a drownin' man's grip round his neck. There seems to be a kind of a lull—kind of a dead calm, *I* call it—in the paint market just now; and then again a ten-hundred-thousand-dollar man don't build a hundred-thousand-dollar house without feeling the drain, unless there's a regular boom. And just now there ain't any boom at all. Oh, I don't say but what the old man's got anchors to windward; guess he *has;* but if he's *goin'* to leave me his money, I wish he'd left it six weeks ago. Yes, sir, I guess there's a cold wave comin'; but you can't generally 'most always tell, as a usual thing, where the old man's concerned, and it's *only* a guess." Walker began to feed in his breaded chop with the same nervous excitement with which he abandoned himself to the slangy and figurative excesses of his talks. Corey had listened with a miserable curiosity and compassion up to a certain moment, when a broad light of hope flashed upon him. It came from Lapham's potential ruin; and the way out of the labyrinth that had hitherto seemed so hopeless was clear enough, if another's disaster would befriend him, and give him the opportunity to prove the unselfishness of his constancy. He thought of the sum of money that was his own, and that he might offer to lend, or practically give, if the time came; and with his crude hopes and purposes formlessly exulting in his heart, he kept on listening with an unchanged countenance.

Walker could not rest till he had developed the whole situation, so far as he knew it. "Look at the stock we've got on hand. There's going to be an awful shrinkage on that, now! And when everybody is shutting down, or running half time, the works up at Lapham are going full chip, just the same as ever. Well, it's his pride. I don't say but what it's a good sort of pride, but he likes to make his brags that the fire's never been out in the works since they started, and that no man's work or wages has ever been cut down yet at Lapham, it don't matter *what* the times are. Of course," explained Walker, "I shouldn't talk so to everybody; don't know as I should talk so to *any*body but you, Mr. Corey."

"Of course," assented Corey.

"Little off your feed to-day," said Walker, glancing at Corey's plate.

"I got up with a headache."

"Well, sir, if you're like me you'll carry it round all day, then. I don't know a much meaner thing than a headache—unless it's earache, or toothache, or some other kind of ache. I'm pretty hard to suit, when it comes to diseases. Notice how yellow the old man looked when he came in this morning? I don't like to see a man of his build look yellow—much."

About the middle of the afternoon the dust-colored face of Rogers, now familiar to Lapham's clerks, showed itself among them. "Has Colonel Lapham returned yet?" he asked, in his dry, wooden tones, of Lapham's boy.

"Yes, he's in his office," said the boy; and as Rogers advanced, he rose and added, "I don't know as you can see him to-day. His orders are not to let anybody in."

"Oh, indeed!" said Rogers; "I think he will see *me!*" and he pressed forward.

"Well, I'll have to ask," returned the boy; and hastily preceding Rogers, he put his head in at Lapham's door, and then withdrew it. "Please to sit down," he said; "he'll see you pretty soon;" and, with an air of some surprise, Rogers obeyed. His sere, dull-brown whiskers and the mustache closing over both lips were incongruously and illogically clerical in effect, and the effect was heightened for no reason by the parchment texture of his skin; the baldness extending to the crown of his head was like a baldness made up for the stage. What his face expressed chiefly was a bland and beneficent caution. Here, you must have said to yourself, is a man of just, sober, and prudent views, fixed purposes, and the good citizenship that avoids debt and hazard of every kind.

"What do you want?" asked Lapham, wheeling round in his swivel-chair as Rogers entered his room, and pushing the door shut with his foot, without rising.

Rogers took the chair that was not offered him, and sat with his hat-brim on his knees, and its crown pointed towards Lapham. "I want to know what you are going to do," he answered, with sufficient self-possession.

"I'll tell you, first, what I've *done*," said Lapham. "I've been to Dubuque, and I've found out all about that milling property you turned in on me. Did you know that the G. L. & P. had leased the P. Y. & X.?"

"I some suspected that it might."

"Did you know it when you turned the property in on me? Did you know that the G. L. & P. wanted to buy the mills?"

"I presumed the road would give a fair price for them," said Rogers, winking his eyes in outward expression of inwardly blinking the point.

"You lie," said Lapham, as quietly as if correcting him in a slight error; and Rogers took the word with equal *sang froid*.[1] "You knew the road wouldn't give a fair price for the mills. You knew it would give what it chose, and that I couldn't help myself, when you let me take them. You're a thief, Milton K. Rogers, and you stole money I lent you." Rogers sat listening, as if respectfully considering the statements. "You knew how I felt about that old matter—or my wife did; and that I wanted to make it up to you, if you felt anyway badly used. And you took advantage of it. You've got money out of me, in the first place, on securities that wa'n't worth thirty-five cents on the dollar, and you've let me in for this thing, and that thing, and you've bled me every time. And all I've got to show for it is a milling property on a line of road that can squeeze me, whenever it wants to, as dry as it pleases. And you want to know what I'm going to do? I'm

1. Cold blood (French, literal trans.); composure, self-control.

going to squeeze *you*. I'm going to sell these collaterals of yours,"—he touched a bundle of papers among others that littered his desk,—"and I'm going to let the mills go for what they'll fetch. *I* ain't going to fight the G. L. & P."[2]

Lapham wheeled about in his chair and turned his burly back on his visitor, who sat wholly unmoved.

"There are some parties," he began, with a dry tranquillity ignoring Lapham's words, as if they had been an outburst against some third person, who probably merited them, but in whom he was so little interested that he had been obliged to use patience in listening to his condemnation,—"there are some English parties who have been making inquiries in regard to those mills."

"I guess you're lying, Rogers," said Lapham, without looking round.

"Well, all that I have to ask is that you will not act hastily."

"I see you don't think I'm in earnest!" cried Lapham, facing fiercely about. "You think I'm fooling, do you?" He struck his bell, and "William," he ordered the boy who answered it, and who stood waiting while he dashed off a note to the brokers and inclosed it with the bundle of securities in a large envelope, "take these down to Gallop & Paddock's, in State street, right away. Now go!" he said to Rogers, when the boy had closed the door after him; and he turned once more to his desk.

Rogers rose from his chair, and stood with his hat in his hand. He was not merely dispassionate in his attitude and expression, he was impartial. He wore the air of a man who was ready to return to business whenever the wayward mood of his interlocutor permitted. "Then I understand," he said, "that you will take no action in regard to the mills till I have seen the parties I speak of."

Lapham faced about once more, and sat looking up into the visage of Rogers in silence. "I wonder what you're up to," he said at last; "I *should* like to know." But as Rogers made no sign of gratifying his curiosity, and treated this last remark of Lapham's as of the irrelevance of all the rest, he said, frowning, "You bring me a party that will give me enough for those mills to clear me of you, and I'll talk to you. But don't you come here with any man of straw. And I'll give you just twenty-four hours to prove yourself a swindler again."

Once more Lapham turned his back, and Rogers, after looking thoughtfully into his hat a moment, cleared his throat, and quietly withdrew, maintaining to the last his unprejudiced demeanor.

Lapham was not again heard from, as Walker phrased it, during the afternoon, except when the last mail was taken in to him; then

2. In essence, Rogers gave Lapham the mill properties as collateral for the loans he received, letting Lapham believe that the mills were worth much more than Rogers knew them to be.

the sound of rending envelopes, mixed with that of what seemed suppressed swearing, penetrated to the outer office. Somewhat earlier than the usual hour for closing, he appeared there with his hat on and his overcoat buttoned about him. He said briefly to his boy, "William, I sha'n't be back again this afternoon," and then went to Miss Dewey and left a number of letters on her table to be copied, and went out. Nothing had been said, but a sense of trouble subtly diffused itself through those who saw him go out.

That evening, as he sat down with his wife alone at tea, he asked, "Ain't Pen coming to supper?"

"No, she ain't," said his wife. "I don't know as I like the way she's going on, any too well. I'm afraid, if she keeps on, she'll be down sick. She's got deeper feelings than Irene."

Lapham said nothing, but, having helped himself to the abundance of his table in his usual fashion, he sat and looked at his plate with an indifference that did not escape the notice of his wife. "What's the matter with *you*?" she asked.

"Nothing. I haven't got any appetite."

"What's the matter?" she persisted.

"Trouble's the matter; bad luck and lots of it's the matter," said Lapham. "I haven't ever hid anything from you, Persis, when you asked me, and it's too late to begin now. I'm in a fix. I'll tell you what kind of a fix, if you think it'll do you any good; but I guess you'll be satisfied to know that it's a fix."

"How much of a one?" she asked, with a look of grave, steady courage in her eyes.

"Well, I don't know as I can tell, just yet," said Lapham, avoiding this look. "Things have been dull all the fall, but I thought they'd brisk up, come winter. They haven't. There have been a lot of failures, and some of 'em owed me, and some of 'em had me on their paper;[3] and——" Lapham stopped.

"And what?" prompted his wife.

He hesitated before he added, "And then—Rogers."

"I'm to blame for that," said Mrs. Lapham. "I forced you to it."

"No; I was as willing to go into it as what you were," answered Lapham. "I don't want to blame anybody."

Mrs. Lapham had a woman's passion for fixing responsibility; she could not help saying, as soon as acquitted, "I warned you against him, Silas. I told you not to let him get in any deeper with you."

"Oh, yes. I had to help him to try to get my money back. I might as well poured water into a sieve. And now——" Lapham stopped.

3. Lapham means that he is being financially squeezed in two ways: businesses to which he has loaned money are unable to repay, and creditors from whom he has borrowed money are demanding repayment.

"Don't be afraid to speak out to me, Silas Lapham. If it comes to the worst, I want to know it—I've got to know it. What did I ever care for the money? I've had a happy home with you ever since we were married, and I guess I shall have as long as you live, whether we go on to the Back Bay, or go back to the old house at Lapham. I know who's to blame, and I blame myself. It was my forcing Rogers on to you." She came back to this, with her helpless longing, inbred in all Puritan souls, to have some one specifically suffer for the evil in the world, even if it must be herself.

"It hasn't come to the worst yet, Persis," said her husband. "But I shall have to hold up on the new house a little while, till I can see where I am."

"I shouldn't care if we had to sell it," cried his wife, in passionate self-condemnation. "I should be *glad* if we had to, as far as I'm concerned."

"I shouldn't," said Lapham.

"I know!" said his wife; and she remembered ruefully how his heart was set on it.

He sat musing. "Well, I guess it's going to come out all right in the end. Or, if it ain't," he sighed, "we can't help it. May be Pen needn't worry so much about Corey, after all," he continued, with a bitter irony new to him. "It's an ill wind that blows nobody good. And there's a chance," he ended, with a still bitterer laugh, "that Rogers will come to time, after all."

"I don't believe it!" exclaimed Mrs. Lapham, with a gleam of hope in her eyes. "What chance?"

"One in ten million," said Lapham; and her face fell again. "He says there are some English parties after him to buy these mills."

"Well?"

"Well, I gave him twenty-four hours to prove himself a liar."

"You don't believe there are any such parties?"

"Not in *this* world."

"But if there were?"

"Well, if there were, Persis——But pshaw!"

"No, no!" she pleaded eagerly. "It don't seem as if he *could* be such a villain. What would be the use of his pretending? If he brought the parties to you——"

"Well," said Lapham scornfully, "I'd let them have the mills at the price Rogers turned 'em in on me at. *I* don't want to make anything on 'em. But guess I shall hear from the G. L. & P. first. And when they make their offer, I guess I'll have to accept it, whatever it is. I don't think they'll have a great many competitors."

Mrs. Lapham could not give up her hope. "If you could get your price from those English parties before they knew that the G. L. & P. wanted to buy the mills, would it let you out with Rogers?"

"Just about," said Lapham.

"Then I know he'll move heaven and earth to bring it about. I *know* you won't be allowed to suffer for doing him a kindness, Silas. He *can't* be so ungrateful! Why, why *should* he pretend to have any such parties in view when he hasn't? Don't you be downhearted, Si. You'll see that he'll be round with them to-morrow."

Lapham laughed, but she urged so many reasons for her belief in Rogers that Lapham began to rekindle his own faith a little. He ended by asking for a hot cup of tea; and Mrs. Lapham sent the pot out and had a fresh one steeped for him. After that he made a hearty supper in the revulsion from his entire despair; and they fell asleep that night talking hopefully of his affairs, which he laid before her fully, as he used to do when he first started in business. That brought the old times back, and he said: "If this had happened then, I shouldn't have cared much. I was young then, and I wasn't afraid of anything. But I noticed that after I passed fifty I began to get scared easier. I don't believe I could pick up, now, from a regular knockdown."

"Pshaw! *You* scared, Silas Lapham?" cried his wife, proudly. "I should like to see the thing that ever scared you; or the knockdown that *you* couldn't pick up from!"

"Is that so, Persis?" he asked, with the joy her courage gave him.

In the middle of the night she called to him, in a voice which the darkness rendered still more deeply troubled: "Are you awake, Silas?"

"Yes; I'm awake."

"I've been thinking about those English parties, Si——"

"So've I."

"And I can't make it out but what you'd be just as bad as Rogers, every bit and grain, if you were to let them have the mills——"

"And not tell 'em what the chances were with the G. L. & P.? I thought of that, and you needn't be afraid."

She began to bewail herself, and to sob convulsively: "Oh, Silas! Oh, Silas!" Heaven knows in what measure the passion of her soul was mixed with pride in her husband's honesty, relief from an apprehended struggle, and pity for him.

"Hush, hush, Persis!" he besought her. "You'll wake Pen if you keep on that way. Don't cry any more! You mustn't."

"Oh, let me cry, Silas! It'll help me. I shall be all right in a minute. Don't you mind." She sobbed herself quiet. "It does seem too hard," she said, when she could speak again, "that you have to give up this chance when Providence had fairly raised it up for you."

"I guess it wa'n't *Providence* raised it up," said Lapham. "Any rate, it's got to go. Most likely Rogers was lyin', and there ain't any such parties; but if there were, they couldn't have the mills from me without the whole story. Don't you be troubled, Persis. I'm going to pull through all right."

"Oh, I ain't afraid. I don't suppose but what there's plenty would help you, if they knew you needed it, Si."

"They would if they knew I *didn't* need it," said Lapham sardonically.

"Did you tell Bill how you stood?"

"No, I couldn't bear to. I've been the rich one so long, that I couldn't bring myself to own up that I was in danger."

"Yes."

"Besides, it didn't look so ugly till to-day. But I guess we sha'n't let ugly looks scare us."

"No."

[NINTH INSTALLMENT—JULY 1885]

XXII.

The morning postman brought Mrs. Lapham a letter from Irene, which was chiefly significant because it made no reference whatever to the writer or her state of mind. It gave the news of her uncle's family; it told of their kindness to her; her cousin Will was going to take her and his sisters ice-boating on the river, when it froze.

By the time this letter came, Lapham had gone to his business, and the mother carried it to Penelope to talk over. "What do you make out of it?" she asked; and without waiting to be answered, she said, "I don't know as I believe in cousins marrying, a great deal; but if Irene and Will were to fix it up between 'em—" She looked vaguely at Penelope.

"It wouldn't make any difference as far as I was concerned," replied the girl, listlessly.

Mrs. Lapham lost her patience.

"Well, then, I'll tell you what, Penelope!" she exclaimed. "Perhaps it'll make a difference to you if you know that your father's in *real* trouble. He's harassed to death, and he was awake half the night, talking about it. That abominable old Rogers has got a lot of money away from him; and he's lost by others that he's helped,"—Mrs. Lapham put it in this way because she had no time to be explicit,—"and I want you should come out of your room now, and try to be of some help and comfort to him when he comes home to-night. I guess Irene wouldn't mope round much, if she was here," she could not help adding.

The girl lifted herself on her elbow. "What's that you say about father?" she demanded, eagerly. "Is he in trouble? Is he going to lose his money? Shall we have to stay in this house?"

"We may be very *glad* to stay in this house," said Mrs. Lapham, half angry with herself for having given cause for the girl's conjectures, and half with the habit of prosperity in her child, which could conceive no better of what adversity was. "And I want you should get up and show that you've got some feeling for somebody in the world besides yourself."

"Oh, I'll get *up!*" said the girl, promptly, almost cheerfully.

"I don't say it's as bad now as it looked a little while ago," said her mother, conscientiously hedging a little from the statement which she had based rather upon her feelings than her facts. "Your father thinks he'll pull through all right, and I don't know but what he will. But I want you should see if you can't do something to cheer him up and keep him from getting so perfectly down-hearted as he seems to get, under the load he's got to carry. And stop thinking about yourself awhile, and behave yourself like a sensible girl."

"Yes, yes," said the girl; "I will. You needn't be troubled about me any more."

Before she left her room she wrote a note, and when she came down she was dressed to go out-of-doors and post it herself. The note was to Corey:

"Do not come to see me any more till you hear from me. I have a reason which I cannot give you now; and you must not ask what it is."

All day she went about in a buoyant desperation, and she came down to meet her father at supper.

"Well, Persis," he said scornfully, as he sat down, "we might as well saved our good resolutions till they were wanted. I guess those English parties have gone back on Rogers."

"Do you mean he didn't come?"

"He hadn't come up to half-past five," said Lapham.

"Tchk!" uttered his wife.

"But I guess I shall pull through without Mr. Rogers," continued Lapham. "A firm that I didn't think *could* weather it is still afloat, and so far forth as the danger goes of being dragged under with it, I'm all right." Penelope came in. "Hello, Pen!" cried her father. "It ain't often I meet *you* nowadays." He put up his hand as she passed his chair, and pulled her down and kissed her.

"No," she said; "but I thought I'd come down to-night and cheer you up a little. I shall not talk; the sight of me will be enough."

Her father laughed out. "Mother been telling you? Well, I *was* pretty blue last night; but I guess I was more scared than hurt. How'd you like to go to the theater to-night? Sellers at the Park.[1] Heigh?"

"Well, I don't know. Don't you think they could get along without me there?"

1. I.e., the Park Theatre on Washington Street in Boston. Colonel Beriah Sellers is a character in the novel *The Gilded Age* (1873), by Mark Twain and Charles Dudley Warner (1829–1900), which Twain later adapted as a play.

"No; couldn't work it at all," cried the Colonel. "Let's all go. Unless," he added, inquiringly, "there's somebody coming here?"

"There's nobody coming," said Penelope.

"Good! Then we'll go. Mother, don't you be late now."

"Oh, *I* sha'n't keep you waiting," said Mrs. Lapham. She had thought of telling what a cheerful letter she had got from Irene; but upon the whole it seemed better not to speak of Irene at all just then. After they returned from the theater, where the Colonel roared through the comedy, with continual reference of his pleasure to Penelope, to make sure that she was enjoying it too, his wife said, as if the whole affair had been for the girl's distraction rather than his, "I don't believe but what it's going to come out all right about the children;" and then she told him of the letter, and the hopes she had founded upon it.

"Well, perhaps you're right, Persis," he consented.

"I haven't seen Pen so much like herself since it happened. I declare, when I see the way she came out to-night, just to please you, I don't know as I want you should get over all your troubles right away."

"I guess there'll be enough to keep Pen going for a while yet," said the Colonel, winding up his watch.

But for a time there was a relief, which Walker noted, in the atmosphere at the office, and then came another cold wave, slighter than the first, but distinctly felt there, and succeeded by another relief. It was like the winter which was wearing on to the end of the year, with alternations of freezing weather, and mild days stretching to weeks, in which the snow and ice wholly disappeared. It was none the less winter, and none the less harassing for these fluctuations, and Lapham showed in his face and temper the effect of like fluctuations in his affairs. He grew thin and old, and both at home and at his office he was irascible to the point of offense. In these days Penelope shared with her mother the burden of their troubled home, and united with her in supporting the silence or the petulance of the gloomy, secret man who replaced the presence of jolly prosperity there. Lapham had now ceased to talk of his troubles, and savagely resented his wife's interference. "You mind your own business, Persis," he said one day, "if you've got any;" and after that she left him mainly to Penelope, who did not think of asking him questions.

"It's pretty hard on you, Pen," she said.

"That makes it easier for me," returned the girl, who did not otherwise refer to her own trouble. In her heart she had wondered a little at the absolute obedience of Corey, who had made no sign since receiving her note. She would have liked to ask her father if Corey was sick; she would have liked him to ask her why Corey did not come any more. Her mother went on:

"I don't believe your father knows *where* he stands. He works away at those papers he brings home here at night, as if he didn't half know what he was about. He always did have that close streak in him, and I don't suppose but what he's been going into things he don't want anybody else to know about, and he's kept these accounts of his own."

Sometimes he gave Penelope figures to work at, which he would not submit to his wife's nimbler arithmetic. Then she went to bed and left them sitting up till midnight, struggling with problems in which they were both weak. But she could see that the girl was a comfort to her father, and that his troubles were a defense and shelter to her. Some nights she could hear them going out together, and then she lay awake for their return from their long walk. When the hour or day of respite came again, the home felt it first. Lapham wanted to know what the news from Irene was; he joined his wife in all her cheerful speculations, and tried to make her amends for his sullen reticence and irritability. Irene was staying on at Dubuque. There came a letter from her, saying that her uncle's people wanted her to spend the winter there. "Well, let her," said Lapham. "It'll be the best thing for her." Lapham himself had letters from his brother at frequent intervals. His brother was watching the G. L. & P., which as yet had made no offer for the mills. Once, when one of these letters came, he submitted to his wife whether, in the absence of any positive information that the road wanted the property, he might not, with a good conscience, dispose of it to the best advantage to anybody who came along.

She looked wistfully at him; it was on the rise from a season of deep depression with him. "No, Si," she said; "I don't see how you could do that."

He did not assent and submit, as he had done at first, but began to rail at the unpracticality of women; and then he shut some papers he had been looking over into his desk, and flung out of the room.

One of the papers had slipped through the crevice of the lid, and lay upon the floor. Mrs. Lapham kept on at her sewing, but after a while she picked the paper up to lay it on the desk. Then she glanced at it, and saw that it was a long column of dates and figures, recording successive sums, never large ones, paid regularly to "Wm. M." The dates covered a year, and the sum amounted at least to several hundreds.

Mrs. Lapham laid the paper down on the desk, and then she took it up again and put it into her work-basket, meaning to give it to him. When he came in she saw him looking absent-mindedly about for something, and then going to work upon his papers, apparently without it. She thought she would wait till he missed it definitely, and then give him the scrap she had picked up. It lay in her basket, and after some days it found its way under the work in it, and she forgot it.

XXIII.

Since New Year's there had scarcely been a mild day, and the streets were full of snow, growing foul under the city feet and hoofs, and renewing its purity from the skies with repeated falls, which in turn lost their whiteness, beaten down, and beaten black and hard into a solid bed like iron. The sleighing was incomparable, and the air was full of the din of bells; but Lapham's turnout was not of those that thronged the Brighton road every afternoon; the man at the livery-stable sent him word that the mare's legs were swelling.

He and Corey had little to do with each other. He did not know how Penelope had arranged it with Corey; his wife said she knew no more than he did, and he did not like to ask the girl herself, especially as Corey no longer came to the house. He saw that she was cheerfuller than she had been, and help-fuller with him and her mother. Now and then Lapham opened his troubled soul to her a little, letting his thought break into speech without preamble or conclusion. Once he said:

"Pen, I presume you know I'm in trouble."

"We all seem to be there," said the girl.

"Yes, but there's a difference between being there by your own fault and being there by somebody else's."

"I don't call it his fault," she said.

"I call it mine," said the Colonel.

The girl laughed. Her thought was of her own care, and her father's wholly of his. She must come to his ground. "What have you been doing wrong?"

"I don't know as you'd call it wrong. It's what people do all the time. But I wish I'd let stocks alone. It's what I always promised your mother I would do. But there's no use cryin' over spilt milk; or watered stock,[1] either."

"I don't think there's much use crying about anything. If it could have been cried straight, it would have been all right from the start," said the girl, going back to her own affair; and if Lapham had not been so deeply engrossed in his, he might have seen how little she cared for all that money could do or undo. He did not observe her enough to see how variable her moods were in those days, and how often she sank from some wild gayety into abject melancholy; how at times she was fiercely defiant of nothing at all, and at others inexplicably humble and patient. But no doubt none of these signs had

1. Stock dishonestly priced higher than its actual value.

passed unnoticed by his wife, to whom Lapham said one day, when he came home, "Persis, what's the reason Pen don't marry Corey?"

"You know as well as I do, Silas," said Mrs. Lapham, with an inquiring look at him for what lay behind his words.

"Well, I think it's all tomfoolery, the way she's going on. There ain't any rhyme nor reason to it." He stopped, and his wife waited. "If she said the word, I could have some help from them." He hung his head, and would not meet his wife's eye.

"I guess you're in a pretty bad way, Si," she said pityingly, "or you wouldn't have come to that."

"I'm in a hole," said Lapham, "and I don't know where to turn. You won't let me do anything about those mills——"

"Yes, I'll let you," said his wife sadly.

He gave a miserable cry. "You know I can't do anything, if you do. Oh, my Lord!"

She had not seen him so low as that before. She did not know what to say. She was frightened, and could only ask, "Has it come to the worst?"

"The new house has got to go," he answered evasively.

She did not say anything. She knew that the work on the house had been stopped since the beginning of the year. Lapham had told the architect that he preferred to leave it unfinished till the spring, as there was no prospect of their being able to get into it that winter; and the architect had agreed with him that it would not hurt it to stand. Her heart was heavy for him, though she could not say so. They sat together at the table, where she had come to be with him at his belated meal. She saw that he did not eat, and she waited for him to speak again, without urging him to take anything. They were past that.

"And I've sent orders to shut down at the Works," he added.

"Shut down at the Works!" she echoed with dismay. She could not take it in. The fire at the Works had never been out before since it was first kindled. She knew how he had prided himself upon that; how he had bragged of it to every listener, and had always lugged the fact in as the last expression of his sense of success. "Oh, Silas!"

"What's the use?" he retorted. "I saw it was coming a month ago. There are some fellows out in West Virginia that have been running the paint as hard as they could. They couldn't do much; they used to put it on the market raw. But lately they got to baking it, and now they've struck a vein of natural gas right by their works, and they pay ten cents for fuel where I pay a dollar, and they make as good a paint. Anybody can see where it's going to end. Besides, the market's overstocked. It's glutted. There wa'n't anything to do but to shut *down*, and I've *shut* down."

"I don't know what's going to become of the hands in the middle of the winter, this way," said Mrs. Lapham, laying hold of one definite thought which she could grasp in the turmoil of ruin that whirled before her eyes.

"I don't care what becomes of the hands," cried Lapham. "They've shared my luck; now let 'em share the other thing. And if you're so very sorry for the hands, I wish you'd keep a little of your pity for *me*. Don't you know what shutting down the Works means?"

"Yes, indeed I do, Silas," said his wife tenderly.

"Well, then!" He rose, leaving his supper untasted, and went into the sitting-room, where she presently found him, with that everlasting confusion of papers before him on the desk. That made her think of the paper in her work-basket, and she decided not to make the careworn, distracted man ask her for it, after all. She brought it to him.

He glanced blankly at it and then caught it from her, turning red and looking foolish. "Where'd you get that?"

"You dropped it on the floor the other night, and I picked it up. Who is 'Wm. M.'?"

" 'Wm. M.'?" he repeated, looking confusedly at her, and then at the paper. "Oh,—it's nothing." He tore the paper into small pieces, and went and dropped them into the fire. When Mrs. Lapham came into the room in the morning, before he was down, she found a scrap of the paper, which must have fluttered to the hearth; and glancing at it she saw that the words were "Mrs. M." She wondered what dealings with a woman her husband could have, and she remembered the confusion he had shown about the paper, and which she had thought was because she had surprised one of his business secrets. She was still thinking of it when he came down to breakfast, heavy-eyed, tremulous, with deep seams and wrinkles in his face.

After a silence which he did not seem inclined to break, "Silas," she asked, "who is 'Mrs. M.'?"

He stared at her. "I don't know what you're talking about."

"Don't you?" she returned mockingly. "When you do, you tell me. Do you want any more coffee?"

"No."

"Well, then, you can ring for Alice when you've finished. I've got some things to attend to." She rose abruptly, and left the room. Lapham looked after her in a dull way, and then went on with his breakfast. While he still sat at his coffee, she flung into the room again, and dashed some papers down beside his plate. "Here are some more things of yours, and I'll thank you to lock them up in your desk and not litter my room with them, if you please." Now he saw that she was angry, and it must be with him. It enraged him that in such a time of trouble she should fly out at him in that way. He left the house without trying to speak to her.

That day Corey came just before closing, and, knocking at Lapham's door, asked if he could speak with him a few moments.

"Yes," said Lapham, wheeling round in his swivel-chair and kicking another towards Corey. "Sit down. I want to talk to you. I'd ought to tell you you're wasting your time here. I spoke the other day about your placin' yourself better, and I can help you to do it, yet. There ain't going to be the outcome for the paint in the foreign markets that we expected, and I guess you better give it up."

"I don't wish to give it up," said the young fellow, setting his lips. "I've as much faith in it as ever; and I want to propose now what I hinted at in the first place. I want to put some money into the business."

"Some money!" Lapham leaned towards him, and frowned as if he had not quite understood, while he clutched the arms of his chair.

"I've got about thirty thousand dollars that I could put in, and if you don't want to consider me a partner—I remember that you objected to a partner—you can let me regard it as an investment. But I think I see the way to doing something at once in Mexico, and I should like to feel that I had something more than a drummer's[2] interest in the venture."

The men sat looking into each other's eyes. Then Lapham leaned back in his chair, and rubbed his hand hard and slowly over his face. His features were still twisted with some strong emotion when he took it away. "Your family know about this?"

"My uncle James knows."

"He thinks it would be a good plan for you?"

"He thought that by this time I ought to be able to trust my own judgment."

"Do you suppose I could see your uncle at his office?"

"I imagine he's there."

"Well, I want to have a talk with him, one of these days." He sat pondering awhile, and then rose, and went with Corey to his door. "I guess I sha'n't change my mind about taking you into the business in that way," he said coldly. "If there was any reason why I shouldn't at first, there's more now."

"Very well, sir," answered the young man, and went to close his desk. The outer office was empty; but while Corey was putting his papers in order it was suddenly invaded by two women, who pushed by the protesting porter on the stairs and made their way towards Lapham's room. One of them was Miss Dewey, the type-writer girl, and the other was a woman whom she would resemble in face and figure twenty years hence, if she led a life of hard work varied by paroxysms of hard drinking.

2. A traveling salesman.

"That his room, Z'rilla?" asked this woman, pointing towards Lapham's door with a hand that had not freed itself from the fringe of dirty shawl under which it had hung. She went forward without waiting for the answer, but before she could reach it the door opened, and Lapham stood filling its space.

"Look here, Colonel Lapham!" began the woman, in a high key of challenge. "I want to know if this is the way you're goin' back on me and Z'rilla?"

"What do you want?" asked Lapham.

"What do I want? What do you s'pose I want? I want the money to pay my month's rent; there ain't a bite to eat in the house; and I want some money to market."

Lapham bent a frown on the woman, under which she shrank back a step. "You've taken the wrong way to get it. Clear out!"

"I *won't* clear out!" said the woman, beginning to whimper.

"Corey!" said Lapham, in the peremptory voice of a master,—he had seemed so indifferent to Corey's presence that the young man thought he must have forgotten he was there,—"is Dennis anywhere round?"

"Yissor," said Dennis, answering for himself from the head of the stairs, and appearing in the wareroom.

Lapham spoke to the woman again. "Do you want I should call a hack, or do you want I should call an officer?"

The woman began to cry into an end of her shawl. "*I* don't know what we're goin' to do."

"You're going to clear out," said Lapham. "Call a hack, Dennis. If you ever come here again, I'll have you arrested. Mind that! Zerrilla, I shall want you early to-morrow morning."

"Yes, sir," said the girl meekly; she and her mother shrank out after the porter.

Lapham shut his door without a word.

At lunch the next day Walker made himself amends for Corey's reticence by talking a great deal. He talked about Lapham, who seemed to have, more than ever since his apparent difficulties began, the fascination of an enigma for his book-keeper, and he ended by asking, "Did you see that little circus last night?"

"What little circus?" asked Corey in his turn.

"Those two women and the old man. Dennis told me about it. I told him if he liked his place he'd better keep his mouth shut."

"That was very good advice," said Corey.

"Oh, all right, if you don't want to talk. Don't know as I should in your place," returned Walker, in the easy security he had long felt that Corey had no intention of putting on airs with him. "But I'll tell you what: the old man can't expect it of everybody. If he keeps this thing up much longer, it's going to be talked about. You can't have a woman walking into your place of business, and trying to bulldoze you before your porter, without setting your porter to thinking. And the last thing you want a porter to do is to think; for when a porter thinks, he thinks wrong."

"I don't see why even a porter couldn't think right about that affair," replied Corey. "I don't know who the woman was, though I believe she was Miss Dewey's mother; but I couldn't see that Colonel Lapham showed anything but a natural resentment of her coming to him in that way. I should have said she was some rather worthless person whom he'd been befriending, and that she had presumed upon his kindness."

"Is that so? What do you think of his never letting Miss Dewey's name go on the books?"

"That it's another proof it's a sort of charity of his. That's the only way to look at it."

"Oh, *I'm* all right." Walker lighted a cigar and began to smoke, with his eyes closed to a fine straight line. "It won't do for a bookkeeper to think wrong, any more than a porter, I suppose. But I guess you and I don't think very different about this thing."

"Not if you think as I do," replied Corey steadily; "and I know you would do that if you had seen the 'circus' yourself. A man doesn't treat people who have a disgraceful hold upon him as he treated them."

"It depends upon who he is," said Walker, taking his cigar from his mouth. "I never said the old man was afraid of anything."

"And character," continued Corey, disdaining to touch the matter further, except in generalities, "must go for something. If it's to be the prey of mere accident and appearance, then it goes for nothing."

"Accidents will happen in the best-regulated families," said Walker, with vulgar, good-humored obtuseness that filled Corey with indignation. Nothing, perhaps, removed his matter-of-fact nature farther from the commonplace than a certain generosity of instinct, which I should not be ready to say was always infallible.

That evening it was Miss Dewey's turn to wait for speech with Lapham after the others were gone. He opened his door at her knock, and stood looking at her with a worried air. "Well, what do you want, Zerrilla?" he asked, with a sort of rough kindness.

"I want to know what I'm going to do about Hen. He's back again; and he and mother have made it up, and they both got to drinking last night after I went home, and carried on so that the neighbors came in."

Lapham passed his hand over his red and heated face. "I don't know what I'm going to do. You're twice the trouble that my own family is, now. But I know what I'd do, mighty quick, if it wasn't for you, Zerrilla," he went on relentingly. "I'd shut your mother up somewheres, and if I could get that fellow off for a three years' voyage——"

"I declare," said Miss Dewey, beginning to whimper, "it seems as if he came back just so often to spite me. He's never gone more than a year at the furthest, and you can't make it out habitual drunkenness, either, when it's just sprees. I'm at my wit's end."

"Oh, well, you mustn't cry around here," said Lapham soothingly.

"I know it," said Miss Dewey. "If I could get rid of Hen, I could manage well enough with mother. Mr. Wemmel would marry me if I could get the divorce. He's said so over and over again."

"I don't know as I like that very well," said Lapham, frowning. "I don't know as I want you should get married in any hurry again. I don't know as I like your going with anybody else just yet."

"Oh, you needn't be afraid but what it'll be all right. It'll be the best thing all round, if I can marry him."

"Well!" said Lapham impatiently; "I can't think about it now. I suppose they've cleaned everything out again?"

"Yes, they have," said Zerrilla; "there isn't a cent left."

"You're a pretty expensive lot," said Lapham. "Well, here!" He took out his pocket-book and gave her a note. "I'll be round to-night and see what can be done."

He shut himself into his room again, and Zerrilla dried her tears, put the note into her bosom, and went her way.

Lapham kept the porter nearly an hour later. It was then six o'clock, the hour at which the Laphams usually had tea; but all custom had been broken up with him during the past months, and he did not go home now. He determined, perhaps in the extremity in which a man finds relief in combating one care with another, to keep his promise to Miss Dewey, and at the moment when he might otherwise have been sitting down at his own table he was climbing the stairs to her lodging in the old-fashioned dwelling which had been portioned off into flats. It was in a region of depots, and of the cheap hotels, and "ladies' and gents'" dining-rooms, and restaurants with bars, which abound near depots; and Lapham followed to Miss Dewey's door a waiter from one of these, who bore on a salver before him a supper covered with a napkin. Zerrilla had admitted them, and at her greeting a young fellow in the shabby shore-suit of a sailor, buttoning imperfectly over the nautical blue flannel of his shirt, got up from where he had been sitting, on one side of the stove, and stood infirmly on his feet, in token of receiving the visitor. The woman who sat on the other side did not rise, but began a shrill, defiant apology.

"Well, I don't suppose but what you'll think we're livin' on the fat o' the land, right straight along, all the while. But it's just like this. When that child came in from her work, she didn't seem to have the spirit to go to cookin' anything, and I had such a bad night last night I was feelin' all broke up, and s'd I, what's the use, anyway? By the time the butcher's heaved in a lot o' bone, and made you pay for the suet he cuts away, it comes to the same thing, and why not *git* it from the rest'rant first off, and save the cost o' your fire? s'd I."

"What have you got there under your apron? A bottle?" demanded Lapham, who stood with his hat on and his hands in his pockets, indifferent alike to the ineffective reception of the sailor and the chair Zerrilla had set him.

"Well, yes, it's a bottle," said the woman, with an assumption of virtuous frankness. "It's whisky; I got to have *some*thing to rub my rheumatism with."

"Humph!" grumbled Lapham. "You've been rubbing *his* rheumatism too, I see."

He twisted his head in the direction of the sailor, now softly and rhythmically waving to and fro on his feet.

"He hain't had a drop to-day in *this* house!" cried the woman.

"What are you doing around here?" said Lapham, turning fiercely upon him. "You've got no business ashore. Where's your ship? Do you think I'm going to let you come here and eat your wife out of house and home, and then give money to keep the concern going?"

"Just the very words I said when he first showed his face here, yist'day. Didn't I, Z'rilla?" said the woman, eagerly joining in the rebuke of her late boon companion. "You got no business here, Hen, s'd I. You can't come here to live on me and Z'rilla, s'd I. You want to go back to your ship, s'd I. That's what I said."

The sailor mumbled, with a smile of tipsy amiability for Lapham, something about the crew being discharged.

"Yes," the woman broke in, "that's always the way with these coasters. Why don't you go off on some them long v'y'ges? s'd I. It's pretty hard, when Mr. Wemmel stands ready to marry Z'rilla and provide a comfortable home for us both,—I hain't got a great many years more to live, and I *should* like to get some satisfaction out of 'em and not be beholden and dependent all my days,—to have Hen, here, blockin' the way. I tell him there'd be more money for him in the end; but he can't seem to make up his mind to it."

"Well, now, look here," said Lapham. "I don't care anything about all that. It's your own business, and I'm not going to meddle with it. But it's my business who lives off me; and so I tell you all three, I'm willing to take care of Zerrilla, and I'm willing to take care of her mother——"

"I guess if it hadn't been for that child's father," the mother interpolated, "you wouldn't been here to tell the tale, Colonel Lapham."

"I know all about that," said Lapham. "But I'll tell you what, Mr. Dewey, I'm not going to support *you*."

"I don't see what Hen's done," said the old woman, impartially.

"He hasn't done anything, and I'm going to stop it. He's got to get a ship, and he's got to get out of this. And Zerrilla needn't come back to work till he does. I'm done with you all."

"Well, I vow," said the mother, "if I ever heard anything like it! Didn't that child's father lay down his life for you? Hain't you said it yourself a hundred times? And don't she work for her money, and slave for it mornin', noon, and night? You talk as if we was beholden to you for the very bread in our mouths. I guess if it hadn't been for Jim, you wouldn't been here crowin' over us."

"You mind what I say. I mean business this time," said Lapham, turning to the door.

The woman rose and followed him, with her bottle in her hand. "Say, Colonel! what should you advise Z'rilla to do about Mr. Wemmel? I tell her there ain't any use goin' to the trouble to git a divorce without she's sure about him. Don't you think we'd ought to git him to sign a paper, or something, that he'll marry her if she gits it? I don't like to have things going at loose ends the way they are. It ain't sense. It ain't right."

Lapham made no answer to the mother anxious for her child's future, and concerned for the moral questions involved. He went out and down the stairs, and on the pavement at the lower door he almost struck against Rogers, who had a bag in his hand, and seemed to be hurrying towards one of the depots. He halted a little, as if to speak to Lapham; but Lapham turned his back abruptly upon him, and took the other direction.

The days were going by in a monotony of adversity to him, from which he could no longer escape, even at home. He attempted once or twice to talk of his troubles to his wife, but she repulsed him sharply; she seemed to despise and hate him; but he set himself doggedly to make a confession to her, and he stopped her one night, as she came into the room where he sat—hastily upon some errand that was to take her directly away again.

"Persis, there's something I've got to tell you."

She stood still, as if fixed against her will, to listen.

"I guess you know something about it already, and I guess it's set you against me."

"Oh, I guess not, Colonel Lapham. You go your way, and I go mine. That's all."

She waited for him to speak, listening with a cold, hard smile on her face.

"I don't say it to make favor with you, because I don't want you to spare me, and I don't ask you; but I got into it through Milton K. Rogers."

"Oh!" said Mrs. Lapham contemptuously.

"I always felt the way I said about it—that it wa'n't any better than gambling, and I say so now. It's like betting on the turn of a card; and I give you my word of honor, Persis, that I never was in it at all till that scoundrel began to load me up with those wild-cat securities[3] of his. Then it seemed to me as if I ought to try to do something to get somewhere even. I know it's no excuse; but watching the market to see what the infernal things were worth from day to day, and seeing it go up, and seeing it go down, was too much for me; and, to make a long story short, I began to buy and sell on a margin[4]—just what I told you I never would do. I seemed to make something—I did make something; and I'd have stopped, I do believe, if I could have reached the figure I'd set in my own mind to start with; but I couldn't fetch it. I began to lose, and then I began to throw good money after bad, just as I always did with everything that Rogers ever came within a mile of. Well, what's the use? I lost the money that would have carried me out of this, and I shouldn't have had to shut down the Works, or sell the house, or——"

Lapham stopped. His wife, who at first had listened with mystification, and then dawning incredulity, changing into a look of relief that was almost triumph, lapsed again into severity. "Silas Lapham, if you was to die the next minute, is this what you started to tell me?"

"Why, of course it is. What did you suppose I started to tell you?"

"And—look me in the eyes!—you haven't got anything else on your mind now?"

"No! There's trouble enough, the Lord knows; but there's nothing else to tell you. I suppose Pen gave you a hint about it. I dropped something to her. I've been feeling bad about it, Persis, a good while, but I hain't had the heart to speak of it. I can't expect you to say you like it. I've been a fool, I'll allow, and I've been something worse, if you choose to say so; but that's all. I haven't hurt anybody but myself—and you and the children."

Mrs. Lapham rose and said, with her face from him, as she turned towards the door, "It's all right, Silas. I sha'n't ever bring it up against you."

She fled out of the room, but all that evening she was very sweet with him, and seemed to wish in all tacit ways to atone for her past unkindness.

She made him talk of his business, and he told her of Corey's offer, and what he had done about it. She did not seem to care for his part in it, however; at which Lapham was silently disappointed a little, for he would have liked her to praise him.

3. Stocks and other financial assets of dubious legitimacy or legality.
4. To buy and sell stocks with money borrowed from a stockbroker. The investor is betting that the stock price will rise, covering his loan and gaining profit, but if the stock price falls, the investor may have to sell at a loss to pay back the loan.

"He did it on account of Pen!'

"Well, he didn't insist upon it, anyway," said Lapham, who must have obscurely expected that Corey would recognize his own magnanimity by repeating his offer. If the doubt that follows a self-devoted action—the question whether it was not after all a needless folly—is mixed, as it was in Lapham's case, with the vague belief that we might have done ourselves a good turn without great risk of hurting any one else by being a little less unselfish, it becomes a regret that is hard to bear. Since Corey spoke to him, some things had happened that gave Lapham hope again.

"I'm going to tell her about it," said his wife, and she showed herself impatient to make up for the time she had lost. "Why didn't you tell me before, Silas?"

"I didn't know we were on speaking terms before," said Lapham sadly.

"Yes, that's true," she admitted, with a conscious flush. "I hope he won't think Pen's known about it all this while."

XXIV.

That evening James Bellingham came to see Corey after dinner, and went to find him in his own room.

"I've come at the instance of Colonel Lapham," said the uncle. "He was at my office to-day, and I had a long talk with him. Did you know that he was in difficulties?"

"I fancied that he was in some sort of trouble. And I had the bookkeeper's conjectures—he doesn't really know much about it."

"Well, he thinks it time—on all accounts—that you should know how he stands, and why he declined that proposition of yours. I must say he has behaved very well—like a gentleman."

"I'm not surprised."

"I am. It's hard to behave like a gentleman where your interest is vitally concerned. And Lapham doesn't strike me as a man who's in the habit of acting from the best in him always."

"Do any of us?" asked Corey.

"Not all of us, at any rate," said Bellingham. "It must have cost him something to say no to you, for he's just in that state when he believes that this or that chance, however small, would save him."

Corey was silent. "Is he really in such a bad way?"

"It's hard to tell just where he stands. I suspect that a hopeful temperament and fondness for round numbers have always caused him to set his figures beyond his actual worth. I don't say that he's been dishonest about it, but he's had a loose way of estimating his assets; he's reckoned his wealth on the basis of his capital, and some of his capital is borrowed. He's lost heavily by some of the recent failures, and there's been a terrible shrinkage in his values. I don't mean merely in the stock of paint on hand, but in a kind of competition which has become very threatening. You know about that West Virginia paint?"

Corey nodded.

"Well, he tells me that they've struck a vein of natural gas out there which will enable them to make as good a paint as his own at a cost of manufacturing so low that they can undersell him everywhere. If this proves to be the case, it will not only drive his paint out of the market, but will reduce the value of his Works—the whole plant—at Lapham to a merely nominal figure."

"I see," said Corey dejectedly. "I've understood that he had put a great deal of money into his Works."

"Yes, and he estimated his mine there at a high figure. Of course it will be worth little or nothing if the West Virginia paint drives his out. Then, besides, Lapham has been into several things outside of his own business, and, like a good many other men who try outside things, he's kept account of them himself; and he's all mixed up about them. He's asked me to look into his affairs with him, and I've promised to do so. Whether he can be tided over his difficulties remains to be seen. I'm afraid it will take a good deal of money to do it—a great deal more than he thinks, at least. He believes comparatively little would do it. I think differently. I think that anything less than a great deal would be thrown away on him. If it were merely a question of a certain sum—even a large sum—to keep him going, it might be managed; but it's much more complicated. And, as I say, it must have been a trial to him to refuse your offer."

This did not seem to be the way in which Bellingham had meant to conclude. But he said no more; and Corey made him no response.

He remained pondering the case, now hopefully, now doubtfully, and wondering, whatever his mood was, whether Penelope knew anything of the fact with which her mother went nearly at the same moment to acquaint her.

"Of course, he's done it on your account," Mrs. Lapham could not help saying.

"Then he was very silly. Does he think I would have let him give father money? And if father lost it for him, does he suppose it would make it any easier for me? I think father acted twice as well. It was very silly."

In repeating the censure, her look was not so severe as her tone; she even smiled a little, and her mother reported to her father that she acted more like herself than she had yet since Corey's offer.

"I think, if he was to repeat his offer, she would have him now," said Mrs. Lapham.

"Well, I'll let her know if he does," said the Colonel.

"I guess he won't do it to you!" she cried.

"Who else will he do it to?" he demanded.

They perceived that they had each been talking of a different offer.

After Lapham went to his business in the morning the postman brought another letter from Irene, which was full of pleasant things that were happening to her; there was a great deal about her cousin Will, as she called him. At the end she had written, "Tell Pen I don't want she should be foolish."

"There!" said Mrs. Lapham. "I guess it's going to come out right, all round;" and it seemed as if even the Colonel's difficulties were past. "When your father gets through this, Pen," she asked impulsively, "what shall you do?"

"What have you been telling Irene about me?"

"Nothing much. What should you do?"

"It would be a good deal easier to say what I should do if father didn't," said the girl.

"I know you think it was nice in him to make your father that offer," urged the mother.

"It was nice, yes; but it was silly," said the girl. "Most nice things are silly, I suppose," she added.

She went to her room and wrote a letter. It was very long, and very carefully written; and when she read it over, she tore it into small pieces. She wrote another one, short and hurried, and tore that up too. Then she went back to her mother, in the family room, and asked to see Irene's letter, and read it over to herself. "Yes, she seems to be having a good time," she sighed. "Mother, do you think I ought to let Mr. Corey know that I know about it?"

"Well, I should think it would be a pleasure to him," said Mrs. Lapham judicially.

"I'm not so sure of that—the way I should have to tell him. I should begin by giving him a scolding. Of course, he meant well by it, but can't you see that it wasn't very flattering? How did he expect it would change me?"

"I don't believe he ever thought of that."

"Don't you? Why?"

"Because you can see that he isn't one of that kind. He might want to please you without wanting to change you by what he did."

"Yes. He must have known that nothing would change me,—at least, nothing that he could do. I thought of that. I shouldn't like him to feel that I couldn't appreciate it, even if I did think it was silly. Should you write to him?"

"I don't see why not."

"It would be too pointed. No, I shall just let it go. I wish he hadn't done it."

"Well, he has done it."

"And I've tried to write to him about it—two letters: one so humble and grateful that it couldn't stand up on its edge, and the other so pert and flippant. Mother, I wish you could have seen those two letters! I wish I had kept them to look at if I ever got to thinking I had any sense again. They would take the conceit out of me."

"What's the reason he don't come here any more?"

"Doesn't he come?" asked Penelope in turn, as if it were something she had not noticed particularly.

"You'd ought to know."

"Yes." She sat silent awhile. "If he doesn't come, I suppose it's because he's offended at something I did."

"What did you do?"

"Nothing. I—wrote to him—a little while ago. I suppose it was very blunt, but I didn't believe he would be angry at it. But this—this that he's done shows he was angry, and that he wasn't just seizing the first chance to get out of it."

"What have you done, Pen?" demanded her mother sharply.

"Oh, I don't know. All the mischief in the world, I suppose. I'll tell you. When you first told me that father was in trouble with his business, I wrote to him not to come any more till I let him. I said I couldn't tell him why, and he hasn't been here since. I'm sure *I* don't know what it means."

Her mother looked at her with angry severity. "Well, Penelope Lapham! For a sensible child, you *are* the greatest goose I ever saw. Did you think he would come here and *see* if you wouldn't let him come?"

"He might have written," urged the girl.

Her mother made that despairing "Tchk!" with her tongue, and fell back in her chair. "I should have *despised* him if he had written. He's acted just exactly right, and you—you've acted—I don't know *how* you've acted. I'm ashamed of you. A girl that could be so sensible for her sister, and always say and do just the right thing, and then when it comes to herself to be such a *disgusting* simpleton!"

"I thought I ought to break with him at once, and not let him suppose that there was any hope for him or me if father was poor. It was my one chance, in this whole business, to do anything heroic, and I jumped at it. You mustn't think, because I can laugh at it now, that I wasn't in earnest, mother! I *was*—dead! But the Colonel has gone to ruin so gradually, that he's spoilt everything. I expected that he would be bankrupt the next day, and that then *he* would understand what I meant. But to have it drag along for a fortnight seems to take all the heroism out of it, and leave it as flat!" She looked at her mother with a smile that shone through her tears, and a pathos that quivered round her jesting lips. "It's easy enough to be sensible for other people. But when it comes to myself, there I am! Especially, when I want to do what I oughtn't so much that it seems as if doing what I didn't want to do *must* be doing what I ought! But it's been a great success one way, mother. It's helped me to keep up before the Colonel. If it hadn't been for Mr. Corey's staying away, and my feeling so indignant with him for having been badly treated by me, I shouldn't have been worth anything at all."

The tears started down her cheeks, but her mother said, "Well, now, go along, and write to him. It don't matter what you say, much; and don't be so very particular."

Her third attempt at a letter pleased her scarcely better than the rest, but she sent it, though it seemed so blunt and awkward. She wrote:

> DEAR FRIEND:
>
> I expected when I sent you that note, that you would understand, almost the next day, why I could not see you any more. You must know now, and you must not think that if anything happened to my father, I should wish you to help him. But that is no reason why I should not thank you, and I do thank you, for offering. It was like you, I will say that.
>
> Yours sincerely, PENELOPE LAPHAM.

She posted her letter, and he sent his reply in the evening, by hand:

> DEAREST:
>
> What I did was nothing, till you praised it. Everything I have and am is yours. Won't you send a line by the bearer, to say that I may come to see you? I know how you feel; but I am sure that I can make you think differently. You must consider that I loved you without a thought of your father's circumstances, and always shall.
>
> T. C.

The generous words were blurred to her eyes by the tears that sprang into them. But she could only write in answer:

> "Please do not come; I have made up my mind. As long as this trouble is hanging over us, I cannot see you. And if father is unfortunate, all is over between us."

She brought his letter to her mother, and told her what she had written in reply. Her mother was thoughtful awhile before she said, with a sigh, "Well, I hope you've begun as you can carry out, Pen."

"Oh, I shall not have to carry out at all. I shall not have to do anything. That's one comfort—the only comfort." She went away to her own room, and when Mrs. Lapham told her husband of the affair, he was silent at first, as she had been. Then he said, "I don't know as I should have wanted her to done differently; I don't know as she could. If I ever come right again, she won't have anything to feel meeching about; and if I don't, I don't want she should be beholden to anybody. And I guess that's the way she feels."

The Coreys in their turn sat in judgment on the fact which their son felt bound to bring to their knowledge.

"She has behaved very well," said Mrs. Corey, to whom her son had spoken.

"My dear," said her husband, with his laugh, "she has behaved *too* well. If she had studied the whole situation with the most artful eye to its mastery, she could not possibly have behaved better."

The process of Lapham's financial disintegration was like the course of some chronic disorder, which has fastened itself upon the constitution, but advances with continual reliefs, with apparent amelioration, and at times seems not to advance at all, when it gives hope of final recovery not only to the sufferer, but to the eye of science itself. There were moments when James Bellingham, seeing Lapham pass this crisis and that, began to fancy that he might pull through altogether; and at these moments, when his adviser could not oppose anything but experience and probability to the evidence of the fact, Lapham was buoyant with courage, and imparted his hopefulness to his household. Our theory of disaster, of sorrow, of affliction, borrowed from the poets and novelists, is that it is incessant; but every passage in our own lives and in the lives of others, so far as we have witnessed them, teaches us that this is false. The house of mourning is decorously darkened to the world, but within itself it is also the house of laughing. Bursts of gayety, as heartfelt as its grief, relieve the gloom, and the stricken survivors have their jests together, in which the thought of the dead is tenderly involved, and a fond sense, not crazier than many others, of sympathy and enjoyment beyond the silence, justifies the sunnier mood before sorrow rushes back, deploring and despairing, and making it all up again with the conventional fitness of things. Lapham's adversity had this quality in common with bereavement. It was not always like the adversity we figure in allegory; it had its moments of being like prosperity, and if upon the whole it was continual, it was not incessant. Sometimes there was a week of repeated reverses, when he had to keep his teeth set and to hold on hard to all his hopefulness; and then days came of negative result or slight success, when he was full of his jokes at the tea-table, and wanted to go to the theater, or to do something to cheer Penelope up. In some miraculous way, by some enormous stroke of success which should eclipse the brightest of his past prosperity, he expected to do what would reconcile all difficulties, not only in his own affairs, but in hers too. "You'll see," he said to his wife; "it's going to come out all right. Irene'll fix it up with Bill's boy, and then she'll be off Pen's mind; and if things go on as they've been going for the last two days, I'm going to be in a position to do the favors myself, and Pen can feel that *she's* makin' a sacrifice, and then I guess may be she'll do it. If things turn out as I expect now, and times ever *do* get any better generally, I can show Corey that I appreciate his offer. I can offer him the partnership myself then."

Even in the other moods, which came when everything had been going wrong, and there seemed no way out of the net, there were points of consolation to Lapham and his wife. They rejoiced that Irene was safe beyond the range of their anxieties, and they had a proud satisfaction that there had been no engagement between Corey and Penelope, and that it was she who had forbidden it. In the closeness of interest and sympathy in which their troubles had reunited them, they confessed to each that nothing would have been more galling to their pride than the idea that Lapham should not have been able to do everything for his daughter that the Coreys might have expected. Whatever happened now, the Coreys could not have it to say that the Laphams had tried to bring any such thing about.

Bellingham had lately suggested an assignment[1] to Lapham, as the best way out of his difficulties. It was evident that he had not the money to meet his liabilities at present, and that he could not raise it without ruinous sacrifices, that might still end in ruin after all. If he made the assignment, Bellingham argued, he could gain time and make terms; the state of things generally would probably improve, since it could not be worse, and the market, which he had glutted with his paint, might recover and he could start again. Lapham had not agreed with him. When his reverses first began, it had seemed easy for him to give up everything, to let the people he owed take all, so only they would let him go out with clean hands; and he had dramatized this feeling in his talk with his wife, when they spoke together of the mills on the G. L. & P. But ever since then it had been growing harder, and he could not consent even to seem to do it now in the proposed assignment. He had not found other men so very liberal or faithful with him; a good many of them appeared to have combined to hunt him down; a sense of enmity towards all his creditors asserted itself in him; he asked himself why they should not suffer a little too. Above all, he shrank from the publicity of the assignment. It was open confession that he had been a fool in some way; he could not bear to have his family—his

1. A way to protect the owner's personal assets by transferring control of his or her business to a second party.

brother the judge, especially, to whom he had always appeared the soul of business wisdom—think him imprudent or stupid. He would make any sacrifice before it came to that. He determined in parting with Bellingham to make the sacrifice which he had oftenest in his mind, because it was the hardest, and to sell his new house. That would cause the least comment. Most people would simply think that he had got a splendid offer, and with his usual luck had made a very good thing of it; others who knew a little more about him would say that he was hauling in his horns, but they could not blame him; a great many other men were doing the same in those hard times—the shrewdest and safest men; it might even have a good effect.

He went straight from Bellingham's office to the real-estate broker in whose hands he meant to put his house, for he was not the sort of man to shilly-shally when he had once made up his mind. But he found it hard to get his voice up out of his throat, when he said he guessed he would get the broker to sell that new house of his on the water side of Beacon. The broker answered cheerfully, yes; he supposed Colonel Lapham knew it was a pretty dull time in real estate? and Lapham said yes, he knew that, but he should not sell at a sacrifice, and he did not care to have the broker name him or describe the house definitely unless parties meant business. Again the broker said yes; and he added, as a joke Lapham would appreciate, that he had half a dozen houses on the water side of Beacon on the same terms; that nobody wanted to be named or to have his property described.

It did, in fact, comfort Lapham a little to find himself in the same boat with so many others; he smiled grimly, and said in his turn, yes, he guessed that was about the size of it with a good many people. But he had not the heart to tell his wife what he had done, and he sat taciturn that whole evening, without even going over his accounts, and went early to bed, where he lay tossing half the night before he fell asleep. He slept at last only upon the promise he made himself that he would withdraw the house from the broker's hands; but he went heavily to his own business in the morning without doing so. There was no such rush, anyhow, he reflected bitterly; there would be time to do that a month later, probably.

It struck him with a sort of dismay when a boy came with a note from the broker, saying that a party who had been over the house in the fall had come to him to know whether it could be bought, and was willing to pay the cost of the house up to the time he had seen it. Lapham took refuge in trying to think who the party could be; he concluded that it must have been somebody who had gone over it with the architect, and he did not like that; but he was aware that this was not an answer to the broker, and he wrote that he would give him an answer in the morning.

Now that it had come to the point, it did not seem to him that he could part with the house. So much of his hope for himself and his children had gone into it that the thought of selling it made him tremulous and sick. He could not keep about his work steadily, and with his nerves shaken by want of sleep, and the shock of this sudden and unexpected question, he left his office early, and went over to look at the house and try to bring himself to some conclusion there. The long procession of lamps on the beautiful street was flaring in the clear red of the sunset towards which it marched, and Lapham, with a lump in his throat, stopped in front of his house and looked at their multitude. They were not merely a part of the landscape; they were a part of his pride and glory, his success, his triumphant life's work which was fading into failure in his helpless hands. He ground his teeth to keep down that lump, but the moisture in his eyes blurred the lamps, and the keen, pale crimson against which it made them flicker. He turned and looked up, as he had so often done, at the window-spaces, neatly glazed for the winter with white linen, and recalled the night when he had stopped with Irene before the house, and she had said that she should never live there, and he had tried to coax her into courage about it. There was no such façade as that on the whole street, to his thinking. Through his long talks with the architect, he had come to feel almost as intimately and fondly as the architect himself the satisfying simplicity of the whole design and the delicacy of its detail. It appealed to him as an exquisite bit of harmony appeals to the unlearned ear, and he recognized the difference between this fine work and the obstreperous pretentiousness of the many overloaded house-fronts which Seymour had made him notice for his instruction elsewhere on the Back Bay. Now, in the depths of his gloom, he tried to think what Italian city it was where Seymour said he had first got the notion of treating brickwork in that way.

He unlocked the temporary door with the key he always carried, so that he could let himself in and out whenever he liked, and entered the house, dim and very cold with the accumulated frigidity of the whole winter in it, and looking as if the arrest of work upon it had taken place a thousand years before. It smelt of the unpainted woods and the clean, hard surfaces of the plaster, where the experiments in decoration had left it untouched; and mingled with these odors was that of some rank pigments and metallic compositions which Seymour had used in trying to realize a certain daring novelty of finish, which had not proved successful. Above all, Lapham detected the peculiar odor of his own paint, with which the architect had been greatly interested one day, when Lapham showed it to him at the office. He had asked Lapham to let him try the Persis Brand in realizing a little idea he had for the finish of Mrs. Lapham's room. If it succeeded, they could tell her what it was, for a surprise.

Lapham glanced at the bay-window in the reception-room, where he sat with his girls on the trestles when Corey first came by; and then he explored the whole house to the attic, in the light faintly admitted through the linen sashes. The floors were strewn with shavings and chips which the carpenters had left, and in the music-room these had been blown into long irregular windrows by the draughts through a wide rent in the linen sash. Lapham tried to pin it up, but failed, and stood looking out of it over the water. The ice had left the river, and the low tide lay smooth and red in the light of the sunset. The Cambridge flats showed the sad, sodden yellow of meadows stripped bare after a long sleep under snow; the hills, the naked trees, the spires and roofs had a black outline, as if they were objects in a landscape of the French school.[2]

The whim seized Lapham to test the chimney in the music-room; it had been tried in the dining-room below, and in his girls' fire-places above, but here the hearth was still clean. He gathered some shavings and blocks together, and kindled them, and as the flame mounted gayly from them, he pulled up a nail-keg which he found there and sat down to watch it. Nothing could have been better; the chimney was a perfect success; and as Lapham glanced out of the torn linen sash he said to himself that that party, whoever he was, who had offered to buy his house might go to the devil; he would never sell it as long as he had a dollar. He said that he should pull through yet; and it suddenly came into his mind that, if he could raise the money to buy out those West Virginia fellows, he should be all right, and would have the whole game in his own hand. He slapped himself on the thigh, and wondered that he had never thought of that before; and then, lighting a cigar with a splinter from the fire, he sat down again to work the scheme out in his own mind.

He did not hear the feet heavily stamping up the stairs, and coming towards the room where he sat; and the policeman to whom the feet belonged had to call out to him, smoking at his chimney-corner, with his back turned to the door, "Hello! what are you doing here?"

"What's that to you?" retorted Lapham, wheeling half round on his nail-keg.

"I'll show you," said the officer, advancing upon him, and then stopping short as he recognized him. "Why, Colonel Lapham! I thought it was some tramp got in here!"

2. A group of painters also known as the Barbizon school, active 1830–1870. Painting landscapes from direct observation of nature, their work marked a turn toward realism and emphasized the solidity of natural forms.

"Have a cigar?" said Lapham hospitably. "Sorry there ain't another nail-keg."

The officer took the cigar. "I'll smoke it outside. I've just come on, and I can't stop. Tryin' your chimney?"

"Yes, I thought I'd see how it would draw, in here. It seems to go first-rate."

The policeman looked about him with an eye of inspection. "You want to get that linen window, there, mended up."

"Yes, I'll speak to the builder about that. It can go for one night."

The policeman went to the window and failed to pin the linen together where Lapham had failed before. "*I* can't fix it." He looked round once more, and saying, "Well, goodnight," went out and down the stairs.

Lapham remained by the fire till he had smoked his cigar; then he rose and stamped upon the embers that still burned with his heavy boots, and went home. He was very cheerful at supper. He told his wife that he guessed he had a sure thing of it now, and in another twenty-four hours he should tell her just how. He made Penelope go to the theater with him, and when they came out, after the play, the night was so fine that he said they must walk round by the new house and take a look at it in the starlight. He said he had been there before he came home, and tried Seymour's chimney in the music-room, and it worked like a charm.

As they drew near Beacon street they were aware of unwonted stir and tumult, and presently the still air transmitted a turmoil of sound, through which a powerful and incessant throbbing made itself felt. The sky had reddened above them, and turning the corner at the Public Garden,[3] they saw a black mass of people obstructing the white perspective of the snowy street, and out of this mass a half dozen engines, whose strong heart-beats had already reached them, sent up volumes of fire-tinged smoke and steam from their funnels. Ladders were planted against the façade of a building, from the roof of which a mass of flame burnt smoothly upward, except where here and there it seemed to pull contemptuously away from the heavy streams of water which the firemen, clinging like great beetles to their ladders, poured in upon it.

Lapham had no need to walk down through the crowd, gazing and gossiping, with shouts and cries and hysterical laughter, before the burning house, to make sure that it was his.

"I guess I done it, Pen," was all he said.

Among the people who were looking at it were a party who seemed to have run out from dinner in some neighboring house; the ladies

3. A large municipal park established in 1837, situated at the western edge of Boston Common, bordered by Beacon Street on the north and the Back Bay neighborhood to the west.

were fantastically wrapped up, as if they had flung on the first things they could seize.

"Isn't it perfectly magnificent!" cried a pretty girl. "I wouldn't have missed it on any account. Thank you *so* much, Mr. Symington, for bringing us out!"

"Ah, I thought you'd like it," said this Mr. Symington, who must have been the host; "and you can enjoy it without the least compunction, Miss Delano, for I happen to know that the house belongs to a man who could afford to burn one up for you once a year."

"Oh, do you think he would, if I came again?"

"I haven't the least doubt of it. We don't do things by halves in Boston."

"He ought to have had a coat of his noncombustible paint on it," said another gentleman of the party.

Penelope pulled her father away toward the first carriage she could reach of a number that had driven up. "Here, father! get into this."

"No, no; I couldn't ride," he answered heavily, and he walked home in silence. He greeted his wife with, "Well, Persis, our house is gone! And I guess I set it on fire myself;" and while he rummaged among the papers in his desk, still with his coat and hat on, his wife got the facts as she could from Penelope. She did not reproach him. Here was a case in which his self-reproach must be sufficiently sharp without any edge from her. Besides, her mind was full of a terrible thought.

"Oh, Silas," she faltered, "they'll think you set it on fire to get the insurance!"

Lapham was staring at a paper which he held in his hand. "I had a builder's risk on it, but it expired last week. It's a dead loss."

"Oh, thank the merciful Lord!" cried his wife.

"Merciful!" said Lapham. "Well, it's a queer way of showing it."

He went to bed, and fell into the deep sleep which sometimes follows a great moral shock. It was perhaps rather a torpor than a sleep.

XXV.

Lapham awoke confused, and in a kind of remoteness from the loss of the night before, through which it loomed mistily. But before he lifted his head from the pillow, it gathered substance and weight against which it needed all his will to bear up and live. In that moment he wished that he had not wakened, that he might never have wakened; but he rose, and faced the day and its cares.

The morning papers brought the report of the fire, and the conjectured loss. The reporters somehow had found out the fact that the loss fell entirely upon Lapham; they lighted up the hackneyed character of their statements with the picturesque interest of the coincidence that the policy had expired only the week before; heaven knows how they knew it. They said that nothing remained of the building but the walls; and Lapham, on his way to business, walked up past the smoke-stained shell. The windows looked like the eye-sockets of a skull down upon the blackened and trampled snow of the street; the pavement was a sheet of ice, and the water from the engines had frozen, like streams of tears, down the face of the house, and hung in icy tags from the window-sills and copings.[1]

He gathered himself up as well as he could, and went on to his office. The chance of retrieval that had flashed upon him, as he sat smoking by that ruined hearth the evening before, stood him in such stead now as a sole hope may; and he said to himself that, having resolved not to sell his house, he was no more crippled by its loss than he would have been by letting his money lie idle in it; what he might have raised by mortgage on it could be made up in some other way; and if they would sell, he could still buy out the whole business of that West Virginia company, mines, plant, stock on hand, good-will, and everything, and unite it with his own. He went early in the afternoon to see Bellingham, whose expressions of condolence for his loss he cut short with as much politeness as he knew how to throw into his impatience. Bellingham seemed at first a little dazzled with the splendid courage of his scheme; it was certainly fine in its way; but then he began to have his misgivings.

"I happen to know that they haven't got much money behind them," urged Lapham. "They'll jump at an offer."

Bellingham shook his head. "If they can show profit on the old manufacture, and prove they can make their paint still cheaper and better hereafter, they can have all the money they want. And it will be very difficult for you to raise it if you're threatened by them. With that competition, you know what your plant at Lapham would be worth, and what the shrinkage on your manufactured stock would be. Better sell out to them," he concluded, "if they will buy."

"There ain't money enough in this country to buy out my paint," said Lapham, buttoning up his coat in a quiver of resentment. "Good-afternoon, sir." Men are but grownup boys, after all. Bellingham watched this perversely proud and obstinate child fling petulantly out of his door, and felt a sympathy for him which was as truly kind as it was helpless.

But Lapham was beginning to see through Bellingham, as he believed. Bellingham was, in his way, part of that conspiracy by which Lapham's creditors were trying to drive him to the wall. More than ever now he was glad that he had nothing to do with that cold-hearted, self-conceited race, and that the favors so far were all

1. Cappings at the tops of walls.

from his side. He was more than ever determined to show them, every one of them, high and low, that he and his children could get along without them, and prosper and triumph without them. He said to himself that if Penelope were engaged to Corey that very minute, he would make her break with him.

He knew what he should do now, and he was going to do it without loss of time. He was going on to New York to see those West Virginia people; they had their principal office there, and he intended to get at their ideas, and then he intended to make them an offer. He managed this business better than could possibly have been expected of a man in his impassioned mood. But when it came really to business, his practical instincts, alert and wary, came to his aid against the passions that lay in wait to betray after they ceased to dominate him. He found the West Virginians full of zeal and hope, but in ten minutes he knew that they had not yet tested their strength in the money market, and had not ascertained how much or how little capital they could command. Lapham himself, if he had had so much, would not have hesitated to put a million dollars into their business. He saw, as they did not see, that they had the game in their own hands, and that if they could raise the money to extend their business, they could ruin him. It was only a question of time, and he was on the ground first. He frankly proposed a union of their interests. He admitted that they had a good thing, and that he should have to fight them hard; but he meant to fight them to the death unless they could come to some sort of terms. Now, the question was whether they had better go on and make a heavy loss for both sides by competition, or whether they had better form a partnership to run both paints and command the whole market. Lapham made them three propositions, each of which was fair and open: to sell out to them altogether; to buy them out altogether; to join facilities and forces with them, and go on in an invulnerable alliance. Let them name a figure at which they would buy, a figure at which they would sell, a figure at which they would combine,—or, in other words, the amount of capital they needed.

They talked all day, going out to lunch together at the Astor House, and sitting with their knees against the counter on a row of stools before it for fifteen minutes of reflection and deglutition,[2] with their hats on, and then returning to the basement from which they emerged. The West Virginia company's name was lettered in gilt on the wide low window, and its paint, in the form of ore, burnt, and mixed, formed a display on the window shelf. Lapham examined it and praised it; from time to time they all recurred to it together; they sent out for some of Lapham's paint and compared it, the West

2. Swallowing. The Astor House was a fashionable New York hotel.

Virginians admitting its former superiority. They were young fellows, and country persons, like Lapham, by origin, and they looked out with the same amused, undaunted, provincial eyes at the myriad metropolitan legs passing on the pavement above the level of their window. He got on well with them. At last, they said what they would do. They said it was nonsense to talk of buying Lapham out, for they had not the money; and as for selling out, they would not do it, for they knew they had a big thing. But they would as soon use his capital to develop it as anybody else's, and if he could put in a certain sum for this purpose, they would go in with him. He should run the works at Lapham and manage the business in Boston, and they would run the works at Kanawha Falls[3] and manage the business in New York. The two brothers with whom Lapham talked named their figure, subject to the approval of another brother at Kanawha Falls, to whom they would write, and who would telegraph his answer, so that Lapham could have it inside of three days. But they felt perfectly sure that he would approve; and Lapham started back on the eleven o'clock train with an elation that gradually left him as he drew near Boston, where the difficulties of raising this sum were to be overcome. It seemed to him, then, that those fellows had put it up on him pretty steep, but he owned to himself that they had a sure thing, and that they were right in believing they could raise the same sum elsewhere; it would take all of it, he admitted, to make their paint pay on the scale they had the right to expect. At their age, he would not have done differently; but when he emerged, old, sore, and sleep broken, from the sleeping-car in the Albany depot at Boston, he wished with a pathetic self-pity that they knew how a man felt at his age. A year ago, six months ago, he would have laughed at the notion that it would be hard to raise the money. But he thought ruefully of that immense stock of paint on hand, which was now a drug in the market, of his losses by Rogers and by the failures of other men, of the fire that had licked up so many thousands in a few hours; he thought with bitterness of the tens of thousands that he had gambled away in stocks, and of the commissions that the brokers had pocketed whether he won or lost; and he could not think of any securities on which he could borrow, except his house in Nankeen Square, or the mine and works at Lapham. He set his teeth in helpless rage when he thought of that property out on the G. L. & P., that ought to be worth so much, and was worth so little if the road chose to say so.

He did not go home, but spent most of the day shinning round, as he would have expressed it, and trying to see if he could raise the

3. A small community on the banks of the Kanawha River in south-central West Virginia.

money. But he found that people of whom he hoped to get it were in the conspiracy which had been formed to drive him to the wall. Somehow, there seemed a sense of his embarrassments abroad. Nobody wanted to lend money on the plant at Lapham without taking time to look into the state of the business; but Lapham had no time to give, and he knew that the state of the business would not bear looking into. He could raise fifteen thousand on his Nankeen Square house, and another fifteen on his Beacon street lot, and this was all that a man who was worth a million by rights could do! He said a million, and he said it in defiance of Bellingham, who had subjected his figures to an analysis which wounded Lapham more than he chose to show at the time, for it proved that he was not so rich and not so wise as he had seemed. His hurt vanity forbade him to go to Bellingham now for help or advice; and if he could have brought himself to ask his brothers for money, it would have been useless; they were simply well-to-do Western people, but not capitalists on the scale he required.

Lapham stood in the isolation to which adversity so often seems to bring men. When its test was applied, practically or theoretically, to all those who had seemed his friends, there was none who bore it; and he thought with bitter self-contempt of the people whom he had befriended in their time of need. He said to himself that he had been a fool for that; and he scorned himself for certain acts of scrupulosity by which he had lost money in the past. Seeing the moral forces all arrayed against him, Lapham said that he would like to have the chance offered him to get even with them again; he thought he should know how to look out for himself. As he understood it, he had several days to turn about in, and he did not let one day's failure dishearten him. The morning after his return he had, in fact, a gleam of luck that gave him the greatest encouragement for the moment. A man came in to inquire about one of Rogers's wild-cat patents,[4] as Lapham called them, and ended by buying it. He got it, of course, for less than Lapham took it for, but Lapham was glad to be rid of it for something, when he had thought it worth nothing; and when the transaction was closed, he asked the purchaser rather eagerly if he knew where Rogers was; it was Lapham's secret belief that Rogers had found there was money in the thing, and had sent the man to buy it. But it appeared that this was a mistake; the man had not come from Rogers, but had heard of the patent in another way; and Lapham was astonished in the afternoon, when his boy came to tell him that Rogers was in the outer office, and wished to speak with him.

4. Speculative investments in patents for ideas or designs that have not yet been developed into products, and may never be.

"All right," said Lapham, and he could not command at once the severity for the reception of Rogers which he would have liked to use. He found himself, in fact, so much relaxed towards him by the morning's touch of prosperity that he asked him to sit down, gruffly, of course, but distinctly; and when Rogers said in his lifeless way, and with the effect of keeping his appointment of a month before, "Those English parties are in town, and would like to talk with you in reference to the mills," Lapham did not turn him out-of-doors.

He sat looking at him, and trying to make out what Rogers was after; for he did not believe that the English parties, if they existed, had any notion of buying his mills.

"What if they are not for sale?" he asked. "You know that I've been expecting an offer from the G. L. & P."

"I've kept watch of that. They haven't made you any offer," said Rogers quietly.

"And did you think," demanded Lapham, firing up, "that I would turn them in on somebody else as you turned them in on me, when the chances are that they won't be worth ten cents on the dollar six months from now?"

"I didn't know what you would do," said Rogers, non-committally. "I've come here to tell you that these parties stand ready to take the mills off your hands at a fair valuation—at the value I put upon them when I turned them in."

"I don't believe you!" cried Lapham brutally, but a wild, predatory hope made his heart leap so that it seemed to turn over in his breast. "I don't believe there are any such parties to begin with; and in the next place, I don't believe they would buy at any such figure; unless—unless you've lied to them, as you've lied to me. Did you tell them about the G. L. & P.?"

Rogers looked compassionately at him, but he answered, with unvaried dryness, "I did not think that necessary."

Lapham had expected this answer, and he had expected or intended to break out in furious denunciation of Rogers when he got it; but he only found himself saying, in a sort of baffled gasp, "I wonder what your game is!"

Rogers did not reply categorically, but he answered, with his impartial calm, and as if Lapham had said nothing to indicate that he differed at all with him as to disposing of the property in the way he had suggested: "If we should succeed in selling, I should be able to repay you your loans, and should have a little capital for a scheme that I think of going into."

"And do you think that I am going to steal these men's money to help you plunder somebody in a new scheme?" answered Lapham. The sneer was on behalf of virtue, but it was still a sneer.

"I suppose the money would be useful to you too, just now."

"Why?"

"Because I know that you have been trying to borrow."

At this proof of wicked omniscience in Rogers, the question whether he had better not regard the affair as a fatality, and yield to his destiny, flashed upon Lapham; but he answered, "I shall want money a great deal worse than I've ever wanted it yet, before I go into such rascally business with you. Don't you know that we might as well knock these parties down on the street, and take the money out of their pockets?"

"They have come on," answered Rogers, "from Portland to see you. I expected them some weeks ago, but they disappointed me. They arrived on the *Circassian* last night; they expected to have got in five days ago, but the passage was very stormy."

"Where are they?" asked Lapham, with helpless irrelevance, and feeling himself somehow drifted from his moorings by Rogers's shipping intelligence.

"They are at Young's.[5] I told them we would call upon them after dinner this evening; they dine late."

"Oh, you did, did you?" asked Lapham, trying to drop another anchor for a fresh clutch on his underlying principles. "Well, now, you go and tell them that I said I wouldn't come."

"Their stay is limited," remarked Rogers. "I mentioned this evening because they were not certain they could remain over another night. But if to-morrow would suit you better——"

"Tell 'em I sha'n't come at all," roared Lapham, as much in terror as defiance, for he felt his anchor dragging. "Tell 'em I sha'n't come at all! Do you understand that?"

"I don't see why you should stickle as to the matter of going to them," said Rogers; "but if you think it will be better to have them approach you, I suppose I can bring them to you."

"No, you can't! I sha'n't let you! I sha'n't see them! I sha'n't have anything to do with them. *Now* do you understand?"

"I inferred from our last interview," persisted Rogers, unmoved by all this violent demonstration of Lapham's, "that you wished to meet these parties. You told me that you would give me time to produce them; and I have promised them that you would meet them; I have committed myself."

It was true that Lapham had defied Rogers to bring on his men, and had implied his willingness to negotiate with them. That was before he had talked the matter over with his wife, and perceived his moral responsibility in it; even she had not seen this at once. He could not enter into this explanation with Rogers; he could only say,

5. A downtown Boston hotel.

"I said I'd give you twenty-four hours to prove yourself a liar, and you did it. I didn't say twenty-four days."

"I don't see the difference," returned Rogers. "The parties are here now, and that proves that I was acting in good faith at the time. There has been no change in the posture of affairs. You don't know now any more than you knew then that the G. L. & P. is going to want the property. If there's any difference, it's in favor of the Road's having changed its mind."

There was some sense in this, and Lapham felt it—felt it only too eagerly, as he recognized the next instant.

Rogers went on quietly: "You're not obliged to sell to these parties when you meet them; but you've allowed me to commit myself to them by the promise that you would talk with them."

"'Twa'n't a promise," said Lapham.

"It was the same thing; they have come out from England on my guaranty that there was such and such an opening for their capital; and now what am I to say to them? It places me in a ridiculous position." Rogers urged his grievance calmly, almost impersonally, making his appeal to Lapham's sense of justice. "I *can't* go back to those parties and tell them you won't see them. It's no answer to make. They've got a right to know *why* you won't see them."

"Very well, then!" cried Lapham; "I'll come and *tell* them why. Who shall I ask for? When shall I be there?"

"At eight o'clock, please," said Rogers, rising, without apparent alarm at his threat, if it was a threat. "And ask for me; I've taken a room at the hotel for the present."

"I won't keep you five minutes when I get there," said Lapham; but he did not come away till ten o'clock.

It appeared to him as if the very devil was in it. The Englishmen treated his downright refusal to sell as a piece of bluff, and talked on as though it were merely the opening of the negotiation. When he became plain with them in his anger, and told them why he would not sell, they seemed to have been prepared for this as a stroke of business, and were ready to meet it.

"Has this fellow," he demanded, twisting his head in the direction of Rogers, but disdaining to notice him otherwise, "been telling you that it's part of my game to say this? Well, sir, I can tell you, on my side, that there isn't a slipperier rascal unhung in America than Milton K. Rogers!"

The Englishmen treated this as a piece of genuine American humor, and returned to the charge with unabated courage. They owned now, that a person interested with them had been out to look at the property, and that they were satisfied with the appearance of things. They developed further the fact that they were not acting solely, or even principally, in their own behalf, but were the agents of people in England who had projected the colonization of a sort of community on the spot, somewhat after the plan of other English dreamers,[6] and that they were satisfied, from a careful inspection, that the resources and facilities were those best calculated to develop the energy and enterprise of the proposed community. They were prepared to meet Mr. Lapham—Colonel, they begged his pardon, at the instance of Rogers—at any reasonable figure, and were quite willing to assume the risks he had pointed out. Something in the eyes of these men, something that lurked at an infinite depth below their speech, and was not really in their eyes when Lapham looked again, had flashed through him a sense of treachery in them. He had thought them the dupes of Rogers; but in that brief instant he had seen them—or thought he had seen them—his accomplices, ready to betray the interests of which they went on to speak with a certain comfortable jocosity, and a certain incredulous slight of his show of integrity. It was a deeper game than Lapham was used to, and he sat looking with a sort of admiration from one Englishman to the other, and then to Rogers, who maintained an exterior of modest neutrality, and whose air said, "I have brought you gentlemen together as the friend of all parties, and I now leave you to settle it among yourselves. I ask nothing, and expect nothing, except the small sum which shall accrue to me after the discharge of my obligations to Colonel Lapham."

While Rogers's presence expressed this, one of the Englishmen was saying, "And if you have any scruple in allowin' us to assume this risk, Colonel Lapham, perhaps you can console yourself with the fact that the loss, if there is to be any, will fall upon people who are able to bear it—upon an association of rich and charitable people. But we're quite satisfied there will be no loss," he added savingly. "All you have to do is to name your price, and we will do our best to meet it."

There was nothing in the Englishman's sophistry very shocking to Lapham. It addressed itself in him to that easy-going, not evilly intentioned, potential immorality which regards common property as common prey, and gives us the most corrupt municipal governments under the sun—which makes the poorest voter, when he has tricked into place, as unscrupulous in regard to others' money as an hereditary prince. Lapham met the Englishman's eye, and with difficulty kept himself from winking. Then he looked away, and tried to find out where he stood, or what he wanted to do. He could hardly tell. He had expected to come into that room and unmask Rogers,

6. Significant numbers of planned communities were founded in the United Sates in the 19th century to further social, political, and moral reform according to a variety of religious or secular utopian ideologies.

and have it over. But he had unmasked Rogers without any effect whatever, and the play had only begun. He had a whimsical and sarcastic sense of its being very different from the plays at the theater. He could not get up and go away in silent contempt; he could not tell the Englishmen that he believed them a pair of scoundrels and should have nothing to do with them; he could no longer treat them as innocent dupes. He remained baffled and perplexed, and the one who had not spoken hitherto remarked:

"Of course we sha'n't 'aggle about a few pound, more or less. If Colonel Lapham's figure should be a little larger than ours, I've no doubt 'e'll not be too 'ard upon us in the end."

Lapham appreciated all the intent of this subtle suggestion, and understood as plainly as if it had been said in so many words, that if they paid him a larger price, it was to be expected that a certain portion of the purchase money was to return to their own hands. Still he could not move; and it seemed to him that he could not speak.

"Ring that bell, Mr. Rogers," said the Englishman who had last spoken, glancing at the annunciator button in the wall near Rogers's head, "and 'ave up something 'ot, can't you? I should like to wet me w'istle, as you say 'ere, and Colonel Lapham seems to find it rather dry work."

Lapham jumped to his feet, and buttoned his overcoat about him. He remembered with terror the dinner at Corey's where he had disgraced and betrayed himself, and if he went into this thing at all, he was going into it sober. "I can't stop," he said, "I must be going."

"But you haven't given us an answer yet, Mr. Lapham," said the first Englishman with a successful show of dignified surprise.

"The only answer I can give you now is, *No*," said Lapham. "If you want another, you must let me have time to think it over."

"But 'ow much time?" said the other Englishman. "We're pressed for time ourselves, and we hoped for an answer—'oped for a hanswer," he corrected himself,[7] "at once. That was our understandin' with Mr. Rogers."

"I can't let you know till morning, anyway," said Lapham, and he went out, as his custom often was, without any parting salutation. He thought Rogers might try to detain him; but Rogers had remained seated when the others got to their feet, and paid no attention to his departure.

He walked out into the night air, every pulse throbbing with the strong temptation. He knew very well those men would wait, and gladly wait, till the morning, and that the whole affair was in his

7. The speaker's self-correction suggests that Rogers's associates are only pretending to be Englishmen.

hands. It made him groan in spirit to think that it was. If he had hoped that some chance might take the decision from him, there was no such chance, in the present or future, that he could see. It was for him alone to commit this rascality—if it was a rascality—or not.

He walked all the way home, letting one car after another pass him on the street, now so empty of other passing, and it was almost eleven o'clock when he reached home. A carriage stood before his house, and when he let himself in with his key, he heard talking in the family-room. It came into his head that Irene had got back unexpectedly, and that the sight of her was somehow going to make it harder for him; then he thought it might be Corey, come upon some desperate pretext to see Penelope; but when he opened the door he saw, with a certain absence of surprise, that it was Rogers. He was standing with his back to the fire-place, talking to Mrs. Lapham, and he had been shedding tears; dry tears they seemed, and they had left a sort of sandy, glistening trace on his cheeks. Apparently he was not ashamed of them, for the expression with which he met Lapham was that of a man making a desperate appeal in his own cause, which was identical with that of humanity, if not that of justice.

"I some expected," began Rogers, "to find you here——"

"No, you didn't," interrupted Lapham; "you wanted to come here and make a poor mouth to Mrs. Lapham before I got home."

"I knew that Mrs. Lapham would know what was going on," said Rogers, more candidly, but not more virtuously, for that he could not, "and I wished her to understand a point that I hadn't put to you at the hotel, and that I want you should consider. And I want you should consider me a little in this business, too; you're not the only one that's concerned, I tell you, and I've been telling Mrs. Lapham that it's my one chance; that if you don't meet me on it, my wife and children will be reduced to beggary."

"So will mine," said Lapham, "or the next thing to it."

"Well, then, I want you to give me this chance to get on my feet again. You've no right to deprive me of it; it's unchristian. In our dealings with each other we should be guided by the Golden Rule, as I was saying to Mrs. Lapham before you came in. I told her that if I knew myself, I should in your place consider the circumstances of a man in mine, who had honorably endeavored to discharge his obligations to me, and had patiently borne my undeserved suspicions. I should consider that man's family, I told Mrs. Lapham."

"Did you tell her that if I went in with you and those fellows, I should be robbing the people who trusted them?"

"I don't see what you've got to do with the people that sent them here. They are rich people, and could bear it if it came to the worst. But there's no likelihood, now, that it will come to the worst; you can see yourself that the Road has changed its mind about buying. And here am I without a cent in the world; and my wife is an invalid. She needs comforts, she needs little luxuries, and she hasn't even the necessaries; and you want to sacrifice her to a mere, idea! You don't know in the first place that the Road will ever want to buy; and if it does, the probability is that with a colony like that planted on its line, it would make very different terms from what it would with you or me. These agents are not afraid, and their principals are rich people; and if there was any loss, it would be divided up amongst them so that they wouldn't any of them feel it."

Lapham stole a troubled glance at his wife, and saw that there was no help in her. Whether she was daunted and confused in her own conscience by the outcome, so evil and disastrous, of the reparation to Rogers which she had forced her husband to make, or whether her perceptions had been blunted and darkened by the appeals which Rogers had now used, it would be difficult to say. Probably there was a mixture of both causes in the effect which her husband felt in her, and from which he turned, girding himself anew, to Rogers.

"I have no wish to recur to the past," continued Rogers, with growing superiority. "You have shown a proper spirit in regard to that, and you have done what you could to wipe it out."

"I should think I had," said Lapham. "I've used up about a hundred and fifty thousand dollars trying."

"Some of my enterprises," Rogers admitted, "have been unfortunate, seemingly; but I have hopes that they will yet turn out well—in time. I can't understand why you should be so mindful of others now, when you showed so little regard for me then. I had come to your aid at a time when you needed help, and when you got on your feet you kicked me out of the business. I don't complain, but that is the fact; and I had to begin again, after I had supposed myself settled in life, and establish myself elsewhere."

Lapham glanced again at his wife; her head had fallen; he could see that she was so rooted in her old remorse for that questionable act of his, amply and more than fully atoned for since, that she was helpless, now in the crucial moment, when he had the utmost need of her insight. He had counted upon her; he perceived now that when he had thought it was for him alone to decide, he had counted upon her just spirit to stay his own in its struggle to be just. He had not forgotten how she held out against him only a little while ago, when he asked her whether he might not rightfully sell in some such contingency as this; and it was not now that she said or even looked anything in favor of Rogers, but that she was silent against him, which dismayed Lapham. He swallowed the lump that rose in his throat, the self-pity, the pity for her, the despair, and said gently, "I guess you better go to bed, Persis. It's pretty late."

She turned towards the door, when Rogers said, with the obvious intention of detaining her through her curiosity:

"But I let that pass. And I don't ask now that you should sell to these men."

Mrs. Lapham paused, irresolute.

"What are you making this bother for, then?" demanded Lapham. "What *do* you want?"

"What I've been telling your wife here. I want you should sell to *me*. I don't say what I'm going to do with the property, and you will not have an iota of responsibility, whatever happens."

Lapham was staggered, and he saw his wife's face light up with eager question.

"I want that property," continued Rogers, "and I've got the money to buy it. What will you take for it? If it's the price you're standing out for——"

"Persis," said Lapham, "go to bed," and he gave her a look that meant obedience for her. She went out of the door, and left him with his tempter.

"If you think I'm going to help you whip the devil round the stump,[8] you're mistaken in your man, Milton Rogers," said Lapham, lighting a cigar. "As soon as I sold to you, you would sell to that other pair of rascals. *I* smelt 'em out in half a minute."

"They are Christian gentlemen," said Rogers. "But I don't purpose defending them; and I don't purpose telling you what I shall or shall not do with the property when it is in my hands again. The question is, Will you sell, and, if so, what is your figure? You have got nothing whatever to do with it after you've sold."

It was perfectly true. Any lawyer would have told him the same. He could not help admiring Rogers for his ingenuity, and every selfish interest of his nature joined with many obvious duties to urge him to consent. He did not see why he should refuse. There was no longer a reason. He was standing out alone for nothing, any one else would say. He smoked on as if Rogers were not there, and Rogers remained before the fire as patient as the clock ticking behind his head on the mantel, and showing the gleam of its pendulum beyond his face on either side. But at last he said, "Well?"

"Well," answered Lapham, "you can't expect me to give you an answer to-night, any more than before. You know that what you've said now hasn't changed the thing a bit. I wish it had. The Lord knows, I want to be rid of the property fast enough."

"Then why don't you sell to me? Can't you see that you will not be responsible for what happens after you have sold?"

"No, I *can't* see that; but if I can by morning, I'll sell."

8. Evade responsibility (idiom).

"Why do you expect to know any better by morning? You're wasting time for nothing!" cried Rogers, in his disappointment. "Why are you so particular? When you drove me out of the business you were not so very particular."

Lapham winced. It was certainly ridiculous for a man who had once so selfishly consulted his own interests to be stickling now about the rights of others.

"I guess nothing's going to happen overnight," he answered sullenly. "Anyway, I sha'n't say what I shall do till morning."

"What time can I see you in the morning?"

"Half-past nine."

Rogers buttoned his coat, and went out of the room without another word. Lapham followed him to close the street-door after him.

His wife called down to him from above as he approached the room again, "Well?"

"I've told him I'd let him know in the morning."

"Want I should come down and talk with you?"

"No," answered Lapham, in the proud bitterness which his isolation brought, "you couldn't do any good." He went in and shut the door, and by and by his wife heard him begin walking up and down; and then the rest of the night she lay awake and listened to him walking up and down. But when the first light whitened the window, the words of the Scripture came into her mind: "And there wrestled a man with him until the breaking of the day. . . . And he said, Let me go, for the day breaketh. And he said, I will not let thee go, except thou bless me."[9]

She could not ask him anything when they met, but he raised his dull eyes after the first silence and said, "*I* don't know what I'm going to say to Rogers."

She could not speak; she did not know what to say, and she saw her husband, when she followed him with her eyes from the window, drag heavily down toward the corner, where he was to take the horse-car.

He arrived rather later than usual at his office, and he found his letters already on his table. There was one, long and official-looking, with a printed letter-heading on the outside, and Lapham had no need to open it in order to know that it was the offer of the Great Lacustrine & Polar Railroad for his mills. But he went mechanically through the verification of his prophetic fear, which was also his sole hope, and then sat looking blankly at it.

Rogers came promptly at the appointed time, and Lapham handed him the letter. He must have taken it all in at a glance, and seen the

9. Genesis 32.24 and 26 relate part of the story of Jacob's nighttime wrestling match with an angel of God.

impossibility of negotiating any further now, even with victims so pliant and willing as those Englishmen.

"You've ruined me!" Rogers broke out. "I haven't a cent left in the world! God help my poor wife!"

He went out, and Lapham remained staring at the door which closed upon him. This was his reward for standing firm for right and justice to his own destruction: to feel like a thief and a murderer.

[TENTH INSTALLMENT—AUGUST 1885]

XXVI.

Later in the forenoon came the dispatch from the West Virginians in New York, saying their brother assented to their agreement; and it now remained for Lapham to fulfill his part of it. He was ludicrously far from able to do this; and unless he could get some extension of time from them, he must lose this chance, his only chance, to retrieve himself. He spent the time in a desperate endeavor to raise the money, but he had not raised the half of it when the banks closed. With shame in his heart he went to Bellingham, from whom he had parted so haughtily, and laid his plan before him. He could not bring himself to ask Bellingham's help, but he told him what he proposed to do. Bellingham pointed out that the whole thing was an experiment, and that the price asked was enormous, unless a great success were morally certain. He advised delay, he advised prudence; he insisted that Lapham ought at least to go out to Kanawha Falls, and see the mines and works, before he put any such sum into the development of the enterprise.

"That's all well enough," cried Lapham; "but if I don't clinch this offer within twenty-four hours, they'll withdraw it, and go into the market; and then where am I?"

"Go on and see them again," said Bellingham. "They can't be so peremptory as that with you. They must give you time to look at what they want to sell. If it turns out what you hope, then—I'll see what can be done. But look into it thoroughly."

"Well!" cried Lapham, helplessly submitting. He took out his watch, and saw that he had forty minutes to catch the four o'clock train. He hurried back to his office, put together some papers preparatory to going, and dispatched a note by his boy to Mrs. Lapham saying that he was starting for New York, and did not know just when he should get back.

The early spring day was raw and cold. As he went out through the office he saw the clerks at work with their street coats and hats on; Miss Dewey had her jacket dragged up on her shoulders and looked particularly comfortless as she operated her machine with her red fingers. "What's up?" asked Lapham, stopping a moment.

"Seems to be something the matter with the steam," she answered, with the air of unmerited wrong habitual with so many pretty women who have to work for a living.

"Well, take your writer into my room; there's a fire in the stove there," said Lapham, passing out.

Half an hour later his wife came into the outer office. She had passed the day in a passion of self-reproach, gradually mounting from the mental numbness in which he had left her, and now she could wait no longer to tell him that she saw how she had forsaken him in his hour of trial and left him to bear it alone. She wondered at herself in shame and dismay; she wondered that she could have been so confused as to the real point by that old wretch of a Rogers, that she could have let him hoodwink her so, even for a moment. It astounded her that such a thing should have happened, for if there was any virtue upon which this good woman prided herself, in which she thought herself superior to her husband, it was her instant and steadfast perception of right and wrong, and the ability to choose the right to her own hurt. But she had now to confess, as each of us has had likewise to confess in his own case, that the very virtue on which she had prided herself was the thing that had played her false; that she had kept her mind so long upon that old wrong which she believed her husband had done this man that she could not detach it, but clung to the thought of reparation for it when she ought to have seen that he was proposing a piece of roguery as the means. The suffering which Lapham must inflict on him if he decided against him had been more to her apprehension than the harm he might do if he decided for him. But now she owned her limitations to herself, and above everything in the world she wished the man whom her conscience had roused and driven on whither her intelligence had not followed, to do right, to do what he felt to be right, and nothing else. She admired and revered him for going beyond her, and she wished to tell him that she did not know what he had determined to do about Rogers, but that she knew it was right, and would gladly abide the consequences with him, whatever they were.

She had not been near his place of business for nearly a year, and her heart smote her tenderly as she looked about her there, and thought of the early days when she knew as much about the paint as he did; she wished that those days were back again. She saw Corey at his desk, and she could not bear to speak to him; she dropped her veil that she need not recognize him, and pushed on to Lapham's room, and, opening the door without knocking, shut it behind her.

Then she became aware with intolerable disappointment that her husband was not there. Instead, a very pretty girl sat at his desk, operating a type-writer. She seemed quite at home, and she paid Mrs. Lapham the scant attention which such young women often bestow upon people not personally interesting to them. It vexed the wife that any one else should seem to be helping her husband about business that she had once been so intimate with; and she did not at all like the girl's indifference to her presence. Her hat and sack hung on a nail in one corner, and Lapham's office coat, looking intensely like him to his wife's familiar eye, hung on a nail in the other corner; and Mrs. Lapham liked even less than the girl's good looks this domestication of her garments in her husband's office. She began to ask herself excitedly why he should be away from his office when she happened to come; and she had not the strength at the moment to reason herself out of her unreasonableness.

"When will Colonel Lapham be in, do you suppose?" she sharply asked of the girl.

"I couldn't say exactly," replied the girl, without looking round.

"Has he been out long?"

"I don't know as I noticed," said the girl, looking up at the clock, without looking at Mrs. Lapham. She went on working her machine.

"Well, I can't wait any longer," said the wife abruptly. "When Colonel Lapham comes in, you please tell him Mrs. Lapham wants to see him."

The girl started to her feet and turned toward Mrs. Lapham with a red and startled face, which she did not lift to confront her. "Yes—yes—I will," she faltered.

The wife went home with a sense of defeat mixed with an irritation about this girl which she could not quell or account for. She found her husband's message, and it seemed intolerable that he should have gone to New York without seeing her; she asked herself in vain what the mysterious business could be that took him away so suddenly. She said to herself that he was neglecting her; he was leaving her out a little too much; and in demanding of herself why he had never mentioned that girl there in his office, she forgot how much she had left herself out of his business life. That was another curse of their prosperity. Well, she was glad the prosperity was going; it had never been happiness. After this she was going to know everything as she used.

She tried to dismiss the whole matter till Lapham returned; and if there had been anything for her to do in that miserable house, as she called it in her thought, she might have succeeded. But again the curse was on her; there was nothing to do; and the looks of that girl kept coming back to her vacancy, her disoccupation. She tried to make herself something to do, but that beauty, which she had not liked, followed her amid the work of overhauling the summer clothing, which Irene had seen to putting away in the fall. Who was the thing, anyway? It was very strange, her being there; why did she jump up in that frightened way when Mrs. Lapham had named herself?

After dark that evening, when the question had worn away its poignancy from mere iteration, a note for Mrs. Lapham was left at the door by a messenger who said there was no answer. "A note for me?" she said, staring at the unknown, and somehow artificial-looking, handwriting of the superscription. Then she opened it and read: "Ask your husband about his lady copying-clerk. A Friend and Well-wisher," who signed the note, gave no other name.

Mrs. Lapham sat helpless with it in her hand. Her brain reeled; she tried to fight the madness off; but before Lapham came back the second morning, it had become, with lessening intervals of sanity and release, a demoniacal possession. She passed the night without sleep, without rest, in the frenzy of the cruelest of the passions, which covers with shame the unhappy soul it possesses, and murderously lusts for the misery of its object. If she had known where to find her husband in New York, she would have followed him; she waited his return in an ecstasy of impatience. In the morning he came back, looking spent and haggard. She saw him drive up to the door, and she ran to let him in herself.

"Who is that girl you've got in your office, Silas Lapham?" she demanded, when her husband entered.

"Girl in my office?"

"Yes! Who is she? What is she doing there?"

"Why, what have you heard about her?"

"Never you mind what I've heard. Who is she? *Is it Mrs. M. that you gave that money to?* I want to know who she is! I want to know what a respectable man, with grown-up girls of his own, is doing with such a looking thing as that in his office! I want to know how long she's been there! I want to know what she's there at all for!"

He had mechanically pushed her before him into the long, darkened parlor, and he shut himself in there with her now, to keep the household from hearing her lifted voice. For a while he stood bewildered, and could not have answered if he would; and then he would not. He merely asked, "Have I ever accused you of anything wrong, Persis?"

"You no need to!" she answered furiously, placing herself against the closed door.

"Did you ever know me to do anything out of the way?"

"That isn't what I asked you."

"Well, I guess you may find out about that girl yourself. Get away from the door."

"I won't get away from the door."

She felt herself set lightly aside, and her husband opened the door and went out. "I *will* find out about her," she screamed after him. "I'll find out, and I'll disgrace you—I'll teach you how to treat me!"

The air blackened round her; she reeled to the sofa; and then she found herself waking from a faint. She did not know how long she had lain there; she did not care. In a moment her madness came whirling back upon her. She rushed up to his room; it was empty; the closet-doors stood ajar and the drawers were open; he must have packed a bag hastily and fled. She went out, and wandered crazily up and down till she found a hack. She gave the driver her husband's business address, and told him to drive there as fast as he could; and three times she lowered the window to put her head out and ask him if he could not hurry. A thousand things thronged into her mind to support her in her evil will. She remembered how glad and proud that man had been to marry her, and how everybody said she was marrying beneath her when she took him. She remembered how good she had always been to him, how perfectly devoted, slaving early and late to advance him, and looking out for his interests in all things, and sparing herself in nothing. If it had not been for her, he might have been driving stage yet; and since their troubles had begun, the troubles which his own folly and imprudence had brought on them, her conduct had been that of a true and faithful wife. Was *he* the sort of man to be allowed to play her false with impunity? She set her teeth and drew her breath sharply through them, when she thought how willingly she had let him befool her and delude her about that memorandum of payments to Mrs. M., because she loved him so much, and pitied him for his cares and anxieties. She recalled his confusion, his guilty looks.

She plunged out of the carriage so hastily when she reached the office that she did not think of paying the driver; and he had to call after her when she had got half-way up the stairs. Then she went straight to Lapham's room, with outrage in her heart. There was again no one there but that type-writer girl; she jumped to her feet in a fright, as Mrs. Lapham dashed the door to behind her and flung up her veil.

The two women confronted each other.

"Why, the good land!" cried Mrs. Lapham, "ain't you Zerrilla Millon?"

"I—I'm married," faltered the girl. "My name's Dewey now."

"You're Jim Millon's daughter, anyway. How long have you been here?"

"I haven't been here regularly; I've been here off and on ever since last May."

"Where's your mother?"

"She's here—in Boston."

Mrs. Lapham kept her eyes on the girl, but she dropped, trembling, into her husband's chair, and a sort of amaze and curiosity were in her voice instead of the fury she had meant to put there.

"The Colonel," continued Zerrilla, "he's been helping us, and he's got me a typewriter, so that I can help myself a little. Mother's doing pretty well now; and when Hen isn't around we can get along."

"That your husband?"

"I never wanted to marry him; but he promised to try to get something to do on shore; and mother was all for it, because he had a little property then, and I thought maybe I'd better. But it's turned out just as I said, and if he don't stay away long enough this time to let me get the divorce,—he's agreed to it, time and again,—I don't know what we're going to do." Zerrilla's voice fell, and the trouble which she could keep out of her face usually, when she was comfortably warmed and fed and prettily dressed, clouded it in the presence of a sympathetic listener. "I saw it was you when you came in the other day," she went on; "but you didn't seem to know me. I suppose the Colonel's told you that there's a gentleman going to marry me—Mr. Wemmel's his name—as soon as I get the divorce; but sometimes I'm completely discouraged; it don't seem as if I ever *could* get it."

Mrs. Lapham would not let her know that she was ignorant of the fact attributed to her knowledge. She remained listening to Zerrilla, and piecing out the whole history of her presence there from the facts of the past, and the traits of her husband's character. One of the things she had always had to fight him about was that idea of his that he was bound to take care of Jim Millon's worthless wife and her child because Millon had got the bullet that was meant for him. It was a perfect superstition of his; she could not beat it out of him; but she had made him promise the last time he had done anything for that woman that it should *be* the last time. He had then got her a little house in one of the fishing ports, where she could take the sailors to board and wash for, and earn an honest living if she would keep straight. That was five or six years ago, and Mrs. Lapham had heard nothing of Mrs. Millon since; she had heard quite enough of her before, and had known her idle and baddish ever since she was the worst little girl at school in Lumberville, and all through her shameful girlhood, and the married days which she had made so miserable to the poor fellow who had given her his decent name and a chance to behave herself. Mrs. Lapham had no mercy on Moll Millon, and she had quarreled often enough with her husband for befriending her. As for the child, if the mother would put Zerrilla out with some respectable family, that would be *one* thing; but as long as she kept Zerrilla with her, she was against letting her husband do anything for either of them. He had done ten times as much for them now as he had any need to, and she had made him give her his solemn word that he would do no more. She saw now that she was wrong to make him give it, and that he must have broken it again and again for the reason that he had given when she once scolded him for throwing away his money on that hussy:

"When I think of Jim Millon, I've *got* to; that's all."

She recalled now that whenever she had brought up the subject of Mrs. Millon and her daughter, he had seemed shy of it, and had dropped it with some guess that they were getting along now. She wondered that she had not thought at once of Mrs. Millon when she saw that memorandum about Mrs. M.; but the woman had passed so entirely out of her life, that she had never dreamt of her in connection with it. Her husband had deceived her, yet her heart was no longer hot against him, but rather tenderly grateful that his deceit was in this sort, and not in that other. All cruel and shameful doubt of him went out of it. She looked at this beautiful girl, who had blossomed out of her knowledge since she saw her last, and she knew that she was only a blossomed weed, of the same worthless root as her mother, and saved, if saved, from the same evil destiny by the good of her father in her; but so far as the girl and her mother were concerned, Mrs. Lapham knew that her husband was to blame for nothing but his willful, wrong-headed kind-heartedness, which her own exactions had turned into deceit. She remained awhile, questioning the girl quietly about herself and her mother, and then, with a better mind towards Zerrilla, at least, than she had ever had before, she rose up and went out. There must have been some outer hint of the exhaustion in which the subsidence of her excitement had left her within, for before she had reached the head of the stairs, Corey came towards her.

"Can I be of any use to you, Mrs. Lapham? The Colonel was here just before you came in, on his way to the train."

"Yes,—yes. I didn't know—I thought perhaps I could catch him here. But it don't matter. I wish you would let some one go with me to get a carriage," she begged feebly.

"I'll go with you myself," said the young fellow, ignoring the strangeness in her manner. He offered her his arm in the twilight of the staircase, and she was glad to put her trembling hand through it, and keep it there till he helped her into a hack which he found for her. He gave the driver her direction, and stood looking a little anxiously at her.

"I thank you; I am all right now," she said, and he bade the man drive on.

When she reached home she went to bed, spent with the tumult of her emotions and sick with shame and self-reproach. She understood now, as clearly as if he had told her in so many words, that if he had befriended these worthless jades—the Millons characterized themselves so, even to Mrs. Lapham's remorse—secretly and in defiance of her, it was because he dreaded her blame, which was so sharp and bitter, for what he could not help doing. It consoled her that he had defied her; deceived her; when he came back she should tell him that; and then it flashed upon her that she did not know where he was gone, or whether he would ever come again. If he never came, it would be no more than she deserved; but she sent for Penelope, and tried to give herself hopes of escape from this just penalty.

Lapham had not told his daughter where he was going; she had heard him packing his bag, and had offered to help him; but he had said he could do it best, and had gone off, as he usually did, without taking leave of any one.

"What were you talking about so loud, down in the parlor," she asked her mother, "just before he came up? Is there any new trouble?"

"No; it was nothing."

"I couldn't tell. Once I thought you were laughing." She went about, closing the curtains on account of her mother's headache, and doing awkwardly and imperfectly the things that Irene would have done so skillfully for her comfort.

The day wore away to nightfall, and then Mrs. Lapham said she *must* know. Penelope said there was no one to ask; the clerks would all be gone home; and her mother said yes, there was Mr. Corey; they could send and ask him; he would know.

The girl hesitated. "Very well," she said then, scarcely above a whisper, and she presently laughed huskily. "Mr. Corey seems fated to come in somewhere. I guess it's a Providence, mother."

She sent off a note, inquiring whether he could tell her just where her father had expected to be that night; and the answer came quickly back that Corey did not know, but would look up the bookkeeper and inquire. This office brought him in person, an hour later, to tell Penelope that the Colonel was to be at Lapham that night and next day.

"He came in from New York in a great hurry, and rushed off as soon as he could pack his bag," Penelope explained, "and we hadn't a chance to ask him where he was to be to-night. And mother wasn't very well, and——"

"I thought she wasn't looking well when she was at the office today; and so I thought I would come rather than send," Corey explained, in his turn.

"Oh, thank you!"

"If there is anything I can do—telegraph Colonel Lapham, or anything?"

"Oh, no, thank you; mother's better now. She merely wanted to be sure where he was."

He did not offer to go upon this conclusion of his business, but hoped he was not keeping her from her mother. She thanked him once again, and said no, that her mother was much better since she had had a cup of tea; and then they looked at each other, and without any apparent exchange of intelligence he remained, and at eleven o'clock he was still there. He was honest in saying he did not know it was so late; but he made no pretense of being sorry, and she took the blame to herself.

"I oughtn't to have let you stay," she said. "But with father gone, and all that trouble hanging over us——"

She was allowing him to hold her hand a moment at the door, to which she had followed him.

"I'm so glad you could let me!" he said; "and I want to ask you now when I may come again. But if you need me, you'll——"

A sharp pull at the door-bell outside made them start asunder, and at a sign from Penelope, who knew that the maids were abed by this time, he opened it.

"Why, Irene!" shrieked the girl.

Irene entered, with the hackman, who had driven her unheard to the door, following with her small bags, and kissed her sister with resolute composure. "That's all," she said to the hackman. "I gave my checks to the expressman," she explained to Penelope.

Corey stood helpless. Irene turned upon him, and gave him her hand. "How do you do, Mr. Corey?" she said, with a courage that sent a thrill of admiring gratitude through him. "Where's mamma, Pen? Papa gone to bed?"

Penelope faltered out some reply embodying the facts, and Irene ran up the stairs to her mother's room. Mrs. Lapham started up in bed at her apparition.

"Irene Lapham!"

"Uncle William thought he ought to tell me the trouble papa was in; and did you think I was going to stay off there junketing, while you were going through all this at home, and Pen acting so silly too? You ought to have been ashamed to let me stay so long! I started just as soon as I could pack. Did you get my dispatch? I telegraphed from Springfield. But it don't matter now. Here I am. And I don't think I need have hurried on Pen's account," she added, with an accent prophetic of the sort of old maid she would become if she happened never to marry.

"Did you see him?" asked her mother. "It's the first time he's been here since she told him he mustn't come."

"I guess it isn't the last time, by the looks," said Irene; and before she took off her bonnet she began to undo some of Penelope's mistaken arrangements of the room.

At breakfast, where Corey and his mother met the next morning before his father and sisters came down, he told her, with embarrassment which told much more, that he wished now that she would go and call upon the Laphams.

Mrs. Corey turned a little pale, but shut her lips tight and mourned in silence whatever hopes she had lately permitted herself. She answered with Roman fortitude: "Of course, if there's anything between you and Miss Lapham, your family ought to recognize it."

"Yes," said Corey.

"You were reluctant to have me call at first, but now if the affair is going on——"

"It is! I hope—yes, it is!"

"Then I ought to go and see her, with your sisters; and she ought to come here and—we ought all to see her and make the matter public. We can't do so too soon. It will seem as if we were ashamed if we don't."

"Yes, you are quite right, mother," said the young man gratefully, "and I feel how kind and good you are. I have tried to consider you in this matter, though I don't seem to have done so; I know what your rights are, and I wish with all my heart that I were meeting even your tastes perfectly. But I know you will like her when you come to know her. It's been very hard for her every way,—about her sister,—and she's made a great sacrifice for me. She's acted nobly."

Mrs Corey, whose thoughts cannot always be reported, said she was sure of it, and that all she desired was her son's happiness.

"She's been very unwilling to consider it an engagement on that account, and on account of Colonel Lapham's difficulties. I should like to have you go, now, for that very reason. I don't know just how serious the trouble is; but it isn't a time when we can seem indifferent."

The logic of this was not perhaps so apparent to the glasses of fifty as to the eyes of twenty-six; but Mrs. Corey, however she viewed it, could not allow herself to blench before the son whom she had taught that to want magnanimity was to be less than gentlemanly. She answered, with what composure she could, "I will take your sisters," and then she made some natural inquiries about Lapham's affairs.

"Oh, I hope it will come out all right," Corey said, with a lover's vague smile, and left her. When his father came down, rubbing his long hands together, and looking aloof from all the cares of the practical world, in an artistic withdrawal, from which his eye ranged over the breakfast-table before he sat down, Mrs. Corey told him what she and their son had been saying.

He laughed, with a delicate impersonal appreciation of the predicament. "Well, Anna, you can't say but if you ever were guilty of supposing yourself porcelain, this is a just punishment of your arrogance. Here you are bound by the very quality on which you've prided yourself to behave well to a bit of earthenware who is apparently in danger of losing the gilding that rendered her tolerable."

"We never cared for the money," said Mrs. Corey. "You know that."

"No; and now we can't seem to care for the loss of it. That would be still worse. Either horn of the dilemma gores us. Well, we still have the comfort we had in the beginning; we can't help ourselves, and we should only make bad worse by trying. Unless we can look to Tom's inamorata[1] herself for help."

Mrs. Corey shook her head so gloomily that her husband broke off with another laugh. But at the continued trouble of her face he said, sympathetically: "My dear, I know it's a very disagreeable affair; and I don't think either of us has failed to see that it was so from the beginning. I have had my way of expressing my sense of it, and you yours, but we have always been of the same mind about it. We would both have preferred to have Tom marry in his own set; the Laphams are about the last set we could have wished him to marry into. They *are* uncultivated people, and, so far as I have seen them, I'm not able to believe that poverty will improve them. Still, it may. Let us hope for the best, and let us behave as well as we know how. I'm sure *you* will behave well, and I shall try. I'm going with you to call on Miss Lapham. This is a thing that can't be done by halves!"

He cut his orange in the Neapolitan manner, and ate it in quarters.

XXVII.

Irene did not leave her mother in any illusion concerning her cousin Will and herself. She said they had all been as nice to her as they could be, and when Mrs. Lapham hinted at what had been in her thoughts,—or her hopes, rather,—Irene severely snubbed the notion. She said that he was as good as engaged to a girl out there, and that he had never dreamt of her. Her mother wondered at her severity; in these few months the girl had toughened and hardened; she had lost all her babyish dependence and pliability; she was like iron; and here and there she was sharpened to a cutting edge. It had been a life and death struggle with her; she had conquered, but she had also necessarily lost much. Perhaps what she had lost was not worth keeping; but at any rate she had lost it.

She required from her mother a strict and accurate account of her father's affairs, so far as Mrs. Lapham knew them; and she showed a business-like quickness in comprehending them that Penelope had never pretended to. With her sister she ignored the past as completely as it was possible to do; and she treated both Corey and Penelope with the justice which their innocence of voluntary offense deserved. It was a difficult part, and she kept away from them as much as she

1. A female sweetheart or lover (Italian).

could. She had been easily excused, on a plea of fatigue from her journey, when Mr. and Mrs. Corey had called the day after her arrival, and, Mrs. Lapham being still unwell, Penelope received them alone.

The girl had instinctively judged best that they should know the worst at once, and she let them have the full brunt of the drawing-room, while she was screwing her courage up to come down and see them. She was afterwards—months afterwards—able to report to Corey that when she entered the room his father was sitting with his hat on his knees, a little tilted away from the Emancipation group, as if he expected the Lincoln to hit him with that lifted hand of benediction; and that Mrs. Corey looked as if she were not sure but the Eagle pecked. But for the time being Penelope was as nearly crazed as might be by the complications of her position, and received her visitors with a piteous distraction which could not fail of touching Bromfield Corey's Italianized sympatheticism. He was very polite and tender with her at first, and ended by making a joke with her, to which Penelope responded in her sort. He said he hoped they parted friends, if not quite acquaintances; and she said she hoped they would be able to recognize each other if they ever met again.

"That is what I meant by her pertness," said Mrs. Corey, when they were driving away.

"Was it very pert?" he queried. "The child had to answer something."

"I would much rather she had answered nothing, under the circumstances," said Mrs. Corey. "However!" she added hopelessly.

"Oh, she's a merry little grig,[1] you can see that, and there's no harm in her. I can understand a little why a formal fellow like Tom should be taken with her. She hasn't the least reverence, I suppose, and joked with the young man from the beginning. You must remember, Anna, that there was a time when you liked my joking."

"It was a very different thing!"

"But that drawing-room!" pursued Corey; "really, I don't see how Tom stands that. Anna, a terrible thought occurs to me! Fancy Tom being married in front of that group, with a floral horse-shoe in tuberoses coming down on either side of it!"

"Bromfield!" cried his wife, "you are unmerciful."

"No, no, my dear," he argued; "merely imaginative. And I can even imagine that little thing finding Tom just the least bit slow at times, if it were not for his goodness. Tom is so kind that I'm convinced he sometimes feels your joke in his heart when his head isn't quite clear about it. Well, we will not despond, my dear."

"Your father seemed actually to like her," Mrs. Corey reported to her daughters, very much shaken in her own prejudices by the fact.

1. A cheerful or lively person.

If the girl were not so offensive to his fastidiousness, there might be some hope that she was not so offensive as Mrs. Corey had thought. "I wonder how she will strike *you*," she concluded, looking from one daughter to another, as if trying to decide which of them would like Penelope least.

Irene's return and the visit of the Coreys formed a distraction for the Laphams in which their impending troubles seemed to hang farther aloof; but it was only one of those reliefs which mark the course of adversity, and it was not one of the cheerful reliefs. At any other time, either incident would have been an anxiety and care for Mrs. Lapham which she would have found hard to bear; but now she almost welcomed them. At the end of three days Lapham returned, and his wife met him as if nothing unusual had marked their parting; she reserved her atonement for a fitter time; he would know now from the way she acted that she felt all right towards him. He took very little note of her manner, but met his family with an austere quiet that puzzled her, and a sort of pensive dignity that refined his rudeness to an effect that sometimes comes to such natures after long sickness, when the animal strength has been taxed and lowered. He sat silent with her at the table after their girls had left them alone; and seeing that he did not mean to speak, she began to explain why Irene had come home, and to praise her.

"Yes, she done right," said Lapham. "It was time for her to come," he added gently.

Then he was silent again, and his wife told him of Corey's having been there, and of his father's and mother's calling. "I guess Pen's concluded to make it up," she said.

"Well, we'll see about that," said Lapham; and now she could no longer forbear to ask him about his affairs.

"I don't know as I've got any right to know anything about it," she said humbly, with remote allusion to her treatment of him. "But I can't help wanting to know. How *are* things going, Si?"

"Bad," he said, pushing his plate from him, and tilting himself back in his chair. "Or they ain't going at all. They've stopped."

"What do you mean, Si?" she persisted tenderly.

"I've got to the end of my string. Tomorrow I shall call a meeting of my creditors, and put myself in their hands. If there's enough left to satisfy them, I'm satisfied." His voice dropped in his throat; he swallowed once or twice, and then did not speak.

"Do you mean that it's all over with you?" she asked fearfully.

He bowed his big head, wrinkled and grizzled; and after a while he said, "It's hard to realize it; but I guess there ain't any doubt about it." He drew a long breath, and then he explained to her about the West Virginia people, and how he had got an extension of the first time they had given him, and had got a man to go up to Lapham with him and look at the works,—a man that had turned up in New York, and wanted to put money in the business. His money would have enabled Lapham to close with the West Virginians. "The devil was in it, right straight along," said Lapham. "All I had to do was to keep quiet about that other company. It was Rogers and his property right over again. He liked the look of things, and he wanted to go into the business, and he had the money—plenty; it would have saved me with those West Virginia folks. But I had to tell him how I stood. I had to tell him all about it, and what I wanted to do. He began to back water in a minute, and the next morning I saw that it was up with him. He's gone back to New York. I've lost my last chance. Now all I've got to do is to save the pieces."

"Will—will—everything go?" she asked.

"I can't tell yet. But they shall have a chance at everything—every dollar, every cent. I'm sorry for you, Persis—and the girls."

"Oh, don't talk of *us!*" She was trying to realize that the simple, rude soul to which her heart clove in her youth, but which she had put to such cruel proof with her unsparing conscience and her unsparing tongue, had been equal to its ordeals, and had come out unscathed and unstained. He was able in his talk to make so little of them; he hardly seemed to see what they were; he was apparently not proud of them, and certainly not glad; if they were victories of any sort, he bore them with the patience of defeat. His wife wished to praise him, but she did not know how; so she offered him a little reproach, in which alone she touched the cause of her behavior at parting. "Silas," she asked after a long gaze at him, "why didn't you tell me you had Jim Millon's girl there?"

"I didn't suppose you'd like it, Persis," he answered. "I did intend to tell you at first, but then I put it off. I thought you'd come round some day, and find it out for yourself."

"I'm punished," said his wife, "for not taking enough interest in your business to even come near it. If we're brought back to the day of small things, I guess it's a lesson for me, Silas."

"Oh, I don't know about the lesson," he said wearily.

That night she showed him the anonymous scrawl which had kindled her fury against him. He turned it listlessly over in his hand. "I guess I know who it's from," he said, giving it back to her, "and I guess you do too, Persis."

"But how—how could he——"

"Mebbe he believed it," said Lapham, with patience that cut her more keenly than any reproach. "*You* did."

Perhaps because the process of his ruin had been so gradual, perhaps because the excitement of preceding events had exhausted their capacity for emotion, the actual consummation of his bankruptcy brought a relief, a repose to Lapham and his family, rather than a fresh sensation of calamity. In the shadow of his disaster they returned to something like their old, united life; they were at least all together again; and it will be intelligible to those whom life has blessed with vicissitude, that Lapham should come home the evening after he had given up everything to his creditors, and should sit down to his supper so cheerful that Penelope could joke him in the old way, and tell him that she thought from his looks they had concluded to pay him a hundred cents on every dollar he owed them.

As James Bellingham had taken so much interest in his troubles from the first, Lapham thought he ought to tell him, before taking the final step, just how things stood with him, and what he meant to do. Bellingham made some futile inquiries about his negotiations with the West Virginians, and Lapham told him they had come to nothing. He spoke of the New York man, and the chance that he might have sold out half his business to him. "But, of course, I had to let him know how it was about those fellows."

"Of course," said Bellingham, not seeing till afterwards the full significance of Lapham's action.

Lapham said nothing about Rogers and the Englishmen. He believed that he had acted right in that matter, and he was satisfied; but he did not care to have Bellingham, or anybody, perhaps think he had been a fool.

All those who were concerned in his affairs said he behaved well, and even more than well, when it came to the worst. The prudence, the good sense, which he had shown in the first years of his success, and of which his great prosperity seemed to have bereft him, came back; and these qualities, used in his own behalf, commended him as much to his creditors as the anxiety he showed that no one should suffer by him; this even made some of them doubtful of his sincerity. They gave him time, and there would have been no trouble in his resuming on the old basis, if the ground had not been cut from under him by the competition of the West Virginia company. He saw himself that it was useless to try to go on in the old way, and he preferred to go back and begin the world anew where he had first begun it, in the hills at Lapham. He put the house at Nankeen Square, with everything else he had, into the payment of his debts, and Mrs. Lapham found it easier to leave it for the old farmstead in Vermont than it would have been to go from that home of many years to the new house on the water side of Beacon. This thing and that is embittered to us, so that we may be willing to relinquish it; the world, life itself, is embittered to most of us, so that we are glad to have done with them at last; and this home was haunted with such memories to each of those who abandoned it that to go was less exile than escape. Mrs. Lapham could not look into Irene's room without seeing the girl there before her glass, tearing the poor little keepsakes of her hapless fancy from their hiding-places to take them and fling them in passionate renunciation upon her sister; she could not come into the sitting-room, where her little ones had grown up, without starting at the thought of her husband sitting so many weary nights at his desk there, trying to fight his way back to hope out of the ruin into which he was slipping. When she remembered that night when Rogers came, she hated the place. Irene accepted her release from the house eagerly, and was glad to go before and prepare for the family at Lapham. Penelope was always ashamed of her engagement there; it must seem better somewhere else, and she was glad to go too. No one but Lapham, in fact, felt the pang of parting in all its keenness. Whatever regret the others had was softened to them by the likeness of their flitting to many of those removals for the summer which they made in the late spring when they left Nankeen Square; they were going directly into the country instead of to the seaside first; but Lapham, who usually remained in town long after they had gone, knew all the difference. For his nerves there was no mechanical sense of coming back; this was as much the end of his proud, prosperous life as death itself could have been. He was returning to begin life anew, but he knew, as well as he knew that he should not find his vanished youth in his native hills, that it could never again be the triumph that it had been. That was impossible, not only in his stiffened and weakened forces, but in the very nature of things. He was going back, by grace of the man whom he owed money, to make what he could out of the one chance which his successful rivals had left him.

In one phase his paint had held its own against bad times and ruinous competition, and it was with the hope of doing still more with the Persis Brand that he now set himself to work. The West Virginia people confessed that they could not produce those fine grades, and they willingly left the field to him. A strange, not ignoble friendliness existed between Lapham and the three brothers; they had used him fairly; it was their facilities that had conquered him, not their ill-will; and he recognized in them without enmity the necessity to which he had yielded. If he succeeded in his efforts to develop his paint in this direction, it must be for a long time on a small scale compared with his former business, which it could never equal, and he brought to them the flagging energies of an elderly man. He was more broken than he knew by his failure; it did not kill, as it often does, but it weakened the spring once so strong and elastic. He lapsed more and more into acquiescence with his changed condition, and that bragging note of his was rarely sounded. He worked faithfully enough in his enterprise, but sometimes he failed to seize occasions that in his younger days he would have turned to golden account. His wife saw in him a daunted look that made her heart ache for him.

One result of his friendly relations with the West Virginia people was that Corey went in with them, and the fact that he did so solely upon Lapham's advice, and by means of his recommendation, was perhaps the Colonel's proudest consolation. Corey knew the business thoroughly, and after half a year at Kanawha Falls and in the office at New York, he went out to Mexico and Central America, to see what could be done for them upon the ground which he had theoretically studied with Lapham.

Before he went he came up to Vermont, and urged Penelope to go with him. He was to be first in the city of Mexico, and if his mission was successful he was to be kept there and in South America several years, watching the new railroad enterprises and the development of mechanical agriculture and whatever other undertakings offered an opening for the introduction of the paint. They were all young men together, and Corey, who had put his money into the company, had a proprietary interest in the success which they were eager to achieve.

"There's no more reason now and no less than ever there was," mused Penelope, in counsel with her mother, "why I should say Yes, or why I should say No. Everything else changes, but this is just where it was a year ago. It don't go backward, and it don't go forward. Mother, I believe I shall take the bit in my teeth—if anybody will put it there!"

"It isn't the same as it was," suggested her mother. "You can see that Irene's all over it."

"That's no credit to me," said Penelope. "I ought to be just as much ashamed as ever."

"You no need ever to be ashamed."

"That's true, too," said the girl. "And I can sneak off to Mexico with a good conscience if I could make up my mind to it." She laughed. "Well, if I could be *sentenced* to be married, or somebody would up and forbid the banns! *I* don't know what to do about it."

Her mother left her to carry her hesitation back to Corey, and she said now they had better go all over it and try to reason it out. "And I hope that whatever I do, it won't be for my own sake, but for—others!"

Corey said he was sure of that, and looked at her with eyes of patient tenderness.

"I don't say it is wrong," she proceeded, rather aimlessly, "but I can't make it seem right. I don't know whether I can make you understand, but the idea of being happy, when everybody else is so miserable, is more than I can endure. It makes me wretched."

"Then perhaps that's your share of the common suffering," suggested Corey, smiling.

"Oh, you know it isn't! You know it's nothing. Oh! One of the reasons is what I told you once before, that as long as father is in trouble I can't let you think of me. Now that he's lost everything——" She bent her eyes inquiringly upon him, as if for the effect of this argument.

"I don't think that's a very good reason," he answered seriously, but smiling still. "Do you believe me when I tell you that I love you?"

"Why, I suppose I must," she said, dropping her eyes.

"Then why shouldn't I think all the more of you on account of your father's loss? You didn't suppose I cared for you because he was prosperous?" There was a shade of reproach, ever so delicate and gentle, in his smiling question, which she felt.

"No, I couldn't think such a thing of you. I—I don't know what I meant. I meant that——" She could not go on and say that she had felt herself more worthy of him because of her father's money; it would not have been true; yet there was no other explanation. She stopped and cast a helpless glance at him.

He came to her aid. "I understand why you shouldn't wish me to suffer by your father's misfortunes."

"Yes, that was it; and there is too great a difference every way. We ought to look at that again. You mustn't pretend that you don't know it, for that wouldn't be true. Your mother will never like me, and perhaps—perhaps I shall not like her."

"Well," said Corey, a little daunted, "you won't have to marry my family."

"Ah, that isn't the point!"

"I know it," he admitted. "I won't pretend that I don't see what you mean; but I'm sure that all the differences would disappear when you came to know my family better. I'm not afraid but you and my mother will like each other—she can't help it!" he exclaimed, less judicially than he had hitherto spoken; and he went on to urge some points of doubtful tenability. "We have our ways, and you have yours; and while I don't say but what you and my mother and sisters would be a little strange together at first, it would soon wear off on both sides. There can't be anything hopelessly different in you all, and if there were it wouldn't be any difference to me."

"Do you think it would be pleasant to have you on my side against your mother?"

"There won't be any sides. Tell me just what it is you're afraid of."

"Afraid?"

"Thinking of, then."

"I don't know. It isn't anything they say or do," she explained, with her eyes intent on his. "It's what they are. I couldn't be natural with them, and if I can't be natural with people, I'm disagreeable."

"Can you be natural with me?"

"Oh, I'm not afraid of you. I never was. That was the trouble from the beginning."

"Well, then, that's all that's necessary. And it never was the least trouble to me!"

"It made me untrue to Irene."

"You mustn't say that! You were always true to her."

"She cared for you first."

"Well, but I never cared for her at all!" he besought her.

"She thought you did."

"That was nobody's fault, and I can't let you make it yours. My dear——"

"Wait. We must understand each other," said Penelope, rising from her seat to prevent an advance he was making from his; "I want you to realize the whole affair. Should you want a girl who hadn't a cent in the world, and felt different in your mother's company, and had cheated and betrayed her own sister?"

"I want you!"

"Very well, then, you can't have me. I should always despise myself. I ought to give you up for all these reasons. Yes, I must." She looked at him intently, and there was a tentative quality in her affirmations.

"Is this your answer?" he said. "I must submit. If I asked too much of you, I was wrong. And—good-bye."

He held out his hand, and she put hers in it. "You think I'm capricious and fickle!" she said. "I can't help it—I don't know myself. I can't keep to one thing for half a day at a time. But it's right for us to part—yes, it must be. It must be," she repeated; "and I shall try to remember that. Good-bye! I will try to keep that in my mind, and you will too—you won't care, very soon! I didn't mean *that*—no; I know how true you are; but you will soon look at me differently, and see that even if there hadn't been this about Irene, I was not the one for you. You do think so, don't you?" she pleaded, clinging to his hand. "I am not at all what they would like—your family; I felt that. I am little, and black, and homely, and they don't understand my way of talking, and now that we've lost everything——No, I'm not fit. Goodbye. You're quite right not to have patience with me any longer. I've tried you enough. I ought to be willing to marry you against their wishes if you want me to, but I can't make the sacrifice—I'm too selfish for that." All at once she flung herself on his breast. "I can't even give you up! I shall never dare look any one in the face again. Go, go! But take me with you! I tried to do without you! I gave it a fair trial, and it was a dead failure. Oh, poor Irene! How could *she* give you up?"

Corey went back to Boston immediately, and left Penelope, as he must, to tell her sister that they were to be married. She was spared from the first advance toward this by an accident or a misunderstanding. Irene came straight to her after Corey was gone, and demanded, "Penelope Lapham, have you been such a ninny as to send that man away on my account?"

Penelope recoiled from this terrible courage; she did not answer directly, and Irene went on, "Because if you did, I'll thank you to bring him back again. I'm not going to have him thinking that I'm dying for a man that never cared for me. It's insulting, and I'm not going to stand it. Now, you just send for him!"

"Oh, I will, 'Rene," gasped Penelope. And then she added, shamed out of her prevarication by Irene's haughty magnanimity, "I have. That is—he's coming back——"

Irene looked at her a moment, and then, whatever thought was in her mind, said fiercely, "Well!" and left her to her dismay—her dismay and her relief, for they both knew that this was the last time they should ever speak of that again.

The marriage came after so much sorrow and trouble, and the fact was received with so much misgiving for the past and future, that it brought Lapham none of the triumph in which he had once exulted at the thought of an alliance with the Coreys. Adversity had so far been his friend that it had taken from him all hope of the social success for which people crawl and truckle, and restored him, through failure and doubt and heartache, the manhood which his prosperity had so nearly stolen from him. Neither he nor his wife thought now that their daughter was marrying a Corey; they thought only that she was giving herself to the man who loved her, and their acquiescence was sobered still further by the presence of Irene. Their hearts were far more with her.

Again and again Mrs. Lapham said she did not see how she could go through it. "I can't make it seem right," she said.

"It *is* right," steadily answered the Colonel.

"Yes, I know. But it don't *seem* so."

It would be easy to point out traits in Penelope's character which finally reconciled all her husband's family and endeared her to them. These things continually happen in novels; and the Coreys, as they had always promised themselves to do, made the best, and not the worst, of Tom's marriage.

They were people who could value Lapham's behavior as Tom reported it to them. They were proud of him, and Bromfield Corey, who found a delicate, æsthetic pleasure in the heroism with which Lapham had withstood Rogers and his temptations,—something finely dramatic and unconsciously effective,—wrote him a letter which would once have flattered the rough soul almost to ecstasy, though now he affected to slight it in showing it. "It's all right if it makes it more comfortable for Pen," he said to his wife.

But the differences remained uneffaced, if not uneffaceable, between the Coreys and Tom Corey's wife. "If he had only married the Colonel!" subtly suggested Nanny Corey.

There was a brief season of civility and forbearance on both sides, when he brought her home before starting for Mexico, and her father-in-law made a sympathetic feint of liking Penelope's way of talking, but it is questionable if even he found it so delightful as her husband did. Lily Corey made a little, ineffectual sketch of her, which she put by with other studies to finish up some time, and found her rather picturesque in some ways. Nanny got on with her better than the rest, and saw possibilities for her in the country to which she was going. "As she's quite unformed socially," she explained to her mother, "there is a chance that she will form herself on the Spanish manner, if she stays there long enough, and that when she comes back she will have the charm of not olives, perhaps, but *tortillas*, whatever they are: something strange and foreign, even if it's borrowed. I'm glad she's going to Mexico. At that distance we can—correspond."

Her mother sighed, and said bravely that she was sure they all got on very pleasantly as it was, and that she was perfectly satisfied if Tom was.

There was, in fact, much truth in what she said of their harmony with Penelope. Having resolved, from the beginning, to make the best of the worst, it might almost be said that they were supported and consoled in their good intentions by a higher power. This marriage had not, thanks to an overruling Providence, brought the succession of Lapham teas upon Bromfield Corey which he had dreaded; the Laphams were far off in their native fastnesses, and neither Lily nor Nanny Corey was obliged to sacrifice herself to the conversation of Irene; they were not even called upon to make a social demonstration for Penelope at a time when, most people being still out of town, it would have been so easy; she and Tom had both begged that there might be nothing of that kind; and though none of the Coreys learned to know her very well in the week she spent with them, they did not find it hard to get on with her. There were even moments when Nanny Corey, like her father, had glimpses of what Tom had called her humor, but it was perhaps too unlike their own to be easily recognizable.

Whether Penelope, on her side, found it more difficult to harmonize, I cannot say. She had much more of the harmonizing to do, since they were four to one; but then she had gone through so much greater trials before. When the door of their carriage closed and it drove off with her and her husband to the station, she fetched a long sigh.

"What is it?" asked Corey, who ought to have known better.

"Oh, nothing. I don't think I shall feel strange amongst the Mexicans now."

He looked at her with a puzzled smile, which grew a little graver, and then he put his arm round her and drew her closer to him. This made her cry on his shoulder. "I only meant that I should have you all to myself." There is no proof that she meant more, but it is certain that our manners and customs go for more in life than our qualities. The price that we pay for civilization is the fine yet impassable differentiation of these. Perhaps we pay too much; but it will not be possible to persuade those who have the difference in their favor that this is so. They may be right; and at any rate the blank misgiving, the recurring sense of disappointment to which the young people's departure left the Coreys is to be considered. That was the end of their son and brother for them; they felt that; and they were not mean or unamiable people.

He remained three years away. Some changes took place in that time. One of these was the purchase by the Kanawha Falls Company of the mines and works at Lapham. The transfer relieved Lapham of the load of debt which he was still laboring under, and gave him an interest in the vaster enterprise of the younger men, which he had once vainly hoped to grasp all in his own hand. He began to tell of this coincidence as something very striking; and pushing on more actively the special branch of the business left to him, he bragged, quite in his old way, of its enormous extension. His son-in-law, he said, was pushing it in Mexico and Central America: an idea that they had originally had in common. Well, young blood was what was wanted in a thing of that kind. Now, those fellows out in West Virginia: all young, and a perfect team!

For himself, he owned that he had made mistakes; he could see just where the mistakes were—put his finger right on them. But one thing he could say: he had been no man's enemy but his own; every dollar, every cent had gone to pay his debts; he had come out with clean hands. He said all this, and much more, to Mr. Sewell the summer after he sold out, when the minister and his wife stopped at Lapham on their way across from the White Mountains to Lake Champlain; Lapham had found them on the cars, and pressed them to stop off.

There were times when Mrs. Lapham had as great pride in the clean-handedness with which Lapham had come out as he had himself, but her satisfaction was not so constant. At those times, knowing the temptations he had resisted, she thought him the noblest and grandest of men; but no woman could endure to live in the same house with a perfect hero, and there were other times when she reminded him that if he had kept his word to her about speculating in stocks, and had looked after the insurance of his property half as carefully as he had looked after a couple of worthless women who had no earthly claim on him, they would not be where they were now. He humbly admitted it all, and left her to think of Rogers herself. She did not fail to do so, and the thought did not fail to restore him to her tenderness again.

I do not know how it is that clergymen and physicians keep from telling their wives the secrets confided to them; perhaps they can trust their wives to find them out for themselves whenever they wish. Sewell had laid before his wife the case of the Laphams after they came to consult with him about Corey's proposal to Penelope, for he wished to be confirmed in his belief that he had advised them soundly; but he had not given her their names, and he had not known Corey's himself. Now he had no compunctions in talking the affair over with her without the veil of ignorance which she had hitherto assumed, for she declared that as soon as she heard of Corey's engagement to Penelope, the whole thing had flashed upon her. "And that night at dinner, I could have told the child that he was in love with her sister by the way he talked about her; I heard him; and if she had not been so blindly in love with him herself, she would have known it too. I must say, I can't help feeling a sort of contempt for her sister."

"Oh, but you must not!" cried Sewell. "That is wrong, cruelly wrong. I'm sure that's out of your novel-reading, my dear, and not out of your heart. Come! it grieves me to hear you say such a thing as that."

"Oh, I dare say this pretty thing has got over it—how much character she has got!—and I suppose she'll see somebody else."

Sewell had to content himself with this partial concession. As a matter of fact, unless it was the young West Virginian who had come on to arrange the purchase of the Works, Irene had not yet seen any one, and whether there was ever anything between them is a fact that would need a separate inquiry. It is certain that at the end of five years after the disappointment which she met so bravely, she was still unmarried. But she was even then still very young, and her life at Lapham had been varied by visits to the West. It had also been varied by an invitation, made with the politest resolution by Mrs. Corey, to visit in Boston, which the girl was equal to refusing in the same spirit.

Sewell was intensely interested in the moral spectacle which Lapham presented under his changed conditions. The Colonel, who was more the Colonel in those hills than he could ever have been on the Back Bay, kept him and Mrs. Sewell over night at his house; and he showed the minister minutely round the Works and drove him all over his farm. For this expedition he employed a lively colt which had not yet come of age, and an open buggy long past its prime, and was no more ashamed of his turnout than of the finest he had ever driven on the Milldam. He was rather shabby and slovenly in dress, and he had fallen unkempt, after the country fashion, as to his hair and beard and boots. The house was plain, and was furnished with the simpler movables out of the house in Nankeen Square. There were certainly all the necessaries, but no luxuries, unless the statues of Prayer and Faith might be so considered. The Laphams now burned kerosene, of course, and they had no furnace in the winter; these were the only hardships the Colonel complained of; but he said that as soon as the company got to paying dividends again,—he was evidently proud of the outlays that for the present prevented this,—he should put in steam-heat and naphtha-gas. He spoke freely of his failure, and with a confidence that seemed inspired by his former trust in Sewell, whom, indeed, he treated like an intimate friend, rather than an acquaintance of two or three meetings. He went back to his first connection with Rogers, and he put before Sewell hypothetically his own conclusions in regard to the matter.

"Sometimes," he said, "I get to thinking it all over, and it seems to me I done wrong about Rogers in the first place; that the whole trouble came from that. It was just like starting a row of bricks. I tried to catch up, and stop 'em from going, but they all tumbled, one after another. It wa'n't in the nature of things that they could be stopped till the last brick went. I don't talk much with my wife any more about it; but I should like to know how it strikes you."

"We can trace the operation of evil in the physical world," replied the minister, "but I'm more and more puzzled about it in the moral world. There its course is often so very obscure; and often it seems to involve, so far as we can see, no penalty whatever. And in your own case, as I understand, you don't admit—you don't feel sure—that you ever actually did wrong this man."

"Well, no; I don't. That is to say——"

He did not continue, and after a while Sewell said, with that subtle kindness of his, "I should be inclined to think—nothing can be thrown quite away; and it can't be that our sins only weaken us—that your fear of having possibly behaved selfishly toward this man kept you on your guard, and strengthened you when you were brought face to face with a greater"—he was going to say temptation, but he saved Lapham's pride, and said—"emergency."

"Do you think so?"

"I think that there may be truth in what I suggest."

"Well, I don't know what it was," said Lapham; "all I know is that when it came to the point, although I could see that I'd got to go under unless I did it, that I couldn't sell out to those Englishmen, and I couldn't let that man put his money into my business without I told him just how things stood."

As Sewell afterwards told his wife, he could see that the loss of his fortune had been a terrible trial to Lapham, just because his prosperity had been so gross and palpable; and he had now a burning desire to know exactly how, at the bottom of his heart, Lapham still felt. "And do you ever have any regrets?" he delicately inquired of him.

"About what I done? Well, it don't always seem as if I done it," replied Lapham. "Seems sometimes as if it was a hole opened for me, and I crept out of it. I don't know," he added thoughtfully, biting the corner of his stiff mustache—"I don't know as I should always say it paid; but if I done it, and the thing was to do over again, right in the same way, I guess I should have to do it."

THE END.

CONTEXTS

A Note on Contexts

The materials assembled in this segment of the book establish some literary contexts for understanding *The Rise of Silas Lapham* before moving on to more broadly cultural and historical contexts. The section "Composition and Publication" begins with an overview of Howells's working methods and habits at this stage of his career by Howells biographer Edwin H. Cady. Two short documents by Howells follow: a brief synopsis of a projected novel to be titled *The Rise of Silas Needham* and an excerpt from the "Savings Bank" notebook that Howells used between 1883 and 1897 to collect incidents, memories, overheard turns of speech, and other materials for potential future use in his writing. These three documents together give a fairly complete account of the process by which the writer developed *Silas Lapham* from idea to outline to finished product. That process is further illuminated by a selection of correspondence written or received by Howells during the process of composition. Letters to his father and to friends and fellow authors Henry James and Samuel L. Clemens (Mark Twain) offer a glimpse into the relation between Howells's professional and personal lives as well as the novelist's unfolding perceptions of the content and concerns of his novel-in-progress. In two of these letters, the author mentions the newly purchased and refurbished Howells residence at 302 Beacon Street ("on the water side of Beacon") in Boston, which provided the author with many of the details of the house Silas Lapham builds during the novel. Further correspondence with his editor and publisher (Richard Watson Gilder and Roswell Smith, respectively) give a sense of the day-to-day routines of authorship as a profession and a business. Smith's overzealous suggestions about new directions Howells might take in the development of this and subsequent novels are particularly revealing of some of the literary and cultural expectations and assumptions from within which Howells's contemporary audience read his work.

Additional publishing correspondence concerning particularly inflammatory aspects of the novel follows in the section titled "Controversial Passages and Textual Variants." Two sets of passages were immediately controversial, causing Howells to make changes in the text of the novel, in one case between magazine and book publication and in the other before magazine publication. The first controversy concerns the content and tenor of Silas and Persis Lapham's conversations about Jews living in their Nankeen Square neighborhood; the other concerns comments made by Bromfield Corey about the possibility that the urban poor might be tempted to dynamite the houses of the Boston upper class. The last item in this subsection is an open letter Howells wrote to readers of *Century* magazine in response to criticisms of perceived anachronisms in his representations of Boston circa 1875. Howells defends himself by explaining his conception of the relation between Realist literary representation and raw factuality, and his letter thus serves as a transition to the next section of contextual materials, "Howells, Literary Realism, and American Literary History."

At the time of writing *The Rise of Silas Lapham*, Howells had already been established in the public mind, along with Henry James, as the chief American proponent and practitioner of the new literary school. He had provoked controversy, particularly in England, with his advocacy of Realist aesthetics in an 1882 *Harper's Weekly* magazine essay, "Henry James, Jr.," excerpted here. Selections from the *Harper's Monthly* "Editor's Study" columns, which Howells began writing the year after completing *Silas Lapham*, articulate literary ideas he was already practicing when he wrote the novel. Excerpts from a lecture Howells delivered on tour near the turn of the century afford additional access to Realist ideas that were already deeply ingrained in his thinking during the writing of *Silas Lapham*. Last, Susan Goodman assesses Howells's lasting influence and importance in American literary history as well as his wildly fluctuating public and scholarly reputation.

A section called "American Society in the Gilded Age" opens a window on the thoroughgoing economic and social upheavals experienced by Americans living during the post–Civil War decades. A condensed but far-ranging account by Jay Martin of the bewildering array of such changes is followed by historian Jackson Lears's exploration of Americans' deeply divided attitudes toward the new modes of business practiced by "robber barons" and entrepreneurs in the burgeoning postwar capitalist economy. Writers wrestle with the nature and meaning of social class in an ostensibly egalitarian and increasingly money-obsessed society (Richard Grant White and Thorstein Veblen) and the troubling moral and ethical implications of modern corporate business practices. Two articles on the latter topic from the *Century* magazine's "Topics of the Time" column are immediately applicable to Silas Lapham's moral decision-making in the latter chapters of the novel as he struggles to reconcile the demands of conscience with his desire to save his business. The section includes selections from a contemporary manners book of the type consulted by the Laphams as they prepare for the ordeal of a society dinner hosted by the Coreys. Robert Tomes's *The Bazar Book of Decorum* is remarkable for its unguarded expressions of disdain for the lower classes and admiration for the genteel classes as well as for its discussion of good manners as a means of social self-improvement in a democracy characterized by the promise of upward economic mobility. A selection from Howells's deliciously sarcastic slap-down of Tomes's pretentiousness in his review of the book closes the section.

One need not read very far in this novel to realize the thoroughness of its permeation with the places, people, public institutions, and history of the city in which it is set. The concluding subsection in "Contexts" is accordingly "Silas Lapham's Boston," which is W. D. Howells's Boston as well. A map and an aerial view of the city dating from about the time of the novel's events are captioned to show key features and locales that figure prominently in the novel. Elif S. Armbruster provides insight into the biographical, aesthetic, and cultural significance of Howells's house at the time of writing the novel: number 302 "on the water side of Beacon" street, the author's model for the centrally symbolic structure that Silas Lapham is having built for his family over the course of the novel.

Composition and Publication

EDWIN H. CADY

[The Professional Man of Letters at Work]†

As a professional man of letters in his early forties he was now ready to establish the habits of life and methods of work which would carry him through the next forty years and sixty-odd books. With essential responsibilities narrowed to his family and writing, he had large vistas of personal freedom in control of his time, his energy, and his place and mode of living. Therefore daily, systematic, hard work became an essential part of his formula. It was one of the family jokes that Elinor Howells said he wrote novels like a man sawing wood. His health had been so good for a decade that he had almost forgotten to be hypochondriac; and his stamina had been proved. And his personal growth, as exemplified for instance in the difference between the mind recorded in the notebook he kept for *Italian Journeys* and *Their Wedding Journey* and the one he kept for *Indian Summer* and later works in the eighties, is really striking. The old self-consciously poetic hypersensitivity and temptation to pose are gone. In their place are a balance of mind and accuracy of perception and response reminiscent of Benjamin Franklin. He was nearing the insight he confided to his father toward the end of the decade—that his enforced self-education had been no disaster: "There are some self-made men in this country who would have done well to spend the time making almost anything else; but on the whole the men made by others are worse."

His work habits became professionally well-grooved, and work became a passion, almost a vice, for a man who loved what he did. Consequently he became contemptuous of the flighty author who must wait on inspiration. Why might the Muse not wait as readily on the man who made a business of wooing her as on the man who mooned about yearning for a miracle? "I sit down at my desk and go

† From *The Road to Realism: The Early Years 1837–1885 of William Dean Howells* (Syracuse, NY: Syracuse UP, 1956), pp. 201–205. Reprinted by permission of the Estate of Edwin H. Cady.

to work as regularly as if I were in a mercantile or banking office," Howells said, ". . . you can work it out by patient and methodical application." The trick was to discipline oneself to free his time and energies for his best effort. Howells got in the habit of rising between seven and seven-thirty in the morning, sitting down to a substantial breakfast at eight, and being at work by nine. Then he wrote until about twelve, never past one o'clock, and had lunch, averaging a thousand to fifteen hundred words of finished production for the day. In a handwriting which deteriorated with the years, he liked to write in extra-large script on half sheets, leaving wide spaces between lines for revisions and piling up huge stacks of paper. He aimed to work three hours a day and sleep eight, and he came to be able to write in trains or hotels, on shipboard, or anywhere there was room. Afternoons he might read or correct proof, but there was always his long constitutional to be walked. Evenings might be given to the theater, to reading aloud with his wife, or to going out.

As Howells' celebrity increased, his public personality continued to be attractive but developed protections. People were surprised on first meeting him to see how quiet, simple, deliberately undistinguished he seemed. He was short, stout, round-shouldered, and peaceable. His "voice had a gentle softness, as though there were twins asleep in the next room." Everyone felt his true kindliness and "absorbent" quality—he seemed really interested in other people and liked to make them talk and unfold themselves rather than parade his own ego. That and his subtle, quick humor gave him great personal charm. But alert observers also saw that in a sense he was armored behind his wit and gentleness. He could not be taken advantage of or pushed into positions he did not like; he was hard to attack. "It is not the attitude of a man who does not think, but more like that of one who does not care always to think aloud," said one sensitive interviewer. "In general he reserves his deeper meditations for himself, as everyone has a right to do. The plane on which he oftenest meets people is one of sensible, considerate, well-balanced reflection on life and books, enlivened by humor and averse to the tediousness of argument." The "colorless Napoleonic face" was full of vitality, the glance of the blue eye exceptionally penetrating; the full mustache was beginning to frost with gray.

All the rest of his career Howells continued to produce plays, essays, poems, reviews, travel pieces—but there was no question about which form enlisted his strongest love. As a brash young interviewer, Van Wyck Brooks[1] "asked him in which, as a man of letters, he took most delight. . . . 'Oh, fiction, fiction,' he replied with a good deal of warmth." Yet, for all his faith in the conscientious application

1. Prominent American writer, biographer, and critic (1886–1963) [*editor's note*].

of the seat of the pants to the chair, Howells was just as dependent on the stirring of the waters, on the mysterious and uncontrollable appearance of the creative impulse from the sub-logical levels of his mind, as any other artist. Fortunately, he suffered from no such poverty of impulse as some other writers, and his method for dealing with the creative impulse toward fiction, when it came, was as well-grooved as his working day.

"My plan is to choose my topic, select the characters I want for the story, choose my locality and time, and then go to work. . . . I generally content myself with choosing the phase of life or the subject that I wish to illustrate, sketch out in mind the principal characters, and then plunge into the work. Most books write themselves when you are fairly started, and I trust to the plot unfolding itself as there may be need. With the portraiture of character it is quite otherwise, and a good deal of reflection is necessary . . ."—thus Howells himself on his method. His system was designed to control himself, not his materials. He was ready to trust his talent and imaginative processes to work out the substance of a book. Academics imagine too much deliberate design in authors, he once protested to Professor Brander Matthews of Columbia: an artist *feels* his way to success; he doesn't *map* it.

For realist Howells, the great thing about fiction was, of course, character. His people absorbed by far the greatest part of his attention and delight. But he rejected the notion that the author is or should be possessed by his characters and lost in his creations: "Never," he said. "The essence of achievement is to keep outside, to be entirely dispassionate, as a sculptor must be, moulding his clay . . ."—or a good actor. By this he did not mean that passion must be absent, but that it must be under artistic command. When the Boston author Robert Grant asked Howells, an old man revisiting the Saturday Club, "how firm a hold he used to have upon his characters," he got a quick, passionate reply: "The grip of a bull dog!" With the characters thus firmly in hand, he could give them their settings and conjecture their fates and significance. All this he could project as a novel: "describe it in 8 or 10 lines, estimate its length, and give its purpose. . . ." But he could go no further except by the process of hard, daily work. He would ordinarily refuse to do that until a magazine editor had agreed to accept the final product; and he would steadfastly refuse to elaborate further. The editor had to take the novel in outline if he took it at all and trust the author's imagination and discipline as the author did.

Of course, Howells was begging part of the question of his creative method when he spoke so easily of "choosing" topic, characters, locale, and all the rest. That leaves untouched the question of how the choices became possible. If anyone in a moment of egomania ever pretended that he could create a work of the literary imagination by simple, arbitrary acts of will and logic, it was Edgar Allan Poe, not Howells. Full understanding of Howells' creative processes will require careful study of his notebooks and manuscripts, not all yet available. But it seems clear that his creative impulses came from an esthetic use of memory. Or that the image of the Well as the source of creativity given in John Livingston Lowes's *The Road to Xanadu* applies to Howells' case. Lowes portrayed Coleridge's creative imagination as a mystic Well into which ideas and images from his wide reading dropped as if they were individual fragments with little hooks attached. In the depths of the Well they somehow, often incongruously, became tangled together. Then, when the mysterious energy of creativity troubled the waters, they rose to the surface in new and unpredictable combinations to make themselves available to the conscious, shaping mind of the skillful artist.

Howells' theory was that "an author is merely one who has had the fortune to remember more . . . than other men. A good many wise critics will tell you that writing is inventing; but I know better than that; it is only remembering . . . the history of your own life." His own memory was, as we have seen, much keener than most people's. But his theory of creativity as memory makes sense (in theory and in conjunction with his own various statements about the creation of literature) only if one takes his "remembering" as roughly equivalent to Lowes's "Well." As Lowes saw Coleridge, he seems to have stocked the Well almost exclusively from reading; Howells stocked his from experience of life as well as books. While memory of specific people and events, or indeed direct observation with literature aforethought, gave him materials for his work, what he remembered or recorded was at least as much the response of his own mind and emotions to places, people, and events as anything "objective"—even supposing a man and artist can really see objects as they are. Urged at the age of forty-nine to write a novel of Washington, D.C., he demurred, "I am too old now. I could not stand the going into society to catch the spirit of things."

Leaving for later discussion the question of how a writer may be imagined actually to have placed a "transcript of life" on his page, one needs to avoid being caught in the trap of supposing that Howells did somehow actually reproduce "real life" as it existed around him. As a realistic theoretician he talked a great deal about doing just that. In practice he found his impulses to creativity just where James or Hawthorne found them—in the "germs," the extraordinarily suggestive moments of experience which could set his imagination in motion and eventually make a work of fiction possible. Some of Howells' effects in his work were importantly different from some of theirs, but that is all. His diaries and notebooks follow an interesting rule of preparation for writing. When there are extensive observations of scenes and people, heavily detailed, these are notes for travel books. The notes for serious fiction are records of inward impulses, stirrings of the creative life shaping the work within. The exception to this rule is the special "study" made to flesh out a structure already given but not complete.

When once Howells had "remembered" the basis for a book, he sometimes had to do research to fill in where memory could not serve. In order not to shatter the illusion of life he was creating by falling into anachronisms, he was often at considerable pains to get things "right." While writing *The Quality of Mercy* he felt he needed to know, for instance, just what the police department of a Canadian city would do about a tip that an American embezzler was living there under cover. So he went to Montreal, walked into police headquarters, and solemnly put a hypothetical question to the chief—who immediately pounded his bell and turned out his detective squad to get a first-hand report on the story and be ready to go right to work.

W. D. HOWELLS

The Rise of Silas Needham†

The story opens with an Interview of Needham by Bartley Hubbard, who includes him in his Solid Men series for the Boston Events. In this interview the outlines of Needham's career are traced from his hard, squalid childhood to the moment of his greatest prosperity as the proprietor and manufacturer of Needham's Mineral Paint (or Stove-Blacking, or Boy's Clothing, etc.). Then the story takes him, and touching the points indicated by the Interview vitalizes them by bringing all into the strongest and most intimate relief. The man's character is carefully studied; his love story is told; the dramatic incidents of his rise are portrayed; an injustice to a partner whom he has crowded out of the business is narrated, and the fact that a sense of his wrong-doing has never ceased to rest heavily on Needham's conscience is indicated.

His family and its social status in Boston is depicted in a series of incidents all bearing on the main story. The romance of his daughter's love-story, and her marriage against his liking is told.

Nothing is spared, good or bad, as to the truth of Needham's life and character; the vulgarity of his nature in some respects is shown;

† This undated manuscript synopsis (mssHM 12428) is in the Howells Family Papers, the Huntington Library, San Marino, California. Transcribed by the editor for this Norton Critical Edition.

his family troubles are dealt with; and the man's essential goodness and patience and moral strength are only covertly indicated.

He abandons his old business after amassing a fortune in it, and goes into speculation. The moment comes when in some railroad adventure, the choice is presented to him of cruelly and oppressively "squeezing" another man, or getting squeezed himself. *He feels the weakening effect of the old wrong that he committed.* The circumstances of his temptation are carefully pointed, and all its incidents. At last, almost by force of "that, not ourselves, which works for righteousness"[1] he resists the temptation and suffers ruin.

His after life of adversity *from which he does not recover,* is sketched. The reader is made to feel that this adversity, consciously and deliberately chosen, is The Rise of Silas Needham.

W. D. HOWELLS

The "Savings Bank" Notebook†

* * *

If the Lapham girls went only to Grammar schools, and they have been taught anything of Eng. Lit. must have a year at private school afterwards.

Lapham vulgar but not sordid.

Make more of the fact that the Laphams don't know what to do with their money.

Say Americans

Corey must make P. own that she loves him. They must talk it out [illegible words] fully. He cannot understand her but submits.

So, she must not own it at first nor let him know why. Perhaps he goes away—to Mexico—mystified. Lapham's difficulty must be pending while his wife's jealousy comes on, and it is harder for him to do the right thing because of his fury at that.—Before this, when

1. A slightly incorrect quotation from *Literature and Dogma* by Matthew Arnold (1822–1888).

† Excerpted from an 80-page manuscript notebook consisting of miscellaneous entries dated as early as 1866 and as late as 1897. Howells Family Papers, 1850–1954 [MS Am 1784.3 (7)], Houghton Library, Harvard University. Transcribed by the editor for this Norton Critical Edition.

it comes out that Corey prefers P. he would naturally insist [illegible words] that Irene must give C., and not stand in her sister's way.

The young trees growing out of the fallen logs in the forest—the new life out of the old. Apply to Lapham's fall.

Reconcile Corey's saying he doesn't like to live upon his father to his having some money of his own.

W. D. HOWELLS

Letter to Richard Watson Gilder†

Wolfeboro, N.H.
July 31, 1884.

My dear Gilder:

I hardly know what advertising material to give you about the story. It will involve more interests, I find, and be more of a love story than I expected, but the main idea of a rude, common, unrefined nature, holding out against a temptation which must beset many business men and accepting ruin rather than inflict it, remains the same. (I wouldn't give this idea away.) The story opens with an interview by Bartley Hubbard, in which the hero's history and character are outlined. The scene is always in Boston, except at the close, when it will be somewhere in Northern New England. I can't think what else to say.

* * *

Yours ever
W. D. Howells

† Letter in the Manuscript Division, New York Public Library. Gilder (1844–1909) was editor of *Century* magazine. Transcription by Don L. Cook, copyright © 1982 by W. W. Norton & Company, Inc. Used by permission of W. W. Norton & Company, Inc.

W. D. HOWELLS

Letter to William Cooper Howells†

Boston, Aug. 10, 1884.

Dear father:

I came down here last Monday to put the house in order—or rather my books—leaving the family at Kennebunkport, Me. (I seem to have written you all this before.) And here I have been hard at work, and lonesome of course. There is not only nobody else in the house, but nobody else that I know sleeps in town. Altogether the effect is queer. There are miles of empty houses all around me. And how unequally things are divided in this world. While these beautiful, airy, wholesome houses are uninhabited, thousands upon thousands of poor creatures are stifling in wretched barracks in the city there, whole families in one room. I wonder that men are as patient with society as they are.

* * *

With love to all, Your aff'te son
Will

W. D. HOWELLS

Letter to Mark Twain‡

Aug. 10, 1884

Dear Clemens:[1]

If I had written half as good a book as Huck Finn, I shouldn't ask anything better than to read the proofs; even as it is I don't. So send them on; they will always find me somewhere. I'm here in town for the present; but I'm going to Kennebunkport where the family are on Tuesday, and then to Campobello, N. B. Back to Boston the last of the month.

† Letter in Howells Family Papers, 1850–1954 [MS Am 1784.1 (78)], Houghton Library, Harvard University. Transcribed by the editor for this Norton Critical Edition. William Cooper Howells (1807–1894) was W. D. Howells's father.

‡ Unpublished letter from the Mark Twain Papers, the Bancroft Library, University of California, Berkeley. Reprinted by permission of the Bancroft Library and the Howells Estate. Transcription by Don L. Cook, copyright © 1982 by W. W. Norton & Company, Inc. Used by permission of W. W. Norton & Company, Inc.

1. Samuel L. Clemens (1835–1910), who adopted the pseudonym Mark Twain, and Howells developed a close, lifelong friendship after their first meeting in 1869 in the offices of the *Atlantic Monthly* magazine, where Howells was assistant editor.

* * *

I'm looking up, for my new story, facts about the general lack of literature in people, and I asked the teacher of a first-class ladies' school here how little literature a girl could carry away from her school. "Some go barely knowing that Shakespeare was an Englishman. One who had read all the 'love-part' of your (my) novels, didn't know that you were an American or a contemporary. We have to fight in eight months against fifteen or twenty years' absolute ignorance of literature."

I've got a mighty pretty house here on the water side of Beacon st., and Mrs. Howells wants Mrs. Clemens and you to consider yourself engaged for a visit to us when my opera comes out in November.[2]

Yours ever
W. D. HOWELLS

W. D. HOWELLS

Letter to Henry James[†]

Kennebunkport, Maine,
Aug. 22, 1884

My Dear James:[1]

It is very good of you to write me when I've so long owed you a letter, and to make my buying a house "on the water side of Beacon" the occasion of forgiving my neglect. The greatest pleasure the house has yet brought me is this; but it is a pretty house and an extremely fine situation, and I hope it is not the only joy I shall have from it. I have spent some desolate weeks in it already, putting my books on their shelves, while the family were away at mountain-side and seaside, and I can speak confidently and authoritatively of the sunsets from the library-windows. The sun goes down over Cambridge with as much apparent interest as if he were a Harvard graduate: possibly he is; and he spreads a glory over the Back Bay that is not to be

2. Howells's collaboration with Georg Henschel (1850–1934), first conductor of the Boston Symphony Orchestra, on a light opera titled *A Sea Change; or, Love's Stowaway* was slated to open in Boston in spring 1884 but was never produced because of the untimely death of the production's manager.

† Letter in Correspondence and journals of Henry James Jr. and other family papers, 1855–1916 [MS Am 1094 (239)], Houghton Library, Harvard University. Transcribed by the editor for this Norton Critical Edition.

1. Novelist Henry James (1843–1916), with whom Howells had established a close personal and professional relationship beginning in 1866, when Howells was working as assistant editor of the *Atlantic Monthly* magazine and James was publishing some of his first short stories there. Their personal and professional relationship lasted until James's death.

equaled by the blush of a Boston Independent for such of us Republicans as are going to vote for Blaine.[2]—Sometimes I feel it an extraordinary thing that I should have been able to buy a house on Beacon str., but I built one on Concord Avenue of nearly the same cost when I had far less money to begin with. In those doubting days I used to go and look at the cellar they were digging, and ask myself, knowing that I had had barely money to pay for the lot, "*Can* blood be got out of a turnip?" Now I know that some divine power loves turnips, and that somehow the blood will be got out of the particular turnip which I represent. Drolly enough, I am writing a story in which the chief personage builds a house "on the water side of Beacon," and I shall be able to use all my experience, down to the quick. Perhaps the novel may pay for the house.

* * *

Yours ever
W. D. Howells

ROSWELL SMITH

Letter to W. D. Howells[†]

Hotel Vendome Boston

Sunday Evig
March 7th. 85

My Dear Howells.

I did not answer your question to day, as to how I like Silas Lapham—I only got ready to answer it—by telling you the critical mood, in which I must necessarily have read it—I have only read to the end of the dinner party—but already I see that your plan was wiser than mine—To lift the average business man it was necessary to go as low down as Silas Lapham—no doubt—You have made him interesting—everybody likes him—as I began to tell you one person going so far as to say he is the only admirable character in the story—I am content—satisfied—more than satisfied—I could not have wished anything better or different—for your sake & in the magazine's

2. James G. Blaine (1830–1893), nominated by the Republican party to stand against the Democrat Grover Cleveland in the presidential election of 1884. Evidence of Blaine's having accepted bribes during his term as congressman, coupled with news of Cleveland's having fathered an illegitimate child, made for a distasteful political choice for Howells and many other voters.

† Letter in Howells Family Papers, 1850–1954 [MS Am 1784 (442)], Houghton Library, Harvard University. Transcribed by the editor for this Norton Critical Edition. New York businessman Roswell Smith (1829–1892), publisher of *Century* magazine, where *The Rise of Silas Lapham* was first published.

interest—than this story to hold & charm our new readers—which must number 500.000—I suspect—I hope each of the new 500.000—will buy and read all your other books—I shall tell Osgood to make a point of advertising your books in May Century—.

Now let me mention what no doubt you have already thought of—"*The Business Career of Tom Corey*"—I think he can be made my ideal business man—Pray pardon the suggestion,—

I will look up English Copyright Law penalties for you—It is specially penal even on private parties, who sing at a public entertainment—a copyright song—

Yours Faithfully
Roswell Smith

ROSWELL SMITH

Letters to W. D. Howells†

THE CENTURY CO.
33 EAST 17TH STREET,
NEW-YORK.

ROSWELL SMITH, President.

March 17. 85

My dear Mr Howells:

I wrote to Mr Warner[1] yesterday with Mr Gilder's approval, suggesting a lay sermon to our British cousins on the London Times' text.

I have read the May installment of "Silas Lapham" with very great pleasure. I do not see how it could be better. It teaches in many ways a much needed lesson—(common sense, as has been aptly said, is the most uncommon sense in the world). Many a time have I, as a lawyer, interposed to prevent a wife from giving up all her property to her husband's creditors with the idea of helping him when he was on the verge of ruin, when the truest kindness to him was that she should keep what she had to enable him to start again.

The great theme I suppose for the coming novel will be the relations of labor and capital. There is room enough for a half dozen authors to write on this subject, and if you ever think of taking it up I should like to talk to you about it. Perhaps there is no country in the world where the abuses of capital are so great as in this country, and

† Letters in Howells Family Papers, 1850–1954 [MS Am 1784 (442)], Houghton Library, Harvard University. Transcribed by the editor for this Norton Critical Edition.

1. Charles Dudley Warner (1829–1900), journalist, editor, and co-author (with his Hartford neighbor Mark Twain) of the novel *The Gilded Age* (1873).

where the strife for wealth is so eager because the opportunities are great, and it is the one god that American society worships. On the other hand, there is no country where what we call Socialism is likely to take so deep a root and flourish and grow strong as here. It has much to feed on, and under our form of government, almost no repression. Just as surely as the relations between labor and capital were all wrong in our Southern states under the system of slavery, just so surely are they wrong today throughout the entire country. We have tried to treat these great questions through narrations of facts. But when we have got at the facts we have found that the articles bristle all over with libel suits, and seem mere personal attacks upon individuals, and, what is worse, were ineffective and uninteresting. Now we are waiting for the coming man to treat them through the medium of fiction. As Dickens[2] reformed the abuses in school life in England, and the Jewish quarter in London, so some writer of fiction may yet do a great service in this country, and help to postpone if not prevent the great impending struggle between labor and capital.

Very truly yours
Roswell Smith

W.D. Howells, Esq.

* * *

THE CENTURY CO.
33 EAST 17TH STREET,
NEW-YORK.

ROSWELL SMITH, President.

Mch. 21. 85

My dear Mr Howells:

Last night Mrs Roswell Smith and I had the great pleasure of reading aloud the June installment of Silas Lapham, and our enthusiasm over it is almost boundless. I think the toning down which you have given the proofs is an improvement. One minor criticism I would make. It seems to me I would not have the mother and daughter go to the druggists to get the bromide—I notice you strike out the laudanum—for there is danger of that sort of suggestion

2. British novelist Charles Dickens (1812–1870). Smith may have had in mind novels like *Dombey and Son* (1848), *David Copperfield* (1850), and *Hard Times* (1854), all of which included social criticism aimed at promoting school reform, and *Our Mutual Friend* (1865), whose sympathetic portrayal of the character Riah may have been designed to atone for the deeply anti-Semitic caricature of Fagin in *Oliver Twist* (1839).

being abused. Is there not a good opportunity to teach the lesson that in cases of such mental trouble, people had better go to the family doctor (Both lessons—The Spiritual advisor has been consulted—The cure of souls—but both are needed to "minister to a mind diseased"—) who would prescribe a simple tonic and sedative, no more important than valerian for example, though I do not suppose it is necessary to give the doctor's prescription. There is a chance even to let the old doctor give a needed word of warning against resorting to such things inadvisedly. I think this story of Silas Lapham is going to be recognized as the "coming novel" we hear so much about. You have him very much in the condition of the of the [*sic*] man who said he was on the frontier with a party, and when they encountered the Indians they all separated like a flock of quails, knowing that was the only chance for any of them to escape. It happened, however, that the entire party of Indians pursued his trail. They followed hum up a ravine, until he came to an impassable wall—There his story ended. One of the excited listeners said—"What did you do?" "Do! Why I died right there,—there was nothing else to do—there was no possible escape"

Now, I do not know what you propose to do with Silas Lapham, but in the whole course of my business experience I never knew but one man who took to speculative gambling in business, and especially when he was in business trouble who did not at the same time begin to drink. I used to know the very beginnings of that sort of thing when I lived at the West, by the hot trembling hand. The only man I ever knew who recovered from the passion was a man of past sixty, and he had only given himself up to it for about two weeks. If you go on to the logical conclusion of Silas Lapham he will drink and go to the devil generally, and he will never give up his passion for gambling in business, pursuing the ignus fatuus[3] hope of recovering prosperity. It seems to me that if he does retrieve his character, the story will fail in the truth of daily experience, and that the opportunity for a splendid lesson will be lost if the story ends too precipitately. It may be that you will have to write the business experience of Tom Corey, by way of showing the long miserable record of Silas Lapham's career as a business gambler. He has got to the point when he will exchange checks when he knows his own check dated ahead is likely to be worthless. When that passion once gets hold of a man it never lets go. I have seen the best and brightest and truest, most honest, upright and conscientious Christian men, who have gone to their death in a few years as the simple result of beginning the career of a business gambler. The demoralization of

3. A misleading or deceptive light or hope (Latin).

conscience that comes from drink is bad enough, but the demoralization from the two—gambling and drink, is something frightful.

Of course I do not know your plans, but I should say that Silas Lapham was getting ready to sell the mill property to the British capitalists, concealing the fact of the railroad, and he might get enough to put him on his feet again, then, having got the passion for gambling, it would be impossible for him to resist trying just once more to make enough money to save the house—the result of course would be that he would lose everything, and then—destruction. Then he is ready to ruin Tom Corey—The story is full of moral lessons and so far, has not a false note in it.

One of the best things in this June installment is the splendid way in which you show up the demoralization of conscience as to divorce. Zerilla and her mother talk about the former getting a divorce and marrying another man as a servant girl and her mother might talk about getting another situation, & in the presence of husband no less! That is a good hit—

For a minor criticism, my wife suggests that when Silas comes home from Dubuque there should be a sentence indicating that he had left Irene at the West. I hope Irene is to marry the fellow who owns the Southern Plantation—

There is an old saw which says advice should not be given unless it be asked. You only asked me to read the installment, and I have volunteered to tell you what I think the situation requires. But now that I have forced myself to write this letter, I am tempted to put it in the fire, which probably you will do when you get it.

Very truly yours
Roswell Smith

W.D. Howells, Esq.

THE CENTURY CO.
33 EAST 17TH STREET,
NEW-YORK.

ROSWELL SMITH, President.

Mch. 24. 85

My dear Mr Howells:

I have your note of March 22d. Yes, there is a divine power which can reach down to us and which we can grasp, that can lift us out of ourselves. Here and there there is a man like Mr Gough[4] who escapes when the disease of drink has fast hold of him. I did not suppose that you proposed to teach that. I rejoice that you do. But this passion for gambling when once it takes hold of a man is more insidious than the passion for drink. It is so difficult to make a man see the wretchedness and wickedness of it, and the line seems to him so vague and uncertain between legitimate business with all its risks, and that which is pure speculation and is condoned to everybody who is "successful" in it. Lest the way of escape should be deemed too easy, I suppose you will take care to make the reader and Lapham realize that in his escape he is one of a thousand—and well nigh a miracle.

Very truly yours
Roswell Smith

When you come on in April come as my guest & bring wife or daughter or both.

W.D. Howells Esq.

4. John Bartholomew Gough (1817–1886), a well-known temperance lecturer.

THE CENTURY CO.
33 EAST 17TH STREET,
NEW-YORK.

ROSWELL SMITH, President.

April 6. 85

My dear Mr Howells:

Somebody said to me the other day that there must be a million of men in this country reading Silas Lapham. I queried the opinion, and he went on to say that of one thing he was sure, namely, that a larger number of persons in this country were reading that serial story than ever read a serial story before.

I send you an item cut from the Tribune of Saturday, which is only another illustration of the sad end of the men who get snared in stock gambling. Probably about the ending of your man Rogers. I did not know this Mr Lawrence, but I knew the firm, and also his brother and his guardian. In this connection it occurs to me to say to you that I knew a man who died of delirium tremens who, it was said, had never been drunk in his life—, and whose own wife did not know that he was in the habit of drinking. Dr. Holland also once told me of a similar case.

Very truly yours
Roswell Smith

W.D. Howells Esq.

When am I to have the expected visit

Controversial Passages and Textual Variants

Textual Variants: Dynamite

These passages from the Corey dinner party conversation in Chapter XIV of the novel are the subject of the following exchange of correspondence between Howells and his *Century* magazine editor and publisher. These passages interpolate into the text of the novel as published in *Century* two sets of alternatives: the text as originally written and set in type but not published before further revision by Howells, and the book version published as the *Century* serialization ended. In each case, the variant texts are presented in chronological order.

Century Version

"That is a very comfortable sentiment, Miss Kingsbury," said Corey, "and must make you feel almost as if you had thrown open No. 931 to the whole North End. But I am serious about this matter. I spend my summers in town, and I occupy my own house, so that I can speak impartially and intelligently; and I tell you that in some of my walks on the Hill and down on the Back Bay, nothing but the surveillance of the local policeman prevents

[**Original, unpublished version**] me from applying dynamite to
[***Century* version**] me from personally affronting
[**Book version**] my offering personal violence to

Century Version

[. . .] those long rows of close-shuttered, handsome, brutally insensible houses. If I were a poor man, with a sick child pining in some garret or cellar at the North End, I should break into one of them, and camp out on the grand piano."

"Surely, Bromfield," said his wife, "you don't consider what havoc such people would make with the furniture of a nice house!"

[**Original, unpublished version**] "That is true," answered Corey, with meek conviction. "I never thought of the furniture. Probably a poor man with a dying child would consider it, and would not break into the house, after all."

"It's wonderful how patient they are," said Mr. Sewell, the minister. "The spectacle of the hopeless luxury and comfort the hard-working poor man sees around him must be hard to bear at times."

[***Century* version**] "That is true," answered Corey, with meek conviction. "I never thought of that."

"And if you were a poor man with a sick child, I doubt if you'd have so much heart for burglary as you have now," said James Bellingham.

"It's wonderful how patient they are," said Mr. Sewell, the minister. "The spectacle of the hopeless luxury and comfort the hard-working poor man sees around him must be hard to bear at times."

[**Book version**] "It's wonderful how patient they are," said Mr. Sewell, the minister. "The spectacle of the hopeless comfort the hard-working poor man sees must be hard to bear."

RICHARD WATSON GILDER

Letter to W. D. Howells†

EDITORIAL DEPARTMENT
THE CENTURY MAGAZINE
UNION SQUARE NEW YORK

Feb. 18. 1885,

My dear Mr. Howells,

The leap made this year in the Century's circulation—up to 210,000 & *still rising*—has thrown upon us, we cannot help feeling, a greater responsibility than ever, & we cannot help being on guard against any false step which may injure our prestige & influence. A week or two ago we cancelled 150,000 pages in an article by Mr. Bigelow[1] (with his consent) in which he quoted an enthusiastic endorsement of dynamite war-fare on the Parliament buildings & reigning

† Letter in Howells Family Papers, 1850–1954 [MS Am 1784 (175)], Houghton Library, Harvard University. Transcribed by the editor for this Norton Critical Edition. Richard Watson Gilder (1844–1909) was the editor of *Century* magazine.

1. Probably John Bigelow (1817–1911), whose article, "Some Recollections of Charles O'Conor," appeared in the March issue of *Century* magazine.

houses generally. We had not objected to this while dynamiting was an insignificant matter; but with recent events[2] before our eyes the paragraph had a new significance—it would doubtless have been copied by dynamite journals as an endorsement of their methods, & possibly might have led to the seizure of the magazine in England.

I hope you will not think us super-sensitive when we call your attention to page 867 of your April installment—where some words written months ago assume a new meaning in the light of new events. It is the very word, *dynamite*, that is now so dangerous for any of us to use, except in condemnation. None but a crank would misinterpret your allusion, but it is the crank who does the deed. The other day it was found that dynamite had been built into all the hearths in a new house!—there is no telling where this sort of thing is going to break out—it is an unknown & horribly inflammable quantity, & we don't want, if we can help it, to be associated with the subject—except as opposing it. I am confident that on reflection you will take this view, & if so can you telegraph (and also write) a line or two to take the place of the phrase which introduces the word "dynamite"? If you cannot make the matter clear (at our expense) by telegraph then please telegraph that you have written. I have asked Mr. Smith to drop you a line to show how the matter struck him. With many regrets at the necessity of troubling you—I remain Sincerely yours

R.W. Gilder

2. Prominent among the "recent events" about which Gilder worried were the series of bombing attacks known as the Fenian Bombing Campaign of 1881–85. Carried out by the Irish Republican Brotherhood (IRB) in support of Irish independence from British rule, these attacks on politically symbolic targets—including, most recently, two January 1885 detonations in the Houses of Parliament and one in the Tower of London—made use of the recently invented explosive, dynamite. Closer to home, a late-January explosion in lower Manhattan had targeted the Garry Brothers dry-goods store, whose clerks' "Equality Association" had been disputing recent layoffs and pay cuts with its owners. Discussion of the potential industrial, military, and political uses and misuses of dynamite was widespread in the mainstream press; *Scientific American*, for instance, published plans for construction of a dynamite bomb as well as articles worrying about the ease with which such devices could be constructed from readily available materials and by people with little technical expertise. The Irish campaign included the creation of bomb-making schools in Brooklyn, New York (whose large Irish-American population had made it a center of Irish Republican activities), supported by lecture series and journal publications promoting the use of the new "scientific warfare" in the cause of Irish independence. Newspapers like the New York-based *Irish World* and the short-lived *Dynamite Monthly*—examples of the "dynamite journals" to which Gilder refers—routinely included news, information, and editorials favorable to the use of dynamite for political purposes. Further anxiety was generated by the efforts of German radical Johann Most (1846–1906), who had emigrated to the United States earlier in the decade and advocated violence as a means of exerting working-class power against the political dominance of Gilded Age robber barons. His pamphlet *The Science of Revolutionary Warfare* (1885) contained instructions for the preparation and use of explosives, including dynamite. The escalating violence of confrontations between labor and capital during the 1870s and 1880s, along with the influence of advocates of political anarchism, nihilism, and socialism within the labor movement, seemed to make dynamite's eventual use for political purposes in America likely.

ROSWELL SMITH

Letter to W. D. Howells†

THE CENTURY CO.
33 EAST 17TH STREET,
NEW-YORK.

ROSWELL SMITH, President.

Febry 18. 85

My dear Howells,

Last night Mrs Roswell Smith read aloud to me, the April installment of Silas Lapham—which we enjoyed greatly—but about noon today I recalled Bromfield Corys [*sic*] utterance on the subject of Dynamite & went back & re-read it. Then I showed it to Buel[1] & Gilder & the result is, we have stopped the Press & taken off the form. We did not feel in justice to you that we could go on with the printing until your attention had been called to it—I know what your first impression will be likely to be—that is simply to let it stand as it is—but when you have thought about it, twenty four hours I am sure you will come to our conclusion—It may be well enough to joke about taking possession of the houses of the rich, &c—but blowing open the shutters with a charge of Dynamite—suggests nihilism, destructiveness—revenge—Etc—which to be sure is not fairly suggested even by the language—nothing worse than getting in is stated—the other is not even fairly suggested—But, think of the recent events[2] in London & elsewhere abroad & in New York—I am sure it won't do—Then I fancy the Law might stop the magazine or make the Publisher trouble in England—ie that, that is among the possibilities—Last month we had to cancel four pages in an article after the sheets had gone to England—& after 150,000—had been printed. Fortunately only 25,000—of this form are printed—& sheets have not gone to England. Please telegraph us whether you decide to change. & send by mail the matter—a single line—or a whole page if you wish that you wish substituted—Gilder agreed two hours ago to write you about it—it comes better from the Editor than the Publisher—but since I have had the honor publicly to differ with you over Mr. Everts—perhaps you will pardon me for

† Letter in Howells Family Papers, 1850–1954 [MS Am 1784 (442)], Houghton Library, Harvard University. Transcribed by the editor for this Norton Critical Edition.

1. Clarence Clough Buel (1850–1933), a *Century* magazine editor.
2. See p. 301, n. 2.

privately calling your attention to what may be a mistake for you & for us—.

I am Always Faithfully Yrs
Roswell Smith

Textual Variants: Portrayal of Jews

These passages from Chapter II of the novel are the subject of the following exchange of correspondence between Howells and Cyrus L. Sulzberger, the editor of the *American Hebrew.* In each case, the passage as originally published in *Century* magazine's serialization of the novel is followed by the revised passage as it appeared in the book version of the novel published as the magazine serialization ended.

Century Version

One of the things which he [Tom Corey] partly said, partly looked, and which was altogether casual, she [Irene Lapham] repeated to her mother, and they canvassed it, as they did all things relating to these new acquaintances, and made it part of a novel point of view which they were acquiring. It was something that Mrs. Lapham especially submitted to her husband when they got home; she asked him if it were true, and if it made any difference.

"It makes a difference in the price of property," replied the Colonel, promptly. "But as long as we don't want to sell, it don't matter."

"Why, Silas Lapham," said his wife, "do you mean to tell me that this house is worth less than we gave for it?"

"It's worth a good deal less. You see, they *have* got in—and pretty thick, too—it's no use denying it. And when they get in, they send down the price of property. Of course, there aint any sense in it; *I* think it's all dumn foolishness. It's cruel, and folks ought to be ashamed. But there it is. You tell folks that the Saviour himself was one, and the twelve apostles, and all the prophets,—I don't know but what Adam was—guess he *was,*—and it don't make a bit of difference. They send down the price of real estate. Prices begin to shade when the first one gets in."

Mrs. Lapham thought the facts over a few moments. "Well, what do we care, so long as we're comfortable in our home? And they're just as nice and as good neighbors as can be."

"Oh, it's all right as far as I'm concerned," said Lapham. "Who did you say those people were that stirred you up about it?"

Mrs. Lapham mentioned their name. Lapham nodded his head. "Do you know them? What business is he in?"

Book Version

Some of the things that he partly said, partly looked, she reported to her mother, and they talked them over, as they did everything relating to these new acquaintances, and wrought them into the novel point of view which they were acquiring. When Mrs. Lapham returned home, she submitted all the accumulated facts of the case, and all her own conjectures, to her husband, and canvassed them anew.

At first he was disposed to regard the whole affair as of small importance, and she had to insist a little beyond her own convictions in order to counteract his indifference.

"Well, I can tell you," she said, "that if you think they were not the nicest people you ever saw, you're mightily mistaken. They had about the best manners; and they had been everywhere, and knew everything. I declare it made me feel as if we had always lived in the backwoods. I don't know but the mother and the daughters would have let you feel so a little, if they'd showed out all they thought; but they never did; and the son—well, I can't express it, Silas! But that young man had about perfect ways."

"Seem struck up on Irene?" asked the Colonel.

"How can I tell? He seemed just about as much struck up on me. Anyway, he paid me as much attention as he did her. Perhaps it's more the way, now, to notice the mother than it used to be."

Lapham ventured no conjecture, but asked, as he had asked already, who the people were.

Mrs. Lapham repeated their name.

Century Version

"Well, I don't want to build on Beacon street, Si," said Mrs. Lapham, gently.

"Just as you please, Persis. I aint in any hurry to leave."

Mrs. Lapham stood flapping the check which she held in her right hand against the edge of her left. "A Mr. Liliengarten has bought the Gordon house across the square," she said, thoughtfully.

"Well, I'm agreeable. I suppose he's got the money to pay for it."

"Oh, yes, they've all got money," sighed Mrs. Lapham. "What are you going to do this afternoon?"

Book Version

"Well, I don't want to build on Beacon street, Si," said Mrs. Lapham, gently.

"Just as you please, Persis. I aint in any hurry to leave."

Mrs. Lapham stood flapping the cheque which she held in her right hand against the edge of her left.

The Colonel still sat looking up at her face, and watching the effect of the poison of ambition which he had artfully instilled into her mind.

She sighed again—a yielding sigh. "What are you going to do this afternoon?"

THE AMERICAN HEBREW

"Silas Lapham" and the Jews†

* * *

The following correspondence between one of the editors of THE AMERICAN HEBREW[1] and Mr. W. D. Howells requires no further explanation.

I.

New York, 12 July, 1885.

Dear Sir:

As "The Rise of Silas Lapham" is about approaching completion and will I presume, soon appear in book form, I beg to call to your notice a slur (in Chapter II.) upon a number of your readers and admirers—a slur as unmerited by the Jewish people as it is unworthy of the author. It is not alone upon the ignorant and uncultured of the Jews that you reflect, for neither "the Saviour himself" nor the twelve apostles, nor the prophets, nor even Adam, were, so far as the records show, of that class which depreciated the value of property when they "got in."

The introduction of the lines in question cannot even be excused on the ground that it serves a literary purpose, for no such end is accomplished. The sentiment is violently dragged in for no other ascertainable reason than to pander to a prejudice against which all educated and cultured Jews must battle. The literary leaders of a country have so great a power in fomenting or in repressing popular prejudice that I make bold to hope that in the permanent form in

† From *The American Hebrew* (September 4, 1885).

1. The unnamed editor in this published exchange of letters is Cyrus L. Sulzberger (1858–1932), a founding editor of the *American Hebrew* (a monthly periodical with a national circulation) and the ancestor of three succeeding generations of *New York Times* publishers.

which "Silas Lapham" will no doubt soon appear, these objectionable lines will be omitted.

I have the honor to be, Sir,

Very respectfully yours,

———————

To W.D. Howells Esq.

II.

Old Orchard Me., July 17, 1885.

My Dear Sir:

I thank you for your frank and manly letter.

I supposed that I was writing in reprobation of the prejudice of which you justly complain, but my irony seems to have fallen short of the mark—so far short that you are not the first Hebrew to accuse me of "pandering" to the stupid and cruel feeling against your race and religion. I will not ask you to read again, in the light of this statement, the passage of my story which you object to, for I have already struck it out of my book, and it will not re-appear. In that passage I merely recognized to rebuke it, the existence of a feeling which civilized men should be ashamed of. But perhaps it is better not to recognize all the facts.

Perhaps, also, you owe me an apology for making an unjust accusation. I leave that to you.

Very truly yours,

W. D. Howells

To ———————

III.

New York, 19 July, 1885

My Dear Sir:

Certainly in view of your kind note of 17 inst., I do owe you an apology. Still, in justification of my own stupidity in missing the point of your irony, I may say that Silias's [sic] admission that "they" do depreciate the value of property when they get in—a fact concerning the financial accuracy of which I have some doubts—seemed to me rather as an endorsement than a rebuke of what you truly call the "stupid and cruel feeling" against us.

I am glad indeed to have your assurance that the passage will not appear in the book and still more pleased to know that the author whom I have so much admired is not to be counted among the number—unfortunately, too large—of Jew-haters in America.

Very truly yours,

———————

To Mr. W. D. Howells
Old Orchard, Maine.

W. D. HOWELLS

Anachronism†

EDITOR OF THE CENTURY:

SIR: I have seen, without the shame and confusion which the fact might have been expected to bring me, a newspaper paragraph convicting me of "anachronism" in the first installment of my current story in your pages. As I may hereafter repeat this cause of offense to accurate minds, perhaps it will be well for me to state the principle upon which I reconcile it to a conscience not void of the usual anxiety. It appears to me that I discharge my whole duty to reality in giving, as well as I can, the complexion of the period of which I write, and I would as lief as not allow one of my persons to speak of Daisy Millerism, even a whole year before Daisy Miller appeared in print, if it gave a characteristic tint in the portraiture. In like manner I would make bold to use a type-writer in 1875, when it had only come into the market in 1874; and if an electric light threw a more impressive glare upon certain aspects of life than the ordinary gasburner, I should have no hesitation in anticipating the inventions of Mr. Edison several months.[1]

† From *The Century Magazine* 29.3 (January 1885): 477.

1. In the first chapter, Lapham says the year is 1875, thus opening the door to readers' quibbles with a number of apparently anachronistic references elsewhere in the novel. The allusion to Henry James's *Daisy Miller* (1878) occurs in Chapter I, to electric lights in Chapters VI and VIII, and to a typewriter in Chapter XXVI. Thomas Alva Edison (1847–1931) invented the first practical electric light bulb in 1879. The first practical, mass-produced typewriter was introduced to the American market in 1874, which, as one sympathetic reader noted in Howells's defense in a letter to the *Critic* magazine, made Howells "'all right' on the type-writer question." Howells wrote his letter to *Century* several months before introducing the alleged typewriter anachronism into the novel. As to Howells's self-defense, not everyone was convinced: Robert Bridges, for instance, writing under the pen name "Droch" in the January 1 issue of *Life*, declared that "Anachronisms are about as consistent with 'contemporaneousness' as thefts with honesty." Detailed discussion of the novel's temporal setting and other anachronisms may be found in Walter J. Meserve's "Introduction" to the *Selected Edition* of the novel.

An artist illustrating my story would put the people in the fashions of 1884, though they actually dressed in those of 1875, and I think he would be right; for it is the effect of contemporaneousness that is to be given, and the general truth is sometimes better than the specific fact.

W. D. Howells.

Howells, Literary Realism, and American Literary History

W. D. HOWELLS

From Henry James, Jr.[†]

* * *

If we take him at all we must take him on his own ground, for clearly he will not come to ours. We must make concessions to him, not in this respect only,[1] but in several others, chief among which is the motive for reading fiction. By example, at least, he teaches that it is the pursuit and not the end which should give us pleasure; for he often prefers to leave us to our own conjectures in regard to the fate of the people in whom he has interested us. There is no question, of course, but he could tell the story of Isabel in "The Portrait of a Lady" to the end, yet he does not tell it.[2] We must agree, then, to take what seems a fragment instead of a whole, and to find, when we can, a name for this new kind in fiction. Evidently it is the character, not the fate, of his people which occupies him; when he has fully developed their character he leaves them to what destiny the reader pleases.

The analytic tendency seems to have increased with him as his work has gone on. Some of the earlier tales were very dramatic: "A Passionate Pilgrim," which I should rank above all his other short stories, and for certain rich poetical qualities, above everything else that he has done, is eminently dramatic. But I do not find much that I should call dramatic in "The Portrait of a Lady," while I do find in it an amount of analysis which I should call superabundance if it were not all such good literature. The novelist's main business is to possess his reader with a due conception of his characters and the

† From *The Century Magazine* 25.1 (November 1882): 26, 28.

1. In the preceding paragraphs, Howells discusses the "artistic impartiality" or objectivity of James's narrators.
2. James's *The Portrait of a Lady* (1881) ends with a degree of plot irresolution atypical of its contemporary novels.

situations in which they find themselves. If he does more or less than this he equally fails. I have sometimes thought that Mr. James's danger was to do more, but when I have been ready to declare this excess an error of his method I have hesitated. Could anything be superfluous that had given me so much pleasure as I read? Certainly from only one point of view, and this a rather narrow, technical one. It seems to me that an enlightened criticism will recognize in Mr. James's fiction a metaphysical genius working to æsthetic results, and will not be disposed to deny it any method it chooses to employ. No other novelist, except George Eliot, has dealt so largely in analysis of motive, has so fully explained and commented upon the springs of action in the persons of the drama, both before and after the facts. These novelists are more alike than any others in their processes, but with George Eliot an ethical purpose is dominant, and with Mr. James an artistic purpose. * * *

* * *

The art of fiction has, in fact, become a finer art in our day than it was with Dickens and Thackeray. We could not suffer the confidential attitude of the latter now, nor the mannerism of the former, any more than we could endure the prolixity of Richardson or the coarseness of Fielding. These great men are of the past—they and their methods and interests; even Trollope and Reade are not of the present. The new school derives from Hawthorne and George Eliot rather than any others; but it studies human nature much more in its wonted aspects, and finds its ethical and dramatic examples in the operation of lighter but not really less vital motives. The moving accident is certainly not its trade; and it prefers to avoid all manner of dire catastrophes. It is largely influenced by French fiction in form; but it is the realism of Daudet rather than the realism of Zola that prevails with it, and it has a soul of its own which is above the business of recording the rather brutish pursuit of a woman by a man, which seems to be the chief end of the French novelist. This school, which is so largely of the future as well as the present, finds its chief exemplar in Mr. James; it is he who is shaping and directing American fiction, at least. It is the ambition of the younger contributors to write like him; he has his following more distinctly recognizable than that of any other English-writing novelist. Whether he will so far control this following as to decide the nature of the novel with us remains to be seen. Will the reader be content to accept a novel which is an analytic study rather than a story, which is apt to leave him arbiter of the destiny of the author's creations? Will he find his account in the unflagging interest of their development? Mr. James's growing popularity seems to suggest that this may be the case; but the work of Mr. James's imitators will have much to do with the final result.

* * *

W. D. HOWELLS

From Editor's Study

[*Classicism, Romance, and Realism*]†

* * *

It is droll to find Balzac,[1] who suffered such bitter scorn and hate for his realism while he was alive, now become a fetich in his turn, to be shaken in the faces of those who will not blindly worship him. But it is no new thing in the history of literature: whatever is established is sacred with those who do not think. At the beginning of the century, when romance was making the same fight against effete classicism which realism is making today against effete romance, the Italian poet Monti[2] declared that "the romantic was the cold grave of the Beautiful," just as the realistic is now supposed to be. The romance of that day and the realism of this are in certain degree the same. Romance then sought, as realism seeks now, to widen the bounds of sympathy, to level every barrier against æsthetic freedom, to escape from the paralysis of tradition. It exhausted itself in this impulse; and it remained for realism to assert that fidelity to experience and probability of motive are essential conditions of a great imaginative literature. It is not a new theory, but it has never before universally characterized literary endeavor. When realism becomes false to itself, when it heaps up facts merely, and maps life instead of picturing it, realism will perish too. Every true realist instinctively knows this, and it is perhaps the reason why he is careful of every fact, and feels himself bound to express or to indicate its meaning at the risk of over-moralizing. In life he finds nothing insignificant; all tells for destiny and character; nothing that God has made is contemptible. He cannot look upon human life and declare this thing or that thing unworthy of notice, any more than the scientist can declare a fact of the material world beneath the dignity of his inquiry. He feels in every nerve the equality of things and the unity of men; his soul is

† From *Harper's New Monthly Magazine* 72.432 (May 1886): 973.
1. Honoré de Balzac (1799–1850), author of a series of fictions collectively titled *La Comédie Humaine*, chronicling a broad spectrum of early-19th-century French social life.
2. Vincenzo Monti (1754–1828), Italian poet and playwright.

exalted, not by vain shows and shadows and ideals, but by realities, in which alone the truth lives. In criticism it is his business to break the images of false gods and misshapen heroes, to take away the poor silly toys that many grown people would still like to play with. * * *

[*The Russian Novel, Realism, and Humanism*]†

The readers of Tourguéneff and of Tolstoy must now add Dostoïevsky[3] to their list if they wish to understand the reasons for the supremacy of the Russians in modern fiction; and we think they must put him beside these two, and not below either, in moral and artistic qualities. They are all so very much more than realists that this name, never satisfactory in regard to any school of writers, seems altogether insufficient for them. They are realists in ascertaining an entire probability of motive and situation in their work; but with them this is only the beginning; they go so far beyond it in purpose and effect that one must cast about for some other word if one would try to define them. Perhaps humanist would be the best phrase in which to clothe the idea of their literary office, if it could be limited to mean their simply, almost humbly, fraternal attitude toward the persons and conditions with which they deal, and again extended to include a profound sense of that individual responsibility from which the common responsibility can free no one. * * *

[*Popular Fiction and the Test of Truth*]‡

* * *

* * * It may be safely assumed that most of the novel-reading which people fancy is an intellectual pastime is the emptiest dissipation, hardly more related to thought or the wholesome exercise of the mental faculties than opium-eating; in either case the brain is drugged, and left weaker and crazier for the debauch. If this may be called the negative result of the fiction habit, the positive injury that most novels work is by no means so easily to be measured in the case of young men whose character they help so much to form or deform, and the women of all ages whom they keep so much in ignorance of the world they misrepresent. Grown men have little harm from them, but in the other cases, which are the vast majority, they hurt because they are not true—not because they are malevolent, but because they are idle lies about human nature and the social fabric, which it behooves us to know and to understand, that we may deal justly with

† From *Harper's New Monthly Magazine* 73.436 (September 1886): 639.

3. Ivan Turgenev (1818–1883), Leo Tolstoy (1828–1910), Fyodor Dostoyevsky (1821–1881), Russian novelists.

‡ From *Harper's New Monthly Magazine* 74.443 (April 1887): 825–26.

ourselves and with one another. One need not go so far as our correspondent, and trace to the fiction habit "whatever is wild and visionary, whatever is untrue, whatever is injurious," in one's life; bad as the fiction habit is, it is probably not responsible for the whole sum of evil in its victims, and we believe that if the reader will use care in choosing from this fungus-growth with which the fields of literature teem every day, he may nourish himself as with the true mushroom, at no risk from the poisonous species.

* * *

Without taking them too seriously, it still must be owned that the "gaudy hero and heroine" are to blame for a great deal of harm in the world. That heroine long taught by example, if not precept, that Love, or the passion or fancy she mistook for it, was the chief interest of a life which is really concerned with a great many other things; that it was lasting in the way she knew it; that it was worthy of every sacrifice, and was altogether a finer thing than prudence, obedience, reason; that love alone was glorious and beautiful, and these were mean and ugly in comparison with it. More lately she has begun to idolize and illustrate Duty, and she is hardly less mischievous in this new rôle, opposing duty, as she did love, to prudence, obedience, and reason. The stock hero, whom, if we met him, we could not fail to see was a most deplorable person, has undoubtedly imposed himself upon the victims of the fiction habit as admirable. With him, too, love was and is the great affair, whether in its old romantic phase of chivalrous achievement or manifold suffering for love's sake, or its more recent development of the "virile," the bullying, and the brutal, or its still more recent agonies of self-sacrifice, as idle and useless as the moral experiences of the insane asylums. With his vain posturings and his ridiculous splendor he is really a painted barbarian, the prey of his passions and his delusions, full of obsolete ideals, and the motives and ethics of a savage, which the guilty author of his being does his best—or his worst—in spite of his own light and knowledge, to foist upon the reader as something generous and noble. We are not merely bringing this charge against that sort of fiction which is beneath literature and outside of it, "the shoreless lakes of ditch-water," whose miasms fill the air below the empyrean where the great ones sit; but we are accusing the work of some of the most famous, who have, in this instance or in that, sinned against the truth, which can alone exalt and purify men. We do not say that they have constantly done so, or even commonly done so; but that they have done so at all marks them as of the past, to be read with the due historical allowance for their epoch and their conditions. For we believe that, while inferior writers will and must continue to imitate them in their foibles and their errors, no one hereafter will be able to achieve greatness who is false to humanity, either in its facts or its duties. * * *

* * *

* * * For our own part we confess that we do not care to judge any work of the imagination without first of all applying this test to it. We must ask ourselves before we ask anything else, Is it true?—true to the motives, the impulses, the principles that shape the life of actual men and women? This truth, which necessarily includes the highest morality and the highest artistry—this truth given, the book *cannot* be wicked and cannot be weak; and without it all graces of style and feats of invention and cunning of construction are so many superfluities of naughtiness. It is well for the truth to have all these, and shine in them, but for falsehood they are merely meretricious, the bedizenment of the wanton; they atone for nothing, they count for nothing. But in fact they come naturally of truth, and grace it without solicitation; they are added unto it. In the whole range of fiction we know of no *true* picture of life—that is, of human nature—which is not also a masterpiece of literature, full of divine and natural beauty. It may have no touch or tint of this special civilization or of that; it had *better* have this local color well ascertained; but the truth is deeper and finer than aspects, and if the book is true to what men and women know of one another's souls it will be true enough, and it will be great and beautiful. It is the conception of literature as something apart from life, super-finely aloof, which makes it really unimportant to the great mass of mankind, without a message or a meaning for them; and it is the notion that a novel may be false in its portrayal of causes and effects that makes literary art contemptible even to those whom it amuses, that forbids them to regard the novelist as a serious or right-minded person. If they do not in some moment of indignation cry out against all novels, as our correspondent does, they remain besotted in the fume of the delusions purveyed to them, with no higher feeling for the author than such maudlin affection as the *habitué* of an opium-joint perhaps knows for the attendant who fills his pipe with the drug.

* * *

[*Fiction and the "Unthinking Multitude"*]†

* * *

Yet even as regards the "unthinking multitude," we believe we are not able to take the attitude of the writer we have quoted.[4] We are

† From *Harper's New Monthly Magazine* 75.448 (September 1887): 638–39.

4. The first section of Howells's essay responds to a writer in another magazine who had asserted as a valid test of a novel's literary excellence its popularity among the "unthinking multitude clamoring about the book counters."

afraid that we respect them more than he would like to have us, though we cannot always respect their taste, any more than that of the "literary elect." We respect them for their good sense in most practical matters; for their laborious, honest lives; for their kindness, their good-will; for that aspiration toward something better than themselves which seems to stir, however dumbly, in every human breast not abandoned to literary pride or other forms of self-righteousness. We find every man interesting, whether he thinks or unthinks, whether he is savage or civilized; for this reason we cannot thank the novelist who teaches us not to know, but to unknow, our kind; and we cannot believe that Miss Murfree[5] will feel herself praised by a critic who says she has made her Tennessee mountaineers acceptable to us because she "has fashioned them as they are not." We believe that she has made them acceptable for exactly the opposite reason, and has taught us to see the inner loveliness and tenderness, however slight and evanescent, of those poor, hard, dull, narrow lives, with an exquisite sympathy which we are afraid must remain unknown to the lovers of the sweet-pretty. The perfect portrayal of what passes even in a soul whose body smokes a cob-pipe or dips snuff, and dwells in a log hut on a mountain-side, would be worth more than all the fancies ever feigned; and we value Miss Murfree's work for the degree in which it approaches this perfection. It is when she seems to have drawn upon romance and tradition rather than life for her colors that we have wished her to "give us her mountain folk as she saw them before her fancy began to work upon them." This may be "babbling folly," and "sheer, unmixed nonsense"; our critic is so sure of himself as to be able to call it so; but we venture to reaffirm it. It appears to us that the opposite position is one of the last refuges of the aristocratic spirit which is disappearing from politics and society, and is now seeking to shelter itself in aesthetics. The pride of caste is becoming the pride of taste; but as before, it is averse to the mass of men; it consents to know them only in some conventionalized and artificial guise. It seeks to withdraw itself, to stand aloof; to be distinguished, and not to be identified. Democracy in literature is the reverse of all this. It wishes to know and to tell the truth, confident that consolation and delight are there; it does not care to paint the marvellous and impossible for the vulgar many, or to sentimentalize and falsify the actual for the vulgar few. Men are more like than unlike one another: let us make them know one another better, that they may be all humbled and strengthened with a sense of their fraternity. Neither arts, nor letters, nor

5. Mary Noailles Murfree (1850–1922), writing under the name Charles Egbert Craddock, published *The Prophet of the Great Smoky Mountains*, which Howells reviewed favorably, in 1885.

sciences, except as they somehow, clearly or obscurely, tend to make the race better and kinder, are to be regarded as serious interests; they are all lower than the rudest crafts that feed and house and clothe, for except they do this office they are idle; and they cannot do this except from and through the truth.

* * *

[*The Ideal and the Real Grasshopper*][†]

* * *

The time is coming, we trust, when each new author, each new artist, will be considered, not in his proportion to any other author or artist, but in his relation to the human nature, known to us all, which it is his privilege, his high duty, to interpret. "The true standard of the artist is in every man's power" already, as Burke says; Michelangelo's "light of the piazza," the glance of the common eye, is and always was the best light on a statue; Goethe's[6] "boys and blackbirds" have in all ages been the real connoisseurs of berries; but hitherto the mass of common men have been afraid to apply their own simplicity, naturalness, and honesty to the appreciation of the beautiful. They have always cast about for the instruction of some one who professed to know better, and who browbeat wholesome common-sense into the self-distrust that ends in sophistication. They have fallen generally to the worst of this bad species, and have been "amused and misled" (how pretty that quaint old use of *amuse* is!) "by the false lights" of critical vanity and self-righteousness. They have been taught to compare what they see and what they read, not with the things that they have observed and known, but with the things that some other artist or writer has done. Especially if they have themselves the artistic impulse in any direction they are taught to form themselves, not upon life, but upon the masters who became masters only by forming themselves upon life. The seeds of death are planted in them, and they can produce only the stillborn, the academic. They are not told to take their work into the public square and see if it seems true to the chance passer, but to test it by the work of the very men who refused and decried any other test of their own work. The young writer who attempts to report the phrase and carriage of every-day life, who tries to tell just how he has heard men talk and seen them look, is made to

† From *Harper's New Monthly Magazine* 76.451 (December 1887): 154–55.

6. Johann Wolfgang von Goethe (1749–1832), foremost writer in the German Romantic movement. Howells quotes part I, section XIX of *A Philosophical Enquiry into the Origin of Our Ideas of the Sublime and Beautiful* (1757) by British aesthetic theorist Edmund Burke (1729–1797). Michelangelo di Lodovico Buonarroti Simoni (1475–1564), Italian Renaissance painter, sculptor, and architect.

feel guilty of something low and unworthy by the stupid people who would like to have him show how Shakespeare's men talked and looked, or Scott's, or Thackeray's, or Balzac's, or Hawthorne's, or Dickens's;[7] he is instructed to idealize his personages; that is, to take the life-likeness out of them, and put the literary-likeness into them. He is approached in the spirit of the wretched pedantry into which learning, much or little, always decays when it withdraws itself and stands apart from experience in an attitude of imagined superiority, and which would say with the same confidence to the scientist: "I see that you are looking at a grasshopper there which you have found in the grass, and I suppose you intend to describe it. Now don't waste your time and sin against culture in *that* way. I've got a grasshopper here, which has been evolved at considerable pains and expense out of the grasshopper in general; in fact, it's a type. It's made up of wire and cardboard, very prettily painted in a conventional tint, and it's perfectly indestructible. It isn't very much like a real grasshopper, but it's a great deal nicer, and it's served to represent the notion of a grasshopper ever since man emerged from barbarism. You may say that it's artificial. Well, it *is* artificial; but then it's ideal too; and what you want to do is to cultivate the ideal. You'll find the books full of my kind of grasshopper, and scarcely a trace of yours in any of them. The thing that you are proposing to do is commonplace; but if you say that it isn't commonplace, for the very reason that it hasn't been done before, you'll have to admit that it's photographic."

As we said, we hope the time is coming when not only the artist, but the common, average man, who always "has the standard of the arts in his power," will have also the courage to apply it, and will reject the ideal grasshopper wherever he finds it, in science, in literature, in art, because it is not "simple, natural, and honest," because it is not like a real grasshopper. But we will own that we think the time is yet far off, and that the people who have been brought up on the ideal grasshopper, the heroic grasshopper, the impassioned grasshopper, the self-devoted, adventureful, good old romantic cardboard grasshopper, must die out before the simple, honest, and natural grasshopper can have a fair field. * * *

7. Sir Walter Scott (1771–1832), William Makepeace Thackeray (1811–1863), Honoré de Balzac (1799–1850), Nathaniel Hawthorne (1804–1864), Charles Dickens (1812–1870), novelists. William Shakespeare (1564–1616), poet and playwright.

W. D. HOWELLS

From Novel-Writing and Novel-Reading: An Impersonal Explanation†

* * *

The reader who is not an author considers what the book is; the author who is a reader, considers, will he, nill he, how the book has been done. It is so in every art. The painter, sculptor, architect, musician feels to his inmost soul the beauty of the picture, statue, edifice, symphony, but he feels still more thoroughly the skill which manifests that beauty. This difference is from everlasting to everlasting, and it disposes instantly of the grotesque pretension that the artist is not the best critic of his art. He is the best of all possible critics. Others may learn to enjoy, to reason and to infer in the presence of a work of art; but he alone who has wrought in the same kind can feel and know concerning it from instinct and from experience. Construction and criticism go hand in hand. No man ever yet imagined beauty without imagining more beauty and less; he *senses*, as the good common phrase has it, the limitations to the expression of beauty; and if he is an artist he puts himself in the place of the man who made the thing of beauty before him, clothes himself in his possibilities, and lives the failure and the success which it records. His word, if honest, is the supreme criticism.

By beauty of course I mean truth, for the one involves the other; it is only the false in art which is ugly, and it is only the false which is immoral. The truth may be indecent, but it cannot be vicious, it can never corrupt or deprave; and I should say this in defence of the grossest material honestly treated in modern novels as against the painted and perfumed meretriciousness of the novels that went before them. I conceive that apart from all the clamor about schools of fiction is the question of truth, how to get it in, so that it may get itself out again as beauty, the divinely living thing, which all men love and worship. So I make truth the prime test of a novel. If I do not find that it is like life, then it does not exist for me as art: it is ugly, it is ludicrous, it is impossible. I do not expect a novel to be wholly true; I have never read one that seemed to me so save Tolstoy's novels; but I expect it to be a constant endeavor for the truth, and I perceive beauty in it so far as it fulfills this endeavor. I am quite willing to recognize and enjoy whatever measure of truth I find in a

† From a manuscript (1896–99?) housed in the Rutherford B. Hayes Presidential Library & Museums, Fremont, OH. Reprinted by permission of the library. Transcribed by the editor for this Norton Critical Edition.

novel that is partly or mainly false; only, if I come upon the falsehood at the outset I am apt not to read that novel. But I do not bear such a grudge against it as I do against the novel which lures me on with a fair face of truth, and drops the mask midway.

* * *

The truth which I mean, the truth which is the only beauty, is truth to human experience, and human experience is so manifold and so recondite, that no scheme can be too remote, too airy for the test. It is a well ascertained fact concerning the imagination that it can work only with the stuff of experience. It can absolutely create nothing; it can only compose. The most fantastic extravagance comes under the same law that exacts likeness to the known as well as the closest and severest study of life. Once for all, then, obedience to this law is the creed of the realist, and rebellion is the creed of the romanticist. Both necessarily work under it, but one willingly, to beautiful effect, and the other unwillingly to ugly effect.

For the reader, whether he is an author too, or not, the only test of a novel's truth is his own knowledge of life. Is it like what he has seen or felt? Then it is true, and for him it cannot otherwise be true, that is to say beautiful. It will not avail that it has style, learning, thinking, feeling; it is no more beautiful without truth than the pretty statue which cannot stand on its feet.

* * *

Of course, there are several ways of regarding life in fiction, and in order to do justice to the different kinds we ought to distinguish very clearly between them. There are three forms, which I think of, and which I will name in the order of their greatness: the novel, the romance, and the romanticistic novel.

The novel I take to be the sincere and conscientious endeavor to picture life just as it is, to deal with character as we witness it in living people, and to record the incidents that grow out of character. This is the supreme form of fiction, and I offer as supreme examples of it, Pride and Prejudice, Middlemarch, Anna Karenina, Fathers and Sons, Doña Perfecta, & Marta y Maria,[1] sufficiently varied in their origin and material and method, but all of the same absolute honesty in their intention. They all rely for their moral effect simply and solely upon their truth to nature.

The romance is of as great purity of intention as the novel, but it deals with life allegorically and not representatively; it employs types

1. Novels, respectively, by Jane Austen (English, 1775–1817), George Eliot (English, 1819–1880), Leo Tolstoy (Russian, 1828–1910), Ivan Turgenev (Russian, 1818–1883), Benito Pérez Galdós (Spanish, 1843–1920), and Armando Palacio Valdés (Spanish, 1853–1938).

rather than characters, and studies them in the ideal rather than the real; it handles the passions broadly. Altogether the greatest in this kind are The Scarlet Letter and The Marble Faun of Hawthorne, which partake of the nature of poems, and which, as they frankly place themselves outside of familiar experience and circumstance, are not to be judged by the rules of criticism that apply to the novel. In this sort, Judd's Margaret is another eminent example that occurs to me; and some of you will think of Mrs. Shelley's Frankenstein, & of Stevenson's Jekyll and Hyde.[2] I suggest also Chamisso's Peter Schlemihl.[3]

The romanticistic novel professes like the real novel to portray actual life, but it does this with an excess of drawing and coloring which are false to nature. It attributes motives to people which do not govern real people, and its characters are of the quality of types; they are heroic, for good or for bad. It seeks effect rather than truth; and endeavors to hide in a cloud of incident the deformity and artificiality of its creations. It revels in the extravagant, the unusual and the bizarre. * * * If you wish to darken council by asking how it is that these inferior romanticists are still incomparably the most popular novelists, I can only whisper, in strict confidence, that by far the greatest number of people in the world, even the civilized world, are people of weak and childish imagination, pleased with gross fables, fond of prodigies, heroes, heroines, portents and improbabilities, without self-knowledge, and without the wish for it. Only in some such exceptional assemblage as the present, do they even prefer truth to lies in art, and it is a great advance for them to prefer the half-lies which they get in romanticistic novels.

I believe, nevertheless, that the novelist has a grave duty to his readers; and I wish his reader realized that he has a grave duty to the novelist, and ought to exact the truth of him. But most readers think that they ought only to exact amusement of him. They are satisfied if they can get that, and often they have to be satisfied without it.

* * *

You will sometimes find it said by the critics that such and such a novel has evidently been written with such and such an object; but unless it is the work of a mere artizan, and no artist at all, I believe this is never the fact. If it is a work of art, it promptly takes itself out of the order of polemics or of ethics, and primarily consents to be nothing if not aesthetical. Its story is the thing that tells, first of all,

2. Sylvester Judd (American, 1813–1853), Mary Wollstonecraft Shelley (English, 1797–1851), and Robert Louis Stevenson (Scottish, 1850–1894).
3. Adelbert von Chamisso (German, 1781–1838).

and if that does not tell, nothing in it tells. It is said that one reason why Tolstoy, when he felt the sorrow of the world laid upon, decided to write no more novels, because no matter how full he filled these with the desire of his soul to help those that have no helper, he found that what went into the minds of most readers was merely the story.

Then shall the novel have no purpose? Shall it not try to do good? Shall this unrivalled, this inapproachable form, beside which epic and drama dwindle to puny dwarfishness, and are so little that they can both be lost in its vast room, shall this do nothing to better men and uplift them? Shall it only amuse them? No, and a thousand times, no! But it shall be a mission to their higher selves only so far as it shall charm their minds and win their hearts. It shall do no good directly. It shall not be the bread, but the grain of wheat which must sprout and grow in the reader's soul, and be harvested in his experience, and in the mills of the gods ground slowly perhaps many years before it shall duly nourish him. I do not mean that there can never be any immediate good from novels. I do not see how any one can read The Scarlet Letter, or Middlemarch, or Romola, without being instantly seized with the dread of falsehood. This is in the way to the love of truth. It is the first step, the indispensable first step towards that love, but it is by no means arrival at it. The novel can teach, and for shame's sake, it must teach, but only by painting life truly. This is what it must above all things strive to do. If it succeeds, every good effect shall come from it: delight, use, wisdom. If it does [not] succeed in this, no good can come of it. Let no reader, and let no intending novelist suppose that this fidelity to life can be carried too far. After all, and when the artist has given his whole might to the realization of his ideal, he will have only an *effect* of life. I think the effect is like that in those cycloramas[4] where up to a certain point there is real ground and real grass, and then carried indivisibly on to the canvass the best that the painter can do to imitate real ground and real grass. We start in our novels with something we have known of life, that is, with life itself; and then we go on and imitate what we have known of life. If we are very skillful and very patient we can *hide the joint*. But the joint is always there, and on one side of it are real ground and real grass, and on the other are the painted images of ground and grass. I do not believe that there was ever any one who longed more strenuously or

4. Popular late-19th-century art form consisting of very large, panoramic paintings depicting landscapes and/or historical events. The panels were arranged in a circle surrounding viewers, typically outdoors and often including real objects in the foreground, creating the illusion for spectators on the inside of the cylinder of being in the midst of the scene depicted. Extant examples of cycloramas depicting Civil War battles are housed in Gettysburg, Pennsylvania, and Atlanta, Georgia.

endeavored more constantly to make the painted ground and grass exactly like the real, than I have done in my cycloramas. But I have to own that I have never yet succeeded to my own satisfaction. Some touch of color, some tone of texture is always wanting; the light is different; it is all in another region. At the same time I have the immense, the sufficient consolation, of knowing that I have not denied such truth as was in me by imitating unreal ground and unreal grass, or even by copying the effect of some other's effort to represent real ground and real grass.

Early in the practice of my art I perceived that what I must do in fiction, if I were to do anything worth while, was to get into it from life the things that had not been got into fiction before. At the very first, of course I tried to do the things that I found done already, or the kind of things especially as I found them in English novels. These had been approved as fit for literature, and they alone were imaginably fit for it. But I tried some other things, and found them fit too. Then I said to myself that I would throw away my English glasses, and look at American life with my own American eyes, and report the things I saw there, whether they were like the things in English fiction or not. In a modest measure this plan succeeded, and I could not commend any other to the American novelist.

I do not mean to say, however, that one's work is always of this intentional, this voluntary sort. On the contrary, there is so much which is unintentional and involuntary, that one might very well believe one's self inspired if one did not know better. For instance, each novel has a law of its own, which it seems to create for itself. Almost from the beginning it has its peculiar temperament and quality, and if you happen to be writing that novel you feel that you must respect its law. You, who are master of the whole affair, cannot violate its law without taking its life.

* * *

When I began to write fiction we were under the romantic superstition that the hero must do something to *win* the heroine; perform some valorous or generous act; save her from danger, as a burning building or a breaking bridge, or the like, or at least be nursed by her through a long and dangerous sickness. In compliance with this burdensome tradition, I had my hero rescue my heroine from a ferocious bulldog, which I remember was thought rather *infra dig.* by some of the critics; but I had no other mortal peril handy, and a bulldog is really a very dangerous animal. This was in my first novel;[5] after that I began to look about me and consider. I observed that none of the loved husbands of the happy wives I knew had done

5. This incident occurs in *A Chance Acquaintance* (1873).

anything to "win" them accept pay a certain number of visits, send them flowers, dance or sit out dances with them at parties, and then muster courage to ask if they would have them. Amongst the young people of my acquaintance, I noticed that this simple and convenient sort of conquest was still going on; and I asked myself why it should be different in books. It was certainly very delightful as I saw it in nature, and why try to paint the lily or tint the rose? After that I let my heroes win my heroines by being as nice fellows as I could make them. But even then I felt that they both expected too much of me; and it was about this time that I had many long and serious talks with my friend, Mr. Henry James, as to how we might eliminate the everlasting young man and young woman, as we called them. We imagined a great many intrigues in which they should *not* be the principal personages; I remember he had one very notable scheme for a novel whose interest should centre about a mother and a son. Still, however, he is writing stories, as I still am about the everlasting man and young woman; though I do think we have managed somewhat to moderate them a little as to their importance in fiction. I suppose we must always have them there, as we must always have them in life, if the race is to go on; but I think the modern novel is more clearly ascertaining their place. Their dominance of course was owing to the belief that young people were the chief readers of fiction. I daresay this is true yet; but I doubt if it is the young people who make the fortune of a novel. Rather, I fancy, its prosperity lies in the favor of women of all ages—and (I was going to say) sexes. These are the most devoted novel-readers, the most intelligent (after the novelists themselves) and the most influential, by far. It is the man of feminine refinement and of feminine culture, with us so much greater than masculine culture, who loves fiction, but amongst other sorts of men I have observed that lawyers are the greatest novel-readers. They read, however, for the story, the distraction, the relief; and after them come physicians, who read novels for much the same reasons, but more for the psychological interest than lawyers. The more liberal sorts of ministers read novels, with an eye to the ethical problems treated; but none of these read so nearly from the novelists' own standpoint as the women. Like the novelists, these read with sympathy for the way the thing is done, with an eye for the shades of character, the distribution of motive, the management of the intrigue, and not merely for the story, or so much for the psychological and ethical aspects of it. Business men, I fancy, seldom read novels at all; they read newspapers.

Fiction is the chief intellectual stimulus of our time, whether we like the fact or not, and taking it in the broad sense if not the deep sense, it is the chief intellectual influence. I should say moral influence, too; but it is often a moral stimulus without being a moral influence; it reaches the mind, and stops short of the conduct. As to the prime fact involved, I think we have but to recall the books of any last year of modern times, and we cannot question it. It is ninety-nine chances out of a hundred that the book which at any given moment is making the world talk, and making the world think is a novel.

* * *

In fine, of the end of the ends, as the Italians say, truth to life is the supreme office of the novel, in whatever form. I am always saying this, and I can say no other. If you like to have it in different words, the business of the novelist is to make you understand the real world through his faithful effigy of it; or, as I have said before, to arrange a perspective for you with everything in its proper relation and proportion to everything else, and this so manifest that you cannot err in it however myopic or astimatic [sic] you may be. It is his function to help you to be kinder to your fellows, juster to yourself, truer to all.

Mostly, I should say, he has failed. I can think of [no] one, except Tolstoy alone, who has met the high requirements of his gift, although I am tempted to add Björnsen[6] in some of his later books. But in spite of his long and almost invariable failure, I have great hopes of the novelist. His art, which is as old as the world, is yet the newest in it, and still very imperfect. But no novelist can think of it without feeling its immeasurable possibilities, without owning that in every instance the weakness, the wrong is in himself, and not in his art.

SUSAN GOODMAN

[Howells's Influence, Importance, and Public Reputation][†]

I

Perhaps no other writer has influenced American letters as much as William Dean Howells (1837–1920) or been so fully forgotten by the novel-reading public he helped to shape. At twenty-three, with some poems and a campaign biography of Abraham Lincoln to his credit, this self-educated Midwesterner made a pilgrimage

6. Bjørnstjerne Bjørnson (1832–1910).

† From "William Dean Howells: The Lessons of a Master," in *Civil Wars: American Novelists and Manners, 1880–1940* (Baltimore: Johns Hopkins UP, 2003), pp. 13–19, 158–59. © 2003 Johns Hopkins University Press. Reprinted by permission of the publisher.

to Boston, then the literary capital of the United States. There he met James Russell Lowell, Nathaniel Hawthorne, Ralph Waldo Emerson, and Oliver Wendell Holmes. Lowell invited him to dinner at the Parker House, which Holmes jokingly proclaimed a version of the apostolic succession. Time proved him nothing less than clairvoyant. Howells succeeded Lowell and James T. Fields to the editor's chair of the *Atlantic Monthly* (1871–81) before moving to New York and *Harper's* in 1885.

The stewardship of the most respected magazines of his day gave Howells tremendous power. Not only did he sway the tastes, values, and mores of a growing middle-class readership, he also brokered literary reputations. Apart from paying well, serialization in the *Atlantic* or *Harper's* created a market for book publication and conferred immediate legitimacy. So did a review by the editor. "Such an encomium from such a source!" is how Charles Chesnutt phrased it when Howells launched his career with a favorable review of *The Conjure Woman* (1899).[1] As Chesnutt knew, Howells possessed an almost unassailable authority, and over three decades of exercising in equal measure ruthlessness and charm, he shaped a canon of American literature that stretched far into the twentieth century.

It is hard to imagine what American culture as well as American literature might have become without Howells, who made both more inclusive and less provincial. He introduced American readers to the work of Thomas Hardy, Émile Zola, Leo Tolstoy, Henrik Ibsen, Björnstjerne Björnson, and Ivan Turgenev, and he championed Henry James when others dismissed him as unreadable and unpatriotic for settling in Europe. Howells remained a fierce enemy of sentimental fiction, though not of female "scribblers," and promoted the careers of regional writers, many of them women. He brought the perspective of African Americans, such as Chesnutt and Paul Laurence Dunbar, into the literary mainstream, arguing, sometimes like a man possessed, that American fiction needed an infusion of "real" life or the very subjects polite society ignored.[2] Looking back to his early years at the *Atlantic*, he explained that the magazine had become southern, midwestern, and far-western in its sympathies without ceasing to be Bostonian at heart. He himself had been much of the reason.

Ironically, Howells's small-town Ohio background and his work for country newspapers, including his father's own *Ashtabula*

1. Charles Chesnutt, "Post-Bellum—Pre-Harlem," in *The Crisis* 40, no. 6 (1931): 194.
2. William Dean Howells, "Novel-Writing and Novel-Reading: An Impersonal Explanation," in *A Selected Edition of William Dean Howells, Selected Literary Criticism* (Bloomington, Indiana University Press, 1993), 3:223.

Howells cited *April Hopes* (1887) as the first time he had a "distinct consciousness" that he was "writing as a realist." See Kermit Vanderbilt, introduction to *April Hopes* (Bloomington: Indiana University Press, 1974), xv.

Sentinel, gave him a cultural perspective that was at once national and international. The story of Howells's childhood reads like an encapsulated history of nineteenth-century America, with its changing demographics, the collapse of the family farm, experiments with communal living, stands against slavery, and the rise of the middle class. Where else save the West of American legend could the son of a man defined by his deficiencies—not a "very good poet, not a very good farmer, not a very good printer, [and] not a very good editor"—ever dream of becoming a consul to Venice or the first president of the American Academy of Arts and Letters?[3]

The subject of manners naturally interested a man intent on bettering his own fortunes and who as a boy had lived on the edge of poverty and respectability. Howells did not know what to say about a man who refused to consider "the things that make for prosperity."[4] And his father did not. William Cooper, a radical in politics, a Swedenborgian by religion, and a failure by habit, had his ten-year-old son setting a thousand ems of type a day, and could barely keep his eight children adequately clothed and fed. The year that Howells turned thirteen, his family, destitute and with no prospects on the horizon, retreated to the wilderness of Eureka Mills on the Little Miami River. Much as Americans might mythologize log cabins as outposts of civilization, these primitive dwellings, surrounded by primeval forests, did produce new visions of democracy and one of America's most literate writers. W. D. Howells always had "prosperity" in mind, married "above" his station, wrote enough books to feed several families (as at least three of his siblings could testify), and went on to become as wealthy perhaps as he was famous. Like Benjamin Franklin, he followed a regimen of self-improvement that would make him a "gentleman," someone "known and respected the moment he is seen" for his "unaffected pride of self . . . tempered with courtesy."[5]

In the many places the Howells family lived (Martin's Ferry, Hamilton, Dayton, Ashtabula, Jefferson, Columbus, and Eureka Mills), they were a class unto themselves. Howells's father employed three journeymen, a boy apprentice, and several girl compositors, but he and his sons also worked with the people he hired. While Howells saw through middle-class trimmings, or "bric-à-brac Jamescracks" as he called them,[6] he also yearned for what they represented, the

3. William Dean Howells, in William Cooper Howells, *Recollections of Life in Ohio from 1813–1840* (Gainesville, Fla.: Scholars' Facsimiles and Reprints, 1963), v.
4. William Dean Howells, *Years of My Youth and Three Essays*, ed. David J. Nordloh (Bloomington: Indiana University Press, 1975), 24.
5. William Dean Howells, *The Early Prose Writings of William Dean Howells, 1852–1861*, ed. Thomas Wortham (Athens: Ohio University Press, 1990), 73–74.
6. William Dean Howells, *A Hazard of New Fortunes*, intro. Everett Carter (Bloomington: Indiana University Press, 1993), 49.

unassailable respectability that came with financial stability. He never worshipped money for its own sake, *and* he never denied its importance. Few people were more aware of or amused by his uncertain social status than Howells himself, who enjoyed the advantages of a class he could not wholly sanction. Howells never entirely resolved his own ambivalence about the groups he liked to call the masses and the classes.[7] As long as both existed, he felt that he could "never be at home anywhere in the world" (*Literature and Life*, 35). To some extent, he remained a feted outsider in the insular world of Harvard-educated Boston, never losing his midwesterner's skepticism about standards and behavior stereotyped as "eastern" (self-consciously intellectual or arty). In "Literary Boston As I Knew It," he remembers his sense of failure when he expressed something "native" to those who accepted only Boston theories and Boston criticisms,[8] which to Howells seemed "Puritanical" or outmoded and sterile.

It should come as no surprise that Howells found most intriguing those times and places where behavior remained indeterminately on the social margin. He brought a unique perspective to the novel when American society was redefining its attitudes about class, a term that became part of the popular lexicon in the early 1900s. Andrew Jackson's presidency (1829–37), which ended in the year of Howells's birth, had inaugurated a new era, symbolized geographically by the building of the Baltimore and Ohio Railroad, and politically by the formation of the Working Men's Party of Philadelphia, a precursor of organized labor. Not only did the United States have to respond to forces from without, particularly waves of European immigrants, it confronted forces from within, when, for example, members of the working urban class made their way into the ranks of businessmen and industrial capitalists. Then, too, the definition of "class" as largely economic became amended by considerations such as the status accorded certain professionals, the descendants of patrician families, or those who accrued public honors. Howells's fiction examines how these and other socioeconomic changes result in what would appear to be contradictory responses: a stricter stratification of classes coupled with a weakening of standards of conduct and social hierarchies. Democracy seemed to Howells at a crucial stage in its history, offering, on the one hand, the promise of true equality; on the other, oligarchy or even anarchy.

7. See William Dean Howells, "The Man of Letters as a Man of Business," *Literature and Life* (New York: Harper & Brothers, 1902), 35.
8. William Dean Howells, *Literary Friends and Acquaintance*, ed. David F. Hiatt and Edwin H. Cady (Bloomington: Indiana University Press, 1968), 100.

Howells's revisioning of the American novel cannot be separated from his understanding of social realism. A Marxist might argue that social and economic forces determined Howells's concept of realism, and in part Howells himself would have agreed. But he refused to see the world from one, limiting perspective. "America is so big and the life here has so many sides," he told an interviewer in 1898, "that a writer can't synthesize it."[9] The conditions of his life, not least of all his Swedenborgian upbringing, made him acutely aware of the tenuous nature of reality. To a Swedenborgian like Howells's father, individual acts of perception make any reality possible, for they reveal a world of inner and outer correspondences. Howells was not a Swedenborgian, yet he did believe people individually responsible for their actions. This affects his view of the possibilities of fiction and the accountability of the artist.

According to Howells's code, anyone who believed that fiction could change people's lives had a civic obligation to tell the "truth," which naturally differed from writer to writer. This may help to explain his wide-ranging generosity, his admiration for fiction as different as Rebecca Harding Davis's *Life in the Iron Mills* (1861) or Stephen Crane's *Maggie: A Girl of the Streets* (1893), and his close friendships with two very different men and writers, Mark Twain and Henry James.

Howells's own books, especially those written after the 1870s, simultaneously salute and deplore the instability of modern life. Their subject is—to borrow from T. S. Eliot's "The Hollow Men"—the shadow that falls between the idea and the reality, that intermediate world of conscience between the emotion and the response. Howells not only wrote about the deepening "sense of unreality" at the heart of his era's middle class life,[1] he embodied it, having suffered from attacks of intense and extended anxiety as an adolescent. During these periods, he became convinced that he had contracted hydrophobia or rabies. Though his symptoms lessened after his marriage in 1862, they never fully disappeared. Whether Howells looked outward or inward, he saw forces, social and hereditary, beyond his control.

Howells believed in those favorite nineteenth-century shibboleths, honor and duty. More than anything, he believed in work. "If you

9. "As Howells Sees Fiction," in [Howells,] *Interviews with William Dean Howells*, ed. Ulrich Halfmann, *American Literary Realism* 6, no. 4 (1973): 335.

1. See Amy Kaplan, *The Social Construction of American Realism* (Chicago: University of Chicago Press, 1988), 9. Kaplan argues that realists like Howells "engage in an enormous act of construction to organize, re-form, and control the social world," which makes it both static and "tentative" (10). See also Donald E. Pease, introduction to *New Essays on "The Rise of Silas Lapham,"* ed. Donald E. Pease (Cambridge: Oxford University Press, 1991), 1–28. Pease gives a historical overview of the critical response to Howells.

can't do all you want to, at present," he advised a younger brother, "don't give up trying to do something. There's a way out of everything. I think hopelessness is about as bad as atheism."[2] He was to need his own advice. Many times, notably after the death of his oldest daughter Winifred in 1889, hopelessness seemed his one reality. Yet Howells chose to emphasize moments of recuperation, as opposed to homogeneity, not because he shied away from truth or lacked courage but because he saw no other alternative.

Howells differs from previous novelists in two evident ways: He emphasized the political and commercial significance of manners; and he assumed their ability to bestow cultural authority. He understood that the tipping of a hat brim might betray an entire system of power. Manners granted a kind of moral sway that those belonging to the "wrong" class had to earn. They placed one in relationship to a whole set of values that Howells himself questioned without abandoning.

When Howells wrested the novel of manners from the upper class (and took the capital S out of society), he operated on the principle that nothing was too common or paltry a subject for fiction. Critics thought his work plotless, it so replicated the eventless rhythms, the humdrum artlessness of daily life. "In defiance of novelistic convention, which asked for elaborate plots, for heroes and crises," his stories seemed to transcend form or tell themselves. Foreshadowing the fiction of Willa Cather, they leave readers with "an impression of outlines not filled in." Howells was a playwright as well as a novelist, and as such he tried to realize "a middle form between narrative and drama, which may be developed into something very pleasant to the reader, and convenient to the fictionalist."[3] The same might be said of his novels, with their resistance to linear plotting, limited characters, and suppressed action. He didn't want "much world, or effect of it," in his fictions,[4] yet how many other writers could make a country picnic carry the social weight of an Academy dinner given by a celebrated Faubourg hostess? Domestic details absorbed his attention. In weekly Sunday letters to his family, he sang the praises of potato cakes, English walnuts, and apricots, and argued the pros and cons of different models of furnaces. Here is a man who, finding the private world of family and friends no less fascinating than the public world of business and politics, belies nineteenth-century stereotypes about gender.[5] Howells did not

2. Letter, William Dean Howells to John Howells, June 1, 1863, in *Selected Letters of W. D. Howells*, ed. George Arms et al. (Boston: Twayne, 1979), 1:152.
3. Letter, William Dean Howells to John Hay, 22 February 1877, in *John Hay-Howells Letters*, ed. George Monterio and Brenda Murphy (Boston: Twayne, 1980), 24.
4. Letter, William Dean Howells to Charles D. Warner, April 1, 1877, in *Selected Letters*, 2:160.
5. See Alfred Habegger, *Gender, Fantasy, and Realism in American Literature* (New York: Columbia University Press, 1982), 62–62, 233.

recognize separate spheres for men and women. Though he could be chauvinistic, he also encouraged his female relatives to pursue careers in literature and the arts. Later writers may have thought his fiction too domesticated or too feminine. A compulsive writer, Howells naturally wrote about everything he knew, and he remained faithful to reality rather than to literary conventions, even those of the realism he popularized.

By expanding the definition of "manners" to include its most unassuming, even vulgar forms, Howells hoped to communicate the entire prospect of American life, or what his friend Henry James described as "our whole democratic light and shade."[6] Anyone who wants to "trace American 'society' in its formative process," advised Thomas Wentworth Higginson in 1880, "must go to Howells. . . . he alone shows you the essential forces in action."[7] Those forces include large cultural patterns and class shifts, from labor unrest in *A Hazard of New Fortunes* (1890) to interracial marriage in *An Imperative Duty* (1891). More personally, they reflect trends in the production and consumption of literature that self-consciously critique Howells's own position as his country's quintessential man of letters.

In an ironic twist of fate, Howells became a victim of his own success. He had hoped to mentor "the whole family" of younger writers—his title for a novel that contained chapters by himself ("The Father") and other well-known authors of his day, including Elizabeth Stuart Phelps ("The Married Daughter"), Henry James ("The Son-In-Law"), and Mary Wilkins Freeman ("The Old-Maid Aunt").[8] Alas (to repeat Wharton), succeeding generations of realists thought his daring hopelessly old-fashioned. No matter that he had exhorted them to expose the "dark places of the soul, the filthy and squalid places of society, high and low" ("Novel-Writing and Novel-Reading," 228), he had become identified with a Victorian gentility bordering on prudishness. Even as old a friend as Wharton accused him of an "incurable moral timidity which again and again checked him on the verge of a masterpiece."[9] Considering the magnitude of his own competitiveness, James remained unwaveringly loyal. He may have harbored private doubts about

6. Henry James, "A Letter to Mr. Howells," *North American Review* 195 (April 1912): 561; published in Michael Anesko, *Letters, Fictions, Lives: Henry James and William Dean Howells* (New York: Oxford University Press, 1997), 452.
7. Thomas Wentworth Higginson, *Short Studies of American Authors* (Boston: Lee & Shepard, 1880), 36–37.
8. See Alfred Bendixen, introduction to *The Whole Family: A Novel by Twelve Authors* (New York: Ungar, 1987), xi, xxxv. *Harper's Bazar* carried the novel from December 1907 to November 1908. See also "Henry James and the *Bazaar* Letters," in *Howells and James: A Double Billing*, ed. Leon Edel and Lyall H. Powers (New York: New York Public Library, 1958), 27–55.
9. Edith Wharton, *A Backward Glance* (New York: Charles Scribner's Sons, 1964), 148.

the "grasping" quality or the depth of Howells's mind, but never his courage or moral resolution.

Howells's dismissal was perhaps inevitable, a case of "the hungry generations" gobbling their elders.[1] It also had something to do with questions of manners. Howells became identified with patrician standards of polite behavior, his books fit reading for young ladies in need of instruction. Howells did voice concerns about the content of fiction, and so did Edith Wharton, Ellen Glasgow, and Jessie Fauset. For him, the problem of aesthetics went beyond matters of sex or personal squeamishness. In fact, Howells, who called himself Victorian in his preference for decency, believed shame to be good in the sense that it kept one honest. "The style is the man," he wrote, for words cannot disguise the "manner of man" within.[2]

Today Howells, who wrote over a hundred books, is most remembered for a single novel, *The Rise of Silas Lapham* (1885). Yet Thomas Higginson's assessment of Howells's contribution to American letters remains as true at the turn of the twenty-first century as it did a century ago. Before James's "Daisy Miller," Howells had studied the "American girl" in Europe and the conflict between distinct cultures. His focus on the middle class, its prejudices and politics, its morals and manners, allowed him to survey a changing American population from its rural and urban poor to its gilded millionaires. "Stroke by stroke and book by book" (James, 561), this historian of culture appraised the character of his compatriots.

1. Letter, Henry James to Sara Norton Darwin, September 11, 1907, in *Henry James Letters*, ed. Leon Edel (Cambridge: Harvard University Press, 1984), 4:504 n. I.
2. William Dean Howells, *My Literary Passions: Criticism and Fiction* (New York: Harper & Brothers, 1895), 15.

American Society in the Gilded Age

JAY MARTIN

From The Massing of Forces—The Forging of Masses†

The changes that took place in America between the Civil War and the First World War were remarkable both for their completeness and for their rapidity. Institutions, systems of belief, ideological and social assumptions, ways of feeling at home in the world—in short, the whole scene of human endeavor and thought—that had existed, as Henry Adams said, since the Middle Ages, now passed away during this fifty-year period. Confusion, resulting from feelings of personal alienation amid the loss of social stability, became more and more apparent. * * *

* * * The characteristics of the period between the wars have been abundantly delineated by contemporary witnesses and the historians who have studied their testimony. A study of them reveals the following as the basic concerns with which the mind, in this age, had to deal.

The Rise of Wealth

Among the best early critics of the age, Henry Adams and Charles Francis Adams, Jr. showed, in their *Chapters of Erie* (1871), that

> the great operations of war, the handling of large masses of men, the influence of discipline, the lavish expenditure of unprecedented sums of money, the immense financial operations, the possibilities of effective co-operation [during the war], were lessons not likely to be lost on men quick to receive and to apply all new ideas.[1]

† From *Harvests of Change: American Literature 1865–1914* (Englewood Cliffs, NJ: Prentice-Hall, 1967), pp. 1–11. Copyright © Jay Martin. Reprinted by permission of the author.

1. *Chapters of Erie and Other Essays* (New York, 1871), p. 135.

Wartime needs in meat-packing, transportation, clothing, and weapons had not only created several millionaires, but also soon engendered, as Rebecca Harding Davis lamented, "the disease of money-getting [that] . . . has infected the nation."[2] The reasons for this astounding growth of wealth are now rather clear. Even before the end of the war, however, Lincoln had expressed his fears for a postwar America that, as Tocqueville had earlier, he now foresaw coming under the domination of a manufacturing aristocracy. To his friend W. R. Ellis, Lincoln wrote prophetically:

> I see in the near future a crisis arising that unnerves me and causes me to tremble for the safety of my country. By a result of the war, corporations have been enthroned, and an era of corruption in high places will follow, and the money power of the country will endeavor to prolong its reign by working upon the prejudices of the people, until all wealth is aggregated in a few hands and the Republic is destroyed.[3]

Not long after, as if in ironic and tragic confirmation of Lincoln's prophecy, Mrs. E. F. Ellet, describing *The Court Circles of the Republic*—itself a revelatory title—noted that despite the recent assassination of President Lincoln, "the fashionable season [in Washington] of 1866 was almost a carnival"[4] in the splendor of its entertainments. The parade of wealth had begun. From a handful of millionaires before the war, the number grew to over 4,000 by the early '90s.[5] With agrarian control of Congress ended by secession, the government was able to enact a series of laws that gave added power to Northern industrial interests. Railroad subsidies, the National Banking Act, the relaxation of immigration laws, increases in the tariff—these not only helped to achieve victory, but continued, after the war, to provide convenient channels for rapid industrial growth.

To compensate for war years of frustration and loss, men hurried to exploit (and exhaust) the natural and human resources of the country. Sensitive contemporary observers remarked the feverish, almost compulsive, intensity of business activity. So obvious were the symptoms of human exhaustion by the '80s that even Herbert Spencer, whose Social Darwinism American businessmen saw as their *apologia,* ironically proposed a "Gospel of Relaxation" to replace the Gospel of Work in America.

2. *Bits of Gossip* (Westminster, England, 1904), p. 138.
3. Quoted in Sylvia Bowman, *The Year 2000: A Critical Biography of Edward Bellamy* (New York, 1958), p. 74.
4. *The Court Circles of the Republic, Or the Beauties and Celebrities of the Nation . . . Sold by Subscription Only* (Hartford, 1869), p. 550.
5. See Edward Chase Kirkland, *Dream and Thought in the Business Community* (Ithaca, 1956), p. 6.

A rapidly increasing passion for frivolous or distracting entertainment also became apparent. Barnum and Beecher and their followers trumpeted their jubilees and hosannas for the populace. Men demanded circuses and popular sermons. They demanded, as well, evidence of increased opulence: palatial architecture—supplied by Richard Morris Hunt and McKim, Mead and White—elegant interiors, the possession of imposing art collections—in short, rich taste. "When the rich man gets good architecture, his neighbors will get it too,"[6] Edith Wharton told her audience in her second book, *The Decoration of Houses* (1897). Increased wealth became the myth of the time, at all levels of society. Citizens of O. Henry's Four Million imagined themselves, like Dreiser's Carrie Meeber, being reborn as denizens of Ward McAllister's Four Hundred.[7]

The Growth of the City

Between the wars city life—and, of course, the mind it fostered—came to dominate American experience. Like the increase in wealth, the city created new aspirations and new ways of satisfying them. Both helped to shape the new, widened consciousness of the age. Nowhere more than in the city were the contrasts between poverty and wealth so appalling; but nowhere else did they hold such fascination. Particularly in America, where man, in the tradition of Jefferson, Emerson, and Whitman, conceived of American destiny in terms of the regenerative frontier, the city symbolized and seemed to embody evil. (In Christian literature, from Dante's Inferno to Bunyan's Vanity Fair, hell was conventionally represented as a crowded city.) But if the city represented something evil for the American, he seemed to feel as well, like Baudelaire at about the same time, that it offered more intense opportunities for human life than possible anywhere else. Both were seeing, as a later American, T. S. Eliot, would interpret Baudelaire's thought, that "it is better, in a paradoxical way, to do evil than to do nothing; at least, we exist."[8] Eliot would make his Waste Land an "Unreal City"; but it was the city as well that in his poem offered the possibility of regeneration. Americans

6. Edith Wharton and Ogden Codman, Jr., *The Decoration of Houses* (New York, 1897), pp. xxi–xxii.
7. The phrase, "The Four Hundred," was said to have been uttered by McAllister, who, requested in 1892 by Mrs. William Astor to draw up a guest list for her annual ball, replied that there were only four hundred socially acceptable people in New York. The phrase and the assumptions which lay behind it were, of course, immediately criticized. Ignatius Donnelly, the Populist lecturer, called the Four Hundred "a hog-show, where men are rated by their financial weight, because it indicates how many shoats they have butted and bumped away from nature's universal trough." See Donnelly, *The Bryan Campaign for the People's Money* (Chicago, 1896), p. 101. The tensions that would arise from four—or forty!—millions of people aspiring to join a Four Hundred—that is, taking wealth as an ideal—are obvious, and make the subject for scores of novels.
8. "Baudelaire" in *Selected Essays* (New York, 1950: "New Edition"), p. 380.

were willing to face evil that they might experience good. Between the wars, while the rural population of America was doubling, urban dwellers multiplied seven times. From a country that was essentially still agrarian in 1865 and, indeed, still contained large unsettled areas, America became, by 1914, bound to cities and city needs. By the time of the First World War, only about 30 per cent of Americans were involved in agriculture; and those, as Sherwood Anderson's books of the grotesque, *Winesburg, Ohio* (1919) and *Poor White* (1920), suggest, were increasingly enfeebled and ineffectual. While Americans were still conceiving of the Middle West as an aspect of the frontier, Ohio and Illinois now had over a hundred towns and cities, including some of the largest in the country. Even in Missouri and Minnesota, three out of every ten inhabitants were townsfolk.[9]

* * *

Immigration

Cities were the first—and most often the last—stop of the waves of immigrants that came to America's shores following the Civil War. Before the War the immigrant was able to adjust to the patterns of rural society with little difficulty. But in the city the problems of adjustment between immigrant and native were more and more intensified. Whitman's multitudinous *Leaves of Grass* and the *Pequod* of Melville's *Moby Dick* (with its English, Dutch, Irish, Portuguese, Sicilian, Danish, Spanish, Negro, and Oriental sailors) had been prophetic of this varied America. Chronicling the march of triumphant democracy in 1885, Andrew Carnegie counted nearly a thousand foreign-language newspapers in the United States.[1] By 1890 a third of all Bostonians were of foreign birth. New York held as many Germans as Hamburg, twice as many Irish as Dublin, and two-and-a-half times as many Jews as Warsaw: it was the greatest immigrant center in the world, with four of every five residents of foreign birth or parentage.[2] The fearful effects of immigration need not be told over. Muckrakers like Jacob Riis and novelists like Stephen Crane vividly portrayed them. It is true that the newcomer to the city was not quite so easily assimilated into American life as, earlier, the Hibernian described in Crèvecoeur's *Letters from an American Farmer* (1782) had been. But immigrants were able, as we can now see, to learn the less obvious patterns of city life almost as readily. It is true as well that the immigrant had in turn decided effects upon

9. See Arthur M. Schlesinger, *The Rise of the City, 1878–1898* (New York, 1933), p. 57.
1. *Triumphant Democracy* (New York, 1886), pp. 344–45.
2. See *ibid.*, pp. 72–3.

the American character. He too, for good or evil, was a force for change. While Immigration Restriction leagues, publicized by Thomas Bailey Aldrich and Henry Cabot Lodge, were lamenting the loss of homogeniety and promulgating a myth of Anglo-Saxon supremacy, immigrants, who for their part, brought with them hopes for a better life, constantly refreshed and revitalized our optimism. The immigrant, who had long used America as a symbol of the Promised Land, helped to produce, as much as the Frontier, the American character. In the period immediately following the Civil War, E. L. Godkin, the Anglo-Irish editor of the *Nation*, embodied the spirit of culture that Lowell, Norton, and Adams were attempting to make American. Later, John Boyle O'Reilly announced that he would run his immigrant paper, *The Pilot*, on "the principles of Democracy as laid down by Jefferson."[3] At the turn of the century, still another immigrant, S. S. McClure, founded the first muckraking magazine, devoted to the analysis and reformation of American industrial and political corruption. "When I came to this country, an immigrant boy, in 1866," he wrote, reflecting his idealism, "I believed that the government of the United States was the flower of all the ages—that nothing could possibly corrupt it."[4] In short, the immigrants to America, along with the American travelers abroad, were making immigration the symbol and occasion for an experience open to the widest and best ideals of culture.

Reform

Writers had to account not only for the uncontrollable forces of change that were altering American culture, but also for those purposeful visions of change that reformers were proposing and seeking to have realized. The triumph of moral idealism in the War left a heritage of reform that conflicted or coalesced with the other elements that have been listed so far. Certainly America seemed to be a land of both promise and broken promises.[5] In 1865, the holy cause of abolition having been won, William Lloyd Garrison suspended publication of *The Liberator*, and, supported by a gift of $30,000

3. O'Reilly created a sensation by the indignation meeting he organized to protest a celebration of the Queen's Jubilee in Boston's Faneuil Hall, where American patriots had spoken during Revolutionary times. To be sure, some of his Irish Anglophobia may have given energy to his indignation; but he protested specifically as an American against this desecration of Revolutionary traditions, and told his audience bitterly: "We must have a hall unpolluted by the breath of Toryism and royalty in Boston." See James Jeffrey Roche, *Life of John Boyle O'Reilly, Together with his Complete Poems and Speeches . . .* (New York, 1891), pp. 347, 307.
4. *My Autobiography* (London, 1914), p. 265.
5. Herbert Croly's *The Promise of American Life* (New York, 1909) summarizes the disillusion of the age in insisting that "the candid reformer can no longer consider the national Promise as destined to automatic fulfillment" (p. 20).

from his admirers, went to Paris.[6] Few prewar reformers, with the exception of Wendell Phillips, carried over their enthusiasm for reform into the new age. And even Phillips faced postwar problems that required for their solution a knowledge of law, economics, sociology, and political science that he did not possess. As Thomas Wentworth Higginson said: "You could not settle the relations of capital and labor off-hand, by saying, as in the case of slavery, 'Let my people go'; the matter was far more complex. It was like trying to adjust a chronometer with no other knowledge than that won by observing a sun-dial."[7] Questions of reform were no longer just abstract or moral; they involved, and demanded knowledge of, the social body. The old reformers—of whom Miss Birdseye in James's *The Bostonians* is a tenderly ironical representative—had no solution; but they lived on and transmitted their moral idealism to the new generation. William Dean Howells—in his protest over the Haymarket Square executions, for instance—found himself treading where older reformers, John Greenleaf Whittier and his peers, could not.[8] Making a science of reform, clergymen, civic organizations, and men of letters from the '70s onward joined as never before to probe and reveal the diseases of the social body. Before the War Rebecca Harding Davis had criticized the "narrow fury" of the Abolitionists, who, "like Saint George . . . thought that one dragon filled the world."[9] But after the War it became increasingly true that reformers were noteworthy precisely for the range of their interests, the ways they were envisioning change on all levels and in all aspects of society. Taken together, the multitude of reformers presented a multiple and magnificent image of the Earthly Paradise, which compelled the mind and held the heart. Almost unbelievably, by the time the First World War began, most of their utopias had become realities.

Education

Part of the program of reform was the argument that increased education was necessary for intelligent participation in political democracy. Congress created the first Department of Education in 1867 to disseminate the gospel of the free-school. In 1872, when the Supreme Court sustained Kalamazoo's right to establish a free high

6. Thomas Beer, *The Mauve Decade: American Life at the End of the Nineteenth Century* (New York, 1926), p. 106.
7. *Contemporaries* (Boston and New York, 1899), p. 276.
8. William Dean Howells remarks bitterly in *Literary Friends and Acquaintance: A Personal Retrospect of American Authorship* (London and New York, 1900) that Whittier had not "appreciated the importance of the social movement" (p. 135).
9. Quoted in [Gerald] Langford, [*The Richard Harding Davis Years: A Biography of Mother and Son* (New York, 1961)], p. 11.

school, Charles Francis Adams, Jr. wrote in *The North American Review*: "The state, therefore, says to the rich: You shall contribute of your abundance for the education of your poor neighbors' children."[1] Nineteen states had adopted compulsory education laws by 1881, and by the time of the First World War, nearly 90 per cent of American children between seven and thirteen were attending school.

Adult education was booming as well. Andrew Carnegie alone gave over $31 million in support of public libraries; and by 1900 the Commissioner of Education reported over 9000 free circulating libraries in the country. Similarly, the Chautauqua movement evoked an astounding response from the adult population. Founded in 1874 by a Methodist minister, John H. Vincent, it spread rapidly until seventy such assemblies were operating at the century's end. Courses in science, literature, music, religion, and government were given. Six presidents of the United States lectured by the shores of Chautauqua Lake. Vincent claimed in 1886 that there were more than "one hundred thousand readers, who for fifty-two weeks in the year turn the pages of useful books, sing songs of college fellowship, [and] think in a larger world."[2] If the Chautauquan might attend swiftly successive Round Tables on Milton, Temperance, and Geology, the thousands who subscribed to winter "star courses" or lecture series were exposed to an even greater variety of entertainment and experience. John L. Stoddard's "travel talks" (illustrated with his double stereopticon), Russell H. Conwell's inspirational "Acres of Diamonds" speech (delivered 5000 times), Will Carleton's recitation of his ballads, Mark Twain, Bill Nye, the Norwegian violinist Ole Bull, George W. Cable (interspersing his tales with Creole melodies), Henry Ward Beecher, the reformed drunkard John B. Gough, Thomas Nast, Henry M. Stanley—these weekly opened up new ranges of experience for an audience whose craving for knowledge seemed hardly satiable. For the first time, a large part of the mass of people was entering, however tentatively, upon the life of the mind.

The Growth of Science and a Naturalistic Test of Truth

While the public school, the Chautauqua movement, free libraries, and lecture series spread knowledge widely, but often thinly, universities were deepening knowledge, particularly along scientific lines, Whereas before the War the president of every important American college had been a clergyman, now scientists, with

1. Quoted in Don M. Wolfe, *The Image of Man in America* (Dallas, 1957), pp. 130–31.
2. *The Chautauqua Movement* (Boston, 1886), p. 35.

John W. Draper's *The Conflict Between Religion and Science* (1874) as their guide, declared war upon religion. In the '60s alone twenty-five scientific schools were founded in a movement which culminated, in 1876, with the establishment of the Johns Hopkins University, which was free from religions obligations.[3] Religion, of course, was not without its champions. One joined in the battle by remarking of Thomas Henry Huxley's address at the opening ceremonies of Johns Hopkins: "It was bad enough to invite Huxley. It were better to have asked God to be present. It would have been absurd to ask them both."[4]

The conspicuous instance of conflict came, of course, in the issue over Darwinism. Between the wars, men were converted—with religious fervor—to the gospel of Darwin. The acceptance of his theory of evolution was part of the general revolt against Calvinism. It assured Americans that Eden was yet to be achieved and that the history of the race was a history of progress. Americans demanded a philosopher of the superman—a Spencer, a Fiske, and later a Nietzsche—to give them a dazzling future, and rejected the philosopher of tragedy like Jonathan Edwards, who offered a glorious, but lost, past. Spencerians, Hegelians, Darwinians, Lamarckians, and catastrophists all spread the excitement, but confused the idea, of evolution. They taught an excited nation how to be modern. In Springfield, Illinois, Lincoln read Darwin and Spencer and "soon grew into the belief in a universal law, evolution." He became, Herndon says, "a warm advocate of the new doctrine."[5] At Yale, President Noah Porter took a volunteer class through Herbert Spencer's *First Principles* with a view toward refuting them; and every member of the class departed a convinced evolutionist.[6] So compellingly did evolution strike the American imagination that, as the Cambridge philosopher Chauncey Wright pointed out, the '70s witnessed the "all but universal" acceptance of a revolutionary doctrine as yet, by rigorous tests of verification, entitled only to be considered a probable hypothesis.[7] No doubt most of the earliest adherents of Darwinism were in the same position as Lady Constance in Benjamin Disraeli's novel *Tancred:*

3. See Stow Persons, *American Minds: A History of Ideas* (New York, 1958), p. 241.
4. Quoted in Richard Hofstadter, *Social Darwinism in American Thought* (New York, 1959: Rev. Ed.), p. 21.
5. William H. Herndon and Jesse W. Weik, *Abraham Lincoln: The True Story of a Great Life* (New York, 1893), Vol. II, p. 148.
6. This is the remembrance of Henry Holt in *Garrulities of an Octogenarian Editor . . .* (Boston and New York, 1923), pp. 49–50. Herbert Spencer was, without question, the philosopher of Americans between the wars, when his books sold with a rapidity unparalleled in philosophic writing—over 370,000 copies in authorized editions between 1860 and 1903.
7. *Philosophical Discussions*, ed. Charles Eliot Norton (New York, 1876), p. 97.

> "You know, all is development. The principle is perpetually going on. First there was nothing; then there was something; then, I forget the next, I think there were shells, then fishes; then we came, let me see, did we come next? Never mind that; we came, at last. And the next change will be something very superior to us, something with wings."[8]

Nevertheless, Americans had committed themselves to science and were ready to follow where it led. Scientific inquiry had not yet outrun common apprehension; and a young diplomat like Henry Adams could make himself an American disciple of Darwinism by his review of Lyell's *Principles* in *The North American Review* for 1868. Adams could feel at home equally with Whitelaw Reid, editor of the *Tribune,* or Clarence King, director of the United States Geological Survey; with political reformers, or with his friends at the Cosmos Club. At the other end of the scale from Adams, John Fiske was defining Darwinism for the masses. His thirty-five Harvard lectures outlining an evolutionary cosmic philosophy were reported verbatim in 1869 to the readers of the New York *World.*[9] In years to come, Fiske's lectures, delivered as far west as Denver, created as much excitement as the arrival of Barnum's circus.

* * *

Technology

In 1874, Mark Twain self-consciously composed a letter on his new $125 typewriter. "I believe it will print faster than I can write," he said proudly. "One may lean back in his chair and work it. It piles an awful stack of words on one page."[1] Inventions were the toys of the age, inventors and industrial promoters its heroes: they seemed to be science incarnate. Technology captured the imagination. Elbert Hubbard's declaration that "a well-appointed factory is a joy" was reechoed in Henry Van Brunt's plea for an architecture of "strict mechanical obedience"; in Washington Gladden's discovery of the "thoughts of God" in "the machine-room of the American Institute" in 1876; in Montgomery Schuyler's analysis of the aesthetics of Brooklyn Bridge; and even in L. H. Morgan's *Ancient Society,* wherein man's progress was measured by invention and discovery, and the railway train thus discovered to be "the triumph of

8. *Tancred, Or the New Crusade* (London, 1847), in *The Works of Benjamin Disraeli* (London, 1927), Vol. X, p. 113.
9. In another striking instance of the news value of science, the New York *Tribune* for September 22, 1876 printed in one extra number all of Huxley's addresses in America.
1. Quoted in Albert Bigelow Paine, *Mark Twain: A Biography* (New York, 1912), Vol. I, p. 537.

civilization."[2] Earlier, in *Walden*, Thoreau had questioned the value of the telegraph; but now technological innovation became an end in itself and compelled, rather than fulfilled, needs.

In a country ostensibly committed to agrarian visions, technology was bound to generate feelings of anxiety.[3] Most of the fears of technology, however, were allayed by the abundance and luxury which seemed to result from it: the Pullman car, with "sofas and arm-chairs, bulging with soft and velvet-bound cushions,"[4] subdued and tranquilized any thought of menace. With the juncture of the Union Pacific and the Central Pacific in 1869, railroads crossed and crisscrossed the West: the Northern Pacific, the Santa Fe, the Rock Island—all were household words. Before and beyond the natural frontier an industrial frontier was arising that would soon replace it.

Rapidly increasing wealth, the rise of the city, expanding immigration, a widened spirit of reform, mass education, a new scientific point of view, and the acceptance of technology as the American way of life—these were the interests that modified, contradicted, or merged with each other in American culture during the period between the wars. So rapid and wholesale were the changes that these made in American culture that the mind found it difficult to accommodate them. As Henry Adams puts this in his *Education* (1918)—one of the books best depicting the impact of change upon a nineteenth-century man—in 1865 he was living in a twentieth-century world with eighteenth-century assumptions about order and purpose in change. What principles of stability he and his peers possessed, he hinted in *Mont-Saint-Michel and Chartres* (1904), were inherited from the Middle Ages. Man had to make his beliefs about his world anew, to accommodate his new circumstances. Certainly the old orders of American culture were dissolving. * * *

2. Elbert Hubbard, *The Romance of Business* (Aurora, New York, 1917), p. 12; Van Brunt quoted in Wayne Andrews, *Architecture, Ambition and Americans* . . . (New York, 1955), p. 150; Washington Gladden, *Working People and their Employers* (New York, 1876), p. 15; and Lewis Henry Morgan, *Ancient Society: Or, Research in the Lines of Human Progress from Savagery Through Barbarism to Civilisation* (New York, 1877), p. 553.
3. These issued into popular myths, such as those of Casey Jones or John Henry, where the individual was destroyed by the machine which he had pitted himself against.
4. [George Makepeace] Towle, *American Society*, [(London, 1870)], Vol. II, p. 180.

JACKSON LEARS

[Capital and Speculation in the Gilded Age]†

* * *

The decades after the Civil War saw the emergence of a freewheeling entrepreneurial society, where capital was unregulated by government and government was manipulated by businessmen to serve their own ends. Crafty speculators, long demonic figures in republican lore, became figures of public fascination and covert admiration—Jay Cooke, the plunger; Jim Fisk, the spender; Jay Gould, the plotter. The great trust builders of the middle and later nineteenth century—Cornelius Vanderbilt, Andrew Carnegie, John D. Rockefeller—enjoyed greater respectability, but they too were little more than freebooting robber barons, in Matthew Josephson's famous phrase. They squeezed competitors dry, smashed unions, and bribed legislatures wholesale. Concentrated capital was responsible only to itself, a raw power that profoundly shaped public policy, influencing every branch of government at every level. Money talked—not for the first time in American politics, but more authoritatively than ever before. No wonder chivalric poseurs succumbed to its insinuations.

Even amid the speculative mania of the Gilded Age, the spread of a money economy was uneven and slow. Farmers and small tradesmen still often resorted to barter. For many Americans in the 1870s, cash was scarce and money exuded an aura of mystery. It could be quantified into apparently precise amounts, yet it remained abstract and arbitrary, a spectral power. This was especially so when it took the form of capital at interest. More than a century earlier, in "Advice to a Young Tradesman" (1748), Benjamin Franklin had summarized the magical power of money to reproduce itself: "Money can beget money, and its offspring can beget more, and so on. Five shillings turned is six, turned again it is seven and threepence, and so on, till it becomes a hundred pounds. The more there is of it, the more it produces every turning, so that profits rise quicker and quicker." Franklin's aphorisms were common currency among Gilded Age Americans. But most could merely dream of quick profits, and only a handful could make money beget money.

Those fortunate few were the capitalists who transformed the American landscape and social order, provoking fascination and

† From *Rebirth of a Nation: The Making of Modern America, 1877–1920* (New York: HarperCollins, 2009), pp. 49–55. Copyright © 2009 by Jackson Lears. Reprinted by permission of HarperCollins Publishers.

fury among the wider population. Despite their attempts to align themselves with the forces of stability, the titans of capital could never quite shake their association with social upheaval. They were magicians of money—to master its mysteries was to exercise an occult power. Nearly all the most successful either had capital to start with or else figured out how to acquire and increase it from an early age. This did not necessarily require hard work, but it did require shrewd bargaining, inside dope, and friends in high places. The spectacle was rarely edifying, but it could be made to seem so. A life of commercial chicanery could be repackaged as a noble assault on adversity. Even P. T. Barnum titled his life story *Struggles and Triumphs.* This was the sort of moral posturing that has given Victorians a bad name. Leading capitalists (including Barnum) shared a fundamental insight with their severest critics (including Karl Marx): they knew that capital, not labor, was the key to economic success. During the first Gilded Age, as in more recent times, moralists penned paeans to work while the rich went about their business, largely oblivious to conventional pieties.

The rest of the population remained divided in mind, fascinated by money but fearful of its corrupting effects. The fascination was all but inevitable. A country lurching headlong into industrial development presented myriad opportunities for the ambitious or the merely greedy. Absence of Old World constraints meant the magic of money was potentially democratized. Longings to experience its transformative effects could be more widely satisfied. Any white male, at least in principle, could take a shot at the main chance. Men and women both could participate in the promise of regeneration through purchase—the fantasy at the heart of the embryonic consumer culture, the faith that paralleled (and sometimes parodied) the older promises of salvation. Peddlers fanned out across the countryside, selling patent medicines and other products that exuded an aura of the mysterious and a prospect of personal transformation.

Still, old suspicions died hard. In popular and often anti-Semitic tradition, money was associated with secret deals, sharp practice, invisible wealth acquired through trickery and guile rather than productive labor. The retail experience of commerce provoked mixed feelings as well. To suspicious customers, selling could seem to be a form of seduction, and peddlers to bring a sexual charge to their transactions with female consumers. Peddlers were often Jews, whose ethnic identity—combined with their mobility and marginality—intensified anxieties about their motives. For many Americans, well into the post–Civil War era, the very act of participating in a market economy was fraught with ambivalent fantasy. Whether it involved speculation in mining or real estate or paper, or simply retail purchase, engagement with the market evoked dreams of sudden self-transformation, and fears that the transaction was nothing more than a trick.

Anxieties surrounding the spread of a market economy focused on the figure of the confidence man, the trickster who manipulated appearances to bilk the unwary and pocket the change. Schemes for making big money overnight pervaded American market culture from earliest colonial days; the European settlement of the New World, despite all the talk about godly communities and holy commonwealths, was mostly little more than a series of risky real estate speculations. But while fascination with fast money was not new, it reached a kind of crescendo during the Gilded Age. So it was altogether fitting that Colonel Beriah Sellers, the protagonist of the novel that gave the age its name, was a purveyor of can't-miss investment scams for everything from Tennessee land to eyewash—a quintessential manipulator of appearances, as Mark Twain and Charles Dudley Warner observed in *The Gilded Age* (1873): "The Colonel's tongue was a magician's wand that turned dried apples into figs and water into wine as easily as it could change a hovel into a palace and present poverty into future riches." This confidence man brings nothing but disaster in his wake for the credulous Squire Hawkins and his son.

The Gilded Age was one of many warnings against misplaced confidence in nineteenth-century American literature, ranging from formulaic moral tracts to the multiplying subtleties of Herman Melville's *The Confidence Man* (1857). As early as 1842, Charles Dickens had found American society pervaded by an atmosphere of "Universal Distrust," and the shape-shifting protagonist of Melville's novel, in his guise as a barber, posts a sign in his shop: "No Trust"—in contemporary parlance, no credit. Yet the other side of universal mistrust was a well-nigh universal need for trust. American entrepreneurs depended heavily on borrowed capital to finance business ventures, as Twain and Warner acknowledged in their ironic peroration: "Beautiful credit! The foundation of modern society. Who shall say that this is not the golden age of mutual trust, of unlimited reliance upon human promises?" Ambitious businessmen were valued in accordance with how much they could be "trusted"—how much, that is, they could persuade a bank to lend them. Indebtedness signified membership in the community of the creditworthy, as the young John D. Rockefeller concluded delightedly after he had been trusted by a Cleveland bank for $2,000. Twain and Warner cite "a distinguished speculator in lands and mines" who remarked: "I wasn't worth a cent two years ago, and now I owe two millions of dollars." The parody left the point intact: an expansive economy required a nearly "unlimited reliance upon human promises."

Yet as the authors of *The Gilded Age* knew, those promises often proved false, and the loans they spawned went bad. A great deal of waste, fraud, and corruption went into the making of the modern American economy, and much of it was concentrated on Wall Street. Railroad stocks, the high-tech stock of the day, epitomized the lurching inefficiency of economic advance. Throughout the 1870s and 1880s, railroads were ridiculously overcapitalized; their stock sold for top dollar while their roadbeds disintegrated and their locomotives lay rusting in ditches. In 1884, *Moody's* reported that $4 billion worth of railroad stock was pure water, in the idiom of the day—that is, artificially inflated beyond its stated ("par") value. But value was an elusive concept. From one point of view, stocks' values depended on what investors would pay for them. In any case, the railroad builders pressed on: between the Civil War and the stock market crash of 1893 they laid 150,000 miles of new track. The transcontinental railroads in particular—the Union Pacific, the Northern Pacific, the Texas and Pacific—continued to capture investors' fancy. Their inflated prices expressed the imperial aspirations of Wall Street financiers after Appomattox.

Out in the countryside, attitudes toward venture capitalism were more complex. During the post–Civil War years, as never before, high-rolling speculation provoked ambivalent fascination among the American populace. Wall Street was a madhouse, a witches' cauldron, critics charged; predatory traders evoked Hobbesian visions of nihilism. Yet there was an undeniable if crude vitality about some of the more fabulous plungers: the tubby womanizer Jim Fisk, a king of the dudes whose "flash" drew a thousand mourners to his funeral; the ferocious Cornelius Vanderbilt, who preferred ruining rivals to suing them. Some, like Vanderbilt and Daniel Drew, a psalm-singing Methodist who made millions by selling watered stock, exuded a risk-taking virility that transformed them from confidence men (at least in the public eye) to Napoleons of finance. Others, like Jay Gould, a sly and secretive man who raised exotic orchids, epitomized the effeminate deceitfulness associated in the male imagination with money manipulators. Whatever their personal style, these capitalists financed a huge industrial explosion even as they systematically corrupted the polity, watering stock and bribing legislatures wholesale, preaching laissez-faire while they depended on government for loans, land, and subsidies.

Such hypocritical freebooters could never be more than temporary heroes. After the stock market crashed in September 1873, the country slipped into five and a half years of the worst depression in its history. Hordes of unemployed men thronged the highways in search of work, while those who kept their jobs faced draconian wage cuts. The big-shot speculators' cultural stock plunged almost as quickly as their portfolios. Even Jay Cooke, who had made himself into a war hero by mass-marketing Union war bonds, became a target of public scorn when his deeply overextended Northern Pacific securities collapsed in price, touching off the panic that led to the crash. By 1877, the Wall Street money men were in bad odor with the rest of the country.

* * *

RICHARD GRANT WHITE

From Class Distinctions in the United States†

* * *

Assuming that no rational person will assert that any form of society can exist without groups of individuals who may be ranked together as possessing common characteristics, and that therefore there must be classes of society, even in the United States, we may yet admit the justice of the often heard protest against their recognition, when we discover what the protesters have in mind. They do not mean classes: they do mean established and privileged classes. There are in the United States no classes of men born, none formed, none recognized in any way, who have the right to do any conceivable thing, to do which all other men have not the right. * * *

The distinctive quality of society in the United States is equality. It is not liberty; still less is it fraternity. Our social and political structure is peculiar among those of the principal communities of the civilized world, not in that here all men's rights are protected,—far from it,—but in that here all men's rights are equal, and not only equal, but absolutely the same. And this equality, or identity, is what the "average American"—be he Irish or German, or born here of Irish or German parents, or of parents native but indefinable—chiefly values. Deny him fraternity if you will; take from him liberty or even property, by form of law, if you can; but leave him equality, and he is measurably content. * * *

* * *

* * * History records no such swift, substantial growth in material prosperity as that of the United States during the last fifty years, and chiefly since the civil war. Men who twenty years ago had

† From *North American Review* 137 (September 1883): 233–46. Richard Grant White (1822–1885) was a prominent social and literary critic and Shakespearean scholar. Notes are by the editor.

nothing have now hundreds of thousands of dollars, millions, tens of millions. And the numbers of those thus suddenly enriched are not hundreds, not thousands or tens of thousands, but hundreds of thousands; while around them are thriving millions in a condition of firm comfort. Upon such a spectacle the sun of prosperity never shone before. Of these men, and of the women who belong to them, very few, in proportion, would be regarded in any other country as educated, still fewer as persons of intellectual or social culture. They have money; nothing more. The result of the forces which have been in operation in this country during the last generation has been to give to this vast multitude two things—unprecedented wealth with absolute equality, likewise without precedent.

* * * Some money is necessary always for the formation and maintenance of a cultivated society; some exclusiveness must be practiced, or your society becomes a general bear-garden.[1] But this society rests upon money only: not upon property, possessions, estates; but upon sheer money, that may be put in a box and carried about, got one day and lost another, like a watch or a toy, and with no more social disturbance; and this exclusiveness excludes only those who have little money, and as to the bears, shuts many of them not out, but in. Let any man who chooses so to spend time and trouble read the highly interesting paragraphs under the "World of Society" and "Circle of Fashion" headings, in three or four of our leading newspapers, and if he has any particular knowledge of society, and a knowledge which extends backward beyond the war, he will see that quite seven-tenths of them relate to people who, at that time, would themselves not have dreamed of themselves as persons of gentility (to use an obsolescent word), not to say of consideration or fashion; people without breeding, without education; whose every word and every tone (surest evidence on such a point) betrays the inferior associations in which they grew up; whose language, whether they speak or write, would be put to shame by that of a well-bred upper servant in England; and whose notions of politeness are confined to the observance of etiquette, which can be taught to a monkey and poured into a man, and yet more easily into a woman, as liquor can be poured out of one vessel into another; who have, indeed, generally a sort of formless, insipid good-nature, but of courtesy, inborn or inbred, no conception whatever. They have simply money,—money which they are ready to spend for their own coarse pleasures; money which they are even willing to give away—for their own aggrandizement; money which they are anxious to use in every

1. A place of chaos and confusion. In the 16th and 17th centuries, bear gardens were public venues constructed for the practice of bear-baiting, wherein dogs were set loose on a chained bear.

mode which will enable them to "get on" and make a figure. Besides these, who are hundreds and thousands, there are others not so prominently rich, who are tens and hundreds of thousands, that are of like origin and social history, and who all more or less affect elegance and "aristocracy," and talk of society and fashion. * * *

* * * The transitory, shifting nature of our newly gotten wealth is one of its most striking and characteristic features. It is not like that of a true aristocracy stayed upon the land, or inwrought with the structure of the Government. * * *

Verily, bats and moles and owls might see that exclusive pretensions and attempts at class distinction in a society based upon wealth acquired by trade or speculation within the memory of living men are too essentially foolish to be worth a moment's respectful consideration. Such pretensions in the United States of to-day are so monstrous, so incongruous, so preposterously absurd, that, if they are continued, some modern Rabelais or Cervantes,[2] looking down upon them from the throne of common sense, and compelled by temptation and material, will dip his pen in ridicule and shake the world with laughter.

Because, however, political or municipal equality is the absolute and unalterable law of the United States of America, now and forever, and because our new "merchant princes" are ridiculous, not as merchants, but as princes, to conclude that we are without a social aristocracy, not unrecognized and not unprized, would show an ignorance worthy of the average European critic of our society. What it is has been hinted in the earlier pages of this article. The several circles which form it in the several centers of society are at once the most reserved and the least pretentious that we have; but access to them is sought and valued by those who are well enough informed in social matters to be aware of their existence. They are confined, of course, to our older commonwealths; for such well-rooted growths do not spring up, even in a republic, in one generation, nor yet in two; and these people were of well-known character and culture and social consideration when even the western part of New York was a savage-haunted wilderness. Some of them have been for a time longer than the age of the United States moderately wealthy, and all of them have been able to command that leisure without which education and social culture are impossible. But wealthy or not, they had such character and such breeding that they were highly considered by their neighbors, who recognized their social superiority, looked up to them as leaders, and sent them as their representatives to the colonial legislatures; and they were judges, ministers, and

2. François Rabelais (French, 1494?–1553) and Miguel de Cervantes (Spanish, 1547?–1616), accomplished writers of social satire [*editor's note*].

clergymen (of the Church of England). Of these people some are now rich, but others are poor (that is, among rich people); but the higher classes, and also the lower, of aristocratic societies detect their quality at once, and are often puzzled by the incongruity of manners and position. * * *

* * * This class realized, as nearly as possible, the ideal of a social aristocracy; for their rule, co-existing with municipal equality, was the social superiority and government of the best. Now, when the best are cast down from their social thrones, their places must be taken by those who are little better than gilded rudesbys and successful sharpers. And, indeed, these social *aristoi*[3] seem to be dwindling in power and importance; beaten down and made comparatively little by the brute power of money in a heterogeneous, half-foreign community, which knows them not, as the Pharaoh arose that knew not Joseph.[4] If the two mingle, the best will surely be debased. That law is absolute. And thus, in any case, it would seem that we are to show that in a perfectly democratic society, where the municipal rights of all are equal and identical, no aristocracy is possible, even in a social sense; but that its seemly and gracious presence must be replaced by a bloated plutocracy, that basest and coarsest and most degrading of social forces.

THORSTEIN VEBLEN

[The Culture of Conspicuous Consumption][†]

Pecuniary Emulation

* * *

The end of acquisition and accumulation is conventionally held to be the consumption of the goods accumulated—whether it is consumption directly by the owner of the goods or by the household attached to him and for this purpose identified with him in theory. This is at least felt to be the economically legitimate end of acquisition, which alone it is incumbent on the theory to take account of. Such consumption may of course be conceived to serve the consumer's physical wants—his physical comfort—or his so-called higher

3. Noblemen in ancient Greece (Greek).
4. In the biblical book of Genesis, the Hebrew Joseph achieves wealth and high rank through service to the Egyptian pharaoh. In the succeeding book of Exodus, however, Joseph's descendants are enslaved by the Egyptians when "there arose up a new king over Egypt, which knew not Joseph" (Exodus 1.8).

† From *The Theory of the Leisure Class: An Economic Study of Institutions* (New York: Macmillan, 1912), pp. 25–26, 36–37, 48–52, 84–86. Thorstein Bunde Veblen (1857–1929) was a contrarian sociologist-economist.

wants—spiritual, æsthetic, intellectual, or what not; the latter class of wants being served indirectly by an expenditure of goods, after the fashion familiar to all economic readers.

But it is only when taken in a sense far removed from its naïve meaning that consumption of goods can be said to afford the incentive from which accumulation invariably proceeds. The motive that lies at the root of ownership is emulation; and the same motive of emulation continues active in the further development of the institution to which it has given rise and in the development of all those features of the social structure which this institution of ownership touches. The possession of wealth confers honour; it is an invidious distinction. Nothing equally cogent can be said for the consumption of goods, nor for any other conceivable incentive to acquisition, and especially not for any incentive to the accumulation of wealth.

It is of course not to be overlooked that in a community where nearly all goods are private property the necessity of earning a livelihood is a powerful and ever-present incentive for the poorer members of the community. The need of subsistence and of an increase of physical comfort may for a time be the dominant motive of acquisition for those classes who are habitually employed at manual labour, whose subsistence is on a precarious footing, who possess little and ordinarily accumulate little; but it will appear in the course of the discussion that even in the case of these impecunious classes the predominance of the motive of physical want is not so decided as has sometimes been assumed. On the other hand, so far as regards those members and classes of the community who are chiefly concerned in the accumulation of wealth, the incentive of subsistence or of physical comfort never plays a considerable part. Ownership began and grew into a human institution on grounds unrelated to the subsistence minimum. The dominant incentive was from the outset the invidious distinction attaching to wealth, and, save temporarily and by exception, no other motive has usurped the primacy at any later stage of the development.

Conspicuous Leisure

* * *

In order to gain and to hold the esteem of men it is not sufficient merely to possess wealth or power. The wealth or power must be put in evidence, for esteem is awarded only on evidence. And not only does the evidence of wealth serve to impress one's importance on others and to keep their sense of his importance alive and alert, but it is of scarcely less use in building up and preserving one's self-complacency. In all but the lowest stages of culture the normally constituted man is comforted and upheld in his self-respect by "decent surroundings" and by exemption from "menial offices." Enforced departure from his habitual standard of decency, either in the paraphernalia of life or in the kind and amount of his every-day activity, is felt to be a slight upon his human dignity, even apart from all conscious consideration of the approval or disapproval of his fellows.

* * *

* * * Refined tastes, manners, and habits of life are a useful evidence of gentility, because good breeding requires time, application, and expense, and can therefore not be compassed by those whose time and energy are taken up with work. A knowledge of good form is *prima facie* evidence that that portion of the well-bred person's life which is not spent under the observation of the spectator has been worthily spent in acquiring accomplishments that are of no lucrative effect. In the last analysis the value of manners lies in the fact that they are the voucher of a life of leisure. Therefore, conversely, since leisure is the conventional means of pecuniary repute, the acquisition of some proficiency in decorum is incumbent on all who aspire to a modicum of pecuniary decency.

So much of the honourable life of leisure as is not spent in the sight of spectators can serve the purposes of reputability only in so far as it leaves a tangible, visible result that can be put in evidence and can be measured and compared with products of the same class exhibited by competing aspirants for repute. Some such effect, in the way of leisurely manners and carriage, etc., follows from simple persistent abstention from work, even where the subject does not take thought of the matter and studiously acquire an air of leisurely opulence and mastery. Especially does it seem to be true that a life of leisure in this way persisted in through several generations will leave a persistent, ascertainable effect in the conformation of the person, and still more in his habitual bearing and demeanour. But all the suggestions of a cumulative life of leisure, and all the proficiency in decorum that comes by the way of passive habituation, may be further improved upon by taking thought and assiduously acquiring the marks of honourable leisure, and then carrying the exhibition of these adventitious marks of exemption from employment out in a strenuous and systematic discipline. Plainly, this is a point at which a diligent application of effort and expenditure may materially further the attainment of a decent proficiency in the leisure-class proprieties. Conversely, the greater the degree of proficiency and the more patent the evidence of a high degree of habituation to observances which serve no lucrative or other directly useful purpose, the greater the consumption of time and substance impliedly involved in their acquisition, and the greater the resultant good repute. Hence, under the competitive struggle for proficiency in good manners, it comes about that much pains is taken with the cultivation of habits of decorum; and hence the details of decorum develop into a comprehensive discipline, conformity to which is required of all who would be held blameless in point of repute. And hence, on the other hand, this conspicuous leisure of which decorum is a ramification grows gradually into a laborious drill in deportment and an education in taste and discrimination as to what articles of consumption are decorous and what are the decorous methods of consuming them.

* * *

There are, moreover, measureable degrees of conformity to the latest accredited code of the punctilios as regards decorous means and methods of consumption. Differences between one person and another in the degree of conformity to the ideal in these respects can be compared, and persons may be graded and scheduled with some accuracy and effect according to a progressive scale of manners and breeding. The award of reputability in this regard is commonly made in good faith, on the ground of conformity to accepted canons of taste in the matters concerned, and without conscious regard to the pecuniary standing or the degree of leisure practised by any given candidate for reputability; but the canons of taste according to which the award is made are constantly under the surveillance of the law of conspicuous leisure, and are indeed constantly undergoing change and revision to bring them into closer conformity with its requirements. So that while the proximate ground of discrimination may be of another kind, still the pervading principle and abiding test of good breeding is the requirement of a substantial and patent waste of time. There may be some considerable range of variation in detail within the scope of this principle, but they are variations of form and expression, not of substance.

* * *

Conspicuous Consumption

* * *

* * * The leisure class stands at the head of the social structure in point of reputability; and its manner of life and its standards of worth therefore afford the norm of reputability for the community. The observance of these standards, in some degree of approximation, becomes incumbent upon all classes lower in the scale. In modern civilized communities the lines of demarcation between social classes have grown vague and transient, and wherever this happens

the norm of reputability imposed by the upper class extends its coercive influence with but slight hindrance down through the social structure to the lowest strata. The result is that the members of each stratum accept as their ideal of decency the scheme of life in vogue in the next higher stratum, and bend their energies to live up to that ideal. On pain of forfeiting their good name and their self-respect in case of failure, they must conform to the accepted code, at least in appearance.

The basis on which good repute in any highly organised industrial community ultimately rests is pecuniary strength; and the means of showing pecuniary strength, and so of gaining or retaining a good name, are leisure and a conspicuous consumption of goods. Accordingly, both of these methods are in vogue as far down the scale as it remains possible; and in the lower strata in which the two methods are employed, both offices are in great part delegated to the wife and children of the household. * * *

From the foregoing survey of the growth of conspicuous leisure and consumption, it appears that the utility of both alike for the purposes of reputability lies in the element of waste that is common to both. In the one case it is a waste of time and effort, in the other it is a waste of goods. Both are methods of demonstrating the possession of wealth, and the two are conventionally accepted as equivalents. The choice between them is a question of advertising expediency simply, except so far as it may be affected by other standards of propriety, springing from a different source. On grounds of expediency the preference may be given to the one or the other at different stages of the economic development. The question is, which of the two methods will most effectively reach the persons whose convictions it is desired to affect. Usage has answered this question in different ways under different circumstances.

* * *

ANONYMOUS

[Dishonesty in Commerce]†

No feature of the present age is more displeasing to the moralist than the dishonesty that so widely prevails in commerce and politics. In whatever direction we turn, this phenomenon meets our eye; and there is no branch of business, no department of

† From "Topics of the Time," *Century Magazine* Vol. 28.3 (July 1884): 463–64.

government, and no class in society in which it does not appear. The forms of commercial dishonesty are almost endless in variety, including not only the old and well-worn tricks of trade, but also some that have been invented or largely developed in recent times. The cases that have been most commented on are the defalcations[1] by presidents, treasurers, and similar persons in charge of the funds of others,—flagrant instances of which have occurred both in this country and in Europe. It may be doubted, however, whether these are the worst or the most common of the dishonest practices of the age,—the malfeasance of the directors of corporations and the cheating on the stock exchanges being probably more flagrantly dishonest and more injurious to the community than are the simple defalcations. The robbery of stockholders and bondholders by their own agents has become a common practice, and some of our leading capitalists seem to make it their principal business. Instances of this sort are so common and so well known that it is not necessary to cite them here, and their pernicious influence is felt both on the commercial prosperity and on the morality of the country.

* * *

It does not necessarily follow that men are more dishonest at heart in our day than in former times; whether they are so or not is difficult to decide, since it is hard to compare the morality of one age with that of another. The spirit of honesty may be as strong as ever, but the temptations to dishonesty are greater than ever before, owing to the immense gains that may often be made by it. It is comparatively easy now for a man in the right position to acquire a large fortune in a few years, by betraying his trust or by prostituting his office to base and unpatriotic uses; and hence a higher morality is required than ever before to keep men in the path of honesty. The greater temptations of the present day demand greater conscientiousness to resist them, and this greater conscientiousness is not always forthcoming. The development of morality has not kept pace with the development of wealth and the facilities for acquiring it; and the result is the dishonesty and corruption that prevail.

* * *

The prime cause of commercial dishonesty and political corruption is a false ideal of life,—an ideal that puts the material interests of man above the spiritual, and makes riches the supreme object of human endeavor; and the only effectual remedy is the establishment of a higher and more spiritual ideal. The facilities for acquiring wealth are, as we have remarked, greater in our time than ever

1. Instances of misappropriation of a business's funds by one of its officers; embezzlement.

before, and men have rushed into the pursuit of it with too little regard for those higher things which, to those capable of appreciating them, make riches of inferior importance. The scramble for wealth thus begun, a paltry emulation has arisen among those engaged in it, so that men who already have more wealth than they know how to enjoy are still eagerly grasping for more, apparently for the mere sake of being richer than their neighbors. And thus avarice has become with multitudes of men an absorbing passion, overbearing the sentiment of justice, and leading to the dishonesty that so widely prevails; and in all probability, so long as this passion is thus dominant, and the pursuit of wealth thus engrosses the minds of men, the dishonest practices will continue, whatever political or legal remedies may be employed to check them.

* * *

The most powerful check upon dishonesty would come, of course, from an increase of the genuine religious spirit, from a deeper love of ideal virtue, and an endeavor, so far as humanity can, to reach it. * * *

Another antidote to dishonesty would be the cultivation among business men of the true business ideal, which consists in a sincere and hearty devotion to the commercial interests of society and the intelligent management of the world's commerce, and not in the mere accumulation of wealth for one's self. Even now this spirit prevails among many of our capitalists, and their example is powerful in making dishonest practices much less frequent than they would otherwise be. Such sentiments as these, if once highly developed in a community, would put a powerful check upon dishonesty in all its forms, and men guilty of it would become the scorn and detestation of their neighbors, and not, as is sometimes the case now, objects of admiration.

* * *

ANONYMOUS

Business Gambling†

Elsewhere in this number of THE CENTURY business gambling is discussed as one of "Three Dangers" which most threaten society, the other two being intemperance and divorce. Perversion of business is certainly the most conspicuous evil, and probably the one from which

† From "Topics of the Time," *Century Magazine* Vol. 28. 4 (August 1884): 629–30.

society has most to fear in the future. Like all other forms of gambling, betting on the future price of stocks and produce is a delusion as a means of money-getting. But it is a delusion which appeals seductively to the popular ambition to get rich easily and quickly. The great exchanges, by letting it in through the same door with honest speculation, and by vouching for the regularity of the gambling transaction, have given the delusion the mask of business. Men of prominence have lent it the mask of respectability. Most of the gigantic fortunes of the country have with their support given it the mask of success. Into the bubble have been drawn "bright" office-boys, "trustworthy" clerks, "sturdy" farmers, "solid" business men, "leading" professional men, "conservative" bank presidents, railway "magnates," and "honored" or "aspiring" statesmen. Those of them who have enjoyed success as fleecers have reasoned that the profits justified the means; and those who have been fleeced have retired on their experience, some maimed, some ruined, and some to nurse the inveterate gambling passion by risking more in the effort to get back what has been lost. Under cover of the enormous gambling transactions, grasping managers of stock companies and dishonest schemers have swelled the bubble with diluted stock and funded moonshine, with the result of breaking down the honest investment market. Such bold-faced robbery as has been practiced in various ways under the name of "stock dividends" could never have happened had not bankers and dealers been demoralized by the profits of illegitimate business.

* * *

ROBERT TOMES

From The Bazar Book of Decorum†

From Chapter I

[THE IMPORTANCE OF MANNERS FOR AMERICAN DEMOCRACY]

* * *

The great purpose of the rules of etiquette is to inculcate good manners, and thus render us mutually agreeable. It is, therefore, especially incumbent upon all Americans to know and obey them, for it is impossible for us to avoid contact. We are all forced, in spite

† From *The Bazar Book of Decorum: The Care of the Person, Manners, Etiquette, and Ceremonials* (New York: Harper & Brothers, 1870), pp. 12–14, 96–97, 127–30, 205–11, 219–22, 235, 238. Notes are by the editor.

of individual objections and protests, to put into practice the national theory of equality. We must mix together, and it therefore behooves us, for our own comfort, to make the mixture as smooth and uniform as possible.

In no country in the world are general good manners so indispensable as in this democratic country. In Europe, where, in society as at the railway stations, different classes are recognized and kept apart by insurmountable barriers and vigilant guards, it is possible, if you happen to be among the high-bred "firsts" or decent "seconds," to endure the existence of the unruly "thirds." These last, in fact, when viewed at a convenient remoteness of distance, are not without their interest. Their unkempt hair, botched and greasy suits, rude manners, and coarse vernacular, are parts of the European picture, and by their own homely raciness, as well as the contrast they afford to the brilliancy of their superiors, seem essential to its effect. To look at a rough and unwashed from the safe distance of European social distinction, by which he is toned down to the picturesqueness of one of Murillo's[1] lousy beggar-boys, is one thing; it is quite another, however, to have him at your elbow on railway and at hotel, where you can hear, feel, and smell him. It is obvious, therefore, that the rough and dirty are quite out of place in this country, where, if they exist, they are sure to be close at your side. Universal cleanliness and good manners are essential to a democracy. This must be generally recognized and acted upon, or the refined will seek in other countries the exclusiveness which will secure for them that nicety of life essential to its enjoyment, and we shall be left alone to wallow in our own brutality and foulness.

There is no reason why propriety of manners should not be as general in the United States as it is exclusive in most countries. With our facility of mixture, any leaven we have can be easily made to pervade the whole mass. There is no vested right, in this country at least, in decency and cleanliness. We can all be, if we please, what we are so fond of calling ourselves, gentlemen and ladies.

* * *

From Chapter VII

[AMERICAN EASE]

With all the faults of manner of the American, no one would think of charging him with a want of ease. Generally feeling at home wherever he goes, he is as apt to be "hale fellow well met" with the king on his throne as with the lackey at the palace door. He is not likely

1. Bartolomé Esteban Murillo (1617–1682), Spanish Baroque painter.

to be taken to account for too much stiffness of body and formality of address. His facility of converse and flexibility of limb are proverbial, and few can equal him in expansiveness of sprawl, reach of boot, and readiness of "jaw." He is unapproachable as an acrobat, and his fine chair balance, or trick of heels up and head down, can not be surpassed by any performer on the social stage. When he presents himself, he is not unlike the clown of our early remembrance, who came with a run, a spring, a somersault, and the shout "Here I am!"

We think that many of our countrymen and countrywomen might be improved by more reserve of manner and less flexibility of limb. Americans can dispense with much freedom of movement and looseness of posture, as indeed of ease of address, without any risk of incurring the imputation of being prigs. In society ordinarily termed good, it is not customary to sit upon more than one chair at a time, nor is the mantelpiece regarded as the proper place for the feet, however well turned the boot or delicately made the shoe. Sprawling of all kinds is avoided by well-bred people, who shun excessive ease as much as excessive formality. It may not be amiss to remind the heedless and the young that, on entering the room of the house of a stranger or that of a visiting acquaintance, it is not becoming to throw themselves at once on the sofa and stretch out their legs, or into the Voltaire or easy-chair, and sink into its luxurious depths. The common seat will be selected by the considerate, and all the exceptional provisions for extra ease and comfort left untouched until the invitation to enjoy them is given.

* * *

From Chapter X

[AMERICAN SPEECH]

Good early culture and habitual association with refined persons are undoubtedly essential to give purity to speech and the highest tone of refinement to conversation. There are many persons who have diligently perfected themselves in a knowledge of the laws of grammar, and become familiar with the style of the chastest writers, and yet can not utter a phrase without betraying the barbarism of a rude origin. It is not uncommon to find people learned in all the rules of syntax, and capable of applying them to the art of writing, who habitually speak incorrectly. Those, too, who are precisians in speech are often ignorant of, and unrestrained by, the laws of grammar in writing. A correct and refined pronunciation, especially, is only to be acquired by hearing it constantly, and from the earliest age, from the lips of those who habitually use it. * * *

Loudness, or what the French call the *criard*, is peculiarly an attribute of American talk, and is not favorable to purity of diction or clearness of thought. This style of conversation is marked by the free use of intense and high-sounding adjectives, generally employed in their superlative degrees. These, moreover, are often most ludicrously misapplied. For example, we hear the "splendidest" weather, the "most beautiful" ice-cream, the "sweetest" clergyman, the "most elegant" sermon, the "awfulest" fine whiskers, the "terrible dress that horrid Miss A——wore," the "dreadfully shocking" hat of Miss B——, and those "magnificent" trowsers of Harry, and "delicious" boots of Tom, gushing from the lips of our young damsels in a torrent of such confused speech that its parts are hardly distinguishable from each other, and form but a turbid mixture of nonsense.

Every few years or so a slang phrase gets somehow or other into vogue. That this should consist merely of the misuse of some familiar term, and not the invention of a new one, like "quiz," for example, shows the comparative poverty of device of us moderns. "Awful" is, for the moment, the abused word, and it is bandied about throughout all the length and breadth of the English language, and consequently all over the globe. For no reason in the world, it has thrown out of usage an appropriate and serviceable adverb, and suddenly taken its place, for which, being an adjective, it is by nature unfit. Wherever the old "very" once becomingly held its own, the impudent interloper "awful" has thrust itself, contrary to all grammatical decorum. Slang of every variety, whether consisting of this absurd abuse of a word, or whatever else, is equally opposed to correctness of speech and propriety of manners.

Profane swearing, or its relatives, the various emphatic expletives, are now never heard in decent society, and people of good breeding are not expected to give pledges of "word" or "honor" as guarantees of their truth and honesty.

* * *

From Chapter XV

[FORMAL DINING]

* * *

The origin of dinner-eating is coeval with the creation of man. Dinner-giving, however, is the later product of advanced civilization. It may be received as an axiom that the social progress of a community is in direct proportion to the number of its dinner-parties. * * * The general tone of science, literature, the fine arts, and taste, is unquestionably sustained by metropolitan social intercourse. If dinner-giving in its capitals were abolished, all Europe, we believe, would relapse into barbarism. In seeking for evidences of American progress in refinement, we should count the number of daily dinner-parties, on the great increase of which of late there is reason to congratulate not only all lovers of good cheer, but friends of their country.

The number of persons at a dinner-party, according to an old saying, should never be "more than the Muses [nine], or less than the Graces [three]." Brillat Savarin[2] says: "Let not the number of the company exceed twelve." He, like all his countrymen, stops suddenly short of the thirteen—an ominous number in the superstitious fancy of the French. Having the belief that this number will be sure to be fatal within the year to some one of the company, it is impossible to persuade thirteen to sit down together at dinner. The host, even, or some accommodating guest, whatever may be the occasion, will be sure to subtract himself from that odd and inauspicious sum, should it be unfortunately cast up at a convivial entertainment.

* * *

The invitations, if the party is a formal one, should be sent about a week or ten days before the dinner. The usual formula is simply this, either written in a note or printed on a card:

"Mr. and Mrs. —— request the pleasure [or honor] of Mr. ——'s company to dinner at — o'clock on ——.

"R. S. V. P."

A formal acceptance should read thus:

"Mr. —— accepts with pleasure Mrs. ——'s invitation to dinner at — o'clock on ——."

All written invitations should be answered immediately in writing, but especially invitations to dinner, and should be complied with at all hazards. If, by any mischance—as the death of a relative, or some other serious cause—the guest, after having once accepted an invitation, is unable to comply with it, he must be careful to send notice of the fact, with his regrets, at the earliest possible moment.

At all dinner-parties the ladies and gentlemen are expected to present themselves in full evening costume. Delicate hosts and hostesses, particularly when the occasion is not a very formal one, will take care to keep their own dresses in due subordination, lest they may possibly outshine too evidently some of their guests, and unnecessarily put them to the blush. Thus a fastidious host will not seldom keep to his frock-coat and black cravat, with a nice consideration for some invited person who may by chance have neglected to put on the swallow-tail and white choker *de rigueur.*

2. Jean Anthelme Brillat-Savarin (1755–1826) published his *The Physiology of Taste, or Meditation on Transcendent Gastronomy* in 1825.

Punctuality is essential to the perfection of dining, as it is to the proper performance of every other social duty. A half hour's grace used to be allowed, and it was not "the thing" to arrive at the exact time appointed. Fashion, however, now sanctions what common sense has always inculcated, and men of society are expected, alike with men of business, to be exact in their engagements.

On reaching the house, the gentleman, if accompanied by a lady, gives her his arm on entering the drawing-room, and the first person addressed should be the hostess. Very fashionable people have a footman at the door to announce the names of the guests as they present themselves. If this is not done, the host or hostess may introduce their visitors to each other, taking care to make as little fuss as possible about it. When introductions are dispensed with, as they may be with propriety, the guests should have no hesitation in conversing freely with each other as mutual acquaintances.

When the dinner is announced, which should be done by the servant simply saying "The dinner is served," a procession is at once formed. The host gives his *right* arm to the female guest who has the precedence from age, rank, or strangeness, and leads her to a place at the dinner-table on his right, he being at the head or at one side. Next comes the most distinguished male guest with the hostess. She seats herself at the other extremity, or at the opposite side of the table, with her cavalier on her right. The rest follow in couples, ranked generally according to age, and as they enter the dining-room are placed so that the host may be flanked on either side by a dame, and the hostess by a cavalier. The rest of the guests are arranged in successive couples, so that each cavalier will be between two dames, and each dame between two cavaliers, provided the sexual proportions of the party allow of such an arrangement. It is usual to separate the husband from his wife, and temporarily sever other domestic relations. This does not seem flattering to the conjugal and family ties, but the practical effect is undoubtedly good.

* * *

From Chapter XVI

[FORMAL DINING, CONTINUED]

At a large dinner-party it is better to confine your powers of entertainment to your immediate neighbors, and avoid bawling out to those opposite or at a considerable distance from you. Where the service is limited, you—if of the masculine gender—must attend constantly to the wants of the dames immediately under your wings. Avoid all gross heaping up of your plate. As a general rule, refuse to be served with more than one kind of meat and vegetable at a time.

There are certain things which are supposed to be sufficiently harmonious for a combination—as, for example, ham and boiled chicken, rice or potatoes and tomatoes. There is one good rule which, if followed, will make you an acceptable guest every where: Be not obtrusive. Do every thing smoothly and quietly. Talk in a low tone of voice, and handle your knife and fork and plate without clatter, and eat without any audible gulping and smacking of the lips.

It was once an essential part of the dinner-table etiquette in England, and in America by inheritance, for the ladies to retire after the dessert and a first round of the wine decanters. The confessed purpose of the practice was to allow the *gentlemen* to indulge freely in strong drink and loose talk, unchecked in their grossness by the restraining influence of refined women. Polished France has given us a lesson of better manners, and the social dinner is now less often marked by this coarse reminder of the divergence of the brutal instincts of one sex from the delicate sentiments of the other. The more refined people in England and the United States now generally adopt the French practice of all rising together from the dinner-table. The effect of this simple change in etiquette has been very great and most beneficial. Drunkenness, once a fashion and almost esteemed a social virtue, is no longer admitted in respectable company, but has been forced to slink away to the bar-room and other haunts of vice.

When the dinner is over and the half of an hour or so has been passed in talk and trifling with the dessert, the hostess gives the signal by rising from the table, and all return to the drawing-room in the order they left. Here coffee and tea are provided, and it is good taste to have them served with as little formality as possible. The less exhibition of the flunkey force on the occasion the better. The tray having been placed by the servant on the table, the dame of the house pours out the beverages, whatever they may be, and invites her guests to partake of them. The gentlemen, of course, take care of the ladies before they take care of themselves, but all is done quite unceremoniously. It is seldom, in fact, that a person takes a seat, but all remain standing, or walk about the drawing-room, conversing or admiring the pictures, articles of *virtù*, and whatever else may invite notice. The visit to the drawing-room, being merely designed to graduate the farewell, and thus render the departure less abrupt, is naturally informal, for it is but a ceremony in an incipient state of dissolution. The stay after dinner, unless additional company has been invited, and there is a supplementary evening party, is seldom prolonged beyond half an hour, when leave is quietly taken.

* * *

From Chapter XVIII

[VISITING]

Every dame nowadays has what is called a visiting list. This is composed of a number of persons of her own sex who spend money, dress, and make calls very much as she herself does. No other sympathy than is indicated by these is required by mutual visitors of the fashionable sort. They need not be friends; it is not, in fact, necessary that they should be acquaintances, and we actually know of two dames who not long since met in the street and looked into each other's face as perfect strangers, though they had been on visiting terms for the last ten years or more. There is so little substance in this kind of social relationship that its obligations can be as well performed by a mere symbol as the person it represents, and thus a bit of card-board, with nothing but a name upon it, frequently serves every purpose.

* * *

There are certain occasions when society exacts the payment of formal visits, as, for example, in exchange for a call of courtesy; after an invitation to a dinner, ball, or other ceremonious entertainment; after weddings, births, and funerals; on any occasion deemed worthy of personal congratulation; on the return of a visiting acquaintance to his residence, whether in town or country; and on the arrival and stay of a visitor at the house of a friend.

* * *

W. D. HOWELLS

From Review of *The Bazar Book of Decorum: The Care of the Person, Manners, Etiquette, and Ceremonials*†

Under many things that otherwise could hardly be borne, the mind is upheld by the hope that in a better state, even on earth, such troubles will be unknown; and we cling to the belief that in a happier and humaner civilization that odious device of society, the polished gentleman, and that invention of the enemy, the accomplished lady, will not exist, and that naturally there will be no books to teach the imitation of their abominable perfection. Men and women born into

† From "Reviews and Literary Notices," *Atlantic Monthly* 26 (July 1870): 122–23.

rich and fashionable society will always be *au fait* in its customs; and people whose wish to rise into that kind of society is cruelly granted will not be kept from betraying their unfashionable origin by all the behavior-books that ever were written. In fact, most behavior-books seem to hint at a pathetic self-consciousness in their authors; they read like the painful warnings of experience, and they are commonly of such a vulgar tone, that it seems better not to seek the difficult circles for which they fit their reader. All the wisdom needed for the career of the ordinary republican[1] aspirant can be condensed into three rules, which he may write down on his reversible paper cuff: 1. Keep out of fine society; 2. Be cleanly, simple, and honest; 3. Never be ashamed of a blunder. Everything beyond these is vanity.

But we suppose that the ordinary republican aspirant will not put up with this succinctness yet a while; and meantime here is happily "The Bazar Book of Decorum," composed in the most elegant language that could be got in the dictionary, and overflowing with fashionable knowledge. The style is really a marvel of genius and learning, and places the ordinary objects in thought and nature in a light so novel and surprising that you feel the freshest interest in them. Would you ever suppose, for example, that you had such a thing as *this* on your face? "The nose, *as is well known*,"—observe the kind intimacy with which this great author stoops to the common mind,—"*is the organ of smell;* for this purpose it is endowed"—now he rises again—"with a pair of nerves, called the olfactory, whose abounding filaments pierce the many holes and cover the multiple surfaces of the light and porous structure termed the spongy bone, which lies at the root of each nostril." We call this a fine diction, and a beautiful use of a familiar object for the illustration of literary power. * * * We must likewise praise him when he calls the female effort to make a small waist, "reducing the centre of the body to an almost impalpable tenuity," as he does in preparing us for a fact that makes us know him at once for a person of the highest breeding: "As we stood admiring that most perfect conception of female grace, the Venus of Milo in the Louvre, we took from the fair woman hanging upon our arm her pocket-handkerchief, and made a comparative measurement of the ancient and modern beauties,"—and did not get his ears boxed, the lucky dog!

Of course, a man who can write like this does not embarrass himself much with the prescription of forms and particular rules for

1. Howells uses the term in its generic sense, referring to a capacious set of ideas about human nature, government, and civic duty that was in wide circulation during the American Revolution and the early years of the American republic and remained influential in the late 19th century. Republican ideology defined the standards of conduct and qualities of character thought to be appropriate to free citizens in a democratic republic, placing equally high values on individual autonomy and public-spiritedness as the surest guarantors of civic virtue in the new American republic.

behavior. He would guard his reader against the habit of passing his pocket-comb through his hair at table, but we believe he nowhere especially tells him not to pick his teeth with his fork. The author is not only a very learned man, as you may judge from his language, but a person of general polite reading, and he chooses to treat mostly of the loftier aspects of his theme, as when, instead of telling us some such thing as that a gentleman always uses his handkerchief in blowing his nose, he touches upon a topic like the control of the emotions and mellifluously polysyllables forth: "A well-bred person is ordinarily disinclined to make a public demonstration of his most affectionate feelings and tenderest sentiments." * * *

We find our author in every way admirable in fact, lofty in thought, proper in sentiment, of a very subtle and characteristic humor, and a severe morality. He is a companion for the toilet and the centre-table, for the study and the drawing-room, in whom we think the reader will find an unfailing pleasure (and profit, of course); and we have quite made up our mind when, in sitting for our mental photograph, we come to that bewildering question, "What book, not the Bible, would you part with last?" to say, "The Bazar Book of Decorum."

Silas Lapham's Boston

Map of Boston, 1875, After the Latest Surveys, with All the Improvements in Progress: A Complete Guide to Strangers, Showing Distinctly the Hotels, Public Buildings, Steam & Horse Rail Roads & Places of Amusement (Boston: L. Prang & Co., 1875). Courtesy of the Norman B. Leventhal Map Center at the Boston Public Library. Call number: G3764.B6 1875 .P7x.

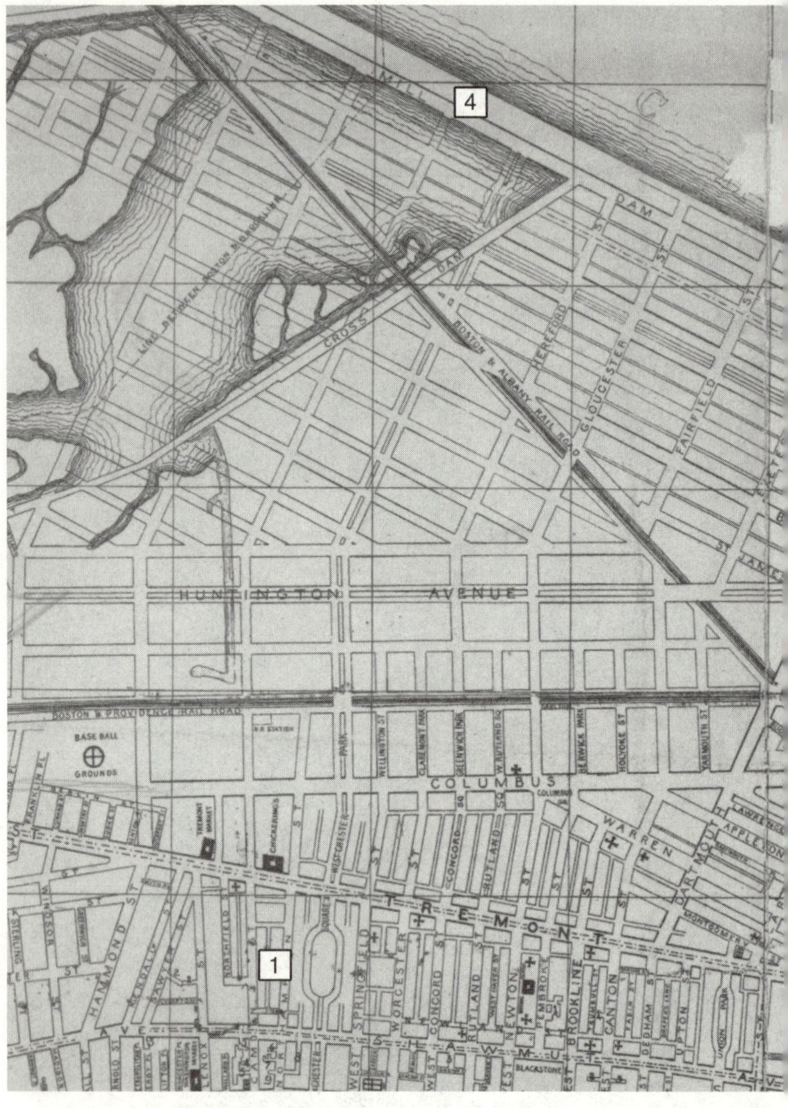

Detail of the map on p. 367, showing places relevant to *The Rise of Silas Lapham*.

1. Chester Square in South Boston, likely the model for Nankeen Square, where the Laphams reside.
2. Location of 302 Beacon Street, "on the water side of Beacon" in the newly filled Back Bay neighborhood: W. D. Howells's residence when writing the novel and the model for the descriptions of the new house Lapham is building. Note the street grid to the west, extending across yet-to-be-filled areas of the bay.

3. Beacon Hill, where the Coreys reside in their house on the fictional Bellingham Place: while Howells leaves the location of their home inexact, internal evidence suggests this location near Mount Vernon and Chestnut Streets and Louisburg Square, where the Howells family lived before purchasing 302 Beacon.
4. The Mill Dam, the westward extension of its successor, Beacon Street, across the unfilled remnant of the Back Bay fens, where Lapham is fond of driving his buggy and sleigh.

F. Fuchs, *View of Boston, July 4, 1870* (Boston: John Weik, 1870). Courtesy of the Norman B. Leventhal Map Center at the Boston Public Library. Call number: G3764.B6A3 1870 .F8. View from the west, down the Charles River toward Beacon Hill,

The Howells Residence (1884–87), 302 Beacon Street in Boston, c. 1885. Courtesy of the Photography Collection, Miriam and Ira D. Wallach Division of Art, Prints and Photographs, The New York Public Library, Astor, Lenox and Tilden Foundations. Image provided to the Library by Mildred Howells, daughter of W. D. Howells.

ELIF S. ARMBRUSTER

From A Crowning Achievement: 302 Beacon Street, 1884–1887†

The Howellses traveled the Northeast and Europe for two years before buying a house on Beacon Street in Boston—one of the city's most expensive addresses. For a hardworking, self-made man like Howells, the purchase of a dignified row house on Beacon Street was the ultimate accomplishment, just as the purchase of a house on the same "water side of Beacon Street" was for Silas Lapham in Howells's novel, *The Rise of Silas Lapham*.

In the 1880s, owning a house on Beacon Street was the surest way to assert one's status and success—the street was arguably one of America's finest. One critic could not understand how it could be so much more attractive than similar streets in New York City: "So much handsomer, neater, more homelike and engaging than our shabby Fifth Avenue," he praised. "Beacon Street is stately; so is Marlborough Street, that runs next parallel it; and even more so is Commonwealth Avenue—with its lines of trees down the center, like a Paris boulevard."[1] Like many of the residential streets in the Back Bay, Beacon Street was lined with rows of impressive brick or brownstone mansions—attached houses that were either made out of or had a façade of brick or reddish brown sandstone called brownstone.[2] Except for corner buildings, the houses had windows on only their narrow ends—the front and back—and were typically twenty-feet wide, in rare cases, twenty-five.

Then, like now, the Back Bay's streets project an air of taste and elegance; yet, many of the neighborhood's houses were constructed quickly in the 1870s and 1880s by speculators who realized the value of the land. One such man by the name of H. Whitwell built the adjacent brick buildings at 300 and 302 Beacon Street; the latter would be inhabited by two great American authors: George Santayana and William Dean Howells. In 1869, when the structures were built, little was done to render them charming. The philosopher and critic, George Santayana, who lived in number 302 as a young boy, offers a compelling snapshot of the place and of the mindset of the speculators in his autobiography, *Persons and Places*:

† From "William Dean Howells: Realism in Transit" in *Domestic Biographies: Stowe, Howells, James, and Wharton at Home* (New York: Peter Lang, 2011), pp. 66–71. Reprinted by permission of the publisher. Page references in brackets refer to this Norton Critical Edition.

1. J. L. and J. B. Gilder, *Authors at Home: Personal and Biographical Sketches of Well-known American Authors* (New York: A. Wessels Company, 1905), 195.
2. Bainbridge Bunting in *Houses of Boston's Back Bay: An Architectural History, 1840–1917* (Cambridge, MA: Belknap Press of Harvard University, 1967), 173.

> Ours was one of two houses exactly alike; yet as they were only two, we could distinguish ours without looking at the number displayed in large figures on the semicircular glass panel over the front door: for ours was the house to the left, not the one to the right. The pair were a product of that 'producer's economy,' then beginning to prevail in America, which first creates articles and then attempts to create a demand for them [. . .] Our twin houses had been designed to attract the buyer, who might sell his bargain again at a profit if he didn't find it satisfactory.[3]

In 1872, when Santayana lived there, many vacant lots surrounded the house, but by 1884, when Howells arrived, the area was far more developed. Aside from the occasional Gothic or Queen Anne style house, the architecture followed a strict pattern: no house of more than five stories, no apartment houses, no fanciful architectural styles.[4] In spite of its prestigious address, Howells's abode at 302 Beacon Street neither "savor[ed] of the architect, nor of the mansion."[5] The narrow, straightforward house featured a reception room and dining room on the ground (or first) floor, front and back parlors on the second floor, two large bedrooms above those, and four small bedrooms on the attic (or fourth) floor; at the time the house was built, there was one bathroom.[6] In the same way he had at Concord Avenue and Redtop, Howells secured a prominent room in the house for his study, using the rear parlor on the second floor for this purpose.

According to Santayana, the redeeming feature of the structure was its "unmistakably impressive" unobstructed view of the Charles River.[7] Paradoxically, though townhouses such as the one that Santayana and Howells lived in were quickly and inexpensively built by profit-conscious speculators, they were also highly desirable and fashionable. Santayana confirms that even in 1872, "The advantages of our house were in the first place social or snobbish, that it was in Beacon Street and on the better or fashionable waterside of that

3. George Santayana, *Persons and Places* (New York: Charles Scribner's Sons, 1944), 141–142. The earliest extant photograph of number 302 dates from 1920 and ran in the *Saturday Evening Transcript* (May 22, 1920), but the building appears to have been altered even by this date. The newspaper's photograph shows four stories plus a basement and attic, while Santayana's and Gilder's descriptions suggest three primary floors, not four.
4. As Bunting confirms, Gothic Styles made up 19 percent of the Back Bay's town houses; while Queen Anne and Romanesque Styles were very infrequent, with 8 and 4 percent of each, respectively. See Bunting, 173.
5. Gilder, 196.
6. Both Gilder, in 1889, and Santayana, from memory, provide detailed descriptions of the building's layout and the surrounding neighborhood. See Gilder, 195–209; and Santayana, 140–147. These chapters remain particularly helpful because the building was entirely remodeled and turned into a five-unit apartment building in 1933 by J. B. Brown (see Bunting, 407).
7. Santayana, 142.

street; which also rendered every room initially attractive, since it had either the sun if in the front, or the view if in the rear."[8]

Silas Lapham, who builds his house on Beacon Street in Howells's eponymous novel, expounds similarly on the street's attributes:

> It's about the sightliest view I know of. I always did like the water side of Beacon. Long before I owned property here, or ever expected to, m'wife and I used to ride down this way, and stop the buggy to get this view over the water . . Commonwealth Avenue don't hold a candle to the water side of Beacon [. . .] No, sir! When you come to the Back Bay at all, give me the water side of Beacon.[9]

Like Lapham, Howells reveled in his accomplishment as he wrote to James: "Sometimes I feel it an extraordinary thing that I should have been able to buy a house on Beacon Street." It was extraordinary. For a self-made man from rural Ohio, who had climbed the ladder of success for the last two decades, there was no point higher than Beacon Street if one lived in Boston—and all before the age of fifty, the age when Harriet Beecher Stowe was building her very first home. Pleased as he was, Howells was reluctant to assign much value to an address because, at least on the outside, he did not want to appear to care too much about such things. In the letter to James, Howells rehearses the details of how he will pay for the home and further justifies the purchase on the basis of its literary utility, as if to counter an assumption that he has become wealthy and self-indulgent; he tells James that he is "writing a story in which the chief personage builds a house 'on the water side of Beacon'" and notes that "I shall be able to use all my experiences down to the quick." Then he adds that the honorable task of writing about the domicile may in fact "pay for the house."[1] Howells's resemblance to Stowe in this regard is telling of the two authors' mutual distrust of consumerism, and even, of success. Unlike James and Wharton who came from wealthy families, Howells and Stowe seem intent upon projecting an image of modesty and frugality, regardless of how they lived and spent in actuality.

The letter to James reveals how quickly Howells shifts from the pleasure of his new home to matters of conscience, as if he must resist too much enjoyment of the material sort for fear of corruption. Howells felt ambivalent about his residence on Beacon

8. Santayana, 142.
9. Howells, *The Rise of Silas Lapham*, (1885; rpt., New York: W. W. Norton & Co., 1982), 49 [43]. All future references to this book are to this edition and are noted parenthetically in the text.
1. WDH to HJ, August 22, 1884, *Selected Letters* [George Arms et al., eds., *Selected Letters of William Dean Howells*. 6 vols. (Boston: Twayne Publishers, 1979–1983)], III: 108–110.

Street—a status symbol enabled by a contract with *Harper's Monthly* signed in 1885 for $13,000 a year. Even though he had the income to live on Beacon Street, he was not one of the people who typically dwelled in the neighborhood. As Bainbridge Bunting points out in his history of the Back Bay, the area was made up of conservative Bostonians of comfortable wealth; within this broad category, there were several implied classes depending upon one's address: "The old rich on Beacon Street, the old poor on Marlborough, the new rich on Commonwealth Avenue, and the new poor on Newbury. Within this hierarchy an even loftier rank was conferred on the 'water side' of Beacon Street or the 'sunny side' of Commonwealth Avenue."[2] Howells was an outsider, a newly wealthy individual from the Midwest, yet the location of his townhouse suggested old money and even more—all because he dwelled on the waterside of Beacon Street.

The tension between new and old money—Howells was of the former group while types like Norton and Lowell (and later, James and Wharton) were of the latter—plagued Howells throughout his life, and seemed to be evident from the moment he entered the right neighborhood in Cambridge when he moved to Berkeley Street. Each house, including the one-of-a-kind bucolic retreat in Belmont and the Beacon Street residence, in its comfort and novelty, contrasted with the modest world of Howells's upbringing. These homes were mixed blessings: on the one hand, signs of accomplishment; on the other, reminders of the family and background he left behind. The impulse to abandon each grand home was there from the moment he moved in. While Howells enjoyed the fruits of his hard work, he could never ignore that back in Ohio, his father and siblings were struggling to make ends meet. Nor could he forget the four-room stone house that his father built with his own hands and in which he and his family of ten grew up. His childhood, though poor, was happy, and as a result, Howells had suspicions of wealth and materialism. Even though, as a young man, he was eager to leave Ohio, see the world, and make his own way, he remained close to his parents and siblings, none of whom achieved the type of success and fame that Howells did. For most of his adult life, he sent money home to help care for his unmarried sisters and his jobless brothers Henry and Sam.

The dis-ease associated with wealth, abundance, and consumption, a disease that Howells struggled to avoid, was a topic making its way into the magazines of the day in the late nineteenth and early

2. Bunting, 20. Bunting's description of the cultural background of the neighborhood reveals that the monotony of the Back Bay's streets matched the conservative, discrete quality of the families with "old money" who lived there. See Bunting, 9–20.

twentieth centuries. Howells's own, the *Atlantic* and *Harper's*, were among the journals that published articles on the risk of losing "health of spirit" to excess. One piece, "The Tyranny of Things," published in the *Atlantic* in 1906, expounded: "The passion for accumulation is upon us [. . .] houses are filled with an undigested mass of things [. . .] But to some of us a day comes when we begin to grow weary of things. We realize that we do not possess them; they possess us."[3] Howells too expressed his amazement at the amount of stuff that crept into his own home and bemoaned the "thousand distractions that ambush me."[4] The Beacon Street house was decorated with all the Victorian embellishment in which Edith Wharton would come of age and soon despise: ornately patterned wallpaper and drapery, heavily carpeted floors, thickly upholstered furniture. In Howells's study alone, six carpets lay overlapped on the floor. Fireplace mantels and walls were crammed with family pictures, Elinor's sketches, and knick-knacks.[5] In spite of his own crowded interiors, Howells advised family members to keep their belongings to a minimum, writing to his sister Annie: "[Sell] all your possessions, or any of them [. . .] Don't let them become obsessions."[6] Howells had felt the effects of his twenty-year career and of the hard work and ambition that resulted in his success. As his literary celebrity grew during his time on Beacon Street, the chasm between his circumstances and those of the poor increasingly troubled him, yet he seemed unable to renounce the comforts that he had earned. He referred ironically to himself, his wife, Mark Twain, and Twain's wife as "theoretical socialists" and "practical aristocrats," adding in a letter to his father, "But it is a comfort to be right theoretically and to be ashamed of oneself practically."[7]

Always an avid walker, Howells could not help but notice the unfortunate who inhabited peripheral Back Bay streets and the area closer to the Boston Common, a hub of transportation. What he saw in his neighborhood troubled him, as he wrote his father in the summer of 1884: "There are miles of empty houses all around me. How unequally things are divided in this world. While these beautiful, airy, wholesome houses are uninhabited, thousands of poor creatures are stifling in wretched barracks in the city here, whole

3. Anon., "The Tyranny of Things," Contributor's Club, *Atlantic Monthly* (January 1906): 715–717.
4. Though Howells wrote these words to his father on August 20, 1869, they were a recurring refrain in his letters until he bought his Maine cottage in 1902.
5. This analysis is drawn from looking at period photographs of the interior of the house that are located in the Howells collection at Houghton and that appear in *Selected Letters* and *Letters of EMH* [Ginette B. Merrill and George Arms, eds., *If Not Literature: Letters of Elinor Mead Howells* (Columbus: Ohio State University Press, 1988)].
6. WDH to Anne Howells Fréchette, Jan. 17, 1913, *Selected Letters*, VI: 27. Emphasis original.
7. WDH to WCH, February 2, 1890, *Selected Letters*, III: 271–272.

families in one room. I wonder that men are so patient with society as they are."[8] These words appeared in slightly different form one year later in a dialogue in *The Rise of Silas Lapham*. Over a sumptuous dinner, Mr. Bromfield Corey and Miss Kingsbury discuss her charity work: "'I have often thought of our great, cool houses standing useless here, and the thousands of poor creatures stifling in their holes and dens, and the little children dying for wholesome shelter. How cruelly selfish we are!" (171 [148]). While Howells notes that the world is "unequal" but its citizens "patient" when he writes his father, in the novel, he confirms the "cruel selfishness" of the wealthy—a group to which he now belonged. Further in the novel, Howells states this message once again: "It is the curse of prosperity that it takes work away from us, and shuts that door to hope and health of spirit" (204 [176]). By the end of the novel, Mrs. Lapham realizes how little happiness her family's newfound wealth has brought her; rather, their affluence has only made her realize her misery. The narrator tells us: "In this house, where everything had come to be done for her, she had no tasks to interpose between her and her despair" (204 [176]). Perhaps Howells felt the same way in the late 1880s: he had over $100,000 in assets—did he even need to work anymore? But his beloved daughter was dead at the age of twenty-five and his wife was routinely bedridden. Life had become increasingly hard for him to enjoy. His misgivings about wealth, materialism, and those less fortunate, as well as his sadness over the death of his father, daughter, and sister, set the stage for a near-religious conversion. Howells was about to change from a man of wealth and status to a man of few needs (family and writing) and ardent political views (socialism).

* * *

8. WDH to WCH, August 10, 1884, *Life in Letters* [Mildred Howells, ed., *Life in Letters of William Dean Howells*. 2 vols. (1928; rpt. New York: Russell & Russell, 1968)], I: 363–364.

CRITICISM

A Note on Criticism

The "Contemporary Responses and Reviews" section here offers an account of the reception of *The Rise of Silas Lapham* by its first generation of readers by way of a selection of responses arranged in generally chronological order. Letters written to Howells during the novel's serial publication establish the predominantly enthusiastic but nonetheless varied responses of friends, protégés, and professional associates. The published reviews that follow begin with responses penned during magazine publication and proceed to essays written after the complete novel had been published as a book. The selection includes responses ranging from "high-cultural," nationally circulated organs of opinion such as the *Atlantic Monthly* and the *Nation* to local daily newspapers, from religious and secular presses on both sides of the Atlantic, and from high moral earnestness (essays in *Andover Review* and *Catholic World*, for instance) to irreverent humor (satiric cartoons and a parody from the weekly humor magazine *Life*).

These reviews are remarkable in the first instance for the frequency with which they agree about the novel's noteworthy features and purposes and, second, for how often and how vehemently they disagree about its artistic success and the validity of Howells's project. Frequently recurring topics in the reviews include the novel's realism, its unusual attention to commonplace people and events, its characteristically American subject matter and perspective, its introduction of the businessman as a new subject for fiction, its balancing of characterization and dialogue with plot, and its moral purposes and effects. Opposing opinions on all of these topics emerged almost immediately as reviewers took sides on the legitimacy of Howells's objectives. Disagreements arose, for instance, about the inherent interest (or lack thereof) of Howells's chosen subject matter, the artistic value of his "scientifically" objective literary representation, his allegedly unsympathetic attitude toward the novel's characters, and the degree (or absence) of "moral uplift" provided by the novel.

In an extreme example, Robert Bridges's two responses in *Life* magazine—one written partway through the novel's serialization and the other a year after its book publication—register as outright self-contradiction the challenge posed by Howells's novel to conventional expectations. But some of the negative reviews (Hamilton Wright Mabie's essay in *Andover Review*, for example) were among the most perceptive about the nature of the novel's achievement even as they questioned or condemned its aesthetic and moral value. The degree of variance in the reviewers' responses reveals the extent to which *Silas Lapham*, which just a generation later would often be seen as a thoroughly conventional work, actively challenged its first readers' shared assumptions about what a novel should be and do: its rightful subject matter and moral purposes, and the mode of its relationship to the world and to its own readers. One way or another, professional reviewers universally recognized that Howells was up to something new and different, but they were unevenly prepared or willing to adopt the new ways of reading that the novel required.

Not coincidentally, the more comprehensive criticisms (including, for instance, essays by Edmund W. Gosse, Horace Scudder, and Hamilton Wright Mabie) both address the immediate task of reviewing the novel and engage in a broader conversation about the purposes, means, and aesthetics of the modern novel in general. This is the case, as well, with the excerpt from Henry James's essay on Howells, which despite its prominent inclusion of *Silas Lapham* is less a book review than a retrospective critical assessment of all Howells's writing to date, discussed in the context of broader artistic trends and questions. These essays participate in a transatlantic discourse already under way when *Silas Lapham* was published and originating in no small part with Howells himself, whose close association with the new Realism in literature was already well established and would escalate in the months and years immediately after publication of his new novel. These reviews, therefore, are usefully read in conversation with the materials in "Howells, Literary Realism, and American Literary History" (pp. 309–31).

The same may be said of the twentieth- and twenty-first-century criticism collected in the "Modern Criticism" section. While these essays and book chapters have been selected to represent the variety of critical approaches that have been brought to bear on Howells's novel over the last half century, the perpetually vital question of the relationship of *The Rise of Silas Lapham* to Howells's literary theory and practice and to literary Realism more generally makes up one of a number of continuities between the concerns of Howells's first readers and those of modern scholars. Contemporary critics continue to read Howells's novel in relation to the novelist's prolific, career-long public theorizing on Realist aesthetics, sharing, whether directly or obliquely, an interest in understanding this novel as a representative Realist work. From the 1980s onward, however, critics availing themselves of the new theoretical tools afforded by the advent of New Historicism in literary studies have reread the novel's Realism as an aesthetic expression of economic and political ideologies formed in response to radical changes in post–Civil War economic and social organization. Their essays represent one of the most far-reaching changes in studies of Howells and of Realism since the first Norton Critical Edition of this novel was published in 1982: a marked turn toward understanding Realism not primarily in terms of its relatively overt critical stance toward the Gilded Age social, political, and economic status quo but instead as a set of texts characterized by deep structural and symbolic complicities with emergent late-nineteenth-century ideologies justifying and bolstering capitalism.

Such essentially economic approaches to *Silas Lapham* carry with them a strong if sometimes submerged element of moral as well as economic critique; more recent responses to first-generation New Historicists further complicate our understanding of the novel's economic and ethical investments in part by exploring the complex *narrativity* of Howells's novel: its sophisticated manipulations of narrative modes and voices to foster a polyvocal and reader-inclusive ethical conversation on the topics (social class, economics, business ethics, gender, literature, and so on) that the novel addresses. This renewed attention to the surprisingly complex nature of Howells's narrative technique (for an author who still bears the stigma of having practiced an allegedly naive and shallowly mimetic realism) underlies most of the recent scholarly work on even the most enduring topics in criticism of *Silas Lapham*.

Questions of social class and ethics are substantively present in virtually all the essays collected here, whether or not they comprise a primary focus. Indeed, the novel's complicated dramatization of personal and public ethics—in Lapham's business-related quandaries and in the family's struggles with the ethics of courtship—continues to draw scholars' attention to issues of personal and public morality just as it did for his earliest readers. Several of the essays collected here register an ongoing debate about the grounds and implications of the novel's system of ethics that has tended over the years toward a wider diversity of opinion and possibility rather than a unifying consensus. Likewise, the novel's grappling with the problems generated by social class difference and upward mobility, along with their moral implications, has continued to generate significant critical discussion and an ever greater multiplicity of approach. Readings focused on the more purely "literary" aspects of the novel are in no short supply, either. The collected essays proceed from critical premises ranging from mid-twentieth-century New Critical formalism, dedicated to finding an underlying structural and thematic unity in a novel that may initially seem sprawling, to more historicized approaches to questions of form, narration, and literary genre that place Howells's novel in conversation with popular, competing genres of nineteenth-century fiction. Such approaches open the door, as well, to renewed consideration of Howells's concerns with the social and moral implications of modern literature's portrayals of gender in a novel that is not only clearly committed to a new kind of literary representation of women but also understands that project in relation to existing literary genres whose appeal to women readers Howells sought to supplant with his own practices.

The selections are loosely arranged according to some long-running and ongoing critical conversations about Howells's novel concerning, respectively: realism, genre, and form; ethics; economics; narrativity; social class; and gender. Within each conversation, items appear in chronological order. These conversations, however, are by no means self-contained; threads of the discussion overlap, disappear, and reemerge throughout the collection, demonstrating and embodying the complexity and vitality of a scholarly interchange of ideas about the aesthetics and ethics of modern fiction, about business and social morality, about social class and wealth in a capitalist democracy, and about gender roles and relationships in *The Rise of Silas Lapham* that shows no signs of abating.

Reception

EDWIN H. CADY

[He Moved a Great Audience with Him][†]

And now as Howells worked he moved a great audience with him. Each new novel became a national event. Once he reminded his father how he had yearned in 1861 to be published in the *Atlantic;* but "now if I were two W.D.H.'s I could not supply the magazines' demand for that writer in England and America," he said. He was becoming a part of the American way of life, in an age when the novel was still the prime resource of domestic cultural life. "When I was a little boy," wrote a nostalgic lover of Howells in 1913, "I used to spend a good deal of time at my grandfather's. There, in the long, cold, quiet evenings of winter, we would play backgammon, we would read aloud, and at ten we would have a collation . . . of cold ham and chicken, cider and mince-pie." And the author most vivid and important to that circle, he remembered was Howells. Hamlin Garland[1] found *The Undiscovered Country* in a frontier store in Osage, Iowa, in 1881 and discovered a new mode in literature. In 1884, when he reached the East, he saw that "all literary Boston was divided into three parts, those who liked [Howells] and read him; those who read him and hated him, and those who just plain hated him."

His next novel, the writing of which may very well have even interpenetrated that of *Indian Summer*, made him still more "controversial." First accepted by Gilder as "The Rise of Silas Needham," *The Rise of Silas Lapham* stirred up a tempest of debate and even abuse when the *Century* began to print it in November, 1884. The Laphams became part of the national consciousness. Out in Indiana, fifteen-year-old Booth Tarkington[2] lay feverishly in wait for the mailman,

† From *The Road to Realism: The Early Years 1837–1885 of William Dean Howells* (Syracuse, NY: Syracuse UP, 1956), pp. 229–232. Reprinted by permission of the Estate of Edwin H. Cady.

1. Hamlin Garland (1860–1940), American novelist, essayist, and short story writer [*editor's note*].
2. Booth Tarkington (1869–1946), American novelist and two-time Pulitzer Prize winner [*editor's note*].

pounced on the *Century*, devoured the latest installment of *Lapham*, and had to run away to hide his tears when forced to tell his sister that Silas had gotten drunk at the Coreys' dinner. People began to notice that certain rich men looked or acted like Silas Lapham. Tourists in Boston asked to be shown his house. A paint company (unsuccessfully) begged permission to use his name on its product. A Methodist clergyman in Indianapolis was disciplined for daring to preach a sermon about him.

* * *

The Rise of Silas Lapham was a big and a controversial book because it spoke directly to the condition of its time. In creating the first important literary projection of the American business man, his mind and his morality, Howells provided symbols of the greatest importance for minds seeking to grasp the new culture. His picture challenged the comfortable optimisms of the Gospel of Wealth and of Social Darwinism[3]—which made it the more important. While unsettling readers with its challenge to the new, however, the book also made its contribution to the advance of the newness. Its author was openly out to demolish what he regarded as the false emotions and outworn clichés of the obsolescent and irrelevant romanticistic past. "The most fiercely debated question in many clubs," reported Garland, was "'Are Howells's heroines true to life or are they merely satiric types?' and most of his feminine critics were fiercely indignant over his 'injustice to women.' 'He never depicts a noble woman,' they declared."

* * *

3. The Gospel of Wealth, a loosely connected array of ideas concerning work, wealth, and morality, was most famously expressed in an essay titled "Wealth," published in 1889 by Gilded Age industrialist Andrew Carnegie (1835–1919). This widely shared cultural myth held that hard work resulted invariably in economic success, that material attainment was closely associated with individual moral rectitude, that income and wealth inequities were ultimately good for society as a whole, and that wealthy people had a social obligation to practice philanthropy. The Gospel of Wealth may be understood as a milder form of Social Darwinism, the sociological theory that class conflict in a society mirrors the processes of natural selection in biology as theorized by Charles Darwin (1809–1882) and his followers. Accordingly, class stratification and wealth disparity were understood as parts of a natural social mechanism ensuring the survival of the fittest individuals and groups in a society, and the upper classes' privileged social position was justified as natural, inevitable, and necessary to the health and progress of society. Consequently, Social Darwinists advocated individualism, competition, and *laissez-faire* political and economic policies. Prominent 19th-century proponents of such ideas included the English philosopher Herbert Spencer (1820–1903), who originated the phrase *survival of the fittest*; Yale University social and economic theorist William Graham Sumner (1840–1910); and American philosopher-historian John Fiske (1842–1901) [*editor's note*].

SUSAN GOODMAN AND CARL DAWSON

[Popularity, Influence, and Appeal]†

Although Howells wrote many novels, his reputation rested for decades on *Silas Lapham.* Hippolyte Taine, the influential French critic, compared it to the work of Honoré de Balzac when recommending its publication. The *Century's* Roswell Smith estimated that more than a million people read the serialized version.[1] In the year after publication, Ticknor printed more than ten thousand copies.[2] In 1911, the novel became required reading in classes at Yale, Columbia, and Cornell.[3] In retrospect it is always difficult to gauge the impact of a book, even on individual readers. This book was different. *Silas Lapham* not only inspired future generations of readers and younger novelists; it also affected disciplines as remote as architectural design. Cass Gilbert, the architect of the Woolworth Building in New York, insisted that Howells did "more to cultivate good taste" in American architecture than any professional then living. "A single sentence in 'Silas Lapham' about [the ugliness of] *black walnut,*" he wrote, "changed the entire trend of thought and made it possible for the architects of the time to stem the turbid tide of brown stone and black walnut so dear to the heart of the American millionaire"—and dear to the Howellses themselves in their house long ago on Sacramento Street.[4] *Silas Lapham* has continued to attract readers because, as Gilbert suggests, it offers them a measure, a way of testing their own standards against those of the Coreys and their cousins in all but name, the Laphams. A domestic drama on a larger scale, the novel addresses the process that turns people like the Laphams into people like the Coreys while showing how little separates any person from another. The ironic design of the book, its appeal to the best and worst tendencies in readers as they shift allegiances from one family to the other—not to mention the insiders' look at how the rich live—have made *Silas Lapham* one of the most enduring of American novels. An additional reason for its popularity is harder to pin down. Unlike *A Hazard of New Fortunes,* the

† From "The Man of Business, 1883–1886" in *William Dean Howells: A Writer's Life* (Berkeley: U of California P, 2005), pp. 258–59. Reprinted by permission of the publisher.

1. [Walter J.] Meserve, "Introduction," *The Rise of Silas Lapham* [introduction and notes by Merserve (Bloomington: Indiana University Press, 1971)], xxiv.
2. David J. Nordloh, "Textual Commentary," *The Rise of Silas Lapham,* 374.
3. Meserve, "Introduction," *The Rise of Silas Lapham,* xxviii.
4. Cass Gilbert to WDH, 10 March 1917, "Tributes to William Dean Howells on the Occasion of his 80th Birthday by His Fellow Craftsmen" (Houghton Library, Harvard University).

novel seems as circumspect as a Jane Austen novel, its emphasis resting almost entirely on personal behavior. Though the setting of *Silas Lapham* is historical and its themes social, readers come back to the book, as Livy Clemens[5] understood, to explore its moral universe.

* * *

5. Olivia Langdon Clemens (1845–1904), wife of Samuel L. Clemens (Mark Twain) [*editor's note*].

Correspondence with Early Readers

JOHN HAY

Letter to W. D. Howells†

Cleveland April 2. [1885]

My dear Howells

I can hardly believe it is I that have so long left a letter of yours unanswered; but I have so many cares of late days that I postpone my pleasures to them.

* * *

Yes, I have read Pepita Jiminez.[1] I like it—but hardly so much as you, and King and Mrs. Adams[2] do. So I conclude the fault is in me. I know Valera a little. He seems to me a dull Spanish Academician.

But Lord love you, the man that wrote Silas Lapham is the man for my money. Mrs. Hay read me the last instalment a few evenings ago, and what with my admiration of the art of it, and my profound sympathy with Silas, I was so wrought up that I felt as if *I* had gone into company too fine for me and got drunk myself. It is awfully good—I am only seized with a terror as to how you are going to keep it up on this level. But of course you know what you are about & it will be a tremendous success.

* * *

Yours faithfully
John Hay

† Letter in Howells Family Papers, 1850–1954 [MS Am 1784 (215)], Houghton Library, Harvard University. Transcribed by the editor for this Norton Critical Edition. Writer and statesman John Hay (1838–1905) served in the presidential administrations of Abraham Lincoln, William McKinley, and Theodore Roosevelt. Howells and Hay developed a lasting friendship based on their shared Midwestern roots, their early support of Lincoln's new Republican Party, and their shared authorial aspirations. Hay had helped Howells secure the American consulship in Venice, where Howells served during the Civil War.

1. A novel by the Spanish writer Juan Valera (1824–1905).
2. Probably Marian "Clover" Hooper Adams (1843–1885), wife of American historian and novelist Henry Adams and leader of Washington, D.C., salon culture. Clarence King (1842–1901), American author and geologist, was a mutual friend of Howells's and Hay's.

HENRY NORMAN

Letter to W. D. Howells†

UNIVERSITY CLUB
Madison Square.

New York, April 14, 1885.

Dear Mr. Howells,

* * *

Will you let me allow me [*sic*] to say to you, *sans phrases*,[1] how extremely good your April instalment of "Silas Lapham" seems to me. I have seen nothing equal to it in modern realistic fiction—which is the only kind of modern fiction we care anything about. You have indeed caught "that intangible essence, the commonplace" (if I quote correctly), which is life. Heaven knows that instalment is pathetic enough, yet I made myself a nuisance to my fellow-travelers in a parlor car by laughing over it, too. And I have heard half a dozen people—literary people and judges of such things—express my own opinion about it.

* * *

Yours faithfully,
Henry Norman.

† Letter in Howells Family Papers, 1850–1954 [MS Am 1784 (346)], Houghton Library, Harvard University. Transcribed by the editor for this Norton Critical Edition. Sir Henry Norman (1858–1939), English politician, journalist, and memoirist.

1. Directly, without extra words (French).

WILLIAM JAMES

Letter to W. D. Howells†

15 Appian Way
Cambridge, Mar 5. 85

My dear Howells,

Harry will no doubt be rather impatient to learn whether he is likely to lose much by Osgood's failure.[1] If you know in your own case how matters are to stand, can't you tip him a line of information? Or can you tell me how to find out?

Which is most diabolical in a publisher, to pay an author a small percentage, or to promise him a large one & fail? They seem to be a fiendish crew anyhow.

You are missed like the d——l at our club dinners. *Pray* come more often! I hope you're all well. I've only read the 1st 3 nos. of Silas Lapham so far, but have squealed with pleasure over every word of it. There isn't a dead line in it—and the endless geniality really nourishes one. I hope you're all well.

Affectly
Wm James

† Letter in Howells Family Papers, 1850–1954 [MS Am 1784 (255)], Houghton Library, Harvard University. Transcribed by the editor for this Norton Critical Edition. Philosopher and psychologist William James (1842–1910), the older brother of novelist Henry James, was a proponent of philosophical pragmatism, whose tenets harmonized with Howells's developing thoughts about literary realism. He and Howells were friends, traveling in the same circles in Boston and Cambridge, and Howells would go on to publish favorable reviews of several of James's books.

1. Both Howells and Henry James (Harry, in this letter) had contracts with James R. Osgood's publishing house, which was then undergoing financial collapse.

HAROLD FREDERIC

Letter to W. D. Howells†

LONDON OFFICE
NEW YORK TIMES.
203, STRAND. W.C.
May 5, 1885:

My dear sir:

At a private dinner here last evening, confined to some dozen professional men of whom I was the only American, the talk turned upon "The Rise of Silas Lapham", and the expressions of delight in it, and of admiration for it, were so cordial and warm that I yield to the temptation to write to you about them. The guests were mainly men of distinction—artists, writers, scientists and so on—and were certainly all men of fine discernment in literature. They talked a long time, upon many subjects, but upon nothing else was there nearly so much unanimity expressed, or feeling shown, as upon the proposition that in choice shading of character, in deftness of analysis of motives and feelings, and in the quality of life in dialogue, the work marked a distinct advance step in fiction.

They were not able to understand as well as I do, I think, how much more there is in the story—to realize that it means the scrutiny of a master turned for almost the first time upon what is the most distinctive phase of American folk-life, but their praise was good to hear, all the same.

I hope you will like my having said this to you. If it impresses you as being a trifle gratuitous, pray explain it on the theory that I haven't borne transplanting very well, and that each one of the eleven months I have spent here has left me more tenaciously fond of all things American, and more intolerant of most things European, than it found me. So that when I *do* hear justice done by Englishmen to the chief of American novelists I am too proud and glad to keep it to myself.

Faithfully Yours
Harold Frederic

† Letter in Howells Family Papers, 1850–1954 [MS Am 1784 (160)], Houghton Library, Harvard University. Transcribed by the editor for this Norton Critical Edition. Journalist and novelist Harold Frederic (1856–1898) is best known for his novel *The Damnation of Theron Ware* (1896).

OWEN WISTER

Letter to W. D. Howells†

402 Walnut St.
Thursday, May 21st. [1885]

My dear Mr. Howells:

* * *

We sit in our drawing room and read Silas Lapham aloud whenever it comes. If you like to hear lay readers give vent to their enthusiasm I wish you could hear my father & mother & all of us—And that clergyman the last time! The direct manner in which his impersonal common sense lays bare the obvious fact to those two poor people who are so involved & bedeviled that they can't see straight! Really, I can not tell you how we enjoy it, & how interested we are. One thing I'm going to ask you. Does young Corry [*sic*] see—or did he in earlier—say Nantasket days—see girls of his own class? Was he in the habit of dropping in to various houses in Beacon St. for 5 o'clock tea &c—or do you mean him so far to have been a man indifferent to female society? I ask this—for you never indicate or allude to any females of Corry's order. That is, I cannot remember any such allusion. I hope this question is not impertinent.

Yours very truly
Owen Wister

† Letter in Howells Family Papers, 1850–1954 [MS Am 1784 (554)], Houghton Library, Harvard University. Transcribed by the editor for this Norton Critical Edition. Owen Wister (1860–1938) would become famous for writing *The Virginian* (1902), the progenitor of the western novel genre.

HENRY JAMES

Letter to W. D. Howells†

St. Alban's Cliff
Bournemouth
May 23d [1885]

My dear Howells—

William enclosed me a note of yours (to him) a few days since in relation to the inquiry he had made of you about the consequences of the wretched Osgood's failure—which gave a point to the sharp desire I already had of writing to express a friendly hope that that catastrophe has not fallen heavily upon *you*. As to this your note (to Wm) gives no information & I wait with some anxiety to learn—praying for you hard in the interval.

* * *

I congratulate you heartily on "Silas Lapham"—it has an immense reality & ranks among your highest flights. It is most remarkable. You do catch hold of life & give its impression.—I am sickened by the idiotic, impudent outcry against my tale in the Century[1]—a thing made up of the thinnest, airiest, rashest *guesswork,* & fancifullest induction from glimpses of New England females in horse-cars 10 & 15 years ago—attacked on the ground of "personality" & invasion of privacy! The fault of my tale is its beastly ignorance & vagueness, as you will easily have perceived. Basta.[2] I hope things are domestically well with you & am ever, with love to your wife very faithfully yours

Henry James

† Letter in Howells Family Papers, 1850–1954 [MS Am 1784 (253)], Houghton Library, Harvard University. Transcribed by the editor for this Norton Critical Edition.

1. James's *The Bostonians* (1885–86) stirred up controversy when Bostonian readers thought they perceived in one of its characters a caricature of Elizabeth Peabody (1804–1894), transcendentalist reformer and sister-in-law of Nathaniel Hawthorne.
2. Enough, stop (interjection; Italian).

Contemporary Reviews

ANONYMOUS

[Really Too Much Realism][†]

In fiction we are having really too much realism. There is reaction in the air, and if some novelist does not give us soon a story with a good, solid murder in it—a murder that never was really murdered and so can be enjoyed conscientiously,—or a tale with at least a 'Crime' or a 'Mystery' in its title, we shall have to give up fiction and take to what is real and not realistic. Who does not wish he could sit down with Poe again and 'sup full with horrors,' after a few hundred pages of glasses of ice-water, South End basements, Back Bay dining-rooms, September weather, etc. Trace, for instance, the progress made this month in the serials: in *The Century*, Mr. Corey calls upon Mr. Lapham, young Mr. Corey calls upon Miss Lapham, Mrs. Corey calls upon Mrs. Lapham. The conversation is realistic, extremely so; it is exactly the way such people would talk under such circumstances. But why, then, call it literature, or spend the time in reading conversation? Why not call on our neighbors in the next street and make our own conversation, retiring with the consciousness of having scored off a social debt or two? * * *

F. E. CHASE

The Rise Of Silas Slap 'Em.
by W. D. Howls[‡]

Chapter I.

When Silas Slap 'Em opened his eyes it was exactly seven o'clock on the authority of the time-piece in the steeple of Park Street Church. The opinion of the Park Street Church clock did not have the same

† Unsigned review from "The Magazines in March," *Critic* 3 (February 28, 1885): 101.
‡ From *Life* 5 (May 7, 1885): 262–63.

weight with Mr. Slap 'Em that a clock striking from Trinity would have had, but it was at least not a South End clock, and so Silas was satisfied that it was really seven.

He was not particularly surprised, however, as it usually *was* seven at about that time every morning.

Silas Slap 'Em was born in Boston, and thereby earned the right to exist. He was unfortunately born at the South End, however, which degraded him far beyond the appreciation of any non-resident. A South Ender sometimes has brains, and may avoid criminal prosecution, but he never can have correct tastes, manners or knowledge of social forms and observances. This is an invariable rule.

Consequently, Silas breathed with difficulty the rarefied air of Beacon street, into which blooded thoroughfare he had been kindly permitted to move when he got to be rich enough.

Silas did not make his money in Atchison, like most Bostonians, but by advertising an unspecified brand of Mineral Paint, just as, some years before, Barthy Hubbub had advertised Tivoli Beer.[1]

Seven o'clock meant business to him, therefore, and he at once prepared to rise. Placing his large, hairy hands upon the floor, he dragged himself head-first over the foot-board. He did not know how to get out of bed properly. This was because he came from the South End.

Some years before Silas had earned the undying gratitude of a certain young Bostonian by mistaking him for an Englishman. In some slight recognition of this great service, the young man had given Silas a few "pointers." It is to this that we owe the astounding circumstance of a South Ender's taking a morning bath. Slap 'Em bathed awkwardly, as a matter of course, but he nevertheless bathed, and then dressed himself. It was a good deal for him to have done this, instead of dressing himself first and bathing afterwards, as he might once have done. In only one thing did his plebeian origin principally betray itself. In breathing his morning prayer to Emerson, he merely knelt, instead of prostrating himself three times.

When Silas lived at the South End he kept a mug at the barber's, but now he shaved himself. His shaving stand stood before the window, and in the process of removing the hair and portions of the cuticle from his countenance, he got certain glimpses of the Common, and further on, of the residences of prominent stock-holders in the Atchison and C. B. and Q. railroads, and the American Bell Telephone Co. On the front door steps of each residence stood the matutinal pot of baked beans.

Thus Silas Slap 'Em rose.

1. In Howells's *A Modern Instance* (1882), Bartley Hubbard developed over several chapters a growing appetite for Tivoli beer. "Atchison": the Atchison, Topeka, and Santa Fe Railroad.

[The other thirty-nine chapters of this remarkable novel we omit, out of consideration for our readers. After an heroic struggle the author gets Silas through breakfast and down town, with the usual number of social solecisms and lapses into alleged South End grammar. Then come variations on the same theme, entitled Luncheon and Dinner. At this latter repast it appears that even alcohol discriminates against a South Ender; though, to tell the truth, we cannot be quite sure whether Silas's confusion of ideas is the result of wine or of the conversation.]

DROCH [ROBERT BRIDGES]

From A Thoroughly American Success†

The increasing excellence and wonderful prosperity of the *Century* are things of which all lovers of American literature should be proud. And it is not the least among the magazine's merits that it is intensely American. The most notable of its recent enterprises is the series of articles on the war epoch of American history. * * *

It is hardly fair to ascribe the whole of that magazine's recent increase in circulation to the war articles. A few thousand at least should be credited to the very clever novel by Mr. Howells, "The Rise of Silas Lapham." It is difficult to recall a better piece of literary workmanship by the same skilful hand. There is more imagination, more delicate fancy and a finer flavor of romance in "The Undiscovered Country:" but in "The Rise of Silas Lapham," the art of character sketching and dialogue is most admirably displayed. Through it all there is a gentle humor which sees the foibles of humanity, and yet forgives them. It is in this direction that the talents of Mr. Howells have, of late years, so markedly developed. With it, as is natural, has developed an insight into the pathos of all lives, even under the most commonplace circumstances.

* * *

† From *Life* 5 (May 14, 1885): 273.

ANONYMOUS

From Mr. Howells's "Rise of Silas Lapham"[†]

* * *

For a long time the mass of Mr. Howells's readers have been complaining that his stories did not "turn out right,"—that is, turned out very much like life itself, instead of like the Dickens Christmas story. Then they have been complained of as vulgar and about vulgar people—as though we had enough of anything but common people in this country about whom to make a true account of life among us—as though life here was ordered on the plan of the English society we have always read about in novels, with its leisured classes distinctly lofty and working classes distinctly low! Descriptions of American society must deal with very "mixed" material, cannot be "writ large" in any such easy fashion. Then his heroines have not been any more satisfying than Thackeray's; they have simply represented the every-day good and pretty American girl as everybody sees her, naturally, without any grand purpose in life or consciousness of heroineship, and happily without any grand consuming passions, but with plenty of amiability and plenty of crudeness, chiefly arising from the easy-going, unsuspicious indiscipline of American home life. In all this Mr. Howells is striving faithfully to be simply true and true to himself and to his art.

In "The Rise of Silas Lapham" he has made, it seems to us, a more ambitious essay than in any previous work—that is, has dealt with more complicated and deeper questions than in any previous story. There are the fine practical and crucial tests of business ethics in Lapham's dealings with his partner, whom he first contrives to leave out of his "big strike," and then, to quiet the nagging of his wife's conscience, takes in again to find that in the early meanness he "started the row of bricks" of his misfortunes—or as he expresses it on the last page of the story: "Sometimes I get to thinking it all over, an' it seems to me I done wrong about Rogers in the first place; that the whole trouble came from that." That covers one great purpose of the novel—to show that there is no escape in this life from a bad action, and that a course such as smart business men every day make a merit of and credit to their smartness is bad and punished by the everlasting law. The other and not less important purpose in hand in this story is to show that money does not make a man and his wife and children over again, that they may build their house on the

† Unsigned review from *Boston Evening Transcript* (August 14, 1885): 4.

water side of Beacon street, but they will have to be born again before gaining social affiliation. It is true that the South End girl is pure gold in character, and in mental equipment fine steel; but when she has spent a week at her Beacon Hill husband's home, and his family have done all that good-breeding and affection for the son would suggest, still, as the bride leaves them she sobs, on Tom's shoulder, in the carriage going to the depot, that she shall not "feel strange amongst the Mexicans now." Here is the real purpose in this great novel—to show that "it is certain that *our manners and customs go for more in life than our qualities*." It is a hard conclusion, but who will venture to contest it? Colonel Lapham, with all his coarseness and offences against taste, is a complete man, as Howells's masterly hand has made him, and one feels that he is a truer gentleman in nature than the somewhat vague and unreal personage born in the purple, and taking nothing seriously but selfish ease and culture, whom the author has created to represent high life at its best. Mr. Howells will be accused of snobbery for this, as he has already been accused of immorality for allowing so good a man as Lapham, at bottom to come to grief, and of vulgarity in dealing with him and his daughters at all.

But Mr. Howells cannot help that; he must go on and put down things as he sees them, whether we like them or no. He does not pretend to be a Hawthorne, creating a remote, poetical, semi-supernatural world to revel in; nor even the son or son-in-law of Hawthorne, with the family note-book at command for characters endowed with supernatural powers, so convenient for thrilling purposes and for romantically or weirdly imagined situations that never existed. Mr. Howells probably made up his mind at the beginning to let all such stories alone. He does us the credit, apparently, of believing that, in this age of our civilization, we care more for conscientious studies of our actual selves. Surely, future historians will think such work as Howells's of more value than most of our histories, because they are the admitted truth, while the histories are all disputed, and have to be rewritten every quarter of a century. "It would be easy," he says, "to point out traits in Penelope's character which finally reconciled all her husband's family and endeared her to them. These things continually happen in *novels*."

* * *

ANONYMOUS

From Mr. Howells's Last Story†

* * *

* * * The story is full of the clear and strong yet delicate analysis and description for which the author has such a gift. * * * But when we have finished the book; when Silas Lapham's rise has been made clear; when we have taken leave of him as, once more withdrawn to the old Vermont homestead, and fallen into somewhat careless personal habits with the decline of vital energy, he answers Sewell's question about the after-effect of his conquest over temptation, why is it that a vague feeling of disappointment and dissatisfaction arises? The feeling is not a new one in connection with Mr. Howells' books, and attempts have been made to explain it in various ways. To us it seems that it is due to a certain deficiency of faith in even his own highest conceptions. To say that he follows his characters with a Mephistophelian sarcasm might be to put the case too strongly; but certainly he does not show that perfect sympathy with them which seems necessary to the display of the best that is in them. And the existence of a doubt whether an author is sincere, or whether he is gibing and sneering at his own characters, must have decidedly unpleasant effects on the reader.

It may be that Mr. Howells really does entertain doubts about his characters; that he really does regard Silas Lapham as a rather poor sort of hero, though not altogether to be denied the possession of heroic qualities; but if this is the case it does not better the situation, for mere cleverness in description and penetration in mental analysis can never compensate for the absence of that fulness of sympathy between author and hero which results in constant insistence upon the latter's best traits, while it by no means involves inattention to his faults. But Mr. Howells treats most of his characters with something of this distant air. He doesn't seem to make up his mind to admit them to his friendship. He is not quite loyal to them, often weakening the effect of his largest concessions by little hints which lower the person in the reader's estimation. * * *

No intelligent reader will deny the power and skill which he manifests in all his books, but few critics will maintain that he is, in the final analysis, a pleasant writer. There are authors who offend through inopportune didacticism, but he is not of them. There are others who annoy by flippant commentary, but he never commits such breaches of good taste. There are some who try the patience

† Unsigned review from *New York Daily Tribune* (August 16, 1885): 8.

of the public by their inability to elucidate their conceptions, but he is ideally lucid. His is indeed no common fault, and yet it is a serious one, implying, as many will be apt to suspect, whether justly or not, a fundamental cynicism and a pessimistic view of life, in the author, which find a more or less veiled reflection in his work. It may be that the philosophy which consciously or unconsciously colors every author's productions, has become too deeply absorbed in Mr. Howells's intellectual system to be eradicated. If so it is a pity, for it seems destined in that case to mar his usefulness very decidedly, and to depreciate the value of what is in many respects the finest and best literary work done in this country.

ANONYMOUS

[A Great Moral Drama]†

The extraordinary impression made by Mr. Howells's history of *The Rise of Silas Lapham* as it appeared from month to month in serial form is more than justified now that we have it before us in its entirety, and are better able to analyze the sources of its unmistakable strength. That its artistic merit rises above any previous work of the author is indisputable. It has the fresh, unsparing, almost pitiless realism of *A Modern Instance*, but it touches throughout a higher plane. In tracing the career of this typical "self-made" American, Mr. Howells omits nothing. All that is crude, hard, and forbidding in his surroundings is portrayed with a fidelity that never wavers; his physical unattractiveness is always insisted on; none of his rude ancestral traits and native awkwardness of body, speech, and thought are glossed over. Uncouth, self-assertive, endowed with a primitive energy of purpose akin to the forces of nature, eager to get and to spend, careless about the minor morals, but with an underlying stratum of honesty in his character able to sustain him in great emergencies, Silas Lapham stands before us a definite creation, a specialized example of a widely existent type. There is no superficial portraiture in this the finest of Mr. Howells's *dramatis persona*—no working from the outside. The keen, far-reaching insight never wavers; every motive is laid bare; all the hesitations, the struggles, the obstinate determinations, are revealed in the mirror-like text, with an accompanying glow of humor that brings out clearly every line and mark—that grim, fatalistic humor latent in every Yankee, but which no other novelist has ever succeeded in transferring to his pages undimmed.

† Unsigned review from *Literary World* 16 (September 5, 1885): 299.

But Silas Lapham is something more than the leading personage in a cleverly contrived story. He is the protagonist in a great moral drama as impressive in its inevitableness as a Greek tragedy. And here is the real strength of the book. It discerns and emphasizes the moral element which exists in every phase of poor humanity. It recognizes that innate desire, weak in some but never wholly wanting, the desire "to do better," the yearning, often vague and unexpressed, yet still a germ of possible effort, to place its possessor on the side of what makes for righteousness. It is this discernment and expression of the truth that art of vital and permanent value can only be attained by a recognition of the underlying moral forces, that constitutes Mr. Howells's triumph.

* * *

Mr. Howells's inadequacy in dealing with women has in some quarters passed into a maxim, but there must be something to say on the other side, for we heard one of the brightest of her sex remark the other day, "I see no reason to condemn him on *that* score; he shows us just about as we are!" And so if the critic finds that Penelope somehow does not verify herself; that Mrs. Corey is little more than an animated shadow; that the pretty Zerilla as a dea ex machina is not altogether justified by necessity; and that only Irene and her mother are after all consistently depicted—he may with advantage remember that the unverified, the shadowy, and the superfluous are not altogether wanting in real life.

* * *

EDMUND W. GOSSE

A Great American Novel†

"Silas Lapham" is undoubtedly up to date the high-water mark of Mr. Howells's great and unique photographic genius. It is a marvellously minute and realistic picture of life in Boston—a miniature of high artistic value, more delicately faithful to the truth of nature than even the average of its author's masterpieces, and yet (for the consolation of the British public we say it) with a little more of romance and plot than Mr. Howells has deigned to bestow upon his inimitable

† From *Pall Mall Gazette* (September 11, 1885): 5. In a letter dated October 26, 1885, Howells thanked his friend Gosse for this review, citing it along with the essay in the *Saturday Review* (which Gosse had mailed to Howells; see p. 410) as having accurately understood his authorial intentions and being "far friendlier than most things on this side" of the Atlantic (see Howells, *Selected Letters*, vol. 3, pp. 132–33, in the *Selected Howells Edition*.

sketches of real contemporary American society. Of course, as always, in the words of the stock English criticism, in Silas Lapham "nothing ever happens." The story is just the simple story of a rough American farmer body who rises from the ranks and never succeeds in getting into society, because he never tries to get into it. To him and his family (of a wife and two charmingly unsophisticated daughters) enter Tom Corey, a representative of Bostonian culture and aristocracy, whom all the Laphams immediately mark out as the possible husband of Irene, the prettiest of the two unsophisticated sisters. There is much pleasant and natural by-play of the mutual distrust of the two families, including such a show of class prejudice as an English novelist in our own society would hardly even have dared to portray; and in the end Tom Corey proposes, not to pretty Irene, but to her plain sister Penelope, whom nobody had ever so much as dreamed of taking into consideration. That is all—that, and a subsequent episode of the fall of the Laphams; and the English critic, who judges novels by the plot alone (as outsiders judge a great picture by the tale it conveys to them), will doubtless always complain that Mr. Howells has intentionally and of set purpose put the unwary off the track (though the skilled reader soon sees through the blind) by making us all fall in love at once with pretty Irene and her coquettish tremors, to the neglect of Penelope and her perverse sardonic New England humorousness. But Mr. Howells knows his own business best. Indeed, it may be laid down as a general rule that the great artist usually knows his own business better than the critic who just glances with a supercilious eye over the work on which the creator has spent in constant consideration whole months or years of patient endeavour.

And Mr. Howells is beyond dispute a great artist. Slowly and by gradual tentative stages even we Philistine English people are beginning with a grudging reluctance to perceive it. The extreme delicacy and lightness of his humour, the exquisitely evanescent aroma of his truly native genius, have prevented a solid, stolid, hard-headed race, brought up on beef and beer and Dickens, from readily appreciating the unrivalled daintiness and gracefulness of his masterly touch. We are as a nation too slow and heavy to rise at once to the airy little bait he dangles so cleverly and fantastically before us. And then, too, he has resolutely and sternly set his face against that last superstition of the dark ages that a novel must necessarily base itself upon a fact or incident utterly unusual in ordinary life. "The story's the thing," is the watchword and creed of the English novel-reader, which means in plain language that the novel must stake its existence on the startling unexpectedness of its central conception. To judge by the average run of British novels, an intelligent inquirer of the twenty-fifth century might come to the conclusion that in the opinion of Englishmen of the age of Gladstone a murder, a bigamy, the forging of a will, or a bank robbery were the only episodes in human life worth a moment's consideration from a rational being. The interest of existence for the modern Englishwoman appears from her favourite writers to be all concentrated upon two poles, one of them crime, and the other the due celebration of holy matrimony. To poison your friend or to marry your choice are the sole recognized aims of romantic humanity. To all this Mr. Howells will have nothing to say. He has never in his life written what the existing school of circulating library critics would call a real, indubitable novel. The interest of his works is entirely dependent upon the fact that every incident and every conversation might really and easily have happened in the actual world as we practically know it. His system is unvarnished naturalism, but naturalism of a healthy, sensible, wholesome kind. He has discovered that a great painter, with a wonderful gift for texture and detail, may paint something besides horrors and nastinesses—may use his skill upon delicate portraits of pure women and solid men, may represent life itself, not its occasional ugly, morbid excrescences.

The novel of pure character is the novel of the future. It is the direction in which all romance has been perpetually travelling, and towards which it still gradually travels. With each half century we are progressively shocked at the clumsy devices, the palpable unreality, the crude and stale machinery, of the preceding age. We get more and more realistic and analytic, we care less and less for the bare plot, the impossible episodes, the terrific encounters, of the older novelists. And of this tendency towards pure character-painting and ordinary incident, Mr. Howells is the furthest living exponent. The consummate perfection of his execution equals the boldness and originality of his simplicity in design. Such a character as that of Bromfield Corey in his present story—an easy-going, ineffective, Massachusetts Chesterfield, the very embodiment of the intulistic, bantering Bostonian scepticism, with his tolerant, well-to-do, well-bred pessimism, and his psychological demolition of struggling, aspiring, human effort—is worth all the murders and secret marriages Miss Braddon and Mrs. Henry Wood in all their lives have ever contrived and perpetrated between them. But the English public only slowly sees it. A generation which swallowed down "Called Back" by the hundred thousand (mostly in the train or on its way home from business) is hardly likely to find much that tickles its dulled palate in "A Chance Acquaintance" or "The Rise of Silas Lapham." Accustomed to the hot and peppery condiments of grown up variants on the pirates and cannibals of the *Boy's Own Journal*,[1]

1. One of a number of magazines and newspapers that included *Boys' Own* in their titles, published in Britain and the United States beginning in the mid-19th century and targeting teen and preteen boys.

it cannot stop to roll on its deadened tongue the delicately flavoured and dainty morsels of the great American master confectioner. It likes its stories hot and spicy: Mr. Howells can only give it the perfection of exquisite and cultivated humour, of admirably true and never overwrought human pathos. The after ages will wonder that we preferred our assassins and our bigamists to the Lady of the Aroostook, just as we ourselves wonder that an age which had Colonel Newcome and Becky Sharpe before its eyes could waste its time on the false, crude, and high-flown romanticism of the first Lord Lytton[2] and his idealistic waxworks.

ANONYMOUS

[A Want of Perception As to Climax]†

In defiance of his own dictum, Mr. Howells has contrived to tell a very good story in 'The Rise of Silas Lapham.' Obviously he has found some difficulty in making the most of it. He seems to have a want of perception us to climax, and consequently he is rather wrong (to use a favourite expression of his) as to the point where he should conclude. The reader shuts the book with a sense of diluted interest, but he cannot say that the character of Silas Lapham is not fully developed. The book is characteristically American. English readers have been made sufficiently familiar with Boston life to appreciate Mr. Howells's picture; but they cannot fail to be amused by the *naïveté* of his hit at what he calls Daisy-Millerism while he is drawing a type which one might imagine to be no less irritating to Americans than the famous Daisy herself. It is, however, impossible to different American sensibilities, and English people must be content to be amused.

* * *

Mr. Howells's careful attention to details and to the machinery of his story is observable throughout. Every character is perfect in its way, and only on a few occasions does the writer slip into the American habit of overdoing the study of a person's state of mind. Once or twice, however, he has seemed to forget the clever little bit of criticism on George Eliot put into the mouth of one of his girls: "I wish she would let you find out a little about the people for yourself."

2. Edward Bulwer-Lytton (1803–1873), popular novelist. Colonel Newcome and Becky Sharp are characters in, respectively, William Makepeace Thackeray's novels *The Newcomes* (1855) and *Vanity Fair* (1848).

† Unsigned review from "Novels of the Week," *Athenaeum* (September 12, 1885): 334.

ANONYMOUS

[Without Any Final Thrill of Delight]†

'The Rise of Silas Lapham' has been read with varying feeling, but it has been read. There can be no doubt that it has been greatly liked, and that in many ways it is extremely likeable. It seems ungracious, since nothing could have kept us from reading it while it was coming out, to lay it down now that it is finished without enthusiasm. Yet it is eminently one of the books that are read with a pleasurable glow from chapter to chapter, but laid down at the end without any final thrill of delight. It is a book that has been enjoyed, but not one that will be remembered. The admirers of Mr. Howells may well claim that as a realistic study it is extremely realistic, but not one of them will regret that in his new novel, 'Indian Summer,' he is returning to the dainty, refined, *spirituel* type of literature which is none the less realistic for dealing with cultivation. Educated people are just as real as uneducated people. The drama of their emotions, the tragedy of their griefs, the significance of their actions, are none the less real for being more complex. * * *

* * * The trouble with Mr. Howells's study of the Laphams is that it is cold. It is not intentionally hard. Mr. Howells means well by Silas. He realizes that his 'rise' was in morals, not in social matters. He wishes us clearly to understand that Silas was greatly to be respected in spite of his uncouth manners. But after all we do not learn to 'tolerate, pity, and love' him. We do not like him any better when we put down the book than we did when we took it up. At the very beginning we had what is known as 'an inkling' that Silas was a good fellow at heart if we could learn to bear with his peculiarities, and after we have heard his story we have not learned to bear with the peculiarities. He is just as much as ever a man whom we should respect, but avoid, in real life. We should be very much more disturbed than even the Coreys were, if any young friend of ours thought of marrying his daughter. Mr. Howells is quite too good-natured to wish to make literary capital out of the frailties of a fellow-man; still, if he can satisfy his literary conscience by being very careful to give even Silas his due, he rather likes to take up Silas's peculiarities for analysis and reproduction. He will not allow himself to make fun of him, but it remains very evident that he is amused by him. He paints in all of Silas' good qualities with faithful conscientiousness, but it was not his good qualities that attracted Mr. Howells to him. He was a good 'subject,' and the author threw a sop to Cerberus by letting him also be a good man.

† Unsigned review from *Critic* 4 (September 12, 1885): 122.

* * *

And yet it is impossible to leave thus lightly a book which after all we have greatly liked. Admirable in its 'touches,' faithful in its efforts to give every one his due, unexceptionable in its moral, and clever in its success in making a 'story' out of everyday effects—very everyday effects—without visible climax for a support, the book is one to interest and to please, even if it does not touch the deepest springs or inspire the most lasting and enthusiastic appreciation.

WILLIAM MORTON PAYNE

[The Business Man's Novel]†

* * *

We are inclined to think that Mr. Howells has never done anything better than this picture of the self-made American. The material offered him was unpromising enough, but he has bestowed upon it the genial touch of the artist, and made of his homely hero something which comes very near to being a veritable creation. It is almost a new species of work—one which might perhaps be styled the business man's novel—that Mr. Howells has done in this story, and the instant recognition which was accorded it even in its early stages indicates the truth and force of the presentation. People who do not care for novels ordinarily can hardly fail to like this one, and may say, with some sort of not unjust reflection upon novel-writing in general, that here at last are such people as one meets in everyday life, and who talk in a natural and familiar way. The interest of such a story is not probably very lasting, but it is very great for the time being, or as long as people continue to talk and act in just the way which it describes.

HORACE SCUDDER

[A Problem Worth Solving]‡

* * *

The novel before us offers a capital example of the difference between the permanent and the transient in art. Had Mr. Howells amused himself and us with a light study of the rise of Silas Lapham in Boston society, what a clever book he might have made of it! We

† From *Dial* 6 (September 1885): 122.
‡ From *Atlantic Monthly* 56 (October 1885): 554–56.

should have chuckled to ourselves over the dismay of the hero at the failure of the etiquette man to solve his problems, and have enjoyed a series of such interior views as we get in the glimpse of Irene "trailing up and down before the long mirror in *her* new dress [Mr. Howells never seems quite sure that we shall put the emphasis where it belongs without his gentle assistance], followed by the seamstress on her knees; the woman had her mouth full of pins, and from time to time she made Irene stop till she could put one of the pins into her train;" we should have followed the fluctuations of pride and affection and fastidiousness in the Corey family, and have sent a final shuddering thought down the vista of endless dinner parties which should await the union of the two houses. All this and much more offered materials for the handling of which we could have trusted Mr. Howells's sense of humor without fear that he would disappoint us.

But all this is in the story; only it occupies the subordinate, not the primary place, and by and by the reader, who has followed the story with delight in the playful art, discovers that Mr. Howells never intended to waste his art on so shallow a scheme, that he was using all this realism of Boston society as a relief to the heavier mass contained in the war which was waged within the conscience of the hero. When in the final sentence he reads: "I don't know as I should always say it paid; but if I done it, and the thing was to do over again, right in the same way, I guess I should have to do it," he recognizes, in this verdict of the faithfully illiterate Colonel, the triumphant because unconscious attainment of a victory which justifies the title of the story. No mere vulgar rise in society through the marriage of a daughter to a son of a social prince, or the possession of a house on the water side of Beacon Street, would serve as a real conclusion to the history of a character like that of Silas Lapham; as if to flout such an idea, the marriage when it comes is stripped of all possible social consequences, and the house is burned to the ground. In place of so trivial an end there is a fine subjection of the mean and ignoble, and as in Balzac's César Birotteau, a man of accidental vulgarity discloses his essential nobility; with this added virtue in the case of Mr. Howells's hero, that we see the achievement of moral solvency unglorified by any material prosperity, and the whole history of the rise unadorned by any decoration of sentiment.

* * *

Nevertheless, though there can be no mistaking Mr. Howells's intention in this novel, and though he uses his material with a firmer hand, we confess, now that we are out of the immediate circle of its charm, that The Rise of Silas Lapham suffers from the same defect as A Modern Instance. The defect is not so obvious, but it arises from the same super-refinement of art. In brief, Silas Lapham, a man of coarse grain and excessive egotism, is, in the crucial scenes, treated as a man of subtlety of thought and feeling. We do not say that the turnings and windings of his conscience, and his sudden encounters with that delicious Mephistopheles, Milton K. Rogers, are not possible and even reasonable; but we complain that the author of his being, instead of preserving him as a rustic piece of Vermont limestone with the soil clinging to it, has insisted upon our seeing into the possibilities of a fine marble statue which reside in the bulk. Moreover, when one comes to think of it, how little the rise of this hero is really connected with the circumstances which make up the main incidents of the story. The relations with Rogers, out of which the moral struggle springs, are scarcely complicated at all by the personal relations with the Corey family arising from the love of young Corey for Penelope Lapham. The Colonel goes through the valley of tribulation almost independently of the fact that he and his are sojourning meanwhile in another half grotesque vale of tears.

This same over-refinement of motive, as supposed in natures which are not presumably subtle, impresses us in the whole history of Penelope's love affair. We feel, rather than are able to say why we feel it, that there is something abnormal in the desolation which falls upon the entire Lapham family in consequence of Irene's blindness and Penelope's over-acuteness. We frankly confess that when reading the scenes, it seemed all right, and we gave ourselves up to the luxury of woe without a doubt as to its reality. But when *thinking* about them (forgive the italics), it seems an exaggeration, a pressing of the relations between these interesting people beyond the bounds of a charitable nature.

But when all is said, we come back with satisfaction to the recollection that Mr. Howells has distinctly set before himself in this book a problem worth solving, and if his statement and solution are presented with an art which has heretofore been so cunning as quite to reconcile one to the fragility of the object under the artist's hand, and this art still seems sometimes to imply the former baselessness, we can at least thank our stars that when we criticise such a book as The Rise of Silas Lapham, we are dealing with a real piece of literature, which surely will not lose its charm when the distinctions of Nankeen Square and Beacon Street have become merely antiquarian nonsense.

ANONYMOUS

[Characteristically American]†

* * *

Any one who wishes to gain an insight into the conditions of life in America, and to peer into its social complexities, cannot do better than to give his days and nights to the study of Mr. Howells's stories in general and of *The Rise of Silas Lapham* in particular. America, and the average American of to-day, are not to be found in the picturesque pages of Mr. Bret Harte or of Mr. George W. Cable, any more than they are to be sought in the *Biglow Papers*, or in Mark Twain's joyful pages, or in the very clever tales of Mr. Henry James.[1] They are here—in the pages of Mr. Howells—as they are to be found nowhere else, except in real life. Mr. Howells has seen and he has understood and he has recorded, and his record is true. Of the truth of the characters in *The Rise of Silas Lapham* there can be no doubt in the mind of any one who knows the American people of to-day. Silas Lapham himself is a type. There are thousands of Silas Laphams throughout the United States. Mr. John T. Raymond, the comedian who acts Colonel Sellers[2] with so comic a zest, has said that there is not a town in the United States in which he has played the part where some one has not represented himself as the original of the sanguine and chivalric speculator. And there is hardly a village in the United States—at least in that part of the United States which is peopled by the original New England stock—where Silas Lapham has not many originals. Strong, gentle, pushing, pertinacious, bragging unconsciously, scrupulous with the scrupulousness of the New England conscience, provincial, limited in his ideas, and yet not hostile to the light in so far as he can perceive it, Silas Lapham is an American type which has never before been so boldly presented. As characteristically American, however, and as true to life, is the elder Corey, the man of family, of breeding, of culture, of inherited traditions; but where there are ten thousand

† From an unsigned review in London's *Saturday Review* 60 (October 17, 1885): 517–18. In a letter to the British writer Edmund W. Gosse dated October 26, 1885, Howells called this article "such a review as I would have written myself. Truly there were just the things said there that I was aching to have said" (see Howells, *Selected Letters*, vol. 3, pp. 132–33, in the *Selected Howells Edition*).

1. Henry James (1843–1916), American novelist; Mark Twain, pen name of American writer and humorist Samuel L. Clemens (1835–1910); *The Biglow Papers*, a verse political satire written in New England dialect by James Russell Lowell (1819–1891); George Washington Cable (1844–1925), New Orleans regionalist novelist and anti-racism reformer; Bret Harte (1836–1902), American writer and humorist.
2. A character in Mark Twain and Charles Dudley Warner's (1829–1900) satirical novel *The Gilded Age* (1873), who became the central figure in Twain's financially successful stage play entitled *Colonel Sellers* (1874).

Silas Laphams there are only a thousand, or perhaps a hundred, Coreys. The contrast between Lapham and Corey, between Mrs. Lapham and Mrs. Corey, between Lapham's daughters and the more remotely presented daughters of Mr. Corey, is admirable in its truth and in its humour. Indeed the humour of Mr. Howells's story is quite as remarkable as its truth. Mr. Howells himself thoroughly understands the Great American Joke. Many, if not most, of his characters have a leaven of comedy—and Mr. Howells's comedy is always delightful. Mr. Corey on one side, and Penelope Lapham on the other, are not only humorous in themselves, but they have a strong sense of humour—and that toleration of others which only a strong sense of humour can give.

* * *

ANONYMOUS

[A Literal, Merciless Representation]†

In 'The Rise of Silas Lapham' Mr. Howells depicts one character distinctively of his time, aggressively of his nation, with a vividness and completeness unapproached in contemporary English fiction, apparently unapproachable by any contemporary writer in the English tongue. Silas Lapham, standing beside Bartley Hubbard, will at least postpone that oblivion which, as a graceful talker in the story says, overwhelms all authors, poor fellows, at last. And perhaps Lapham and Hubbard will get their full meed of praise from remote posterity only. Just now, with so many of them about, it is difficult to find a large public able to appreciate them unreservedly without doing violence to domestic affections. For Lapham is no more a creature of the imagination than Hubbard. He is a literal, merciless representation. With the representation is blended a searching and comprehensive interpretation. Directing and perfecting both is the quick, subtle, mocking spirit of the author, flashing in a phrase or comparison, gleaming in a jest at the sober unconsciousness of the subject who provides the opportunity. From the cleverness of Lapham as literary work it is as impossible to detract as it is to dispute the antipathy his personality excites in people of good taste, or to deny his practical virtues. His almost unmitigated offensiveness is a large part of his truth. His vulgarity is neither exaggerated nor underestimated. * * *

What has been said of the perfection of Lapham's delineation cannot be applied to all the characters of the novel. Bromfield Corey is

† Unsigned review from *Nation* (October 22, 1885): 347–48.

a charming contrasting figure, but touched very lightly. Tom Corey, too, commands respect for his persistence in an unpromising love-affair, if not for his taste in the choice of a sweetheart. But the women, especially the young women, are deplorably unattractive, and, moreover, if they represent any truth, it is only half a truth, and the worst half at that. If the young women introduced by Mr. Howells in the novels wherein he stands committed to Realism are representative, the "Woman Movement" in New England should be towards reform of temper and restriction of the freedom of the tongue. But we are disposed to imagine that Boston girls are neither dolts nor vixens, that the passion of jealousy does not rage in their breasts to the exclusion of any other, and that all, whether well-bred Coreys or Laphams of no breeding at all, are not habitually impertinent to their elders, more especially to their helpless, hapless mothers. Here the most unpleasant and the most unnatural girl is Penelope Lapham. Mrs. Corey said she was a "thoroughly disagreeable young woman," and Mrs. Corey did not know that what is called her "drolling" was most brilliant when she was ironically snubbing her relations, or urging her sister to inextinguishable laughter by mimicking their father. Irene Lapham, the beauty, is probably the most extraordinary girl ever graduated from a Boston grammar-school. She mentally connected Sir Walter Scott with a school-fellow who, she said, had a habit of apostrophizing him, prefixing "great" to his name, and she but vaguely conjectured that he was not an American. In a recent speech before a woman's college, Mr. Lowell said, encouragingly, that he believed they could educate women there who would know the difference between literature and books. If Irene Lapham is not a gross caricature, that college must beware of girls from the Boston grammar-schools, else fulfilment of Mr. Lowell's rosy vision is far off indeed.

* * *

ANONYMOUS

[Tenderness and True Pathos][†]

Those determined people who will not read a serial story in sections may now take their comfort in an easy-chair with this novel in book form. Many thousands of readers have been following the fortunes of the sturdy Silas through the numbers of the *Century* since last winter, and various have been the opinions passed upon this latest

† Unsigned review from "The Bookshelf," *Cottage Hearth* 11 (October 1885): 326.

creation of Mr. Howells. Few, we think, will deny that it is the finest thing he has done. When "Polly" was "Among the Catskills"[1] a few months ago, COTTAGE HEARTH readers will recall her wish that this author would interest himself in the noble and lovable traits of character shown in common people, rather than dwell upon their failings and awkward manners. In "Silas Lapham" exactly this has been done. The hero is common, and he has big, country hands; but he is a hero for all that, and his true "Rise" is in his persistent adherence to truth and honor, his surmounting of the one great temptation of his life. The introduction of the "pretty type-writer" and the jealously [*sic*] of Mrs. Lapham regarding her, seems too much apart from the man interest of the story, too hastily and meagrely sketched, to be thoroughly artistic. The girl may have been needed to fully bring out the benevolent merchant's character, but we cannot help believing that the author intended to do more with the character and that branch of the plot, when he first introduced her. The little love-affair of Irene and Tom is one of the most exquisite pieces of dainty writing Mr. Howells has given us. It seems impossible that any one but a woman could have conceived the episode of the pine shaving, and its subsequent appearance with a bit of ribbon knotted fantastically about it. Penelope, too, is natural to the least detail, and Bromfield Corey is consistent, with his Neapolitan orange, to the last. Of all Mr. Howells' novels, this story of American life seems quite the most likely to stand the rest of time, and to rank close beside the classic productions of the English writers of fiction of the last generation. Tenderness and true pathos have not heretofore characterized his work, but the "Rise of Silas Lapham" abounds in such gentle and kindly passages full of human feeling, as have brought the more thoughtful works of Dickens and Thackeray—especially the former—very near to the hearts of the people.

ANONYMOUS

From Novel-Writing as a Science[†]

* * *

The revolution attempted by Mr. Howells is as simple as it is great. He regards novel-writing as science and not as art.

1. "Polly among the Catskills," a short story by Willis Boyd Allen, had appeared in the July 1885 issue of *Cottage Hearth*.

† Unsigned review from *Catholic World* 42 (November 1885): 274–80.

This is, perhaps, a natural outcome of what Mr. Spencer[1] would call heredity and environment. The Puritan mind is scientific, analytical. It is too severe and cold and suspicious to fuse into the constructive enthusiasm of art. And the last thing it would dream of would be to pursue art for art's sake, or even science for the sake of science alone. It must have an object in view, some useful end to serve. Thus it is curious to note how the Puritan mind in Mr. Howells, finding itself, by a freak of circumstance, working at an art, takes it strongly in its hands and transforms it into a science, and a science intended to have a useful application.

Two men study some object in nature, say a plant. One of them will drink in with his eye all its visible beauty, its form, its color, the stirring of the wind and the delicate play of light and shade among its leaves. He seizes a brush and with a few bold strokes reproduces all these traits upon a canvas. That is Art. The other observer plucks up the plant by the roots and brings it home to his herbarium. There he makes minute and careful diagrams of it, probably with the aid of a camera. He measures it and weighs it. He cuts it up into sections and makes drawings of the sections. He analyzes the clay at its roots, he counts its juices and tests for acids in them. That is Science; and therein lies the difference between the novel-writing of, say, Nathaniel Hawthorne and novel-writing as Mr. Howells pursues it.

In this way Mr. Howells has produced the most scientifically realistic novel that has yet been written. M. Zola's[2] books are as the awkward gropings of an amateur compared with this finished treatise. The field that Mr. Howells takes for his investigation is, he tells us, "the commonplace." By studying "the common feelings of common people" he believes he "solves the riddle of the painful earth."

Silas Lapham is a type of the self-made American. He has grown rich through the instrumentality of a mineral paint of which he is the proprietor. He lives in Boston and entertains social ambitions for his wife and two daughters. Bromfield Corey is a Boston aristocrat with a wife, two daughters, and a son. The Laphams and the Coreys are thrown together in consequence of a contemplated misalliance between young Corey and one of the Lapham daughters; and in the contrasts and developments that appear among all these "types" is supposed to consist the main interest of the story. There are no incidents that are not sternly commonplace, but everything connected with these incidents and their psychological effect on the actors is analyzed and detailed with microscopic accuracy.

* * *

1. Herbert Spencer (1820–1903), English philosopher (see p. 368, n.3).
2. Émile Zola (1840–1902), French novelist and a leading proponent of literary Naturalism, an aesthetic movement closely related to literary Realism.

* * * Now, Mr. Howells, though a mechanic—an anatomist, shall we say?—of exquisite skill, despises art. Therefore his work should be compared rather to a series of scientific diagrams than to photographs. It is not Mr. Howells' details that offend the artistic eye; it is the plans, the sections, the front elevations, the isometric projections he gives of his subjects.

He studies men and women as a naturalist does insects. We read his book on the manners, habits, sensations, nerves of a certain set of people as we might a treatise on the coleoptera. And he investigates and expounds his theme with the same soullessness and absence of all emotion. Even Mr. Henry James, beside this chilly *savant*, appears quite a child of sentiment. He is capable of receiving "impressions"—which, in Mr. Howells' eyes, would be a most unscientific weakness—and he manages to retain some smack of art about the work he does.

Is this kind of novel-writing an elevating pursuit? and is the reading of it beneficial? To these two queries the answer must be emphatically, No.

Novels like *Silas Lapham* mark a descent, a degradation. Of course art is debased when it has fallen so low into realism. Art is ever pointing upward, and the influence of true art upon man is to make him look upward, too, to that vast where his Ideal sits,

"—pinnacled in the lofty ether dim,"

where all is beautiful, but where all is immeasurable by him until he beholds it with his glorified intelligence. Science points downward, and when science is unguided by religion it leads its followers lower and lower into the mud beneath their feet. And even as we see some scientists making a distinct "progress" downward from the study of the higher to that of the lower forms of animal life, so in the novel-writing of Mr. Howells we can already mark this scientific decadence. He began with people who were not quite commonplace, whose motives and acts and ideas were a little bit above the common. He now declares that nothing is worthy to be studied but the common feelings of common people; and having begun *Silas Lapham* with people who were inoffensively commonplace, he was unable to finish the book without falling a stage lower. Towards the end he introduces a young woman who speaks thus of her husband: "If I could get rid of Hen I could manage well enough with mother. Mr. Wemmel would marry me if I could get the divorce. He said so over and over again." He introduces a scene in which this young woman, her tipsy sailor-husband, her drunken mother, and Silas Lapham as the family benefactor, figure—a scene that, for hopeless depravity both in the author and subject, out-Zolas Zola. The old woman, who has a bottle in her hand, complains of her son-in-law not giving the daughter an opportunity to obtain a divorce. "'Why don't you go off on some them long v'y'ges?' s'd I. It's pretty hard when Mr. Wemmel stands ready to marry Z'rilla and provide a comfortable home for us both—I han't got a great many years more to live, and I *should* like to get more satisfaction out of 'em and not be beholden and dependent all my days—to have Hen, here, blockin' the way. I tell him there'd be more money for him in the end; but he can't seem to make up his mind to it." Again says this old harridan: "Say, Colonel, what should you advise Z'rilla do about Mr. Wemmel? I tell her there an't any use goin' to the trouble to git a divorce without she's sure about him. Don't you think we'd ought to git him to sign a paper, or something, that he'll marry her if she gits it? I don't like to have things goin' at loose ends the way they are. It an't sense. It an't right." Before Mr. Howells reaches the end of the book he makes even the worthy Mrs. Lapham suspect her husband of infidelity and make a scene, accusing him, in the hearing of her children. It has seldom been our duty to read a book whose moral tone was so unpleasantly, so hopelessly bad; it is a book without heart or soul, neither illumined by religion nor warmed by human sympathy. This is all the more astonishing that Mr. Howells seems convinced that he is fulfilling a high moral purpose in writing it. It might be explicable on the theory that it was the legitimate outcome of the doctrine of total depravity; but it is more probably the logic of the downward progress of godless science. We shall not be surprised if the next book of Mr. Howells deal with characters and feelings that shall be so far below the commonplace from which he has already fallen that even M. de Goncourt will not enjoy reading about them. It is the progress from man to the apes, from the apes to the worms, from the worms to bacteria, from bacteria to—mud. It is the descent to dirt.

* * *

HAMILTON WRIGHT MABIE

From A Typical Novel†

In "The Rise of Silas Lapham" Mr. Howells has given us his best and his most characteristic work; none of his earlier stories discloses so clearly the quality and resources of his gift or his conception of the novelist's art. As an expression of personal power and as a type

† From *Andover Review* 4 (November 1885): 417–29.

of the dominant school of contemporary fiction in this country and in France, whence the special impulse of recent realism has come, this latest work of a very accomplished and conscientious writer deserves the most careful and dispassionate study. If Mr. Howells's work possessed no higher claim upon attention, its evident fidelity to a constantly advancing ideal of workmanship would command genuine respect and admiration; whatever else one misses in it, there is no lack of the earnestness which concentrates a man's full power on the thing in hand, nor of the sensitive literary conscience which permits no relaxation of strength on subordinate parts, but exacts in every detail the skill and care which are lavished on the most critical unfoldings of plot or disclosures of character. Mr. Howells evidently leaves nothing to the chance suggestion of an inspired moment, and takes nothing for granted; he verifies every insight by observation, fortifies every general statement by careful study of facts, and puts his whole force into every detail of his work. In spite of its evident danger in any save the strongest hands, there is a tonic quality in this exacting conscientiousness which writers of a different school often lack, and the absence of which is betrayed by hasty, unbalanced, and incomplete workmanship. It is this quality which discovers itself more and more distinctly in Mr. Howells's novels in a constant development of native gifts, a stronger grasp of facts, and a more comprehensive dealing with the problems of character and social life to which he has given attention. In fact, this popular novelist is giving thoughtful readers of his books a kind of inspiration in the quiet but resolute progress of his gift and his art; a progress stimulated, no doubt, by success, but made possible and constant by fidelity to a high and disinterested ideal.

Nor has Mr. Howells spent his whole force on mere workmanship; he has made a no less strenuous endeavor to enlarge his knowledge of life, his grasp of its complicated problems, his insight into the forces and impulses which are the sources of action and character. If he has failed to touch the deepest issues, and to lay bare the more obscure and subtle movements of passion and purpose, it has been through no intellectual willfulness or lassitude; he has patiently and unweariedly followed such clews as he has been able to discover, and he has resolutely held himself open to the claims of new themes and the revelations of fresh contacts with life. The limitations of his work are also the limitations of his insight and his imagination, and this fact, fully understood in all its bearings, makes any effort to point out those limitations ungracious in appearance and distasteful in performance; if personal feeling were to control in such matters, one would content himself with an expression of hearty admiration for work so full of character, and of sincere gratitude for a delicate intellectual pleasure so varied and so sustained. * * * His purpose grows steadily more serious, and his work gains correspondingly in substance and solidity. The problems of character which he sets before himself for solution become more complex and difficult, and, while there is nowhere a really decisive closing with life in a determined struggle to wring from it its secret, there is an evident purpose to grapple with realities and to keep in sympathy and touch with vital experiences.

In "The Rise of Silas Lapham" Mr. Howells has made a study of social conditions and contrasts everywhere present in society in this country; not, perhaps, so sharply defined elsewhere as in Boston, but to be discovered with more or less definiteness of outline in all our older communities. His quick instinct has fastened upon a stage of social evolution with which every body is familiar and in which everybody is interested. The aspect of social life presented in this story is well-nigh universal; it is real, it is vital, and it is not without deep significance; in dealing with it Mr. Howells has approached actual life more nearly, touched it more deeply, and expressed it more strongly than in any of his previous stories. The skill of his earliest work loses nothing in his latest; it is less evident because it is more unconscious and, therefore, more genuine and effective. There is the same humor, restrained and held in check by the major interests of the story, but touching here and there an idiosyncrasy, an inconsistency, a weakness, with all the old pungency and charm; a humor which is, in fact, the most real and the most distinctive of all Mr. Howells's gifts. There is, also, stronger grasp of situations, bolder portraiture of character, more rapid and dramatic movement of narrative. Still more important is the fact that in this novel life is presented with more of dramatic dignity and completeness than in any of Mr. Howells's other stories; there is a truer and nobler movement of human nature in it; and the characters are far less superficial, inconsequential, and unimportant than their predecessors; if not the highest types, they have a certain force and dignity which make us respect them, and make it worth while to write about them. Add to these characterizations of "The Rise of Silas Lapham" the statement that Mr. Howells has never shown more complete mastery of his art in dealing with his materials; that his style has never had more simplicity and directness, more solidity and substance, and it will be conceded that the sum total of excellence which even a reader who dissents from its underlying conception and method discovers in this story is by no means inconsiderable; is, indeed, such as to entitle it to very high praise, and to give added permanence and expansion to a literary reputation which, from the standpoint of popularity at least, stood in small need of these things.

And yet, when all this has been said, and said heartily, it must be added that "The Rise of Silas Lapham" is an unsatisfactory story;

defective in power, in reality, and in the vitalizing atmosphere of imagination. No one is absorbed by it, nor moved by it; one takes it up with pleasure, reads it with interest, and lays it down without regret. It throws no spell over us; creates no illusion for us, leaves us indifferent spectators of an entertaining drama of social life. The novelist wrote it in a cool, deliberate mood, and it leaves the reader cold when he has finished it. The appearance and action of life are in it, but not the warmth; the frame, the organism, are admirable, but the divine inbreathing which would have given the body a soul has been withheld. Everything that art could do has been done, but the vital spark has not been transmitted. Mr. Howells never identifies himself with his characters; never becomes one with them in the vital fellowship and communion of the imagination; he constructs them with infinite patience and skill, but he never, for a moment, loses consciousness of his own individuality. He is cool and collected in all the emotional crises of his stories; indeed, it is often at such moments that one feels the presence of a diffused satire, as if the weakness of the men and women whom he is describing excited a little scorn in the critical mind of the novelist. The severest penalty of the persistent analytic mood is borne by the writer in the slight paralysis of feeling which comes upon him at the very moment when the pulse should beat a little faster of its own motion; in the subtle skepticism which pervades his work, unconsciously to himself, and like a slight frost takes the bloom off all fine emotions and actions. There are passages in Mr. Howells's stories in reading which one cannot repress a feeling of honest indignation at what is nothing more nor less than a refined parody of genuine feeling, sometimes of the most pathetic experience. Is Mr. Howells ashamed of life in its outcries of pain and regret? Does he shrink from these unpremeditated and unconventional revelations of character as vulgar, provincial, inartistic; or does he fail to comprehend them? Certainly the cool, skillful hand which lifts the curtain upon Silas Lapham's weakness and sorrows does not tremble for an instant with any contagious emotion; and whenever the reader begins to warm a little, a slight turn of satire, a cool phrase or two of analysis, a faint suggestion that the writer doubts whether it is worth while, clears the air again. Perhaps nothing more decisive on this point could be said of Mr. Howells's stories than that one can read them aloud without faltering at the most pathetic passages; the latent distrust of all strong feeling in them makes one a little shy of his own emotion.

This failure to close with the facts of life, to press one's heart against them as well as to pursue and penetrate them with one's thought; this lack of unforced and triumphant faith in the worth, the dignity, and the significance for art of human experience in its whole range; this failure of the imagination to bridge the chasm between the real and the fictitious reproduction of it, are simply fatal to all great and abiding work. Without faith, which is the very ground upon which the true artist stands; without love, which is both inspiration and revelation to him, a true art is impossible. * * *

* * * The method of the realism illustrated in "The Rise of Silas Lapham" is external, and, so far as any strong grasp of life is concerned, necessarily superficial. It is an endeavor to enter into the recesses of character, and learn its secret, not by insight, the method of the imagination, but by observation, the method of science; and it is an endeavor to reproduce that character under the forms of art, not by identification with it, and the genuine and almost unconscious evolution which follows, but by skillful adjustment of traits, emotions, passions, and activities which are the result of studies more or less conscientiously carried on. The patience and work involved in the making of some novels constructed on this method are beyond praise; but they must not make us blind to the fact that no method can take the place of original power, and that genius in some form—faith, sympathy, insight, imagination—is absolutely essential in all true art. The hesitation, the repression of emotion, the absence of color, are significant, not of a noble restraint of power, a wise husbanding of resources for the critical moment and situation, but of a lack of the spontaneity and overflow of a great force. Ruskin finely says that when we stand before a true work of art we feel ourselves in the presence, not of a great effort, but of a great force. In most of the novels of realism it is the effort which impresses us, and not the power. * * *

Mr. Howells has said, in substance, that realism is the only literary movement of the day which has any vitality in it, and certainly no one represents this tendency on its finer side more perfectly than himself. Its virtues and its defects are very clearly brought out in his work: its clearness of sight, its fixed adherence to fact, its reliance upon honest work; and, on the other hand, its hardness, its lack of vitality, its paralysis of the finer feelings and higher aspirations, its fundamental defect on the side of the imagination. Realism is crowding the world of fiction with commonplace people; people whom one would positively avoid coming in contact with in real life; people without native sweetness or strength, without acquired culture or accomplishment, without that touch of the ideal which makes the commonplace significant and worthy of study. To the large, typical characters of the older novels has succeeded a generation of feeble, irresolute, unimportant men and women whose careers are of no moment to themselves, and wholly destitute of interest to us. The analysis of motives that were never worth an hour's serious study, the grave portraiture of frivolous, superficial, and often vulgar conceptions of life, the careful scrutiny of characters without force, beauty, aspiration, or any of the elements which touch and teach men, has become wearisome, and will sooner or later set in motion a powerful reaction. One cannot but regret such a comparative waste of delicate, and often genuine, art; it is as if Michael Angelo had given us the meaningless faces of the Roman fops of his time instead of the heads of Moses and Hercules.

* * *

The older art of the world is based on the conception that life is at bottom a revelation; that human growth under all conditions has a spiritual law back of it; that human relations of all kinds have spiritual types behind them; and that the discovery of these universal facts, and the clear, noble embodiment of them in various forms, is the office of genius and the end of art. * * * But modern realism knows nothing of any revelation in human life; of any spiritual facts of which its facts are significant; of any spiritual laws to which they conform in the unbroken order of the Universe. It does more than ignore these things; it denies them. Under the conditions which it imposes art can see nothing but the isolated physical fact before it; there are no mysterious forces in the soil under it; there is no infinite blue heaven over it. It forms no part of a universal order; it discovers no common law; it can never be a type of a great class. It is, in a word, practical atheism applied to art. It not only empties the world of the Ideal, but, as Zola frankly says, it denies "the good God;" it dismisses the old heaven of aspiration and possible fulfillment as an idle dream; it destroys the significance of life and the interpretative quality of art.

* * *

* * * We are in great danger of coming to accept as work of the first order that which has no claim to any such distinction, and adopt as the standards of the noblest literary art the very delightful but very inadequate creations of some of our contemporary writers. It is always wisest to face the truth; if the poets of the time lack the qualities which go to the making of great singers, let us acknowledge the fact and make the best of it; if our realistic novelists are more skillful than powerful, more adroit and entertaining than original and inspiring, let us admit this fact also. But, in the name and for the sake of art, let us decline to accept these charming storytellers as the peers of the great masters, and, above all, let us refuse to impose their individual limitations upon the great novelists of the future. "The Rise of Silas Lapham" and the novels of its class are

additions to the literature of fiction for which we are grateful; but it is a great injustice to them and to their writers to insist upon placing them side by side with the great novels of the past.

What is needed now, in fiction as in poetry, is a revitalization of the imagination and a return to implicit and triumphant faith in it. The results of the scientific movement are misread by men of literary genius no less than by religious people; in the end, they will be found to serve the noblest uses of art no less than of religion. * * *

HENRY JAMES
From William Dean Howells†

* * *

* * * [Howells] had the good fortune of not approaching the novel until he had lived considerably, until his inclination for it had ripened. His attitude was as little as possible that of the gifted young person who, at twenty, puts forth a work of imagination of which the merit is mainly in its establishing the presumption that the next one will be better. It is my impression that long after he was twenty he still cultivated the belief that the faculty of the novelist was not in him, and was even capable of producing certain unfinished chapters (in the candor of his good faith he would sometimes communicate them to a listener) in triumphant support of this contention. He believed, in particular, that he could not make people talk, and such have been the revenges of time that a cynical critic might almost say of him to-day that he cannot make them keep silent. It was life itself that finally dissipated his doubts, life that reasoned with him and persuaded him. The feeling of life is strong in all his tales, and any one of them has this rare (always rarer) and indispensable sign of a happy origin, that it is an impression at first hand. Mr. Howells is literary, on certain sides exquisitely so, though with a singular and not unamiable perversity he sometimes endeavors not to be; but his vision of the human scene is never a literary reminiscence, a reflection of books and pictures, of tradition and fashion and hearsay. I know of no English novelist of our hour whose work is so exclusively a matter of painting what he sees and who is so sure of what he sees. People are always wanting a writer of Mr. Howells's temperament to see certain things that he doesn't (that he doesn't sometimes even want to), but I must content myself with congratulating the author of *A Modern Instance* and *Silas Lapham*

† From *Harper's Weekly* 30 (June 19, 1886): 394–95.

on the admirable quality of his vision. The American life which he for the most part depicts is certainly neither very rich nor very fair, but it is tremendously positive, and as his manner of presenting it is as little as possible conventional, the reader can have no doubt about it. This is an immense luxury; the ingenuous character of the witness (I can give it no higher praise) deepens the value of the report.

Mr. Howells has gone from one success to another, has taken possession of the field, and has become copious without detriment to his freshness. I need not enumerate his works in their order, for, both in America and in England (where it is a marked feature of the growing curiosity felt about American life that they are constantly referred to for information and verification), they have long been in everybody's hands. Quietly and steadily they have become better and better; one may like some of them more than others, but it is noticeable that from effort to effort the author has constantly enlarged his scope. His work is of a kind of which it is good that there should be much today—work of observation, of patient and definite notation. Neither in theory nor in practice is Mr. Howells a romancer; but the romancers can spare him; there will always be plenty of people to do their work. He has definite and downright convictions on the subject of the work that calls out to be done in opposition to theirs, and this fact is a source of much of the interest that he excites.

It is a singular circumstance that to know what one wishes to do should be, in the field of art, a rare distinction; but it is incontestable that, as one looks about in our English and American fiction, one does not perceive any very striking examples of a vivifying faith. There is no discussion of the great question of how best to write, no exchange of ideas, no vivacity nor variety of experiment. A vivifying faith Mr. Howells may distinctly be said to possess, and he conceals it so little as to afford every facility to those people who are anxious to prove that it is the wrong one. He is animated by a love of the common, the immediate, the familiar and vulgar elements of life, and holds that in proportion as we move into the rare and strange we become vague and arbitrary; that truth of representation, in a word, can be achieved only so long as it is in our power to test and measure it. He thinks scarcely anything too paltry to be interesting, that the small and the vulgar have been terribly neglected, and would rather see an exact account of a sentiment or a character he stumbles against every day than a brilliant evocation of a passion or a type he has never seen and does not even particularly believe in. He adores the real, the natural, the colloquial, the moderate, the optimistic, the domestic, and the democratic; looking askance at exceptions and perversities and superiorities, at surprising and incongruous phenomena in general. One must have seen a great deal before one concludes; the world is very large, and life is a mixture of many things; she by no means eschews the strange, and often risks combinations and effects that make one rub one's eyes. Nevertheless, Mr. Howells's standpoint is an excellent one for seeing a large part of the truth, and even if it were less advantageous, there would be a great deal to admire in the firmness with which he has planted himself. He hates a "story," and (this private feat is not impossible) has probably made up his mind very definitely as to what the pestilent thing consists of. In this respect he is more logical than M. Émile Zola, who partakes of the same averision, but has greater lapses as well as greater audacities. Mr. Howells hates an artificial fable and a *dénouement* that is pressed into the service; he likes things to occur as they occur in life, where the manner of a great many of them is not to occur at all. He has observed that heroic emotion and brilliant opportunity are not particularly interwoven with our days, and indeed, in the way of omission, he *has* often practised in his pages a very considerable boldness. It has not, however, made what we find there any less interesting and less human.

The picture of American life on Mr. Howells's canvas is not of a dazzling brightness and many readers have probably wondered why it is that (among a sensitive people) he has so successfully escaped the imputation of a want of patriotism. The manners he describes—the desolation of the whole social prospect in *A Modern Instance* is perhaps the strongest expression of those influences—are eminently of a nature to discourage the intending visitor, and yet the westward pilgrim continues to arrive, in spite of the Bartley Hubbards and the Laphams, and the terrible practices at the country hotel in *Doctor Breen*, and at the Boston boarding-house in *A Woman's Reason*. This tolerance of depressing revelations is explained partly, no doubt, by the fact that Mr. Howells's truthfulness imposes itself—the representation is so vivid that the reader accepts it as he accepts, in his own affairs, the mystery of fate—and partly by a very different consideration, which is simply that if many of his characters are disagreeable, almost all of them are extraordinarily good, and with a goodness which is a ground for national complacency. If American life is on the whole, as I make no doubt whatever, more innocent than that of any other country, nowhere is the fact more patent than in Mr. Howells's novels, which exhibit so constant a study of the actual and so small a perception of evil. His women, in particular, are of the best—except, indeed, in the sense of being the best to live with. Purity of life, fineness of conscience, benevolence of motive, decency of speech, good-nature, kindness, charity, tolerance (though, indeed, there is little but each other's manners for the people to tolerate), govern all the scene; the only immoralities are aberrations of thought, like that of Silas Lapham, or excesses of beer, like that of Bartley Hubbard. In the gallery of Mr. Howells's portraits there are none more living than the admirable, humorous images of those two ineffectual sinners. Lapham, in particular, is magnificent, understood down to the ground, inside and out—a creation which does Mr. Howells the highest honor. I do not say that the figure of his wife is as good as his own, only because I wish to say that it is as good as that of the minister's wife in the history of *Lemuel Barker*,[1] which is unfolding itself from month to month at the moment I write. These two ladies are exhaustive renderings of the type of virtue that worries. But everything in *Silas Lapham* is superior—nothing more so than the whole picture of casual female youth and contemporaneous "engaging" one's self, in the daughters of the proprietor of the mineral paint.

This production had struck me as the author's high-water mark, until I opened the monthly sheets of *Lemuel Barker*, in which the art of imparting a palpitating interest to common things and unheroic lives is pursued (or is destined, apparently, to be pursued) to an even higher point. The four (or is it eight?) repeated "good-mornings" between the liberated Lemuel and the shopgirl who has crudely been the cause of his being locked up by the police all night are a poem, an idyl, a trait of genius, and a compendium of American good-nature. The whole episode is inimitable, and I know fellow-novelists of Mr. Howells's who would have given their eyes to produce that interchange of salutations, which only an American reader, I think, can understand. Indeed, the only limitation, in general, to his extreme truthfulness is, I will not say his constant sense of the comedy of life, for that is irresistible, but the verbal drollery of many of his people. It is extreme and perpetual, but I fear the reader will find it a venial sin. Theodore Colville, in *Indian Summer*, is so irrepressibly and happily facetious as to make one wonder whether the author is not prompting him a little, and whether he could be quite so amusing without help from outside. This criticism, however, is the only one I find it urgent to make, and Mr. Howells doubtless will not suffer from my saying that, being a humorist himself, he is strong in the representation of humorists. There are other reflections that I might indulge in if I had more space. I should like, for instance, to allude in passing, for purposes of respectful remonstrance, to a phrase that he suffered the other day to fall from his pen (in a periodical, but not in a novel), to the effect that the style of a work of fiction is a thing that matters less and less all the while. Why less and less? It seems to me as great a mistake to say so as it would be to say that it matters more and more. It is difficult to see how it can matter either less or more. The style of a novel is a part of the

1. *The Minister's Charge, Or The Apprenticeship of Lemuel Barker* ran in *Century* magazine from February through December 1886.

execution of a work of art; the execution of a work of art is a part of its very essence, and that, it seems to me, must have mattered in all ages in exactly the same degree, and be destined always to do so. I can conceive of no state of civilization in which it shall not be deemed important, though of course there are states in which executants are clumsy. I should also venture to express a certain regret that Mr. Howells (whose style, in practice, after all, as I have intimated, treats itself to felicities which his theory perhaps would condemn) should appear increasingly to hold composition too cheap—by which I mean, should neglect the effect that comes from alternation, distribution, relief. He has an increasing tendency to tell his story altogether in conversations, so that a critical reader sometimes wishes, not that the dialogue might be suppressed (it is too good for that), but that it might be distributed, interspaced with narrative and pictorial matter. The author forgets sometimes to paint, to evoke the conditions and appearances, to build in the subject. He is doubtless afraid of doing these things in excess, having seen in other hands what disastrous effects that error may have; but all the same I cannot help thinking that the divinest thing in a valid novel is the compendious, descriptive, pictorial touch, *à la Daudet.*

It would be absurd to speak of Mr. Howells to-day in the encouraging tone that one would apply to a young writer who had given fine pledges, and one feels half guilty of that mistake if one makes a cheerful remark about his future. And yet we cannot pretend not to take a still more lively interest in his future than we have done in his past. It is hard to see how it can help being more and more fruitful, for his face is turned in the right direction, and his work is fed from sources which play us no tricks.

DROCH [ROBERT BRIDGES]

Social Contempt in Fiction†

Moral indifference and social contempt are the dominant qualities in that school of fiction writers of which Mr. Howells is the head. These realists are in doubt as to what is wholly admirable in life, because, like many people in this transition period, they are giving up the old forms of faith, and have not grasped the significance and responsibilities of the new. As a recent essayist has said: "They have not made up their own minds as to what they shall admire, what they shall detest, what they shall excuse, and what they shall commiserate." There is no

† From *Life* 8 (September 2, 1886): 132.

dignity in moral heroism, no worth in self-sacrifice, no merit in endurance, no romance in love with such a creed.

The old Puritan censoriousness which formerly expended its venom and severity on the morals of men now attacks without mercy their manners. It can find an apology for crime, but shudders at a breach of etiquette and heaps contempt on common life.

With a keen appreciation of this attitude of Social Contempt, a newspaper writer has called the novels of Mr. Howells "Studies of American Vulgarity." Though trying to appreciate all that is sincere in American life, Mr. Howells and his imitators approach perilously near the Snob's standard of judgment. Nine-tenths of his readers must mentally squirm as they listen to his merciless dissection of their peculiarities of dress, speech, and manner.

And some of them feel and know that the qualities which make Mr. Howells the genial and polished gentleman of Beacon Street, Boston, were equally the charm of the boy who "sorted slugs" in an Ohio newspaper office.

The glory of American life is that it is possible for men to rise, and the hope of it has vitalized us. To ridicule the incongruities of such transitions is to throw a damper on honest American ambition.

There is so much that is gross, bad and demoralizing about American success which is a fitting target for the keenest ridicule and satire, that it is a deplorable waste of energy to expend them on the eccentricities of manner with which birth has loaded so many of our worthy countrymen.

In hundreds of villages where the leading magazines are considered the standard measure of literature and life by most estimable people, false distinctions of class and rank are being inculcated by these subtle analyses of American Vulgarity.

W. A. Rogers, “The Modern Novel,” *Life* 7 (May 20, 1886): 288–89. Courtesy of the Watkinson Library, Trinity College, Hartford, CT. The cartoon pictures Howells and Henry James as brain surgeons, with a caption reading:

Do these gentlemen find what they are hunting for? / Oh, yes. / What is it? / Nothing.

Modern Criticism

BRENDA MURPHY

From Howells and the Popular Story Paradigm: Reading *Silas Lapham*'s Proairetic Code†

* * *

Silas Lapham's structure is fundamentally a "correction"[1] of two popular nineteenth-century story paradigms, the rags-to-riches "success myth" and the sentimental novel of self-sacrifice, two story paradigms which the realist Howells rejected as false representations of reality. The overwhelming import of the novel's proairetic code is that the truth, the representation of reality the novel embodies, is only to be found in disruption of the conventional story paradigm, and that the false representation prevailing in popular literature not only is simple-minded and silly, but is cynically manipulated by its purveyors for their own profit, to the deep injury of its audience. Reading the proairetic code[2] in *The Rise of Silas Lapham* brings Howells' polemic opposition to the falsity of contemporary popular narratives into sharper focus than has occurred with previous analysis and adds one more "voice," as Barthes would say, to the articulation of meaning in *Silas Lapham*.[3]

† From *American Literary Realism, 1870–1910* 21.2 (Winter 1989): 22–33. Reprinted by permission of *American Literary Realism*. Page references in brackets refer to this Norton Critical Edition.

1. I use the term "correction" here in the sense developed by Alfred Habegger, that realism "bore in part an adversary or corrective relation to a major type of novel, woman's fiction. . . . The detailed verisimilitude, close social notion, analysis of motives, and unhappy endings were all part of a strategy of argument, an adversary polemic" (*Gender, Fantasy, and Realism in American Literature,* New York: Columbia Univ. Press, 1982, p. 106).
2. Murphy borrows this term from Roland Barthes's *S/Z,* where, she says, "he defined it loosely as the 'code of actions and behavior,'" composing "'one of the voices out of which the text is woven'" [*editor's note*].
3. Previous analyses of *Silas Lapham's* plot have chiefly revolved around two issues: the relation of its two story-lines or plots to each other and to the novel as a whole, and the nature of its form, archetype, or genre. The most influential views on the first issue have been Donald Pizer's contention in "The Ethical Unity of *The Rise of Silas Lapham,*" *American Literature,* 32 (November 1960), 322–27, that the two plots function together to elucidate "the ethical core of the novel"; Kermit Vanderbilt's view in *The*

The most significant cultural paradigm that Howells addresses in *Silas Lapham* is, of course, the success myth, a universal popular property since Benjamin Franklin's formulation of it in his autobiography and *Poor Richard's Almanac,* revised slightly by Horatio Alger during the eighteen-sixties, seventies, and eighties. In Kenneth Lynn's estimation, "the Alger hero represents a triumphant combination—and reduction to the lowest common denominator—of the most widely accepted concepts in nineteenth-century American society. The belief in the potential greatness of the common man, the glorification of individual effort and accomplishment, the equation of the pursuit of money with the pursuit of happiness and of business success with spiritual grace."[4] While more recent scholarship on Alger has modified the view of the pursuit of money as the endpoint of a single-minded life of striving that Lynn's analysis implies, it is consistent with Michael Zuckerman's formulation of Alger's version of business success: "As Alger would have it . . . success follows dependability and a desire to serve others. It attends those who obey orders cheerfully and serve others willingly. And it is available to all, for Alger posited no pinnacle of preeminence for which many compete and few prove fit."[5] The paradigm for the American success story pervaded Howells' culture, and it does not take much investigation to see the forms in which he encountered it.

* * *

In *The Self-Made Man in America*, Irvin Wylie laid out the five sequences of events in the biography of a self-made man that were necessary to the success cult's ideology: origin in poverty, a rural childhood, migration to the city, a mother's moral influence that

Achievement of William Dean Howells (Princeton: Princeton Univ. Press, 1968) that the two story-lines are not a main plot and a subplot but "co-plots"; and G. Thomas Tanselle's careful reading of the novel's five "movements" and its rhythm, based on the seasons of the year, in "The Architecture of *The Rise of Silas Lapham,*" *American Literature,* 37 (January 1966), 430–57. About the second issue there is real disagreement, and critical views range from George C. Carrington's in *The Immense Complex Drama: The World and Art of the Howells Novel* (Columbus: Ohio State Univ. Press, 1966) that the novel is satire, to the opposing camps which claim that it is romance—John E. Hart, "The Commonplace as Heroic in *The Rise of Silas Lapham,*" *Modern Fiction Studies,* 8 (Winter 1963), 375–83; and S. Foster, "W. D. Howells: *The Rise of Silas Lapham*" in *The Monster in the Mirror,* ed. D. A. Williams (Oxford: Oxford Univ. Press, 1978); or that it is anti-romance—Robert Lee Hough, "William Dean Howells, *The Rise of Silas Lapham,*" in *The American Novel*, ed. Wallace Stegner (New York: Basic Books, 1965).

4. *The Dream of Success: A Study of the Modern American Imagination* (Boston: Little, Brown, 1955), p. 7.
5. "The Nursery Tales of Horatio Alger," *American Quarterly* 24 (1972), 191–210. For a full discussion of the Alger stories and their interrelation with American culture, see Gary Scharnhorst and Jack Bales, *The Lost Life of Horatio Alger, Jr.* (Bloomington: Indiana Univ. Press, 1985) and John Cawelti, *Apostles of the Self Made Man* (Chicago: Univ. of Chicago Press, 1965).

lasted for a lifetime, and marriage to a good woman who was an unfailing support to her husband.[6] Howells' understanding of the rags-to-riches story paradigm and the cultural forces that manipulated it is abundantly clear in the opening of the novel. In the narrative of the interview between Bartley Hubbard and Silas Lapham, Howells carefully interweaves four distinct levels of discourse which articulate four levels of cultural awareness about the success myth. The first is the discourse of Silas' ingenuously egotistical narrative, delivered in his own language and in his own style. To him his story is personal and unique, a simple narration of what happened in his life. The second is the discourse of the newspaper article, Bartley's public reformulation of Lapham's story in accord with the cultural paradigm. The third is Bartley's cynical commentary on the story, reflecting his awareness that he is dealing in the culture's popular fictions rather than reality, and his willingness to manipulate both the story and Lapham for his own profit. The fourth is the narrator's commentary, the moral voice that represents Bartley to the reader as the "potential reprobate" (24 [7]), weak and amoral.

All four of these levels are at work in the presentation of Lapham's early rural poverty. Lapham has been told to begin at the beginning:

> "Well, say I'm fifty-five years old; and I've *lived* 'em too; not an hour of waste time about *me*, anywheres! I was born on a farm, and—" [1]
>
> "Worked in the fields summers and went to school winters: regulation thing?" [3] Bartley cut in. [4]
>
> "Regulation thing," [1] said Lapham, accepting this irreverent version of his history somewhat dryly. [4]
>
> "Parents poor, of course," [3] suggested the journalist. [4] "Any barefoot business? Early deprivations of any kind, that would encourage the youthful reader to go and do likewise? Orphan myself, you know," [3] said Bartley, with a smile of cynical good-comradery. [4]
>
> Lapham looked at him silently, and then said with quiet self-respect, [4] "I guess if you see these things as a joke, my life won't interest you." [1] (5 [4])

Thus the first and third levels of awareness are set up for the reader: Silas' straightforward belief in the "real" events of his life, and the reporter's sense of them as material he can manipulate in order to fulfill the public's expectation of a familiar and satisfying story-line. Demonstrating the extent of this manipulation, and of Bartley's cynicism, Howells juxtaposes the second level, the text of the newspaper interview, with the conversation:

6. *The Self-Made Man in America* (New York: Macmillan, 1954), pp. 21–31.

> Mr. Lapham . . . passed rapidly over the story of his early life, its poverty and its hardships, sweetened, however, by the recollections of a devoted mother, and a father who, if somewhat her inferior in education, was no less ambitious for the advancement of his children. They were quiet, unpretentious people, religious, after the fashion of that time, and of sterling morality, and they taught their children the simple virtues of the Old Testament and Poor Richard's Almanac (5 [5]).

Finally, the voice of the narrator comes in, revealing in its commentary a knowledge of Silas' simplicity, the public's acquiescence in the newspaper's formulaic discourse, the falsity of the formula's representation of reality, and the cynicism with which the reporter presents it: "Bartley could not deny himself this gibe; but he trusted to Lapham's unliterary habit of mind for his security in making it, and most other people would consider it sincere reporter's rhetoric" (5 [5]).

By manipulating these four levels of discourse, Howells maintains a triple irony in the narrative. It is of course Bartley whose amoral cynicism comes under sharpest attack. Being shown a picture of Irene Lapham, for example, "'She's a good-looking chap,' said Bartley, with prompt irreverence. He hastened to add, at the frown which gathered between Lapham's eyes, 'What a beautiful creature she is! What a lovely, refined sensitive face! And she looks *good*, too . . . And, after all, that's about the best thing in a woman,' said the potential reprobate" (8 [7]). But the narrative treatment of both the formula's bland hypocrisy and Lapham's egotistical naiveté is ironic as well. The passage from Bartley's newspaper piece shows Howells' ironic treatment of the formula's hypocritical pretense of morality. As if the juxtaposition of the Old Testament and Poor Richard's Almanac were not enough, the glaring absence of the New Testament in the moral life of these supposed Christians sharply defines the limits of the success myth's morality. Lapham's inability to see "where the joke comes in" in his painting "Lapham's Mineral Paint—Specimen" on every available board-fence, bridge girder, dead wall, barn, or face of rock is a good example of the narrative irony with which he is treated. "I say the landscape was made for man, and not man for the landscape," he says. Whereupon Bartley replies, "Yes . . . it was made for the stove-polish man and the kidney-cure man," and Silas remains "insensible to Bartley's irony" (15 [12–13]).

The pervasive irony of this opening chapter has an unsettling effect on the reader, who has not been directed clearly by its multilevel discourse into what perspective to take on Silas Lapham and his story. Howells settles this doubt in Chapter II, with a long narrative passage about the Laphams, and the truth about the lives of "successful" Americans. He takes up the "reality" of their lives where the paradigm for the success story ends, with the achievement of wealth and ease. What do these simple, hard-working and virtuous rural people do with their money after they've earned it? This, Howells suggests, is where the formula fails.

> Suddenly the money began to come so abundantly that [Mrs. Lapham] need not save; and then they did not know what to do with it. A certain amount could be spent on horses, and Lapham spent it; his wife spent in rich and rather ugly clothes and a luxury of household appointments. Lapham had not yet reached the picture-buying stage of the rich man's development, but they decorated their house with the costliest and most abominable frescoes; they went upon journeys, and lavished upon cars and hotels; they gave with both hands to their church and to all the charities it brought them acquainted with; but they did not know how to spend on society. (25 [20])

And this is the rub in their so-called success, for the Laphams find that they have put themselves in a social no-man's land where it will be impossible to find husbands for their daughters. They are too wealthy to seek out friends and acquaintances in the simple country fashion that is the only way the elder Laphams know, and in their ignorance they have violated the rigid codes of the society they hope to enter by sending their daughters to the "wrong" schools and not introducing them as children to the complexities of Boston social connections. The picture Howells paints is that of a family left completely to itself because its money has thrust it out of the class it belongs to but has not been sufficient to impel it into another. In social terms, Howells implies, success is a disaster. This is the part of the story that the success myth of the previous chapter omits.

The introduction of the Lapham family provides the link to the second major story-line in the novel, the action involving the Lapham sisters and Tom Corey that is Howells' treatment of the self-sacrifice paradigm in nineteenth-century popular fiction. Howells was never shy about showing the disgust with which he encountered the "gaudy hero and heroine" of popular sentimental fiction. He especially berated the heroine who "taught by example, if not precept, that Love, or the passion or fancy she mistook for it, was the chief interest of a life, which is really concerned with a great many other things . . . More lately she has begun to idolize and illustrate Duty, and she is hardly less mischievous in this new role, opposing duty, as she did love, to prudence, obedience, and reason."[7] His *bete noire* in this

7. *Criticism and Fiction,* 1891; rpt. ed. Clara and Rudolf Kirk (New York: New York Univ. Press, 1959), pp. 47–48.

idolization of Duty was the cult of self-sacrifice, and his attack on it in his fiction has received cogent analysis, most recently by Alfred Habegger, who has argued that "in attacking the ideal of self-sacrifice Howells was aiming at the dead center of American life—the negative, passive, self-denying life that women were expected to lead."[8]

In his study of the sentimental popular paradigm for what he calls loosely "women's fiction," Habegger has put his finger on precisely the aspect of these sentimentally idealized fantasies about self-sacrifice that Howells represents as so destructive to their readers. "Ultimately, the reason why novels encouraged the reader to identify herself with an altogether superior heroine was to make possible the intensely pleasurable pay-off at the end, a climax not considered successful unless it produced a physical effect—happy tears."[9] The danger came precisely with this sense of identity, for "this gender identity was at one and the same time very private and very public—private because it formed the individual's goal or idealized self or wished-for image; public, because it was after all a kind of copy of cultural norms. Fantasy, then, was nothing less than a private drama in which one put oneself into the ideal gender role. And the popular novel was a prop for standard fantasies."[1]

In foregrounding his presentation of the popular version of self-sacrifice, the imaginary novel *Tears, Idle Tears*, Howells was attempting to expose these standard fantasies to his readers for what they were, and in the story-line depicting Penelope's behavior in her dilemma, he was correcting the popular story paradigm, first by showing that romantic self-sacrifice was not heroic but silly and hurtful, and second by showing that the reality of human behavior was a good deal more complicated than the popular paradigm suggested.

Howells introduces the issue by presenting the paradigm and the standard reaction to it that Habegger describes. At the dinner party, the good-hearted but rather silly and emotional Clara Kingsbury brings up *Tears, Idle Tears* as a topic of conversation: "It's perfectly heart-breaking, as you'll imagine from the name; but there's such a dear old-fashioned hero and heroine in it, who keep dying for each other all the way through, and making the most wildly satisfactory and unnecessary sacrifices for each other. You feel as if you'd done them yourself" (197 [150–51]). At this point, the narrative

8. "The Autistic Tyrant: Howells' Self-Sacrificial Woman and Jamesian Renunciation," *Novel*, 10 (Fall 1976), 32. Other analyses of Howells's treatment of self-sacrifice may be found in Edwin H. Cady, *The Realist at War* (Syracuse: Syracuse Univ. Press, 1958), pp. 232–35; John Roland Dove, "Howells' Irrational Heroines," *Texas Studies in English*, 35 (1956), 64–80; and Habegger, *Gender, Fantasy, and Realism in American Literature*, pp. 190–92 and passim.

9. *Gender, Fantasy, and Realism*, p. 6.

1. Ibid., p. 10.

confronts the popular sentiment directly, with Nanny Corey's comment that the novel ought to have been called *Slop, Silly Slop* and the Reverend Mr. Sewall's condemnation: "The self-sacrifice painted in most novels like this . . . is nothing but psychical suicide, and is as wholly immoral as the spectacle of a man falling on his sword" (198 [151]). The crucial foregrounding of the conventional paradigm comes, however, in the discussion Tom and Penelope have of the book just before his proposal prompts her own struggle with self-sacrifice. Learning that Penelope has just read *Tears, Idle Tears*, Tom remarks:

> "It's a famous book with ladies. They break their hearts over it. Did it make you cry?"
>
> "Oh, it's pretty easy to cry over a book," said Penelope, laughing; "and that one *is* very natural till you come to the main point. Then the naturalness of all the rest makes that seem natural too; but I guess it's rather forced."
>
> "Her giving him up to the other one?"
>
> "Yes; simply because she happened to know that the other one had cared for him first. Why should she have done it? What right had she?"
>
> "I don't know. I suppose that the self-sacrifice—"
>
> "But it *wasn't* self-sacrifice—or not self-sacrifice alone. She was sacrificing him too; and for someone who couldn't appreciate him half as much as she could. I'm provoked with myself when I think how I cried over that book—for I did cry. It's silly—it's wicked for anyone to do what that girl did. Why can't they let people have a chance to behave reasonably in stories?"
>
> "Perhaps they couldn't make it so attractive," suggested Corey, with a smile. (217 [166])

Foregrounding the story paradigm in this way, Howells was sure of at least getting his readers to think about the falseness of the ideal that it preached and of the harm that identification with the heroine could do to the readers of sentimental popular fiction. It also prepared his readers for the realistic correction he was about to offer, the sequence of events portraying 1) the pain that not only Penelope and Tom, but Irene, the elder Laphams, and even the Coreys had to endure; 2) the gradual conviction, largely through Sewall's agency, in all of them that Penelope could only do wrong to give Tom up because Irene had fancied him first; 3) the slow recovery of Irene from the pain of her rejection; and 4) the more or less happy union of Tom and Penelope. The "more or less" is important here, for Howells was representing real life. Penelope's final course is far from the noble and selfless decision of the sentimental heroine in her world of simple black-and-white choices. At the end of her year of trial, she complains, "'There's no more reason now and no less than ever there was . . . why I should say Yes, or why I should say No . . . if I could be *sentenced* to be married, or somebody would up and forbid the banns! *I* don't know what to do about it'" (354–55 [267]).

In the end, Penelope marries Tom because she loves him and he loves her and they want to be married, but she still feels guilty because, Howells has strongly implied, of that fantastic and silly popular ideal. Nor does Howells allow the romantic implication that all will be happy-ever-after romantic bliss following the wedding trip to slip into his love story.

> It would be easy to point out traits in Penelope's character which finally reconciled all her husband's family and endeared her to them. These things continually happen in novels; and the Coreys, as they had always promised themselves to do, made the best, and not the worst of Tom's marriage. . . . But the differences remained uneffaced, if not uneffaceable, between the Coreys and Tom Corey's wife. . . . That was the end of their son and brother for them; they felt that; and they were not mean or unamiable people. (359–61 [272])

Howells' correction of the popular sentimental story paradigm implies a new, "truer" one based on the faithful representation of what he saw in the world rather than on the confirmation of the prevailing popular fantasy. The primary characteristic of this new narrative structure is that its impelling logic, the logic of human behavior, is not simple and one-dimensional, but complex, not ideally heroic but human.

Howells makes a similar correction of the conventional paradigm with the business story-line. Not only is success not what it's cracked up to be in the popular fantasy, as he demonstrates in depicting the Laphams' relations with the Coreys, but business success is neither the assured reward of hard work nor a synonym for virtue. Lapham, of course, loses his wealth and most of his business, partly through human frailty, partly through virtue, and partly through chance. He lends more money than he should to Rogers to ease his conscience about ill-treating him, and he spends more on his house than he should, mostly out of vanity. It is partly greed, partly excitement over an early gain, partly bad judgment that makes for his heavy losses in the stock market, and it is a combination of vanity and Yankee closeness about his affairs that keeps him from seeking expert help when his financial dealings get too complicated for him. It is a combination of chance and his own carelessness that causes the fire which destroys his house, a week after the insurance has expired. Finally, it is his conscience and his wife's that keeps him from taking the business chance that might save him by either deceiving the prospective buyers of his mill properties or helping Rogers to do so.

Again the novel's proairetic logic is no less complex than that which impels the events in life, although Howells isolates one strand of it in the telling. Silas has risen morally at the end of this sequence of events. He had learned from his earlier mistreatment of Rogers that morality does have force in business dealings, and he will have to square his behavior with both his conscience and his wife's. This knowledge leads him to behave morally, even when he is sorely tested, and he comes out of the trial with an easy conscience, though a considerably reduced fortune.

What does Howells' realistic correction of these two popular story paradigms amount to? Essentially, his narrative structure conveys the same message that he transmits in every other way in his fiction—that life is not as simple as sentimental popular fiction would have it; that moral behavior and moral decisions are immensely complicated; that the actions of people are governed neither by nobly heroic virtue nor by simple malevolence, but by a complex congeries of forces, internal and external; that fiction which seeks to represent truth cannot be satisfied with the quick fix of emotional satisfaction provided by the reinforcement of popular fantasies in popular novels; that these popular lies are harmful and need to be corrected. The action of *Silas Lapham*, like the action of Howells' other novels, is primarily a disruption of conventional expectations and assumptions, a statement that the action of life is not so simple as novelists who live off these expectations and assumptions, and readers who escape to them, would like to make it.

* * *

G. THOMAS TANSELLE

From The Architecture of *The Rise of Silas Lapham*†

When the architect Seymour, in Chapter 3 of *The Rise of Silas Lapham*, is discussing with the Laphams their plans for a new house, he suggests a dining room behind the hall because such an arrangement "gets you rid of one of those long, straight, ugly staircases . . .

† From *American Literature* 37.4 (January 1966): 430–36, 442–46. Copyright © 1966, Duke University Press. All rights reserved. Reprinted by permission of the copyright holder, Duke UP.

and gives you an effect of amplitude and space." He also hopes that Silas will not insist on a flamboyant material like black walnut, for which there has recently been "a great craze." After all, as a paint manufacturer ought to know, a more everyday material will be just as effective in the end; indeed, "there is really nothing like white paint" for simple dignity. So Howells knew, and he constructed, on a small foundation and with common materials, scrupulously following his blueprint, a house of "amplitude and space" which contains, not a "long, straight, ugly" staircase, but rather two staircases that intersect in many ingenious ways before they finally come together at the upper level.

It is, in fact, this double "staircase," or plot, that has caused more disagreement than anything else about the relative merits of *Lapham*. Any reader sees immediately that the book is made up of two strands which can be referred to roughly as the "bankruptcy" plot and the "love" plot and that certain characters are involved in both. But the love story is sometimes thought of as not integrally related to the main story of Silas's financial downfall and ethical rise; it has been considered Howells's concession to the public demand for romance. Oscar Firkins once went so far as to say that the two plots "do not concern each other" (though he admitted, "Structurally perhaps [*Lapham*] is the shapeliest of the novels");[1] Howard Mumford Jones has suggested that "possibly [Howells's] two plots interfere with each other";[2] and Harry Hartwick believes that the book "is weakened by Howells's inevitable intrusion of a love affair."[3] The fact that a manuscript summary of the original idea for *Lapham* contains only two sentences referring to the "subplot" has been

1. *William Dean Howells: A Study* (Cambridge, Mass., 1924), pp. 71, 112. In fairness to Firkins, one should also quote his statement that "the story of the business difficulties of the father is united to this love-tale by ties which a logician might blame as inadequate, but which, in an age in which art measures its prosperity by its indifference to logic, criticism must not hasten to condemn" (p. 112).
2. Introduction to the World's Classics edition of *Lapham* (London, 1948), pp. x–xi. Jones explains that "once Howells has got Tom down to Nahant, the conditions of the plot compel him to lose interest in the hero [Tom] as a person; he becomes merely the occasion of tension in the Lapham family and quite fades out at the end. The management of the plot is, I think, the real weakness here." But even as "the occasion of tension" he is serving his function and helping make the two plots work together. A more serious objection to the Corey plot consists of the "good many loose ends" Jones notices in the handling of the Coreys: that Bromfield is too "passive to be effective except as a commentator"; that, although the Corey fortunes shrink, nothing "follows from what would appear to be a plot datum of significance"; and that the two Corey daughters remain shadowy (pp. vii–viii). One may concede, however, that these are undeveloped possibilities for parallelism without detracting from the impressiveness of the plot integration that is actually achieved.
3. *The Foreground of American Fiction* (New York, 1934), pp. 324–325; at the same time, he alludes to Howells's "able construction of plot," which he considers a "delight." That the romantic element is an "intrusion" is also suggested by Marcus Cunliffe, who talks of what led Howells "to contrive a subplot that seems a little implausible" (*The Literature of the United States*, London, 1954, p. 198).

used by both the detractors of the novel and its defenders.[4] The former consider this document proof that the Penelope-Tom plot, as it finally turned out, is an excrescence which Howells allowed to develop during the composition of the novel but which was not in his mind originally as an important part of the book; the latter, on the contrary, assert that the very development of the second plot beyond the proportions suggested by the synopsis reveals how essential and integral it is—Howells saw that he could not get along without it. Whichever way one argues, it is clear that any final evaluation of *Lapham* as a work of art must meet this question of its basic unity and that any meaningful answer must come from an examination of the work itself as we have it.

The presence of the word "rise" in the title naturally draws attention to the rise-and-fall pattern, and critics have most frequently looked at the structure of the novel in these terms—a social and materialistic rise accompanied by a moral descent in the first part of the book, which reverses itself to become a worldly failure and an ethical success in the last part.[5] But this approach is not entirely successful in showing the relevance of the secondary plot: in fact, although most commentators do feel the need to say something about the construction of the book and usually praise it in general terms, one is surprised to observe how rarely they actually analyze the precise degree of integration of the two plots.[6] There should be

4. Clara and Rudolf Kirk were the first to describe and comment on this manuscript synopsis of "The Rise of Silas Needham" in their introduction to the American Writers Series, *Howells: Representative Selections* (New York, 1950), pp. cix–cx. Everett Carter, in the introduction to the Harper's Modern Classics edition (New York, 1958), reprints this synopsis (pp. xiv–xv). Recently Kermit Vanderbilt, in "Howells Among the Brahmins: Why 'The Bottom Dropped Out' During *The Rise of Silas Lapham*," *New England Quarterly*, XXXV, 291–317 (Sept., 1962), has analyzed some of the changes made in the novel from the Needham synopsis to the *Century* serialization to the published book; see especially Part IV (pp. 308–313), where he discusses the enlargement of the "subplot" to such an extent that the book becomes a "general inquiry into the social structure of a new era in America."
5. Besides Howells's famous comment to Francis Parkman (who had misunderstood the title) that he supposed Lapham's rise to be a moral one, see his remark in a letter to Professor William Strunk that Lapham "was finding out, against his selfish ambition and temptations, what a true rise was"—a letter published by Paul Carter in "A Howells Letter," *New England Quarterly*, XXVIII, 93–96 (March, 1955).
6. The major discussions of *Lapham* will be referred to in later parts of this article, but many briefer comments on the book allude to its structure: Carl Van Doren in *Cambridge History of American Literature* (New York, 1917–1921), III, 80; Alexander Harvey, *William Dean Howells* (New York, 1917), pp. 54, 147; D. G. Cooke, *William Dean Howells* (New York, 1922), p. 248; Ludwig Lewisohn, *Expression in America* (New York, 1932), p. 253; Booth Tarkington in the Centenary edition of *Lapham* (Boston, 1937), p. xi; Carl Van Doren, *The American Novel* (rev. ed.; New York, 1940), p. 127; Gordon S. Haight in *Literary History of the United States* (New York, 1948), p. 892; Alexander Cowie, *The Rise of the American Novel* (New York, 1948), p. 670; Van Wyck Brooks, *Howells: His Life and World* (New York, 1959), p. 162; Edwin T. Bowden, *The Dungeon of the Heart* (New York, 1961), pp. 108–109; Rudolf and Clara Kirk in the Collier edition of *Lapham* (New York, 1962), p. 9; and in *William Dean Howells* (New York, 1962), p. 106.

some value, therefore, in examining the structure of *Lapham* in detail, for only then shall we have a factual basis for evaluating the two contradictory traditions: that of commending the book's finely wrought structure and of criticizing its superfluous plot. Only then shall we know whether the edifice can support the burden it has to bear or whether it will collapse as a result of inexpert draftsmanship.

I

We may begin, in order to see each part of the book in its proper perspective, by making a quick survey of the over-all plan of the novel before going in more detail into the various parts. *Lapham* falls, quite naturally, into five large movements. One notices, first of all, that the dinner party comes in Chapter 14 and that, since the book contains twenty-seven chapters, this is the exact center, with thirteen chapters on each side. That everything radiates from this central chapter is not a new idea—almost all commentators have observed it. But there is no general agreement from there on as to how the book is divided. George Arms says that the "second part," Chapters 11 to 19, "consists of one highly concentrated sequence, the dinner party and the events anticipating and following it." But it is not clear why one should consider the discussion about what Penelope is to do (in Chaps. 16–19) or Corey's visit to Lapham's office (Chap. 11) as more closely associated with the dinner party than other events earlier or later. It seems best, therefore, to limit the dinner party sequence to three chapters—Chapter 14, the one preceding it, and the one following. In Chapter 13 the invitations are sent, the Laphams receive them, and they prepare to go; in Chapter 15 Lapham the next day apologizes to Tom for the way he behaved at the party. These three chapters bear a direct relation to the party, then, and together may be taken as the central pivot.

We are now left with twelve chapters before, and twelve after, this central section. Each of these groups of twelve falls symmetrically into two parts, one of four chapters and the other of eight. In the first half, Chapters 1–4 concern the Lapham family and portray Silas's materialistic "rise"—the interview, plans for the house, and a visit to the house. Beginning with Chapter 5, there are eight chapters devoted mainly to the Corey family, introduced by the conversation between Tom and his father about what work Tom is going to do (Chap. 5). The question of Tom's job, in fact, is the unifying force of this section and brings the Coreys into contact with the Laphams, as their relationship is explored in terms of Tom's romantic interest in one of the Lapham daughters. It is worth observing that, up to this halfway point in the book, one has no basis for referring to the love story as the "subplot" since more than half of the chapters, quantitatively, have been given over to it.

The second half of the novel breaks into the same kind of grouping, though with the opposite emphasis—a four-chapter section (Chaps. 16–19) dealing with the love plot and an eight-chapter portion (Chaps. 20–27) dealing with the bankruptcy plot. This half of the book shows, in both plots, an ethical choice being faced and made. In Chapter 16 Tom declares his love, and in the succeeding three chapters Penelope tries to decide what to do. After she refuses Tom in Chapter 19 (in the vein of romantic self-sacrifice discussed at the dinner party), attention turns to the business plot with Silas's revelation of Rogers's treachery (Chap. 20). The Laphams now discuss the Rogers matter, just as they had wrestled with Penelope's choice earlier, until events reach a crisis, and Lapham, deciding to sacrifice personal financial gain, finds himself in bankruptcy (Chap. 27). The visit of the Reverend Mr. Sewell in the last chapter is not only to be contrasted to the Hubbard interview of the first chapter but is also to be compared with the earlier visit in Chapter 18. That Sewell should be consulted in both the Penelope-Tom affair and in the Lapham-Rogers matter is indicative of the parallelism with which the climactic events of each plot are handled.

Such a way of schematizing the novel brings out the care Howells has taken to keep the two plots in balance. Twelve chapters are dominated by each plot, and they are arranged around the dinner-party chapters with regard for both symmetry and emphasis. It does make sense to speak of the romance as a subplot to the extent that it is placed in the middle of the book, leaving the emphatic positions at beginning and end for the other plot. After we witness Silas as a boasting self-made businessman at the opening, we shift our attention to Tom Corey, so that we are fully prepared for the climax of the theme of "social rise" at the dinner party; then we watch Penelope making her decision (and thus get most of the love plot out of the way in the middle of the book) before turning to Silas's parallel problem in the last block of chapters.[7] The two plots support each other, but the decision in the love plot does seem to be serving as a

7. Similarly, Donald Pizer, in "The Ethical Unity of *The Rise of Silas Lapham*," *American Literature*, XXXII, 322–327 (Nov., 1960), says that the love plot contributes to Lapham's education because, "Dominating the center of the novel, it is solved before the full exposition of Lapham's business career" (p. 324). Vanderbilt, too, recognizes that "subplot" is not quite the right term (pp. 310–312).

preparation for Silas's final decision. It may perhaps be convenient to summarize this approach diagrammatically.[8]

Chapters			
I. 1–4	(4) Business	Materialistic rise	Discussions about house
II. 5–12	(8) Love	Social rise	Discussions about marriage
III. 13–15	(3) Dinner	Equilibrium of elements	
IV. 16–19	(4) Love	Social fall	Ethical choice: Penelope
V. 20–27	(8) Business	Materialistic fall	Ethical choice: Silas

The centrality of social relationships and conventions to both plots is evidenced not only by the central position of the dinner party (with its emphasis on etiquette and the relationship between social classes) but also by the general progression of the seasons, against which all the events of the novel are set. As we move into the summer of 1875 in the early part of the book and then through fall into winter and back around to summer at the end, we watch the fashionable classes leaving Boston for their summer homes and gradually returning again. This is the large rhythmic pattern that informs every individual incident and plays a crucial role in determining the date for the dinner party.

The outline of *Lapham* set forth here has the merit of dealing with both plots and of giving each an equal place in the structure: in short, of finding that a symmetrical arrangement of chapters

8. It should be noted that the divisions of the novel for serial publication in the *Century* do not coincide, except in one instance (Chapter 12 is the end of the fifth instalment), with the outline suggested in this paper. Though it seems undeniable that serial publication affects structure (when a work is specifically written with such publication in mind), the serial divisions of *Lapham* do not appear to correspond to plot movement so much as to achieve an apportioning into ten fairly equal segments. The ten monthly instalments (from November, 1884, through August, 1885) divide the chapters in the following manner (with the number of pages covered given in parentheses, those in the *Century* before the oblique line, those in the first edition afterward): (1) Chapters 1–2 (14/52); (2) Chapters 3–5 (13/47); (3) Chapters 6–8 (15/52); (4) Chapters 9–10 (12/41); (5) Chapters 11–12 (14/50); (6) Chapters 13–14 (15/52); (7) Chapters 15–18 (13/47); (8) Chapters 19–21 (15/54); (9) Chapters 22–25 (21/74); (10) Chapters 26–27 (13/46). The only division which is out of proportion is the ninth, but if Chapter 25 had been held over, the tenth instalment would have been equally out of proportion. The slight pattern created by the fact that the first and last instalments, as well as the three middle ones (4, 5, 6), each consist of two chapters, is coincidental and of little significance when one considers some of the breaking points these divisions produce: for example, Penelope's refusal of Tom (Chap. 19), surely a climax to be compared with Silas's later decision, is the *first* chapter of an instalment, followed by two others which shift the subject to Rogers and to Silas's financial problems. The division is more understandable, then, as the strategy of a magazine editor (who not only would hope for equal instalments but would try to end an instalment *before* a climactic incident in order to build up interest in the forthcoming issue) than as a guide to the structure of the novel.

coincides with the pattern of movement between the plots. This is not to deny the value of such a plan as George Arms's three-part division (after Chaps. 10 and 19); what he describes as the "essential movement" of the book—a rising toward material success, followed by two failures, first in "social ambitions" and then in business—is certainly there and is a helpful way of seeing the overall pattern, but it is most applicable to the bankruptcy plot.[9] One must agree with Arms that there is "a sense of form in *The Rise of Silas Lapham* that is notably fine and in last analysis renders the novel a work of art"; but one must realize that any attempt to examine what creates that sense of form has to show, in addition to the movement of the whole, the inextricability and interrelationship of the parts—in this case, the two plots. One can then discern—to use Mark Twain's phrase about Howells's style—the "architectural felicities of construction" in *Lapham*.

* * *

IV

The center of the novel, in every respect, occurs in the three chapters dealing with the dinner, and it is not surprising that the dinner party has been the most frequently discussed scene in the book and the one that remains in the memory as somehow symbolizing the whole work.[1] Chapter 13 begins with a metaphor that expresses the Coreys' feelings about the dinner in business terms: "Not only the principal of their debt of gratitude remained, but the accruing interest" (p. 242). The tying together of elements, suggested by this sort of metaphor, reaches its highest point in these chapters. The first takes up the Coreys' selection of guests and the Laphams' preparations for attending. Chapter 14 is the dinner itself, memorable largely because of Howells's skill in selecting exactly the right

9. Arms, in his introduction to the Rinehart edition (New York, 1951), pp. xiv–xv, defines his division further (p. xv) by saying that the first part contains "four main sequences" (not specified), the second "one highly concentrated sequence" (the dinner), and the third "a series of hopes and disappointments"; the final moral rise he finds occurring in "two steps": resistance to temptations, then the "testing of [Lapham's] sensibility by Sewell." He also talks of the "pleasing symmetry" of the Hubbard interview at the beginning and the Sewell visit at the end, but he believes finally that Howells "does not achieve a richly satisfying relationship between the daughter's conduct in love and the father's in business." John E. Hart, in "The Commonplace as Heroic in *The Rise of Silas Lapham*," *Modern Fiction Studies*, VIII, 375–383 (1962–1963), also points out that an interview opens and closes the book (in addition to commenting on the symbols of houses and paint).
1. [Everett] Carter ([*Howells and the Age of Realism* (Philadelphia, 1954),] pp. 166–67) and [George N.] Bennett ([*William Dean Howells: The Development of a Novelist* (Norman, OK: 1959),] p. 160), for example, point out the centrality of the dinner party; Booth Tarkington, in his introduction to the Centenary edition, comments on the impression which that scene made on him when he first read it (p. xv); and a dinner scene is used as the jacket decoration for the Modern Library edition.

details (Lapham's trouble with his gloves, his leg falling asleep, his cigar ashes on the plate, and the like)—but hardly less so because of Howells's courage in tackling the difficult task of presenting such a climactic scene directly and of giving us the actual conversation. For the structure of the book, this scene is a necessity; Howells's great accomplishment can be measured by the fact that the scene does not strike most readers as a disappointment but rather as an admirable fulfilment of its role as keystone. And Chapter 15 (the shortest and perhaps the most intense in the book), in which Lapham the following day apologizes to Tom for his drunkenness and lack of refinement, does not come as an anticlimax but instead reveals how well the dinner has served as a means of turning the direction of the story.

The dinner is a point of equilibrium with the Coreys and the Laphams meeting ostensibly as equals, and the conversation there draws together all the threads of the book. Since Seymour is present, Silas's new house comes up for discussion (p. 269), and the talk moves on to the Coreys' place, which is in "perfect taste," as the description of its classic simplicity at the beginning of the chapter suggests (pp. 263–264);[2] and from there the conversation takes a natural turn into architecture in general, which leads to matters of taste in the other arts as well. Before the subject of architecture is passed, however, it is skilfully connected with social distinctions based on wealth and on summers in the country: Bromfield suggests, half seriously, that the "deserving poor of neat habits" might be able to make use of "all the beautiful, airy, wholesome

2. The Coreys' house in "Bellingham Place" is based, according to Howells's daughter, on one built by Thomas Buckminster Curtis at 45 Mount Vernon Street, "where my father often dined in his earlier Boston days" (Centenary edition, p. v). In her foreword, Mildred Howells also refers to the autobiographical basis of the novel—extending even to the seasonal pattern. Howells had bought in 1884 "a small house on the water side of Beacon Street"; and, "as there were various alterations to be made in it, he spent most of the summer there overseeing them, while he sent the rest of the family to the country" (p. v). Clara and Rudolf Kirk quote Howells's letter to his father in the summer of 1884 (from *Life in Letters*, Garden City, N. Y., 1928, I, 363–364), commenting on the "miles of empty houses all round me" and on the fact that "nobody else I know sleeps in town"—a letter which the dinner-party conversation in *Lapham* echoes almost verbatim. The Kirks also discuss the connection between Howells's move to Beacon Street from Louisburg Square and Lapham's similar move (*William Dean Howells*, pp. 104–106)—though Lapham's "Nankeen Square" cannot be identified with Louisburg Square, because it is in the South End just off Washington Street (see the opening of Chap. 2). It seems most reasonable to equate "Nankeen Square" with Chester Square, as Clark does in his introduction (p. vii) and James M. Spinning in his notes (p. 518) to the Riverside Literature Series edition (Boston, 1928), or with Canton Square, as Mildred Howells does (p. v). According to Walter Muir Whitehill, in *Boston: A Topographical History* (Cambridge, Mass., 1959), Chester Square was established in 1850 (p. 127), and the wider land in the Neck south of Dover Street rapidly grew in population in the 1850's (p. 122); but by the mid-1860's the flight to the Back Bay was already occurring with such precipitance that people like the Laphams could find many good buys in the area (p. 120). The Laphams bought their Nankeen house in 1863, since, in 1875, they had lived there twelve years (p. 31).

houses that stand empty the whole summer long, while their owners are away in their lowly cots beside the sea" (p. 273), mansions that appear at that season as "long rows of close-shuttered, handsome, brutally insensible houses"—and he can put forward this idea, like Swift's modest proposer, because, as he says, "I spend my summers in town, and I occupy my own house, so that I can speak impartially and intelligently."

The main topic is literature, particularly popular novels like *Tears, Idle Tears,* in which the hero and heroine make "the most wildly satisfactory and unnecessary sacrifices for each other" (p. 277)—"you can't put a more popular thing than self-sacrifice into a novel." It is here that Howells inserts, in the words of the Reverend Mr. Sewell, his first explicit comments on self-sacrifice and on the relation of fiction to life; to Sewell the unrealistic self-sacrifice in sentimental novels is "psychical suicide," and the effect of the novels is "ruinous." After the ladies leave the room, the conversation turns to reminiscences of the Civil War and the subject of heroism—and sacrifice. Sewell again sums up the general feeling when he says that until a new occasion for heroism arises, "we must content ourselves with the everyday generosities and sacrifices" (p. 284). This brings the group back to the lack of realism in literature, and then Silas, who is always a step behind in the conversation, tells of a war experience that illustrates sacrifice. His story about Jim Millon not only furnishes us with the background information for the Zerrilla episode (and we learn at the end of this chapter that Zerrilla is the Miss Dewey of Silas's office) but shows that Silas himself is indebted to someone else for saving his life (just as Mrs. Corey feels an obligation to Mrs. Lapham for saving hers). Silas's drunken rambling also includes references to Rogers, to the Lapham paint, to Mrs. Corey's charity drive, to the library in his new house, and so on—all of which brings to mind important earlier episodes.

The short chapter which follows is a necessary coda to the dinner scene. In it we witness the beginnings of humility and compassion, not merely in Silas, but in Tom as well. Silas's apology, almost groveling, is perhaps rather extreme, but at least no one can fail to see the difference between this Silas and the boastful man of the first half of the book. The earlier Silas had been saying to his family just the opposite of what he now says to Tom: "you're a gentleman, and I'm not, and it ain't right I should be over you" (p. 295). Silas recognizes that money alone does not make him a gentleman, and Tom is struck by "the tragic humility of his appeal" (p. 296). But Tom, too, has some misgivings, and the last part of the chapter focuses on Tom's reactions to Silas's apology, as a preparation for the ensuing group of chapters which deal (even more intensely than the eight preceding the dinner) with Tom's courtship of Penelope.

While Silas is humbling himself, Tom's special interest in the Laphams is revealed by his interruptions ("I have my reasons for refusing to hear you," p. 296) and by his thoughts ("It had become a vital necessity with him to think the best of Lapham," p. 297). He sees Silas as an "offensive boor"; yet he remembers "that which must control him at last," speaking to him "almost with the girl's voice" (p. 298). It is then, in thinking the matter over, that Tom understands how he, too, needs to be humbler, for he had met Lapham's apology "on the gentlemanly ground," selfishly sparing his own feelings, "asserting the superiority of his sort," and "superfinely standing aloof." He also recognizes his family's legitimate concern: "Often he could not make it appear right that he should merely please himself in what chiefly concerned himself" (p. 299); there was even the possibility of an "injury he might be doing to some one besides his family and himself" (p. 300). All these thoughts border on self-sacrifice; certainly Tom is beginning to be more considerate of others. Just as the two plots involve a similar kind of decision about self-sacrifice, so here, in this one chapter, we observe both Tom and Silas going through a similar change of attitude. The chapter ends with Tom, like Silas, "far as might be from vain confidence" (a surprising position for both of them); and Tom decides to go to Silas to offer "reparation" for the "want of sympathy—of humanity—which he had shown" (p. 300). Tom is now ready to apologize, as Silas was at the beginning of the chapter.

To have accomplished so much in three chapters should be regarded as an astonishing technical performance. It would be difficult to find reasons for concurring in O. W. Firkins's complaint about the "leisurely pace" of the book in which "thirty-one pages are allotted to a dinner at which nothing decisive occurs, to say nothing of the assignment of from twenty to twenty-five pages to the elaboration of pre-prandial arrangements" (p. 113). That "nothing decisive occurs" may be partly true in terms of physical actions, but one cannot deny that a great deal happens here in terms of feelings and attitudes. When Tom thinks of the "chaos" of experience, which at times seems "ruin" and at other times appears to be "the materials out of which fine actions and a happy life might be shaped" (p. 299), he is also describing, one may imagine, the process of the novel itself, by which the disorganized impressions and incidents of life are structured. Once the "form" and "content" are seen as inseparable, the indispensability of these chapters is also recognized; and, conversely, the success of these chapters is that they prove the artificiality of any such division as "form" and "content."

It is not surprising, then, that architecture is a prominent subject in the dinner chapter. One would expect matters related to the major symbol to enter the central chapter; but, beyond that, if *Lapham* is a demonstration of the theory of fiction set forth within it (as it manifestly is), the comments on architecture may be applied to the art of fiction as well. In the literary discussion of Chapter 14 the emphasis (as in *Criticism and Fiction*) is on proportion; Howells realizes that even "realistic" art involves selection—arrangement of details so as to suggest "true proportion and relation" and not "monstrous disproportion" (p. 279). Therefore, despite Corey's belief that novelists (who "try to imitate") are very different from architects (who "create form"), the words Howells puts into Seymour's mouth, comparing present architects with those of the past, may be applied to the artistry of *Lapham* itself: "I think we may claim a better feeling for structure. We use better material, and more wisely; and by and by we shall work out something more characteristic and original" (p. 270). The center of the book well illustrates how the "material" of everyday life, arranged in "characteristic" proportion, can be "original" through the illuminating metamorphosis that "structure" and form provide.

* * *

DONALD PIZER

The Ethical Unity of *The Rise of Silas Lapham*†

Critics of Howells's *The Rise of Silas Lapham* have usually examined its subplot as an excrescence arising from a need to satisfy the popular demand for a romantic entanglement, as a digressive attack on the sentimental self-sacrifice of the "Tears, Idle Tears" variety, or as an overexpansion of the comedy of manners strain in the novel. Each of these points of view has a certain validity. But it is also true that the subplot and main plot have fundamentally similar themes, and that an examination of the thematic function of the subplot will elucidate both the ethical core of the novel and the relationship of that core to a prominent theme in Howells's later economic novels.[1]

† From *American Literature* 32.3 (November 1960): 322–27. Copyright © 1960, Duke University Press. All rights reserved. Reprinted by permission of the copyright holder, Duke UP. Page references in brackets refer to this Norton Critical Edition.

1. The most satisfying explications of the novel are by George Arms, *The Rise of Silas Lapham,* Rinehart Editions (New York, 1949), pp. v–xvi; Everett Carter, *Howells and the Age of Realism* (Philadelphia, 1954), pp. 164–169; Edwin H. Cady, *The Road to Realism* (Syracuse, 1956), pp. 230–240; and George N. Bennett, *William Dean Howells: The Development of a Novelist* (Norman, Okla., 1959), pp. 150–161. Cady and Carter have also written excellent introductions to reprints of the novel in the Riverside Editions and Harper's Modern Classics series, respectively. Carter comes closest to discussing the theme of the novel as I do, though he defines it differently and does not analyze the relationship between the main plot and the subplot.

I

The main plot of *The Rise of Silas Lapham* concerns Silas's financial fall and moral rise. It revolves around his business affairs and social aspirations, and it concludes with his decision to sacrifice wealth and position rather than engage in business duplicity. The subplot centers on the triangle of Tom Corey and Irene and Penelope Lapham. Tom is mistakenly believed by all to be in love with Irene. The dilemma caused by his revelation that he loves Penelope is resolved when Irene is informed of the error. Irene then withdraws, leaving Tom and Penelope free to marry.

The dilemma or conflict within the subplot is solved by the use of an "economy of pain" formula.[2] Despite Penelope's willingness to sacrifice herself, Irene must be told of Corey's true sentiments, and Penelope and Corey must be encouraged to fulfil their love. In this way Irene suffers but Penelope and Tom are spared the pain of thwarted love. One rather than three suffers lasting pain. Of the three characters who determine the resolution of the subplot, Lapham realizes instinctively the correct course of action, Mrs. Lapham is helpless and hesitant—this despite her moralizing throughout the novel—and the clergyman Sewell articulates the principle involved and confirms Lapham's choice.

The problem which Silas must solve in the main plot parallels that in the subplot. The three groups who will be affected by his decision are he and his family (Lapham is a participant now as well as an arbiter), Rogers and his family, and the English agents who wish to purchase Lapham's depreciated mill.[3] The crucial point is that the Englishmen are more than mere scoundrels and more than the agents for an "association of rich and charitable people";[4] they also represent society at large. This fact is somewhat obscured in the context of the financial trickery involved in the sale, since the agents are willing to be cheated. But Howells indicated the social implications of the sale when he immediately compared it to the defrauding of municipal governments. In both instances wealth and anonymity encourage dishonesty, and in both instances dishonesty undermines that which is necessary for the maintenance of the common good—effective city governments on the one hand, fair play and honest dealings in business affairs on the other. Lapham's refusal to sell therefore ultimately contributes to the well-being of society as a whole.

2. *The Rise of Silas Lapham* (Boston, 1885), p. 338 [183].
3. Although Howells hints that the agents are counterfeit rather than real Englishmen, I have followed him in designating them as English.
4. *The Rise of Silas Lapham*, p. 458 [245].

The thematic similarity in the two plots is that both involve a principle of morality which requires that the individual determine correct action by reference to the common good rather than to an individual need. Within the subplot this principle requires Lapham to choose on the basis of an "economy of pain" formula in which the fewest suffer. Within the main plot it requires him to weigh his own and Rogers's personal needs against the greater need of all men for decency and honesty. His "rise" is posited exactly in these terms, for at one point in the events leading up to his rejection of the Englishmen's offer he reflects quizzically that "It was certainly ridiculous for a man who had once so selfishly consulted his own interests to be stickling now about the rights of others."[5]

The method used to achieve moral insight is also similar in both plots. What is required is the ability to project oneself out of the immediate problem in which the personal, emotionally compelling need or desire is seen out of proportion to the need of the larger unit. In the subplot Mrs. Lapham finds this difficult, and Sewell asks her, " 'What do you think some one else ought to do in your place?' "[6] In the main plot it is no doubt Silas's realization of the honesty that he would ask of other men in a similar situation which aids him in making the same demand of himself. Lastly, as in the subplot, Silas is capable of moral insight, Mrs. Lapham again falters, and Sewell (at the end of the novel) attempts explanations.

One of the functions of the subplot is therefore to "double" the moral theme of the novel, to intensify and clarify it by introducing it within a narrower, more transparent dilemma. The subplot also plays other important roles. Dominating the center of the novel, it is solved before the full exposition of Lapham's business crisis.[7] It occurs, in other words, between Howells's early remark that Lapham "could not rise"[8] to unselfishness in his dealings with Rogers and Lapham's own words at the close which indicate a concern for the "rights of others." The subplot thus contributes to the "education" of Lapham in the correct solution of moral problems. His moral rise is the product of more than a conscience troubled by his earlier treatment of Rogers. It is also the result of his ready absorption of the "economy of pain" formula as a moral guide in the subplot, a formula which he later translates into its exact corollary, the greatest happiness for the greatest number, when he is faced in the main plot with the more difficult problem of the ethical relationship of the individual to

5. *Ibid.*, p. 466 [250].
6. *Ibid.*, p. 338 [449].
7. By the close of Chapter XIX Irene has been told of Tom's preference, Lapham has given Tom permission to continue courting Penelope, and Penelope has indicated (in the final words of Chapter XIX) that it will only be a matter of time before she will accept Tom. The problem of the depreciated mill is introduced in the next chapter.
8. *The Rise of Silas Lapham*, p. 67 [39].

society. To sum up, the subplot of *The Rise of Silas Lapham* serves the functions of doubling the statement of the novel's theme, of foreshadowing the moral principle governing the main plot, and of introducing Lapham to the correct solution of moral problems.[9]

II

It is possible, at this point, to suggest that the ethical core of the novel can be described as utilitarianism (as interpreted by John Stuart Mill), since both plots dramatize a moral principle in which the correct action is that which results in the greatest happiness for the greatest number. I do not wish to intimate that Howells consciously employed the ethical ideas of Mill. Rather, I believe that the similarity between Mill's utilitarianism and the ethical principles of *The Rise of Silas Lapham* is probably the result of parallel attempts to introduce the ethical teachings of Christ within social contexts and yet avoid supernatural sanctions. Howells's emerging Christian socialism in the late 1880's is well known,[1] and Mill wrote:

> I must again repeat . . . that the happiness which forms the utilitarian standard of what is right in conduct, is not the agent's own happiness, but that of all concerned. . . . In the golden rule of Jesus of Nazareth, we read the complete spirit of the ethics of utility. To do as you would be done by, and to love your neighbour as yourself, constitute the ideal perfection of utilitarian morality.[2]

That Howells was conscious of the applicability of the Golden Rule to the theme of *The Rise of Silas Lapham* is clear, I believe, from his ironic use of it in connection with Rogers. When Rogers senses that Lapham may reject the Englishmen's offer, his appeal to Lapham is based on the premise that

> In our dealings with each other we should be guided by the Golden Rule, as I was saying to Mrs. Lapham before you came in. I told her that if I knew myself, I should in your place consider the circumstances of a man in mine, who had honourably endeavoured to discharge his obligations to me, and had patiently borne my undeserved suspicions. I should consider that man's family, I told Mrs. Lapham.

9. Mrs. Lapham's ethical values are a foil to those which Lapham ultimately practices. Her moral beliefs are strongly held but are fragmented; she is helpless and uncertain when a conflict of interests is present and a universal moral criterion is needed.
1. See particularly Clara and Rudolph Kirk, "Howells and the Church of the Carpenter," *New England Quarterly*, XXXII, 185-206 (June, 1959).
2. *Utilitarianism, Liberty, and Representative Government*, Everyman's Library, p. 16.

But Lapham's answer is the response of a man who is aware of the sophistry of a narrow use of the Golden Rule and who recognizes the necessity for the consideration of a wider range of obligation than individual need. "'Did you tell her,'" he asks Rogers, "'that if I went in with you and those fellows, I should be robbing the people who trusted them?'"[3]

III

There is a twofold advantage in viewing the main and subplots of *The Rise of Silas Lapham* as controlled by a similar conception of moral behavior. First, the novel takes on a thematic unity and structural symmetry. It is within a single moral system, for example, that the apparent conflict between the attack on self-sacrifice in the subplot and Lapham's self-sacrifice in the main plot is reconciled. Penelope's self-sacrifice would diminish the sum total of happiness of those affected by her action, and therefore is wrong; Silas's self-sacrifice increases the happiness of mankind collectively, and therefore is right.[4] Secondly, the theme of the novel anticipates Howells's acceptance of Tolstoy's ethical ideals within the next few years and helps explain his response to those ideals once he encountered them. For in the two plots of *The Rise of Silas Lapham* Howells had already begun working out a belief that man must rise above himself and view life, as, he later explained, Tolstoy had taught him to view life, "not as a chase of a forever impossible personal happiness, but as a field for endeavor toward the happiness of the whole human family."[5] The conviction that man's primary commitment is to mankind was to be one of the themes which Howells emphasized in the series of novels from *Annie Kilburn* (1888) to *A Traveler from Altruria* (1894). In *The Rise of Silas Lapham* that theme appears in a less obvious social context (Howells had to strain for the connection between the English agents and society) and—more importantly—as an obligation which the average individual can grasp and fulfil. His novels during the years following the Haymarket crisis were to examine the theme of man's duty to his fellow men more intensively but less hopefully.

3. *The Rise of Silas Lapham,* p. 462 [247].
4. Cf. Mill, *Utilitarianism,* pp. 15–16: "The utilitarian morality does recognize in human beings the power of sacrificing their greatest good for the good of others. It only refuses to admit that the sacrifice is itself a good. A sacrifice which does not increase, or tend to increase, the sum total of happiness, it considers as wasted. The only self-renunciation which it applauds, is devotion to the happiness, or to some of the means of happiness, of others; either of mankind collectively, or of individuals within the limits imposed by the collective interests of mankind."
5. Howells, *My Literary Passions* (New York, 1895), p. 251.

FRITZ OEHLSCHLAGER

From An Ethic of Responsibility in *The Rise of Silas Lapham*†

At the end of *The Rise of Silas Lapham*, Lapham explains to Mr. Sewell, the minister, why he was unable to sell his depreciated mill property to the English agents whom Rogers had brought to him, and why he informed the New York investor interested in putting needed capital into his paint mine of his business' failing position in the market:

> "All I know is that when it came to the point, although I could see that I'd got to go under unless I did it—that I couldn't sell out to those Englishmen, and I couldn't let that man put his money into my business without I told him just how things stood."[1]

Noteworthy by its absence here is any mention on Lapham's part of a rational calculation of consequences. He does not remember appealing in these ethical dilemmas to the "economy of pain" formula advocated by Sewell as a way to resolve the ethical problem of the novel's love plot, or, indeed, to any utilitarian or consequentialist principle. Rather than suggesting utilitarianism's image of man-the-maker calculating the future balance of good and evil to be achieved by his free acts,[2] the language of Lapham's ethical self-reflection emphasizes constraint: he "couldn't" do certain things. Lapham's sense that he "couldn't" do certain things points to the centrality of conscience in his ethical decision-making. His comment reflects the negative function of conscience illuminated by Hannah Arendt in her summary of the rules of conscience drawn from Socrates: "They do not say what to do; they say what not to do. They do not spell out certain principles for taking action; they lay down boundaries no act should transgress. They say: Don't do wrong, for then you will have to live together with a wrong doer."[3] We should remember that when Lapham is tempted by Rogers, he does nothing definitive to resolve the crisis: he goes to bed and by the next

† From *American Literary Realism* 23.2 (Winter 1991): 20–34. Reprinted by permission of *American Literary Realism*. Page references in brackets refer to this Norton Critical Edition.

1. William Dean Howells, *The Rise of Silas Lapham,* ed. Don L. Cook (New York: Norton, 1982), p. 320 [274–75]. Future citations are to this edition; they are given parenthetically.
2. H. Richard Niebuhr, *The Responsible Self: An Essay in Christian Moral Philosophy* (New York: Harper & Row, 1963), pp. 48–52, especially.
3. Hannah Arendt, *Crises of the Republic* (New York: Harcourt Brace Jovanovich, 1972), p. 63.

morning finds that he can no longer sell the mills anyway. What matters is what he has not done: he has not given in to Rogers' imploring him to sell the property he knows to be worthless.

By refusing to sell the mills, Lapham avoids having to live with a wrongdoer. Implicit in his comments about what he "couldn't" do is the concern for integrity or wholeness of the person who has faced a conflict of conscience. Lapham's comments are a way of saying that he could not live with himself or even be himself if he had deceived either the English or the New York investors. As I hope to demonstrate, he also "couldn't" do certain things because of what had been done to him and for him by others. The past—the specific history within which he has lived—makes claims on Lapham and makes it impossible for him to engage in the deceptions without violating himself. Of great specific importance in Lapham's past are his forcing Rogers out of the paint business and his attempting later to make reparation for that act. Even though his attempt at reparation is a practical failure, it reveals Lapham's capacity for guilt and thus for change. Even more important is Lapham's fidelity to Jim Millon and Millon's family, which he has identified as something he must maintain. What ethicist James F. Childress has said of conscience can be of great value in establishing the connection between Lapham's fidelity to Millon and his refusal to deceive the investors: "The self over time acting in real situations and imagining others comes to associate th[e] admonition about integrity with particular moral requirements that it has identified as matters of conscience."[4] Lapham hears the "admonition about integrity" in the "real situation" of his relationship to the Millons, and he responds with fidelity. Because he does so, he is able to "imagine" other situations, like those in which he confronts the English agents or the New York investor, in such a way that he similarly hears the same admonition. The language of Lapham's ethical self-reflection clearly points to this connection between his fidelity to the Millons and his refusal to deceive the investors. When Persis reproves him for throwing away money on the Millons, he responds in language that expresses the same sense of constraint that we have seen in his final self-explanation to Sewell: "When I think of Jim Millon, I've *got* to; that's all" (299 [257]). In the one case, "all" he knows is that he "couldn't"; in the other, "he's *got* to, that's all."

What I hope to have demonstrated thus far is our need to look beyond utilitarianism as a way to characterize Howells' moral vision in *The Rise of Silas Lapham.* * * *

First, as we have seen, the language of utilitarian decision-making, with its rational calculation of consequences, bears little relation to

4. James F. Childress, "Appeals to Conscience," *Ethics,* 89 (1979), 322.

Silas' ethical reflection, with its emphasis on constraint, integrity, and respect for persons. Second, the way Howells works out the Laphams' reaction to Pen's contemplated self-sacrifice indicates that even Sewell's celebrated "economy of pain" is not a purely utilitarian formula. Moreover, the quandary that Lapham faces when tempted by Rogers cannot really be resolved by appeal to utilitarian principles. Indeed, it reads almost like the kind of example moral philosophers devise when they explore the limits of utilitarianism. Third, the novel seemingly undercuts utilitarianism's assumptions about the predictability of the future. Whereas utilitarianism depends on the assumptions that one can reasonably predict the future consequences of one's actions, *The Rise of Silas Lapham* repeatedly reveals that the consequences of actions are quite different from anything that any of the actors plots. The most obvious example of this lies in the story of Lapham's own salvation through the destruction of his plans and the loss of his fortune. Fourth, and finally, the novel emphasizes the influence of the past on ethical decision-making in a way that utilitarianism does not. * * * In supporting Millon's family, Lapham is acting in a particular way because he has been acted upon. His action is in response to a pattern of action within which he finds himself. Indeed, as I will argue, the ethics that *The Rise of Silas Lapham* adumbrates has much less in common with utilitarianism than it does with an ethics of response and responsibility like that developed by theologian H. Richard Niebuhr.[5]

Since I have already looked at Lapham's ethical self-reflection at some length, I propose here to take up the second of the ways enumerated above in which the novel's ethical vision departs from utilitarianism. This will involve analysis both of the way the "economy of pain" functions in the love plot, and of the problem that Lapham faces when Rogers brings him the English agents who want to buy the depreciated mill property. Two points are especially important about the way the Laphams resolve the dilemma of the love triangle involving Tom Corey, Penelope, and Irene. First, Sewell's "economy of pain" formula is not a purely utilitarian one. He argues that it is "sense" and "justice" that "one suffer instead of three, *if none is to*

5. Niebuhr distinguishes his ethic from teleological and deontological systems by focusing on the central metaphors of each. Teleological ethics depend on the metaphor of the person-as-maker, for whom the moral question is "What is my goal, ideal, or telos?" At the heart of deontological ethics is the metaphor of the person-as-citizen, who asks "What is the law and what is the first law of my life?" Niebuhr finds both of these fundamental conceptions insufficient; he proposes instead the metaphor of "man-the-answerer, man engaged in dialogue, man acting in response to action upon him." For the responsible self, the first question in any situation seeks to understand "What is going on?" See Niebuhr, pp. 56, 60.

blame" (212 [183]). If his were a purely utilitarian scheme, the italicized clause would be irrelevant; the decision would be made purely on the basis of a cost-benefit analysis of present and future good and harm to be produced by the available courses of action. Sewell's comment reveals that even for him the past makes claims on the present; responsibility must be considered a significant factor in ethical decision-making. If responsibility can be put aside in resolving the dilemma of the love plot, it is only because the dilemma has arisen in a purely fortuitous manner: Tom has fallen in love with Penelope rather than Irene.

Second, and more important to the novel's ethical core, is the way Silas and Persis actually determine what to do about the love triangle. They do not make their decision by referring to the "economy of pain" formula as an abstract moral principle separable from time and circumstance and to which all cases are to be referred. Instead, Sewell only uses the "economy of pain" to help them have confidence in the moral judgments that they have already made. In short, Howells is careful to show that both Persis and Silas made the "right" judgments prior to any introduction to Sewell's formula. Moral action and judgment precede reflection and spring from the character of the Laphams and from their whole understanding of the story of their life together. That they go to Sewell for advice and confirmation reflects their loss of confidence in one another, a loss occasioned primarily by Silas' departure from the common purpose of their marriage as he seeks the approval of the Coreys.

When Penelope first hints to her mother that she will give up Tom in an act of self-sacrifice, Persis repudiates the idea, appealing to the wisdom of her husband and expressing a conviction that is very like what Sewell later thematizes as his "economy of pain": "Your father would think you were a fool . . . No! If there's to be any giving up, let it be by the one that sha'n't make anybody but herself suffer. There's trouble and sorrow enough in the world, without *making* it on purpose!" (203 [175]). Similarly, when Lapham first learns of the complications of the love triangle, he rejects the suggestion of the by now confused Persis that Pen should sacrifice herself in order to avoid future remorse: "If he wants her, and she wants him, I don't see what that's got to do with it" (209 [180]). Silas sees the essentials, he sees what ought to be done, and he does so because he reflects on the matter within the purpose of his and Persis' life together: "We don't either of us want anything but the children's good. What's it all of it for, if it ain't for that?" (208 [179]). Persis suspects, however, that part of "what it's all for" to Lapham is obtaining Tom Corey as a son-in-law, and thus she cannot see the rightness of Lapham's judgment. When they meet Sewell, he merely leads them back to the original moral insight that both had expressed. After mentioning the "economy of pain," he asks each of them successively:

> "Tell me, Mrs. Lapham, didn't this come into your mind when you first learned how matters stood?"
>
> "Why, yes, it flashed across me. But I didn't think it could be right."
>
> "And how was it with you, Mr. Lapham?"
>
> "Why, that's what I thought, of course. But I didn't see my way—" (212–13 [183]).

This is a crucial passage for understanding the ethical reality of *The Rise of Silas Lapham*, for it suggests the moral resources available to the Laphams on the level of habit, character, and virtue. Its language is that of moral insight and vision rather than the rational calculus of utilitarianism. Sewell closes this discussion by imploring the Laphams to believe their "common sense." What he gives the Laphams, in short, is not a new moral formula capable of resolving all dilemmas but a renewed confidence in the wisdom of the story that has formed their lives.

Howells further explores the limitations of the "economy of pain" in the quandary Lapham faces over selling the depreciated mills. This quandary cannot be resolved by reference to a principle like Mill's "greatest happiness for the greatest number." If Lapham sells the mills, he will greatly benefit his own and Rogers' family while harming a larger group, an "association of rich and charitable people" who "are able to bear it" (285–86 [245]). Lapham, can, in short, produce a great amount of good for a limited number of people while inflicting only minimal harm on a larger group. * * *

If we feel, as we surely do, that Silas ought not to sell the mills no matter how much good he would do for his and Rogers' families, it is because we are moved by a principle of justice that is quite independent of utilitarian calculation. The point here can be clarified by a hypothetical example from W. K. Frankena's widely influential *Ethics*. In assessing rule-utilitarianism, Frankena posits a situation much like that which Howells creates for Lapham. Frankena supposes two rules, R1 and R2, both of which create the same balance of good over evil in the universe. R1, like Silas' selling the mills to benefit his and Rogers' families, "may give all of the good to a relatively small group of people without any merit on their part." Acting on R2 would, on the other hand, "spread the good more equally over a large part of the population," as Silas does by refusing to sell the mills, thereby benefiting the English investors, at least to the extent of not doing them harm, and the wider society by contributing to the climate of trust needed for all contractual relationships.

Frankena argues that we "must and would say that R1 is an unjust rule and that R2 is morally preferable." The conclusion that he draws is "that the operation of a rule may be beneficent, that is, it may maximize the sum of good in the world, and yet be unjust in the way it distributes this sum, so that a less beneficent rule which is more just may be preferable." Frankena's conclusion parallels and illumines our intuitive reaction to Silas' quandary. Even if his selling the mills were to "maximize the sum of good in the world," we would prefer that he not do so, that he take the less beneficent course because it is more just. In drawing this conclusion, we go beyond utilitarianism, for, as Frankena says, we appeal to a principle of justice that is "independent of the principle of utility."[6]

An even more important distinction needs to be made at this point, however, for to some extent our weighing of the relative beneficence of Silas' options obscures morally relevant features of his dilemma. By selling the mills, Silas would benefit his and Rogers' families, but only by intentionally doing positive harm to innocent people. Howells has placed Lapham, in short, in a position where one course of action involves active maleficence. * * * That this is Howells' real moral emphasis is suggested by the way he arranges the next crisis Lapham faces. When the New York investor expresses an interest in putting money into Lapham's mine, the Colonel again confronts the possibility of inflicting harm on the innocent. He cannot do this, and the course he chooses is to remove the man's vulnerability by informing him of his financial difficulties. In doing so he appeals to no utilitarian calculus but acts instead from something much more like a Kantian respect for persons: "But I had to tell him how I stood. I had to tell him all about it, and what I wanted to do" (307 [264]). To do less would have been to treat the man as less than an equal, or in Kant's language, as a means rather than an end in himself.

To some deontologists, utilitarianism seems to make a "fundamental mistake" in the way it conceives the moral life as a matter of means and ends. Utilitarianism seems to them "to presuppose a greater capacity to predict and control than we actually have."[7] Such criticisms point further to the inadequacy of utilitarianism as a description of the ethics of *The Rise of Silas Lapham*, for the novel insists repeatedly on its characters' inability to control the future. Indeed, what Silas must learn as much as anything else is to relinquish his attempt to control the future. The Laphams project and plan a romance between Irene and Tom Corey; Tom falls in love instead with Penelope. The Laphams look on Irene's failure to win

6. William K. Frankena, *Ethics* (Englewood Cliffs, NJ: Prentice-Hall, 1963), p. 33.
7. Tom L. Beauchamp and James F. Childress, *Principles of Biomedical Ethics* (New York: Oxford Univ. Press, 1983), p. 39.

Tom as the shattering of her world, and Penelope nearly sacrifices herself in a misguided attempt to save her sister. Instead, the pain she suffers creates a strength and independence in Irene that she would never have achieved if she had been simply passed from the protection of the Laphams to the protection of Tom Corey. Lapham plans to build the house on Back Bay and to realize a social triumph; he is thwarted by the completely fortuitous discovery of gas near the paint mine of the West Virginians. Lapham's rise in the first half of the novel, when he enjoys his greatest control of events, is really a moral fall; his fall in the latter half, as he increasingly loses control of events, is really a moral rise. These reversals in the novel are simply inconsistent with a conception of the moral life as primarily a matter of means and ends. The pattern of his characters' lives suggest that Howells simply does not share the utilitarian faith in the human ability to predict and control the future.

If utilitarianism overestimates the agent's control of the future, it also seriously underestimates the claim of the past on moral behavior. In the past lie the real sources of Lapham's integrity, though what the novel dramatizes is Silas' nearly destructive attempt to escape that past. * * *

Lapham has, of course, been the beneficiary of a gift in the paint itself, "found" by his father "in a hole made by a tree blowing down" (8 [6]). Yet despite this revealed quality of the paint's origin, Lapham comes to think of the paint as exclusively his own. When Persis challenges the rightness of his forcing Rogers out of the business just as a market rise promises to bring him a huge advantage, Lapham responds, "I had a right to it. I made the success" (42 [38]). Lapham has "made" the success only if one forgets the tree's blowing down, his father's discovery of and faith in the paint, and the contribution of Rogers' capital, itself representing the accumulated energy, labor, and blood of others. Lapham's insistence on his own making of the success springs from that part of him which would deny the past as a source either of gift or claim. Persis says of him, with theological precision, that he has made his paint his "god," and cannot "bear to let anybody else share in its blessings" (42 [37]). Interestingly, Lapham justifies his squeezing Rogers out as an entirely legal and standard business practice, precisely the kind of justification he refuses to hide behind when he is later approached by Rogers about selling the depreciated mills. Moreover, what Lapham does in forcing Rogers out is what he declines to do when approached by the investor from New York: he takes advantage of another man's vulnerability. This pair of antitheses between the first half of the novel and the second help to define Silas' moral rise. By the time of his later decisions, Lapham has moved toward a morality that is beyond self-justification and has arrived at a perception of the vulnerability of all, in part through his remembering Jim Millon and in part through the destruction of his own plans.

It is entirely appropriate that Rogers reenter the life of the Laphams at the new house on Back Bay, for that house represents the culmination of Lapham's drive to break with the past. Building the house is to confirm Lapham's success, to signal his eligibility for admission to the highest reaches of Boston society, and to give his daughters a base from which to work in their pursuit of husbands. In an extremely suggestive image, Howells describes Lapham's joy at watching the pilings being driven for the new house. That house is to be on "New Land," land created out of what was originally salt marsh, rather than on the kind of solid foundation on which Lapham's ancestors had built. The driving of piles in the salt marsh stands in direct opposition to the image of the earth's opening to reveal the paint mine. Lapham's fortune was founded on the earth's own gracious opening, but the confirmation of his success is his own self-founded project, the Back Bay house. Lapham is seeking to found a house, too, in the lineal sense, as is suggested by his not very subtle pursuit of a son in the figure of Tom Corey.

When Lapham's fortunes begin to fail, the house becomes the focus of his attempts to control his destiny. Its place in his life project is never clearer than on the night in which he burns it down. By this point in the novel, Lapham has become increasingly entangled in a pattern of events which are in large measure beyond his control. But being in the house leads to a new surge of confidence; he reflects that he can yet "buy out those West Virginia fellows" and "have the whole game in his own hand" (274 [235]). He has not yet learned what his decline eventually forces him to recognize: that moral action consists of action in response to actions upon one rather than in efforts to control the whole game. Indeed, utlimately he will decide to put himself in the "hands" of his creditors (307 [263]) rather than seek to have others in his hands. What destroys the house specifically is a "whim" that seizes Lapham, leading him "to test the chimney in the music–room" (274 [235]). * * * Lapham glories in a proud moment of self-possession, but it is precisely his whim that leads to the burning of the house, the destruction symbolically of his attempt to live free of time and a narrative identity.

But while Silas is impelled on one level to live free of time, death, and a story-formed identity, there is also in him the strong countermotive of fidelity: to the parents he describes at the novel's outset, to Persis and his children, to his friend Jim Millon. Emerson may declare, again in "Self-Reliance," that he "keeps no covenants but proximities,"[8] but Lapham is one who enters into covenants and knows himself ultimately through his fidelity to them. Such covenant fidelity and the closely related idea of responsibility account for Lapham's ethical strength in the latter half of the novel. Lapham resists deceiving the investors because to do so would be to violate the self he has acquired through living a particular history in faithful response to others. The moral value of Lapham's loan to Rogers, pragmatically an utter failure, derives from the fidelity the act evinces. In making the loan, Lapham asserts the continuity of his life's narrative at the very time at which that continuity is being disrupted by his social pretensions and his building the Back Bay house (where, as we remember, Rogers reappears). Lapham's act binds time. Though he continues to maintain his innocence of wrongdoing toward Rogers, his act acknowledges that what he is in the present is related to what he has been in the past, that the way he acts now is related to how he acted then. The importance of the act to Lapham's temporal continuity is set off by Persis' naive failure to understand it. After congratulating him for taking the "one *speck*" off his soul, she reassures him that "it's all past and gone now, anyway; and I don't want you should think anything more about it" (116 [101]). It is not all "past and gone," for Silas has reaffirmed the place of his actions toward Rogers in his personal history. Through his doing so that history becomes a moral resource, a source of the ability to later imagine concrete situations in such a way that he hears in them what Childress calls the "admonition about integrity." In his final summary comments, Sewell points toward such a reading of the relation between Lapham's wronging Rogers and his later refusal to wrong others: "'I should be inclined to think—nothing can be thrown quite away; and it can't be that our sins only weaken us—that your fear of having possibly behaved selfishly toward this man kept you on your guard, and strengthened you when you were brought face to face with a greater'—he was going to say temptation, but he saved Lapham's pride, and said—'emergency'" (320 [274]).

What also strengthens Silas in his "emergency" is his fidelity to Jim Millon. Silas tells the story of Millon's death after dinner and just before the disaster at the Coreys'. The scene perhaps suggests Howells' own effort to find a narrative that could serve to unify a society obviously in process of polarization. Through the men's sharing of the story of the Civil War and of the "commonplace" heroism of the ordinary soldier, Howells suggests a shared ground of allegiance and value for a democratic society. War, as it has so often,

8. "Self-Reliance," in *The Selected Writings of Ralph Waldo Emerson,* ed. Brooks Atkinson (New York: The Modern Library, 1940), p. 160.

provides a sacred story binding the present to the past. Lapham's telling of Millon's story points toward his own deepest allegiance, revealed in the second half of the novel through his efforts to help Zerrilla and her mother. * * * [W]hat seems incontestable to me is that Lapham identifies his integrity with Jim Millon and faithfulness to Millon's family, that when he stands before Rogers during the temptation or before the New York investor, he stands also in relation to, perhaps even in the presence of, Jim Millon. To deceive the investors would be to violate the self he has become by acting faithfully in response to Millon. Fidelity to Millon helps him to imagine what faithfulness to other human beings means. His glimpse of Millon's death has given him an insight into human vulnerability, and it is precisely the vulnerability of others that he refuses to exploit in the latter half of the novel. It should be noted that Silas' assistance of Zerrilla and her mother, like his loaning money to Rogers, is pragmatically less than successful. What this suggests again is that Howells is pressing toward a vision of the moral life as more than a matter of means and ends.

The end of the novel places Silas within the story of his family again. He returns to Vermont, to the place he had originally "hung on to . . . not because the paint-mine was on it, but because the old house was—and the graves" (7 [6]). He has returned to living in temporality directed toward death (though not as an absolute horizon), as is suggested too by the fact that the Persis brand of paint is the one thing he retains from his once thriving enterprise. What endures derives from his marriage, with all that it implies about temporality, about the complex rhythm of change and fidelity of two people in response to one another. To be married is to move through time; perhaps it is to consent to move through time. When Lapham is asked whether he has any regrets about what he has done, he says only that "it don't always seem as if I done it" (321 [275]). While Howells does not, of course, specifically thematize Christ's role in mediating the work of grace, Lapham's remark nevertheless sounds like nothing quite so much as Paul's reflections on the alien righteousness of the justified sinner.[9] In one sense, Lapham does not "do it"; instead he opens himself in trust to the working of power that he has come to regard as gracious. He will put himself in the

9. Cf. especially *Galatians* 2: 18–20, but much of both *Romans* and *Galatians* is, of course, relevant. See too Howells' comment in the manuscript synopsis for the novel, which at the time he planned to call *The Rise of Silas Needham:* "At last, almost by force of 'that, not ourselves, which works for righteousness' he resists the temptation and suffers ruin." Don L. Cook notes that Howells seems to be "quoting loosely" from Matthew Arnold's *Literature and Dogma,* but clearly both Arnold and Howells are quoting loosely from Paul. The synopsis, which predates Howells' beginning to work on the novel, appears in *The Rise of Silas Lapham,* ed. Don L. Cook (New York: Norton, 1982), p. 328.

hands of his creditors rather than violate himself or victimize others. The language Lapham uses to describe his coming through his crisis is very explicitly religious: "Seems sometimes as if it was a hole opened for me, and I crept out of it" (321 [275]). The image is of resurrection, the passing from death to life.

Such language may very well reflect Howells' own experience during the writing of *Silas Lapham*. We know he began the book with characteristically great energy, but then, to use his phrase, "the bottom dropped out."[1] Later he told Owen Wister about a "sort of religious experience" he had during this period at his own grand new Beacon Street house. One day people from the alley kept climbing on his fence to see the rowing on the river. A "policeman was busy making them get off" until Howells "sent for him, and thanked him." After the policeman left, "it came over me," Howells recalled, "what better right had I than they to sit comfortably in this room when they were out on the fence?"[2] The logic of Howells' "religious experience" destroys Lapham's own house—his "whim" perhaps even representing a subconscious wish for such destruction—for that house is built on the assumption that the rich man has the right to his success, that the earth belongs to the one who is strong enough and cunning enough to exploit it. But the language of Howells' experience may also suggest the ground of his recovery from his psychic depression. In its acknowledgment of others' claims and denial of exclusive property rights, the experience implies a deep recognition of ultimate dependence, and with it, the need to abandon the driven *causa sui* project (represented in the novel by the building of the house) for a life lived with others in mutual dependence and basic trust.

* * *

PATRICK DOOLEY

From Nineteenth Century Business Ethics and *The Rise of Silas Lapham*[†]

It is most obvious to twentieth-century readers of *The Rise of Silas Lapham* that William Dean Howells intends to provide moral education. To this end, he utilizes two plots: a love story and a

1. Marrion Wilcox, "Works of William Dean Howells," *Harper's Weekly,* 40 (July 4, 1896), 656.
2. Edwin H. Cady, *The Road to Realism: The Early Years of William Dean Howells* (Syracuse: Syracuse Univ. Press, 1956), p. 245.

† From *American Studies* 21.2 (Fall 1980): 79, 85–93. Reprinted by permission of *American Studies*. Page references in brackets refer to this Norton Critical Edition.

bankruptcy to explore the tensions involved in both a private and a social moral dilemma. What is surprising is that Howells' point was frequently missed by the first readers of this novel. They focused on the love plot, all but ignored the bankruptcy plot, and had difficulty discerning any moral lesson in the novel.[1]

* * *

* * * Why did earlier reviewers, Howells' Bostonian friends like Parkman and critics like Harvey and Firkins, misperceive the novel?

I am sure several accounts are possible. For example, one might explain that Howells was attempting to recast the very nature and purpose of novels. His contemporaries did not recognize, let alone appreciate, the sort of innovation Howells contemplated. Certainly many of the reviewers cited above seem to fit this explanation. I do not wish to dispute such accounts. I will, however, advance a non-literary, complementary explanation: *Silas Lapham* was misread for although Howells saw business and ethics as connected, very many of his contemporaries did not. An analysis of moral philosophy texts from 1835–1895 reveals the very slow emergence and eventual acceptance of business ethics. At first, no special ethical demands were associated with business; next, a confused mixture of legal principles and accepted practices were applied to moral conflicts in business; and finally, a genuine business ethic was worked out. Early readers of *Silas Lapham* had not yet caught up to this third stage so they misread the book; later readers were accustomed to the concept of business ethics so they found Howells' moral point obvious.

In the six decades from 1835 to 1895 American moral philosophy was dominated by three college president-moral philosophers: Francis Wayland of Brown University and Asa Mahan and James H. Fairchild of Oberlin College. All three men wrote popular and well-regarded textbooks. The most popular of all was Wayland's *The Elements of Moral Science*.[2] It went through four editions in its first two years and sold 200,000 in the sixty years mentioned above. All three men used their college presidencies to exert influence on the ethical questions of the day. All were highly visible, all were anti-slavery and Mahan and Fairchild were active abolitionists.

There were, however, important differences in the moral positions advanced by these ethicists. In regard to business ethics, Mahan's

1. The following section of Dooley's essay analyzes contemporary reviews of the novel, many of which are included elsewhere in this volume. Treating them in order from "most superficial" to "most perceptive," Dooley concludes that "only two of Howells's initial three dozen reviewers understood his moral point" [*editor's note*].
2. Francis Wayland, *The Elements of Moral Science*, edited by Joseph Blau (Cambridge Mass., 1963). Although originally published in 1835, Blau here reprints Wayland's 1847 fourth and standard edition.

A Science of Moral Philosophy all but ignored the topic,[3] Wayland's *The Elements of Moral Science* presented a simplistic and confused position and Fairchild's *Moral Philosophy: The Science of Obligation* laid out a clear, sophisticated and practical set of moral principles as they apply to business.[4]

a) General moral obligations. Before we look at business ethics, a brief comment on nineteenth-century moral philosophy is in order. A typical moral philosophy of this period would devote most of its attention to personal and interpersonal ethical obligations but practically none to civil and social duties. The divorce of the private from the public and the separation of personal from social duties was not accidental or unconscious. Especially in view of the slavery issue, nineteenth-century moral philosophers worried a great deal about the ethical obligations of individual citizens. What should a moral man do in the concrete?

The most influential of these three moral philosophers, Wayland, advanced the standard, conservative position in his *The Limitations of Human Responsibility* in 1838.[5] After a lengthy caution about the dangers of moral fanaticism and excessive zeal (he cites temperance societies), Wayland states his central principle: "our responsibility for the *temper of mind* is *unlimited* and *universal,* our responsibility for the *outward act* is *limited* and *special*" (19). That is, we are responsible for intentions (motives), not consequences (results). Therefore, we are obliged to preach the gospel; we are not obligated to convert our fellow men. As to slavery, it is clearly evil. However the issue is what mean should be used: "what *manner* it be proper [to use] to remove or to arrest the evil . . ." (162). Wayland offers the advice to preach the immorality to the slave holder and leave the rest to God:

> They (the slave holders) have as good a right to their ears, as we have to our tongues. Hence, if they will not hear us, our responsibility is at an end. We have no right to force our instructions upon them, either by conversation, or by lectures, or by the mail. If they still determine to go on, in what we believe to be wrong, we must leave them to God, who is perfectly capable of vindicating his own laws, and executing justice among the children of men. If they will not hear us, the indication is plain, that God does not mean to use *our* instrumentality in this affair. We must retire and leave the case in his hands, and turn our attention to the doing of good, in some other way (185).

3. Asa Mahan, *A Science of Moral Philosophy* (Oberlin, Ohio, 1848).
4. James H. Fairchild, *Moral Philosophy: The Science of Obligation* (New York, 1869).
5. Francis Wayland, *The Limitations of Human Responsibility* (Boston, 1838). Subsequent references cited parenthetically in the text.

Wayland then opts for a narrow and limited zone of personal responsibility.[6] Just how limited this responsibility is can be seen in another concrete moral assessment he makes.

Exactly what is involved in our duty to tell the truth? Wayland gives an interesting answer. Not only is this answer repeated in his ethical textbook, *The Elements of Moral Science,* it is exactly the same *moral* advice that Rogers will give to Silas regarding the mills and the English buyers. Wayland's advice, "the moral precept respecting veracity, is not a positive but merely a negative precept. It does not command us *to bear witness,* it merely forbids us to bear *false witness.*"[7] More of this and its application to *Silas Lapham* below.

Two aspects of an individual's moral obligations need to be stressed. First, according to Wayland those obligations are very limited. Second, and more important, the demeanor of the moral agent is passive and not active, "Don't be immoral but then again don't crusade!"

If the nineteenth-century reader was accustomed to thinking of morality as limited to personal, even private, matters, does it not seem natural for that reader to focus on the love story and the ethical questions involved in the Tom-Irene-Penelope triangle? Would not that reader, like the reviewers cited above, either see Lapham's bankruptcy as a superfluous plot or fail to perceive the ethical dilemmas which confront Lapham in his business dealing with Rogers? Let us now turn to the matter of business ethics. I will confine my treatment to Wayland and Fairchild since Mahan did not develop a formal position on these matters.[8]

b) Business ethics. Francis Wayland's treatment of business ethics occurs in the section of *The Elements of Moral Science* entitled, "Justice in Respect to Property,"[9] especially in a subsection called, "modes in which the right of property may be violated by the individual" (216). Although this subsection is detailed and gives a wide assortment of concrete examples, the principles espoused by Wayland are shifting and vague. In the last analysis, it is clear that the principles of Wayland's business ethics are *non*-moral. Wayland is

6. For a more detailed analysis of this work by Wayland see: Edward H. Madden, "Francis Wayland and the Limits of Moral Responsibility," *Proceedings of the American Philosophical Society,* 106 (1962), pp. 348–359. For more on the issue of slavery and northern moral philosophers (some 48 are treated) see: Wilson Smith, *Professors and Public Ethics: Studies of Northern Moral Philosophers before the Civil War* (Ithaca, New York, 1956). Smith observes, citing H. R. Niebuhr, "Protestant churches and churchmen in America have been concerned primarily with the problems of the individual in society rather than with the problems of society as a whole" (197).
7. Wayland, *The Limitations of Human Responsibility, op. cit.,* 68.
8. Mahan does make scattered observations on ethics and business, but his comments are unsystematic and usually amount to disclaimers. For instance, he explains that a contract, business or otherwise, is only a mutual promise and hence needs no special treatment beyond what he has already given concerning promises, see: Mahan, *op. cit.,* 367–369.
9. Wayland, *The Elements of Moral Science, op. cit.,* 210, subsequent references cited parenthetically in the text.

candid: both the buyer and the seller know the business of business and each knows he must look after his own interest, "hence . . . a seller . . . is under no obligation to assist the judgement of the buyer *unless* the article for sale is defective, and then he is under obligation to reveal it" (219, emphasis added). But even this proviso about declaring defects is suspended in cases where known risk is involved, say, at an auction or in a speculative enterprise. Apparently buying mills in a foreign country would be just such a speculative enterprise. Later Wayland asserts: "while the seller is under no obligation to set forth the quality of his merchandise, yet he is at liberty to do so, confining himself to the truth" (220). However, in the examples which Wayland analyzes to illustrate his truth-in-merchandising principle, his advice is quite simple: one must not lie but one need not volunteer information. As above, no need to bear witness!

The tenor of Wayland's business ethics is most clear in his position on three issues: liability for the delivery of defective goods, exorbitant interest rates and bankruptcy. In the case of the delivery of defective goods he concludes, "[liability] must be settled by precedent; and can rarely be known in any country until a decision is had in the courts of law" (223). As for exorbitant interest rates:

> If it be said, men may charge exorbitant interest, I reply, so they may charge exorbitant rent for houses and exorbitant hire for horses. And, I ask, how is the evil or exorbitant charges . . . [to be] remedied? The answer is plain. We allow a perfectly free competition. . . . (224).

Finally as to bankruptcy, "the question is often asked whether a debtor is *morally* liberated by an act of insolvency" (226, emphasis added). Wayland's reply is tentative and qualified, "I *think* not, if he ever afterward have the means of repayment" (226, emphasis added). Notice that in all three of these issues it is not a moral principle but either a practical consideration or a legal precedent which furnished the "moral" solution. What is even more surprising is that Wayland himself seems not to have noticed his slippage from morality to legality or practicality; he does not even notice that he is no longer functioning as a moral philosopher. He is codifying existing business practice, not furnishing a business ethic.

Wayland pawns off another descriptive and legal treatment of business as a normative and ethical treatment in a second, well-known textbook, *The Elements of Political Economy.* This book was first published in 1837 and by 1860 it had sold 30,000 copies. Here again Wayland convolutes values and facts:

> The principles of Political Economy are so closely analogous to those of Moral Philosophy, that almost every question in one, may be argued on ground belonging to the other.

However, business practices not moral principles are primary. On the question of whether contracts are binding he explains, "with this question, Political Economy has nothing to do. Its only business is, to decide whether a given contract were or were not *wise*."[1] In other words, in business the prudential is the moral. Further, the prudential is what is customarily allowed and legally permitted. For Wayland, then, writing a business ethics is not a normative project; it is a descriptive one.

James H. Fairchild's *Moral Philosophy: The Science of Obligation* is very different in tone and result. He is very precise in his separation of the realms of morality and legality. He carefully and consistently maintains that, in business, what is legal may have little or nothing to do with what is ethical. His premise is the opposite of Wayland's: "The ordinary business maxim, to assume that every man in trade will attend to his own interests, is, by no means, a safe [that is, an acceptable ethical] principle of conduct."[2] When Fairchild treats the duties of sellers, he does not waver; he speaks of "commercial honesty," "an honest bargain" and "true commercial integrity" (247–248). He judges monopolies, artificial shortages and market glutting as "utterly unjustifiable" (249). Whereas Wayland only tentatively and reluctantly linked morality and bankruptcy, Fairchild does so without doubts or reservations:

> Morally, debts are never outlawed . . . There is, doubtless, propriety in the law which set a limit to the collectability of a debt, but such a law cannot discharge the moral obligation. The proper force of bankrupt laws, is not in any power to release the debtor from his moral obligation. They have no such power; but it is in the protection they afford to the debtor, in his effort to recover himself, and acquire the ability to meet his obligations. The release from indebtedness is technical and legal, not real (253).

Thus with regard to bankruptcy, conduct morally permissible to Wayland would be immoral for Fairchild. The difference between Wayland and Fairchild is vast. In the end it comes to this: Wayland sees business in legal not moral terms, while Fairchild holds that there are moral obligations in business which are more extensive and much more binding than *merely* legal obligations. In a work, Wayland is concerned with avoiding fraud; Fairchild seeks to promote honor and honesty.

In any number of situations wherein Fairchild would see a moral duty, Wayland would judge the situation in practical and legal, that

1. Francis Wayland, *The Elements of Political Economy* (New York, 1837), vi.
2. James H. Fairchild, *op. cit.* 248. Subsequent page references are cited parenthetically in the text.

is, in *amoral* terms. Chapter XXI of *Silas Lapham* describes such a situation. Rogers announces to Lapham that he has found some English parties interested in buying the mills. Lapham explodes: why had Rogers not told him that the railroad intended to buy the mills? "You lie . . . you're a thief . . . you stole."[3] Through all of this Rogers maintains "self-possession" (385 [207]). After he is called a liar, Rogers calmly sits:

> . . . listening, as if respectfully considering the statements . . . [He] sat wholly unmoved . . . with dry tranquility ignoring Lapham's words, as if they had been an outburst against some third person, who probably merited them, but in whom he was so little interested that he had been obliged to use patience in listening to his condemnation. . . . (385–86 [208]).

The fact that those details about the railroads had not been volunteered is, for Rogers (as for Wayland), a practical matter, a matter of business acumen and shrewdness. If Lapham had only bothered to ask, Rogers might have complied; but as it stood it was Lapham's, not Rogers', responsibility. However, for Lapham (and for Fairchild), Rogers' craftiness is immoral and despicable. Thus the same action, viewed by two different persons from the perspective of two different ethical systems, is either highly unethical or blandly amoral. Perhaps Rogers is not putting up a front at all; perhaps he is not morally callous. He can confront Lapham with "dry tranquility" for although Lapham finds Rogers' conduct morally outrageous, Rogers himself sees it as standard business practice.

Lapham himself had advanced an identical argument earlier. In Chapter III, Persis attempts to prick Silas' conscience on the matter of his buying out Rogers. Silas claims that his conscience is clear: "It was a business chance . . . it's a thing that's done every day" (63–64 [38]). Lapham fails to see the obvious parallel: Rogers had turned over the mills to Lapham just before they became practically worthless; earlier, Lapham had forced Rogers out just before the paint business became highly profitable. Persis observes, "you unloaded [your partner, Rogers] just at the time when *you knew* that your paint was going to be worth about twice what it ever had been" (64 [38], emphasis added). Howells' tit-for-tat is very neat: Silas had not alerted Rogers to his paint's imminent boom; Rogers had not warned Silas of his mills' impending bust!

Finally, witness Rogers' notion of the limits of personal responsibility. In Chapter XXV Lapham will not sell the mills. Rogers offers a way out: "then why don't you sell to me? Can't you see that you will not be responsible for what happens after you have sold?" (466

3. William Dean Howells, *The Rise of Silas Lapham* (Boston, 1885), 385 [207]. Subsequent page references are cited parenthetically in the text.

[249]). Clearly, Rogers is appealing to Wayland's concept of limited personal responsibility.

If Rogers dramatizes the ethical stance of Wayland, then Lapham amounts to a moral exemplar for Fairchild. Lapham is clear about legal and about moral responsibilities and because he responds to the latter not the former he loses his fortune. Much has been written about the moral quandries and ethical calculations of Lapham. My point is more basic. Lapham's ethical intuitions are sometimes clear and decisive, at other times clouded and halting. But his eventual actions are clearly ethical as opposed to prudential or legal; Lapham responds to *a business ethic*.

I will cite only three examples. First, although Lapham claims that his "conscience is easy" (63 [37]) about buying Rogers out of the business, his conscience was not clear. Listening to it and to his wife lead him to loan Rogers the money which initiated Lapham's financial plunge. Although it took him a while to see it, he did do his moral duty. Afterwards (Chapter X) he and his wife, "did not celebrate his reconciliation with his old enemy . . . by any show of joy or affection. . . . She was content to have told him that he had done his duty, and he was content with her saying that" (186 [101]).

Again, in the climactic Chapter XXV, after the meeting with the English parties, Rogers comes to the Lapham home with a final offer. If Lapham would sell the mills to Rogers the matter (and the responsibility) would be out of Lapham's hands:

> It was perfectly true. Any lawyer would have told him the same. He could not help admiring Rogers for his ingenuity, and every selfish interest of his nature joined with many obvious duties to urge him to consent. He did not see why he should refuse. There was no longer a reason. He was standing alone for nothing . . . (466 [249]).

But after wrestling through the night, Lapham ended by "standing firm for right and justice [even] to his own destruction" (468 [251]).

Third, in the concluding Chapter XXVII, Lapham and his family lived in near poverty until "every dollar, every cent, had gone to pay his debts; he had come out with clean hands" (510 [272]). Lapham has not sought, in Fairchild's words the technical and legal release of bankruptcy! Lapham had discharged the real, moral responsibility of his debts.

* * *

So I maintain that the moral point of *Silas Lapham* was frequently missed by its early readers. If they liked the book, they saw it as a love story with a happy ending; if they didn't, they saw it as decadent realism. The moral dilemma involved in the bankruptcy plot escaped them. I have argued that a lack of awareness of changing moral standards, especially in business ethics best explains this blind spot. Early readers, not yet accustomed to connecting business and ethics, saw bankruptcy plot as a financial not a moral matter. Only the more perceptive, and ethically sensitized readers and critics appreciated the moral drama of *Silas Lapham.* Following the lead of the moralist James Fairchild, business ethics gradually gained popular awareness and support. So too, the moral drama of *Silas Lapham* came to be widely appreciated. Eventually it was regarded as the main message of the novel.

What of shallow readings given by current readers? The figure of Rogers is the key here. Rogers is quickly and universally dismissed as a scoundrel. Rogers, if he is noticed, is seen as the ignoble foil of the exemplary Lapham. Such a reading fails to capture the complexity of Howells' task. Howells was quite aware that in the eyes of his contemporaries, Rogers could be crafty and moral at the same time. In Francis Wayland's views of personal responsibility and ethical practices in business, Rogers' schemes *are* moral. Howells strongly disagrees. He writes this novel to convince his contemporaries to reject Wayland's hair-splitting, casuistic morality. Howells and moralists like Fairchild were successful. They were so successful that it is difficult to fathom Rogers as a moral figure. But that must have been as obvious to the nineteenth-century reader as Lapham's moral excellence is to us. In *The Rise of Silas Lapham,* William Dean Howells was attempting to change theory in novel writing and ethical practice in business. His success in *both* tasks deserves acknowledgment.

WAI CHEE DIMOCK

From The Economy of Pain: The Case of Howells†

At one of the most touching moments in William Dean Howells's novel *The Rise of Silas Lapham*, the Laphams, feeling wretched about the drastic new development in their daughters' marital fortunes, consult the Reverend Sewell. The minister offers his counsel in the form of a hypothetical question. If somebody else had come to them with the same unhappy discovery that the presumptive suitor of one daughter was really courting the other, what would they have said? Wouldn't they have come up with some kind of moral

† From "The Economy of Pain: The Case of Howells," *Raritan* 9.4 (Spring 1990): 99–104, 107–19. Reprinted by permission of the publisher, Rutgers University.

arithmetic to solve the problem? As Sewell sees it, that arithmetic is one that would seek to minimize pain:

> "One suffer instead of three, if none is to blame?" suggested Sewell. "That's sense, and that's justice. It's the economy of pain which naturally suggests itself, and which would insist upon itself, if we were not all perverted by traditions which are the figment of the shallowest sentimentality."

As a way of managing the suffering of others, Sewell's "economy of pain" is a truly indispensable vehicle. The sentient and the economic are not usually seen in such close conjunction; Sewell not only mentions them in the same breath, but also uses them to justify and reinforce each other. If his concern with pain reflects a humane sensibility, his emphasis on economy, on the distribution and management of pain, bespeaks another influence as well. Neither strictly a model for moral conduct nor strictly a model for economic organization, Sewell's "economy of pain" works, instead, as a combination of the two. We might think of it as a kind of moral economy, a model whose claim to "justice" rests on its ability to conjoin the moral and the economic, or rather, on the fact that, under its dispensation, the moral and the economic need no conjoining at all, because they are already one and the same: what is economic here is also what is moral. This neat arrangement comes about because, according to Sewell, suffering can become morally acceptable only when it is economically organized. Its rationale rests on its rationality. Such a model obviously tries to minimize pain, but even as it does so, it also confers legitimacy on what it minimizes. Because one is inflicting as little pain as possible, what one does inflict becomes correspondingly acceptable. In Sewell's model, then, resource allocation and moral adjudication turn out to be identical activities, because in perfecting the former one also enforces the latter.

Sewell's economy of pain appears, on this occasion, as a modest proposal concerning only the Laphams. Still, as a way of calibrating, distributing, and legitimizing suffering, its sphere of application would seem much wider. In fact, such a way of thinking about pain has a history of its own outside fiction. Simon Nelson Patten, the turn-of-the-century economist and social Darwinist, would soon speak, in terms strikingly similar to Sewell's, of a "Pain Economy," to be replaced by a "Pleasure Economy" as society progressed. Less sanguine about such progress, Patten's more famous associate William Graham Sumner, perhaps the best-known social Darwinist in America, concentrated instead on economics of the less pleasurable sort. "Who pays for it?" he asks, repeatedly and always in a tone of gloating malice, in his well-known essay of 1883, "The Forgotten Man." "Paying" is what someone always ends up doing, Sumner argues, because society works by "the balance of the account," and "the advantage of some is won by an equivalent loss of others." * * * The preoccupation with suffering—with its distribution and legitimacy—was very much a nineteenth-century preoccupation, shared by people of all ideological shades and stripes. * * *

Such a widespread interest in pain was not altogether surprising. The nineteenth century, an age of rapid industrial expansion, was also an age of industrial poverty and urban slums, haunted both by the growing proximity and visibility of human suffering and by the perception that this suffering was not just an isolated phenomenon but part of a symptomatic network. Such a perception, which emphasized the connections among things, was especially important to the nineteenth century, so much so that we might think of it as a nineteenth-century cognitive style. This is especially true of late nineteenth-century America, which, as historians tell us, was rapidly transformed from a nation of "island communities" to a nation of corporate interdependence, organized into a vast interlocking network by the advent of the railroad, the emergence of government bureaucracy, and the growth of big business. As local livelihood became tied to distant events—to the Wall Street crash of 1873, for instance, or the bitter railroad strikes of 1877—local welfare also seemed bound up with the welfare of strangers, strangers unknown, unloved, unconscionably numerous. Nineteenth-century Americans, in short, had to adapt not only to an expanded geographical universe but also, even more crucially, to an expanded causal universe, in which human agency, social relations, and moral responsibility all had to be redefined. An ever-widening field of causality could be both inspiring and scary, and those confronted with it reacted variously, often antithetically. Nativist sentiments, noticeably strong during this period, registered one kind of response: immigrants, after all, embodied all that was alien and threatening in a world grown too large and complex. Humanitarian sentiments, equally strong during the period, registered another kind of response: accepting causal connections even among the seemingly unconnected, reformers proceeded to act upon them, treating the welfare of the poor and weak as their own responsibility.

Howells himself would write about this sense of human connectedness in his next book of 1886, *The Minister's Charge*. Published just a year after *The Rise of Silas Lapham*, this novel shares some of the themes and characters of its predecessor, and, as it happens, it is once again the Reverend Sewell who is made to deliver the book's central statement. "Everybody's mixed up with everybody else," he observes with admirable succinctness in a sermon entitled "Complicity." Complicity, the condition of being all mixed up, is indeed an inescapable fact in Howells, and the agonizing problems of both *The Minister's Charge* and *The Rise of Silas Lapham* can all be traced to it. Those problems, in turn, inspire Sewell to come up with a vehicle of arbitration: an economy of pain. Even within the space of these two novels, then, a double pattern begins to emerge: a problem and a solution, something that produces moral entanglements and something that releases those entanglements. Within the terms of our discussion, we might say that, on the one hand, there is a movement toward expanded connectedness, which implicates everyone and makes everyone responsible for everyone else. Complementing it, however, is a movement in the opposite direction, a movement that restores limits, that tries to minimize not only suffering but also the obligations that suffering entails.

Taken together, these double motions in Howells would seem to constitute a self-limiting cognitive structure that not only honors moral responsibilities but also makes sure that they will be kept within bounds. Such a structure casts an interesting light on the recent debate among historians about the cognitive conditions for moral responsibility, a debate that has ignited the pages of the *American Historical Review*. What sparked it off was an important theoretical essay, "Capitalism and the Origins of the Humanitarian Sensibility," by Thomas Haskell. Haskell argues that a particular form of moral sensibility—in this case, a capacity for humanitarian action—can flourish only within the cognitive universe of a particular form of economic life—in this case, capitalism. Capitalism rewards those who can think in terms of distant events, who can connect things across space and time, and, in doing so, it helps to enlarge not only "the range of causal perceptions" but also the range of assumed obligations. What capitalism accomplishes is not just an economic revolution but, even more crucially, a cognitive revolution. Out of this revolution, Haskell argues, a "new moral universe" is born, where "failing to go to the aid of a suffering stranger might become an unconscionable act." * * * Without disagreeing with Haskell, then, I would like to complicate his model by suggesting one such collateral provision: one that posits capitalism not only as an *enabling* influence on humanitarianism but also as a *limiting* condition, not only its cognitive ground but also its cognitive boundary. There is a limit beyond which humanitarianism will not go. And, to see how that limit works, and how it is instituted as a cognitive provision, it is useful, I think, to look at the economy of pain, because such an economy, in its ability to minimize not only suffering but also obligation, is also a crucial instrument for establishing boundaries and maintaining limits. It is a crucial instrument, we might say, for preventing moral responsibilities from becoming moral liabilities.

Such a safety mechanism is central, I suggest, to the workings of capitalism.

* * *

The same self-limiting structure—the same double provision for expanded commitments and curtailed obligations—governs the realistic novel as well. * * * Given these dual aspects of the novel—its plenitude as well as its regimentation—we might think of it as an uneasy compromise between two contending forces: between the claims of expanded connectedness on the one hand and the claims of reinstated boundaries on the other, or, within the terms of our discussion, between the claims of moral responsibility and the claims of limited liability.

In the very form of the novel, in its web of causality and its need for closure, we see a universe of alternating expansion and contraction that would seem to correspond, more or less, to the alternately expanding and contracting cognitive universe that facilitates both capitalism and humanitarianism. * * *

In their semidetached state, Rogers and Miss Dewey would seem to confirm our usual view of the realistic novel as a commodious vessel whose formal identity lies in the abundance, perhaps even superfluity, of its details. And yet, if we think of the subplot not as a thematic appendage to the main plot but as its structural complement, the seemingly gratuitous complications turn out to be not gratuitous but necessary, if only as the negative condition of possibility for the main plot. For the subplot, in its unwieldly, unwarranted complications, would seem to represent the very circumstances—an expanded, and ultimately untenable, radius of pertinence—which the main plot must rectify, contain, counteract. Within the terms of this essay, we might also say that the subplot, as a field of ever-widening entanglements, is also the formal register of the novel's humanitarian impulse: a network of causal connections as well as moral obligations which must ultimately be kept in check. That double movement—an initial expansiveness as well as an eventual retrenchment—is exactly how the two subplots work in *The Rise of Silas Lapham*.

The tenuous ties that connect Rogers and Miss Dewey to the story are important, then, precisely because they *are* tenuous, because they define a radius of pertinence so wide as to appear limitless. In such a world of causal infinitude, human responsibility becomes infinitely problematic. Is Lapham still responsible for the fate of

Rogers, after all these years? How long should he keep on making amends, and how far must he go? That is the very question Mrs. Lapham asks, and her answer is unequivocal. "I want you should ask yourself," she urges her husband, "whether Rogers would ever have gone wrong, or got into these ways of his, if it hadn't been for your forcing him out of the business when you did. I want you should think whether you're not responsible for everything he's done since."

Mrs. Lapham has "a woman's passion for fixing responsibility," Howells tells us, and she certainly seems to be indulging it on this occasion. Still, her passion turns out to be more sporadic than we might think. She has no desire to "fix responsibility," for instance, when the responsibility involves taking care of the widow and child of a dead army buddy. In fact, she is as vehemently opposed, on this point, as she is vehemently insistent on the other. "One of the things she had to fight [Lapham] about was that idea of his that he was bound to take care of Jim Millon's worthless wife and her child because Millon had got the bullet that was meant for him." As far as she is concerned, this is just "willful, wrong-headed kind-heartedness" on Lapham's part because he has no moral responsibility to speak of in this case, and no reason to "look after a couple of worthless women who had no earthly claim on him." Fight as she does, however, she cannot "beat [the idea] out of" her husband, because, on this occasion at least, Lapham is operating in a wider causal universe than her own. Seeing himself as the cause of Jim Millon's death, he puts himself under a moral obligation toward the dead man's family. That is why Miss Dewey is in his office to begin with: she is Jim Millon's daughter, and Lapham feels "bound to take care of" her and her mother. The subplot revolving around the typist, then, turns out to be exactly analogous to the one revolving around Rogers. In both cases, a distant event is evoked to reveal a network of complications and entanglements, giving rise to a universe of ever-receding and ever-expanding causality: a universe of unlimited connections and unlimited liability.

It is the unlimited liability, of course, that precipitates Lapham's downfall. The causal universe he inhabits is not only fearfully expansive but also fatally expensive. Moral responsibilities here have a way of becoming financial liabilities because both Rogers and Miss Dewey (as well as her mother) use their moral claims to ask for money—a fact significant in itself and suggestive of the problematic Howells means to set up. Lapham speaks both too prophetically and too soon, then, when he says, "I'm glad to have that old trouble healed up. I don't think I ever did Rogers any wrong . . . but if I *did* do it—if I did—I'm willing to call it square, if I never see a cent of my money back again." The money that he will never see a cent of back again turns out to be the sum total of his fortune, for Milton K. Rogers, Lapham later realizes, "let me in for this thing, and that thing, and bled me every time." Lapham's moral economy is, without question, an economy of expenditure, and even though Howells approves of it, at least in this particular instance, it is ultimately untenable as anything other than a cautionary tale, something others must try to avoid. Lapham himself suggests as much. All his troubles began with "Rogers in the first place," he says. "It was just like starting a row of bricks. I tried to catch up, and stop 'em from going, but they all tumbled, one after another. It wasn't in the nature of things that they could be stopped till the last brick went."

A domino theory of moral responsibility is clearly a frightening prospect. But if so, the very terms of Howells's problematic would seem already to suggest a remedy. If moral responsibilities tend to get out of hand by mutating into financial liabilities, then the solution must work in the opposite direction, which is to say, it must try to rectify the moral by way of the economic. In short, by dramatizing the permeable relation between the moral and the economic, and by focusing on liability as a problem in moral conduct, Howells not only makes morality a vital issue in business dealings, he also makes economics a vital instrument in moral arbitration. The Reverend Sewell is speaking not just for himself, then, but equally for Howells when he urges upon the Laphams an economy of pain. Such an economy, in its ability to manage both suffering and obligation, would have saved Lapham not only from his financial woes but also from his moral agonies.

Of course, it is not Lapham's good fortune to benefit from such an economy, nor is he the intended beneficiary. Sewell has in mind a different problem and a different set of clients. Not the Laphams themselves, but their offspring, Penelope, and not the elder Coreys either, but their offspring, Tom, will stand to benefit, both from Sewell's proposed economy of pain and from the actual novelistic economy that is *The Rise of Silas Lapham*. Such a differential pattern in the assignment of benefits is itself interesting, but even more interesting is its double effect of at once minimizing and legitimizing pain. * * *

To the extent that the novel is itself an economy, our usual emphasis on its *thematic* referentiality would seem quite inadequate. What we need as well, I think, is a theory about its *formal* referentiality: a theory about the novel form as a system of distribution and adequation and about its relation, as such, to the more general system of distribution and adequation that obtains outside the province of fiction. We might even argue for a direct link between the formal arrangements inside a novel, arrangements that guarantee its "poetic justice," and the social arrangements outside a novel, arrangements designed for the same end. From the standpoint of practical criticism, what this suggests is that we might want to focus less on the actions and psychologies of individual characters and more on their aggregate configuration: their mutualities and equivalences within a pattern of correlated gain and loss.

Some such pattern, in fact, is what Tom Corey notices, and what gives him hope, as he contemplates the synchronized gain and loss that seem to have overtaken himself and his employer, Silas Lapham. "Lapham's potential ruin" might turn out to be his own salvation, Tom thinks, because this is a case where "another's disaster would befriend him, and give him the opportunity to prove the unselfishness of his constancy." This is not just wishful thinking either, because it in fact happens: Lapham's downfall does indeed "befriend" Corey, and his marriage to Penelope does indeed take place, to the tune of his father-in-law's financial disaster. In some mysterious fashion, then, the two events seem to have balanced out each other in a kind of trade-off, a remote and yet correlated proportionality. And yet, simply to note that fact does not quite settle the question because, from our perspective, what is most interesting is not so much the proportionality itself as the ground on which it is computed: the ground on which one event is judged the equivalent of the other. In what sense, and by what calculus, does Lapham's financial disaster (not to mention the elder Coreys' afflicted sensibility) answer to the marital bliss of Tom and Penelope? What rate of exchange—to put the question most bluntly—measures those two events and certifies their proportionality?

To ask such questions is obviously to think of the novel form as a system of symbolic equivalents, in which disparate events tally with each other, compensate for each other, and balance out each other, both as a matter of figuration and as a matter of configuration. * * * In short, in thinking about the novel as a system of symbolic equivalents, we might also be able to think, more generally, about the grounds for equivalence that govern both the narrative arrangements inside fiction and the social arrangements outside it.

In *The Rise of Silas Lapham*, the grounds for equivalence are especially interesting because they require the yoking together of pleasure and pain in a kind of narrative balance. Such an arrangement (whose goal, after all, is to make the pleasure of some characters equivalent to the pain of others) might seem bizarre in one sense, but it is by no means unthinkable because, as we shall see, neither the pain nor the pleasure here turns out to be unmixed, and, being so compounded and confounded, they are also infinitely fluid and infinitely amenable to the postulate of equivalence. Positing equivalences, I would argue, is the central task of *The Rise of Silas Lapham*, just as it is, more generally, the task of the realistic novel. This impulse, to create identity out of difference, explains, I think, why the nineteenth-century novel gives us so few straightforward "happy endings" and why the ones that we do get are often so tepid and so unsatisfactory—so much so that their pleasure seems virtually a kind of pain. The well-known marriages that conclude nineteenth-century novels—between Fanny Price and Edmund Bertram, between Jane Eyre and Mr. Rochester, between Dorothea Brooke and Will Ladislaw—are happy endings only in form; in any other respect they hardly deserve the title. Within this context, the famous last line of *The Bostonians* must serve as an extreme epigraph to the genre. When Verena goes off with Basil Ransom, she is discovered, James tells us, to be "in tears." And he goes on, "It is to be feared that with the union, so far from brilliant, into which she was about to enter, these were not the last she was destined to shed."

Howells does not say that about Penelope, of course, and we have every expectation that she will fare better than Verena Tarrant. And yet it is interesting that, even in *The Rise of Silas Lapham*, a book that otherwise has little in common with *The Bostonians*, Howells should find it incumbent upon himself to supply his happy ending with some measure of unhappiness. "The marriage came after so much sorrow and trouble," Howells tells us, "and the fact was received with so much misgiving for the past and future, that it brought Lapham none of the triumph." The same is true, needless to say, on the side of the Coreys: polite tolerance is all they can muster toward their new in-law. As for Penelope herself, when she is finally allowed to go off with Tom, she too, strangely enough, is seen crying on his shoulder. That activity is perhaps more appropriate to Verena, but it is not entirely out of place in Penelope either, because her case, as we have seen, is one of mixed blessing, of "painful pleasure," something nineteenth-century novelists apparently feel obligated to concoct at the end of their stories.

But if pleasure shows up in the realistic novel as mixed pleasure, the obverse is just as true. By the same logic, pain also will not be unadulterated pain, or at least it will not register as such. Instead, it too will bring along a kind of compensation, so that, far from being an unmitigated disaster, it might seem a blessing in disguise. To be crude about it, we might even say that in many nineteenth-century novels, there is a kind of trade-off between suffering and edification: pain is the "price" one has to pay in exchange for a certain moral elevation. This phenomenon is probably familiar enough to need no illustration. Within this context, *The Rise of Silas Lapham* must seem an exemplary story because the "rise" that is advertised in the title—the moral ascent of its main character—is of course predicated on (and purchased by) the pain that character is made to endure. What makes Lapham's fictive trajectory possible, then, is a crucial and animating process of exchange: an exchange between beginnings and endings, between what he starts out with and what he ends up with.

From this perspective, Lapham's beginnings—the assets that accompany him when he first appears—are especially worthy of notice. And *assets* is the right word because, in the first part of the book, Lapham is noticeably well endowed: endowed, that is, with bodily parts that are not only conspicuous, but downright obtrusive. Over and over again, we hear about his "bulk," his "huge foot," his "No. 10 boots." He is in the habit of pounding "with his great hairy fist," and, instead of closing the door with his hands, he uses "his huge foot" instead. When he talks to Bartley Hubbard, he puts "his huge foot close to Bartley's thigh." Lapham's body is prominently on display in the opening chapter, and the rest of the book bears out this initial portrait. We continue to hear about his "hairy paws," his "ponderous fore-arms," and his "large fists" hanging down "like canvased hams." It is inconceivable that Bromfield Corey would have appeared in this light, not because Boston Brahmins do not have "hairy paws," but because Boston Brahmins are not described in bodily terms at all. Lapham's attributes, then, turn out to be less a matter of neutral portrayal than of strategic representation. He comes with a body, a body grossly physical and grossly visible, and that is the most significant fact about him. His physicality stands as the sum and measure of who he is.

In this context, it is especially ominous that Lapham's body is so often linked with his failures to "rise"—failures first literal and then not so literal. When Bartley Hubbard shows up at the office, for instance, Lapham "did not rise from the desk at which he was writing, but he gave Bartley his left hand for welcome, and he rolled his large head in the direction of a vacant chair." Similarly, when he needs to close the door, he does not rise, but puts out "his huge foot" to push it shut. So far, Lapham's failure to rise is literally just that: he does not get up from his chair, his body stays put. Things become more worrisome, however, when this bodily inertia becomes metaphorical: Lapham's head, we are told, rests on "a short neck, which does not trouble itself to rise far." Some tyranny of physique seems to be keeping him down, and so we are not surprised to learn that he had failed to rise on another occasion as well, when it would have behooved his moral character to do so. Years ago, when he had to decide whether to keep Rogers on or to force him out, Lapham found that he could not "choose the ideal, the unselfish part in such an exigency"—in short, that he "could not rise to it." It is a fatal mistake, of course, although, given his beginnings, given the negative assets that dominate him from the first, it is no more than what we might expect. With a body like his, failure to rise is all but a foregone conclusion.

And yet Lapham does eventually rise, and indeed is destined to do so, as the title promises. Between the unrisen Lapham at the beginning of the book and the risen Lapham at the end, some momentous change has taken place. We might think of it, in fact, not just as a change but as an exchange—an exchange of personality traits—because he is able to rise only insofar as he is able to trade one set of attributes for another. What he possesses at the end is no longer the gross animal vitality he once flaunted, but rather "a sort of pensive dignity that . . . sometimes comes to such natures after long sickness, when the animal strength has been taxed and lowered." In short, a gain and a loss seem to have occurred somewhere, "taxing" and "lowering" Lapham's animal strength to augment his moral capital.

Exchange of this sort is what constitutes a moral economy in Howells, I would suggest, and the mechanics for it turns out to be straightforward enough. As Howells's allusion to "long sickness" suggests, what facilitates the exchange—the conversion from the animal to the moral—is a severe affliction, a just measure of pain, we might even say. Of course, as we also know, the "long sickness" in question is not physical sickness, but mental agony, the sort of sickness that befalls us when all our money disappears, a conceit borne out by Lapham's complaint that Rogers has "bled" him. Bloodletting, it would seem, is the means to moral elevation because, according to the internal economy that regulates Lapham's being, animal strength and moral capital turn out to be symbolic equivalents, and the gain in one cannot be effected without a corresponding loss in the other. Suffering ennobles, then, precisely because, by virtue of the loss that it entails, it is also able to bring forth a new ratio in one's composition of character, a new balance of attributes, and a gain commensurate with the loss. Understood as such, suffering never exists in isolation, but always in partnership with something else. It is only half the equation, as it were, in an economy of pain, the other half being not only its complement but also its compensation.

We have arrived then, once again, at a paradoxical situation where things are strangely mixed up, where pain seems indistinguishable from pleasure. This is the mirror image, of course, of the economy of pleasure we discussed earlier. Just as the latter mixes pleasure with pain and turns every happy ending into a tearful event, so the former mixes pain with pleasure and turns every disaster into a hidden blessing. It is just this sort of logic that makes Lapham's story a comedy, in spite of its palpable hardships. From one point of view, of course, Lapham has suffered much: he has gone bankrupt, and his paint business has fallen apart. From another point of view, however, such suffering might look like a kind of miraculous salvation. It is the miraculous salvation, in fact, that Lapham notices when he talks the matter over with the Reverend Sewell at the end of the book: "Seems sometimes as if it was a hole opened for me, and I crept out of it."

Lapham's misfortune turns out not only to have "befriended" Tom Corey, it seems also to have befriended the sufferer himself. Just like pleasure, which is always appropriately diluted, pain too seems to carry its organic anodyne. In this curious mixing of attributes, we see perhaps the most powerful mechanism that secures for the novel its "poetic justice," that makes its unequal distribution of benefits morally acceptable. Since pleasure here has more than its share of pain, and pain more than its share of pleasure, the two are all but similar: they can be tabulated as such, and, more to the point, they can be distributed as such. Penelope going off to Mexico in her painful pleasure and Lapham going back to Vermont in his pleasurable pain are doing the same thing, after all. Their disparate fortunes bespeak no inequity in resource management because those fortunes, properly tallied, turn out to be pretty much alike.

If we might speak of the "cultural work" of the realistic novel, a crucial part of that work is surely to educate our moral sensibility, to instill in us a capacity for outrage as well as a capacity for acquiescence. In teaching us, as *The Rise of Silas Lapham* does, to think about pleasure and pain not as stark opposites but as ambiguous compounds, it no doubt helps us to cope with our own suffering. But it helps us too, it would seem, to cope with the suffering of others: cope with it, in the sense of acceding to it, accounting for it, and learning to see it, as Howells says, in its "true proportion." Suffering measured by such a calculus can no longer be a reproach, and the realistic novel, operating as an economy of pain, turns out to honor the dictates of both capitalism and humanitarianism. Even as it faithfully represents human sufferings, it just as faithfully prevents those sufferings from becoming liabilities.

BROOK THOMAS

From The Risky Business of Accessing the Economy of Howells's Realism in *The Rise of Silas Lapham*†

As Tom Corey goes to work for Silas Lapham, his mother worries about his seeming attraction to Silas's daughter, Irene. While not

† From *REAL: Yearbook of Research in English and American Literature, Vol. 11: The Historical and Political Turn in Literary Studies*, ed. Winfried Fluck (Tübingen: Gunter Narr Verlag Tübingen, 1995), pp. 229–51. Reprinted by permission of the author. Page references in brackets refer to this Norton Critical Edition.

admitting her motive to herself or others, Mrs. Corey decides to pay a second visit to the Laphams, telling her daughter that "it seemed she ought somehow to recognize the business relation that Tom had formed with the father; they must not think that his family disapproved of what he had done.

'Yes, business is business,' said Nanny, with a laugh. 'Do you wish us to go with you again?'"[1]

The Rise of Silas Lapham is often called the first realistic portrayal of a businessman in American literature, but Nanny Corey's laughing response to her mother calls attention to a problem that occupies most critics of the novel: how does its business plot relate to the love plot involving Tom and Silas's daughters? Nanny's identification of business with business would seem to imply that the business plot could be marked off as a self-contained entity. But the effect of her laugh is to undercut any such tautological identification. Business, her laugh suggests, is not quite identical to business. Mrs. Corey may claim that her visit to the Laphams is to recognize her son's business relation, but if business were completely confined to the world of business, she would have no obligation to do so. Instead, her "business" as mother is to give her son's relation her blessing, a reminder that business relations are legitimated by more than purely market relations.

And there is more. Mrs. Corey claims to be visiting the Laphams on business matters, but, as her daughter knows, her visit involves more serious business: the possible romantic relation between Tom and Irene. Woman's business may focus on personal relations whereas man's business focuses on market relations, but Howells's plot makes it impossible completely to separate the two. Howells dramatizes that impossibility by self-consciously using the word "business" in non-business contexts. For Mrs. Corey the confusion about the object of her son's affections is the Laphams' "terrible business" (265 [201]). Silas reminds Penelope that her actions in the matter are "my business and your mother's business, as well as yours" (252 [191]). When his wife wants to know about his deteriorating business affairs, Silas rebukes her with, "You mind your own business, Persis" (284 [214]). Asked by Jim Millon's wife what he thinks about the possibility of her daughter getting a divorce, Silas responds, "I don't care anything about all that. It's your own business, and I'm not going to meddle with it. But it's my business who lives off me" (296 [223]).

And just as "when it came really to business" (317 [239]), "business" moves into all realms of the novel, so romance comes to inhabit the

1. William Dean Howells, *The Rise of Silas Lapham* (Bloomington: Indiana U.P., 1971; rpt. 1885), p. 163 [124]. Future references to this edition will be cited parenthetically.

realm of business. Money, Bromfield Corey claims, "is the romance, the poetry of our age" (64 [49]). Silas's paint is "more than a business to him; it was a sentiment, almost a passion" (50 [39]).

Confronted with this seepage of one plot into another, critics have sought ways to balance the two. For instance, G. Thomas Tanselle refers to "the care Howells has taken to keep the two plots in balance," whereas Wai-chee Dimock wants us to think of "the novel form as a system of symbolic equivalents, in which disparate events tally with each other, compensate for each other, and balance each other out."[2] What these efforts fail to take into account, however, is an imbalance at the heart of Howells's novel, an imbalance that makes itself felt in even the simple effort to make business equivalent to itself. If formalist critics attempted to stabilize that imbalance by offering a reading of the novel as a whole, recent historical critics have tried to stabilize it by expanding the scope of their reading to situate Howells's text within its cultural context. Dimock, for instance, argues that Howells's balancing of "formal arrangements inside [the] novel" has a "direct link" to "social arrangements outside" it and thus reveals the novelist's effort to dispense "poetic justice."[3]

Howells did see a relationship between a work's formal structure and questions of justice, but it is much more complicated than new historicists allow. The most influential new historicist reading of Howells is Walter Benn Michaels's. Michaels's account is, as he acknowledges, indebted to Leo Bersani. Working within a framework established by Roland Barthes, Bersani challenges arguments like Georg Lukacs's that champion nineteenth-century realism for opposing the fragmented world created by capitalism. Admitting that the realistic novel can offer valuable social criticism by exposing contradictions, Bersani claims that, nonetheless, its final sense of cohesion offers implicit reassurance that those contradictions can be contained within a significantly ordered structure inherent in society. Naturalizing the historically-constructed relations under capitalism as "the real," realism's balanced formal order serves the status quo by castrating desire for an alternative social order.[4]

Michaels accepts Bersani's account of realism's efforts to achieve a balanced economy within a balanced formal structure, but he offers

2. Thomas G. Tanselle, "The Architecture of *The Rise of Silas Lapham*," *American Literature* 27 (1966), 434, and Wai-chee Dimock, "The Economy of Pain: The Case of Howells," *Raritan* 9 (1990), 113.
3. Dimock, 112–3. The "myth and symbol school" is supposedly out of fashion, but symbolic analysis seems to be back in favor. In addition to Dimock's "system of symbolic equivalents" there is Sacvan Bercovitch's use of "cultural symbology" to examine "art as ideological mimesis." *The Office of "The Scarlet Letter"* (Baltimore: The Johns Hopkins U.P., 1991), pp. xvii, xxii. If symbol is back, is myth back under the guise of ideology?
4. Leo Bersani, *A Future for Astyanax* (Boston: Little Brown, 1976) and "The Subject of Power," *Diacritics* (1977), 2–21.

a different account of capitalism. Capitalism, he argues, does not castrate desire; it functions by generating it. Consumer capitalism, after all, works by producing and reproducing subjects with an endless desire to be what they are not. That desire is generated by an economy based on speculation. Building his argument on the precarious foundation of this speculative economy, Michaels performs a dazzling balancing act that links business and love plots through their fear of speculation. The love plot, he argues, warns against sentimental fiction whose lack of anchor in reality arouses dangerous speculative desire, whereas the business plot warns against a capitalist economy that rewards earnings gained through speculation rather than "real" labor. In this reading Howells opposes the dangers of speculation with the agrarian values of self-sufficiency and balance that led to Silas's initial rise and to which he returns at the end of the novel. Aligning Howells's realism with this premarket notion of character, Michaels claims that Howells thinks of both as sources of inherent values that resist the flux of an inequitable capitalist economy. In contrast, Michaels champions *Sister Carrie* whose dramatization of the "almost structural impossibility of equilibrium" endorses (against Dreiser's own intentions) "the popular economy" of capitalism.[5]

* * *

For Michaels, naturalism's "realistic" relation to consumer capitalism does not come from its accurate representation of reality. On the contrary, within the "logic" of naturalism there is an inevitable gap between a work of art and what it would represent. It is, however, precisely this imbalance between life and art that serves the interests of capitalism, for it helps to generate mimetic desire, a desire to be what one is not. In naturalism "the relation between art and desire is . . . very different from Howells's in *The Rise of Silas Lapham*, where art, like character, was seen as a kind of still point, a repository of values that resisted the fluctuations and inequalities of industrial capitalism."[6] In contrast, naturalism is both about and produces ideal subjects for consumer capitalism, subjects constituted by a desire to imitate what they cannot be.

One problem with Michaels's account of Howells's realism is that he along with most critics are misled by Howells's statements that the function of fiction is to portray men and women as "they really are." Such an aesthetic, Michaels argues, is essentially a painter's aesthetic. To be sure, in *Silas Lapham* the Reverend Sewell proclaims that "The novelists might be the greatest help to us if they painted

5. Walter Benn Michaels, *The Gold Standard and the Logic of Naturalism* (Berkeley: U. of California P., 1987), p. 42.
6. Michaels, p. 46.

life as it is, and human feelings in their true proportion and relation" (197 [152]). But a call to paint "life as it is" is somewhat ironic in a novel in which Silas uses his paint to cover the natural landscape with advertisements for itself. Paint seems as capable of covering up the world as accurately imitating it. Granted, Silas's commercial use of paint needs to be distinguished from aesthetic uses of it, such as those of Bromfield Corey. For instance, in a statement that Michaels quotes to represent Howells's aesthetic, Corey asserts that "You never hear of values in a picture shrinking; but rents, stocks, real estate—all these shrink abominably" (95–6 [73]). Corey does see art as an escape from the speculative fluctuations of the market. But Corey's theory of art should not be taken as Howells's. Within the dramatic context of the novel it has problems of its own.

Causing Corey to respond to a "shrinkage in values" (95 [73]) by investing "his values into pictures" (96 [73]), it contributes to the decline in Corey's and his family's fortunes. Its concept of imitation has also robbed Corey of the originality necessary for him to develop as a painter. The limits of Corey's otherwise admirable taste are further suggested in the conversation about his house during the book's central dinner scene. Built in "perfect taste" (192 [146]) and embodying its architect's "preference for the classic" (187 [142]), the house is, according to Silas's architect, neither as "original" (192 [146]) nor as well-built as the structure that Silas's "practical sympathy" (191 [146]) has allowed him to construct. The point is not that the Corey house lacks aesthetic value. Howells continues to value taste, just as he continues to value human "character." The house does create a space for impeccable taste and trustworthy character. But in protecting itself from "modern fuss" (191 [146]), it shuts out the temporality necessary for the *development* of character.[7]

* * * Corey's classical, "painterly" aesthetic assumes, like the Greeks, that the real is stable and unchanging. In contrast, Howells's novelistic aesthetic assumes a world in which temporality has become a component part of reality, one in which a future reality is always capable of rendering an existing reality unreal. Incapable of expression by spatial metaphors, this sense of reality plays havoc with balancing efforts that depend on foundational thought.

Michaels argues that Howells's realism rests on the solid foundation of stable values of morality and art. But Howells is at pains to undercut Silas's efforts to establish firm foundations. For instance, in contrast to his speculation in the stock market, Silas's investment in his house would seem to be a stable investment. Indeed, the house is

7. Corey's position is, in fact, even more conservative than I suggest. The house discussed is Mrs. Corey's. "*My* ancestral halls," he insists, "are in Salem, and I'm told you couldn't drive a nail into their timbers" (SL 192 [146]). Solid as that structure might be, it is located in Salem, which declined when Boston took away its commerce.

an attempt to establish foundations in a variety of ways. Most obvious is the metaphor of foundation itself. A house is constructed on a foundation rooted in the earth. It is built on a piece of *real* estate. But Silas's investment in his house is also an investment in the social status of his daughters. He first considers building it after Mrs. Corey's visit to their Nankeen Square house and her remark that "'Nearly all our friends are on the New Land or on the Hill.'" (29 [23]). Mrs. Lapham, who at first resists the notion of building on Silas's Back Bay lot, ponders the consequences for her daughters and grants that, "'we ought to do the best we can for the children, in every way.'" (29 [24]). The Back Bay location will provide the daughters with a social foundation lacking in their Nankeen Square address.

The speculative nature of this investment is dramatically indicated when the house goes up in flames. But even before this spectacular event, Howells hints at the investment's shaky foundation. Houses in Back Bay are built on top of a salt marsh, so that "before they began to put in the piles for the foundation they had to pump. The neighborhood smelt like the hold of a ship after a three years' voyage. People who had cast their fortunes with the New Land went by professing not to notice it; people who still 'hung onto the Hill' put their handkerchiefs to their noses, and told each other the old terrible stories of the material used in filling up the Back Bay" (43 [35]). As in the case of his paint "farm," Silas invests in a piece of land with a hole in it whose value is subject to market fluctuations. Significantly, Silas loses the entire investment in his house because the passage of time causes his insurance policy to lapse.

A world in which temporality is a component part of reality, Howells recognizes, greatly complicates the novelist's task to, as Dimock puts it, dispense "poetic justice." In the Western tradition justice has been associated with balancing, as indicated by the metaphor of the scales.[8] But in a temporal world there is no simple way to balance the "formal arrangements inside" a novel with "social arrangements outside" it. Instead, as *Silas Lapham* demonstrates, the desire for balance more often than not results in further unbalancing. Thus, those critics, like Dimock, who attempt to come up with balanced readings end up repeating the efforts of Silas, who continually strives to balance his accounts, but usually fails. That repetition is especially apparent in new historicist efforts to provide balance by appealing to the book's cultural context since they, like Silas, mistake the temporal aspects of the period's economy.

Most critics trying to balance love and business plots appeal, as Donald Pizer did years ago, to the "economy of pain" articulated by

8. Dennis E. Curtis and Judith Resnick, "Images of Justice," *Yale Law Journal* 96 (1987), 1727–72.

Reverend Sewell to solve the dilemma in the love plot when Tom declares his love for Penelope, not Irene.[9] Confronted by one heart-broken daughter and one full of guilt, who refuses to see Tom, the Laphams seek Sewell's counsel. Sewell advises Penelope to overcome her false sense of duty that he blames on sentimental novels and accept Tom's offer to marry. For him the solution is pure common sense:

> "One suffer instead of three, if none is to blame. . . . That's sense, and that's justice. It's the economy of pain which naturally suggests itself, and which would insist upon itself, if we were not all perverted by traditions which are the figment of the shallowest sentimentality" (241 [183]).

Sewell's advice does seem to work for this particular situation. It does not, however, apply to all events in the novel. Silas's transactions with Rogers, for instance, do not adhere to its logic.

In the story's moral climax, Silas refuses to sell potentially worthless stock to his ex-partner, even though doing so would, without violating the business ethics of his day, save his financial empire and satisfy his wife, who feels that Silas owes Rogers a moral debt. Silas has scruples because he knows that Rogers plans to unload the stock on unsuspecting Englishmen, ill-served by morally questionable agents acting on their behalf. Pleading that the sale is "my one chance; that if [Lapham doesn't] meet me on it, my wife and children will be reduced to beggary" (327 [247]), Rogers accuses Silas of wanting "to sacrifice [Rogers's wife] to a mere idea" (328 [248]). Of course, according to Sewell this is precisely the problem with Penelope's refusal to marry Tom. Her "false ideal of self-sacrifice" (241 [183]) causes unnecessary suffering. In both plots agreements could be reached that would minimize suffering for everyone except a third party, in one case Irene, in the other rich men who can well afford the financial losses that they might suffer. But for some reason the economic logic of the love plot does not work for the business plot.

If most critics turn to an "economy" to unite the book's action, Donald Pease turns to the logic of family relations. Noting that, "Throughout the novel the different subject positions Silas Lapham occupied in different social narratives produced mobile social energies transgressive of any single social logic," Pease finds himself, nonetheless, compelled to offer such a single logic. He finds it in Silas's refusal to sell to Rogers. According to Pease, by treating English strangers "as if they were family members rather than business partners," Silas "enacts a scene that refuses the difference

9. Donald Pizer, "The Ethical Unity of *The Rise of Silas Lapham*," *American Literature* 32 (1960), 322–27.

between business transactions and family relations out of which all of these narratives were constructed."[1] But Pease's reading also raises questions. Why, for instance, does Silas protect the interests of his adopted English "family" at the expense of his real family (or even that of Rogers)? Furthermore, how does this logic square with the logic of Sewell's economy of pain, which advises Penelope to construct a new family by discounting the suffering of her closest family member—her sister?

Howells does, as Pease suggests, invite us and Silas to bring the different social narratives in which Silas is placed "into relationship with one another."[2] But in doing so we need to resist the temptation to erase their differences so as to fit them under a single logic. The difference between Penelope's and Silas's dilemmas seems to be that one results from what in *A Hazard of New Fortunes* Basil March calls the chance world of God, whereas the other results from the economic chance world of men. In the love plot no one, as Sewell insists, is to blame. No one can account for why Tom loves Penelope rather than Irene. The distribution of affections is not something that we can control. In contrast, Silas's actions are not blameless. The distribution of economic opportunity does seem to involve questions of blame and responsibility.

This difference affects the meaning of self-sacrifice in the two situations. Even though she is not to blame, Penelope adheres to a "false ideal of self-sacrifice" (241 [183]) in refusing Tom, whereas Silas is incapable of the proper "measure of self-sacrifice" (50 [39]) in his dealings with Rogers, even though he is potentially to blame for Rogers's fate. In one case self-sacrifice is folly, in the other it is called for.

The distinction between the two plots does not rule out similarities between Silas's and Penelope's dilemmas. What is common, however, is that a perfect balance cannot be found in either situation. The love plot suggests why. Balancing the interests of all involved is impossible because it is the nature of a triangular affair to leave an odd person out. The plot of *Silas Lapham* consists of one incident after another in which attempts to balance accounts leave something or someone unaccounted for. We could even say that the plot is driven by Silas's failed desire to make things come out even. Nonetheless, his desire is understandable. Silas does not want to feel in anyone's debt. His image of himself as a self-sufficient, self-made man depends upon keeping balanced accounts, especially moral ones.

1. Donald E. Pease, "Introduction," *New Essays on "The Rise of Silas Lapham,"* ed. Donald E. Pease (New York: Cambridge U.P., 1991), p. 20.
2. Pease, p. 20.

The image of balance brings us back to the relationship between the formal structure of Howells's novel and the world in which it is produced. If the late nineteenth-century economy disrupted efforts to balance one's accounts, the ideology legitimating that economy depended on various images of balance. One involved the balancing of different social spheres. Another involved contractual relations among supposedly equal economic individuals. We can start with contractual relations.

According to laissez-faire thinking the economy operated most efficiently and for the benefit of all when it was generated by mutually agreed-upon contractual relations between autonomous, self-possessed individuals. Two images of balance lie at the heart of this vision. The first is that such an economy, left to regulate itself, will generate a natural balance among its individual members. The second, that a contractual society corrects the undemocratic hierarchies of traditional society by granting all of its members equal standing and weight in economic exchanges. For instance, the nineteenth-century British legal historian Sir Henry Maine argued that, "The movement in progressive societies . . . has been from Status to Contract," by which he meant that in a contractual society duties and obligations were not preassigned according to one's status but negotiated by contract.[3]

If contract contributed to modernization by undermining economic relations of hierarchical status, it also generated new anxieties. Traditional societies may have been hierarchical, but the status assigned to various members was part of an intricate, interconnected network of spiritual and symbolic relations that linked the social system to a cosmic order. Influenced by Maine, Ferdinand Tönnies compared the traditional community (*Gemeinschaft*) with the modern society (*Gesellschaft*).[4] Loosening the traditional communal bonds of *Gemeinschaft*, contract threatened to produce what Emile Durkheim called anomie by atomizing society.[5] That atomization was marked by both a celebration of the individual and the dissociation of institutional spheres from one another.

The image of balanced social spheres is important because it helped to combat this sense of atomization. The various social spheres of modern societies may not be organically interconnected, yet ideally they are held together by a delicate, organic balance.

It is a mistake to assume, as too many do, that late nineteenth-century laissez-faire theorists confined themselves to market relations.

3. Sir Henry Maine, *Ancient Law: Its Connection with the Early History of Society and Its Relation to Modern Ideas* (New York: Dorset, 1986; rpt. 1861), p. 141.
4. For Maine's influence on Tönnies see George Feaver, *From Status to Contract* (London: Longmans, 1969).
5. Emile Durkheim, *Le Suicide* (Paris: Presses Universitaires de France, 1960; rpt. 1897).

Recognizing that human society could not be accounted for solely in terms of "economic man," they assumed that society consisted of more economics than a market economy. For instance, there was also the domestic economy, an economy that comes closer to the word's original meaning, which is the control or management of a household. The order of the domestic economy was, however, different from that of the market economy. The difference is obvious if we compare the contract constituting the domestic economy—the marriage contract—with the business contract. If business contracts undermined traditional relations of status by assuming that contracting parties had equal standing and weight in economic exchanges, the marriage contract constructed a relation of status that determined the proper duties and obligations of husband and wife. Furthermore, if in the business realm responsibility was for the most part limited to the contracting parties, in the domestic realm responsibility extended to all members of the corporate body making up the family.

Contemporary social theorists tend to explain the simultaneous existence of these two spheres in terms of the uneven development of residual, dominant, and emergent forces.[6] The domestic sphere seems to be a residual form, left over from a previous form of social relations. But laissez-faire theory dealt with it through what recent legal historians have described as "boundary ideology."[7] Relying on science, legal scholars tried to identify the natural boundaries between different spheres of human interaction. To identify and establish such boundaries was to minimize governmental interference, for individuals would be free to act in accordance with laws of natural necessity *appropriate to each sphere* rather than be controlled by government. In other words, laissez-faire legal science hoped to create conditions in which the social system would, more or less, run by itself.[8] The promise of boundary ideology, like the promise of contract, depended on an image of balance. Just as in contract self-sufficient individuals came together to join in mutually beneficial relations, so various self-contained spheres balanced one another to generate a smoothly running society. Modern societies may have broken down the sense of an interconnected *Gemeinschaft*, but the image of balance allowed boundary theorists to retain the sense of an organic, if differentiated, society.

6. On "residual, dominant, and emergent," see Raymond Williams, *Marxism and Literature* (New York: Oxford U.P., 1977). An example of the use of the notion of "uneven development" is Mary Poovey, *Uneven Developments: The Ideological Work of Gender in Mid-Victorian England* (Chicago: U. of Chicago P., 1988).
7. Al Katz, "Studies in Boundary Theory: Three Essays in Adjudication and Politics," *Buffalo Law Review* 28 (1979), 383–435.
8. Robert Gordon, "Legal Thought and Legal Practice in the Age of American Enterprise, 1870–1920," *Professions and Professional Ideologies in America*, ed. Gerald L. Geison (Chapel Hill: U. of North Carolina P., 1983), pp. 70–110.

Howells's relationship to boundary ideology is extremely complicated. On the one hand, he seems to share the laissez-faire assumption that different situations generate different logics. For instance, the logic of the love plot cannot simply be imposed on the logic of the business plot. On the other, the seepage of one plot into the other suggests that the boundaries separating different spheres are fluid, not fixed. For instance, Dominick La Capra argues that "The saying 'Business is business' was a meaningful tautological expression" of the doctrine of separate spheres.[9] But, as we have seen, the plot of *Silas Lapham* is generated by the inability to confine business strictly to business. That inability unbalances the balance sought by boundary ideology. We can see how by looking at Silas's unsatisfactory account of the transaction that ended his partnership with Rogers.

Silas absolves himself of any responsibility in forcing Rogers out of partnership by arguing that they agreed to a balanced exchange between free and equal individuals. According to Silas their exchange was a "perfectly square thing." Rogers "got his money out and more too." Mrs. Lapham, of course, does not consider their accounts balanced. When she objects that Rogers's lack of money unbalanced their exchange, Silas reverts to the laissez-faire vocabulary of free will. Rogers had a "choice: buy out or go out." When Persis further objects that, "It was no choice at all" (46 [39]), Silas asserts that Rogers's choice was determined by natural laws of economics. Silas had not taken unfair "advantage," he had simply exploited a "business chance." Mrs. Lapham's rebuke that, "It was no chance at all" (47 [37]) threatens Silas because it implies that the transaction was not square. Her response so throws him off balance that he closes off discussion by dogmatically appealing to the separation of domestic and business spheres. "'I'm sick of this,' said Lapham. 'If you'll tend to the house, I'll manage my business without your help'" (47 [37]). The book goes on to show the impossibility of keeping those two spheres separate, all the while resisting efforts to collapse them into one another.

* * *

Howells presents us with a social world, not united by a common logic, but one in which the "logics" governing individual spheres are simultaneously different and related. They are, it might seem, in a relation of "relative autonomy." But even this extremely sophisticated formulation fails to do justice to Howells's presentation of social relations. Louis Althusser drew upon it to offer a structuralist revision to Marx's theory of economic determinism.[1] What it

9. Dominick La Capra, *Emile Durkheim* (Ithaca: Cornell U.P., 1972), p. 108.
1. For a use of the notion, of relative autonomy prior to Althusser see Jean-Paul Sartre, *Search for a Method*, trans. Hazel E. Barnes (New York: Vintage P., 1968), pp. 48, 66, 111.

lacks is an adequate account of temporality. To be sure, notions of spheres and boundaries involve space. Nonetheless, the relations among spheres in Howells's novel need to be understood temporally in at least two ways. First, efforts to apply the logic of one sphere to another involve an act of translation, an act with a temporal dimension. Second, the various spheres are not, as boundary ideologists assumed, fixed over time, but subject to revision.

* * *

* * * In *Silas Lapham* there is no imagined synthesis of contradictions. Rather than an *Überwindung* of contradictions, he presents us with what Martin Heidegger calls a *Verwindung*.[2] The aesthetic counterpart to such a *Verwindung* is not a balanced formal structure that contains all of the individual elements of its plot. It is instead a work of fiction in which the plot's temporal movement disrupts efforts, including its author's, to achieve formal balance. This disruption is apparent in the novel's third plot.

Akin to the third party that gets left out in a triangular affair, the third plot has caused problems for those intent on balancing the book's main plots. For instance, for Tanselle it is a "serious problem" because it "remains an element not smoothly blended into the larger structure."[3] But Howells's realism delights in forcing us to face such problems, even if they are not easy to account for.

The third plot involves Zerrilla Dewey, the daughter of Jim Millon who sacrificed himself in the Civil War so that Silas could live. Feeling infinitely indebted to Jim, Silas supports his wife and daughter by employing Zerrilla as a secretary. This support becomes increasingly expensive because Zerrilla is married to a sailor who shares Zerrilla's mother's alcoholism.

Bucking the trend of critics who tend to ignore or discount this plot, Dimock argues that its importance *is* its tenuousness. Tenuously connected to the main plots, but revealing a "network of complications and entanglements," it suggests "a world of causal infinitude" in which "human responsibility becomes infinitely problematic." According to Dimock, Silas's decline is precipitated by this dilemma of "unlimited liability," because "the causal universe he inhabits is not

2. On Heidegger's *Verwindung* see Gianni Vattimo, *The End of Modernity*, trans. Jon R. Snyder (Cambridge: Polity P., 1988). Vattimo uses *Verwindung* to characterize a postmodern era, one that is "post-historical." My use of *Verwindung* to describe an effect of Howells's novels suggests that *Verwindung* need not indicate an end to modernity. Indeed, we might need to rethink what we mean by modernity. Not all notions of modernity need be teleological. See, for instance, Hans Blumenberg, *The Legitimacy of the Modern Age*, trans. Robert Wallace (Cambridge: MIT Press, 1983). According to my reading Howells's realism is intricately linked to a modern sense of temporality as described by both Blumenberg and Koselleck. See n. 6 on p. 498. This modern sense of temporality should not be confused with literary "modernism."

3. Tanselle, 482–3.

only fearfully expansive but also fatally expensive. Moral responsibilities here have a way of becoming financial liabilities." Though this "domino theory of moral responsibility" proves frightening, Dimock argues that Howells's problematic suggests a remedy. "If moral responsibilities tend to get out of hand by mutating into financial liabilities, then the solution *must* work in the opposite direction, which is to say, it *must* try to rectify the moral by way of the economic" (my emphasis). She finds this solution in the familiar appeal to the economy of pain," an economy that not only helps us to "cope with our own suffering," but also "with the suffering of others: cope with it, in the sense of acceding to it, accounting for it, and learning to see it, as Howells says in its 'true proportion.'"[4]

Dimock, then, provides us with a subtle version of the police academy version of realism. Howells's economy of pain is so embracing that it even contains the tenuous or the contingent, thus helping readers account for suffering. But as powerful as her reading is, Dimock miscalculates the proportion between the third plot and the rest of the story. To be sure, Silas tries to isolate it. He even records his payments in a separate account book. Nonetheless, Zerrilla's story does not present us with actions almost "completely superfluous" that can eventually be accounted for by an economy of pain. Instead, it presents us with vitally connected actions that, nonetheless, painfully force us to face our inability fully to account for them. For instance, Zerrilla does more than "provoke Mrs. Lapham into a fit of unfounded jealousy"; her story brings aspects of the two main plots into direct conflict with one another.[5] Those conflicts undermine efforts neatly to balance the business and love plots.

As a working wife Zerrilla occupies a space that stretches the period's belief in contract to its conceptual limits by threatening the delicate balance that laissez-faire thinkers had maintained between the business and domestic economies. On the one hand, the business realm depended upon honoring the right of individuals to contract out their labor for pay. On the other, the domestic realm depended upon a contract in which a woman forfeited her right to enter into business contracts because her husband became her legal representative. As more and more women entered the work force, legal thinkers were forced to face the problem of who owned her earnings. The solution did not lend itself to simple balancing.[6]

* * *

4. Dimock, 110, 111, 111, 111, 119.
5. Dimock, 109.
6. Amy Stanley, "Conjugal Bonds and Wage Labor: Rights of Contract in the Age of Emancipation," *The Journal of American History* 75 (1988), 471–500.

The main love plot is special because it involves no breaking of contractual promises. If Tom and Penelope's pursuit of their love violated vows made to Irene in courtship or marriage, Sewell could not so easily have declared that "none is to blame" (241 [183]). Indeed, by placing Zerrilla in a situation in which she can assert her rights only by breaking the vows of marriage, Howells calls into question the logic of Sewell's economy of pain. By suggesting that human conditions sometimes necessitate a renegotiation of even the "sacred bond" (49 [38]) of an institution partaking of "divinity" (49 [38]), the issue of divorce even questions the distinction that Basil March will make between the chance worlds of God and humankind. The third plot dramatizes the difficulty of maintaining even that distinction.

Displaying a generosity that he refuses to share with Rogers, who, his wife claims, also "saved [him]" (47 [37]), Silas tries to pay back what he considers to be an infinite debt to Jim Millon by economically supporting his wife and daughter. Infinite as it might be, that debt has little to do with blame. Just as Tom is not responsible for the distribution of his affections, so Silas is not responsible for Jim's fate, which belongs to the chance world of life and death. Silas's debt is linked to that world.

Silas tells Jim's story at the dinner party to illustrate Corey's remark that an individual may go into war "simply and purely for his country's sake, not knowing whether, if he laid down his life, he should ever find it again, or whether, if he took it up hereafter, he should take it up in heaven or hell" (202 [155]). Such sacrifice, Sewell admits, helps us "to imagine what God must be" (202 [155]). Recalling the ultimate sacrifice, Jim's death calls attention to humanity's infinite debt to Christ, whose story dramatizes how the world of God, while different from that of humankind, intersects with it. As a result, Jim's story confirms what Sewell in *The Minister's Charge* calls the doctrine of Complicity. Linked to a longstanding belief in "the old Christ-humanity," Complicity means that "no one for good or for evil, for sorrow or joy, for sickness or health, stood apart from his fellows, but each was bound by the ties that centered in the hand of God."[7] But if Jim's story dramatizes human beings' infinite responsibility, his daughter's dramatizes the impossibility of paying back an infinite debt such as the one owed to Christ or Jim.

As the alcoholism of Zerrilla's mother and husband becomes a bottomless hole, absorbing all the money that Silas can give, Silas is forced to realize, contrary to Dimock's argument, that he can no more successfully translate his moral debts into economic ones than

7. William Dean Howells, *The Minister's Charge; or The Apprenticeship of Lemuel Barker* (Bloomington: Indiana U. P., 1978; rpt. 1886), p. 341.

he can successfully buy status in Boston society. The economic factors influence these other realms and vice versa, but they are not equivalent. Furthermore, Silas must learn that as a mere human being he cannot pay back all of his moral debts. To live in a historical world once inhabited by Christ may mean that people live with an infinite debt, but when Silas acts to cut off support to Zerrilla's husband, he dramatizes a paradox: to be a responsible human agent one must draw limits to one's responsibility. Not to do so is to pretend to be a divine rather than a human agent. Such pretense is not, according to Howells, very responsible.[8]

In order to function every society constructs narratives that establish what it considers responsible limits to responsibility. As we have seen, some do so by assigning people clearly defined sets of duties and obligations based on status, while others limit obligations to terms negotiated by contracting parties. When Howells insists that people have an infinite debt that can never be fulfilled, he draws attention to the contingency by which such limits are drawn. By presenting us with situations in which people must act in order to be responsible, he confronts us with the necessity of drawing them. By imagining novel situations that cannot be accounted for by agreed-upon limits, he forces us to reconsider and perhaps redefine them, just as the "flawed" third plot of his novel does.

Any consideration of how the formal structure of Howells's fiction relates to questions of justice needs to take into account his concern with such novel situations; that is, situations that cannot be accounted for by existing formal structures or a Hegelian dialectic. Critics who believe that Howells's realism is simply an effort to copy life as it is assume that Howells endorses Corey's claim that "You architects and musicians are the true and only artistic creators. All the rest of us, sculptors, painters, novelists, and tailors, deal with forms that we have before us; we try to imitate, we try to represent. But you two sorts of artists create form (192 [147])."[9] The dramatic context in which Corey makes his remark suggests, however, that Howells's practice is more complicated. A novelist might work with given forms, but he still needs to place them in relation so as to create "novel" forms. This creative act is crucial for the novelist's fulfillment of his moral responsibility, because by forcing us to revise fixed notions about the nature of what is real it contributes to what Everett

8. Silas's decision to cut off support for Zerrilla's husband might seem to be dictated by the logic of an economy of pain since once again two benefit while one is left out. But pain has little to do with Silas's decision. Zerrilla's mother will continue to suffer because of her alcoholism as much as Zerrilla's husband. Silas draws the limit in this case in terms of immediate blood relation to Jim.

9. A recent critic whose account of realism suffers from granting it a naïve attempt to imitate life is Michael Davitt Bell, *The Problem of American Realism* (Chicago: U. of Chicago P., 1993).

Carter calls, Howells's "criticism of unexamined 'fixed principles'" and "closed systems of morality."[1]

The assessment of responsibility for Howells is a formal one, and his responsibility as a novelist is the formal one of bringing different spheres of action into proportionate relation. But for a novelist to fulfill that responsibility in a temporal world subject to chance, he cannot rest content with finding a form that "captures" reality either through spatial images or a dialectical logic. Instead, starting with existing forms, he must continually work to rearrange and reorder them. If in constructing a form that brings actions into proportionate relation Howells helps us to see how one should act in a given situation, he also knows that the "logic" growing out of that situation is not self-contained. Instead, a responsible action in one situation helps to generate new situations that unbalance whatever tentative balance might have been achieved. Every formal solution, in other words, requires endless revisions, which in Howells's case leads to the Balzacian strategy of interweaving various works, an interweaving necessitated by Howells's need both to supplement his balancing efforts in one work with new situations in another and to remind us that, as "novel" as those situations are, they should not be seen in isolation from related ones. Thus, *The Rise of Silas Lapham* is followed by *The Minister's Charge*, peopled with characters from the previous work who are confronted by another triangular love affair, but one that cannot be solved by Sewells's "economy of pain." Actions in one situation help to generate actions in another, but precisely because the new situation is a novel one, the solution applied to the previous one cannot be simply translated to the other without some form of revision.

When Howells's fictional strategies are successful, the requirement for continual revision is transferred to readers, who are confronted with a work that forces them to be prepared to revise their existing notions about virtuous action.[2] One way in which Howells forces readers to take the responsibility to judge responsible action is through a self-conscious manipulation of point of view that undermines any illusion of a transcendental perspective that he might have created. If Flaubert begins *Madame Bovary* with a first-person narrator who shortly gives way to the Godlike perspective of third-person omniscience, Howells begins with third-person narrative only to introduce a first-person narrator late in his novel. That narrator's first comment is about the possible fallibility of Tom Corey's "generosity of instinct" (293 [221]). Indeed, in his few intrusions Howells's narrator calls attention to his inability to penetrate the interior of characters in

1. Everett Carter, *Howells and the Age of Realism* (Philadelphia: Lippincott, 1954), p. 154.
2. Winfried Fluck, *Inszenierte Wirklichkeit: Der Amerikanische Realismus, 1865–1900* (Munich: Wilhelm Fink Verlag, 1992).

order to report their feelings and intentions (359, 360, 362 [271, 272, 273]). Thus, readers are forced to make judgments about them based on the results of actions, not motives. Rather than link an omniscient perspective to God, Howells speaks of a "wicked omniscience in Rogers" (321 [243]), a character whose first name of Milton recalls *Paradise Lost* and Satan's attempt to usurp God's role. Appropriately, the last sentence in which the narrator speaks in the first person begins, "I do not know . . ." (362 [273]). In undermining his narrative omniscience, Howells invites readers to enter a contingent world of chance, in which determination of responsibility is risky business because it can never be made with certainty.[3]

Early critics recognized the dangers of entering such a world, but refused to accept its challenges and instead complained that Howells's realism offered no models for virtuous action. Michaels offers a new historicist twist to their argument. According to him, Howells faults sentimental writers, not only because they offer bad models, but, more importantly, because they offer any models at all. "Realism, defined by its fidelity to things as they are, can never in principle serve as a model, good or bad, since only when art is *not* like life can life attempt to be like art. The true scandal of sentimentality is thus its inversion of the proper relation of life to art, an inversion made possible only by the introduction of a discrepancy between the two terms."[4]

Michaels's argument follows from his assumption that Howells's realism is based on a balanced economy of equivalents. "Realism," he claims, "is Howells's literary equivalent of the Lapham's domestic economy and of the Reverend Sewell's 'economy of pain.'" There is, however, a contradiction within Michaels's argument. For him Howells's realism is a "fundamentally agrarian, anticapitalist vision of the world" because it endorses the firmly rooted, natural values from which Silas has strayed during his financial rise and to which he returns at the end of the novel. But, if Howells endorses such values, they clearly become models for how to act. Indeed, Michaels associates Howells with the "genteel/progressive view" that "important works of art" are capable of "transcending or opposing the market"

3. Joel Porte sees Howells's "wobbling point of view . . . caused presumably by Howells' own social anxieties" as "one of his great formal weaknesses as a novelist," "Manners, Morals, and Mince Pie: Howells's America Revisited," *Prospects* 10 (1987), 447. I see his use of point of view as calculated to create effects on his readers that cannot be accounted for totally by irony as Arlene Young attempts to do in "The Triumph of Irony in *The Rise of Silas Lapham*," *Studies in American Fiction* 20 (1992), 45–55. Instead, as Fluck brilliantly argues, such techniques helped the realists transform the ideal role of the literary text from that of a guardian figure to one of a conversational partner. Janet Holmgren McKay details Howells's use of point of view in relation to James and Twain in *Narration and Discourse in American Realistic Fiction* (Philadelphia: U. of Pennsylvania P., 1982).
4. Michaels, p. 36.

precisely because he supposedly partakes of such moralism.[5] Dimock's description of how Howells's attempt to dispense poetic justice establishes a formal equivalent with the reigning logic of the market expands this aspect of Michaels's argument, for if such an equivalence exists Howells's fiction cannot be said to transcend or oppose the capitalist culture that produced it.

The flaw in such new historicist readings is their acceptance of both the New Critics's and Lukacs's view that realism is a formally balanced organicism. On the contrary, Howells presents us with a temporal world in which the business of life is not even equivalent to itself because it is always subject to revision. In such a world there is inevitably a discrepancy (not equivalency) between life and art. Even so, not all discrepancies are the same. Howells's problem with sentimental fiction is not that it presents us with a discrepancy between life and art and thus offers itself as a model. All fiction, because it will never be completely equivalent to life, has the capacity to be used as a model. What is at stake is the nature of the discrepancy that it presents between itself and life and thus the type of model that it offers. Assuming the existence of transcendental values outside the contingent world of time in which human beings live, sentimental fiction offers models of behavior based on fixed principles of morality. In contrast, Howells's realism serves pragmatically as equipment for living precisely because it forces readers to face the moral complexity of living in a world without fixed or transcendent principles.

The discrepancy between life and art dramatized by Howells's realism is not between a fallen world of history and a transcendental world of permanent values. It instead results from what Reinhart Koselleck calls an asymmetry between our space of experience and our horizon of expectations. This asymmetry, according to Koselleck, is constitutive of a modern sense of temporality, one that is future-oriented because the future may always bring about events that present or past experience cannot account for.[6] In such a world people are continually challenged to reconstruct and reorder social arrangements and to reconsider the nature of virtuous action.

At the end of his novel Howells does not return us nostalgically to a precapitalist agrarian economy founded on a set of natural values. Nor in his attempt to dispense poetic justice has he created a system of symbolic equivalents that balances aesthetic form and existing social structures. Instead, he presents us with a world that looks forward to new forms of social and economic organization, as Silas's business has been absorbed by a newly formed corporation. This

5. Michaels, pp. 41, 41, 14 n. 16.
6. Reinhart Koselleck, *Futures Past*, trans. Keith Tribe (Cambridge: MIT Press, 1985).

corporation is not, as Pease mistakenly argues, "Lapham and Son, the business corporation that tacitly resulted from Penelope's marriage to Tom Corey." It is not, "structured like Lapham's ideal for the family, combining the commercial interests of a growing enterprise with the trustworthy self-reliance of its founder."[7] Instead, starting as a family enterprise by brothers from West Virginia, it becomes, as we learn in the sequel, a publicly-traded corporation on Wall Street, one intent on opening new markets in an expanding global economy. The social and moral consequences of an economy dominated by such corporate, rather than individually-owned, businesses are unclear at the end of the book.

Similarly, the status of Silas's past behavior remains unresolved. For many critics Silas's moral rise begins when he balances his earlier ruthless treatment of Rogers with his seemingly moral refusal late in the book to unload worthless stock on British businessmen. But Silas, at least, does not share this reading. On the one hand, he refuses to admit to any wrong-doing in his early affairs with Rogers. On the other, he explains the latter act to Sewell with, "Seems sometimes as if it was a hole opened for me, and I crept out" (365 [275]).[8]

Indeed, in a number of ways Silas's early and late actions are similar. Both work against Rogers's interests. Far from balancing Silas's accounts with Rogers, as his wife with her fixed moral sense desires, the second adds to the unbalance. In addition, in both Silas takes advantage of chance. Forcing Rogers out of business, Silas takes advantage of a "business chance," whereas in not selling worthless stock Silas simply takes advantage of a chance presented to him. One action may seem moral opportunism and the other immoral; nonetheless, as the image of the hole evoked in Silas's response to Sewell suggests, to enter Howells's fictional world is to be born into a world in which there is no solid ground to measure with certainty why one action has more moral standing than another. Did Jim Millon receive a bullet aimed at Silas because he happened to be standing where he was, or did he self-consciously position himself to save his friend? Did Silas not sell worthless stock back to Rogers because he stood "firm for right and justice" (332 [251]) or because by chance the railroad's offer for the mills came in the next morning's mail?[9]

In a static world of status, in which responsibilities and duties are determined by one's standing in society, the morality of various

7. Pease, p. 21.
8. See John Seeyle, "The Hole in Howells/The Lapse in *Silas Lapham*," in *New Essays*, pp. 47–65.
9. Fritz Oehlschager, "An Ethic of Responsibility in *The Rise of Silas Lapham*," *American Literary Realism, 1870–1910* 23 (1991), 20–34, and Kermit Vanderbilt, "Introduction," *The Rise of Silas Lapham* (New York: Penguin, 1986), pp. vii–xxviii. Vanderbilt is especially well-tuned to the complications that Howells presents to anyone seeking certain moral judgments of his characters.

actions is relatively clear. In a world of contract judgments of morality are instead continually open to negotiations and exchange. Dimock, unlike Michaels, recognizes the importance of exchange in Howells's "moral economy." But the exchanges that he presents are not of the type that she describes. The change in Silas's personality that marks his moral rise, she argues, needs to be seen as an exchange, the exchange of one set of personality traits for another. But, as we have seen, exchanges in Howells's world are not so clear-cut. There is always something left over, something unaccounted for. One reason that it is so hard to come up with balanced exchanges is that in Howells's world status has not been completely replaced by contract. Instead, status persists in both the domestic economy and the social world of Boston and continues to influence exchanges in an economic realm that can never be quite identical with itself. Unbalanced exchanges, in turn, unsettle attempts to construct simple linear narratives of progress, whether they be Maine's about the movement from status to contract or ones of individual moral development that Dimock attributes to Howells.

The point is not that Howells rules out possibilities of moral development. On the contrary, in his world one can develop as a moral character only by accepting the risks of acting and judging in a world without clear-cut moral guidelines. But those actions and judgments are risky precisely because, on the one hand, they generate future actions and judgments that no existing set of principles can account for, and, on the other, they leave something behind that no dialectical process of history can translate into the future. Howells's realism busies itself with the moral dilemmas faced by people living in a world in which necessarily future-oriented actions leave behind something that persists to raise questions about the direction the future has taken.

GEORDIE HAMILTON

[Howells's Narrator and Narrative Polyphony]†

Americanist literary scholars have long considered W. D. Howells the central theorist and practitioner of American realism. The most frequently cited text from this late nineteenth-century genre is probably Howells' novel *The Rise of Silas Lapham*. Well into the twentieth century, American realism was frequently understood as a

† From *American Literary Realism* 42.1 (Fall 2009): 13–14, 26–30, 33–35. Copyright © 2009 by the Board of Trustees of the University of Illinois. Reprinted by permission of the publisher, U of Illinois P. Page references in brackets refer to this Norton Critical Edition.

politically progressive genre that sought to mimetically represent all levels of society and all manner of social issues. American realism was contrasted with the genre of romance, which was said to avoid depicting society as it was, in favor of depicting society as authors (and specific audiences) believed society should be.[1]

However, many Americanist scholars of the late-twentieth century have come to understand American realism quite differently. Among these scholars, Amy Kaplan influentially argues in *The Social Construction of American Realism* that "realism has turned into a conservative force whose very act of exposure reveals its complicity with the structures of power." As part of the voluminous evidence used to support this central claim, Kaplan cites the end of *Silas Lapham*. Kaplan notes that the final pages render Silas—the novel's central and working-class character—"more ungrammatical and inarticulate than ever." Kaplan refers here to some of the points of character—poor grammar and diction—that mark Silas' class position: markers that the narrator of *Silas Lapham* repeatedly requires the reader to notice. Kaplan goes on to claim that the narrative "returns [Silas] to his origins in a kind of wish-fulfillment to undo his entire life story."[2] In the course of the novel Silas rises from impoverished rural obscurity to urban fame and wealth and comes close to attaining higher social position. By the end of the novel Silas sinks back into relative poverty and returns to his farm. Kaplan is thinking of Howells when she describes Silas' financial and social decline in terms of "wish fulfillment," and Kaplan is theorizing that the whole genre of American realism, while consciously intended to be politically progressive, is in fact a reactionary literature. Kaplan's reading suggests that the upper-class-sympathetic Howells constructed not only a single novel, but an entire literary movement untrue to its conscious political aims.

Though Kaplan published her book twenty years ago, we still have much to learn from her arguments and those of similarly-minded scholars about the place of American realism in literary history. However, this paper adopts an opposing thesis: *Silas Lapham* is an artfully designed narrative that does not hold a significant upper-class bias. Howells' novel is—as the existing work of many scholars already suggests—the rhetorical communication of a moral message. This message is contained in the actions of a working-class hero, Silas, whom Howells directs the authorial audience to admire. Most important to my argument about the egalitarian message of *Silas Lapham* is the explanation of *how* Howells constructs his narrative

1. See Daniel H. Borus, *Writing Realism: Howells, James, and Norris in the Mass Market* (Chapel Hill: Univ. of North Carolina Press, 1989), pp. 12–26.
2. Amy Kaplan, *The Social Construction of American Realism* (Chicago: Univ. of Chicago Press, 1988), pp. 1, 42.

progression. *Silas Lapham,* as several scholars already note, is a polyphony of character voices, none of whom serves as a direct representative for the author.[3] Furthermore, I argue that the usually reliable narrator is deliberately designed to act as part of the character polyphony: we make a mistake if we try to read the narrator as a constantly reliable representative of Howells. * * *

* * *

In *Writing Realism,* Daniel Borus tells us that American realist authors like the flesh-and-blood Howells wanted to construct a "common culture" in which all classes could participate. The realist culture of literature was intended to speak to and for all Americans, and in doing this the realist novel was intended to unify the nation. To do this, the realists sought to create a distinct kind of narrator. The ideal realist narrator does not intervene to pause and comment upon the action. Instead, the realist narrator is "a removed and unacknowledged intelligence" that controls the course of narrative events. Borus calls the omniscient, nonintrusive and neutral narrator the "crucial litmus test" of realist fiction. However, Borus also admits that even the most classic American realist texts spend almost as much time violating as abiding by this theory of narration.[4]

As I am sure Borus would happily concede, the narrator of *Silas Lapham* frequently acts as an exception to the realist rules of narration. Therefore, one of three conclusions must follow: 1) *Silas Lapham* is not realist fiction; 2) Howells is out of control; or 3) Howells is in control and the formal rules of realist narration need modification. Neither Borus nor any other scholar of American realism is likely to admit the first conclusion. *Silas Lapham* will probably remain a classic text of American realism, and against the second conclusion we have the judgment of more than one critic. Manierre claims that Howells is highly conscious of the benefits to be had from proper control of narrative perspective, while Barton characterizes *Silas Lapham's* "intrusive" narrator as a classic element of Howellsian realism.[5] I submit that the third conclusion is correct. Howells' narrator *is* a crucial part of Howells' realist technique and performs a specific role in creating a text that seeks to speak for and even create a democratically-inclined reading audience, while

3. For a definition of "polyphony," see *Routledge Encyclopedia of Narrative Theory,* ed. David Herman, Manfred Jahn, and Marie-Laure Ryan (London and New York: Routledge, 2005), pp. 443–44.
4. Borus, pp. 4, 23, 96, 97, 17.
5. [William] Manierre ["*The Rise of Silas Lapham*: Retrospective Discussion as Dramatic Technique," *College English* XXIII (Feb. 1962)], p. 357; [John Cyril] Barton, ["Howells's Rhetoric of Realism: The Economy of Pain(t) and Social Complicity in *The Rise of Silas Lapham* and *The Minister's Charge,*" *Studies in American Fiction* 29 (Autumn 2001)], pp. 170–71.

at the same time acknowledging the upper-class biases present in much of Howells' actual nineteenth-century reading public.

Young notes that as Silas is ethically tested and proved during his financial decline, the narrator becomes gentler with Silas, drastically reducing the number of occasions in which the narrator makes upper-class-biased remarks on Silas' lower-class characteristics.[6] Young's comment helps us to notice that the narrator's snarky attacks on the Laphams are mostly frontloaded into the first half or two-thirds of the narrative. Howells' goal, as we saw in the first section, is to introduce the reader into a storyworld with a clear protagonist but without a clear moral hero. This is one reason why the narrator occasionally expresses negative judgments about Silas and Persis: judgments that are clearly tinged with a class-bias favorable to the Coreys, but judgments that, as we have seen, are not necessarily shared by Howells. By my reading, the occasional distance between the narrator and Howells is a deliberate tactic. The narrator is a tool that Howells uses to appeal to the upper-class cultural standards of his actual nineteenth-century audience, subtly leading the actual audience to believe that the narrator guiding them through the storyworld of *Silas Lapham* is one of their own. If the narrator shares many of the actual audience's cherished biases, then the effect is for the actual audience to, perhaps unconsciously, place an increased amount of faith in the narrator's judgments. Silas—the narrator, narratee and actual audience conclude in the beginning and middle of the narrative—is something of a clown. Yet he is also admirable, and the actual audience sees that he is admirable even when viewed through the lens of their own class prejudice.

As the narrative progresses and Howells feels that the narrator has captured the trust of the actual audience, the narrator begins to abandon his original class biases. If one were to look for a turning point in the narrator's class-biased address to the narratee, one could do worse than to point to an incident that occurs in chapter 18. In this chapter Silas and Persis go for a drive: both want to talk about family problems. Silas wants to talk about his financial difficulties, while Persis wants to discuss the problem of both their daughters being in love with the same man. Persis prefers to drive quietly so they can speak without distraction, but Silas says, "When I can't drive this mare and talk too, I'll sell out altogether" [177]. This line is significant, because a few pages later Silas crashes the buggy [180]. From this chapter forward, Silas does in fact move towards selling out altogether, though his final bankruptcy does not occur until chapter 27. Along the way, Silas forgets his social

6. [Arlene] Young, ["The Triumph of Irony in *The Rise of Silas Lapham*," *Studies in American Fiction* 20 (Spring 1992)], p. 53.

ambition and focuses his attention on the dual goals of saving his financial situation using only ethical business practice and providing for the emotional well-being of his daughters. Silas becomes an increasingly admirable character at the same time that the narrator drops his class biases. The actual audience—habituated by the first half of the narrative to trust the narrator's judgments—is perhaps also persuaded to consider Silas' increasingly obvious merits from a more egalitarian point of view.

In order to achieve this final effect, Howells is careful to appeal to the actual audience's class biases before chapter 18. Howells deliberately designs a narrator who occasionally addresses a narratee with clear upper-class bias. In one instance at the opening of chapter 10, second-person pronouns show us the class position of the narratee:

> It was June, almost July, when Corey took up his life in Boston again, where the summer slips away so easily. If you go out of town early, it seems a very long summer when you come back in October; but if you stay, it passes swiftly, and, seen foreshortened in its flight, seems scarcely a month's length. [96]

In the storyworld of *Silas Lapham,* as in actual nineteenth-century Boston, only the well-to-do are able to afford to leave town for the summer months. The narrator's "you" clearly marks the narratee as a member of the upper class. Here, I would argue, the flesh-and-blood Howells is attempting to remind his presumed flesh-and-blood readers of their privileged class position and, consequently, of their allegiance to the standards of social judgment shared in common with the upper-class Coreys, not the working-class-origin Laphams. Likewise, at the opening of chapter 14 the narrator appeals to a narratee whose sympathies run towards the upper class:

> The Coreys were one of the few old families who lingered in Bellingham place, the handsome, quiet old street which the sympathetic observer must grieve to see abandoned to boarding-houses. The dwellings are stately and tall, and the whole place wears an air of aristocratic seclusion, which Mrs. Corey's father might well have thought assured when he left her his house there at his death. . . . It has a wooden portico, with slender fluted columns . . . nothing could be simpler, and nothing could be better. . . . the simple adequacy of the architectural intention had been respected, and the place looked bare to the eyes of the Laphams as they entered. [142–43]

The narratee is the "sympathetic observer," and the narratee is sympathetic both to the "aristocratic seclusion" and aesthetic perfection of the Corey home: an aesthetic perfection to which the Laphams are conspicuously blind. Again, I would argue that the flesh-and-blood Howells is attempting to remind the actual audience of their class allegiance to the Coreys. Howells' occasional manipulation of the narrator/narratee relationship prior to chapter 18 is a rhetorical device by which he seeks to temporarily reduce the actual audience's sympathy for the Laphams while simultaneously increasing their confidence in the judgments of the narrator.

As the instability of Silas' financial difficulties moves towards resolution, Howells puts Silas through the moral tests from which he will emerge as a hero—albeit a hero that Howells tries to cut down to what he believes are limited, human proportions. After chapter 18 the narrator seems to lose most of his bias in favor of the upper-class. If anything, the narratee seems to have changed from an aristocrat into a democrat. When Persis and Silas consult with Sewell, the narrator reminds the narratee that "each one of us must suffer long to himself before he can learn that he is but one in a great community of wretchedness which has been pitilessly repeating itself from the foundation of the world" [182]. Not much seems to remain of the narratee's prior class bias: now the narratee is reminded only of their place in an undifferentiated mass of humanity. The narratee is asked to identify with Persis as she prepares to leave Boston in the wake of Silas' bankruptcy: "This thing and that is embittered to us, so that we may be willing to relinquish it; the world, life itself, is embittered to most of us, so that we are glad to have done with them at last; and this home was haunted with such memories to each of those who abandoned it that to go was less exile than escape" [265]. Again, the narrator appeals to a narratee in terms of a common human experience of suffering rather than to an elite experience of privilege.

Howells no longer seeks to appeal as strongly to the class biases of the actual audience as we approach the end of the narrative. Previous details that the once upper-class-biased narrator used against the Laphams now turn into information damaging to the Coreys. For example, we have already seen that the narrator makes negative judgments of the aesthetic value of decoration of the Laphams' original Boston home [164]. The narrator particularly turns up his nose at some statuary in the Laphams' drawing-room: "an Italian conception of Lincoln Freeing the Slaves." But by chapter 27 we notice that the narrator no longer attacks the aesthetics of this statuary. Free indirect discourse tells the reader that Penelope understands Bromfield and Anna Corey to perceive the statuary as hopelessly gauche, but the narrator has conspicuously detached himself from sharing the Coreys' class-tinged aesthetic judgment [262]. Moreover, chapter 26 concludes with the narrator remarking that Bromfield Corey eats an orange in the "Neapolitan" manner [261].

Here Howells reminds us that Bromfield's sense of aesthetics was primarily cultivated in Italy, the very country that has produced the statuary Bromfield finds so abhorrent. Bromfield does not catch the irony implicit in his snobbery, but that irony has been carefully placed by Howells. From using the narrator to make overt judgments damaging to the Laphams, Howells has now switched to using the narrator to make covert judgments against the Coreys.

Howells concludes the narrative addressing a narratee who occupies an indeterminate social position. In the last passage in which the second-person is used, the narrator states, "it is certain that our manners and customs go for more in life than our qualities. The price that we pay for civilization is the fine yet impassable differentiation of these. Perhaps we pay too much; but it will not be possible to persuade those who have the difference in their favor that this is so. They may be right" [272]. The passage begins by assuming a narratee who is receptive to the idea that civilization depends on counting "manners and customs" as more important than a person's "qualities." If the narratee agrees that, if this is the case, we "pay too much" for civilization, then this judgment is democratic in nature. But the narrator's qualifying "perhaps" is vital to our sense of the narratee, who consequently does not know for certain whether or not we *do* pay too high a price for civilization. The narrator refuses to answer the question for certain, implying that there is something to be said for the aristocrats, who "may be right" that civilization is after all worth the price of valuing a person's manners over their moral worth. This seemingly impartial ending is appropriate to Howells' realist project, which attempts to speak to and for the entire nation. But the authorial audience recalls the relatively democratically-biased narratee present in the second half of *Silas Lapham* and understands that Howells has directed the majority of our sympathy towards the working-class Silas and Persis. Indeed, the entire trend of the narrative is a subtle movement away from the upper-class biases of Howells' actual audience. By this reading, *Silas Lapham*'s narrator spends the first half of the novel capturing the trust of the actual audience, in part by playing on their class prejudices. In the second half of the novel, Howells uses the narrator to subtly modify the actual audience's class perspective, bringing the narratee and actual audience into alignment with the authorial audience's more democratic values.

* * *

HILDEGARD HOELLER

From Capitalism, Fiction, and the Inevitable, (Im)Possible, Maddening Importance of the Gift†

> *The thing as given thing, the given of the gift arrives, if it arrives, only in narrative.*
>
> —Jacques Derrida, *Given Time* (41)

> *At present business is the only human solidarity; we are all bound together with that chain, whatever interests, tastes, and principles separate us.* —William Dean Howells, "The Man of Letters as a Man of Business" (4)

When the subject is the relation between capitalism and American literature, few novels come more readily to mind than William Dean Howells's 1885 *The Rise of Silas Lapham.* "Published at the height of America's industrial expansion," writes Wayne Westbrook in a typical assessment, it "pictures an era and personifies a type. The Era is the Gilded Age. The type is the American businessman" (59). But for a novel self-consciously focused on business, *The Rise of Silas Lapham* is surprisingly interested in the gift. Counter to Howells's famous later assertion that "[a]t present business is the only human solidarity," the gift turns out to be the sole "chain" uniting Howells's characters against whatever interests, tastes, and principles separate them. Hidden in plain sight, the main plot of the novel delineates the awkward yet ultimately binding relations between the Brahmin Coreys and the rising Lapham family, which come about not because the Laphams "buy their way into society" (Michaels 40) but because they give the Coreys a gift so true and so large that it must be recognized and reciprocated. When the women of both families happen to be staying at a Canadian resort, Mrs. Lapham spontaneously comes to Mrs. Corey's rescue and, as a French doctor later makes uncomfortably explicit, saves Mrs. Corey's life. "A certain intimacy inevitably followed," Howells writes, as the Coreys are "gratefully recognizant" of the gift and their "singular obligation" to the Laphams (24–25 [20]). This gift has received no critical attention[1] even though it engenders the main plot of the novel as the initial "helplessly contracted" (172 [131]) obligation

† From *PMLA* 127.1 (January 2012): 131–36. Reprinted by permission of copyright owner, the Modern Language Association of America. Page references in brackets are to this Norton Critical Edition.

1. A recent, typical summary of the novel is entirely based on its business plot and does not mention the two parallel gift plots between the Laphams and the Coreys and the Laphams and the Deweys (Goodman and Dawson 258).

leads to further contact between the families, from dinner to business dealings to marriage. None of these consequences are comfortable; indeed, each of them is excruciating and poses one of the text's central questions: how does one reciprocate such an impossibly large gift when one shares no interests or tastes with the people to whom one is now bound by gratitude and debt? Mrs. Lapham's gift to Mrs. Corey not only transforms the Coreys' life forever (in a way, they pay with their son for the mother's life), but it also transforms Howells's novel from a novel about business to a narrative about gifts. This is far from incidental. Howells doubles the Corey-Lapham plot as Silas Lapham, in turn, believes that he owes his life to Jim Millon, who, during the Civil War, took a bullet for Lapham and died. The Laphams equally struggle with their own uncomfortable obligation to the working-class Deweys. While neither the Coreys nor the Laphams can figure out how to respond to impossibly large gifts given to them by people with whom they share nothing else, they do know instinctively that they must do so and reciprocate in one way or another. Howells's novel tells the story of these gifts and their confusing, maddening, and binding obligations. Indeed, Howells's supposed business novel can only spin itself out on these gifts, given and recognized as such.[2]

The novel's strangely dangling first chapter proves that point. Depicting an encounter between Silas Lapham and the journalist Bartley Hubbard in Lapham's office, it seems a more appropriate beginning for a novel about business than does Mrs. Lapham's saving Mrs. Corey's life in the Canadian wilderness, but the relations between the two men fail to launch a narrative because of unrecognized, rejected gifts. The encounter is odd from the start since Howells's man of letters turns out to be a thorough man of business,[3] there only to make a sellable story out of Lapham's life, while the businessman Lapham thinks almost exclusively in terms of gifts—about his business, his family, and his appointment with Hubbard. Ignoring Hubbard's business-mindedness,[4] Lapham again and again tries to turn the encounter into a personal affair, not only by "turning himself

2. This essay is merely suggestive. For a fuller treatment of the gift in narratives and in relation to capitalism and for readings of the entire novel and Howells's essays "The Man of Letters as a Man of Business" and "Tribulations of a Cheerful Giver," as well as texts by Hannah Foster, Lydia Maria Child, Susan Warner, Herman Melville, William Wells Brown, and Frank Norris, see my forthcoming book *From Gift to Commodity: Capitalism and the Spirit of the Gift in Nineteenth-Century American Fiction* (U of New England P, 2012). For a similar economic reading, see also my essay on Zora Neale Hurston's short story "The Gilded Six-Bits."
3. An issue over which Howells struggles considerably in his essay about the man of letters as a man of business.
4. Moreover, Hubbard fakes personal interest in the service of business. He seduces Lapham to some degree, knowing that Lapham's story can be elicited only through this personal touch.

inside out" (21 [18]) but also by sending the journalist later a gift of his most cherished paint. Hubbard's wife is moved to tears by the "goodness" of Lapham's gift, but Hubbard only sneers at the "old fool" (22–23 [19]) and, consequently, exits the novel.[5] No relations ensue. And so Howells starts his novel again, this time with Mrs. Lapham's gift to Mrs. Corey, and, the gift being recognized this time, a narrative unfolds. Howells offers us two opening chapters: one in which gifts are rejected in the light of a pure business logic and another in which they are recognized and lead to obligations and ultimately a strained solidarity. The first story, the business story, dies a sudden death; the next story, the gift story, becomes Howells's novel.

The Rise of Silas Lapham illustrates that capitalism has a hard time telling stories about itself and that any consideration of capitalism and literature should relate them to the gift. Narratives cannot exist without gift giving, whether they are about capitalism or not. But we rarely look at texts about capitalism through theorizations of the gift perhaps because our Marxist training has obscured our vision in this regard.[6] It is remarkable, for example, how little notice the central gift plots in Howells's novel have attracted, but it is not in the least exceptional. Gifts abound in American fiction and especially American fiction about capitalism, yet they are rarely explored. Approaching texts about capitalism through gift theory allows us to understand the inevitable, (im)possible—to use Derrida's term—even maddening role gifts play in these narratives; it helps us see that, on the one hand, gifts are the very vehicles that allow writers to tell stories about capitalism while, on the other, they also bring those narratives to the brink of reason and reveal their aporias.

When Jacques Derrida notes that "the thing as given thing, the given of the gift arrives, if it arrives, only in narrative," he acknowledges the intricate relation between gifts and narratives. In his own work on the gift, he is responding to Marcel Mauss's seminal *Essai sur le don* (1924), in which Mauss insists that gifts—far from being pure—are part of an economy that depends on the obligations to give, receive, and repay (37–41). In Mary Douglas's words, Mauss insists that "there should not be any free gifts. . . . A free gift that does nothing to enhance solidarity is a contradiction" (vii). Gifts bind people together by being recognized and then by being reciprocated in time. The ensuing "solidarity"—such as the relations between the Laphams and the Coreys—creates narratives. But while Mauss can

5. Herman Melville repeated that pattern obsessively in his novel *The Confidence-Man*, having the narrative abort itself in each chapter over the (im)possibility of the gift.
6. Theoretical approaches to literature through the gift tend to focus on medieval and Renaissance texts, and they are entirely absent from discussions of 19th-century American literature.

demystify the gift and analyze how it circulates according to patterns of obligation he cannot quite account for why the gift circulates at any given moment. Mauss argues that among the Maori it is the *hau*, the spirit of the gift, but he can only accept the *hau* as a testimony without being able to explain it. In response, Pierre Bourdieu shows convincingly that the "logic of practice" of the gift is different; gift exchange happens in time and with an indeterminate time lag between giving and receiving back and therefore differs from an anthropological description of a gift economy that turns gift giving into a reciprocal logic of gift and countergift. "Do you think it amounts to a dinner?" Tom asks his mother when she considers paying back her debt to the Laphams. The question is both laughable and serious. The Coreys know that a dinner invitation seems absurdly small in return for a saved life, but they are also aware that a dinner will create lasting relations between the two families and thus may be too high a price to pay. "I don't know," Mrs. Corey responds—and then invites them (174–75 [133]). Maddeningly, one cannot know how to repay such a large gift, nor can one do so without getting entangled even further. And equally maddening, and evident in Howells's novel, the moment of decision remains unknowable, outside language. Bourdieu rightly points out that "the most ordinary and even the seemingly most routine exchanges of ordinary life, like the 'little gifts' that 'bind friendship,' presuppose an improvisation and therefore a constant uncertainty, which, as we say, make all their *charm*, and hence all their social efficacy" (191). This uncertainty, the very moment of giving, which is Derrida's focus as well, cannot be explained through the "mechanical laws" of the "cycle of reciprocity" that Mauss posits, and therefore, Bourdieu argues, the uncertainty is "sufficient to change the whole experience of practice, and, by the same token, its logic" (191). Thus, the "practical logic manifests itself in a kind of stylistic unity," while there is no "strict, regular coherence" (194) since gifts can remain unreciprocated (as in Hubbard's case) and our decision to give is unaccountable (as in Mrs. Corey's case). Were we to read *The Rise of Silas Lapham* backward, we could see indeed that the gift of life that Mrs. Lapham gives to Mrs. Corey results in the Coreys' giving their son to the Laphams, but the story is as much about the many excruciating moments of reflecting on, being unsure about, and being maddened, or brought to the point of unreason, by the obligation of the gift. I think both these aspects of the gift are necessary for an understanding of narratives: the obligations and rules that bind people in relations to one another and give narratives "stylistic unity" and the mystery, unpredictability, even (im)possibility of the gift, which keep us reading and wondering and point to the unaccountability, the aporia, of narratives.

* * *

The gift can also be said to have this (im)possible value for narratives about capitalism—it disrupts the logos of capitalism, brings us to the brink of its reason and language, and therefore opens an aporic space that gestures toward something other outside capitalism's logos. Consider Howells's novel once again. On the surface, it aims to be sensible, proposing as its plot resolution a common sense "economy of pain" (241 [183]) that would regulate unnecessary gift giving and sacrifice. But, as many critics have pointed out, the novel belies that formulaic, rational solution and swirls into aporia, a kind of madness outside logos.[7] Faced with gifts and the logos of capitalism, characters become speechless and clueless, "grotesquely confused" as Howells puts it ("Man" 1). Dashes and ellipses abound, and silences happen in mid-sentence. While the gift engenders the narrative, it also brings it to its knees, propels it into nonsense, alogos. For example, when the Laphams learn that Tom Corey has been courting their elder daughter, Penelope, and not—as they all assumed—the younger, prettier Irene, they seek the advice of Minister Sewell about what to do. Should Penelope sacrifice her love for Corey to Irene? Sewell assumes the voice of a rational *homo economicus* who advises the Laphams that their romantic and emotional dilemma can be solved through the logic of an economy of pain: "one [should] suffer instead of three, if none is to blame" (241 [183]). In the end Sewell's logical advice makes sense but does not feel right to anyone. "I must say, I can't help feeling a sort of contempt for her sister," Mrs. Sewell admits to her husband; Penelope, like Lapham when he does the right thing in business, admits that she feels like a "thief" (363, 252 [251, 191]). And, in an often overlooked moment, Howells for once lets the omniscient third-person narrative voice break into the first person as the narrator all of a sudden confesses, "I cannot say" how Penelope managed to "harmonize" with her new family (360 [271]). Everyone, narrator and characters alike, appears at a loss for words and explanations, perhaps even confused about how to account for the outcome of his tale. Even the author seemingly cannot handle the marriage between Corey and Penelope, as he awkwardly exoticizes Penelope and sends his lovers to Mexico, across the border and outside the realm of his novelistic vision. Part of the confusion comes from the fact that the marriage between Tom and Penelope is made possible by the logic of an economy of pain, the conscious rational counting of pain that Sewell suggests, but it is ultimately caused by a deeper and less conscious economy, the gift economy that brought the two lovers together and indebted Tom and his family in the first

7. See, e.g., Crowley 165–66, Hamilton 18, Nettels 69, and Forster 218.

place. The sense that Sewell propagates as a solution, which is portrayed as the hallmark of American realism and a corrective to sentimental fiction, is ultimately perhaps more a marketing ploy than a sense Howells embraces; but it is one that Howells can present in his novel as an economy with rules and reasons that his characters can utter. The logic of the gift, on the other hand, which drives Howells's plot, remains paradoxically unutterable; it leaves the narrator as much as his characters at a loss for words.

* * *

Works Cited

Bourdieu, Pierre. "Selections of *The Logic of Practice*." *The Logic of the Gift: Toward an Ethic of Generosity*. Ed. Alan D. Schrift. New York: Routledge, 1997. 190–230. Print.

Crowley, John W. "An Introduction to *The Rise of Silas Lapham*." *American Literary Realism* 42.2 (2010): 151–73. Print.

Derrida, Jacques. *Given Time: I. Counterfeit Money*. Chicago: U of Chicago P, 1992. Print.

Douglas, Mary. Foreword. Mauss vii–xviii.

Forster, Sophia. "Americanist Literary Realism: Howells, Historicism, and American Exceptionalism." *Modern Fiction Studies* 55.2 (2009): 216–41. Print.

Goodman, Susan, and Carl Dawson. *William Dean Howells: A Writer's Life*. Berkeley: U of California P, 2005. Print.

Hamilton, Geordie. "Rethinking the Politics of American Realism through the Narrative Form and Moral Rhetoric of W. D. Howells' *The Rise of Silas Lapham*." *American Literary Realism* 42.1 (2009): 13–35. Print.

Howells, William Dean. "The Man of Letters as a Man of Business." *Literature and Life*. New York: Harper, 1902. 1–33. Print.

———. *The Rise of Silas Lapham*. 1885. New York: Penguin, 1971. Print.

———. "Tribulations of a Cheerful Giver." *Century* June and July 1895: 181–85, 417–21. Print.

Mauss, Marcel. *The Gift*. 1950. New York: Norton, 1990. Print.

Michaels, Walter Benn. *The Gold Standard and the Logic of Naturalism*. Berkeley: U of California P, 1987. Print.

Nettels, Elsa. *Language, Race, and Social Class in Howells's America*. Lexington: UP of Kentucky, 1988. Print.

Westbrook, Wayne W. *Wall Street in the American Novel*. New York: New York UP, 1980. Print.

JOEL PORTE

[Republican Individualism and Social Class][†]

* * *

I have been pointing to what we may now call the Twain-impulse in Howells, though we may also call it the Lincoln-impulse (we recall Howells's celebrated sentence at the end of *My Mark Twain*, where he refers to Clemens as "the Lincoln of our literature"). It is the impulse to rebel, as Howells averred Twain did, "against the social stupidities and cruelties" in the name of an autochthonous authenticity. It rages against distinctions of class and caste, though finally it may have to pronounce itself baffled at the persistence of such distinctions in our democratic republic. This impulse, I want to insist, laces the pages of many of Howells's best novels, most notably *The Rise of Silas Lapham*. Indeed, Silas is precisely a version of that "ordinary republican aspirant" to whom Howells had addressed himself in his review of *The Bazar Book of Decorum*.[1] The rise and fall chronicled in the novel fundamentally concerns not Lapham's success and failure in business, but his social aspirations, which lead his forthright Vermont soul into the toils of the Back Bay and Boston's polite society. Howells's story verges on being a parable of rustic America—the America of Lincoln and Twain—confronting the values and vagaries of a superficially attractive but finally deceitful and destructive patriciate. As may well be imagined, this was a very touchy subject for the western-born autodidact who had made his own uncertain way among Boston's finicky intelligentsia and found himself, as he began writing the book, installed in a house on Beacon Street only two doors away from the autocrat of the breakfast table.

Howells's uneasiness with the vulgarly pushy side of the upwardly aspiring Laphams is easy to spot in the book, though it is not clear whether Howells meant to emphasize the pathos or the futility of their ludicrous attempts at bettering themselves and penetrating good society. When Howells comments on the Laphams' "rich and rather ugly clothes" or on the costly "and most abominable frescoes" with which they decorated their house, or notes that "they had a

† From "Manners, Morals, and Mince Pie: Howells's America Revisited" in *Prospects: An Annual Journal of American Cultural Studies* 10 (October 1985): 446–51. Copyright © 1985 Cambridge University Press. Reprinted by permission of the publisher, Cambridge UP.

1. Excerpts from Tomes's book and Howells's review of it are reprinted on pp. 357–64 and pp. 364–66, respectively. See also p. 365, n. 1 for Howells's use of the term *republican* [*editor's note*].

crude taste in architecture, and . . . admired the worst" and, moreover, drank Oolong tea because "none of them had a sufficiently cultivated palate for Souchong," he comes perilously close to adopting the patronizing tones of *The Bazar Book of Decorum* (which, it is clear, the Laphams themselves consult in their frantic preparations for the Corey dinner party). These are not sympathetic remarks and suggest nothing but Howells's unfortunate desire to flatter the prejudices of his polite readers by occasionally ridiculing the brave Vermonters who represent, after all, the moral center of Howells's vision. It is precisely this wobbling point of view, caused presumably by Howells's own social anxieties, that constitutes one of his great formal weaknesses as a novelist.

But the fundamental contours of Howells's fable are not compromised by such lapses. The book opens with a masterful chapter in which the morally sleazy newspaperman of *A Modern Instance*, Bartley Hubbard, has come to interview Lapham in preparation for sketching Lapham's life in the "Solid Men of Boston" series published by his journal. Bartley, who has fallen into the nasty habit of treating everyone, including himself, with a kind of easy contempt, tends to think of Lapham, cynically, in terms of a stereotypical American success story that clearly seems to him little more than a literary convention. His sketch of Lapham as "one of nature's noblemen"—that is his phrase—is completed, as Howells tells us, "with a good deal of inward derision." But we are made to understand that Bartley's contemptuous treatment both of Lapham and the American fable he exemplifies is a measure only of Hubbard's own moral debasement, for the class of natural noblemen to which Lapham belongs is dignified by Howells in a significant way. When Lapham shows Bartley the minie-ball that is embedded in his leg, he remarks: "Gettysburg. That's my thermometer. If it wa'n't for that, I shouldn't know enough to come in when it rains." Bartley laughs away the story as a hackneyed joke, but Howells clearly intends that we should pick up the moral rather than the meteorological significance of the remark. Indeed, since Howells has previously allowed Lapham to relate the tale of his decent poverty-stricken rural childhood, presided over by a pious, self-sacrificing angel-mother, we have already been prepared for this alignment of Lapham and Lincoln. (It is interesting to note that the original synopsis for the book was entitled "The Rise of Silas Needham"; the metamorphosis of Silas's name hardly seems accidental.)[2] At this point the student of Howells's career will remember that the author's first prose work was a short campaign biography of Lincoln published in 1860 that

2. For information about the synopsis I am indebted to Kermit Vanderbilt, *The Achievement of William Dean Howells* (Princeton, N.J.: Princeton University Press, 1968).

undoubtedly served as the lingering paradigm for the kind of hagiographic portrait being attempted here. Howells always regretted that he had passed up the opportunity to interview Lincoln himself (it was done by a young law student whom Howells knew) and therefore managed to compensate himself imaginatively for the loss by replaying the event in the Hubbard/Lapham confrontation.

Howells's understated association of Lapham with the egalitarian spirit of America's most distinguished natural nobleman is amusingly reinforced, and indeed given point, late in the book, when the unregenerately snobbish Coreys pay an agonizing courtesy call on Penelope Lapham, whom their son improbably insists on marrying. Howells has already described, presumably as part of his satire of the Laphams' bad taste, a piece of imported statuary located in their drawing-room: "a white marble group of several figures, expressing an Italian conception of Lincoln Freeing the Slaves . . . with our Eagle flapping his wings in approval, at Lincoln's feet." As so often in Howells, it would be a mistake to conclude that the author's critical view of his characters' taste in interior decorations necessarily implies a negative judgment on their moral standards. Indeed, the sad lesson that Howells explicitly draws at the end of the book tells us that in a so-called civilized world our manners unfortunately count for more than our qualities. However profound we may come to feel are the Laphams' virtues, they can scarcely outweigh their aesthetic failings in the eyes of proper Boston. But that piece of statuary is not as lifeless or ineffectual as it first appears, for when Penelope descends to the drawing-room she discovers the elder Coreys engaged in a kind of moral combat with the Lincoln scene: Mr. Corey "was sitting . . . a little tilted away from the Emancipation group, as if he expected the Lincoln to hit him, with that lifted hand of benediction; and . . . Mrs. Corey looked as if she were not sure but the Eagle pecked." Thus does the lesson of Lincoln come to active judgment on the frigid exclusiveness of Boston society! Here and elsewhere, one can hardly overemphasize the fierceness with which Howells adhered to the western democratic spirit exemplified for him by the linked figures of Lincoln and Twain. As Howells would write in *My Mark Twain*, "his books witness how he abhorred the dreadful fools who through some chance of birth or wealth hold themselves different from other men."

The spirit of Twain, in fact, hovers as firmly over *The Rise of Silas Lapham* as does that of Lincoln. One astute Howells scholar, Kermit Vanderbilt, has noticed that there is a striking parallel between Lapham's embarrassing performance at the Coreys' dinner party and Mark Twain's disastrous speech at the Whittier Day dinner in 1877. Both situations concern an *Auslander*, as Vanderbilt notes, "talking endlessly and indecorously before an apparently unamused audience of entrenched Bostonians."[3] Twain's speech, in substance at least, was very different from Lapham's boorish boasting and back-slapping, for Twain used the occasion to take a very pointed swipe at the New England literary establishment by portraying Emerson, Longfellow, and Holmes as three deadbeats victimizing a prospector in the California Sierras. The aim of Twain's burlesque (and he does not shrink from turning it against himself at the end) was not to prove that the three worthies in question were frauds but rather to take the notion of respectability, literary or otherwise, down a few pegs. New England's pantheon was being invited to let a little of the starch out and laugh at itself for a few minutes. Indeed, even a few *seconds* of mirth would have satisfied Twain, for the icy silence in which his joke was received made it clear that this decorous Boston audience were no more prepared to have their collective cultural noses tweaked by a rough western wit than were Bromfield Corey and company to accept Lapham's cozying up to them in his drunken euphoria. But though Twain, like Lapham, seems initially to have been abysmally ashamed of his blunder, it is interesting to observe, in Howells's own account of the event, that Twain soon repented of his repentance, insisting, "with all his fierceness, 'But I don't admit that it *was* a mistake.'" Did Howells remember, as he set down Twain's uncompromising words, his own rule for the "ordinary republican aspirant"—"Never be ashamed of a blunder?" Twain thus stands out as a shining exemplar of the true republican's determination to hold his ground in the face of genteel criticism.

Although we do not have sufficient evidence to decide whether Howells had this episode subliminally or even consciously in mind as he wrote of Lapham's behavior at the Coreys', Vanderbilt's conjecture may be strengthened by another, and I think more striking, instance of Howells's associating the Lapham family with the spirit of Twain. To my knowledge, no other commentator on the book has noticed that Howells's true Penelope—to paraphrase Pound on Mauberley—is Twain.[4] As the elder Corey notes, without entire sympathy, Penelope is "a merry little grig." His son Tom reports approvingly that she is "humorous" and has "a sort of droll way of

3. *Ibid.*, p. 135.
4. Alfred Habegger comes close in his "Nineteenth-Century American Humor: Easygoing Males, Anxious Ladies, and Penelope Lapham," *PMLA*, 91, 5 (October 1976), 884–99: "Inevitably, American humor was masculine. Only by grasping that fact can we understand the significance of Penelope Lapham. . . . Penelope is a female humorist who marches to a different drum from that heard by the genteel feminine humorists [of her time]. . . . She has the horse sense of the lengendary self-taught, self-reliant American man; and in contrast to her sister, the pattern of femininity, she has an odd and active sense of humor. . . . Penelope has the manner of a vernacular male storyteller. . . . She may not prop her feet on the rail, but in her improprieties of posture, bearing, and diction she clearly bears the distinctive marks of the proverbial male humorist. . . . Penelope is in the mainstream of vernacular male humor."

looking at things . . . she tells what she's seen, and mimics a little." Later, the Laphams themselves expand on their elder daughter's gift for doing impressions and spinning tales. "'That girl can talk for twenty, right straight along. She's better than a circus any day. I wonder what she's up to now,'" Silas asks his wife. "'Oh, she's probably getting off some of those yarns of hers, or telling about some people,'" responds Persis.

> She can't step out of the house without coming back with more things to talk about than most folks would bring back from Japan. There ain't a ridiculous person she's ever seen but what she's got something from them to make you laugh at; and I don't believe we've ever had anybody in the house since the girl could talk that she hain't got some saying from, or some trick that'll paint 'em out so 't you can see 'em and hear 'em. Sometimes I want to stop her; but when she gets into one of her gales there ain't any standing up against her.

It is thus sufficiently clear that "Pen"—as she is significantly called—has the makings of a first-class American humorist in the mode of Samuel Clemens. Indeed, we do not have to guess where she has formed her own literary manners since early on in the book Howells offers this example of Penelope's banter. Teasing her sister Irene about Tom Corey's unexpected visit to their less than fashionable summer home at Nantasket, the irrepressible wag breaks out: "'Why shouldn't he come down with father, if father asked him? and he'd be sure to if he thought of it. I don't see any p'ints about that frog that's any better than any other frog.'" Howells, to be sure, has tidied up the language a bit here—Twain wrote "I don't see *no* p'ints about that frog that's any better'n any other frog"—but Penelope's appropriation of the punch line from "The Notorious Jumping Frog of Calaveras County" would hardly have been missed by any contemporary reader of Howells's novel, nor should we miss the implications of Howells's allusion. Penelope's humor, like Twain's, is aimed at puncturing pretension and snobbishness and at obliterating invidious distinctions. This frog may be called Tom Corey, or Dan'l Webster, or any other impressive name, but if he can't move faster than an ordinary swamp-frog, he might just as well be called Mud.

"In the light of the more modern appreciation," Howells was to write with regard to the growing tendency to read Twain parabolically,

> we elders may be able to see some things seriously that we once thought pure drolling, and from our experience his younger admirers may learn to receive as drolling some things that they might otherwise accept as preaching. What we all should wish to do is to keep Mark Twain what he has always been: a comic force unique in the power of charming us out of our cares and

> troubles, united with as potent an ethic sense of the duties, public and private, which no man denies in himself without being false to other men. I think we may hope for the best he can do to help us deserve our self-respect, without forming Mark Twain societies to read philanthropic meanings into his jokes, or studying the "Jumping Frog" as the allegory of an imperializing Republic.[5]

Howells's point is well taken, though it no more denies significance in Twain's drolling than it does in Penelope's. "'I am little, and black, and homely, and they don't understand my way of talking,'" she explains to Tom in an attempt to dissuade him from a marriage that can only horrify his Brahmin family. Penelope's pert Twainisms are no more acceptable to polite Boston than are her curious person and her dubious social credentials, and Howells leaves us with no illusions about the promise of this improbable union between republican America and the exclusive precincts of Beacon Hill. "It is certain," he concludes, "that our manners and customs go for more in life than our qualities. The price that we pay for civilization is the fine yet impassable differentiation of these." At this point in his career, Howells felt obliged to ask whether this was too high a price for America to pay, since it involved the compromise of a fundamental principle: the right of all individuals to make their way on the strength of intrinsic worth rather than according to the accidents of birth and breeding.

As I have been arguing, a painful awareness of class and caste is one of the prime motivating forces in Howells's writing. Accordingly, he hoped to find, and indeed would help to create, a literary tradition in America capable of transcending—or better, *leveling*—such distinctions by means of its inclusiveness and sheer humanity. Howells most lovingly identifies not with social climbers but with figures firmly centered in their own self-worth who render the whole notion of "making it" in polite society nugatory. Such figures typically reconcile in themselves the opposed claims of nature and breeding. Howells delights in the wise autodidact, the rustic who is innately refined, the Harvard graduate who is not ashamed to spend his life in Walden woods, or run a country hotel, or entertain his friends by imitating a black uncle's shuffle and breakdown. Some cultural figures who were paradigmatic in this regard, as we have seen, were Lincoln and Twain. In addition, they were humorists, capable of deflating pretension and affectation with a thrust of wit or an incongruous or unexpected gesture or remark. Above all, they gloried in the commonplace, elevating what was mean, as Emerson said, through the force of their own

5. [Edwin H.] Cady [ed., *W. D. Howells as Critic* (London and Boston: Routledge and Kegan Paul, 1973)], p. 351.

example. This was the American tradition Howells most profoundly admired and was determined to champion, transmit, and emulate. To be sure, as a country boy dropped down in the hub of the universe, Howells was forever anxious about his own position and manners. The drama of Howells's life, in literature and out of it, lay in the stresses and strains created by warring impulses: the need to be admired by his betters, and the determination to impose his democratic values without apology on all his compatriots.

ALFRED HABEGGER

[Gender, Humor, and Penelope Lapham]†

Penelope Lapham in *The Rise of Silas Lapham* (1885) is the first humorous romantic female lead in a novel by an American man. The one character who considers this humorist marriageable is the man who loves her, Tom Corey. Everyone else, including Penelope herself, assumes that Tom prefers her sister Irene, a beautiful blonde who, as of chapter 7, hasn't heard of George Eliot. Not until Tom proposes does it become clear that he loves Penelope, who has not only read *Middlemarch* but shares Howells' view of Eliot's narrative technique: "I wish she would let you find out a little about the people for yourself."[1]

Penelope is sane, shrewd, unfashionable, and not pretty; she has the horse sense of the legendary self-taught, self-reliant American man; and in contrast to her sister, the pattern of femininity, she has an odd and active sense of humor. A few critics have dismissed the "subplot" of *Silas Lapham* as an unrealistic contrivance.[2] And except for Henry James, nobody has considered the character of Penelope to be a major achievement.[3] But this self-made girl is a triumph of American realistic art and as important a creation as any of Howells' and James's many American girls. Penelope is an authentic person, but one who was required by everything in her culture to make herself invisible; "'You never thought of me!' cried the girl, with a

† From Gender, *Fantasy, and Realism in American Literature* (New York: Columbia UP, 1982), pp. 115, 184–95, 329–30, 344–36. Copyright © 1982 Columbia University Press. Reprinted by permission of the publisher. Page references in brackets refer to this Norton Critical Edition.

1. *The Rise of Silas Lapham*, Walter J. Meserve and David J. Nordloh, eds. (Bloomington: Indiana University Press, 1971), p. 88 [67]. Subsequent references are to this edition.
2. See, e. g., Marcus Cunliffe, *The Literature of the United States* (Baltimore: Penguin, 1961), p. 198; Howells "contrive[s] a subplot that seems a little implausible."
3. James's praise ("Everything in *Silas Lapham* is superior—nothing more so than the whole picture of casual, female youth and contemporaneous 'engaging' one's self") points to Penelope more than to anyone else. Cited from "William Dean Howells," *Harper's Weekly*, (1886), 30:394. One of the rare reviews that praised Penelope's humor was in the British *Saturday Review*, (1885), 60:517.

bitterness that reached her mother's heart. 'I was nobody! I couldn't feel! No one could care for me!'" (p. 226 [172]).

* * *

The subplot of *The Rise of Silas Lapham* gives a perfect aesthetic form to the invisibility of the independent, humorous girl. Nobody imagines that Tom could possibly prefer Penelope to her beautiful sister. The tired old device of mistaken courtship acquires a rich contemporary meaning.

Nowhere outside the novel itself—neither in his prospectus, his "Savings Bank" Diary, or his correspondence—did Howells suggest that Penelope would be humorous.[4] The articles on women's sense of humor that appeared in the *Critic* shortly before Howells began writing *Silas Lapham* may have led him to make the female lead a humorist. It happens that the editors of the *Critic*, Jeannette and Joseph B. Gilder, were sister and brother of the editor of the *Century*, which serialized Howells' novel. But quite apart from the possibility of direct influence, it is clear that as Howells got to work on the novel in the summer of 1884, the question of women's humor was in the air. During the next summer Kate Sanborn would compile her anthology, *The Wit of Women*; just one year earlier, *The Hidden Hand* had appeared for the third and last time in the *New York Ledger*. Most important of all, Howells' work on *Mark Twain's Library of Humor* in the months before he began *Silas Lapham* had given him a detailed and crystalline overview of American humor.[5]

What kind of humorist is Penelope? It seems clear that she does not have the civilized feminine wit that had been so highly praised in the *Critic* articles and in *The Wit of Women*.[6] In fact, we are explicitly told (p. 134 [102]) that Penelope does not make epigrams. Rather, she seems to follow the advice Howells gave Annie in 1872: "keep the tone low, and let the reader do all the laughing."[7] Instead of scattering bright replies in high-toned drawing rooms, she entertains her family at home, often as a monologist. Sitting on the veranda at the Nantasket cottage, she holds Tom Corey and Irene spellbound with her "drolling" and "funning." As these unusual words suggest, her humor hardly conforms

4. According to Walter J. Meserve's introduction to *The Rise of Silas Lapham* (Bloomington: Indiana University Press, 1971), p. xvi, Howells began the novel in July 1884. All quotations come from this edition.
5. *Mark Twain—Howells Letters*, Henry Nash Smith and William M. Gibson, ed. (Cambridge: Harvard University Press, 1960), 2:492–493.
6. The *Critic* treated *Silas Lapham* rather coolly: "In fiction we are having really too much realism" (February 28, 1885, N.S. 3, p. 101, as quoted in Clayton L. Eichelberger, *Published Comment on William Dean Howells Through 1920: A Research Bibliography* [Boston: Hall, 1976], p. 52). Significantly, the *Critic* found it "beyond belief" that Tom should love "the half-cultivated" Penelope (September 12, 1885, N.S. 4, p. 122). See also item 327 in Eichelberger.
7. Howells, *Selected Letters* (Boston: Twayne, 1979), 1:396.

to standards of good breeding and propriety. In fact, Penelope has the manner of a vernacular male storyteller. She speaks slowly, with a "drawl" (p. 37 [31]), and her face has an "arch, lazy look" (p. 218 [167]). She sits "leaning forward lazily and running on, as the phrase is" (p. 133 [102]). To Corey, "her talk was very unliterary, and its effect seemed hardly conscious" (p. 133 [102]). She may not prop her feet on the rail, but in her improprieties of posture, bearing, and diction she clearly bears the distinctive marks of the proverbial male humorist.

Penelope is a male impersonator, yet her act is anything but a self-conscious or artificial pose. Her humor is part and parcel of an easygoing temperament that will not be hassled. When the strenuous Mrs. Corey decides she must invite the Laphams to dinner, Penelope wisely avoids the pointless ordeal and stays home. She feels oppressed by the decorum Mrs. Corey imposes. Her imagination has a kind of Wild West freedom, a feeling for improvisation and roughing it. Tired of all the talk about her father's new house, Penelope thinks "it would be a sort of relief to go and live in tents for a while" (p. 57 [44]). She enjoys Lapham's uncouth bragging, and she also enjoys mimicking and making fun of him. She has a wonderful gift for parodying the formulas of politeness and reducing them to nonsense. Thus, when Tom expresses his regret that Penelope missed the dinner, she slyly trips him up:

> "We all missed you very much."
>
> "Oh, thank you! I'm afraid you wouldn't have missed me if I had been there."
>
> "Oh, yes, we should," said Corey, "I assure you."
>
> They looked at each other, (p. 216 [165])

Here Penelope does the same sort of job on Tom Corey as Ferris does on nervous Mrs. Vervain in *A Foregone Conclusion*:

> "I'm *so* pleased!" said Mrs. Vervain, rising when Ferris said that he must go. . . .
>
> "Thank you, Mrs. Vervain; I could have gone before, if I'd thought you would have liked it," answered the painter.[8]

As the contrast between these two exchanges suggests, there is less animus in Penelope than in Ferris, who gets genuinely irritated with Mrs. Vervain. Yet both Penelope and Ferris are doing essentially the same thing—burlesquing polite manners. This would be a male activity in a culture that makes etiquette feminine.

Given the masculine qualities of Penelope's humor, it is fitting that in one exchange with her father she actually threatens to become a man, and a lazy one at that. Her father says:

8. Howells, *A Foregone Conclusion* (Boston: Osgood, 1875), p. 66.

> "Now, I suppose that fellow belongs to two or three clubs, and hangs around 'em all day, lookin' out the window,—I've seen 'em,—instead of tryin' to hunt up something to do for an honest livin'."
>
> "If I was a young man," Penelope struck in, "I would belong to twenty clubs, if I could find them, and I would hang around them all, and look out the window till I dropped."
>
> "Oh, you would, would you?" demanded her father, delighted with her defiance, and twisting his fat head around over his shoulder to look at her. "Well, you wouldn't do it on *my* money, if you were a son of *mine*, young lady."
>
> "Oh, you wait and see," retorted the girl. (p. 58 [45])

Like Capitola, Penelope sasses back the bullheaded old man who assumes authority over her. Unlike Southworth's heroine, however, Penelope evinces no sexual or generational bitterness. She does not make her father fear that she may cut his throat, does not show any real desire to become a boy. When she threatens to turn into the idle son who squanders the old man's money, she is giving free rein to her protean independence. Of course, there is a serious layer here: she is taking down her father for complacently sounding off on "honest livin'." Also, she is sticking up for her sister by defending the man she's presumed to be interested in (and Irene thanks Penelope for this loyalty later on). But basically, Penelope's "Oh, you wait and see" is an expression of a contented femininity that feels no pressure whatever: she feels free to do and become whatever she wants. Also, she is well aware how much her defiance pleases her father. Similarly, she flashes her wit at Tom on purpose to fascinate and attract him, and eventually she realizes this: "I know now that I tried to make him think that I was pretty and—funny" (p. 229 [174]). Her funniness *is* her beauty and the basis of her charm. Ideal femininity, as embodied by Irene, proves much less sexy than the vagrant, individual humor of a free spirit.

Penelope is a tomboy who does not dislike being female. The heroines closest to her would seem to be those of Mary Jane Holmes, with their untrammeled and slightly wayward manners. Penelope also resembles a character in Adeline D. T. Whitney's *The Gayworthys*, Joanna, who entertains others with monologues poking fun at conventional matters. But Penelope is even more original or queer than these heroines from the 1850s and 60s: "She had a slow, quaint way of talking, that seemed a pleasant personal modification of some ancestral Yankee drawl, and her voice was low and cozy, and so far from being nasal that it was a little hoarse" (p. 37 [31]). Like any successful performer, Penelope is like nobody else. She seems to be partly a throwback to an older, preindustrial New England; there is an archaic Yankee quality about her, slow but trenchant. (Her first name is so "old-fashioned" that it has often been "mocked"—p. 255 [193]). Yet she does not have a nasal voice, nor does she speak in dialect. The adjectives that describe her voice—low, cozy, and hoarse—suggest the throaty, even sexy, quality of Adah Isaacs Menken's voice.

Is it any surprise that the man who falls in love with Penelope does not happen to "get on" with "cultivated" (p. 170 [130]) Bostonians? Tom is fascinated by Penelope's humor and finds it impossible to describe:

> She never says anything that you can remember; nothing in flashes or ripples; nothing the least literary. But it's a sort of droll way of looking at things; or a droll medium through which things present themselves. I don't know. She tells what she's seen, and mimics a little. (p. 100 [76])

This humor, which the young man here struggles to convey to his mother, is obviously anything but verbal or formulaic. The quality that seems to appeal most of all to Tom is the droll representational aspect. *Things* seem to present themselves in a new way in Penelope's speech and manner, which constitute a sort of medium, a magic mirror whose surface is so revealing and whose pantomimic working so impenetrable. It looks as if Penelope has the same master passions as the realistic novelist who invented her: she wants to see and then make others see. She educates herself, as did Howells, by reading and attending lectures and looking out the window. She is an observer on a "self-guided search for self-improvement" (p. 26 [21]) and she resents it when in *Middlemarch* George Eliot instructs the reader what to think about the characters: "I wish she would let you find out a little about the people for yourself" (p. 88 [67]). The fact that Penelope does not attend a fashionable school or move in good society confers on her the freedom to make sense of the world. Her humor is thus to some extent a function of her parents' social isolation in modern Boston and her own totally unconscious alienation. It is because she is on the sidelines that she gets high on reality and then on miming it for the amusement of others.

The one person in the novel who actively dislikes this free spirit is Mrs. Corey. The antagonism between her and Penelope goes much deeper than the clash of personality. Mrs. Corey is the feminine ruling class. She is a sober, responsible, devious manipulator. Like Margaret Dumont in the Marx Brothers films, she has a commonplace mind and expects a rigid adherence to the rules. When the hapless Mrs. Lapham has to confess that Penelope has not come to dinner, Mrs. Corey makes her suffer by publicly branding her with a letter which is almost as painful as Hester Prynne's "A"; "Mrs. Corey emitted a very small 'O!'—very small, very cold—which began to grow larger and hotter and to burn into Mrs. Lapham's soul" (p. 190 [144]). Mrs. Corey has taken upon herself the burden of regulating society. Her husband, who carries no burdens whatever, regards a formal dinner as an occasion for witty conversation. He is an inactive man who does not work and has no place in the world of men, staying at home while his wife goes out. He seems to bear the stigma of the subject husband, as he addresses his wife only in tones of irony. Mrs. Corey tolerates his wit and even tries to smile, but she cannot abide Penelope's humor, which seems rude and disrespectful to her. Like the bad girl in "Little Orphant Annie," Penelope is "pert," a "thoroughly disagreeable young woman" who "says things to puzzle you and put you out" (p. 169 [129]). Mrs. Corey refers to her as "the plain sister" (p. 99 [76]), as "little and dark" (p. 170 [130]). There is no social contract between the two women; they are necessarily enemies; and when the younger one takes away the older one's son by marrying him, it is abject defeat for an old-fashioned foot-bound mandarin.[9]

The differences between Irene and Penelope derive from an inner conflict in the Lapham family and the vernacular culture they represent. Both parents encourage the doll-like femininity of Irene and parade her before others as the warrant of their genteel social value. But they are also proud of Penelope's humor, wide reading, independence, and toughness. Lapham is "delighted with her defiance" of the values he thinks he believes in. The contrast between the two girls reflects his inner confusion. He wants a mansion on the water side of Beacon Street, and in his parlor at Nankeen Square he has installed "a white marble group of several figures, expressing an Italian conception of Lincoln Freeing the Slaves,—a Latin negro and his wife,—with our Eagle flapping his wings in approval, at Lincoln's feet" (p. 215 [164]). As we see, the most showy and spurious excesses of the post-Civil War period have invaded Silas Lapham's home. The source of his wealth—paint, which he advertises by painting

9. The reviewer for the *Nation* shared Mrs. Corey's distaste: "The most unpleasant and the most unnatural girl is Penelope Lapham . . . , ironically snubbing her relations, or urging her sister to inextinguishable laughter by mimicking their father" (October 22, 1885, 41:348). Actually, this highbrow reviewer disliked Penelope *because* she was natural. In *Cottage-Hearth: A Magazine of Home Arts and Home Culture*, the reviewer who considered Penelope "natural to the least detail" (October 1885, 11:326) wrote with greater accuracy. In Miriam Harris' popular novel, *Rutledge* (New York: Derby & Jackson, 1860), drawling speech is a salient trait in the disagreeable Grace, who, in the narrator's eyes, has "a sort of gutta-percha insensibility, a lazy coolness that I had not expected from her drawling, listless way" (p. 221). The narrator notices Grace's "pertness" (pp. 218, 221, 235) and sees her as pre-feminine: "nothing of the woman seemed developed in her but the sharpness." *Rutledge* is an extremely well-bred novel; it offers precisely the view of Grace that Mrs. Corey takes of Penelope.

the landscape—shows that he himself has helped make it a Gilded Age,[1] a cheaply colored "Chromo-civilization" in E. L. Godkin's famous phrase. And yet Lapham is also an aboriginal, freedom-loving, plainspoken Yankee with big fists and an ancestral honesty and simplicity. The terrible marble group is about liberation, after all, and Lapham himself had volunteered in the Civil War. Poor pretty Irene is the product of his phony values, and Penelope the product of the old and real ones. Irene conforms to a "gilded" standard of femininity and effaces her own individuality. But her plain dark sister is free to develop her mind, her pantomimic skill, and her odd way of talking because she is a total failure at conforming to the ideal gender role. Similarly, Lapham saves himself only by failing in business. In a civilization that goes wrong by "gilding" nature, humor and integrity are both incompatible with success.

But Penelope is the offspring of her mother as well as her father. Persis—Howells had used this name in *The Lady of the Aroostook* for the wife of the bluff New England captain—comes from Vermont and has the true native gumption, but she has been softened by life in Boston. She no longer has anything to do with Silas' work. In his crisis she abandons him. The jealousy that overcomes her is a symptom of the growing separation between husband and wife. Fortunately the chasm closes; Silas and Persis reach an understanding after their last bitter quarrel; and they return to the old place in the country. This return to the land has an entirely different meaning here from what it had in *A Modern Instance*. In the earlier novel Marcia's return is part of an unqualified defeat, but the Laphams' return puts them back in touch with an honest way of life. Silas puts on his comfortable old clothes again and seems "more the Colonel in those hills than he could ever have been on the Back Bay" (p. 363 [273]). And Persis can at least resume the character revealed by her spunky arguments with her husband and the name he affectionately gives her.

"Pert"—the word Mrs. Corey applies to Penelope's sassy quickness—happens, not by accident, to be identical with Mrs. Lapham's nickname. The word merits more than passing attention. To be pert was to be humorously self-assertive and cheeky in a feminine way. Neither a pert girl nor a pert woman could ever be a proper lady. Howells himself spoke for genteel decorum when he ridiculed a statue of the madonna in *Venetian Life* for its "pert

1. Lapham "knew who the Coreys were . . . and . . . had long hated their name as a symbol of splendor which, unless he should live to see at least three generations of his descendants *gilded* with mineral paint, he could not hope to realize in his own" (p. 92; italics mine). In *The World of Chance* (New York: Harper, 1893), p. 350, a publisher announces the extent to which he intends to promote a possible bestseller by saying, "I'm simply going to paint the universe red."

smile."[2] Yet there was a strong tendency in vernacular American culture to approve of pertness in women. Often spelled *peart*, the word was applied to women in a complimentary way by many different kinds of speakers, rich and poor, Southern or Northern, black or white, male or female. In Albion Tourgee's *Bricks without Straw* a North Carolina planter says to one of his female slaves, "I'm very well, thank ye, Lorency, an' glad to see you looking so peart."[3] In Mary Jane Holmes's *Tempest and Sunshine* a black auntie in Kentucky praises Fanny, a white girl, by saying she "allus was peart like and forrud."[4] In Sarah Orne Jewett's first book, *Deephaven*, the narrator joins in the laughter at a story told by the energetic Mrs. Bonny and then writes: "One might have ventured to call her 'peart,' I think."[5] In *Silas Lapham* Howells returned to the popular rural valuation of the lighthearted gutsy equality of which pertness was the expression. More than that, Howells revealed the continuity between the humor that defines Penelope and the country spunk and sauciness of her mother. Yet he did not make Penelope a country hoyden but an odd amalgam of old New England and big city anonymity and alienation. Just as Jewett's narrator, who was also from Boston, had to distance herself from "peart" by means of quotation marks, Howells would show that Penelope's inheritance of her mother's pertness would be in grave disharmony with modern urban life.

If wealth, the move from country to city, and the historic changes of the Gilded Age have deposited a terrible contradiction in the older Laphams, these forces practically destroy Penelope. The crisis begins at the moment when Tom Corey's declaration of love brings Penelope's girlhood to an end. Just before this moment Penelope seems as rational as ever. Her opinion of the popular novel *Tears, Idle Tears* is as level-headed as any of her ideas. She sees the hollowness of the heroine's self-sacrificial refusal to marry the man she loves just because he happened to love another woman first: "But it *wasn't* self-sacrifice," says Penelope, "or not self-sacrifice alone. She was sacrificing him too; and for someone who couldn't appreciate him half as much as she could." Tom calls this popular novel "a famous book with ladies" and says, "they break their hearts over it" (p. 217 [166]). Is Penelope one of these ladies or is she still the laughing girl? She

2. Howells, *Venetian Life* (Boston: Osgood, 1875), p. 162.
3. Albion Tourgee, *Bricks without Straw: A Novel* (New York: Fords, Howard, & Hulbert, 1880), p. 19. "Peart" is applied to a man on p. 192.
4. Mary Jane Holmes, *Tempest and Sunshine* (New York: Appleton, 1854). An earlier novel, Caroline Lee Hentz's *Rena; or, the Snow Bird* (Philadelphia: Hart, 1851) seems close to Howells with its black-haired tomboy heroine contrasted with a blonde, conniving beauty.
5. Sarah Orne Jewett, *Deephaven and Other Stories* (New Haven: College and University Press, 1966), p, 137. First published in book form in 1877. In Marietta Holley, *Samantha among the Brethren* (New York: Funk and Wagnalls, 1890), pp. 190, 183, 191, a woman who is "pert," has common sense, and "likes a joke," is praised for being "smart to answer back and joke."

answers this question herself in admitting that she has not only read the book more than once but has cried over it. Evidently, Penelope is not so exclusively the bystander as she has appeared. In fact, like the man in the prison chant, she has a long chain on and from now on will feel its drag and attempt to behave in precisely the same manner as the heroine of the silly novel she couldn't help crying over. After Corey's proposal Penelope speaks like a tragedy queen: "Life has got to go on. It does when there's a death in the house, and this is only a little worse" (p. 230 [175]). She exacts a lofty promise from Tom, then gives him a despairing embrace. Craziest of all, she insists that even though she and Tom want each other, it is impossible for them to marry—because of Irene.

Penelope's trouble goes very deep. In giving way to the feeling that self-denial is better than happiness, she is doing more than succumbing to popular sentimentality as embodied in *Tears, Idle Tears*. Her heart has been corrupted by her culture. Her lofty renunciation is nothing less than a misguided attempt to be feminine in the approved way. The reason Howells preached against self-sacrifice in so many novels was that self-sacrifice was the essence of femininity, which defined woman as being-for-others and not being-for-herself.[6] Irene sitting at the Corey dinner, a beautiful and silent mannequin, is being-for-others. Penelope, defined by her perception, her comic sensibility, is being-for-herself. Self-sacrifice, the ultimate form of being-for-others, has a persistent and dangerous appeal for Howells' heroines—Helen Harkness, Imogene Graham, Alice Pasmer, Hermia Faulkner. If these ladies are so rigid, irrational, and solemn, it is because they lack that confidence in their inner value that allows men to take it easy. Self-sacrifice is both the ultimate expression of their sense of worthlessness and an attempt to influence—to control—the real world *in some way*. In passing from girlhood to womanhood, Penelope has to overcome the temptation to throw herself away. She has to stifle the false inner voice that tells her she cannot respect herself unless she destroys herself.

Tom's love makes Penelope conscious for the first time in her life of "the sense of sex"[7] and her own reciprocal feelings; yet the sense of

6. On women and self-sacrifice, see Edwin H. Cady, *The Road to Realism: The Early Years, 1837–1885, of William Dean Howells* (Syracuse: Syracuse University Press, 1956), pp. 232–234. For general discussions of Howells' women, see Edward Wagenknecht, *William Dean Howells: The Friendly Eye* (New York: Oxford University Press, 1969), pp. 156–170; William Wasserstrom, *Heiress of All the Ages* (Minneapolis: University of Minnesota Press, 1959); and Paul John Eakin, *The New England Girl: Cultural Ideals in Hawthorne, Stowe, Howells and James* (Athens: University of Georgia Press, 1974).
7. Henry James, *Watch and Ward*, *Atlantic* (August 1871), 28:245. Eakin's explanation for Penelope's melodramatic self-sacrifice is superficial. He suggests it is "the psychology of the plain girl"—a "desire to become through identification with the heroines of fiction, the pretty girl she isn't in real life" (*New England Girl*, p. 122). One might believe this if Penelope tried to make herself prettier during her self-sacrificial phase. But prettiness seems the last thing on her mind.

sex also dictates self-denial. And if this double bind were not enough, Penelope has another serious problem. The fact that up to now she has been a kind of male impersonator means that, her femaleness notwithstanding, her public self has basically been masculine. The sudden necessity to define a public feminine role destroys her self-confidence and brings about a temporary breakdown.[8] For a period of weeks or months, she rarely leaves the house. She has a "wan face." In her mother's words, she "just sits in her room and mopes" (p. 259 [196]). She even gives up reading. When she tries to write a note to Tom, her inability to assume a public role or style leads her to tear up one draft after another. Her mother says: "A girl that could be so sensible for her sister, and always say and do just the right thing, and then when it comes to herself to be such a *disgusting* simpleton!" (p. 304 [229]). With her usual shrewdness, Mrs. Lapham senses that Penelope has always projected her own femininity onto Irene. Now that Pen must be her own woman, she can't help falling apart.

Fortunately, Penelope fights back, regains her old sanity, and marries the man she wants. But it is clear that there is no place for her in Bostonian society. After she has spent a week with the Coreys she is glad to leave for Mexico City. Not even Bromfield Corey could appreciate her humor. Howells' last word on Penelope is a dry speculation that "our manners and customs go for more in life than our qualities" (p. 361 [272]). What this means apparently is that society cannot accommodate Penelope, no matter how fine her individual qualities may be. Howells condemns society for excluding her and suggests that we "pay too much" for "civilization." And then he hedges and speaks for the Coreys:

> But it will not be possible to persuade those who have the difference in their favor that this is so. They may be right; and at any rate the blank misgiving, the recurring sense of disappointment to which the young people's departure left the Coreys is to be considered. That was the end of their son and brother for them; they felt that; and they were not mean or unamiable people. (p. 361 [272])

This important passage reveals one of many major differences between *Silas Lapham* and the novel that was serialized simultaneously in the *Century, Adventures of Huckleberry Finn*. Huck is the orphan saint whose ingenuousness exposes the absurdity or evil of society. But *Silas Lapham* is a more urbane novel, and does not accord any one character, either Penelope or her father, the kind of moral authority Huck enjoys. There is something to be said, after all, for the Coreys. The character of Penelope may represent the sort

8. For a rendering of a different sort of feminine nervous breakdown, see Howells' *A Counterfeit Presentment* and *The Kentons*.

of freshness that society inevitably stifles; yet for all this Howells refuses finally to side with her against the Coreys (or with the Coreys against her). To fail to see this, as one critic has failed,[9] is to miss the basic point about Howells' novels: they seek to represent the totality of contemporary society, imperfect as it is, and not to transcend it. Francis Hackett grasped this point in writing about *The Rise of Silas Lapham* in 1918: "It is the main achievement of this novel that it drives us to realize the inexorable necessity and the equally inexorable cruelty of exclusiveness, social and sexual, in direct proportion as we have imagination."[1]

One of the basic reasons why Howells was a great realistic writer was that he did not indulge the transcendent allegiances that permit such sweeping dismissals of society as one finds in Thoreau or Mark Twain. As a man, Howells belonged to the contemporary world. The novel in which the hero finds virtue only by renouncing his Back Bay social ambitions and returning to the ancestral home in the country actually helped pay for Howells' own new mansion on Beacon Street. Even as Howells decided to make his female lead an unconventional vernacular humorist, and then audaciously married her to a Brahmin scion, he was anticipating the Boston debut of his daughter Winifred. Still, I see no sufficient reason for judging Howells a hypocrite in these instances. Like any member of a changing society, he was full of contradictions. Yet he succeeded in holding on to his basic decency and his broad sympathy for various categories of people. One of the remarkable aspects of the composition of *Silas Lapham* is that an author fastidious enough to flesh out Bromfield Corey could give such a profound and sympathetic portrait of a vernacular rebel like Penelope. It was, however, precisely this sort of personal amplitude that enabled Howells at one and the same time to dream up a wonderfully pert and perverse humorist and move toward a more complete representation of the American scene than any novelist before him.

* * *

Finally, Penelope is not a person but a fragment of her creator, who admitted late in life that a writer's characters "all come out of himself."[2] She was to some extent Howells' comic mask, just as Artemus Ward and Petroleum V. Nasby were the easygoing alter egos of

9. Myself, in the original version of this chapter: "Nothing more is said of Penelope in the novel. Howells whisks her away by sleight of hand while distracting us with those timid social pieties that make us see that, finally, we cannot respect this man as we respect Thoreau. Worse, Howells invokes our pity for the Coreys' loss of their son in order to make us sympathize with their social rigidity." Alfred Habegger, "Nineteenth-Century American Humor: Easygoing Males, Anxious Ladies, and Penelope Lapham," *PMLA* (October 1976), 91:896.
1. Francis Hackett, *Horizons: A Book of Criticism* (New York: Huebsch, 1918), p. 24.
2. Howells, *Literature and Life: Studies* (New York: Harper, 1902), p. 29.

more exacting and successful men and not real men themselves. Those countrified, old-fashioned losers who made men laugh were as out of place in America as Penelope Lapham. They represented a submerged self in their creators and audiences, a self that was sent under in proportion as traditional rural life was destroyed. The American humorist was by definition insincere, not even trying to integrate his odd mask with the rest of himself. Howells was not spared the male schizophrenia that was epidemic in the nineteenth century. In the character of Penelope, he dredged up an alternative self that spoke with an "ancestral Yankee drawl," and then he sent her into southern exile. Penelope represented a way of seeing, thinking, and talking that was a very important part of the enormously complex and successful person who created her. But she was only a part, and in the end it was impossible for Howells, like all the other upward bound men, to heal his schizophrenia. There was no prevention. Laughter was the only medicine.

DAWN HENWOOD

From Complications of Heroinism: Gender, Power, and the Romance of Self-Sacrifice in *The Rise of Silas Lapham*†

The ethical debate at the center of so many discussions within and about *The Rise of Silas Lapham* is really only part of a broader cultural debate with which Howells' novel grapples at a more fundamental, formalistic level. The Reverend Sewell's controversial "economy of pain" is, at bottom, a literary rather than a moral manifesto. * * *

As critics, Sewell and Howells seem to share a mixed moral and aesthetic outrage which is, as Lawrence Levine has established, symptomatic of their era.[1] Sewell's attack on the contaminating influence of popular fiction takes its slightly hysterical tone from an emergent elitist paranoia over the control of "culture" in America. In *Silas Lapham*, romance's perennial threat to cultural segregation is doubly disconcerting to Sewell, the self-appointed cultural custodian, because it calls into question criteria of gender as well as

† From *American Literary Realism, 1870–1910* 30.3 (Spring 1998): 14–21, 27–30. Reprinted by permission of *American Literary Realism*. Henwood's original references to the novel are to the 1983 Viking Penguin edition; page references in brackets refer to this Norton Critical Edition.

1. Lawrence W. Levine, *Highbrow/Lowbrow: The Emergence of Cultural Hierarchy in America* (Cambridge: Harvard Univ. Press, 1988). According to Levine, the late nineteenth century witnessed a "cultural bifurcation" (8) in American society, as Americans began to develop for the first time a distinct notion of a "highbrow" aesthetic that separated certain kinds of artistic experiences from other, more popular varieties.

taste. The plebeian fiction that infects Penelope Lapham with an absurdly "false ideal of self-sacrifice," is, tellingly, "a famous book with ladies" (217 [166]).

Within the narrative of *Silas Lapham*, Penelope's story is framed by recurring references to two famous books representing opposite cultural poles: the vulgar romance, *Tears, Idle Tears*, and the intellectual realist masterpiece, *Middlemarch*.[2] These two novels are not, however, as ideologically far apart as Sewell's worries and Mrs. Corey's literary snobbery might initially encourage us to think. Not only do both works struggle with the central dilemma of Howells' plot—the ethics of self-sacrifice—but they both also explore the powerful, paradoxical appeal of feminine self-sacrifice. Behind the sentimental "slop" that appeals to Penelope Lapham and her sister heroines lurk deep-seated conflicts over gender and power that the enlightened realist imagination is able neither to resist nor resolve.

Laurie Langbauer has observed that the novel conventionally uses Romance as "a lightning rod for the anxieties about gender at the heart of every depiction of the sexes."[3] *Silas Lapham* is no exception to the trend. At the heart of the novel's ethical debate and Sewell's rationalistic moral economics, gender surfaces as a decisive and disruptive factor. Most commentators on the novel have remarked that self-sacrifice is not, for Sewell or Howells, inherently ridiculous. Within the context of the novel, it is not silly for Silas to regain his dignity through personal sacrifice, or for Tom to put his love for Pen above his family's social sensibilities, or for Irene to swallow stoically her disappointment. What Sewell attacks, then, in his social criticism is not the idea of self-sacrifice *per se* but rather the misapplication of the concept by a would-be literary heroine. Self-immolation becomes, in Sewell's view, as "noxious" as the novelists who promote it when it becomes an excuse for female martyrdom.

Female martyr-heroinism arouses Sewell's ire, I shall argue, because it masks a threatening attempt at willful self-assertion. The female romance of self-sacrifice—which entrances Eliot's Dorothea Brooke just as it does the nameless stock-heroine Penelope imitates—offers a model of feminine power that inverts, even as it adheres to, traditional notions of womanly submissiveness. The title of Howells' imaginary archetype of uncultured, feminine literature, *Tears, Idle*

2. Howells cited *Middlemarch* as a premier example of the "novel," which he defined in opposition to Hawthornesque "romance" and the vulgar "romanticistic novel": "The novel I take to be the sincere and conscientious endeavor to picture life just as it is, to deal with character as we witness it in living people, and to record the incidents that grow out of character. This is the supreme form of fiction." "Novel-Writing and Novel-Reading: An Impersonal Explanation," *Selected Literary Criticism*, Vol. III: 1898–1920 (Bloomington: Indiana Univ. Press, 1993), 218.
3. Laurie Langbauer, *Women and Romance: The Consolations of Gender in the English Novel* (Ithaca: Cornell Univ. Press, 1990), p. 66.

Tears, highlights the paradoxical attraction of passive-aggressive heroinism for nineteenth-century women readers. The lachrymose title is the first line of a seemingly soothing Tennysonian lyric. The lyric appeared, however, as Howells well knew, in the extremely controversial poem "The Princess," Tennyson's most ambitious attempt to deal with what his age euphemistically called "the woman question." Behind the mawkish title looms the imposing figure of an Amazonian heroine, Princess Ida, and the threat of nothing less than full-scale gender warfare. Larger than life, Ida embraces and embodies an ardent vision of female power through personal sacrifice.

When Charles Bellingham remarks at the Coreys' dinner party, "you can't put a more popular thing than self-sacrifice in a novel" (197 [151]), he points to the very element later commentators on the popular romance have identified as the paradoxical but enduring lure of the genre for women. Although Penelope is intelligent enough to know better—she reads Eliot, after all—she is not alone among Howells' heroines in succumbing to the appeal of "Slop, Silly Slop." Like Imogene Graham of *Indian Summer* and Alice Pasmer of *April Hopes*, heroines who resurrect the romance-reading female quixotes of the eighteenth century,[4] Pen turns to a world of blatant emotional excess and exaggerated idealism in order to live the fantasy of controlling her own destiny, by whatever desperate or self-destructive means.

Despite her ironic humor, Penelope enjoys the reading experience Rachel Brownstein describes as "getting as it were high on heroines."[5] Because Silas' attitude towards Pen encourages us to see her as a quick-witted, independent-minded young woman, it is easy for the reader to overlook the irreverent comic's more conventional side. Persis furnishes an important insight into Pen's character near the beginning of the novel when she wonders aloud: "I don't know as it's good for a girl to read so much . . . , especially novels. I don't want she [Penelope] should get notions" (135 [103]).

Persis is able to see, as her husband is not, that Pen is the "dreamer" in the family (135–36 [103]). Irene, who is repeatedly referred to as a "child" and who has "an innocence almost vegetable" (27 [22]), is, according to Persis, the more "wide-awake" of the two sisters (136 [103]). In the family photograph that Lapham shows Bartley Hubbard, Penelope's face wears a look of "singular gravity" (8 [7]), owing, the narrator later explains, to the "mooning" (36 [29]) expression

4. Paul John Eakin, *The New England Girl: Cultural Ideals in Hawthorne, Stowe, Howells and James* (Athens: Univ. of Georgia Press, 1976), p. 122. Arabella of Charlotte Lennox's *Female Quixote* (1752) is one of the most prominent of such deluded heroines.
5. Rachel M. Brownstein, *Becoming a Heroine: Reading About Women in Novels*, 2nd ed. (New York: Columbia Univ. Press, 1994), p. xx.

of the girl's short-sighted eyes. If she were a young man, Pen jests, she would rather spend her time day-dreaming at a club window than pursuing a business man's life of mundane activity.[6] Popular novels, which formed the collective day-dream of nineteenth-century young women,[7] appeal to the dreamy, idealizing tendency beneath the humorist's habitual irony. Moreover, they offer Penelope a vision of self-fulfillment and empowerment that she, the often overlooked "plain" sister (99 [76]), does not find available in her everyday social reality.

* * *

The highly emotional style of nineteenth-century popular novelists allowed women like Penelope to identify intensely with the female saint triumphant. Clara Kingsbury captures the seductive immediacy of *Tears, Idle Tears* when she gushes: "It's perfectly heartbreaking, as you'll imagine from the name; but there's such a dear old-fashioned hero and heroine in it, who keep dying for each other all the way through and making the most wildly satisfactory and unnecessary sacrifices for each other. You feel as if you'd done them yourself" (197 [150–51]). This sense of vicarious heroinism, or living the plot oneself, is exactly what Penelope, who succumbs to the lachrymose appeal of *Tears*, finds missing from *Middlemarch*. "I wish," she says, "she [Eliot] would let you find out a little about the people for yourself" (88 [67]).

In *Becoming a Heroine*, Brownstein describes the essence of heroinism as a character's realization of her own self-worth and claims that "to want to become a heroine, to have a sense of the possibility of being one, is to develop the beginnings of what feminists call a 'raised' consciousness."[8] In order to grasp the mysterious appeal of the bathetic behavior of *Tears*, a novel Pen dismisses as "silly" (217 [166]) yet reads (and weeps over) twice, we have to first understand her frustration with the conventional social script in which she is trapped. Following the flirting between Irene and Corey over a wood shaving in the new Lapham house, Pen reflects wryly on the inertia enjoined on women by the courtship ritual: "Well, 'Rene, *you* haven't got to do *any*thing. That's one advantage girls have got—if it *is* an advantage. *I'm not always sure*" (122 [94]). The "trouble" that flits over Pen's face as she speaks these thoughts passionately erupts later in the novel when she gives way before her mother to a plain girl's frustration: "'You never thought of me!' cried the girl,

6. Whereas Alfred Habegger interprets Penelope's joke as evidence of an iconoclastic spirit that makes her a "male impersonator," it seems to me that, as is the case with most of Pen's jokes, this jest is half-serious. Habegger, *Gender, Fantasy and Realism in American Literature* (New York: Columbia Univ. Press, 1982), p. 185.
7. Habegger, pp. 3–14.
8. Brownstein, p. xix.

with a bitterness that reached her mother's heart. 'I was nobody! I couldn't feel! No one could care for me!' The turmoil of despair, of triumph, of remorse and resentment, which filled her soul, tried to express itself in the words" (226 [172]). Since she is, to borrow Mrs. Corey's unflattering language, a "little, black, odd creature" (264 [200]), Penelope has not even the conventional tools of beauty or coquetry to attract a potential husband. To an even greater extent than Irene, she must resign herself to a passive part in the mating game, and, like her mythical namesake, sit and wait.

Pen's discontent with the yoke of powerlessness, with doing nothing, finds an outlet in her empathy with the dramatic heroine of *Tears*, who, according to Clara Kingsbury, engages in an excess of action, carrying out with the hero a succession of "wildly satisfactory and unnecessary sacrifices" (197 [150–51]). Like Imogene Graham in Howells' *Indian Summer*, Penelope tries to make herself into a heroine who is empowered to do something, to take control of circumstances and people. Self-inflicted suffering becomes for the would-be romantic heroine a form of action. * * *

Penelope's sudden determination to throw herself into the shoes of a "silly" heroine and her persistent clinging to the role long after her family has become reconciled to Corey's choice can be partly explained by the effect the self-sacrificial pose has on her lover. Tom may smile at some of Penelope's more melodramatic moments but, overall, her exaggerated gestures of self-devotion clearly attract him to her. As he confesses to his mother, her suffering attitude makes him "prouder and fonder of her"; her self-chastising cements the appeal she has for him, rouses his admiration to passion. If, before Tom declared himself, Penelope was simply "fascinating," her subsequent self-torment makes her seem so "patient" and "good" that Tom is moved to declare: "There never was any one like her—so brave, so true, so noble. I won't give her up—I can't" (265–66 [201]).

Tom, too, it seems, falls under the influence of romantic ideals of self-forgetful womanliness, worshipping the woman he believes has "acted nobly" under difficult circumstances and "made a great sacrifice" of her principles by agreeing to marry him (345 [260]). Romantic martyrdom is perhaps, Tom's enthusiasm seems to indicate, a plain girl's substitute for erotic magnetism. As Paul John Eakin suggests, Penelope's addiction to sentimental novels may hint at "her desire to become, through identification with the heroines of fiction, the pretty girl she isn't in real life."[9] * * *

The erotic powers of the self-sacrificing heroine must appeal to "plain" Penelope, who clearly resents being seen as "little, and black, and homely" (358 [269]). Her bitter outburst before her mother, "I

9. Eakin, p. 122.

was nobody! . . . No one could care for me!," reveals the pain and anger she must long have felt at being persistently disregarded as a possible object of sexual interest. Whether Pen consciously realizes it or not, the role of female martyr gives her a new kind of hold over Tom's emotions that more than compensates for her lingering insecurity regarding her physical attractions. Howells thus portrays the sentimental romance plot rooted in the heroics of female selflessness as socially endorsed by both male and female delusions. Artificially inspired martyrdom acts in Howells' fiction as a kind of costume in which suppressed eroticism, latent hostility, and passive aggressiveness can walk through genteel society discreetly disguised.

Unlike Alice Pasmer,[1] Penelope comes to share Howells' realization that the obsession with selflessness is essentially self-centered. When she has exhausted her arguments for giving Tom up because of Irene and because of the Laphams' financial disgrace, Penelope discovers that, despite her noble aims, she cannot bring herself to make the one sacrifice that is really demanded of her. She cannot, she thinks, manage to sacrifice her own pride by marrying into a family that does not appreciate her. "I'm too selfish for that," she declares (358 [269]). Only when Penelope recognizes the truth of her own so-called "selfishness," which is really another word for her own will, can she abandon the pose of self-sacrifice, take responsibility for her actions, and commit herself to Corey once and for all.

* * *

Howells, Henry James determined, "is one of the few writers who hold a key to feminine logic and detect a method in feminine madness."[2] The obsession with self-sacrifice accounts largely for the so-called "feminine madness" that led James to the conclusion that Howells' overly-conscientious women characters "are of the best—except, indeed, in the sense of being the best to live with."[3] But, if Howells' heroines are not always easy to live with, neither is the web of cultural narratives in whose entangling "meshes" (the image is Sewell's) they are trying to find their footing. More far-seeing than his representative moralist Sewell, Howells recognizes that the invisible snares of romantic "madness" are inescapable because they are deeply and dangerously involved with real social problems. The so-called "hyperliterariness"[4] of *Silas Lapham*—its deliberate

1. The heroine in Howells's *April Hopes* (1888).
2. Henry James, *Literary Reviews and Essays*, ed. Albert Mordell (New York; Twayne, 1957), p. 207.
3. James, "William Dean Howells," *The American Essays*, ed. Leon Edel (New York: Vintage, 1956), p. 153.
4. [John] Seelye ["The Hole in the Howells / The Lapse in *Silas Lapham*," in *New Essays on "The Rise of Silas Lapham,"* ed. Donald Pease (New York: Cambridge University Press, 1991)], p. 53.

juxtaposition of literary paradigms and specific literary works—enables its author to explore the complex matrix of forces that shape the social distribution of power and, consequently, social identities. The intertextual disturbances Howells invites into his novel reflect his essential empathy with all those who find themselves living in an unstable world of shifting fictions, roles and power structures—a world where romantic nonsense can sometimes appear more relevant to real life than common sense likes to admit.

W. D. Howells: A Chronology

1837 William Dean Howells (WDH) born March 1 in Martinsville (now Martins Ferry), Ohio, across the Ohio River from Wheeling, Virginia (now West Virginia). "Will" is the second of eight children of Mary Dean Howells (1812–1868), of Irish and Pennsylvania German stock, and William Cooper Howells (1807–1894), a Welsh-born itinerant printer-publisher-editor, abolitionist, and adherent of the mystical Swedenborgian New Church.

1840–48 Family moves to Hamilton, Ohio, in the southwest corner of the state north of Cincinnati, when printer-publisher William Cooper Howells (WCH) buys the *Hamilton Intelligencer*, a local newspaper affiliated with the recently formed Whig Party. WDH learns to set type and begins self-education in the "poor boy's college" of the print shop.

1848–52 WCH, increasingly at odds with the Whigs over the Mexican War and expansion of slavery into the western territories, is forced to sell *Intelligencer*. Family moves to Dayton, Ohio, where WCH's new venture, the *Dayton Transcript*, quickly fails, as does his attempt to establish a utopian community with his brothers at Eureka Mills, Ohio. Family moves to state capital, Columbus, where WCH works as legislative reporter while WDH becomes printer's apprentice and reads voraciously.

1852–57 WCH accepts editorship of abolitionist *Ashtabula Sentinel* in the politically open-minded "Western Reserve" of northeast Ohio, eventually settling family in Jefferson, the county seat. WDH works as typesetter, undertakes extensive self-education, including European languages and literatures and, briefly, law, while writing poems, essays, and journalism for local and regional publication. He experiences recurring migraines and episodes of extreme anxiety and hypochondria, which he gradually learns to manage.

1858–60 WDH begins work as editor and writer for the *Ohio State Journal* in Columbus, entering city society and association with newly formed Republican Party. Writing begins to gain wider attention with placement of work in national publications, including the prestigious *Atlantic Monthly*, where he publishes the antislavery poem "The Pilot's Story." Publishes his first book, *Poems of Two Friends* (1859), with John James Piatt. Meets future wife, Elinor Mead, of Brattleboro, Vermont, during her visit to the family of a recently deceased cousin, the sister of future U.S. President Rutherford B. Hayes. WDH writes biography for successful presidential candidacy of Abraham Lincoln, and on the proceeds makes pilgrimage east through Canada to New England and New York. In Boston he dines with literary luminaries, including *Atlantic* editor James Russell Lowell, *Atlantic* owner James T. Fields, and Oliver Wendell Holmes Sr., who quips that the meeting "is something like the apostolic succession . . . the laying on of hands." In Concord he meets Ralph Waldo Emerson, Henry David Thoreau, and Nathaniel Hawthorne, and in New York, Walt Whitman.

1861–65 As reward for Lincoln campaign biography, WDH posted to Venice, Italy as U.S. consul. Epistolary courtship with Elinor Mead culminates in December 1862 wedding in Paris. First daughter, Winifred ("Winny"), born 1863 in Venice. Howellses begin lifelong pattern of clumsy household management and frequent changes of residence.

1865–70 After return to United States and brief employment as book reviewer and columnist for the newly founded *Nation* magazine in New York, WDH assumes assistant editorship of the *Atlantic* in Boston, writing numerous essay-length book reviews evaluating and promoting new American writers. Establishes numerous relationships with contemporary authors, including enduring friendships with novelists Mark Twain (Samuel L. Clemens) and Henry James and philosopher-psychologist William James. Son, John Mead Howells, born 1868. Publishes *Venetian Life* (1866) and *Italian Journeys* (1867) based on recent sojourn in Italy, and *Suburban Sketches* (1870) based on family's experiences in Cambridge, Massachusetts.

1871–80 Promoted to editorship of the *Atlantic*, continues campaign for new American fiction while introducing American readers to contemporary European writing and new work in science, philosophy, and social and economic theory. Builds and occupies house on Concord Avenue in Cambridge, Massachusetts, then another, Redtop, on Somerset Street in Belmont, one town to the west. Third and final child, Mildred ("Pilla"), born 1872. Makes transition from travel writing to fiction with *Their Wedding Journey* (1872), followed by novels, including *A Foregone Conclusion* (1874), *The Lady of the Aroostook* (1879), and *The Undiscovered Country* (1880). Begins writing popular short plays intended for amateur home performance and continues torrent of essays and reviews.

1881–84 Resigns from the *Atlantic* to write fiction full time. Daughter Winifred suffers increasingly frequent bouts of illness consistently misdiagnosed as neurasthenia or "hysteria," a complex of symptoms including fatigue, depression, and loss of appetite usually understood as specific to women and psychosomatic in origin. WDH provokes international controversy when his *Century* essay on Henry James (1882) devalues some British novelists in comparison with James and other contemporary literary realists. In 1884, buys and extensively refurbishes a house at 302 Beacon Street, on the Charles River in Boston's fashionable Back Bay neighborhood, then undergoing ongoing reclamation from tidal marshland. Publishes novels, including *Dr. Breen's Practice* (1881), and experiences major success with *A Modern Instance* (1882). Negotiates publishing contract for new novel late in 1882, begins planning during 1883–84, and completes the first installment by August 1884. Serial publication in *Century* magazine begins in November 1884.

1885–86 During the writing of *The Rise of Silas Lapham*, WDH experiences a spiritual-existential crisis apparently brought on by the combined effects of Winny's continuing decline and worsening Gilded Age socioeconomic inequities and injustices. Increasing interest in socialism and extensive, systematic reading of Tolstoy. Serialization of *The Rise of Silas Lapham* ends with the August issue of *Century*, almost simultaneously with first book publication of the completed novel. In both forms, the novel is a large financial success. WDH signs lucrative contract with Harper Brothers publishing house, agreeing to produce a book a year and "Editor's Study" column for *Harper's Monthly* magazine (1886–92), wherein he will continue public campaign for literary Realism and progressive social, economic, and political reform.

1887–91	In 1887, risks career by defending, alone among prominent American writers, anarchists sentenced to death in a politically charged trial for their unproven connections to a fatal bomb detonation at a pro-labor demonstration in Chicago's Haymarket Square the previous year. Widespread public backlash. Winny dies, March 1889, of causes belatedly revealed as organic rather than psychosomatic, causing WDH lifelong feelings of grief and guilt. WDH publishes succession of major novels of economic and social criticism, including *The Minister's Charge* (1886), *Annie Kilburn* (1888), *A Hazard of New Fortunes* (1889), and *An Imperative Duty* (1891), along with works of psychological fiction (*The Shadow of a Dream*, 1890), literary theory (*Criticism and Fiction*, 1892) and autobiography (*A Boy's Town*, 1890).
1891–98	In December, moves to New York City, occupying the first in a long series of apartments that will serve as primary residences for the next decade. Briefly assumes editorship of socially radical *Cosmopolitan* magazine before falling out with its millionaire owner. Protests Spanish-American War and begins long-term campaign against American and European imperialism. Publishes novels, including *The Quality of Mercy* (1892), *The World of Chance* (1893), *The Coast of Bohemia* (1893), and *The Landlord at Lion's Head* (1897); children's fiction (*Christmas Every Day*, 1892); autobiography (*My Year in a Log Cabin*, 1893); a socialist-utopian novel (*A Traveler from Altruria*, 1894); poetry (*Stops of Various Quills*, 1895), and numerous essays.
1899–1909	Begins decade-long tenure in the "Editor's Easy Chair" column of *Harper's Monthly*. Continues progressive social criticism and advocacy for new American realist writers. Undertakes lecture tour of Midwest, 1899. Buys summer house in Kittery Point, Maine, 1902, where he will spend most summers until Elinor Howells's death. Awarded an honorary Litt. D. from Oxford University in 1904. Elected first president of newly formed American Academy of Arts and Letters, 1908, a post WDH will hold until his death. Continues prolific publishing schedule, including fiction in genres ranging from supernatural fiction (*Questionable Shapes*, 1903; *Between the Dark and the Daylight*, 1907) to utopian political fantasy (*Through*

the Eye of the Needle, 1907) and an experimental multiauthored collaborative novel (*The Whole Family*, 1908), as well as more conventional novels such as *The Kentons* (1902) and *The Son of Royal Langbrith* (1904), along with numerous works of travel writing, memoir, and criticism.

1910–19 Mark Twain dies in April 1910, followed by Elinor Mead Howells in May and William James in August. WDH continues peripatetic living habits, spending most summers in York Harbor, Maine, and most winters in Florida or Georgia, with frequent trips abroad, including Europe and Bermuda. The first six volumes of a projected multivolume "Library Edition" of Howells's collected works appear in 1911 before the project is abandoned because of publishers' disputes over publication rights and fees. Attends seventy-fifth birthday dinner at Sherry's restaurant in New York, along with four hundred guests including President William H. Taft. Despite longstanding antiwar position, WDH supports Allies in Great War, seeing Germany as a threat to civilization itself. The National Institute of Arts and Letters (parent organization of the American Academy of Arts and Letters) awards the first Gold Medal for fiction to WDH in 1915; the prize for a distinguished American novel will be renamed the Howells Medal and awarded quinquennially beginning in 1925. Henry James dies, 1916. Publishes *My Mark Twain* (1910), novels including *New Leaf Mills* (1913) and *The Leatherwood God* (1916), and further works of travel and autobiography.

1920 WDH dies of pneumonia in New York, May 11, at the age of eighty-three, and is buried in Cambridge Cemetery, Massachusetts. *The Vacation of the Kelwyns* (novel) published posthumously.

Selected Bibliography

• indicates works included or excerpted in this Norton Critical Edition.

Works by W. D. Howells

The Rise of Silas Lapham (1885). *A Selected Edition of W. D. Howells*. Ed. Walter J. Meserve and David J. Nordloh. Vol. 12. Bloomington: Indiana UP, 1971. (This authoritative scholarly edition of the novel includes all textual variants and emendations, as well as definitive information about the novel's composition and publication history.)

OTHER MAJOR NOVELS

A Modern Instance (1882)
Indian Summer (1886)
The Minister's Charge (1887)
Annie Kilburn (1888)
A Hazard of New Fortunes (1889)
An Imperative Duty (1891)
The Shadow of a Dream (1890)
The Landlord at Lion's Head (1897)
The Leatherwood God (1916)

SELECTED EDITIONS OF WORKS BY HOWELLS

A Selected Edition of W. D. Howells. Gen. ed. Edwin H. Cady, Ronald M. Gottesman, Don L. Cook, and David J. Nordloh. Bloomington: Indiana UP, 1968–97.

Novels 1875–1886. New York: Library of America, 1982. (Includes *A Foregone Conclusion, A Modern Instance, Indian Summer, The Rise of Silas Lapham.*)

Novels 1886–1888. New York: Library of America, 1989. (Includes *The Minister's Charge, April Hopes, Annie Kilburn.*)

Selected Short Stories of William Dean Howells. Ed. Ruth Bardon. Athens, Ohio: Ohio UP, 1997.

Pebbles, Monochromes, and Other Modern Poems, 1891–1916. Ed. Edwin H. Cady. Athens, Ohio: Ohio UP, 2000.

Web Resource

William Dean Howells Society. www.howellssociety.org.

Biography

Cady, Edwin H. *The Realist at War: The Mature Years 1885–1920 of William Dean Howells*. Syracuse, NY: Syracuse UP, 1958.

• ———. *The Road to Realism: The Early Years 1837–1885 of William Dean Howells*. Syracuse, NY: Syracuse UP, 1956.
• Goodman, Susan, and Carl Dawson. *William Dean Howells: A Writer's Life*. Berkeley: U of California P, 2005.
Lynn, Kenneth S. *William Dean Howells: An American Life*. New York: Harcourt Brace Jovanovich, 1970.

Criticism

Alexander, William. *William Dean Howells: The Realist as Humanist*. New York: Burt Franklin, 1981.
• Armbruster, Elif S. *Domestic Biographies: Stowe, Howells, James, and Wharton at Home*. New York: Peter Lang, 2011.
Arms, George, and William M. Gibson. "*Silas Lapham*, 'Daisy Miller,' and The Jews." *New England Quarterly* 16.1 (1943): 118–22.
Barrish, Phillip. *American Literary Realism, Critical Theory, and Intellectual Prestige, 1880–1995*. Cambridge: Cambridge UP, 2001.
Barton, John Cyril. "Howells's Rhetoric of Realism: The Economy of Pain(t) and Social Complicity in *The Rise of Silas Lapham* and *The Minister's Charge*." *Studies in American Fiction* 29.2 (2001): 159–87.
Beckman, John. "The Church of Fact: Genre Hybridity in *Huckleberry Finn* and *Silas Lapham*." *Arizona Quarterly* 69.3 (2013): 23–47.
Bennett, George N. *William Dean Howells: The Development of a Novelist*. Norman: U of Oklahoma P, 1959.
Blair, Amy. *Reading Up: Middle-Class Readers and the Culture of Success in the Early Twentieth-Century United States*. Philadelphia: Temple UP, 2011.
Borus, Daniel. *Writing Realism: Howells, James, and Norris in the Mass Market*. Chapel Hill: U of North Carolina P, 1989.
Cady, Edwin H. *The Light of Common Day: Realism in American Fiction*. Bloomington: Indiana UP, 1971.
Cady, Edwin H., and Louis J. Budd, eds. *On Howells: The Best from* American Literature. Durham, NC: Duke UP, 1993.
Cady, Edwin H., and Norma W. Cady, eds. *Critical Essays on W.D. Howells, 1866–1920*. Boston: G. K. Hall, 1983.
Campbell, Charles L. "Realism and the Romance of Real Life: Multiple Fictional Worlds in Howells' Novels." *Modern Fiction Studies* 16.3 (1970): 280–302.
Carrington, George. *The Immense Complex Drama*. Athens: Ohio State UP, 1966.
Carter, Everett. *Howells and the Age of Realism*. Philadelphia: Lippincott, 1954.
Claybaugh, Amanda. "The Autobiography of a Substitute: Trauma, History, Howells." *Yale Journal of Criticism* 18.1 (2005): 45–65.
Crowley, John W. "An Introduction to *The Rise of Silas Lapham*." *American Literary Realism* 42.2 (2010): 151–73.
———. *The Mask of Fiction: Essays on W. D. Howells*. Amherst: U of Massachusetts P, 1989.
———. "*The Portrait of a Lady* and *The Rise of Silas Lapham*: The Company They Kept." In *Cambridge Companion to American Literary Realism and Naturalism*. Ed. Donald Pizer. Cambridge: Cambridge UP, 1995, pp. 117–37.
• Dimock, Wai Chee. "The Economy of Pain: The Case of Howells." *Raritan* 9.4 (1990): 99–119. Republished as "The Economy of Pain: Capitalism, Humanitarianism, and the Realistic Novel" in *New Essays on* The Rise of Silas Lapham. Ed. Donald Pease. Cambridge: Cambridge UP, 1991, pp. 67–90.
• Dooley, Patrick. "Nineteenth-Century Business Ethics in *The Rise of Silas Lapham*." *American* Studies 21.2 (Fall 1980): 79–93.
Dooley, Patrick K. *A Community of Inquiry: Conversations between Classical American Philosophy and American Literature*. Kent, OH: Kent State UP, 2008.

Eby, Clare Virginia. "Compromise and Complicity in *The Rise of Silas Lapham*." *American Literary Realism* 24.1 (1991): 39–53.

Foster, S. "W. D. Howells: *The Rise of Silas Lapham*." In *The Monster in the Mirror: Studies in Nineteenth-Century Realism*. Ed. David Anthony Williams. Oxford: Oxford UP, 1978, pp. 149–78.

Goldman, Irene C. "Business Made Her Nervous: The Fall of Persis Lapham." *Old Northwest* 13.4 (1986): 419–38.

Goodman, Susan. *Civil Wars: American Novelists and Manners, 1880–1940*. Baltimore: Johns Hopkins UP, 2003.

Gross, Seymour, and Rosalie Murphy. "Commonplace Reality and the Romantic Phantoms: Howells' *A Modern Instance* and *The Rise of Silas Lapham*." *Studies in American Fiction* 4.1 (1976): 1–14.

Habegger, Alfred. "The Autistic Tyrant: Howells' Self-Sacrificial Woman and Jamesian Renunciation." *Novel* 10.1 (1976): 27–39.

• ———. *Gender, Fantasy, and Realism in American Literature*. New York: Columbia UP, 1982.

• Hamilton, Geordie. "Rethinking the Politics of American Realism Through the Narrative Form and Moral Rhetoric of W. D. Howells' *The Rise of Silas Lapham*." *American Literary Realism* 42.1 (2009): 13–35.

Hart, John E. "The Commonplace as Heroic in *The Rise of Silas Lapham*." *Modern Fiction Studies* 8 (1963): 375–83.

Hedges, Elaine R. "César Birotteau and *The Rise of Silas Lapham*: A Study in Parallels." *Nineteenth-Century Fiction* 17.2 (1962): 163–74.

• Henwood, Dawn. "Complications of Heroinism: Gender, Power, and the Romance of Self-Sacrifice in *The Rise of Silas Lapham*." *American Literary Realism* 30.3 (1998): 14–30.

• Hoeller, Hildegard. "Capitalism, Fiction, and the Inevitable, (Im)Possible, Maddening Importance of the Gift." *PMLA* 127.1 (2012): 131–36.

———. *From Gift to Commodity: Capitalism and the Spirit of the Gift in Nineteenth-Century American Fiction*. Durham: UP of New Hampshire, 2012.

Jackson, Fleda Brown. "A Sermon without Exegesis: The Achievement of Stasis in *The Rise of Silas Lapham*." *Journal of Narrative Technique* 16.2 (1986): 131–47.

Kaplan, Amy. *The Social Construction of American Realism*. Chicago: U of Chicago P, 1988.

Kohler, Michelle. "Realism and The Perception of Romance in *The Rise of Silas Lapham*." *American Literary Realism* 38.3 (2006): 223–38.

Kolb, Harold. *The Illusion of Life*. Charlottesville: UP of Virginia, 1969.

Lavin, Matthew J. "Clean Hands and an Iron Face: Frontier Masculinity and Boston Manliness in *The Rise of Silas Lapham*." *Western American Literature* 45.4 (2011): 362–82.

Ludwig, Sämi. *Pragmatist Realism: The Cognitive Paradigm in American Realist Texts*. Madison: U of Wisconsin P, 2002.

Manierre, William R. II. "*The Rise of Silas Lapham*: Retrospective Discussion as Dramatic Technique." *College English* 23.5 (1962): 357–61.

Marchand, Mary. "Faking It: Social Bluffing and Class Difference in Howells's *The Rise of Silas Lapham*." *New England Quarterly* 83.2 (2010): 283–312.

McKay, Janet. *Narration and Discourse in American Realistic Fiction*. Philadelphia: U of Penn P, 1982.

McMurray, William. *The Literary Realism of William Dean Howells*. Carbondale: Southern Illinois UP, 1967.

Michaels, Walter Benn. "Sister Carrie's Popular Economy." *Critical Inquiry* 7 (1980): 373–90. Republished in *The Gold Standard and the Logic of Naturalism*. Berkeley: U of California P, 1987, pp. 31–58.

• Murphy, Brenda. "Howells and the Popular Story Paradigm: Reading *Silas Lapham*'s Proairetic Code." *American Literary Realism* 21.2 (1989): 21–33.

Nettels, Elsa. *Language, Race and Social Class in Howells's America*. Lexington: U of Kentucky P, 1988.

• Oehlschlager, Fritz. "An Ethic of Responsibility in *The Rise of Silas Lapham*." *American Literary Realism* 23.2 (1991): 20–34.

Pease, Donald, ed. *New Essays on* The Rise of Silas Lapham. Cambridge: Cambridge UP, 1991.

• Pizer, Donald. "The Ethical Unity of *The Rise of Silas Lapham*." *American Literature* 32.3 (1960): 322–27. Republished in *Realism and Naturalism in Nineteenth-Century American Literature*. Carbondale: Southern Illinois UP, 1966 (2nd ed., 1984, pp. 121–26).

• Porte, Joel. "Manners, Morals, and Mince Pie: Howells' America Revisited." *Prospects* 10 (1985): 443–60.

Prioleau, Elizabeth Stevens. *The Circle of Eros: Sexuality in the Work of William Dean Howells*. Durham, NC: Duke UP, 1983.

• Tanselle, G. Thomas. "The Architecture of *The Rise of Silas Lapham*." *American Literature* 37.4 (1966): 430–57.

———. "The Boston Seasons of Silas Lapham." *Studies in the Novel* 1.1 (1969): 60–66.

• Thomas, Brook. "The Risky Business of Accessing the Economy of Howells's Realism in *The Rise of Silas Lapham*." In *REAL: Yearbook of Research in English and American Literature*, Vol. 11. Ed. Winfried Fluck. Tübingen: Gunter Narr Verlag Tübingen, 1995. Republished as "*The Rise of Silas Lapham* and the Hazards of Realistic Development" in *American Literary Realism and the Failed Promise of Contract*. Berkeley: U of California P, 1997, pp. 122–55.

Thompson, Graham. *Male Sexuality under Surveillance: The Office in American Literature*. Iowa City: U of Iowa P, 2003.

Trachtenberg, Alan. *The Incorporation of America: Culture and Society in the Gilded Age*. New York: Hill and Wang, 1982.

Trilling, Lionel. "W. D. Howells and the Roots of Modern Taste." *Partisan Review* 18 (1951): 516–36. Republished in *The Opposing Self*. New York: Viking, 1955, pp. 76–103.

Tuttleton, James W. *The Novel of Manners in America*. Chapel Hill: U of North Carolina P, 1972.

Vanderbilt, Kermit. *The Achievement of William Dean Howells*. Princeton: Princeton UP, 1968.

Wadsworth, Sarah. *In the Company of Books: Literature and Its "Classes" in Nineteenth-Century America*. Amherst: U of Massachusetts P, 2006.

Wasserstrom, William. "Howells and the High Cost of Junk." *Old Northwest* 10.1 (1984): 77–90.

Westbrook, Wayne. *Wall Street in the American Novel*. New York: New York UP, 1980.

Young, Arlene. "The Triumph of Irony in *The Rise of Silas Lapham*." *Studies in American Fiction* 20.1 (1992): 45–55.